Defect
Detect

DUmps Binaries Logs INternals
School of Security

Rust

Windows Memory Dump Analysis

Accelerated

Dmitry Vostokov
Software Diagnostics Services

Published by OpenTask, Republic of Ireland

Product and company names mentioned in this book may be trademarks of their owners.

OpenTask books and magazines are available through booksellers and distributors worldwide. For further information or comments, send requests to press@opentask.com.

A CIP catalog record for this book is available from the British Library.

ISBN-l3: 978-1-912636-89-1 (Paperback)

Revision 1.01 (December 2024)

Contents

About the Author

Dmitry Vostokov is an internationally recognized expert, speaker, educator, scientist, inventor, and author. He founded the pattern-oriented software diagnostics, forensics, and prognostics discipline (Systematic Software Diagnostics) and Software Diagnostics Institute (DA+TA: DumpAnalysis.org + TraceAnalysis.org). Vostokov has also authored over 50 books on software diagnostics, anomaly detection and analysis, software and memory forensics, root cause analysis and problem solving, memory dump analysis, debugging, software trace and log analysis, reverse engineering, and malware analysis. He has over 30 years of experience in software architecture, design, development, and maintenance in various industries, including leadership, technical, and people management roles. Dmitry founded OpenTask Iterative and Incremental Publishing (OpenTask.com) and Software Diagnostics Technology and Services (former Memory Dump Analysis Services) PatternDiagnostics.com. In his spare time, he explores Software Narratology and Quantum Software Diagnostics. His interest areas are theoretical software diagnostics and its mathematical and computer science foundations, application of formal logic, semiotics, artificial intelligence, machine learning, and data mining to diagnostics and anomaly detection, software diagnostics engineering and diagnostics-driven development, diagnostics workflow and interaction. Recent interest areas also include functional programming, cloud native computing, monitoring, observability, visualization, security, automation, applications of category theory to software diagnostics, development and big data, and diagnostics of artificial intelligence.

Presentation Slides and Transcript

Rust
Windows Memory Dump Analysis
Accelerated

Dmitry Vostokov
Software Diagnostics Services

Hello, everyone, my name is Dmitry Vostokov, and I teach this training course.

Prerequisites

- Basic Windows troubleshooting

- Basic Rust knowledge

These prerequisites are hard to define. Some of you have software development experience, and some do not. However, one thing is certain: to get most of this training, you are expected to have basic Windows troubleshooting experience—another thing I expect you to be familiar with Rust. The ability to read assembly language has some advantages but is not necessary for most of this training.

Training Goals

- Review fundamentals

- Review x64 disassembly

- Learn how to analyze process dumps

- Learn how to analyze complete (physical memory) dumps

Our primary goal is to learn Rust Windows memory dump analysis in an accelerated fashion. So first, we review absolutely essential fundamentals necessary for memory dump analysis, including x64 disassembly. Then, we learn how to analyze different types of memory dumps: process memory dumps and complete (physical memory) dumps. We also review memory dump collection methods.

Training Principles

◎ Talk only about what I can show

◎ Lots of pictures

◎ Lots of examples

◎ Original content and examples

There were many training formats to consider, and I decided that the best way is to concentrate on exercises. Specifically, for this training, I developed 10 of them.

Fundamentals

So now I show you some pictures.

Process Space (x64)

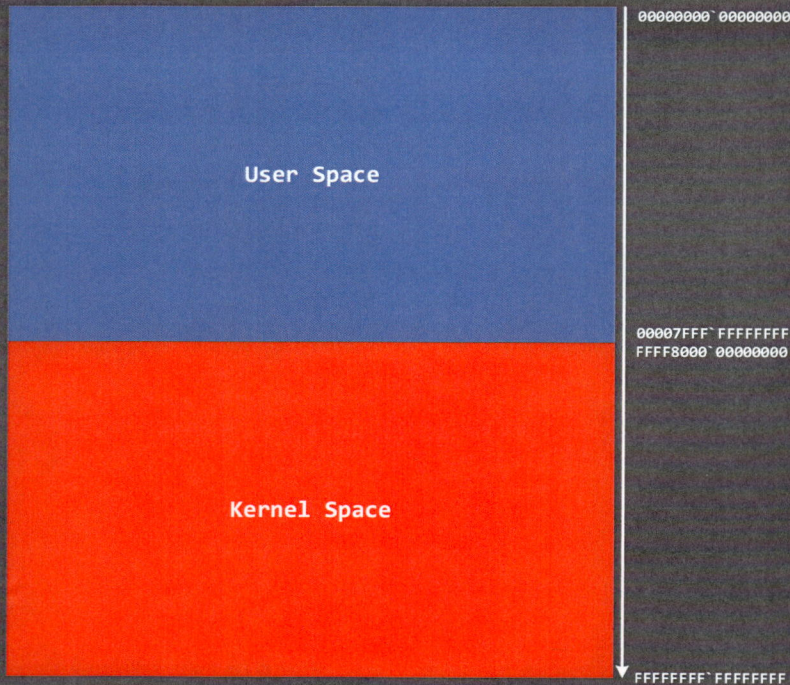

User Space

Kernel Space

```
00000000`00000000

00007FFF`FFFFFFFF
FFFF8000`00000000

FFFFFFFF`FFFFFFFF
```

© 2025 Software Diagnostics Services

Windows process memory range is divided into kernel space and user space parts for every process. I follow the tradition of using red for the kernel and blue for the user part. Please note that there is a difference between space and mode. The mode is the execution privilege attribute; for example, code running in kernel space has higher execution privilege than in user space. However, kernel code can access user space and access data there. We say that such code is running in kernel mode. On the contrary, the application code from user space is running in user mode, and because of its lower privilege, it cannot access kernel space. This division prevents accidental kernel modifications. Otherwise, you could easily crash your system. I put addresses on the right, and on 64-bit systems, all kernel addresses start with a hexadecimal digit "F." This uniform memory space is called virtual process space because it is an abstraction that allows us to analyze memory dumps without thinking about how it is all organized in physical memory. We are concerned with virtual space only when we look at process dumps.

Application/Process/Module (x64)

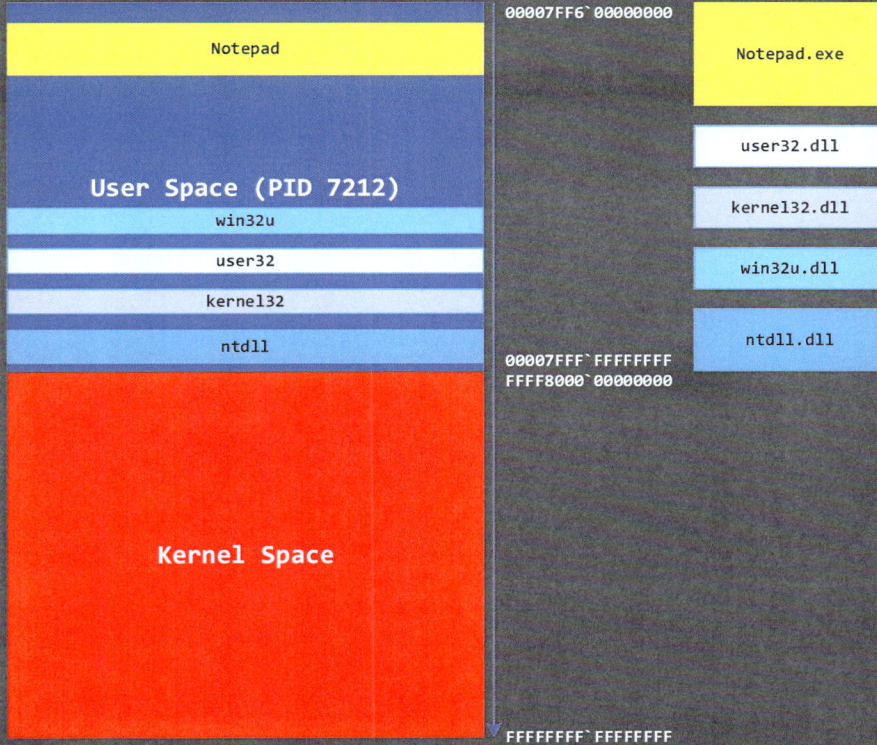

00007FF6`00000000

Notepad

User Space (PID 7212)

win32u
user32
kernel32
ntdll

Notepad.exe

user32.dll

kernel32.dll

win32u.dll

ntdll.dll

00007FFF`FFFFFFFF
FFFF8000`00000000

Kernel Space

FFFFFFFF`FFFFFFFF

When an application is loaded, all modules (an executable image on a disk and associated DLLs) are organized sequentially in virtual memory space. Some modules can also be loaded twice at different virtual memory locations. A process is then set up for running, and a process ID is assigned to it. If you run another such process, it has a different virtual memory space (it could be exactly the same in layout, but most recent Windows versions put modules in a different order). We see that the main application executable module is usually loaded above the 00007FF0`00000000 address (subject to change with every major update).

15

Process Virtual Space (x64)

Let's now see the big picture: the whole virtual process memory space and how it all maps to memory dumps.

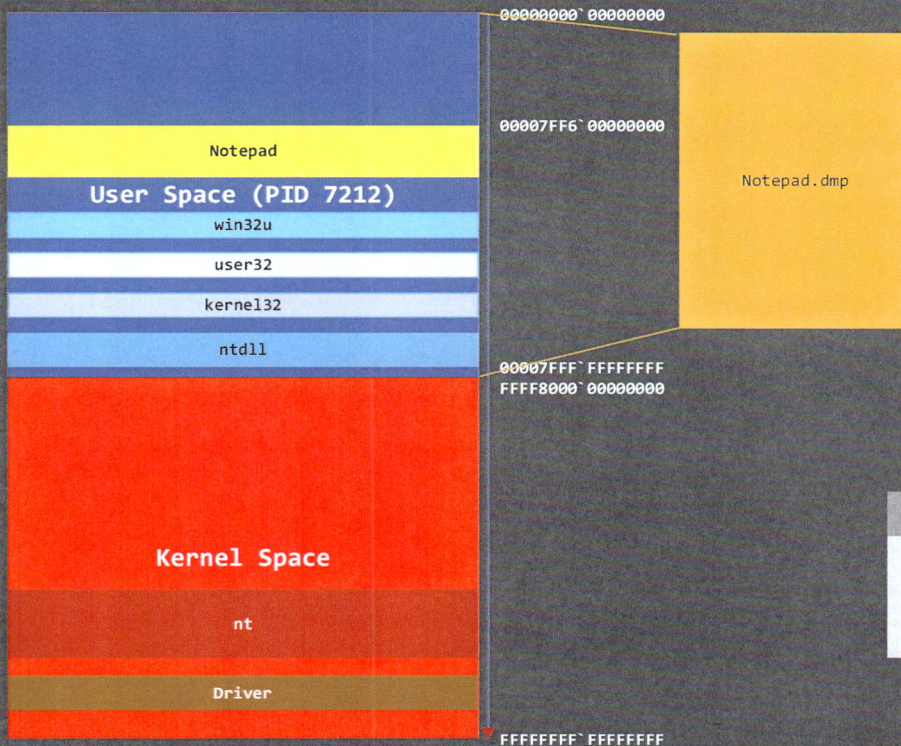

Process Memory Dump (x64)

```
00000000`00000000
00007FF6`00000000

Notepad.dmp

00007FFF`FFFFFFFF
FFFF8000`00000000

FFFFFFFF`FFFFFFFF
```

Notepad

User Space (PID 7212)

win32u

user32

kernel32

ntdll

Kernel Space

nt

Driver

WinDbg Commands

lmv command lists modules and their description

When we save a process memory dump, a user space portion of the application virtual process space is saved without any kernel virtual space stuff. However, we usually don't see process memory dumps of several gigabytes in size unless we have memory leaks. This is because process space has gaps unfilled with modules and data. These unallocated parts are not saved in a memory dump. However, if some parts were paged out and now reside in a page file, they are usually brought back before saving a memory dump. You may have noticed that sometimes, when you save a dump file, for example, by using Task Manager, process memory consumption increases.

Complete Memory Dump (x64)

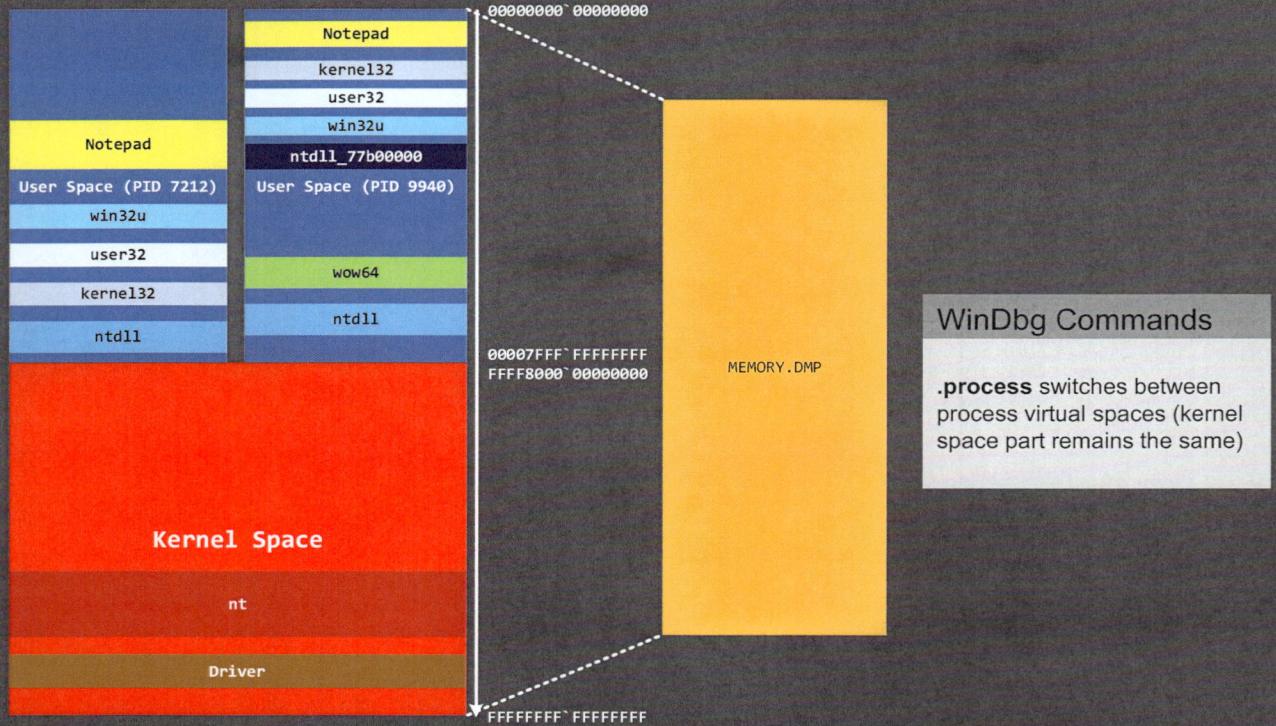

The complete memory dump is a dump file containing only physical memory contents. One of the tasks of WinDbg is to provide you with an abstraction of process virtual address space and give you commands to navigate between such spaces. Note that the kernel part never changes when switching between different process spaces while looking at a complete memory dump. Therefore, when we look at complete memory dumps, we would learn how to navigate and switch between different process virtual memory spaces.

Process Threads

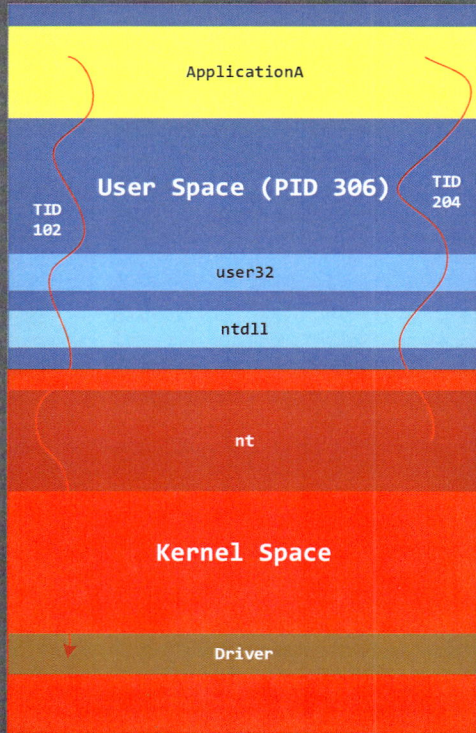

ApplicationA

User Space (PID 306)

TID 102

TID 204

user32

ntdll

nt

Kernel Space

Driver

WinDbg Commands

Process dumps:
~<n>s switches between threads

Now, we come to another important fundamental concept in Windows memory dump analysis: a thread. It is basically a unit of execution, and many threads can be in a given process. Every thread executes some code and performs various tasks; for example, in Microsoft Edge, one thread can download a page, another thread responds to parse JavaScript on a different page, and other threads can support Java or .NET virtual machine and execute graphics code. Every thread has its ID. In this training, we also learn how to navigate between process threads. They are called process threads because they originate in user space.

Thread Stack Raw Data

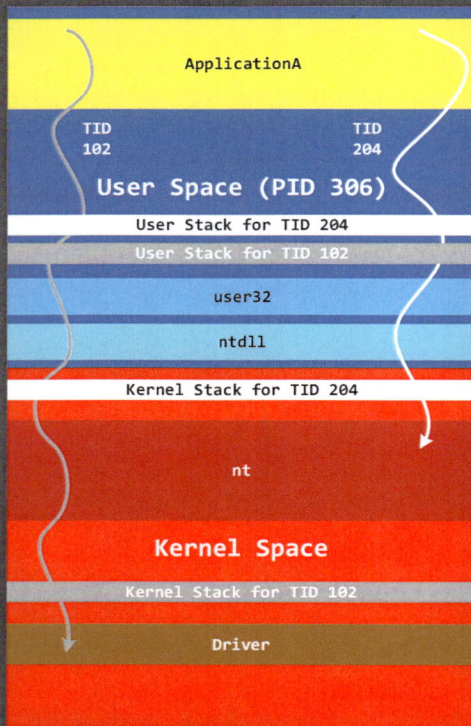

ApplicationA

TID 102   TID 204

User Space (PID 306)

User Stack for TID 204

User Stack for TID 102

user32

ntdll

Kernel Stack for TID 204

nt

Kernel Space

Kernel Stack for TID 102

Driver

WinDbg Commands

Process dumps:
!teb

Data:
dc / dps / dpp / dpa / dpu

© 2025 Software Diagnostics Services

Every thread needs a temporary memory region to store its execution history and temporary data. This region is called a thread stack. To avoid conflict, OS designers split the thread stack into 2 parts: user and kernel. You see them for both threads with TID 102 and 204 in the picture. Please note that the stack region is just any other memory region, and you can use any WinDbg data dumping commands there. We also learn how to get the thread stack region address range. Examining raw stack data can hint at the past system behavior: the so-called **Execution Residue** pattern.

Thread Stack Trace

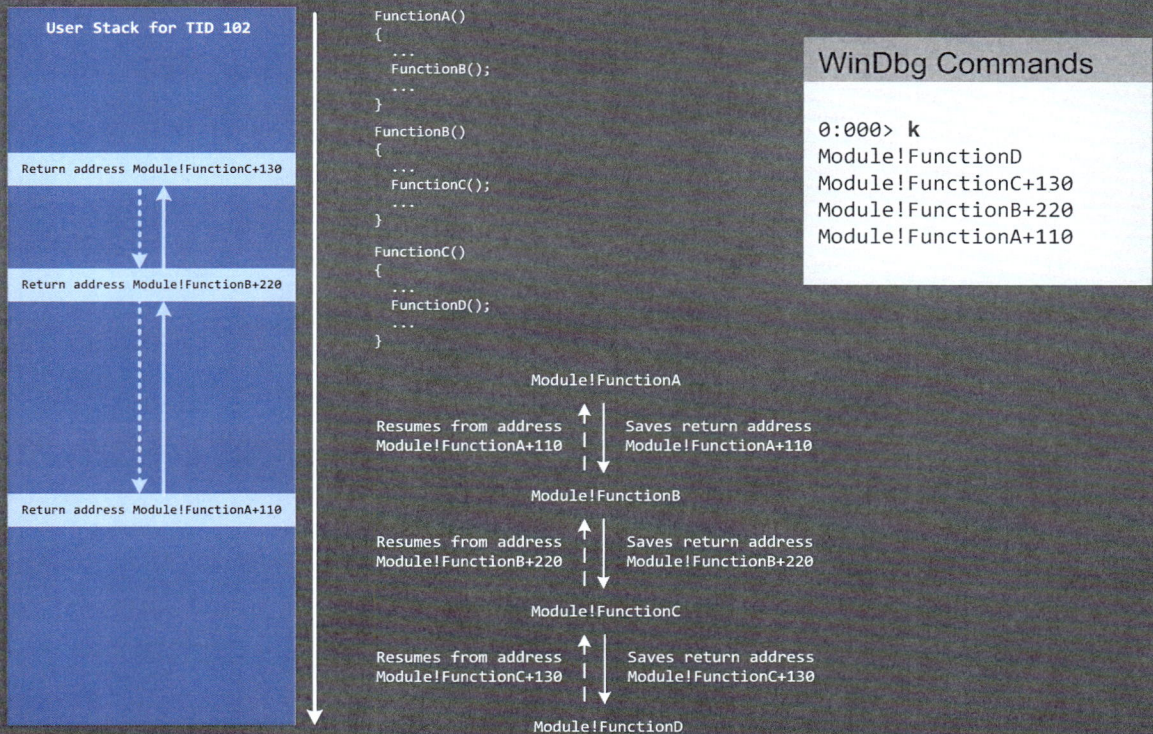

User Stack for TID 102

Return address Module!FunctionC+130

Return address Module!FunctionB+220

Return address Module!FunctionA+110

```
FunctionA()
{
    ...
    FunctionB();
    ...
}
FunctionB()
{
    ...
    FunctionC();
    ...
}
FunctionC()
{
    ...
    FunctionD();
    ...
}
```

Module!FunctionA

Resumes from address   Saves return address
Module!FunctionA+110   Module!FunctionA+110

Module!FunctionB

Resumes from address   Saves return address
Module!FunctionB+220   Module!FunctionB+220

Module!FunctionC

Resumes from address   Saves return address
Module!FunctionC+130   Module!FunctionC+130

Module!FunctionD

WinDbg Commands

```
0:000> k
Module!FunctionD
Module!FunctionC+130
Module!FunctionB+220
Module!FunctionA+110
```

Now, we explain thread stack traces. Suppose we have source code where *FunctionA* calls *FunctionB* at some point, *FunctionB* calls *FunctionC,* and so on: a thread of execution. If *FunctionA* calls *FunctionB*, you expect the execution thread to return to the same place where it left and then resume from there. It is achieved by saving a return address in the thread stack region. So every return address is saved and then restored during the course of thread execution. Although the memory addresses grow from top to bottom in this picture, return addresses are saved from bottom to top: the stack grows from higher to lower addresses. It might seem counter-intuitive to all previous pictures, but this is how you would see the output from WinDbg commands. What WinDbg does when you instruct it to dump a stack trace from a given thread is to analyze thread raw stack data and figure out return addresses, map them to symbolic form according to symbol files and show them from top to bottom. Note that *FunctionD* is not present in the raw stack data on the left because the thread is currently executing the function *FunctionD* called from *FunctionC*. However, *FunctionC* called *FunctionD,* and the return address of *FunctionC* was saved. In the gray box on the right, we see the results of the WinDbg command.

Thread Stack Trace (no PDB)

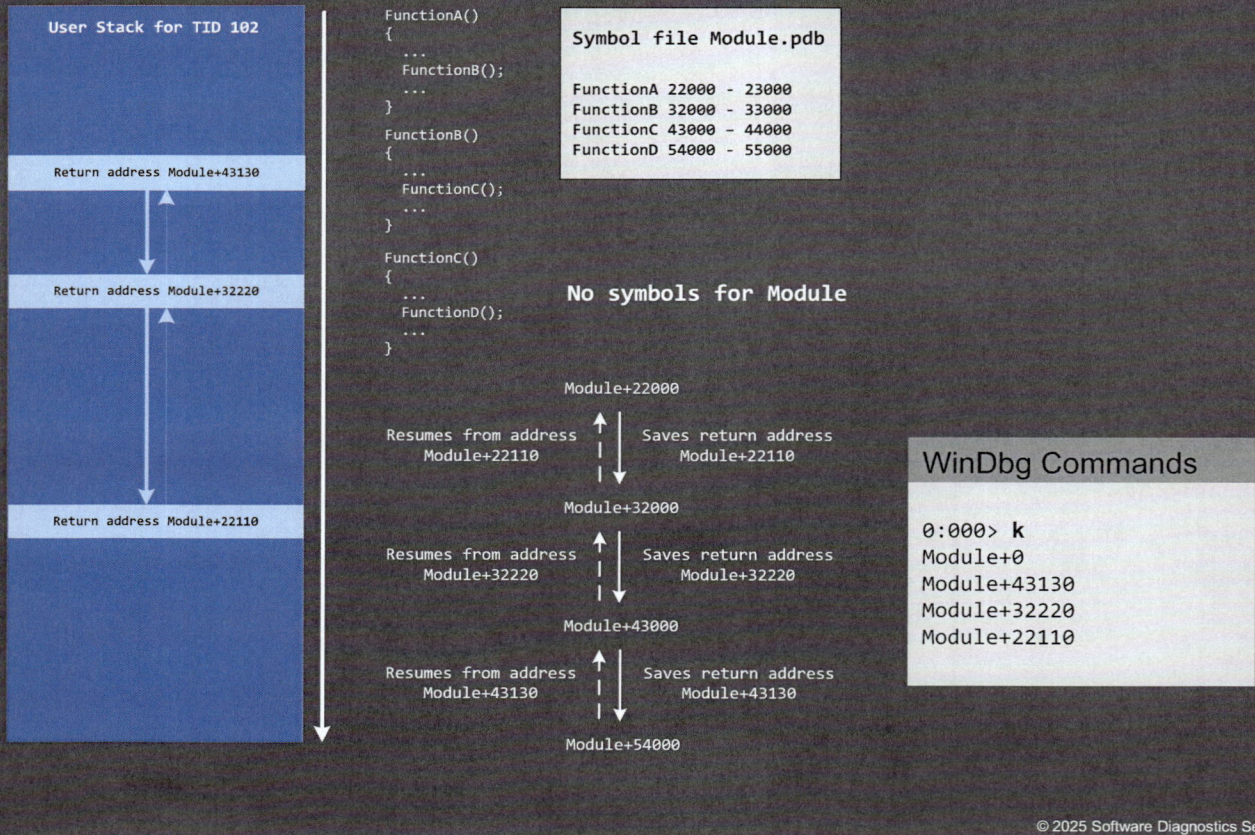

```
User Stack for TID 102


  Return address Module+43130


  Return address Module+32220


  Return address Module+22110
```

```
FunctionA()
{
  ...
  FunctionB();
  ...
}
FunctionB()
{
  ...
  FunctionC();
  ...
}
FunctionC()
{
  ...
  FunctionD();
  ...
}
```

```
Symbol file Module.pdb

FunctionA 22000 - 23000
FunctionB 32000 - 33000
FunctionC 43000 - 44000
FunctionD 54000 - 55000
```

No symbols for Module

```
                          Module+22000
Resumes from address  ↑   Saves return address
     Module+22110     |        Module+22110
                      ↓
                          Module+32000
Resumes from address  ↑   Saves return address
     Module+32220     |        Module+32220
                      ↓
                          Module+43000
Resumes from address  ↑   Saves return address
     Module+43130     |        Module+43130
                      ↓
                          Module+54000
```

WinDbg Commands

```
0:000> k
Module+0
Module+43130
Module+32220
Module+22110
```

© 2025 Software Diagnostics Services

Here, I'd like to show you why symbol files are important and what stack traces you get without them. Symbol files just provide mappings between memory address ranges and associated symbols, like a table of contents in a book. So, in the absence of symbols, we are left with bare module names that are saved in a dump.

Exceptions (Access Violation)

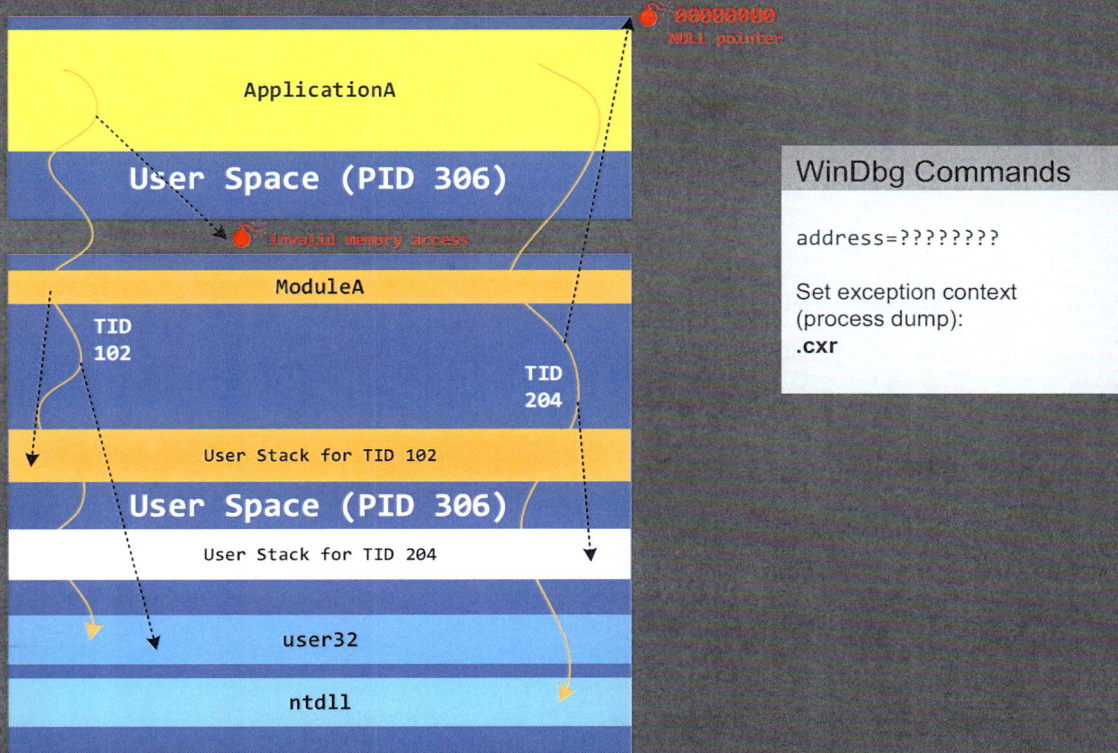

ApplicationA

User Space (PID 306)

invalid memory access

ModuleA

TID 102

TID 204

User Stack for TID 102

User Space (PID 306)

User Stack for TID 204

user32

ntdll

00000000 NULL pointer

WinDbg Commands

address=????????

Set exception context (process dump):
.cxr

Now, we talk about access violation exceptions. During thread execution, it accesses various memory addresses doing reads and writes. Sometimes the memory is absent due to gaps in virtual address space or different protection levels like read-only or no execute memory regions. If a thread tries to violate that, we get an exception, or it is often called fault or trap in kernel space. OS stores an exception context and transfers execution to exception processing code. In practical exercises, we would see how to recover that information because WinDbg is just a tool with its own assumptions and often is wrong in its conclusions when you just execute the default analysis command !analyze –v. Certain regions are forbidden to read and write, such as near-zero addresses. If we have an access violation there, it is called NULL pointer access. Note that every thread can have an exception, and multiple exceptions are often stored in a dump file.

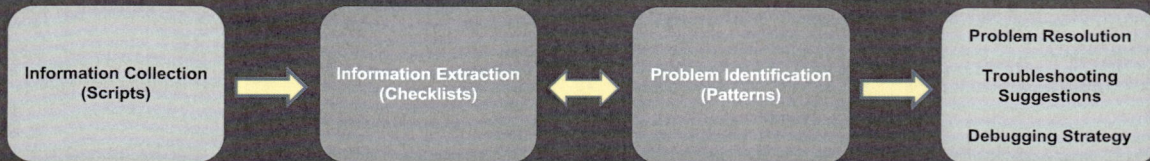

Pattern-Oriented Diagnostic Analysis

Diagnostic Pattern: a common recurrent identifiable problem together with a set of recommendations and possible solutions to apply in a specific context.

Diagnostic Problem: a set of indicators (symptoms, signs) describing a problem.

Diagnostic Analysis Pattern: a common recurrent analysis technique and method of diagnostic pattern identification in a specific context.

Diagnostics Pattern Language: common names of diagnostic and diagnostic analysis patterns. The same language for any operating system: Windows, Mac OS X, Linux, ...

| Information Collection (Scripts) | → | Information Extraction (Checklists) | ↔ | Problem Identification (Patterns) | → | Problem Resolution / Troubleshooting Suggestions / Debugging Strategy |

Checklist: http://www.dumpanalysis.org/windows-memory-analysis-checklist

Patterns: http://www.dumpanalysis.org/blog/index.php/crash-dump-analysis-patterns/

A few words about logs, checklists, and patterns: memory dump analysis is usually an analysis of a text for the presence of diagnostic patterns. We run commands; they output text, and then we look at that textual output, and when we find suspicious diagnostic indicators, we execute more commands. Here, checklists can be very useful. One such checklist is provided as a link. In some cases (such as complete memory dumps), collecting information into one huge log file by running several commands one by one (like a script) and then doing the first-order analysis is beneficial.

Checklist: https://www.dumpanalysis.org/windows-memory-analysis-checklist

Patterns: https://www.dumpanalysis.org/blog/index.php/crash-dump-analysis-patterns/

Memory Dump Collection

Memory Dump Collection

Process Dump Generation

- ⊙ **Crash or Hang, ... ?**

  PID in Task Manager

- ⊙ **Windows W10, W11**

  - Crash: LocalDumps
  - Hang / Leak / Spike: Task Manager, procdump -ma

Local Dumps
https://learn.microsoft.com/en-gb/windows/win32/wer/collecting-user-mode-dumps

procdump -ma
https://learn.microsoft.com/en-us/sysinternals/downloads/procdump

Complete Dump Setup

- View Advanced System Settings (Control Panel)
- Page file size > physical memory + 100 MB

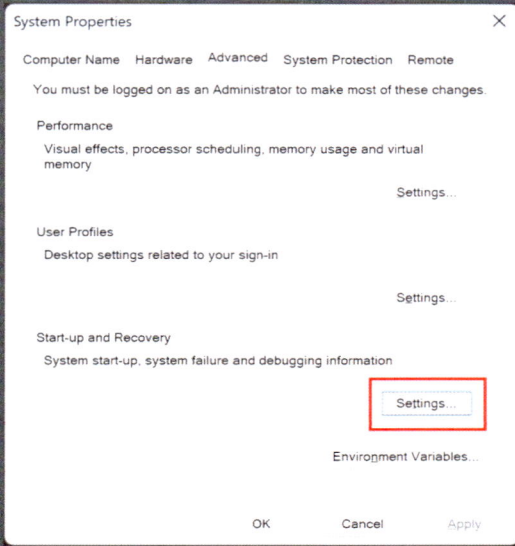

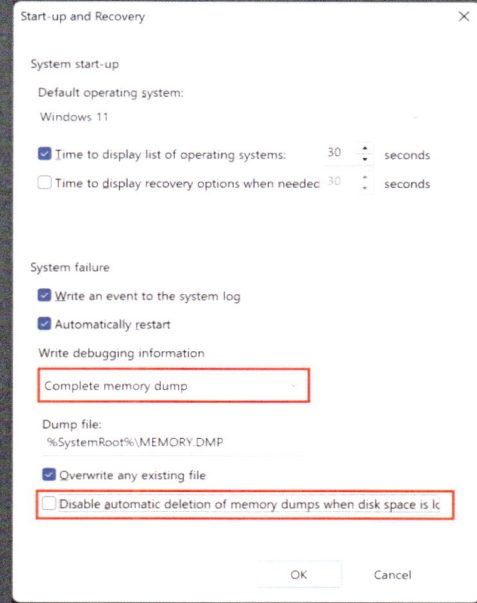

Complete Dump Generation

- Keyboard, NMI button

- Tools: NotMyFault

- VMware memory snapshot + vmss2core

Keyboard
https://learn.microsoft.com/en-us/windows-hardware/drivers/debugger/forcing-a-system-crash-from-the-keyboard

NMI button
https://learn.microsoft.com/en-us/troubleshoot/windows-client/performance/generate-a-kernel-or-complete-crash-dump

NotMyFault
https://learn.microsoft.com/en-us/sysinternals/downloads/notmyfault

vmss2core
https://knowledge.broadcom.com/external/article/323788/converting-a-snapshot-file-to-memory-dum.html

Common Issues

- Truncated complete dumps

- No "Complete memory dump" option

  HKLM \ SYSTEM \ CurrentControlSet \ Control \ CrashControl
  CrashDumpEnabled = 1 (DWORD)

Review of x64 Disassembly

x64 Disassembly

This section provides an overview of disassembly for the x64 platform. Linux developers who know the x64 assembly language may benefit because we use a different flavor than the default in Linux GDB.

x64 CPU Registers

- RAX ⊃ EAX ⊃ AX ⊇ {AH, AL}

RAX 64-bit	EAX 32-bit

- ALU: **RAX**, **RDX**

- Counter: **RCX**

- Memory copy: **RSI** (src), **RDI** (dst)

- Stack: **RSP**

- Frame Pointer: **RSP**, **RBP**

- Next instruction: **RIP**

- New: **R8** – **R15**, **Rx(D|W|B)**

There are familiar 32-bit CPU register names, such as **EAX,** that are extended to 64-bit names, such as **RAX**. Most of them are traditionally specialized, such as ALU, counter, and memory copy registers. Although, now they all can be used as general-purpose registers. There is, of course, a stack pointer, **RSP**, and it also takes the role of a frame pointer, which is also used to address local variables and saved parameters. It can be used for stack reconstruction. In Microsoft compiler code generation implementations, **RBP** is also used as a general-purpose register. An instruction pointer **RIP** is saved in the stack memory region with every function call, then restored on return from the called function. In addition, the x64 platform features another eight general-purpose registers, from **R8** to **R15**.

Instructions and Registers

- Opcode DST, SRC

- Examples:

```
mov    rax, 10h              ; RAX ← 0x10
mov    r13, rdx              ; R13 ← RDX
add    r10, 10h              ; R10 ← R10 + 0x10
imul   edx, ecx             ; EDX ← EDX * ECX
call   rdx                  ; RDX already contains
                            ;    the address of func (&func)
                            ; PUSH RIP; RIP ← &func
sub    rsp, 30h             ; RSP ← RSP-0x30
                            ; make room for local variables
```

This slide shows a few examples of CPU instructions involving operations with registers, such as moving a value and doing arithmetic. The direction of operands is opposite to the AT&T x64 disassembly flavor if you are accustomed to default GDB disassembly on Linux.

Memory and Stack Addressing

Lower addresses   Values

Stack grows

RSP-0x20 →   [RSP-0x20]

RSP-0x18 →   [RSP-0x18]

RSP-0x10 →   [RSP-0x10]

RSP-0x8 →   [RSP-0x8]

RSP →   [RSP]

RSP+0x8 →   [RSP+0x8]

RSP+0x10 →   [RSP+0x10]

RSP+0x18 →   [RSP+0x18]

RSP+0x20 →   [RSP+0x20]

Higher addresses

Before we look at operations with memory, let's look at a graphical representation of memory addressing where for simplicity, I use 64-bit (or 8-byte) memory cells. A thread stack is just any other memory region, so instead of **RSP,** any other register can be used. Please note that the stack grows towards lower addresses, so to access the previously pushed values, you need to use positive offsets from **RSP**.

Memory Cell Sizes

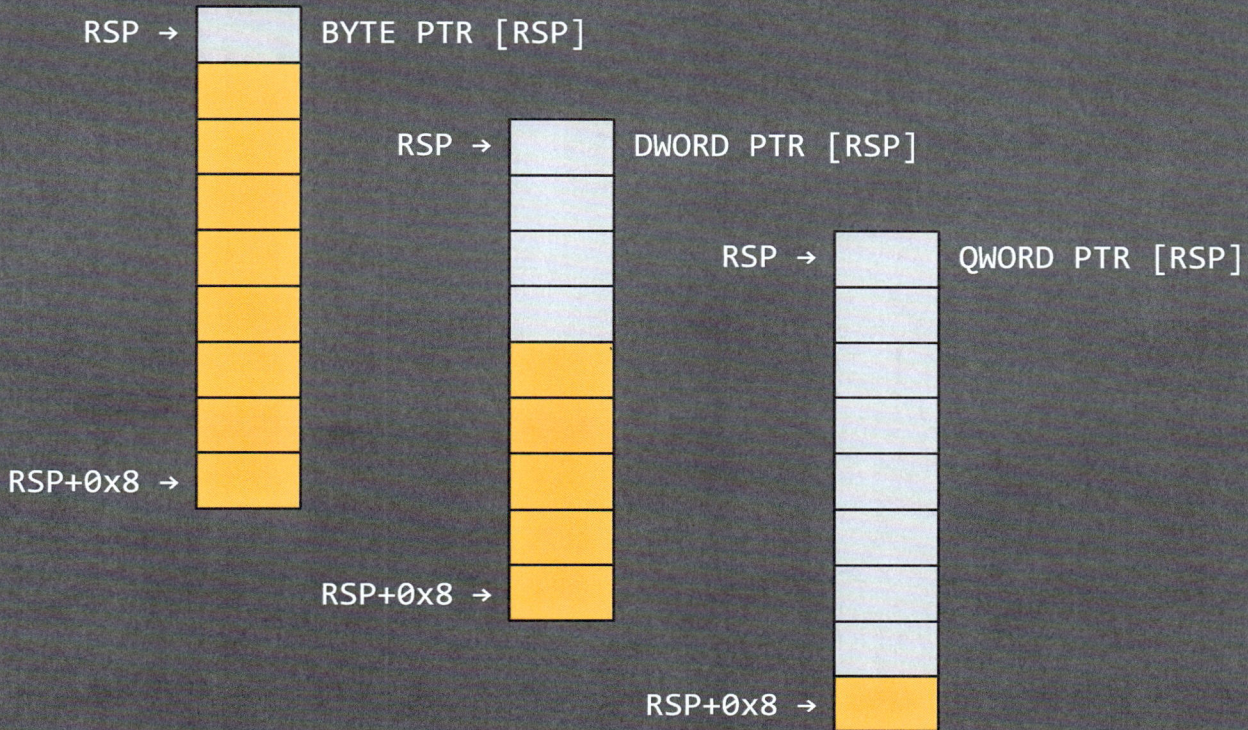

RSP → BYTE PTR [RSP]

RSP+0x8 →

RSP → DWORD PTR [RSP]

RSP+0x8 →

RSP → QWORD PTR [RSP]

RSP+0x8 →

© 2025 Software Diagnostics Services

Here, each memory cell is 8-bit (or one byte). When we have a register pointing to memory, and we want to work with the value at that address, we need to specify the size of memory cells to work with, for example, **BYTE PTR** if we want to work with a byte, **DWORD PTR** if we want to work with 32-bit double words, and **QWORD PTR** if we want to work with 64-bit quad words. There's also **WORD PTR** for 16-bit values. This notation differs from Linux GDB, where we have bytes, half-words, words, and double words.

Memory Load Instructions

- Opcode DST, PTR [SRC+Offset]

- Opcode DST

- Examples:

```
mov    rax, qword ptr [rsp+10h]  ; RAX ←
                                 ; 64-bit value at address RSP+0x10
mov    ecx, dword ptr [20]       ; ECX ←
                                 ; 32-bit value at address 0x20
pop    rdi                       ; RDI ← value at address RSP
                                 ; RSP ← RSP + 8
lea    r8, [rsp+20h]             ; R8 ← address RSP+0x20
```

Constants are encoded in instructions, but if we need arbitrary values, we must get them from memory. Square brackets show memory access relative to an address stored in a register.

Memory Store Instructions

- Opcode PTR [DST+Offset], SRC

- Opcode DST|SRC

- Examples:

```
mov   qword ptr [rbp-20h], rcx ; 64-bit value at address RBP-0x20
                               ;    ← RCX
mov   byte ptr [0], 1          ; 8-bit value at address 0 ← 1
push  rsi                      ; RSP ← RSP - 8
                               ; value at address RSP ← RSI
inc   dword ptr [rcx]          ; 32-bit value at address RCX ←
                               ;    1 + 32-bit value at address RCX
```

Storing is similar to loading.

Flow Instructions

- Opcode DST

- Opcode PTR [DST]

- Examples:

```
jmp    00007ff6`9ef2f008   ; RIP ← 0x7ff69ef2f008
                           ; ("goto" 0x7ff69ef2f008)
jmp    qword ptr [rax+10h] ; RIP ← value at address RAX+0x10
call   00007ff6`9ef21400   ; RSP ← RSP - 8
00007ff6`9ef21057:         ; value at address RSP ← 0x7ff69ef21057
                           ; RIP ← 0x7ff69ef21400
                           ; ("goto" 0x7ff69ef21400)
```

Goto (an unconditional jump) is implemented via the **JMP** instruction. Function calls are implemented via **CALL** instruction. For conditional branches, please look at the official Intel documentation. We don't use these instructions in our exercises.

Function Parameters

- fn func(...);

- Left to right via RCX, RDX, R8, R9, stack

- stack: [RSP+20], [RSP+28], [RSP+30], ...

On the x64 platform, the first 4 Rust function parameters from left to right are moved to CPU registers, and the rest are passed via stack locations.

Struct Function Parameters

- **RCX**

  Implicit struct object memory address (&myStruct)

  ```
  let myStruct: Struct = ...;
  myStruct.func(...);
  ```

- **RDX, R8, R9, stack**

  The rest of the struct function parameters

  ```
  impl Struct {
    fn func(&self, ...);
  }
  ```

When a struct function is called, the first parameter is implicit. It is an object address to help functions differentiate between objects of the same struct type and reference correct fields' memory. The rest of the parameters are passed as usual.

Windows API Parameters

x64: Left to right RCX, RDX, R8, R9, stack

Args to Child are not parameters

```
WinDbg Commands

0:000> kv
 # Child-SP    RetAddr   : Args to Child   : Call Site
...
```

Additional calling convention explanation slides are available from the "Accelerated Windows API for Software Diagnostics" presentation:

https://www.patterndiagnostics.com/Training/Accelerated-Windows-API-Slides.pdf

Practice Exercises

Practice Exercises

Now we come to practice. The goal is to show you important commands and how their output helps recognize abnormal software structure and behavior patterns.

Links

⊙ **Memory Dumps:**

Included in Exercise RW1

⊙ **Exercise Transcripts:**

Included in this book

Process Memory Dumps

Exercises RW1 – RW8

All exercises were modeled on real-life examples using specially constructed applications. All process dumps were saved from the Windows 11 system. We learn more than 35 memory analysis patterns.

Exercise RW1

- **Goal:** Learn how to see dump file type and version, get a stack trace, check its correctness, perform default analysis, list threads and modules, check module version information, dump module data, and check the process environment

- **Patterns:** Manual Dump (Process); Incorrect Stack Trace; Stack Trace; Stack Trace Collection (Unmanaged Space); Main Thread; System Call; Not My Version (Software); Environment Hint; Unknown Component

- \ARWMDA-Dumps\Exercise-RW1.pdf

Exercise RW1

Goal: Learn how to see dump file type and version, get a stack trace, check its correctness, perform default analysis, list threads and modules, check module version information, dump module data, and check the process environment.

Patterns: Manual Dump (Process); Incorrect Stack Trace; Stack Trace; Stack Trace Collection (Unmanaged Space); Main Thread; System Call; Not My Version (Software); Environment Hint; Unknown Component.

0.   Download the archive with memory dumps, symbols, and source code:
https://www.patterndiagnostics.com/Training/ARWMDA/ARWMDA-Dumps.zip
https://www.patterndiagnostics.com/Training/ARWMDA/ARWMDA-Dumps2.zip
https://www.patterndiagnostics.com/Training/ARWMDA/ARWMDA-Dumps3.zip

1.   Install WinDbg (or upgrade existing WinDbg Preview) from https://learn.microsoft.com/en-gb/windows-hardware/drivers/debugger. Launch WinDbg.

2.   Open \ARWMDA-Dumps\Process\normal-release.DMP.

3.   We get the dump file loaded:

```
Microsoft (R) Windows Debugger Version 10.0.27725.1000 AMD64
Copyright (c) Microsoft Corporation. All rights reserved.


Loading Dump File [C:\ARWMDA-Dumps\Process\normal-release.DMP]
User Mini Dump File with Full Memory: Only application data is available


************* Path validation summary **************
Response                        Time (ms)      Location
Deferred                                       srv*
Symbol search path is: srv*
Executable search path is:
Windows 10 Version 22000 UP Free x64
Product: WinNt, suite: SingleUserTS
Edition build lab: 22000.1.amd64fre.co_release.210604-1628
Debug session time: Sun Oct 13 18:22:13.000 2024 (UTC + 1:00)
System Uptime: 0 days 0:07:15.310
Process Uptime: 0 days 0:01:25.000
.......
For analysis of this file, run !analyze -v
ntdll!NtDeviceIoControlFile+0x14:
00007fff`ea0a4164 ret
```

4.   Open a log file to save all future output using the **.logopen** command:

```
0:000> .logopen C:\ARWMDA-Dumps\RW1.log
Opened log file 'C:\ARWMDA-Dumps\RW1.log'
```

5.　　　Type **k** command to verify the correctness of the stack trace:

```
0:000> k
 # Child-SP          RetAddr           Call Site
00 00000032`2394cec8 00007fff`e7914da5 ntdll!NtDeviceIoControlFile+0x14
01 00000032`2394ced0 00007fff`e7994c5d KERNELBASE!ConsoleCallServerGeneric+0xe9
02 00000032`2394d030 00007fff`e7994aba KERNELBASE!ReadConsoleInternal+0x18d
03 00000032`2394d180 00007ff7`fe66dc8b KERNELBASE!ReadConsoleW+0x1a
04 00000032`2394d1c0 00007ff7`fe66da5f normal+0xdc8b
05 00000032`2394d270 00007ff7`fe668677 normal+0xda5f
06 00000032`2394f310 00007ff7`fe666d25 normal+0x8677
07 00000032`2394f3b0 00007ff7`fe6635b1 normal+0x6d25
08 00000032`2394f450 00007ff7`fe6620a2 normal+0x35b1
09 00000032`2394f4e0 00007ff7`fe6610e6 normal+0x20a2
0a 00000032`2394f600 00007ff7`fe6610cc normal+0x10e6
0b 00000032`2394f630 00007ff7`fe6652b9 normal+0x10cc
0c 00000032`2394f660 00007ff7`fe66233c normal+0x52b9
0d 00000032`2394f720 00007ff7`fe67b56c normal+0x233c
0e 00000032`2394f760 00007fff`e89d53e0 normal+0x1b56c
0f 00000032`2394f7a0 00007fff`ea00485b kernel32!BaseThreadInitThunk+0x10
10 00000032`2394f7d0 00000000`00000000 ntdll!RtlUserThreadStart+0x2b
```

6.　　　The required system modules symbol files are also available – downloaded automatically from the Microsoft symbol server:

```
0:000> lm
start             end               module name
00007ff7`fe660000 00007ff7`fe68d000 normal    C (no symbols)
00007fff`d7e40000 00007fff`d7e5b000 VCRUNTIME140   (deferred)
00007fff`e4800000 00007fff`e4891000 apphelp    (deferred)
00007fff`e78e0000 00007fff`e7c65000 KERNELBASE   (pdb symbols)    C:\ProgramData\Dbg\sym\kernelbase.pdb\94E7C4F93A4BDBF6F1873AD3B38C08D01\kernelbase.pdb
00007fff`e7d40000 00007fff`e7e51000 ucrtbase   (deferred)
00007fff`e89c0000 00007fff`e8a7d000 kernel32   (pdb symbols)    C:\ProgramData\Dbg\sym\kernel32.pdb\6A245216BEF1B5AC632AF386769C84C61\kernel32.pdb
00007fff`ea000000 00007fff`ea20a000 ntdll     (pdb symbols)    C:\ProgramData\Dbg\sym\ntdll.pdb\50746DC2F3CCE545AC017E855F45C3031\ntdll.pdb
```

Note: To simulate the absence of system symbol files, we can delete the highlighted files, turn off the internet connection, and reload symbol files:

```
0:000> .reload
.......

************* Symbol Loading Error Summary **************
Module name                Error
ntdll                      The system cannot find the file specified
KERNELBASE                 The system cannot find the file specified

You can troubleshoot most symbol related issues by turning on symbol loading diagnostics (!sym
noisy) and repeating the command that caused symbols to be loaded.
You should also verify that your symbol search path (.sympath) is correct.

0:000> k
00 00000032`2394cec8 00007fff`e7914da5 ntdll!NtDeviceIoControlFile+0x14
01 00000032`2394ced0 00007fff`e7994c5d KERNELBASE!WriteConsoleW+0x1d5
02 00000032`2394d030 00007fff`e7994aba KERNELBASE!ReadConsoleW+0x1bd
03 00000032`2394d180 00007ff7`fe66dc8b KERNELBASE!ReadConsoleW+0x1a
04 00000032`2394d1c0 00007ff7`fe66da5f normal+0xdc8b
05 00000032`2394d270 00007ff7`fe668677 normal+0xda5f
06 00000032`2394f310 00007ff7`fe666d25 normal+0x8677
07 00000032`2394f3b0 00007ff7`fe6635b1 normal+0x6d25
```

```
08  00000032`2394f450 00007ff7`fe6620a2   normal+0x35b1
09  00000032`2394f4e0 00007ff7`fe6610e6   normal+0x20a2
0a  00000032`2394f600 00007ff7`fe6610cc   normal+0x10e6
0b  00000032`2394f630 00007ff7`fe6652b9   normal+0x10cc
0c  00000032`2394f660 00007ff7`fe66233c   normal+0x52b9
0d  00000032`2394f720 00007ff7`fe67b56c   normal+0x233c
0e  00000032`2394f760 00007fff`e89d53e0   normal+0x1b56c
0f  00000032`2394f7a0 00007fff`ea00485b   kernel32!BaseThreadInitThunk+0x10
10  00000032`2394f7d0 00000000`00000000   ntdll!RtlUserThreadStart+0x2b

0:000> lm
start             end               module name
00007ff7`fe660000 00007ff7`fe68d000   normal    C (no symbols)
00007fff`d7e40000 00007fff`d7e5b000   VCRUNTIME140   (deferred)
00007fff`e4800000 00007fff`e4891000   apphelp    (deferred)
00007fff`e78e0000 00007fff`e7c65000   KERNELBASE   (export symbols)     KERNELBASE.dll
00007fff`e7d40000 00007fff`e7e51000   ucrtbase   (deferred)
00007fff`e89c0000 00007fff`e8a7d000   kernel32   (export symbols)     kernel32.dll
00007fff`ea000000 00007fff`ea20a000   ntdll     (export symbols)     ntdll.dll
```

Note: Without symbol files, WinDbg uses approximate export function addresses.

7.   After enabling the internet connection again, we can restore symbol file mappings (WinDbg also shows them as being downloaded in the bottom status bar):

```
0:000> .reload
.......

0:000> k
 # Child-SP          RetAddr           Call Site
00  00000032`2394cec8 00007fff`e7914da5   ntdll!NtDeviceIoControlFile+0x14
01  00000032`2394ced0 00007fff`e7994c5d   KERNELBASE!ConsoleCallServerGeneric+0xe9
02  00000032`2394d030 00007fff`e7994aba   KERNELBASE!ReadConsoleInternal+0x18d
03  00000032`2394d180 00007ff7`fe66dc8b   KERNELBASE!ReadConsoleW+0x1a
04  00000032`2394d1c0 00007ff7`fe66da5f   normal+0xdc8b
05  00000032`2394d270 00007ff7`fe668677   normal+0xda5f
06  00000032`2394f310 00007ff7`fe666d25   normal+0x8677
07  00000032`2394f3b0 00007ff7`fe6635b1   normal+0x6d25
08  00000032`2394f450 00007ff7`fe6620a2   normal+0x35b1
09  00000032`2394f4e0 00007ff7`fe6610e6   normal+0x20a2
0a  00000032`2394f600 00007ff7`fe6610cc   normal+0x10e6
0b  00000032`2394f630 00007ff7`fe6652b9   normal+0x10cc
0c  00000032`2394f660 00007ff7`fe66233c   normal+0x52b9
0d  00000032`2394f720 00007ff7`fe67b56c   normal+0x233c
0e  00000032`2394f760 00007fff`e89d53e0   normal+0x1b56c
0f  00000032`2394f7a0 00007fff`ea00485b   kernel32!BaseThreadInitThunk+0x10
10  00000032`2394f7d0 00000000`00000000   ntdll!RtlUserThreadStart+0x2b
```

8.   Type the **version** command to get the OS version, system and process uptimes, the dump file timestamp, and its type:

```
0:000> version
Windows 10 Version 22000 UP Free x64
Product: WinNt, suite: SingleUserTS
Edition build lab: 22000.1.amd64fre.co_release.210604-1628
Debug session time: Sun Oct 13 18:22:13.000 2024 (UTC + 1:00)
System Uptime: 0 days 0:07:15.310
```

```
Process Uptime: 0 days 0:01:25.000
  Kernel time: 0 days 0:00:00.000
  User time: 0 days 0:00:00.000
Full memory user mini dump: C:\ARWMDA-Dumps\Process\normal-release.DMP

Microsoft (R) Windows Debugger Version 10.0.27725.1000 AMD64
Copyright (c) Microsoft Corporation. All rights reserved.

command line: '"C:\Program Files\WindowsApps\Microsoft.WinDbg_1.2410.11001.0_x64__8wekyb3d8bbwe\amd64\EngHost.exe"
npipe:pipe=DbgX_c51204472d9b4803a9514664d3a13fe8,password=9455d47b9137 "C:\Program
Files\WindowsApps\Microsoft.WinDbg_1.2410.11001.0_x64__8wekyb3d8bbwe\amd64" "C:\ProgramData\Dbg"' Debugger Process 0x33E4
dbgeng:  image 10.0.27725.1000,
         [path: C:\Program Files\WindowsApps\Microsoft.WinDbg_1.2410.11001.0_x64__8wekyb3d8bbwe\amd64\dbgeng.dll]
dbghelp: image 10.0.27725.1000,
         [path: C:\Program Files\WindowsApps\Microsoft.WinDbg_1.2410.11001.0_x64__8wekyb3d8bbwe\amd64\dbghelp.dll]
         DIA version: 0
Extension DLL search Path:
[...]
Extension DLL chain:
    DbgEngCoreDMExt: image 10.0.27725.1000, API 0.0.0,
         [path: C:\Program Files\WindowsApps\Microsoft.WinDbg_1.2410.11001.0_x64__8wekyb3d8bbwe\amd64\winext\DbgEngCoreDMExt.dll]
    MachOBinComposition: image 10.0.27725.1000, API 0.0.0,
         [path: C:\Program Files\WindowsApps\Microsoft.WinDbg_1.2410.11001.0_x64__8wekyb3d8bbwe\amd64\winext\MachOBinComposition.dll]
    ELFBinComposition: image 10.0.27725.1000, API 0.0.0,
         [path: C:\Program Files\WindowsApps\Microsoft.WinDbg_1.2410.11001.0_x64__8wekyb3d8bbwe\amd64\winext\ELFBinComposition.dll]
    dbghelp: image 10.0.27725.1000, API 10.0.6,
         [path: C:\Program Files\WindowsApps\Microsoft.WinDbg_1.2410.11001.0_x64__8wekyb3d8bbwe\amd64\dbghelp.dll]
    exts: image 10.0.27725.1000, API 1.0.0,
         [path: C:\Program Files\WindowsApps\Microsoft.WinDbg_1.2410.11001.0_x64__8wekyb3d8bbwe\amd64\WINXP\exts.dll]
    uext: image 10.0.27725.1000, API 1.0.0,
         [path: C:\Program Files\WindowsApps\Microsoft.WinDbg_1.2410.11001.0_x64__8wekyb3d8bbwe\amd64\winext\uext.dll]
    ntsdexts: image 10.0.27725.1000, API 1.0.0,
         [path: C:\Program Files\WindowsApps\Microsoft.WinDbg_1.2410.11001.0_x64__8wekyb3d8bbwe\amd64\WINXP\ntsdexts.dll]
```

Note: Debug session time is when the dump was generated. Although the dump is called a "mini dump," it is a full memory user dump with all process memory included.

9.   Type the default analysis command **!analyze -v**:

Note: This command may take some time initially as symbols may be downloaded from the symbol server:

```
0:000> !analyze -v
*******************************************************************************
*                                                                             *
*                        Exception Analysis                                   *
*                                                                             *
*******************************************************************************

KEY_VALUES_STRING: 1

    Key  : Analysis.CPU.mSec
    Value: 343

    Key  : Analysis.Elapsed.mSec
    Value: 610

    Key  : Analysis.IO.Other.Mb
    Value: 7

    Key  : Analysis.IO.Read.Mb
    Value: 2

    Key  : Analysis.IO.Write.Mb
    Value: 30

    Key  : Analysis.Init.CPU.mSec
    Value: 1062

    Key  : Analysis.Init.Elapsed.mSec
    Value: 3604428

    Key  : Analysis.Memory.CommitPeak.Mb
    Value: 224

    Key  : Analysis.Version.DbgEng
    Value: 10.0.27725.1000

    Key  : Analysis.Version.Description
    Value: 10.2408.27.01 amd64fre

    Key  : Analysis.Version.Ext
    Value: 1.2408.27.1

    Key  : Failure.Bucket
```

```
        Value: BREAKPOINT_80000003_normal.exe!Unknown

        Key  : Failure.Hash
        Value: {ff10f8cc-0ad0-4798-64ca-b7e4bab5b164}

        Key  : Timeline.OS.Boot.DeltaSec
        Value: 435

        Key  : Timeline.Process.Start.DeltaSec
        Value: 85

        Key  : WER.OS.Branch
        Value: co_release

        Key  : WER.OS.Version
        Value: 10.0.22000.1


FILE_IN_CAB:  normal-release.DMP

NTGLOBALFLAG:  0

APPLICATION_VERIFIER_FLAGS:  0

EXCEPTION_RECORD:  (.exr -1)
ExceptionAddress: 0000000000000000
   ExceptionCode: 80000003 (Break instruction exception)
  ExceptionFlags: 00000000
NumberParameters: 0

FAULTING_THREAD:  000026e4

PROCESS_NAME:  normal.exe

ERROR_CODE: (NTSTATUS) 0x80000003 - {EXCEPTION}  Breakpoint  A breakpoint has been reached.

EXCEPTION_CODE_STR:  80000003

STACK_TEXT:
00000032`2394cec8 00007fff`e7914da5     : 00000032`2394cff0 00007fff`e7914c3a 00000000`00000000 00007ff7`fe67f870 : ntdll!NtDeviceIoControlFile+0x14
00000032`2394ced0 00007fff`e7994c5d     : 00000000`00000000 005f0064`006f006d 0020003a`00610061`0063006e`00750066 : KERNELBASE!ConsoleCallServerGeneric+0xe9
00000032`2394d030 00007fff`e7994aba     : 00000000`00000000 00000000`00000000 00000058`00000001`00000001 : KERNELBASE!ReadConsoleInternal+0x18d
00000032`2394d180 00007ff7`fe66dc8b     : 00000000`00000000 00000000`00000000 000001f6`536e0000 00000000`00000002 : KERNELBASE!ReadConsoleW+0x1a
00000032`2394d1c0 00007ff7`fe66da5f     : 00000032`2394d2b0 000001f6`00000030 00007ff7`fe689188 000001f6`536f3380 : normal+0xdc8b
00000032`2394d270 00007ff7`fe668677     : 00000032`2394f380 00007ff7`fe67cf35 00000032`00000000 00000032`2394f348 : normal+0xda5f
00000032`2394f310 00007ff7`fe666d25     : 00000000`00000005 00000000`00000005 00000032`2394f410 00007ff7`fe67c55f : normal+0x8677
00000032`2394f3b0 00007ff7`fe6635b1     : 00000000`00000000 00000000`00000000 00000032`2394f560 00007ff7`fe6634e8 : normal+0x6d25
00000032`2394f450 00007ff7`fe6620a2     : 000001f6`536e2450 00007ff7`fe66ed10 00000032`2394f570 00007ff7`fe66ee10 : normal+0x35b1
00000032`2394f4e0 00007ff7`fe6610e6     : 00000000`00150014 00007ff7`fe680000 ffffffff`ffffffe 000001f6`536e5b30 : normal+0x20a2
00000032`2394f600 00007ff7`fe6610cc     : 01000032`2394f640 01ffffff`ffffffe ffffffff`ffffffe 00007ff7`fe67e4e0 : normal+0x10e6
00000032`2394f630 00007ff7`fe6652b9     : 000001f6`536f1bd0 00007ff7`fe67e4e0 00000032`2394f750 00007fff`ea006800 : normal+0x10cc
00000032`2394f660 00007ff7`fe66233c     : 00007ff7`fe67e328 00007ff7`fe67b801 00000000`00000007 00000000`00000000 : normal+0x52b9
00000032`2394f720 00007ff7`fe67b56c     : 00000000`00000000 00007ff7`fe67b5e5 00000000`00000000 00000000`00000000 : normal+0x233c
00000032`2394f760 00007fff`e89d53e0     : 00000000`00000000 00000000`00000000 00000000`00000000 00000000`00000000 : normal+0x1b56c
00000032`2394f7a0 00007fff`ea00485b     : 00000000`00000000 00000000`00000000 00000000`00000000 00000000`00000000 : kernel32!BaseThreadInitThunk+0x10
00000032`2394f7d0 00000000`00000000     : 00000000`00000000 00000000`00000000 00000000`00000000 00000000`00000000 : ntdll!RtlUserThreadStart+0x2b


STACK_COMMAND:  ~0s; .ecxr ; kb

SYMBOL_NAME:  normal+dc8b

MODULE_NAME: normal

IMAGE_NAME:  normal.exe

FAILURE_BUCKET_ID:  BREAKPOINT_80000003_normal.exe!Unknown

OS_VERSION:  10.0.22000.1

BUILDLAB_STR:  co_release

OSPLATFORM_TYPE:  x64

OSNAME:  Windows 10

FAILURE_ID_HASH:  {ff10f8cc-0ad0-4798-64ca-b7e4bab5b164}

Followup:     MachineOwner
---------
```

Note: "Break instruction exception" can be the sign of a **Manual Dump** pattern, but often WinDbg cannot figure out an exception that may be on another thread or hidden. **STACK_COMMAND** shows the sequence commands that WinDbg executed to get **STACK_TEXT**.

10.   Now we check how many threads there are by using the ~ command:

```
0:000> ~
.  0  Id: 26e0.26e4 Suspend: 0 Teb: 00000032`23ba7000 Unfrozen "main"
```

```
1  Id: 26e0.270c Suspend: 0 Teb: 00000032`23bab000 Unfrozen
2  Id: 26e0.2710 Suspend: 0 Teb: 00000032`23bad000 Unfrozen
3  Id: 26e0.2714 Suspend: 0 Teb: 00000032`23baf000 Unfrozen
4  Id: 26e0.2718 Suspend: 0 Teb: 00000032`23bb1000 Unfrozen
5  Id: 26e0.271c Suspend: 0 Teb: 00000032`23bb3000 Unfrozen
```

Note: 26e0 is Process ID (PID), and 26e4 is Thread ID (TID). 26e0.26e4 is called CID (Client ID). Threads may also have names.

11.   Now we dump a stack trace using the **kc** command (only modules and symbols):

```
0:000> kc
 # Call Site
00 ntdll!NtDeviceIoControlFile
01 KERNELBASE!ConsoleCallServerGeneric
02 KERNELBASE!ReadConsoleInternal
03 KERNELBASE!ReadConsoleW
04 normal
05 normal
06 normal
07 normal
08 normal
09 normal
0a normal
0b normal
0c normal
0d normal
0e normal
0f kernel32!BaseThreadInitThunk
10 ntdll!RtlUserThreadStart
```

12.   We can also dump the stack trace of any valid thread number or TID:

```
0:000> ~1k
 # Child-SP          RetAddr               Call Site
00 00000032`23eff898 00007fff`e79310ee     ntdll!NtWaitForSingleObject+0x14
01 00000032`23eff8a0 00007ff7`fe6658dd     KERNELBASE!WaitForSingleObjectEx+0x8e
02 00000032`23eff940 00007ff7`fe66110c     normal+0x58dd
03 00000032`23eff9b0 00007ff7`fe662bcb     normal+0x110c
04 00000032`23eff9e0 00007ff7`fe66df8d     normal+0x2bcb
05 00000032`23effa80 00007fff`e89d53e0     normal+0xdf8d
06 00000032`23effae0 00007fff`ea00485b     kernel32!BaseThreadInitThunk+0x10
07 00000032`23effb10 00000000`00000000     ntdll!RtlUserThreadStart+0x2b
```

```
0:000> ~~[2710]k
 # Child-SP          RetAddr               Call Site
00 00000032`240ffb88 00007fff`e79310ee     ntdll!NtWaitForSingleObject+0x14
01 00000032`240ffb90 00007ff7`fe6658dd     KERNELBASE!WaitForSingleObjectEx+0x8e
02 00000032`240ffc30 00007ff7`fe66110c     normal+0x58dd
03 00000032`240ffca0 00007ff7`fe662bcb     normal+0x110c
04 00000032`240ffcd0 00007ff7`fe66df8d     normal+0x2bcb
05 00000032`240ffd70 00007fff`e89d53e0     normal+0xdf8d
06 00000032`240ffdd0 00007fff`ea00485b     kernel32!BaseThreadInitThunk+0x10
07 00000032`240ffe00 00000000`00000000     ntdll!RtlUserThreadStart+0x2b
```

13.   We can dump stack traces of all threads:

```
0:000> ~*k

.  0  Id: 26e0.26e4 Suspend: 0 Teb: 00000032`23ba7000 Unfrozen "main"
 # Child-SP          RetAddr               Call Site
00 00000032`2394cec8 00007fff`e7914da5     ntdll!NtDeviceIoControlFile+0x14
01 00000032`2394ced0 00007fff`e7994c5d     KERNELBASE!ConsoleCallServerGeneric+0xe9
02 00000032`2394d030 00007fff`e7994aba     KERNELBASE!ReadConsoleInternal+0x18d
03 00000032`2394d180 00007ff7`fe66dc8b     KERNELBASE!ReadConsoleW+0x1a
04 00000032`2394d1c0 00007ff7`fe66da5f     normal+0xdc8b
05 00000032`2394d270 00007ff7`fe668677     normal+0xda5f
06 00000032`2394f310 00007ff7`fe666d25     normal+0x8677
07 00000032`2394f3b0 00007ff7`fe6635b1     normal+0x6d25
08 00000032`2394f450 00007ff7`fe6620a2     normal+0x35b1
09 00000032`2394f4e0 00007ff7`fe6610e6     normal+0x20a2
0a 00000032`2394f600 00007ff7`fe6610cc     normal+0x10e6
0b 00000032`2394f630 00007ff7`fe6652b9     normal+0x10cc
0c 00000032`2394f660 00007ff7`fe66233c     normal+0x52b9
0d 00000032`2394f720 00007ff7`fe67b56c     normal+0x233c
0e 00000032`2394f760 00007fff`e89d53e0     normal+0x1b56c
0f 00000032`2394f7a0 00007fff`ea00485b     kernel32!BaseThreadInitThunk+0x10
10 00000032`2394f7d0 00000000`00000000     ntdll!RtlUserThreadStart+0x2b

   1  Id: 26e0.270c Suspend: 0 Teb: 00000032`23bab000 Unfrozen
 # Child-SP          RetAddr               Call Site
00 00000032`23eff898 00007fff`e79310ee     ntdll!NtWaitForSingleObject+0x14
01 00000032`23eff8a0 00007ff7`fe6658dd     KERNELBASE!WaitForSingleObjectEx+0x8e
02 00000032`23eff940 00007ff7`fe66110c     normal+0x58dd
03 00000032`23eff9b0 00007ff7`fe662bcb     normal+0x110c
04 00000032`23eff9e0 00007ff7`fe66df8d     normal+0x2bcb
05 00000032`23effa80 00007fff`e89d53e0     normal+0xdf8d
06 00000032`23effae0 00007fff`ea00485b     kernel32!BaseThreadInitThunk+0x10
07 00000032`23effb10 00000000`00000000     ntdll!RtlUserThreadStart+0x2b

   2  Id: 26e0.2710 Suspend: 0 Teb: 00000032`23bad000 Unfrozen
 # Child-SP          RetAddr               Call Site
00 00000032`240ffb88 00007fff`e79310ee     ntdll!NtWaitForSingleObject+0x14
01 00000032`240ffb90 00007ff7`fe6658dd     KERNELBASE!WaitForSingleObjectEx+0x8e
02 00000032`240ffc30 00007ff7`fe66110c     normal+0x58dd
03 00000032`240ffca0 00007ff7`fe662bcb     normal+0x110c
04 00000032`240ffcd0 00007ff7`fe66df8d     normal+0x2bcb
05 00000032`240ffd70 00007fff`e89d53e0     normal+0xdf8d
06 00000032`240ffdd0 00007fff`ea00485b     kernel32!BaseThreadInitThunk+0x10
07 00000032`240ffe00 00000000`00000000     ntdll!RtlUserThreadStart+0x2b

   3  Id: 26e0.2714 Suspend: 0 Teb: 00000032`23baf000 Unfrozen
 # Child-SP          RetAddr               Call Site
00 00000032`242ff7e8 00007fff`e79310ee     ntdll!NtWaitForSingleObject+0x14
01 00000032`242ff7f0 00007ff7`fe6658dd     KERNELBASE!WaitForSingleObjectEx+0x8e
02 00000032`242ff890 00007ff7`fe66110c     normal+0x58dd
03 00000032`242ff900 00007ff7`fe662bcb     normal+0x110c
04 00000032`242ff930 00007ff7`fe66df8d     normal+0x2bcb
05 00000032`242ff9d0 00007fff`e89d53e0     normal+0xdf8d
06 00000032`242ffa30 00007fff`ea00485b     kernel32!BaseThreadInitThunk+0x10
07 00000032`242ffa60 00000000`00000000     ntdll!RtlUserThreadStart+0x2b

   4  Id: 26e0.2718 Suspend: 0 Teb: 00000032`23bb1000 Unfrozen
```

```
 # Child-SP          RetAddr              Call Site
00 00000032`244ffc08 00007fff`e79310ee   ntdll!NtWaitForSingleObject+0x14
01 00000032`244ffc10 00007ff7`fe6658dd   KERNELBASE!WaitForSingleObjectEx+0x8e
02 00000032`244ffcb0 00007ff7`fe66110c   normal+0x58dd
03 00000032`244ffd20 00007ff7`fe662bcb   normal+0x110c
04 00000032`244ffd50 00007ff7`fe66df8d   normal+0x2bcb
05 00000032`244ffdf0 00007fff`e89d53e0   normal+0xdf8d
06 00000032`244ffe50 00007fff`ea00485b   kernel32!BaseThreadInitThunk+0x10
07 00000032`244ffe80 00000000`00000000   ntdll!RtlUserThreadStart+0x2b

   5  Id: 26e0.271c Suspend: 0 Teb: 00000032`23bb3000 Unfrozen
 # Child-SP          RetAddr              Call Site
00 00000032`246ff568 00007fff`e79310ee   ntdll!NtWaitForSingleObject+0x14
01 00000032`246ff570 00007ff7`fe6658dd   KERNELBASE!WaitForSingleObjectEx+0x8e
02 00000032`246ff610 00007ff7`fe66110c   normal+0x58dd
03 00000032`246ff680 00007ff7`fe662bcb   normal+0x110c
04 00000032`246ff6b0 00007ff7`fe66df8d   normal+0x2bcb
05 00000032`246ff750 00007fff`e89d53e0   normal+0xdf8d
06 00000032`246ff7b0 00007fff`ea00485b   kernel32!BaseThreadInitThunk+0x10
07 00000032`246ff7e0 00000000`00000000   ntdll!RtlUserThreadStart+0x2b
```

14.   We can check how much time each thread had spent in kernel and user modes and also how much time had elapsed since the thread was created by using the **!runaway f** command:

```
0:001> !runaway f
User Mode Time
  Thread       Time
    5:271c     0 days 0:00:00.000
    4:2718     0 days 0:00:00.000
    3:2714     0 days 0:00:00.000
    2:2710     0 days 0:00:00.000
    1:270c     0 days 0:00:00.000
    0:26e4     0 days 0:00:00.000
Kernel Mode Time
  Thread       Time
    0:26e4     0 days 0:00:00.015
    5:271c     0 days 0:00:00.000
    4:2718     0 days 0:00:00.000
    3:2714     0 days 0:00:00.000
    2:2710     0 days 0:00:00.000
    1:270c     0 days 0:00:00.000
Elapsed Time
  Thread       Time
    0:26e4     0 days 0:01:24.002
    1:270c     0 days 0:01:23.607
    2:2710     0 days 0:01:23.607
    3:2714     0 days 0:01:23.607
    4:2718     0 days 0:01:23.607
    5:271c     0 days 0:01:23.607
```

15.   Now we dump the stack trace of the current thread again using the **k** command to explore return addresses:

```
0:000> k
 # Child-SP          RetAddr              Call Site
00 00000032`2394cec8 00007fff`e7914da5   ntdll!NtDeviceIoControlFile+0x14
01 00000032`2394ced0 00007fff`e7994c5d   KERNELBASE!ConsoleCallServerGeneric+0xe9
02 00000032`2394d030 00007fff`e7994aba   KERNELBASE! +0x18d
03 00000032`2394d180 00007ff7`fe66dc8b   KERNELBASE!ReadConsoleW+0x1a
04 00000032`2394d1c0 00007ff7`fe66da5f   normal+0xdc8b
```

```
05 00000032`2394d270 00007ff7`fe668677     normal+0xda5f
06 00000032`2394f310 00007ff7`fe666d25     normal+0x8677
07 00000032`2394f3b0 00007ff7`fe6635b1     normal+0x6d25
08 00000032`2394f450 00007ff7`fe6620a2     normal+0x35b1
09 00000032`2394f4e0 00007ff7`fe6610e6     normal+0x20a2
0a 00000032`2394f600 00007ff7`fe6610cc     normal+0x10e6
0b 00000032`2394f630 00007ff7`fe6652b9     normal+0x10cc
0c 00000032`2394f660 00007ff7`fe66233c     normal+0x52b9
0d 00000032`2394f720 00007ff7`fe67b56c     normal+0x233c
0e 00000032`2394f760 00007fff`e89d53e0     normal+0x1b56c
0f 00000032`2394f7a0 00007fff`ea00485b     kernel32!BaseThreadInitThunk+0x10
10 00000032`2394f7d0 00000000`00000000     ntdll!RtlUserThreadStart+0x2b
```

Hint: How to check that the stack trace is correct. Use the **ub** command (**u**nassemble **b**ackward) to check if there is a *call* instruction. We check that the *ConsoleCallServerGeneric* function was called from the *ReadConsoleInternal* function:

```
0:000> k
 # Child-SP          RetAddr               Call Site
00 00000032`2394cec8 00007fff`e7914da5     ntdll!NtDeviceIoControlFile+0x14
01 00000032`2394ced0 00007fff`e7994c5d     KERNELBASE!ConsoleCallServerGeneric+0xe9
02 00000032`2394d030 00007fff`e7994aba     KERNELBASE!ReadConsoleInternal+0x18d
03 00000032`2394d180 00007ff7`fe66dc8b     KERNELBASE!ReadConsoleW+0x1a
04 00000032`2394d1c0 00007ff7`fe66da5f     normal+0xdc8b
05 00000032`2394d270 00007ff7`fe668677     normal+0xda5f
06 00000032`2394f310 00007ff7`fe666d25     normal+0x8677
07 00000032`2394f3b0 00007ff7`fe6635b1     normal+0x6d25
08 00000032`2394f450 00007ff7`fe6620a2     normal+0x35b1
09 00000032`2394f4e0 00007ff7`fe6610e6     normal+0x20a2
0a 00000032`2394f600 00007ff7`fe6610cc     normal+0x10e6
0b 00000032`2394f630 00007ff7`fe6652b9     normal+0x10cc
0c 00000032`2394f660 00007ff7`fe66233c     normal+0x52b9
0d 00000032`2394f720 00007ff7`fe67b56c     normal+0x233c
0e 00000032`2394f760 00007fff`e89d53e0     normal+0x1b56c
0f 00000032`2394f7a0 00007fff`ea00485b     kernel32!BaseThreadInitThunk+0x10
10 00000032`2394f7d0 00000000`00000000     ntdll!RtlUserThreadStart+0x2b
```

```
0:000> ub 00007fff`e7994c5d
KERNELBASE!ReadConsoleInternal+0x163:
00007fff`e7994c33 lea     rax,[rsp+80h]
00007fff`e7994c3b mov     qword ptr [rsp+28h],rax
00007fff`e7994c40 mov     dword ptr [rsp+20h],14h
00007fff`e7994c48 mov     r9d,1000005h
00007fff`e7994c4e lea     r8,[rsp+50h]
00007fff`e7994c53 xor     edx,edx
00007fff`e7994c55 mov     rcx,r13
00007fff`e7994c58 call    KERNELBASE!ConsoleCallServerGeneric (00007fff`e7914cbc)
```

Then we check that the *NtDeviceIoControlFile* function was called from the *ConsoleCallServerGeneric* function:

```
0:000> k
 # Child-SP          RetAddr               Call Site
00 00000032`2394cec8 00007fff`e7914da5     ntdll!NtDeviceIoControlFile+0x14
01 00000032`2394ced0 00007fff`e7994c5d     KERNELBASE!ConsoleCallServerGeneric+0xe9
02 00000032`2394d030 00007fff`e7994aba     KERNELBASE!ReadConsoleInternal+0x18d
03 00000032`2394d180 00007ff7`fe66dc8b     KERNELBASE!ReadConsoleW+0x1a
04 00000032`2394d1c0 00007ff7`fe66da5f     normal+0xdc8b
```

```
05 00000032`2394d270 00007ff7`fe668677     normal+0xda5f
06 00000032`2394f310 00007ff7`fe666d25     normal+0x8677
07 00000032`2394f3b0 00007ff7`fe6635b1     normal+0x6d25
08 00000032`2394f450 00007ff7`fe6620a2     normal+0x35b1
09 00000032`2394f4e0 00007ff7`fe6610e6     normal+0x20a2
0a 00000032`2394f600 00007ff7`fe6610cc     normal+0x10e6
0b 00000032`2394f630 00007ff7`fe6652b9     normal+0x10cc
0c 00000032`2394f660 00007ff7`fe66233c     normal+0x52b9
0d 00000032`2394f720 00007ff7`fe67b56c     normal+0x233c
0e 00000032`2394f760 00007fff`e89d53e0     normal+0x1b56c
0f 00000032`2394f7a0 00007fff`ea00485b     kernel32!BaseThreadInitThunk+0x10
10 00000032`2394f7d0 00000000`00000000     ntdll!RtlUserThreadStart+0x2b
```

```
0:000> ub 00007fff`e7914da5
KERNELBASE!ConsoleCallServerGeneric+0xc1:
00007fff`e7914d7d xor     edx,edx
00007fff`e7914d7f lea     rax,[rsp+60h]
00007fff`e7914d84 mov     rcx,rdi
00007fff`e7914d87 mov     qword ptr [rsp+30h],rax
00007fff`e7914d8c lea     rax,[rsp+50h]
00007fff`e7914d91 mov     dword ptr [rsp+28h],500016h
00007fff`e7914d99 mov     qword ptr [rsp+20h],rax
00007fff`e7914d9e call    qword ptr [KERNELBASE!_imp_NtDeviceIoControlFile (00007fff`e7b2baf8)]
```

```
0:000> dps 00007fff`e7b2baf8 L1
00007fff`e7b2baf8  00007fff`ea0a4150 ntdll!NtDeviceIoControlFile
```

Note: Remember the functions call each other from bottom to top. The topmost function from the stack trace is the last one that was called. **ExceptionAddress** may point to the last one. We will come to this in the real exception process dumps later.

16.   Now we check the list of loaded modules again but with timestamp information:

```
0:000> lmt
start             end               module name
00007ff7`fe660000 00007ff7`fe68d000   normal      Sun Oct 13 16:19:53 2024 (670BE519)
00007fff`d7e40000 00007fff`d7e5b000   VCRUNTIME140  006CB796 (This is a reproducible build file hash, not a timestamp)
00007fff`e4800000 00007fff`e4891000   apphelp     F8DFA076 (This is a reproducible build file hash, not a timestamp)
00007fff`e78e0000 00007fff`e7c65000   KERNELBASE  3739E3D8 (This is a reproducible build file hash, not a timestamp)
00007fff`e7d40000 00007fff`e7e51000   ucrtbase    00E78CE9 (This is a reproducible build file hash, not a timestamp)
00007fff`e89c0000 00007fff`e8a7d000   kernel32    1B24EDA6 (This is a reproducible build file hash, not a timestamp)
00007fff`ea000000 00007fff`ea20a000   ntdll       77DA5A19 (This is a reproducible build file hash, not a timestamp)
```

Note: **start** and **end** addresses show where modules are loaded in process virtual memory. You can see the module contents by using the **dc** command (**Unknown Component** pattern):

```
0:000> dc 00007ff7`fe660000 00007ff7`fe68d000
00007ff7`fe660000  00905a4d 00000003 00000004 0000ffff  MZ..............
00007ff7`fe660010  000000b8 00000000 00000040 00000000  ........@.......
00007ff7`fe660020  00000000 00000000 00000000 00000000  ................
00007ff7`fe660030  00000000 00000000 00000000 000000e8  ................
00007ff7`fe660040  0eba1f0e cd09b400 4c01b821 685421cd  ........!..L.!Th
00007ff7`fe660050  70207369 72676f72 63206d61 6f6e6e61  is program canno
00007ff7`fe660060  65622074 6e757220 206e6920 20534f44  t be run in DOS
00007ff7`fe660070  65646f6d 0a0d0d2e 00000024 00000000  mode....$.......
00007ff7`fe660080  73198c7b 2077ed3f 2077ed3f 2077ed3f  {..s?.w ?.w ?.w
00007ff7`fe660090  20e49536 2077ed33 2176692f 2077ed3d  6.. 3.w /iv!=.w
```

62

```
00007ff7`fe6600a0  2174692f 2077ed3c 2173692f 2077ed36  /it!<.w /is!6.w
00007ff7`fe6600b0  2172692f 2077ed28 21769574 2077ed37  /ir!(.w t.v!7.w
00007ff7`fe6600c0  2076ed3f 2077ed91 2077ed3f 2077ed2d  ?.v ..w ?.w -.w
00007ff7`fe6600d0  21756877 2077ed3e 68636952 2077ed3f  whu!>.w Rich?.w
00007ff7`fe6600e0  00000000 00000000 00004550 00058664  ........PE..d...
00007ff7`fe6600f0  670be519 00000000 00000000 002200f0  ...g..........".
00007ff7`fe660100  290e020b 0001ce00 0000d200 00000000  ...)............
00007ff7`fe660110  0001b5dc 00001000 fe660000 00007ff7  ..........f.....
[...]
00007ff7`fe68cf90  00000000 00000000 00000000 00000000  ................
00007ff7`fe68cfa0  00000000 00000000 00000000 00000000  ................
00007ff7`fe68cfb0  00000000 00000000 00000000 00000000  ................
00007ff7`fe68cfc0  00000000 00000000 00000000 00000000  ................
00007ff7`fe68cfd0  00000000 00000000 00000000 00000000  ................
00007ff7`fe68cfe0  00000000 00000000 00000000 00000000  ................
00007ff7`fe68cff0  00000000 00000000 00000000 00000000  ................
00007ff7`fe68d000  ????????                             ????
```

Note: It is also possible to filter ASCII and UNICODE strings using these commands:

```
0:000> s-sa 00007ff7`fe660000 00007ff7`fe68d000
...
00007ff7`fe67eb30  "called `Result::unwrap()` on an "
00007ff7`fe67eb50  "`Err` value"
...

0:000> s-su 00007ff7`fe660000 00007ff7`fe68d000
...
00007ff7`fe680600  "NTDLL.DLL"
...
```

17.   We can check verbose module information using the **lmv** command or use **lmv m** *<module name>* to check an individual module (**Not My Version** pattern):

```
0:000> lmv m normal
Browse full module list
start             end                 module name
00007ff7`fe660000 00007ff7`fe68d000   normal     C (no symbols)
    Loaded symbol image file: normal.exe
    Image path: C:\Work\normal.exe
    Image name: normal.exe
    Browse all global symbols  functions  data  Symbol Reload
    Timestamp:        Sun Oct 13 16:19:53 2024 (670BE519)
    CheckSum:         00000000
    ImageSize:        0002D000
    Translations:     0000.04b0 0000.04e4 0409.04b0 0409.04e4
    Information from resource tables:
```

18.   Sometimes, the **lmv** command doesn't show much, and the **!lmi** command might give extra information:

```
0:000> !lmi normal
Loaded Module Info: [normal]
        Module: normal
  Base Address: 00007ff7fe660000
    Image Name: normal.exe
  Machine Type: 34404 (X64)
```

```
      Time Stamp: 670be519 Sun Oct 13 16:19:53 2024
            Size: 2d000
        CheckSum: 0
 Characteristics: 22
Debug Data Dirs: Type   Size     VA   Pointer
                 CODEVIEW    23, 24874,   23a74 RSDS - GUID: {58764FCF-8A76-49AF-818F-C14AE9FEF9B4}
                 Age: 1, Pdb: normal.pdb
                 VC_FEATURE   14, 24898,   23a98 [Data not mapped]
                 POGO        330, 248ac,   23aac [Data not mapped]
      Image Type: MEMORY   - Image read successfully from loaded memory.
     Symbol Type: NONE     - PDB not found from symbol server.
     Load Report: no symbols loaded
```

Note: We can use the **lmt** command if we are interested in timestamps only.

19.   Sometimes **Environment Hint** pattern can give troubleshooting suggestions related to environment variables and DLL paths. **!peb** command (**P**rocess **E**nvironment **B**lock):

```
0:000> !peb
PEB at 0000003223ba6000
    InheritedAddressSpace:    No
    ReadImageFileExecOptions: No
    BeingDebugged:            No
    ImageBaseAddress:         00007ff7fe660000
    NtGlobalFlag:             0
    NtGlobalFlag2:            0
    Ldr                       00007fffea17a140
    Ldr.Initialized:          Yes
    Ldr.InInitializationOrderModuleList: 000001f6536e2070 . 000001f6536ec140
    Ldr.InLoadOrderModuleList:           000001f6536e21f0 . 000001f6536ec120
    Ldr.InMemoryOrderModuleList:         000001f6536e2200 . 000001f6536ec130
              Base TimeStamp                     Module
        7ff7fe660000 670be519 Oct 13 16:19:53 2024 C:\Work\normal.exe
        7fffea000000 77da5a19 Sep 20 04:10:17 2033 C:\WINDOWS\SYSTEM32\ntdll.dll
        7fffe89c0000 1b24eda6 Jun 06 22:22:46 1984 C:\WINDOWS\System32\KERNEL32.DLL
        7fffe78e0000 3739e3d8 May 12 21:26:00 1999 C:\WINDOWS\System32\KERNELBASE.dll
        7fffe4800000 f8dfa076 Apr 25 11:46:14 2102 C:\WINDOWS\SYSTEM32\apphelp.dll
        7fffe7d40000 00e78ce9 Jun 25 16:14:49 1970 C:\WINDOWS\System32\ucrtbase.dll
        7fffd7e40000 006cb796 Mar 24 11:08:06 1970 C:\WINDOWS\SYSTEM32\VCRUNTIME140.dll
    SubSystemData:      0000000000000000
    ProcessHeap:        000001f6536e0000
    ProcessParameters:  000001f6536e6570
    CurrentDirectory:   'C:\Work\'
    WindowTitle:  'C:\Work\normal.exe'
    ImageFile:    'C:\Work\normal.exe'
    CommandLine:  '"C:\Work\normal.exe" '
    DllPath:      '< Name not readable >'
    Environment:  000001f6536e11f0
        =::=::\
        ALLUSERSPROFILE=C:\ProgramData
        APPDATA=C:\Users\User\AppData\Roaming
        CommonProgramFiles=C:\Program Files\Common Files
        CommonProgramFiles(x86)=C:\Program Files (x86)\Common Files
        CommonProgramW6432=C:\Program Files\Common Files
        COMPUTERNAME=WINDEV2204EVAL
        ComSpec=C:\WINDOWS\system32\cmd.exe
        DriverData=C:\Windows\System32\Drivers\DriverData
        FPS_BROWSER_APP_PROFILE_STRING=Internet Explorer
        FPS_BROWSER_USER_PROFILE_STRING=Default
        HOMEDRIVE=C:
        HOMEPATH=\Users\User
        LOCALAPPDATA=C:\Users\User\AppData\Local
        LOGONSERVER=\\WINDEV2204EVAL
        NUMBER_OF_PROCESSORS=1
        OneDrive=C:\Users\User\OneDrive
        OS=Windows_NT
```

```
Path=C:\Windows\system32;C:\Windows;C:\Windows\System32\Wbem;C:\Windows\System32\WindowsPowerShell\v1.0\;C:\Windows\Sy
stem32\OpenSSH\;C:\Program Files\Microsoft SQL Server\150\Tools\Binn\;C:\Program Files\Microsoft SQL Server\Client
SDK\ODBC\170\Tools\Binn\;C:\Program
Files\dotnet\;C:\Users\User\AppData\Local\Microsoft\WindowsApps;C:\Users\User\.dotnet\tools
        PATHEXT=.COM;.EXE;.BAT;.CMD;.VBS;.VBE;.JS;.JSE;.WSF;.WSH;.MSC
        PROCESSOR_ARCHITECTURE=AMD64
        PROCESSOR_IDENTIFIER=Intel64 Family 6 Model 142 Stepping 10, GenuineIntel
        PROCESSOR_LEVEL=6
        PROCESSOR_REVISION=8e0a
        ProgramData=C:\ProgramData
        ProgramFiles=C:\Program Files
        ProgramFiles(x86)=C:\Program Files (x86)
        ProgramW6432=C:\Program Files
        PSModulePath=C:\Program Files\WindowsPowerShell\Modules;C:\WINDOWS\system32\WindowsPowerShell\v1.0\Modules
        PUBLIC=C:\Users\Public
        SESSIONNAME=Console
        SystemDrive=C:
        SystemRoot=C:\WINDOWS
        TEMP=C:\Users\User\AppData\Local\Temp
        TMP=C:\Users\User\AppData\Local\Temp
        USERDOMAIN=WINDEV2204EVAL
        USERDOMAIN_ROAMINGPROFILE=WINDEV2204EVAL
        USERNAME=User
        USERPROFILE=C:\Users\User
        windir=C:\WINDOWS
```

20.   To launch classic help from the WinDbg app, type the **.hh** command.

21.   We close logging before exiting WinDbg:


```
0:000> .logclose
Closing open log file C:\ARWMDA-Dumps\RW1.log
```

Note: If you close a log and later reopen it using the **.logopen** command, its contents will be lost. To append new output to an already existing log, please use the **.logappend** WinDbg command.

Supportability Best Practice

Keep PDB files from each release

Exercise RW2

- **Goal:** Learn how to analyze stack traces from debug versions

- **Patterns:** Technology-Specific Subtrace (Rust)

- \ARWMDA-Dumps\Exercise-RW2.pdf

Goal: Learn how to analyze stack traces from debug versions.

Patterns: Technology-Specific Subtrace (Rust).

1.   Launch WinDbg.

2.   Open \ARWMDA-Dumps\Process\normal-debug.DMP.

3.   We get the dump file loaded:

```
Microsoft (R) Windows Debugger Version 10.0.27725.1000 AMD64
Copyright (c) Microsoft Corporation. All rights reserved.


Loading Dump File [C:\ARWMDA-Dumps\Process\normal-debug.DMP]
User Mini Dump File with Full Memory: Only application data is available


************* Path validation summary **************
Response                        Time (ms)     Location
Deferred                                      srv*
Symbol search path is: srv*
Executable search path is:
Windows 10 Version 22000 UP Free x64
Product: WinNt, suite: SingleUserTS
Edition build lab: 22000.1.amd64fre.co_release.210604-1628
Debug session time: Sun Oct 13 18:23:56.000 2024 (UTC + 1:00)
System Uptime: 0 days 0:08:57.906
Process Uptime: 0 days 0:00:12.000
.......
For analysis of this file, run !analyze -v
ntdll!NtDeviceIoControlFile+0x14:
00007fff`ea0a4164 ret
```

4.   Open a log file to save all future output using the **.logopen** command:

```
0:000> .logopen C:\ARWMDA-Dumps\RW2.log
Opened log file 'C:\ARWMDA-Dumps\RW2.log'
```

5.   Type the **k** command to verify the correctness of the stack trace:

```
0:000> k
 # Child-SP          RetAddr               Call Site
00 00000059`41cfd3d8 00007fff`e7914da5     ntdll!NtDeviceIoControlFile+0x14
01 00000059`41cfd3e0 00007fff`e7994c5d     KERNELBASE!ConsoleCallServerGeneric+0xe9
02 00000059`41cfd540 00007fff`e7994aba     KERNELBASE!ReadConsoleInternal+0x18d
03 00000059`41cfd690 00007ff6`bb5343cb     KERNELBASE!ReadConsoleW+0x1a
04 00000059`41cfd6d0 00007ff6`bb53419f     normal+0x143cb
05 00000059`41cfd780 00007ff6`bb52ed57     normal+0x1419f
06 00000059`41cff820 00007ff6`bb52d3f5     normal+0xed57
07 00000059`41cff8c0 00007ff6`bb52936e     normal+0xd3f5
```

```
08 00000059`41cff960 00007ff6`bb528dde     normal+0x936e
09 00000059`41cffa20 00007ff6`bb5226f4     normal+0x8dde
0a 00000059`41cffa80 00007ff6`bb522fb4     normal+0x26f4
0b 00000059`41cffae0 00007ff6`bb526780     normal+0x2fb4
0c 00000059`41cffb40 00007ff6`bb5274db     normal+0x6780
0d 00000059`41cffcb0 00007ff6`bb52184e     normal+0x74db
0e 00000059`41cffcf0 00007ff6`bb5263d1     normal+0x184e
0f 00000059`41cffd30 00007ff6`bb52b909     normal+0x63d1
10 00000059`41cffd70 00007ff6`bb5263aa     normal+0xb909
11 00000059`41cffe30 00007ff6`bb526979     normal+0x63aa
12 00000059`41cffea0 00007ff6`bb541d8c     normal+0x6979
13 00000059`41cffed0 00007fff`e89d53e0     normal+0x21d8c
14 00000059`41cfff10 00007fff`ea00485b     kernel32!BaseThreadInitThunk+0x10
15 00000059`41cfff40 00000000`00000000     ntdll!RtlUserThreadStart+0x2b
```

6.   We now specify a path to the symbol file for the *normal* module:

```
0:000> .sympath+ C:\ARWMDA-Dumps\Symbols\debug
Symbol search path is: srv*;C:\ARWMDA-Dumps\Symbols\debug
Expanded Symbol search path is:
cache*;SRV*https://msdl.microsoft.com/download/symbols;c:\arwmda-dumps\symbols\debug


************* Path validation summary **************
Response                        Time (ms)     Location
Deferred                                      srv*
OK                                            C:\ARWMDA-Dumps\Symbols\debug


0:000> k
 # Child-SP          RetAddr               Call Site
00 00000059`41cfd3d8 00007fff`e7914da5     ntdll!NtDeviceIoControlFile+0x14
01 00000059`41cfd3e0 00007fff`e7994c5d     KERNELBASE!ConsoleCallServerGeneric+0xe9
02 00000059`41cfd540 00007fff`e7994aba     KERNELBASE!ReadConsoleInternal+0x18d
03 00000059`41cfd690 00007ff6`bb5343cb     KERNELBASE!ReadConsoleW+0x1a
04 (Inline Function) --------`--------     normal!std::sys::pal::windows::stdio::read_u16s+0x4e [/rustc/eeb90cda1969383f56a2637cbd3037bdf598841c/library/std/src/sys/pal/windows/stdio.rs @
352]
05 00000059`41cfd6d0 00007ff6`bb53419f     normal!std::sys::pal::windows::stdio::read_u16s_fixup_surrogates+0xcb
[/rustc/eeb90cda1969383f56a2637cbd3037bdf598841c/library/std/src/sys/pal/windows/stdio.rs @ 318]
06 00000059`41cfd780 00007ff6`bb52ed57     normal!std::sys::pal::windows::stdio::impl$2::read+0x19f [/rustc/eeb90cda1969383f56a2637cbd3037bdf598841c/library/std/src/sys/pal/windows/stdio.rs
@ 284]
07 (Inline Function) --------`--------     normal!std::io::Read::read_buf::closure$0+0xb [/rustc/eeb90cda1969383f56a2637cbd3037bdf598841c/library/std/src/io/mod.rs @ 973]
08 (Inline Function) --------`--------     normal!std::io::default_read_buf+0x1f [/rustc/eeb90cda1969383f56a2637cbd3037bdf598841c/library/std/src/io/mod.rs @ 574]
09 (Inline Function) --------`--------     normal!std::io::Read::read_buf+0x1f [/rustc/eeb90cda1969383f56a2637cbd3037bdf598841c/library/std/src/io/mod.rs @ 973]
0a (Inline Function) --------`--------     normal!std::io::stdio::impl$0::read_buf+0x1f [/rustc/eeb90cda1969383f56a2637cbd3037bdf598841c/library/std/src/io/stdio.rs @ 105]
0b (Inline Function) --------`--------     normal!std::io::impl$1::read_buf+0x1f [/rustc/eeb90cda1969383f56a2637cbd3037bdf598841c/library/std/src/io/impls.rs @ 24]
0c (Inline Function) --------`--------     normal!std::io::buffered::bufreader::Buffer::fill_buf+0x3b
[/rustc/eeb90cda1969383f56a2637cbd3037bdf598841c/library/std/src/io/buffered/bufreader/buffer.rs @ 115]
0d (Inline Function) --------`--------     normal!std::io::buffered::impl$5::fill_buf+0x3b
[/rustc/eeb90cda1969383f56a2637cbd3037bdf598841c/library/std/src/io/buffered/bufreader.rs @ 396]
0e 00000059`41cff820 00007ff6`bb52d3f5     normal!std::io::read_until<std::io::buffered::bufreader::BufReader<std::io::stdio::StdinRaw> >+0x67
[/rustc/eeb90cda1969383f56a2637cbd3037bdf598841c/library/std/src/io/mod.rs @ 2091]
0f (Inline Function) --------`--------     normal!std::io::stdio::impl$9::read_line+0x1a [/rustc/eeb90cda1969383f56a2637cbd3037bdf598841c/library/std/src/io/stdio.rs @ 555]
10 00000059`41cff8c0 00007ff6`bb52936e     normal!std::io::stdio::Stdin::read_line+0x65 [/rustc/eeb90cda1969383f56a2637cbd3037bdf598841c/library/std/src/io/stdio.rs @ 399]
11 00000059`41cff960 00007ff6`bb528dde     normal!crate_c::mod_cb::func+0x5e [C:\ARWMDA-Dumps\normal\crate_c\src\mod_cb.rs @ 6]
12 00000059`41cffa20 00007ff6`bb5226f4     normal!crate_b::mod_b::func+0x2e [C:\ARWMDA-Dumps\normal\crate_b\src\mod_b.rs @ 11]
13 00000059`41cffa80 00007ff6`bb522fb4     normal!normal::mod_aa::func+0x24 [C:\ARWMDA-Dumps\normal\normal\src\mod_aa.rs @ 6]
14 00000059`41cffae0 00007ff6`bb526780     normal!normal::mod_ab::func+0x24 [C:\ARWMDA-Dumps\normal\normal\src\mod_ab.rs @ 6]
15 00000059`41cffb40 00007ff6`bb5274db     normal!normal::main+0x90 [C:\ARWMDA-Dumps\normal\normal\src\main.rs @ 20]
16 00000059`41cffcb0 00007ff6`bb52184e     normal!core::ops::function::FnOnce::call_once<void (*)(),tuple$<> >+0xb
[/rustc/eeb90cda1969383f56a2637cbd3037bdf598841c\library\core\src\ops\function.rs @ 250]
17 (Inline Function) --------`--------     normal!core::hint::black_box+0xa [/rustc/eeb90cda1969383f56a2637cbd3037bdf598841c\library\core\src\hint.rs @ 389]
18 00000059`41cffcf0 00007ff6`bb5263d1     normal!std::sys::backtrace::__rust_begin_short_backtrace<void (*)(),tuple$<> >+0xe
[/rustc/eeb90cda1969383f56a2637cbd3037bdf598841c\library\std\src\sys\backtrace.rs @ 155]
19 00000059`41cffd30 00007ff6`bb52b909     normal!std::rt::lang_start::closure$0<tuple$<> >+0x11 [/rustc/eeb90cda1969383f56a2637cbd3037bdf598841c\library\std\src\rt.rs @ 162]
1a (Inline Function) --------`--------     normal!std::rt::lang_start_internal::closure$2+0x6 [/rustc/eeb90cda1969383f56a2637cbd3037bdf598841c\library\std\src\rt.rs @ 141]
1b (Inline Function) --------`--------     normal!std::panicking::try::do_call+0x6 [/rustc/eeb90cda1969383f56a2637cbd3037bdf598841c\library\std\src\panicking.rs @ 557]
1c (Inline Function) --------`--------     normal!std::panicking::try+0x6 [/rustc/eeb90cda1969383f56a2637cbd3037bdf598841c\library\std\src\panicking.rs @ 521]
1d (Inline Function) --------`--------     normal!std::panic::catch_unwind+0x6 [/rustc/eeb90cda1969383f56a2637cbd3037bdf598841c\library\std\src\panic.rs @ 350]
1e 00000059`41cffd70 00007ff6`bb5263aa     normal!std::rt::lang_start_internal+0x79 [/rustc/eeb90cda1969383f56a2637cbd3037bdf598841c\library\std\src\rt.rs @ 141]
1f 00000059`41cffe30 00007ff6`bb526979     normal!std::rt::lang_start<tuple$<> >+0x3a [/rustc/eeb90cda1969383f56a2637cbd3037bdf598841c\library\std\src\rt.rs @ 161]
20 00000059`41cffea0 00007ff6`bb541d8c     normal!main+0x19
21 (Inline Function) --------`--------     normal!invoke_main+0x22 [D:\a\_work\1\s\src\vctools\crt\vcstartup\src\startup\exe_common.inl @ 78]
22 00000059`41cffed0 00007fff`e89d53e0     normal!__scrt_common_main_seh+0x10c [D:\a\_work\1\s\src\vctools\crt\vcstartup\src\startup\exe_common.inl @ 288]
23 00000059`41cfff10 00007fff`ea00485b     kernel32!BaseThreadInitThunk+0x10
24 00000059`41cfff40 00000000`00000000     ntdll!RtlUserThreadStart+0x2b
```

Note: We can make the stack trace output less cluttered by omitting source code references:

```
0:000> kL
 # Child-SP          RetAddr               Call Site
00 00000059`41cfd3d8 00007fff`e7914da5     ntdll!NtDeviceIoControlFile+0x14
01 00000059`41cfd3e0 00007fff`e7994c5d     KERNELBASE!ConsoleCallServerGeneric+0xe9
02 00000059`41cfd540 00007fff`e7994aba     KERNELBASE!ReadConsoleInternal+0x18d
```

```
03 00000059`41cfd690 00007ff6`bb5343cb     KERNELBASE!ReadConsoleW+0x1a
04 (Inline Function) --------`--------     normal!std::sys::pal::windows::stdio::read_u16s+0x4e
05 00000059`41cfd6d0 00007ff6`bb53419f     normal!std::sys::pal::windows::stdio::read_u16s_fixup_surrogates+0xcb
06 00000059`41cfd780 00007ff6`bb52ed57     normal!std::sys::pal::windows::stdio::impl$2::read+0x19f
07 (Inline Function) --------`--------     normal!std::io::Read::read_buf::closure$0+0xb
08 (Inline Function) --------`--------     normal!std::io::default_read_buf+0x1f
09 (Inline Function) --------`--------     normal!std::io::Read::read_buf+0x1f
0a (Inline Function) --------`--------     normal!std::io::stdio::impl$0::read_buf+0x1f
0b (Inline Function) --------`--------     normal!std::io::impls::impl$0::read_buf+0x1f
0c (Inline Function) --------`--------     normal!std::io::buffered::bufreader::buffer::Buffer::fill_buf+0x3b
0d (Inline Function) --------`--------     normal!std::io::buffered::bufreader::impl$5::fill_buf+0x3b
0e 00000059`41cff820 00007ff6`bb52d3f5     normal!std::io::read_until<std::io::buffered::bufreader::BufReader<std::io::stdio::StdinRaw> >+0x67
0f (Inline Function) --------`--------     normal!std::io::stdio::impl$9::read_line+0x1a
10 00000059`41cff8c0 00007ff6`bb52936e     normal!std::io::stdio::Stdin::read_line+0x65
11 00000059`41cff960 00007ff6`bb528dde     normal!crate_c::mod_cb::func+0x5e
12 00000059`41cffa20 00007ff6`bb5226f4     normal!crate_b::mod_b::func+0x2e
13 00000059`41cffa80 00007ff6`bb522fb4     normal!normal::mod_aa::func+0x24
14 00000059`41cffae0 00007ff6`bb526780     normal!normal::mod_ab::func+0x24
15 00000059`41cffb40 00007ff6`bb5274db     normal!normal::main+0x90
16 00000059`41cffcb0 00007ff6`bb52184e     normal!core::ops::function::FnOnce::call_once<void (*)(),tuple$<> >+0xb
17 (Inline Function) --------`--------     normal!core::hint::black_box+0xa
18 00000059`41cffcf0 00007ff6`bb5263d1     normal!std::sys::backtrace::__rust_begin_short_backtrace<void (*)(),tuple$<> >+0xe
19 00000059`41cffd30 00007ff6`bb52b909     normal!std::rt::lang_start::closure$0<tuple$<> >+0x11
1a (Inline Function) --------`--------     normal!std::rt::lang_start_internal::closure$2+0x6
1b (Inline Function) --------`--------     normal!std::panicking::try::do_call+0x6
1c (Inline Function) --------`--------     normal!std::panicking::try+0x6
1d (Inline Function) --------`--------     normal!std::panic::catch_unwind+0x6
1e 00000059`41cffd70 00007ff6`bb5263aa     normal!std::rt::lang_start_internal+0x79
1f 00000059`41cffe30 00007ff6`bb526979     normal!std::rt::lang_start<tuple$<> >+0x3a
20 00000059`41cffea0 00007ff6`bb541d8c     normal!main+0x19
21 (Inline Function) --------`--------     normal!invoke_main+0x22
22 00000059`41cffed0 00007fff`e89d53e0     normal!__scrt_common_main_seh+0x10c
23 00000059`41cfff10 00007fff`ea00485b     kernel32!BaseThreadInitThunk+0x10
24 00000059`41cfff40 00000000`00000000     ntdll!RtlUserThreadStart+0x2b
```

Note: The Rust source code *main* function differs from the C runtime *main* function: *normal!normal::main* vs. *normal!main*.

7.   We can switch to any stack trace frame of interest:

```
0:000> .frame 15
15 00000059`41cffb40 00007ff6`bb5274db     normal!normal::main+0x90 [C:\ARWMDA-Dumps\normal\normal\src\main.rs @ 20]
```

Note: To see the source code, we need to set the source code path if it is different from the source code path specified in symbol files:

```
0:000> .scrpath+ C:\ARWMDA-Dumps\Source\normal
Source search path is: SRV*;C:\ARWMDA-Dumps\Source\normal

************* Path validation summary **************
Response                        Time (ms)     Location
Deferred                                      SRV*
OK                                            C:\ARWMDA-Dumps\Source\normal
```

We now see the source code window:

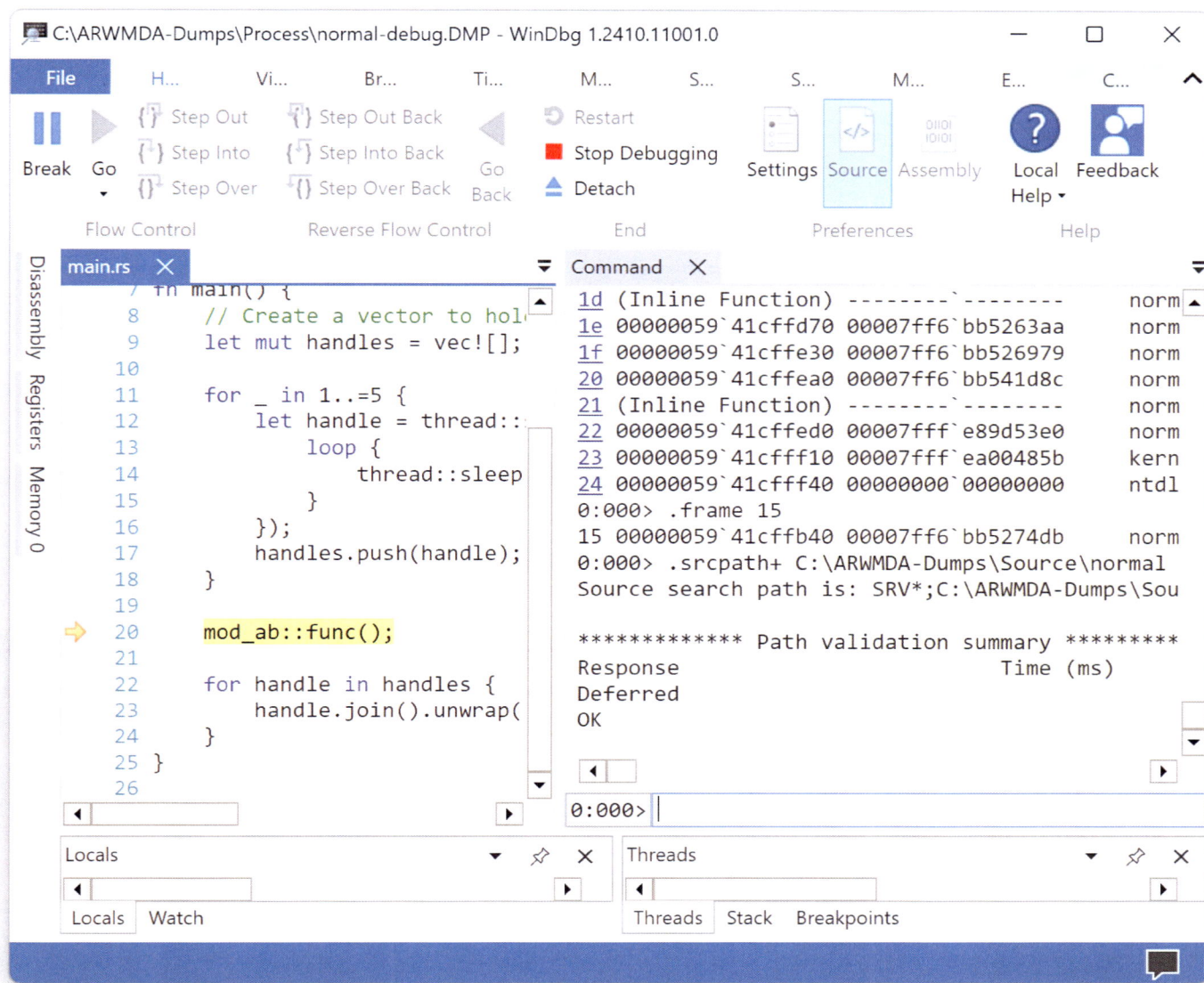

8.   It is also possible to check local variables in the current context:

```
0:000> dv /i /V
prv local  00000059`41cffb80 @rbp-0x0040         handles = { len=0x5 }
prv local  <unavailable>     <unavailable>            iter = <value unavailable>
prv local  <unavailable>     <unavailable>            iter = <value unavailable>
prv local  <unavailable>     <unavailable>          handle = <value unavailable>

0:000> dt handles
Local var @ 0x5941cffb80 Type alloc::vec::Vec<std::thread::JoinHandle<tuple$<> >,alloc::alloc::Global>
   +0x000 buf              : alloc::raw_vec::RawVec<std::thread::JoinHandle<tuple$<> >,alloc::alloc::Global>
   +0x010 len              : 5

0:000> dt -r handles
Local var @ 0x5941cffb80 Type alloc::vec::Vec<std::thread::JoinHandle<tuple$<> >,alloc::alloc::Global>
   +0x000 buf              : alloc::raw_vec::RawVec<std::thread::JoinHandle<tuple$<> >,alloc::alloc::Global>
      +0x008 ptr              : core::ptr::unique::Unique<std::thread::JoinHandle<tuple$<> > >
         +0x000 pointer          : core::ptr::non_null::NonNull<std::thread::JoinHandle<tuple$<> > >
```

```
                      +0x008 _marker          : core::marker::PhantomData<std::thread::JoinHandle<tuple$<> > >
                   +0x000 cap             : alloc::raw_vec::Cap
                      +0x000 __0            : 8
                   +0x010 alloc           : alloc::alloc::Global
                +0x010 len            : 5
```

```
0:000> dx handles
```

```
handles                  : { len=0x5 } [Type: alloc::vec::Vec<std::thread::JoinHandle<tuple$<> >,alloc::alloc::Global>]
    [<Raw View>]          [Type: alloc::vec::Vec<std::thread::JoinHandle<tuple$<> >,alloc::alloc::Global>]
    [len]           : 0x5 [Type: unsigned __int64]
    [capacity]      : 0x8 [Type: unsigned __int64]
    [0]             [Type: std::thread::JoinHandle<tuple$<> >]
    [1]             [Type: std::thread::JoinHandle<tuple$<> >]
    [2]             [Type: std::thread::JoinHandle<tuple$<> >]
    [3]             [Type: std::thread::JoinHandle<tuple$<> >]
    [4]             [Type: std::thread::JoinHandle<tuple$<> >]
```

9.   Let's now look at all thread stack traces:

```
0:000> ~*kL
```

```
.  0  Id: afc.2830 Suspend: 0 Teb: 00000059`41aa5000 Unfrozen "main"
 # Child-SP          RetAddr           Call Site
00 00000059`41cfd3d8 00007fff`e7914da5 ntdll!NtDeviceIoControlFile+0x14
01 00000059`41cfd3e0 00007fff`e7994c5d KERNELBASE!ConsoleCallServerGeneric+0xe9
02 00000059`41cfd540 00007fff`e7994aba KERNELBASE!ReadConsoleInternal+0x18d
03 00000059`41cfd690 00007ff6`bb5343cb KERNELBASE!ReadConsoleW+0x1a
04 (Inline Function) --------`-------- normal!std::sys::pal::windows::stdio::read_u16s+0x4e
05 00000059`41cfd6d0 00007ff6`bb53419f normal!std::sys::pal::windows::stdio::read_u16s_fixup_surrogates+0xcb
06 00000059`41cfd780 00007ff6`bb52ed57 normal!std::sys::pal::windows::stdio::impl$2::read+0x19f
07 (Inline Function) --------`-------- normal!std::io::Read::read_buf::closure$0+0xb
08 (Inline Function) --------`-------- normal!std::io::default_read_buf+0x1f
09 (Inline Function) --------`-------- normal!std::io::Read::read_buf+0x1f
0a (Inline Function) --------`-------- normal!std::io::stdio::impl$0::read_buf+0x1f
0b (Inline Function) --------`-------- normal!std::io::impls::impl$5::read_buf+0x1f
0c (Inline Function) --------`-------- normal!std::io::buffered::bufreader::buffer::Buffer::fill_buf+0x3b
0d (Inline Function) --------`-------- normal!std::io::buffered::impl$5::fill_buf+0x1f
0e 00000059`41cff820 00007ff6`bb52d3f5 normal!std::io::read_until<std::io::buffered::bufreader::BufReader<std::io::stdio::StdinRaw> >+0x67
0f (Inline Function) --------`-------- normal!std::io::stdio::impl$9::read_line+0x1a
10 00000059`41cff8c0 00007ff6`bb52936e normal!std::io::stdio::Stdin::read_line+0x65
11 00000059`41cff960 00007ff6`bb528dde normal!crate_c::mod_cb::func+0x5e
12 00000059`41cffa20 00007ff6`bb5226f4 normal!crate_b::mod_b::func+0x2e
13 00000059`41cffa80 00007ff6`bb522fb4 normal!normal::mod_aa::func+0x24
14 00000059`41cffae0 00007ff6`bb526780 normal!normal::mod_ab::func+0x24
15 00000059`41cffb40 00007ff6`bb5274db normal!normal::main+0x90
16 00000059`41cffcb0 00007ff6`bb52184e normal!core::ops::function::FnOnce::call_once<void (*)(),tuple$<> >+0xb
17 (Inline Function) --------`-------- normal!core::hint::black_box+0xa
18 00000059`41cffcf0 00007ff6`bb5263d1 normal!std::sys::backtrace::__rust_begin_short_backtrace<void (*)(),tuple$<> >+0xe
19 00000059`41cffd30 00007ff6`bb52b909 normal!std::rt::lang_start::closure$0<tuple$<> >+0x11
1a (Inline Function) --------`-------- normal!std::rt::lang_start_internal::closure$2+0x6
1b (Inline Function) --------`-------- normal!std::panicking::try::do_call+0x6
1c (Inline Function) --------`-------- normal!std::panicking::try+0x6
1d (Inline Function) --------`-------- normal!std::panic::catch_unwind+0x6
1e 00000059`41cffd70 00007ff6`bb5263aa normal!std::rt::lang_start_internal+0x79
1f 00000059`41cffe30 00007ff6`bb526979 normal!std::rt::lang_start<tuple$<> >+0x3a
20 00000059`41cffea0 00007ff6`bb541d8c normal!main+0x19
21 (Inline Function) --------`-------- normal!invoke_main+0x22
22 00000059`41cffed0 00007fff`e89d53e0 normal!__scrt_common_main_seh+0x10c
23 00000059`41cfff10 00007fff`ea00485b kernel32!BaseThreadInitThunk+0x10
24 00000059`41cfff40 00000000`00000000 ntdll!RtlUserThreadStart+0x2b

   1  Id: afc.1d60 Suspend: 0 Teb: 00000059`41aa7000 Unfrozen
 # Child-SP          RetAddr           Call Site
00 00000059`41dff948 00007fff`ea016cdf ntdll!NtWaitForWorkViaWorkerFactory+0x14
01 00000059`41dff950 00007fff`e89d53e0 ntdll!TppWorkerThread+0x2df
02 00000059`41dffc40 00007fff`ea00485b kernel32!BaseThreadInitThunk+0x10
03 00000059`41dffc70 00000000`00000000 ntdll!RtlUserThreadStart+0x2b

   2  Id: afc.2820 Suspend: 0 Teb: 00000059`41aa9000 Unfrozen
 # Child-SP          RetAddr           Call Site
00 00000059`41fff978 00007fff`e79310ee ntdll!NtWaitForSingleObject+0x14
01 00000059`41fff980 00007ff6`bb52bf2d KERNELBASE!WaitForSingleObjectEx+0x8e
02 (Inline Function) --------`-------- normal!std::sys::pal::windows::time::WaitableTimer::wait+0xe
03 (Inline Function) --------`-------- normal!std::sys::pal::windows::thread::impl$0::sleep::high_precision_sleep+0x7c
04 (Inline Function) --------`-------- normal!std::sys::pal::windows::thread::Thread::sleep+0x89
05 00000059`41fffa20 00007ff6`bb526036 normal!std::thread::sleep+0x9d
06 00000059`41fffa90 00007ff6`bb521869 normal!normal::main::closure$0+0x16
07 (Inline Function) --------`-------- normal!core::hint::black_box
08 00000059`41fffac0 00007ff6`bb524f69 normal!std::sys::backtrace::__rust_begin_short_backtrace<normal::main::closure_env$0,tuple$<> >+0x9
09 00000059`41fffaf0 00007ff6`bb521759 normal!std::thread::impl$0::spawn_unchecked_::closure$1::closure$0<normal::main::closure_env$0,tuple$<> >+0x9
0a 00000059`41fffb20 00007ff6`bb52285d normal!core::panic::unwind_safe::impl$25::call_once<tuple$<>,std::thread::impl$0::spawn_unchecked_::closure$1::closure_env$0<normal::main::closure_env$0,tuple$<> > >+0x9
0b 00000059`41fffb50 00007ff6`bb525153 normal!std::panicking::try::do_call<core::panic::unwind_safe::AssertUnwindSafe<std::thread::impl$0::spawn_unchecked_::closure$1::closure_env$0<normal::main::closure_env$0,tuple$<> > >,tuple$<> >+0x1d
0c 00000059`41fffba0 00007ff6`bb524dc4 normal!std::thread::impl$7::drop::closure$0<tuple$<> >+0xb3
0d (Inline Function) --------`-------- normal!std::panicking::try+0x1f
0e (Inline Function) --------`-------- normal!std::panic::catch_unwind+0x1f
0f 00000059`41fffbf0 00007ff6`bb52743e normal!std::thread::impl$0::spawn_unchecked_::closure$1<normal::main::closure_env$0,tuple$<> >+0x114
10 00000059`41fffd40 00007ff6`bb5346dd normal!core::ops::function::FnOnce::call_once<std::thread::impl$0::spawn_unchecked_::closure_env$1<normal::main::closure_env$0,tuple$<> >,tuple$<> >+0xe
11 (Inline Function) --------`-------- normal!alloc::boxed::impl$48::call_once+0xb
12 (Inline Function) --------`-------- normal!alloc::boxed::impl$48::call_once+0x16
13 00000059`41fffd80 00007fff`e89d53e0 normal!std::sys::pal::windows::thread::impl$0::new::thread_start+0x3d
14 00000059`41fffde0 00007fff`ea00485b kernel32!BaseThreadInitThunk+0x10
15 00000059`41fffe10 00000000`00000000 ntdll!RtlUserThreadStart+0x2b

   3  Id: afc.287c Suspend: 0 Teb: 00000059`41aab000 Unfrozen
 # Child-SP          RetAddr           Call Site
00 00000059`421ffa78 00007fff`e79310ee ntdll!NtWaitForSingleObject+0x14
01 00000059`421ffa80 00007ff6`bb52bf2d KERNELBASE!WaitForSingleObjectEx+0x8e
02 (Inline Function) --------`-------- normal!std::sys::pal::windows::time::WaitableTimer::wait+0xe
```

```
03 (Inline Function) --------`--------    normal!std::sys::pal::windows::thread::impl$0::sleep::high_precision_sleep+0x7c
04 (Inline Function) --------`--------    normal!std::sys::pal::windows::thread::Thread::sleep+0x89
05 00000059`421ffb20 00007ff6`bb526036   normal!std::thread::sleep+0x9d
06 00000059`421ffb90 00007ff6`bb521869   normal!normal::main::closure$0+0x16
07 (Inline Function) --------`--------    normal!core::hint::black_box
08 00000059`421ffbc0 00007ff6`bb524f69   normal!std::sys::backtrace::__rust_begin_short_backtrace<normal::main::closure_env$0,tuple$<> >+0x9
09 00000059`421ffbf0 00007ff6`bb521759   normal!std::thread::impl$0::spawn_unchecked_::closure$1::closure$0<normal::main::closure_env$0,tuple$<> >+0x9
0a 00000059`421ffc20 00007ff6`bb52285d
normal!core::panic::unwind_safe::impl$25::call_once<tuple$<>,std::thread::impl$0::spawn_unchecked_::closure$1::closure_env$0<normal::main::closure_env$0,tuple$<> > >+0x9
0b 00000059`421ffc50 00007ff6`bb525153
normal!std::panicking::try::do_call<core::panic::unwind_safe::AssertUnwindSafe<std::thread::impl$0::spawn_unchecked_::closure$1::closure_env$0<normal::main::closure_env$0,tuple$<> >
>,tuple$<> >+0x1d
0c 00000059`421ffca0 00007ff6`bb524dc4   normal!std::thread::impl$7::drop::closure$0<tuple$<> >+0xb3
0d (Inline Function) --------`--------    normal!std::panicking::try+0x1f
0e (Inline Function) --------`--------    normal!std::panic::catch_unwind+0x1f
0f 00000059`421ffcf0 00007ff6`bb52743e   normal!std::thread::impl$0::spawn_unchecked_::closure$1<normal::main::closure_env$0,tuple$<> >+0x114
10 00000059`421ffe40 00007ff6`bb5346dd   normal!core::ops::function::FnOnce::call_once<std::thread::impl$0::spawn_unchecked_::closure$1<normal::main::closure_env$0,tuple$<> >,tuple$<>
>+0xe
11 (Inline Function) --------`--------    normal!alloc::boxed::impl$48::call_once+0xb
12 (Inline Function) --------`--------    normal!alloc::boxed::impl$48::call_once+0x16
13 00000059`421ffe80 00007fff`e89d53e0   normal!std::sys::pal::windows::thread::impl$0::new::thread_start+0x3d
14 00000059`421ffee0 00007fff`ea00485b   kernel32!BaseThreadInitThunk+0x10
15 00000059`421fff10 00000000`00000000   ntdll!RtlUserThreadStart+0x2b

   4  Id: afc.282c Suspend: 0 Teb: 00000059`41aad000 Unfrozen
 # Child-SP          RetAddr               Call Site
00 00000059`423ff338 00007fff`e79310ee   ntdll!NtWaitForSingleObject+0x14
01 00000059`423ff340 00007ff6`bb52bf2d   KERNELBASE!WaitForSingleObjectEx+0x8e
02 (Inline Function) --------`--------    normal!std::sys::pal::windows::time::WaitableTimer::wait+0xe
03 (Inline Function) --------`--------    normal!std::sys::pal::windows::thread::impl$0::sleep::high_precision_sleep+0x7c
04 (Inline Function) --------`--------    normal!std::sys::pal::windows::thread::Thread::sleep+0x89
05 00000059`423ff3e0 00007ff6`bb526036   normal!std::thread::sleep+0x9d
06 00000059`423ff450 00007ff6`bb521869   normal!normal::main::closure$0+0x16
07 (Inline Function) --------`--------    normal!core::hint::black_box
08 00000059`423ff480 00007ff6`bb524f69   normal!std::sys::backtrace::__rust_begin_short_backtrace<normal::main::closure_env$0,tuple$<> >+0x9
09 00000059`423ff4b0 00007ff6`bb521759   normal!std::thread::impl$0::spawn_unchecked_::closure$1::closure$0<normal::main::closure_env$0,tuple$<> >+0x9
0a 00000059`423ff4e0 00007ff6`bb52285d
normal!core::panic::unwind_safe::impl$25::call_once<tuple$<>,std::thread::impl$0::spawn_unchecked_::closure$1::closure_env$0<normal::main::closure_env$0,tuple$<> > >+0x9
0b 00000059`423ff510 00007ff6`bb525153
normal!std::panicking::try::do_call<core::panic::unwind_safe::AssertUnwindSafe<std::thread::impl$0::spawn_unchecked_::closure$1::closure_env$0<normal::main::closure_env$0,tuple$<> >
>,tuple$<> >+0x1d
0c 00000059`423ff560 00007ff6`bb524dc4   normal!std::thread::impl$7::drop::closure$0<tuple$<> >+0xb3
0d (Inline Function) --------`--------    normal!std::panicking::try+0x1f
0e (Inline Function) --------`--------    normal!std::panic::catch_unwind+0x1f
0f 00000059`423ff5b0 00007ff6`bb52743e   normal!std::thread::impl$0::spawn_unchecked_::closure$1<normal::main::closure_env$0,tuple$<> >+0x114
10 00000059`423ff700 00007ff6`bb5346dd   normal!core::ops::function::FnOnce::call_once<std::thread::impl$0::spawn_unchecked_::closure$1<normal::main::closure_env$0,tuple$<> >,tuple$<>
>+0xe
11 (Inline Function) --------`--------    normal!alloc::boxed::impl$48::call_once+0xb
12 (Inline Function) --------`--------    normal!alloc::boxed::impl$48::call_once+0x16
13 00000059`423ff740 00007fff`e89d53e0   normal!std::sys::pal::windows::thread::impl$0::new::thread_start+0x3d
14 00000059`423ff7a0 00007fff`ea00485b   kernel32!BaseThreadInitThunk+0x10
15 00000059`423ff7d0 00000000`00000000   ntdll!RtlUserThreadStart+0x2b

   5  Id: afc.13d0 Suspend: 0 Teb: 00000059`41aaf000 Unfrozen
 # Child-SP          RetAddr               Call Site
00 00000059`425ff428 00007fff`e79310ee   ntdll!NtWaitForSingleObject+0x14
01 00000059`425ff430 00007ff6`bb52bf2d   KERNELBASE!WaitForSingleObjectEx+0x8e
02 (Inline Function) --------`--------    normal!std::sys::pal::windows::time::WaitableTimer::wait+0xe
03 (Inline Function) --------`--------    normal!std::sys::pal::windows::thread::impl$0::sleep::high_precision_sleep+0x7c
04 (Inline Function) --------`--------    normal!std::sys::pal::windows::thread::Thread::sleep+0x89
05 00000059`425ff4d0 00007ff6`bb526036   normal!std::thread::sleep+0x9d
06 00000059`425ff540 00007ff6`bb521869   normal!normal::main::closure$0+0x16
07 (Inline Function) --------`--------    normal!core::hint::black_box
08 00000059`425ff570 00007ff6`bb524f69   normal!std::sys::backtrace::__rust_begin_short_backtrace<normal::main::closure_env$0,tuple$<> >+0x9
09 00000059`425ff5a0 00007ff6`bb521759   normal!std::thread::impl$0::spawn_unchecked_::closure$1::closure$0<normal::main::closure_env$0,tuple$<> >+0x9
0a 00000059`425ff5d0 00007ff6`bb52285d
normal!core::panic::unwind_safe::impl$25::call_once<tuple$<>,std::thread::impl$0::spawn_unchecked_::closure$1::closure_env$0<normal::main::closure_env$0,tuple$<> > >+0x9
0b 00000059`425ff600 00007ff6`bb525153
normal!std::panicking::try::do_call<core::panic::unwind_safe::AssertUnwindSafe<std::thread::impl$0::spawn_unchecked_::closure$1::closure_env$0<normal::main::closure_env$0,tuple$<> >
>,tuple$<> >+0x1d
0c 00000059`425ff650 00007ff6`bb524dc4   normal!std::thread::impl$7::drop::closure$0<tuple$<> >+0xb3
0d (Inline Function) --------`--------    normal!std::panicking::try+0x1f
0e (Inline Function) --------`--------    normal!std::panic::catch_unwind+0x1f
0f 00000059`425ff6a0 00007ff6`bb52743e   normal!std::thread::impl$0::spawn_unchecked_::closure$1<normal::main::closure_env$0,tuple$<> >+0x114
10 00000059`425ff7f0 00007ff6`bb5346dd   normal!core::ops::function::FnOnce::call_once<std::thread::impl$0::spawn_unchecked_::closure$1<normal::main::closure_env$0,tuple$<> >,tuple$<> >
>+0xe
11 (Inline Function) --------`--------    normal!alloc::boxed::impl$48::call_once+0xb
12 (Inline Function) --------`--------    normal!alloc::boxed::impl$48::call_once+0x16
13 00000059`425ff830 00007fff`e89d53e0   normal!std::sys::pal::windows::thread::impl$0::new::thread_start+0x3d
14 00000059`425ff890 00007fff`ea00485b   kernel32!BaseThreadInitThunk+0x10
15 00000059`425ff8c0 00000000`00000000   ntdll!RtlUserThreadStart+0x2b

   6  Id: afc.2890 Suspend: 0 Teb: 00000059`41ab1000 Unfrozen
 # Child-SP          RetAddr               Call Site
00 00000059`427ff558 00007fff`e79310ee   ntdll!NtWaitForSingleObject+0x14
01 00000059`427ff560 00007ff6`bb52bf2d   KERNELBASE!WaitForSingleObjectEx+0x8e
02 (Inline Function) --------`--------    normal!std::sys::pal::windows::time::WaitableTimer::wait+0xe
03 (Inline Function) --------`--------    normal!std::sys::pal::windows::thread::impl$0::sleep::high_precision_sleep+0x7c
04 (Inline Function) --------`--------    normal!std::sys::pal::windows::thread::Thread::sleep+0x89
05 00000059`427ff600 00007ff6`bb526036   normal!std::thread::sleep+0x9d
06 00000059`427ff670 00007ff6`bb521869   normal!normal::main::closure$0+0x16
07 (Inline Function) --------`--------    normal!core::hint::black_box
08 00000059`427ff6a0 00007ff6`bb524f69   normal!std::sys::backtrace::__rust_begin_short_backtrace<normal::main::closure_env$0,tuple$<> >+0x9
...
0c 00000059`427ff780 00007ff6`bb524dc4   normal!std::thread::impl$7::drop::closure$0<tuple$<> >+0xb3
0d (Inline Function) --------`--------    normal!std::panicking::try+0x1f
0e (Inline Function) --------`--------    normal!std::panic::catch_unwind+0x1f
0f 00000059`427ff7d0 00007ff6`bb52743e   normal!std::thread::impl$0::spawn_unchecked_::closure$1<normal::main::closure_env$0,tuple$<> >+0x114
10 00000059`427ff920 00007ff6`bb5346dd   normal!core::ops::function::FnOnce::call_once<std::thread::impl$0::spawn_unchecked_::closure$1<normal::main::closure_env$0,tuple$<> >,tuple$<> >
>+0xe
11 (Inline Function) --------`--------    normal!alloc::boxed::impl$48::call_once+0xb
12 (Inline Function) --------`--------    normal!alloc::boxed::impl$48::call_once+0x16
13 00000059`427ff960 00007fff`e89d53e0   normal!std::sys::pal::windows::thread::impl$0::new::thread_start+0x3d
14 00000059`427ff9c0 00007fff`ea00485b   kernel32!BaseThreadInitThunk+0x10
15 00000059`427ff9f0 00000000`00000000   ntdll!RtlUserThreadStart+0x2b
```

Note: Module names and functions can give us an idea of what every thread was doing. For example, thread #0 was waiting for user input. Other threads are blocked while sleeping. If we have a lot of similar thread stack traces, we can significantly reduce the output by executing the **!uniqstack** command:

```
0:000> !uniqstack
Processing 7 threads, please wait

. 0 Id: afc.2830 Suspend: 0 Teb: 00000059`41aa5000 Unfrozen "main"
     Start: normal!mainCRTStartup (00007ff6`bb541dfc)
     Priority: 0  Priority class: 32  Affinity: 1
# Child-SP          RetAddr           Call Site
00 00000059`41cfd3d8 00007fff`e7914da5 ntdll!NtDeviceIoControlFile+0x14
01 00000059`41cfd3e0 00007fff`e7994c5d KERNELBASE!ConsoleCallServerGeneric+0xe9
02 00000059`41cfd540 00007fff`e7994aba KERNELBASE!ReadConsoleInternal+0x18d
03 00000059`41cfd690 00007ff6`bb5343cb KERNELBASE!ReadConsoleW+0x1a
04 (Inline Function) --------`-------- normal!std::sys::pal::windows::stdio::read_u16s+0x4e [/rustc/eeb90cda1969383f56a2637cbd3037bdf598841c/library\std\src\sys\pal\windows\stdio.rs @
352]
05 00000059`41cfd6d0 00007ff6`bb53419f normal!std::sys::pal::windows::stdio::read_u16s_fixup_surrogates+0xcb
[/rustc/eeb90cda1969383f56a2637cbd3037bdf598841c/library\std\src\sys\pal\windows\stdio.rs @ 318]
06 00000059`41cfd780 00007ff6`bb52ed57 normal!std::sys::pal::windows::stdio::impl$2::read+0x19f [/rustc/eeb90cda1969383f56a2637cbd3037bdf598841c/library\std\src\sys\pal\windows\stdio.rs
@ 284]
07 (Inline Function) --------`-------- normal!std::io::Read::read_buf::closure$0+0xb [/rustc/eeb90cda1969383f56a2637cbd3037bdf598841c/library\std\src\io\mod.rs @ 973]
08 (Inline Function) --------`-------- normal!std::io::default_read_buf+0x1f [/rustc/eeb90cda1969383f56a2637cbd3037bdf598841c/library\std\src\io\mod.rs @ 574]
09 (Inline Function) --------`-------- normal!std::io::Read::read_buf+0x1f [/rustc/eeb90cda1969383f56a2637cbd3037bdf598841c/library\std\src\io\mod.rs @ 973]
0a (Inline Function) --------`-------- normal!std::io::stdio::impl$0::read_buf+0x1f [/rustc/eeb90cda1969383f56a2637cbd3037bdf598841c/library\std\src\io\stdio.rs @ 105]
0b (Inline Function) --------`-------- normal!std::io::impls::impl$0::read_buf+0x1f [/rustc/eeb90cda1969383f56a2637cbd3037bdf598841c/library\std\src\io\impls.rs @ 24]
0c (Inline Function) --------`-------- normal!std::io::buffered::bufreader::buffer::Buffer::fill_buf+0x3b
[/rustc/eeb90cda1969383f56a2637cbd3037bdf598841c/library\std\src\io\buffered\bufreader\buffer.rs @ 115]
0d (Inline Function) --------`-------- normal!std::io::buffered::bufreader::impl$5::fill_buf+0x3b
[/rustc/eeb90cda1969383f56a2637cbd3037bdf598841c/library\std\src\io\buffered\bufreader.rs @ 396]
0e 00000059`41cff820 00007ff6`bb52d3f5 normal!std::io::read_until<std::io::buffered::bufreader::BufReader<std::io::stdio::StdinRaw> >+0x67
[/rustc/eeb90cda1969383f56a2637cbd3037bdf598841c/library\std\src\io\mod.rs @ 2091]
0f (Inline Function) --------`-------- normal!std::io::stdio::impl$9::read_line+0x1a [/rustc/eeb90cda1969383f56a2637cbd3037bdf598841c/library\std\src\io\stdio.rs @ 555]
10 00000059`41cff8c0 00007ff6`bb52936e normal!std::io::Stdin::read_line+0x65 [/rustc/eeb90cda1969383f56a2637cbd3037bdf598841c/library\std\src\io\stdio.rs @ 399]
11 00000059`41cff960 00007ff6`bb528dde normal!crate_c::mod_cb::func+0x5e [C:\ARWMDA-Dumps\normal\crate_c\src\mod_cb.rs @ 6]
12 00000059`41cffa20 00007ff6`bb5226f4 normal!crate_b::mod_b::func+0x2e [C:\ARWMDA-Dumps\normal\crate_b\src\mod_b.rs @ 11]
13 00000059`41cffa80 00007ff6`bb522fb4 normal!normal::mod_aa::func+0x24 [C:\ARWMDA-Dumps\normal\normal\src\mod_aa.rs @ 6]
14 00000059`41cffae0 00007ff6`bb526780 normal!normal::mod_ab::func+0x24 [C:\ARWMDA-Dumps\normal\normal\src\mod_ab.rs @ 6]
15 00000059`41cffb40 00007ff6`bb5274db normal!main+0x90 [C:\ARWMDA-Dumps\normal\normal\src\main.rs @ 20]
16 00000059`41cffcb0 00007ff6`bb52184e normal!core::ops::function::FnOnce::call_once<void (*)(),tuple$<> >+0xb
[/rustc/eeb90cda1969383f56a2637cbd3037bdf598841c/library\core\src\ops\function.rs @ 250]
17 (Inline Function) --------`-------- normal!core::hint::black_box+0xa [/rustc/eeb90cda1969383f56a2637cbd3037bdf598841c/library\core\src\hint.rs @ 389]
18 00000059`41cffcf0 00007ff6`bb5263d1 normal!std::sys::backtrace::__rust_begin_short_backtrace<void (*)(),tuple$<> >+0xe
[/rustc/eeb90cda1969383f56a2637cbd3037bdf598841c/library\std\src\sys\backtrace.rs @ 155]
19 00000059`41cffd30 00007ff6`bb52b909 normal!std::rt::lang_start::closure$0<tuple$<> >+0x11 [/rustc/eeb90cda1969383f56a2637cbd3037bdf598841c/library\std\src\rt.rs @ 162]
1a (Inline Function) --------`-------- normal!std::rt::lang_start_internal::closure$2+0x6 [/rustc/eeb90cda1969383f56a2637cbd3037bdf598841c/library\std\src\rt.rs @ 141]
1b (Inline Function) --------`-------- normal!std::panicking::try::do_call+0x6 [/rustc/eeb90cda1969383f56a2637cbd3037bdf598841c/library\std\src\panicking.rs @ 557]
1c (Inline Function) --------`-------- normal!std::panicking::try+0x6 [/rustc/eeb90cda1969383f56a2637cbd3037bdf598841c/library\std\src\panicking.rs @ 521]
1d (Inline Function) --------`-------- normal!std::panic::catch_unwind+0x6 [/rustc/eeb90cda1969383f56a2637cbd3037bdf598841c/library\std\src\panic.rs @ 350]
1e 00000059`41cffd70 00007ff6`bb5263aa normal!std::rt::lang_start_internal+0x79 [/rustc/eeb90cda1969383f56a2637cbd3037bdf598841c/library\std\src\rt.rs @ 141]
1f 00000059`41cffe30 00007ff6`bb526979 normal!std::rt::lang_start<tuple$<> >+0x3a [/rustc/eeb90cda1969383f56a2637cbd3037bdf598841c/library\std\src\rt.rs @ 161]
20 00000059`41cffea0 00007ff6`bb541d8c normal!main+0x19
21 (Inline Function) --------`-------- normal!invoke_main+0x22 [D:\a\_work\1\s\src\vctools\crt\vcstartup\src\startup\exe_common.inl @ 78]
22 00000059`41cffed0 00007fff`e89d53e0 normal!__scrt_common_main_seh+0x10c [D:\a\_work\1\s\src\vctools\crt\vcstartup\src\startup\exe_common.inl @ 288]
23 00000059`41cfff10 00007fff`ea00485b kernel32!BaseThreadInitThunk+0x10
24 00000059`41cfff40 00000000`00000000 ntdll!RtlUserThreadStart+0x2b

. 1 Id: afc.1d60 Suspend: 0 Teb: 00000059`41aa7000 Unfrozen
     Start: ntdll!TppWorkerThread (00007fff`ea016a00)
     Priority: 0  Priority class: 32  Affinity: 1
# Child-SP          RetAddr           Call Site
00 00000059`41dff948 00007fff`ea016cdf ntdll!NtWaitForWorkViaWorkerFactory+0x14
01 00000059`41dff950 00007fff`e89d53e0 ntdll!TppWorkerThread+0x2df
02 00000059`41dffc40 00007fff`ea00485b kernel32!BaseThreadInitThunk+0x10
03 00000059`41dffc70 00000000`00000000 ntdll!RtlUserThreadStart+0x2b

. 2 Id: afc.2820 Suspend: 0 Teb: 00000059`41aa9000 Unfrozen
     Start: normal!std::sys::pal::windows::thread::impl$0::new::thread_start (00007ff6`bb5346a0)
     Priority: 0  Priority class: 32  Affinity: 1
# Child-SP          RetAddr           Call Site
00 00000059`41fff978 00007fff`e79310ee ntdll!NtWaitForSingleObject+0x14
01 00000059`41fff980 00007ff6`bb52bf2d KERNELBASE!WaitForSingleObjectEx+0x8e
02 (Inline Function) --------`-------- normal!std::sys::pal::windows::time::WaitableTimer::wait+0xe
[/rustc/eeb90cda1969383f56a2637cbd3037bdf598841c/library\std\src\sys\pal\windows\time.rs @ 254]
03 (Inline Function) --------`-------- normal!std::sys::pal::windows::thread::impl$0::sleep::high_precision_sleep+0x7c
[/rustc/eeb90cda1969383f56a2637cbd3037bdf598841c/library\std\src\sys\pal\windows\thread.rs @ 101]
04 (Inline Function) --------`-------- normal!std::sys::pal::windows::thread::Thread::sleep+0x89
[/rustc/eeb90cda1969383f56a2637cbd3037bdf598841c/library\std\src\sys\pal\windows\thread.rs @ 106]
05 00000059`41fffa20 00007ff6`bb526036 normal!std::thread::sleep+0x9d [/rustc/eeb90cda1969383f56a2637cbd3037bdf598841c/library\std\src\thread\mod.rs @ 930]
06 00000059`41fffa90 00007ff6`bb521869 normal!normal::main::closure$0+0x16 [C:\ARWMDA-Dumps\normal\normal\src\main.rs @ 14]
07 (Inline Function) --------`-------- normal!core::hint::black_box [/rustc/eeb90cda1969383f56a2637cbd3037bdf598841c/library\core\src\hint.rs @ 389]
08 00000059`41fffac0 00007ff6`bb524f69 normal!std::sys::backtrace::__rust_begin_short_backtrace<normal::main::closure_env$0,tuple$<> >+0x9
[/rustc/eeb90cda1969383f56a2637cbd3037bdf598841c/library\std\src\sys\backtrace.rs @ 155]
09 00000059`41fffaf0 00007ff6`bb521759 normal!std::thread::impl$0::spawn_unchecked_::closure$1::closure$0<normal::main::closure_env$0,tuple$<> >+0x9
[/rustc/eeb90cda1969383f56a2637cbd3037bdf598841c/library\std\src\thread\mod.rs @ 539]
0a 00000059`41fffb20 00007ff6`bb52285d
normal!core::panic::unwind_safe::impl$25::call_once<tuple$<>,std::thread::impl$0::spawn_unchecked_::closure$1::closure_env$0<normal::main::closure_env$0,tuple$<> > >+0x9
[/rustc/eeb90cda1969383f56a2637cbd3037bdf598841c/library\core\src\panic\unwind_safe.rs @ 273]
0b 00000059`41fffb50 00007ff6`bb525153
normal!std::panicking::try::do_call<core::panic::unwind_safe::AssertUnwindSafe<std::thread::impl$0::spawn_unchecked_::closure$1::closure_env$0<normal::main::closure_env$0,tuple$<> >
>,tuple$<> >+0x1d [/rustc/eeb90cda1969383f56a2637cbd3037bdf598841c/library\std\src\panicking.rs @ 557]
0c 00000059`41fffba0 00007ff6`bb524dc4 normal!std::thread::impl$7::drop::closure$0<tuple$<> >+0xb3
0d (Inline Function) --------`-------- normal!std::panicking::try+0x1f [/rustc/eeb90cda1969383f56a2637cbd3037bdf598841c/library\std\src\panicking.rs @ 521]
0e (Inline Function) --------`-------- normal!std::panic::catch_unwind+0x1f [/rustc/eeb90cda1969383f56a2637cbd3037bdf598841c/library\std\src\panic.rs @ 350]
0f 00000059`41fffbf0 00007ff6`bb52743e normal!std::thread::impl$0::spawn_unchecked_::closure$1<normal::main::closure_env$0,tuple$<> >+0x114
[/rustc/eeb90cda1969383f56a2637cbd3037bdf598841c/library\std\src\thread\mod.rs @ 537]
10 00000059`41fffd40 00007ff6`bb5346dd normal!core::ops::function::FnOnce::call_once<std::thread::impl$0::spawn_unchecked_::closure_env$1<normal::main::closure_env$0,tuple$<> >,tuple$<>
>+0xe [/rustc/eeb90cda1969383f56a2637cbd3037bdf598841c/library\core\src\ops\function.rs @ 250]
11 (Inline Function) --------`-------- normal!alloc::boxed::impl$48::call_once+0xb [/rustc/eeb90cda1969383f56a2637cbd3037bdf598841c/library\alloc\src\boxed.rs @ 2070]
12 (Inline Function) --------`-------- normal!alloc::boxed::impl$48::call_once+0x16 [/rustc/eeb90cda1969383f56a2637cbd3037bdf598841c/library\alloc\src\boxed.rs @ 2070]
13 00000059`41fffd80 00007fff`e89d53e0 normal!std::sys::pal::windows::thread::impl$0::new::thread_start+0x3d
[/rustc/eeb90cda1969383f56a2637cbd3037bdf598841c/library\std\src\sys\pal\windows\thread.rs @ 58]
14 00000059`41fffde0 00007fff`ea00485b kernel32!BaseThreadInitThunk+0x10
15 00000059`41fffe10 00000000`00000000 ntdll!RtlUserThreadStart+0x2b

Total threads: 7
Duplicate callstacks: 4 (windbg thread #s follow):
3, 4, 5, 6
```

10.   We close logging before exiting WinDbg:

```
0:000> .logclose
Closing open log file C:\ARWMDA-Dumps\RW2.log
```

Exercise RW3

- **Goal:** Learn how to analyze stack traces from release versions

- **Patterns:** Adjoint Stack Trace; Hidden Frame; Inline Function Optimization (Unmanaged Code)

- \ARWMDA-Dumps\Exercise-RW3.pdf

Goal: Learn how to analyze stack traces from release versions.

Patterns: Adjoint Stack Trace; Hidden Frame; Inline Function Optimization (Unmanaged Code).

1.   Launch WinDbg.

2.   Open \ARWMDA-Dumps\Process\normal-release.DMP.

3.   We get the dump file loaded:

```
Microsoft (R) Windows Debugger Version 10.0.27725.1000 AMD64
Copyright (c) Microsoft Corporation. All rights reserved.


Loading Dump File [C:\ARWMDA-Dumps\Process\normal-release.DMP]
User Mini Dump File with Full Memory: Only application data is available


************* Path validation summary **************
Response                        Time (ms)     Location
Deferred                                      srv*
Symbol search path is: srv*
Executable search path is:
Windows 10 Version 22000 UP Free x64
Product: WinNt, suite: SingleUserTS
Edition build lab: 22000.1.amd64fre.co_release.210604-1628
Debug session time: Sun Oct 13 18:22:13.000 2024 (UTC + 1:00)
System Uptime: 0 days 0:07:15.310
Process Uptime: 0 days 0:01:25.000
.......
For analysis of this file, run !analyze -v
ntdll!NtDeviceIoControlFile+0x14:
00007fff`ea0a4164 ret
```

4.   Open a log file to save all future output using the **.logopen** command:

```
0:000> .logopen C:\ARWMDA-Dumps\RW3.log
Opened log file 'C:\ARWMDA-Dumps\RW3.log'
```

5.   Type the **k** command to verify the correctness of the stack trace:

```
0:000> k
 # Child-SP          RetAddr               Call Site
00 00000032`2394cec8 00007fff`e7914da5     ntdll!NtDeviceIoControlFile+0x14
01 00000032`2394ced0 00007fff`e7994c5d     KERNELBASE!ConsoleCallServerGeneric+0xe9
02 00000032`2394d030 00007fff`e7994aba     KERNELBASE!ReadConsoleInternal+0x18d
03 00000032`2394d180 00007ff7`fe66dc8b     KERNELBASE!ReadConsoleW+0x1a
04 00000032`2394d1c0 00007ff7`fe66da5f     normal+0xdc8b
05 00000032`2394d270 00007ff7`fe668677     normal+0xda5f
06 00000032`2394f310 00007ff7`fe666d25     normal+0x8677
07 00000032`2394f3b0 00007ff7`fe6635b1     normal+0x6d25
```

```
08 00000032`2394f450 00007ff7`fe6620a2     normal+0x35b1
09 00000032`2394f4e0 00007ff7`fe6610e6     normal+0x20a2
0a 00000032`2394f600 00007ff7`fe6610cc     normal+0x10e6
0b 00000032`2394f630 00007ff7`fe6652b9     normal+0x10cc
0c 00000032`2394f660 00007ff7`fe66233c     normal+0x52b9
0d 00000032`2394f720 00007ff7`fe67b56c     normal+0x233c
0e 00000032`2394f760 00007fff`e89d53e0     normal+0x1b56c
0f 00000032`2394f7a0 00007fff`ea00485b     kernel32!BaseThreadInitThunk+0x10
10 00000032`2394f7d0 00000000`00000000     ntdll!RtlUserThreadStart+0x2b
```

6.   We now specify a path to the symbol file for the *normal* module:

```
0:000> .sympath+ C:\ARWMDA-Dumps\Symbols\release
Symbol search path is: srv*;C:\ARWMDA-Dumps\Symbols\release
Expanded Symbol search path is:
cache*;SRV*https://msdl.microsoft.com/download/symbols;c:\arwmda-dumps\symbols\release

************* Path validation summary **************
Response                        Time (ms)    Location
Deferred                                     srv*
OK                                           C:\ARWMDA-Dumps\Symbols\release
```

```
0:000> kL
# Child-SP          RetAddr               Call Site
00 00000032`2394cec8 00007fff`e7914da5    ntdll!NtDeviceIoControlFile+0x14
01 00000032`2394ced0 00007fff`e7994c5d    KERNELBASE!ConsoleCallServerGeneric+0xe9
02 00000032`2394d030 00007fff`e7994aba    KERNELBASE!ReadConsoleInternal+0x18d
03 00000032`2394d180 00007ff7`fe66dc8b    KERNELBASE!ReadConsoleW+0x1a
04 (Inline Function) --------`--------    normal!std::sys::pal::windows::stdio::read_u16s+0x4e
05 00000032`2394d1c0 00007ff7`fe66da5f    normal!std::sys::pal::windows::stdio::read_u16s_fixup_surrogates+0xcb
06 00000032`2394d270 00007ff7`fe668677    normal!std::sys::pal::windows::stdio::impl$2::read+0x19f
07 (Inline Function) --------`--------    normal!std::io::Read::read_buf::closure$0+0xb
08 (Inline Function) --------`--------    normal!std::io::default_read_buf+0x1f
09 (Inline Function) --------`--------    normal!std::io::Read::read_buf+0x1f
0a (Inline Function) --------`--------    normal!std::io::stdio::impl$0::read_buf+0x1f
0b (Inline Function) --------`--------    normal!std::io::impls::impl$0::read_buf+0x1f
0c (Inline Function) --------`--------    normal!std::io::buffered::bufreader::buffer::Buffer::fill_buf+0x3b
0d (Inline Function) --------`--------    normal!std::io::buffered::bufreader::impl$5::fill_buf+0x3b
0e 00000032`2394f310 00007ff7`fe666d25    normal!std::io::read_until<std::io::buffered::bufreader::BufReader<std::io::stdio::StdinRaw> >+0x67
0f (Inline Function) --------`--------    normal!std::io::stdio::impl$9::read_line+0x1a
10 00000032`2394f3b0 00007ff7`fe6635b1    normal!std::io::stdio::Stdin::read_line+0x65
11 00000032`2394f450 00007ff7`fe6620a2    normal!ZN7crate_c6mod_cb4func17h8ed23eaf84b3cc6bE+0x71
12 00000032`2394f4e0 00007ff7`fe6610e6
normal!ZN86_$LT$alloc..vec..into_iter..IntoIter$LT$T$C$A$GT$$u20$as$u20$core..ops..drop..Drop$GT$4drop17h8c50d4e5a113a5afE+0x812
13 00000032`2394f600 00007ff7`fe6610cc
normal!ZN3std2rt10lang_start28_$u7b$$u7b$closure$u7d$$u7d$17h0b755b328912fb54E.llvm.17425134955195048245+0x26
14 00000032`2394f630 00007ff7`fe6652b9
normal!ZN3std2rt10lang_start28_$u7b$$u7b$closure$u7d$$u7d$17h0b755b328912fb54E.llvm.17425134955195048245+0xc
15 (Inline Function) --------`--------    normal!std::rt::lang_start_internal::closure$2+0x6
16 (Inline Function) --------`--------    normal!std::panicking::try::do_call+0x6
17 (Inline Function) --------`--------    normal!std::panicking::try+0x6
18 (Inline Function) --------`--------    normal!std::panic::catch_unwind+0x6
19 00000032`2394f660 00007ff7`fe66233c    normal!std::rt::lang_start_internal+0x79
1a 00000032`2394f720 00007ff7`fe67b56c    normal!main+0x2c
1b (Inline Function) --------`--------    normal!invoke_main+0x22
1c 00000032`2394f760 00007fff`e89d53e0    normal!__scrt_common_main_seh+0x10c
1d 00000032`2394f7a0 00007fff`ea00485b    kernel32!BaseThreadInitThunk+0x10
1e 00000032`2394f7d0 00000000`00000000    ntdll!RtlUserThreadStart+0x2b
```

Note: We see only the *crate_c::mod_cb::func* function call on the stack trace
(*normal!ZN7**crate_c6mod_cb4func**17h8ed23eaf84b3cc6bE*) compared to the debug version from the previous
exercise:

```
11 00000059`41cff960 00007ff6`bb528dde    normal!crate_c::mod_cb::func+0x5e
12 00000059`41cffa20 00007ff6`bb5226f4    normal!crate_b::mod_b::func+0x2e
13 00000059`41cffa80 00007ff6`bb522fb4    normal!normal::mod_aa::func+0x24
14 00000059`41cffae0 00007ff6`bb526780    normal!normal::mod_ab::func+0x24
15 00000059`41cffb40 00007ff6`bb5274db    normal!normal::main+0x90
```

7.   Let's look at the return address **00007ff7`fe6620a2**:

```
0:000> ub 00007ff7`fe6620a2
normal!ZN86_$LT$alloc..vec..into_iter..IntoIter$LT$T$C$A$GT$$u20$as$u20$core..ops..drop..Drop$G
T$4drop17h8c50d4e5a113a5afE+0x7e8:
00007ff7`fe662078 mov      qword ptr [rbp-10h],1
00007ff7`fe662080 mov      qword ptr [rbp-8],8
00007ff7`fe662088 movups   xmmword ptr [rbp],xmm6
00007ff7`fe66208c mov      byte ptr [rbp+37h],1
00007ff7`fe662090 lea      rcx,[rbp-18h]
00007ff7`fe662094 call     normal!std::io::stdio::_print (00007ff7`fe667700)
00007ff7`fe662099 mov      byte ptr [rbp+37h],1
00007ff7`fe66209d call     normal!ZN7crate_b5mod_b4func17h2c4118b811a7b92cE (00007ff7`fe663450)
```

Note: We see that a different function *crate_b::mod_b::func* was called instead. However, when we disassemble it, we see that it jumps to the *crate_c::mod_cb::func* function we see on the stack trace:

```
0:000> uf 00007ff7`fe663450
normal!ZN7crate_b5mod_b4func17h2c4118b811a7b92cE:
00007ff7`fe663450 sub      rsp,68h
00007ff7`fe663454 movaps   xmmword ptr [rsp+50h],xmm6
00007ff7`fe663459 lea      rax,[normal!anon.27261d7dec9111478dd8cf11a98650d5.2.llvm.5820089071535542758+0xd8
(00007ff7`fe67e860)]
00007ff7`fe663460 mov      qword ptr [rsp+20h],rax
00007ff7`fe663465 mov      qword ptr [rsp+28h],1
00007ff7`fe66346e mov      qword ptr [rsp+30h],8
00007ff7`fe663477 xorps    xmm6,xmm6
00007ff7`fe66347a movups   xmmword ptr [rsp+38h],xmm6
00007ff7`fe66347f lea      rcx,[rsp+20h]
00007ff7`fe663484 call     normal!std::io::stdio::_print (00007ff7`fe667700)
00007ff7`fe663489 lea      rax,[normal!anon.27261d7dec9111478dd8cf11a98650d5.2.llvm.5820089071535542758+0xa0
(00007ff7`fe67e828)]
00007ff7`fe663490 mov      qword ptr [rsp+20h],rax
00007ff7`fe663495 mov      qword ptr [rsp+28h],1
00007ff7`fe66349e mov      qword ptr [rsp+30h],8
00007ff7`fe6634a7 movups   xmmword ptr [rsp+38h],xmm6
00007ff7`fe6634ac lea      rcx,[rsp+20h]
00007ff7`fe6634b1 call     normal!std::io::stdio::_print (00007ff7`fe667700)
00007ff7`fe6634b6 lea      rax,[normal!anon.27261d7dec9111478dd8cf11a98650d5.2.llvm.5820089071535542758+0xb8
(00007ff7`fe67e840)]
00007ff7`fe6634bd mov      qword ptr [rsp+20h],rax
00007ff7`fe6634c2 mov      qword ptr [rsp+28h],1
00007ff7`fe6634cb mov      qword ptr [rsp+30h],8
00007ff7`fe6634d4 movups   xmmword ptr [rsp+38h],xmm6
00007ff7`fe6634d9 lea      rcx,[rsp+20h]
00007ff7`fe6634de call     normal!std::io::stdio::_print (00007ff7`fe667700)
00007ff7`fe6634e3 call     normal!ZN7crate_c6mod_ca4func17h8bb43d8048892409E (00007ff7`fe663500)
00007ff7`fe6634e8 movaps   xmm6,xmmword ptr [rsp+50h]
00007ff7`fe6634ed add      rsp,68h
00007ff7`fe6634f1 jmp      normal!ZN7crate_c6mod_cb4func17h8ed23eaf84b3cc6bE (00007ff7`fe663540)  Branch

normal!ZN7crate_c6mod_cb4func17h8ed23eaf84b3cc6bE:
00007ff7`fe663540 push     rbp
00007ff7`fe663541 sub      rsp,80h
00007ff7`fe663548 lea      rbp,[rsp+80h]
00007ff7`fe663550 mov      qword ptr [rbp-8],0FFFFFFFFFFFFFFFEh
00007ff7`fe663558 lea      rax,[normal!anon.27261d7dec9111478dd8cf11a98650d5.2.llvm.5820089071535542758+0x118
(00007ff7`fe67e8a0)]
00007ff7`fe66355f mov      qword ptr [rbp-50h],rax
00007ff7`fe663563 mov      qword ptr [rbp-48h],1
00007ff7`fe66356b mov      qword ptr [rbp-40h],8
00007ff7`fe663573 xorps    xmm0,xmm0
00007ff7`fe663576 movups   xmmword ptr [rbp-38h],xmm0
00007ff7`fe66357a lea      rcx,[rbp-50h]
00007ff7`fe66357e call     normal!std::io::stdio::_print (00007ff7`fe667700)
00007ff7`fe663583 mov      qword ptr [rbp-50h],0
00007ff7`fe66358b mov      qword ptr [rbp-48h],1
```

```
00007ff7`fe663593 mov      qword ptr [rbp-40h],0
00007ff7`fe66359b call     normal!std::io::stdio::stdin (00007ff7`fe666c90)
00007ff7`fe6635a0 mov      qword ptr [rbp-58h],rax
00007ff7`fe6635a4 lea      rcx,[rbp-58h]
00007ff7`fe6635a8 lea      rdx,[rbp-50h]
00007ff7`fe6635ac call     normal!std::io::stdio::Stdin::read_line (00007ff7`fe666cc0)
00007ff7`fe6635b1 test     rax,rax
00007ff7`fe6635b4 je       normal!ZN7crate_c6mod_cb4func17h8ed23eaf84b3cc6bE+0xe0 (00007ff7`fe663620)   Branch

normal!ZN7crate_c6mod_cb4func17h8ed23eaf84b3cc6bE+0x76:
00007ff7`fe6635b6 mov      eax,edx
00007ff7`fe6635b8 and      eax,3
00007ff7`fe6635bb lea      rcx,[rax-2]
00007ff7`fe6635bf cmp      rcx,2
00007ff7`fe6635c3 jb       normal!ZN7crate_c6mod_cb4func17h8ed23eaf84b3cc6bE+0xe0 (00007ff7`fe663620)   Branch

normal!ZN7crate_c6mod_cb4func17h8ed23eaf84b3cc6bE+0x85:
00007ff7`fe6635c5 test     rax,rax
00007ff7`fe6635c8 je       normal!ZN7crate_c6mod_cb4func17h8ed23eaf84b3cc6bE+0xe0 (00007ff7`fe663620)   Branch

normal!ZN7crate_c6mod_cb4func17h8ed23eaf84b3cc6bE+0x8a:
00007ff7`fe6635ca mov      rax,rdx
00007ff7`fe6635cd dec      rax
00007ff7`fe6635d0 mov      qword ptr [rbp-20h],rax
00007ff7`fe6635d4 mov      rax,qword ptr [rdx-1]
00007ff7`fe6635d8 mov      qword ptr [rbp-18h],rax
00007ff7`fe6635dc mov      rax,qword ptr [rdx+7]
00007ff7`fe6635e0 mov      qword ptr [rbp-10h],rax
00007ff7`fe6635e4 mov      rax,qword ptr [rax]
00007ff7`fe6635e7 test     rax,rax
00007ff7`fe6635ea je       normal!ZN7crate_c6mod_cb4func17h8ed23eaf84b3cc6bE+0xb2 (00007ff7`fe6635f2)   Branch

normal!ZN7crate_c6mod_cb4func17h8ed23eaf84b3cc6bE+0xac:
00007ff7`fe6635ec mov      rcx,qword ptr [rbp-18h]
00007ff7`fe6635f0 call     rax

normal!ZN7crate_c6mod_cb4func17h8ed23eaf84b3cc6bE+0xb2:
00007ff7`fe6635f2 mov      rcx,qword ptr [rbp-18h]
00007ff7`fe6635f6 mov      rax,qword ptr [rbp-10h]
00007ff7`fe6635fa mov      rdx,qword ptr [rax+8]
00007ff7`fe6635fe test     rdx,rdx
00007ff7`fe663601 je       normal!ZN7crate_c6mod_cb4func17h8ed23eaf84b3cc6bE+0xcc (00007ff7`fe66360c)   Branch

normal!ZN7crate_c6mod_cb4func17h8ed23eaf84b3cc6bE+0xc3:
00007ff7`fe663603 mov      r8,qword ptr [rax+10h]
00007ff7`fe663607 call     normal!_rust_dealloc (00007ff7`fe663420)

normal!ZN7crate_c6mod_cb4func17h8ed23eaf84b3cc6bE+0xcc:
00007ff7`fe66360c mov      edx,18h
00007ff7`fe663611 mov      r8d,8
00007ff7`fe663617 mov      rcx,qword ptr [rbp-20h]
00007ff7`fe66361b call     normal!_rust_dealloc (00007ff7`fe663420)

normal!ZN7crate_c6mod_cb4func17h8ed23eaf84b3cc6bE+0xe0:
00007ff7`fe663620 mov      rdx,qword ptr [rbp-50h]
00007ff7`fe663624 test     rdx,rdx
00007ff7`fe663627 je       normal!ZN7crate_c6mod_cb4func17h8ed23eaf84b3cc6bE+0xf8 (00007ff7`fe663638)   Branch

normal!ZN7crate_c6mod_cb4func17h8ed23eaf84b3cc6bE+0xe9:
00007ff7`fe663629 mov      rcx,qword ptr [rbp-48h]
00007ff7`fe66362d mov      r8d,1
00007ff7`fe663633 call     normal!_rust_dealloc (00007ff7`fe663420)

normal!ZN7crate_c6mod_cb4func17h8ed23eaf84b3cc6bE+0xf8:
00007ff7`fe663638 nop
00007ff7`fe663639 add      rsp,80h
00007ff7`fe663640 pop      rbp
00007ff7`fe663641 ret
```

Note: Despite being concatenated, the *normal!ZN7**crate_c6mod_cb4func***17h8ed23eaf84b3cc6bE* function is a real function:

```
0:000> x normal!*crate_*
00007ff7`fe663450 normal!ZN7crate_b5mod_b4func17h2c4118b811a7b92cE (_ZN7crate_b5mod_b4func17h2c4118b811a7b92cE)
00007ff7`fe663500 normal!ZN7crate_c6mod_ca4func17h8bb43d8048892409E (_ZN7crate_c6mod_ca4func17h8bb43d8048892409E)
00007ff7`fe663540 normal!ZN7crate_c6mod_cb4func17h8ed23eaf84b3cc6bE (_ZN7crate_c6mod_cb4func17h8ed23eaf84b3cc6bE)
```

8.   We call two stack traces adjoint when we move between both back and forth to facilitate understanding. In our case: both release and debug versions. In our case, we compare these:

```
; release
...
0f normal!std::io::stdio::impl$9::read_line
10 normal!std::io::stdio::Stdin::read_line
11 normal!ZN7crate_c6mod_cb4func17h8ed23eaf84b3cc6bE
; Hidden Frame
12
normal!ZN86_$LT$alloc..vec..into_iter..IntoIter$LT$T$C$A$GT$$u20$as$u20$core..ops..drop..Drop$G
T$4drop17h8c50d4e5a113a5afE
...

; debug
...
0f normal!std::io::stdio::impl$9::read_line
10 normal!std::io::stdio::Stdin::read_line
11 normal!crate_c::mod_cb::func
12 normal!crate_b::mod_b::func
13 normal!normal::mod_aa::func
14 normal!normal::mod_ab::func
15 normal!normal::main
16 normal!core::ops::function::FnOnce::call_once<void (*)(),tuple$<> >
...
```

Another example of adjoint stack traces is two successive process executions with different collected stack traces.

9.   We close logging before exiting WinDbg:

```
0:000> .logclose
Closing open log file C:\ARWMDA-Dumps\RW3.log
```

Exercise RW4

- **Goal:** Learn to recognize exceptions in process memory dumps and get their context

- **Patterns:** Exception Stack Trace; Exception Module; Multiple Exceptions (User Mode); NULL Pointer (Data); Invalid Pointer (General); NULL Pointer (Code)

- \ARWMDA-Dumps\Exercise-RW4.pdf

Exercise RW4

Goal: Learn to recognize exceptions in process memory dumps and get their context.

Patterns: Exception Stack Trace; Multiple Exceptions (User Mode); NULL Pointer (Data); Invalid Pointer (General); NULL Pointer (Code).

1.   Launch WinDbg.

2.   Open \AWMDA-Dumps\Process\multiple-exceptions.exe.344.dmp.

3.   We get the dump file loaded:

```
Microsoft (R) Windows Debugger Version 10.0.27725.1000 AMD64
Copyright (c) Microsoft Corporation. All rights reserved.


Loading Dump File [C:\ARWMDA-Dumps\Process\multiple-exceptions.exe.344.dmp]
User Mini Dump File with Full Memory: Only application data is available


************* Path validation summary **************
Response                         Time (ms)      Location
Deferred                                        srv*
Symbol search path is: srv*
Executable search path is:
Windows 10 Version 22000 UP Free x64
Product: WinNt, suite: SingleUserTS
Edition build lab: 22000.1.amd64fre.co_release.210604-1628
Debug session time: Mon Oct 28 14:36:16.000 2024 (UTC + 0:00)
System Uptime: 0 days 0:08:18.877
Process Uptime: 0 days 0:00:03.000
......
This dump file has an exception of interest stored in it.
The stored exception information can be accessed via .ecxr
(158.1ac8): Access violation - code c0000005 (first/second chance not available)
For analysis of this file, run !analyze -v
ntdll!NtWaitForMultipleObjects+0x14:
00007ff9`20f24bd4 ret
```

4.   Open a log file using the **.logopen** command:

```
0:000> .logopen C:\ARWMDA-Dumps\RW4.log
Opened log file 'C:\ARWMDA-Dumps\RW4.log'
```

5.   Type the **k** command to verify the correctness of the stack trace:

```
0:003> k
 # Child-SP          RetAddr           Call Site
00 000000bb`24efe318 00007ff9`1e46dcd0  ntdll!NtWaitForMultipleObjects+0x14
01 000000bb`24efe320 00007ff9`1e46dbce  KERNELBASE!WaitForMultipleObjectsEx+0xf0
02 000000bb`24efe610 00007ff9`1f8ef087  KERNELBASE!WaitForMultipleObjects+0xe
03 000000bb`24efe650 00007ff9`1f8eeac6  kernel32!WerpReportFaultInternal+0x587
04 000000bb`24efe770 00007ff9`1e55e503  kernel32!WerpReportFault+0xbe
```

82

```
05 000000bb`24efe7b0 00007ff9`20f2b0ec   KERNELBASE!UnhandledExceptionFilter+0x3e3
06 000000bb`24efe8d0 00007ff9`20f140f6   ntdll!RtlUserThreadStart$filt$0+0xac
07 000000bb`24efe910 00007ff9`20f2906f   ntdll!_C_specific_handler+0x96
08 000000bb`24efe980 00007ff9`20eb5bea   ntdll!RtlpExecuteHandlerForException+0xf
09 000000bb`24efe9b0 00007ff9`20f2805e   ntdll!RtlDispatchException+0x25a
0a 000000bb`24eff100 00007ff6`a4ce10ee   ntdll!KiUserExceptionDispatch+0x2e
0b 000000bb`24eff820 00007ff6`a4ce2c30   multiple_exceptions+0x10ee
0c 000000bb`24eff850 00007ff6`a4ced1cd   multiple_exceptions+0x2c30
0d 000000bb`24eff8f0 00007ff9`1f8953e0   multiple_exceptions+0xd1cd
0e 000000bb`24eff950 00007ff9`20e8485b   kernel32!BaseThreadInitThunk+0x10
0f 000000bb`24eff980 00000000`00000000   ntdll!RtlUserThreadStart+0x2b
```

Note: The symbols were loaded correctly for MS modules but not for the 3rd-party *multiple_exceptions*. This is a normal real-life scenario where symbols are not available. We also see that the current thread is #3, and it does exception processing from the exception module *multiple_exceptions,* including fault reporting.

6.   Type default analysis command **!analyze -v**:

```
0:003> !analyze -v
*******************************************************************
*                                                                 *
*                        Exception Analysis                       *
*                                                                 *
*******************************************************************


KEY_VALUES_STRING: 1

    Key  : AV.Dereference
    Value: NullClassPtr

    Key  : AV.Fault
    Value: Write

    Key  : Analysis.CPU.mSec
    Value: 265

    Key  : Analysis.Elapsed.mSec
    Value: 1419

    Key  : Analysis.IO.Other.Mb
    Value: 0

    Key  : Analysis.IO.Read.Mb
    Value: 1

    Key  : Analysis.IO.Write.Mb
    Value: 0

    Key  : Analysis.Init.CPU.mSec
    Value: 562

    Key  : Analysis.Init.Elapsed.mSec
    Value: 396849

    Key  : Analysis.Memory.CommitPeak.Mb
    Value: 224

    Key  : Analysis.Version.DbgEng
    Value: 10.0.27725.1000

    Key  : Analysis.Version.Description
    Value: 10.2408.27.01 amd64fre

    Key  : Analysis.Version.Ext
    Value: 1.2408.27.1

    Key  : Failure.Bucket
    Value: NULL_CLASS_PTR_WRITE_c0000005_multiple-exceptions.exe!Unknown

    Key  : Failure.Hash
    Value: {f26697c8-a666-47fd-51b6-192d6c42204a}

    Key  : Timeline.OS.Boot.DeltaSec
    Value: 498

    Key  : Timeline.Process.Start.DeltaSec
    Value: 3

    Key  : WER.OS.Branch
    Value: co_release

    Key  : WER.OS.Version
    Value: 10.0.22000.1
```

```
FILE_IN_CAB:  multiple-exceptions.exe.344.dmp

NTGLOBALFLAG:  0

APPLICATION_VERIFIER_FLAGS:  0

CONTEXT:  (.ecxr)
rax=0000029e1e70e8e0 rbx=0000000000000000 rcx=0000000000000002
rdx=0000000000000000 rsi=0000000000000002 rdi=0000000000000000
rip=00007ff6a4ce10ee rsp=000000bb24eff820 rbp=000000bb24eff8c0
 r8=0000000000000050  r9=0000000000000001 r10=0000000000000001
r11=000000bb24eff260 r12=0000000000000000 r13=0000000000000000
r14=0000000000000000 r15=0000000000000000
iopl=0          nv up ei pl zr na po nc
cs=0033  ss=002b  ds=002b  es=002b  fs=0053  gs=002b          efl=00010246
multiple_exceptions+0x10ee:
00007ff6`a4ce10ee mov     dword ptr [1],0       ds:00000000`00000001=????????
Resetting default scope

EXCEPTION_RECORD:  (.exr -1)
ExceptionAddress: 00007ff6a4ce10ee (multiple_exceptions+0x00000000000010ee)
   ExceptionCode: c0000005 (Access violation)
  ExceptionFlags: 00000000
NumberParameters: 2
   Parameter[0]: 0000000000000001
   Parameter[1]: 0000000000000001
Attempt to write to address 0000000000000001

PROCESS_NAME:  multiple-exceptions.exe

WRITE_ADDRESS:  0000000000000001

ERROR_CODE: (NTSTATUS) 0xc0000005 - The instruction at 0x%p referenced memory at 0x%p. The memory could not be %s.

EXCEPTION_CODE_STR:  c0000005

EXCEPTION_PARAMETER1:  0000000000000001

EXCEPTION_PARAMETER2:  0000000000000001

STACK_TEXT:
000000bb`24eff820 00007ff6`a4ce2c30     : 00000000`00000000 00000000`00000000 00000000`00000000 00000000`00000000 : multiple_exceptions+0x10ee
000000bb`24eff850 00007ff6`a4ced1cd     : 00000000`00000000 0000029e`1e70cb00 00000000`00000000 00000000`00000000 : multiple_exceptions+0x2c30
000000bb`24eff8f0 00007ff9`1f8953e0     : 00000000`00000000 00000000`00000000 00000000`00000000 00000000`00000000 : multiple_exceptions+0xd1cd
000000bb`24eff950 00007ff9`20e8485b     : 00000000`00000000 00000000`00000000 00000000`00000000 00000000`00000000 : kernel32!BaseThreadInitThunk+0x10
000000bb`24eff980 00000000`00000000     : 00000000`00000000 00000000`00000000 00000000`00000000 00000000`00000000 : ntdll!RtlUserThreadStart+0x2b

STACK_COMMAND:  ~3s; .ecxr ; kb

SYMBOL_NAME:  multiple_exceptions+10ee

MODULE_NAME: multiple_exceptions

IMAGE_NAME:  multiple-exceptions.exe

FAILURE_BUCKET_ID:  NULL_CLASS_PTR_WRITE_c0000005_multiple-exceptions.exe!Unknown

OS_VERSION:  10.0.22000.1

BUILDLAB_STR:  co_release

OSPLATFORM_TYPE:  x64

OSNAME:  Windows 10

FAILURE_ID_HASH:  {f26697c8-a666-47fd-51b6-192d6c42204a}

Followup:     MachineOwner
---------
```

Note: We see that WinDbg identified a null pointer write and provided the stack trace (that we show in smaller font below):

Attempt to write to address 0000000000000001

```
STACK_TEXT:
000000bb`24eff820 00007ff6`a4ce2c30     : 00000000`00000000 00000000`00000000 00000000`00000000 00000000`00000000 : multiple_exceptions+0x10ee
000000bb`24eff850 00007ff6`a4ced1cd     : 00000000`00000000 0000029e`1e70cb00 00000000`00000000 00000000`00000000 : multiple_exceptions+0x2c30
000000bb`24eff8f0 00007ff9`1f8953e0     : 00000000`00000000 00000000`00000000 00000000`00000000 00000000`00000000 : multiple_exceptions+0xd1cd
000000bb`24eff950 00007ff9`20e8485b     : 00000000`00000000 00000000`00000000 00000000`00000000 00000000`00000000 : kernel32!BaseThreadInitThunk+0x10
000000bb`24eff980 00000000`00000000     : 00000000`00000000 00000000`00000000 00000000`00000000 00000000`00000000 : ntdll!RtlUserThreadStart+0x2b
```

7. Let's check that WinDbg conclusion was correct:

```
0:003> k
 # Child-SP          RetAddr             Call Site
00 000000bb`24efe318 00007ff9`1e46dcd0   ntdll!NtWaitForMultipleObjects+0x14
01 000000bb`24efe320 00007ff9`1e46dbce   KERNELBASE!WaitForMultipleObjectsEx+0xf0
02 000000bb`24efe610 00007ff9`1f8ef087   KERNELBASE!WaitForMultipleObjects+0xe
03 000000bb`24efe650 00007ff9`1f8eeac6   kernel32!WerpReportFaultInternal+0x587
04 000000bb`24efe770 00007ff9`1e55e503   kernel32!WerpReportFault+0xbe
05 000000bb`24efe7b0 00007ff9`20f2b0ec   KERNELBASE!UnhandledExceptionFilter+0x3e3
06 000000bb`24efe8d0 00007ff9`20f140f6   ntdll!RtlUserThreadStart$filt$0+0xac
07 000000bb`24efe910 00007ff9`20f2906f   ntdll!_C_specific_handler+0x96
08 000000bb`24efe980 00007ff9`20eb5bea   ntdll!RtlpExecuteHandlerForException+0xf
09 000000bb`24efe9b0 00007ff9`20f2805e   ntdll!RtlDispatchException+0x25a
0a 000000bb`24eff100 00007ff6`a4ce10ee   ntdll!KiUserExceptionDispatch+0x2e
0b 000000bb`24eff820 00007ff6`a4ce2c30   multiple_exceptions+0x10ee
0c 000000bb`24eff850 00007ff6`a4ced1cd   multiple_exceptions+0x2c30
0d 000000bb`24eff8f0 00007ff9`1f8953e0   multiple_exceptions+0xd1cd
0e 000000bb`24eff950 00007ff9`20e8485b   kernel32!BaseThreadInitThunk+0x10
0f 000000bb`24eff980 00000000`00000000   ntdll!RtlUserThreadStart+0x2b

0:003> u 00007ff6`a4ce10ee
multiple_exceptions+0x10ee:
00007ff6`a4ce10ee mov     dword ptr [1],0
00007ff6`a4ce10f9 jmp     multiple_exceptions+0x1102 (00007ff6`a4ce1102)
00007ff6`a4ce10fb mov     eax,12345678h
00007ff6`a4ce1100 call    rax
00007ff6`a4ce1102 call    multiple_exceptions+0x57b0 (00007ff6`a4ce57b0)
00007ff6`a4ce1107 nop
00007ff6`a4ce1108 add     rsp,28h
00007ff6`a4ce110c ret
```

Note: The return address for *ntdll!KiUserExceptionDispatch+0x2e* is not an address after the *call* instruction but the address of an instruction that caused the exception. This is why we use the **u** command, not the **ub** command, as we did in the previous exercises.

8. We can set the exception context manually to replicate the **!analyze -v** output:

```
0:003> .ecxr
rax=0000029e1e70e8e0 rbx=0000000000000000 rcx=0000000000000002
rdx=0000000000000000 rsi=0000000000000002 rdi=0000000000000000
rip=00007ff6a4ce10ee rsp=000000bb24eff820 rbp=000000bb24eff8c0
 r8=0000000000000050  r9=0000000000000000 r10=0000000000000001
r11=000000bb24eff260 r12=0000000000000000 r13=0000000000000000
r14=0000000000000000 r15=0000000000000000
iopl=0         nv up ei pl zr na po nc
cs=0033  ss=002b  ds=002b  es=002b  fs=0053  gs=002b            efl=00010246
multiple_exceptions+0x10ee:
00007ff6`a4ce10ee mov     dword ptr [1],0         ds:00000000`00000001=????????

0:003> k
  *** Stack trace for last set context - .thread/.cxr resets it
 # Child-SP          RetAddr             Call Site
00 000000bb`24eff820 00007ff6`a4ce2c30   multiple_exceptions+0x10ee
01 000000bb`24eff850 00007ff6`a4ced1cd   multiple_exceptions+0x2c30
02 000000bb`24eff8f0 00007ff9`1f8953e0   multiple_exceptions+0xd1cd
03 000000bb`24eff950 00007ff9`20e8485b   kernel32!BaseThreadInitThunk+0x10
```

```
04 000000bb`24eff980 00000000`00000000     ntdll!RtlUserThreadStart+0x2b
```

Note: To restore the previous default context, use the **.cxr** command:

```
0:003> .cxr
Resetting default scope

0:003> k
 # Child-SP          RetAddr               Call Site
00 000000bb`24efe318 00007ff9`1e46dcd0     ntdll!NtWaitForMultipleObjects+0x14
01 000000bb`24efe320 00007ff9`1e46dbce     KERNELBASE!WaitForMultipleObjectsEx+0xf0
02 000000bb`24efe610 00007ff9`1f8ef087     KERNELBASE!WaitForMultipleObjects+0xe
03 000000bb`24efe650 00007ff9`1f8eeac6     kernel32!WerpReportFaultInternal+0x587
04 000000bb`24efe770 00007ff9`1e55e503     kernel32!WerpReportFault+0xbe
05 000000bb`24efe7b0 00007ff9`20f2b0ec     KERNELBASE!UnhandledExceptionFilter+0x3e3
06 000000bb`24efe8d0 00007ff9`20f140f6     ntdll!RtlUserThreadStart$filt$0+0xac
07 000000bb`24efe910 00007ff9`20f2906f     ntdll!_C_specific_handler+0x96
08 000000bb`24efe980 00007ff9`20eb5bea     ntdll!RtlpExecuteHandlerForException+0xf
09 000000bb`24efe9b0 00007ff9`20f2805e     ntdll!RtlDispatchException+0x25a
0a 000000bb`24eff100 00007ff6`a4ce10ee     ntdll!KiUserExceptionDispatch+0x2e
0b 000000bb`24eff820 00007ff6`a4ce2c30     multiple_exceptions+0x10ee
0c 000000bb`24eff850 00007ff6`a4ced1cd     multiple_exceptions+0x2c30
0d 000000bb`24eff8f0 00007ff9`1f8953e0     multiple_exceptions+0xd1cd
0e 000000bb`24eff950 00007ff9`20e8485b     kernel32!BaseThreadInitThunk+0x10
0f 000000bb`24eff980 00000000`00000000     ntdll!RtlUserThreadStart+0x2b
```

9.   Now we check how many threads we have by using the ~ command:

```
0:003> ~
   0  Id: 158.ffc Suspend: 0 Teb: 000000bb`248e6000 Unfrozen "main"
   1  Id: 158.ca8 Suspend: 0 Teb: 000000bb`248e8000 Unfrozen
   2  Id: 158.1b04 Suspend: 0 Teb: 000000bb`248ea000 Unfrozen
.  3  Id: 158.1ac8 Suspend: 0 Teb: 000000bb`248ec000 Unfrozen
   4  Id: 158.1ad4 Suspend: 0 Teb: 000000bb`248ee000 Unfrozen
   5  Id: 158.1acc Suspend: 0 Teb: 000000bb`248f0000 Unfrozen
   6  Id: 158.2090 Suspend: 0 Teb: 000000bb`248f2000 Unfrozen
```

Note: Exceptions and faults are per thread. There can be other exceptions from other threads. It is usually the case that WinDbg recognizes the first exception but misses the subsequent ones being processed at the time of the first exception.

10.   We get stack traces from all threads at once using the **~*k** command:

```
0:003> ~*k

   0  Id: 158.ffc Suspend: 0 Teb: 000000bb`248e6000 Unfrozen "main"
 # Child-SP          RetAddr               Call Site
00 000000bb`2477f768 00007ff9`1e4610ee     ntdll!NtWaitForSingleObject+0x14
01 000000bb`2477f770 00007ff6`a4ced331     KERNELBASE!WaitForSingleObjectEx+0x8e
02 000000bb`2477f810 00007ff6`a4ce2381     multiple_exceptions+0xd331
03 000000bb`2477f8a0 00007ff6`a4ce2108     multiple_exceptions+0x2381
04 000000bb`2477f900 00007ff6`a4ce1116     multiple_exceptions+0x2108
05 000000bb`2477fa20 00007ff6`a4ce10cc     multiple_exceptions+0x1116
06 000000bb`2477fa50 00007ff6`a4ce5229     multiple_exceptions+0x10cc
07 000000bb`2477fa80 00007ff6`a4ce234c     multiple_exceptions+0x5229
08 000000bb`2477fb40 00007ff6`a4cfa7ac     multiple_exceptions+0x234c
09 000000bb`2477fb80 00007ff9`1f8953e0     multiple_exceptions+0x1a7ac
```

```
0a  000000bb`2477fbc0  00007ff9`20e8485b     kernel32!BaseThreadInitThunk+0x10
0b  000000bb`2477fbf0  00000000`00000000     ntdll!RtlUserThreadStart+0x2b

    1  Id: 158.ca8 Suspend: 0 Teb: 000000bb`248e8000 Unfrozen
 # Child-SP          RetAddr               Call Site
00  000000bb`24aff548  00007ff9`20e96cdf     ntdll!NtWaitForWorkViaWorkerFactory+0x14
01  000000bb`24aff550  00007ff9`1f8953e0     ntdll!TppWorkerThread+0x2df
02  000000bb`24aff840  00007ff9`20e8485b     kernel32!BaseThreadInitThunk+0x10
03  000000bb`24aff870  00000000`00000000     ntdll!RtlUserThreadStart+0x2b

    2  Id: 158.1b04 Suspend: 0 Teb: 000000bb`248ea000 Unfrozen
 # Child-SP          RetAddr               Call Site
00  000000bb`24cff818  00007ff9`20e9d89d     ntdll!NtWaitForAlertByThreadId+0x14
01  000000bb`24cff820  00007ff9`20edb3fe     ntdll!RtlpWaitOnAddressWithTimeout+0x81
02  000000bb`24cff850  00007ff9`20edb343     ntdll!RtlpWaitOnAddress+0xae
03  000000bb`24cff8c0  00007ff9`1e47dd9f     ntdll!RtlWaitOnAddress+0x13
04  000000bb`24cff900  00007ff6`a4ce5901     KERNELBASE!WaitOnAddress+0x2f
05  000000bb`24cff940  00007ff6`a4ce1107     multiple_exceptions+0x5901
06  000000bb`24cff9b0  00007ff6`a4ce2c30     multiple_exceptions+0x1107
07  000000bb`24cff9e0  00007ff6`a4ced1cd     multiple_exceptions+0x2c30
08  000000bb`24cffa80  00007ff9`1f8953e0     multiple_exceptions+0xd1cd
09  000000bb`24cffae0  00007ff9`20e8485b     kernel32!BaseThreadInitThunk+0x10
0a  000000bb`24cffb10  00000000`00000000     ntdll!RtlUserThreadStart+0x2b

 #  3  Id: 158.1ac8 Suspend: 0 Teb: 000000bb`248ec000 Unfrozen
 # Child-SP          RetAddr               Call Site
00  000000bb`24efe318  00007ff9`1e46dcd0     ntdll!NtWaitForMultipleObjects+0x14
01  000000bb`24efe320  00007ff9`1e46dbce     KERNELBASE!WaitForMultipleObjectsEx+0xf0
02  000000bb`24efe610  00007ff9`1f8ef087     KERNELBASE!WaitForMultipleObjects+0xe
```

```
03  000000bb`24efe650  00007ff9`1f8eeac6     kernel32!WerpReportFaultInternal+0x587
04  000000bb`24efe770  00007ff9`1e55e503     kernel32!WerpReportFault+0xbe
05  000000bb`24efe7b0  00007ff9`20f2b0ec     KERNELBASE!UnhandledExceptionFilter+0x3e3
06  000000bb`24efe8d0  00007ff9`20f140f6     ntdll!RtlUserThreadStart$filt$0+0xac
07  000000bb`24efe910  00007ff9`20f2906f     ntdll!_C_specific_handler+0x96
08  000000bb`24efe980  00007ff9`20eb5bea     ntdll!RtlpExecuteHandlerForException+0xf
09  000000bb`24efe9b0  00007ff9`20f2805e     ntdll!RtlDispatchException+0x25a
0a  000000bb`24eff100  00007ff6`a4ce10ee     ntdll!KiUserExceptionDispatch+0x2e
```

```
0b  000000bb`24eff820  00007ff6`a4ce2c30     multiple_exceptions+0x10ee
0c  000000bb`24eff850  00007ff6`a4ced1cd     multiple_exceptions+0x2c30
0d  000000bb`24eff8f0  00007ff9`1f8953e0     multiple_exceptions+0xd1cd
0e  000000bb`24eff950  00007ff9`20e8485b     kernel32!BaseThreadInitThunk+0x10
0f  000000bb`24eff980  00000000`00000000     ntdll!RtlUserThreadStart+0x2b

    4  Id: 158.1ad4 Suspend: 0 Teb: 000000bb`248ee000 Unfrozen
 # Child-SP          RetAddr               Call Site
00  000000bb`250ffab8  00007ff9`20e9d89d     ntdll!NtWaitForAlertByThreadId+0x14
01  000000bb`250ffac0  00007ff9`20edb3fe     ntdll!RtlpWaitOnAddressWithTimeout+0x81
02  000000bb`250ffaf0  00007ff9`20edb343     ntdll!RtlpWaitOnAddress+0xae
03  000000bb`250ffb60  00007ff9`1e47dd9f     ntdll!RtlWaitOnAddress+0x13
04  000000bb`250ffba0  00007ff6`a4ce5901     KERNELBASE!WaitOnAddress+0x2f
05  000000bb`250ffbe0  00007ff6`a4ce1107     multiple_exceptions+0x5901
06  000000bb`250ffc50  00007ff6`a4ce2c30     multiple_exceptions+0x1107
07  000000bb`250ffc80  00007ff6`a4ced1cd     multiple_exceptions+0x2c30
08  000000bb`250ffd20  00007ff9`1f8953e0     multiple_exceptions+0xd1cd
09  000000bb`250ffd80  00007ff9`20e8485b     kernel32!BaseThreadInitThunk+0x10
0a  000000bb`250ffdb0  00000000`00000000     ntdll!RtlUserThreadStart+0x2b

    5  Id: 158.1acc Suspend: 0 Teb: 000000bb`248f0000 Unfrozen
 # Child-SP          RetAddr               Call Site
```

```
00 000000bb`252feab8 00007ff9`20edb903     ntdll!NtDelayExecution+0x14
01 000000bb`252feac0 00007ff9`1e43d051     ntdll!RtlDelayExecution+0x43
02 000000bb`252feaf0 00007ff9`1f8eeaac     KERNELBASE!SleepEx+0x71
03 000000bb`252feb70 00007ff9`1e55e503     kernel32!WerpReportFault+0xa4
04 000000bb`252febb0 00007ff9`20f2b0ec     KERNELBASE!UnhandledExceptionFilter+0x3e3
05 000000bb`252fecd0 00007ff9`20f140f6     ntdll!RtlUserThreadStart$filt$0+0xac
06 000000bb`252fed10 00007ff9`20f2906f     ntdll!_C_specific_handler+0x96
07 000000bb`252fed80 00007ff9`20eb5bea     ntdll!RtlpExecuteHandlerForException+0xf
08 000000bb`252fedb0 00007ff9`20f2805e     ntdll!RtlDispatchException+0x25a
09 000000bb`252ff500 00000000`12345678     ntdll!KiUserExceptionDispatch+0x2e
0a 000000bb`252ffc18 00007ff6`a4ce1102     0x12345678
0b 000000bb`252ffc20 00007ff6`a4ce2c30     multiple_exceptions+0x1102
0c 000000bb`252ffc50 00007ff6`a4ced1cd     multiple_exceptions+0x2c30
0d 000000bb`252ffcf0 00007ff9`1f8953e0     multiple_exceptions+0xd1cd
0e 000000bb`252ffd50 00007ff9`20e8485b     kernel32!BaseThreadInitThunk+0x10
0f 000000bb`252ffd80 00000000`00000000     ntdll!RtlUserThreadStart+0x2b

   6  Id: 158.2090 Suspend: 0 Teb: 000000bb`248f2000 Unfrozen
 # Child-SP          RetAddr               Call Site
00 000000bb`254ffbd8 00007ff9`20e9d89d     ntdll!NtWaitForAlertByThreadId+0x14
01 000000bb`254ffbe0 00007ff9`20edb3fe     ntdll!RtlpWaitOnAddressWithTimeout+0x81
02 000000bb`254ffc10 00007ff9`20edb343     ntdll!RtlpWaitOnAddress+0xae
03 000000bb`254ffc80 00007ff9`1e47dd9f     ntdll!RtlWaitOnAddress+0x13
04 000000bb`254ffcc0 00007ff6`a4ce5901     KERNELBASE!WaitOnAddress+0x2f
05 000000bb`254ffd00 00007ff6`a4ce1107     multiple_exceptions+0x5901
06 000000bb`254ffd70 00007ff6`a4ce2c30     multiple_exceptions+0x1107
07 000000bb`254ffda0 00007ff6`a4ced1cd     multiple_exceptions+0x2c30
08 000000bb`254ffe40 00007ff9`1f8953e0     multiple_exceptions+0xd1cd
09 000000bb`254ffea0 00007ff9`20e8485b     kernel32!BaseThreadInitThunk+0x10
0a 000000bb`254ffed0 00000000`00000000     ntdll!RtlUserThreadStart+0x2b
```

Note: We see an exception on another thread.

11.   We switch to the second exception (#5, threads are numbered from #0) thread and get its verbose stack trace (**~1s** and **k** commands, the stack trace is shown in smaller font for readability):

```
0:003> ~5s
ntdll!NtDelayExecution+0x14:
00007ff9`20f24704 ret
```

```
0:005> kv
# Child-SP          RetAddr          : Args to Child                                                                              : Call Site
00 000000bb`252feab8 00007ff9`20edb903 : 00007ff9`20fb11f8 000000bb`00000279 00000000`00000001 00000000`00000000 : ntdll!NtDelayExecution+0x14
01 000000bb`252feac0 00007ff9`1e43d051 : 00000000`00000000 00000000`00000000 00000000`00000000 00000000`00000000 : ntdll!RtlDelayExecution+0x43
02 000000bb`252feaf0 00007ff9`1f8eeaac : 00000000`00000000 00007ff9`00000000 ffffffff`ff676980 00000000`00002000 : KERNELBASE!SleepEx+0x71
03 000000bb`252feb70 00007ff9`1e55e503 : 00000000`00000000 000000bb`252ffd80 00007ff9`1f880000 00000000`00000000 : kernel32!WerpReportFault+0xa4
04 000000bb`252febb0 00007ff9`20f2b0ec : 00007ff9`210001ec 00007ff9`20fd0928 00000000`00000000 00000000`00000000 : KERNELBASE!UnhandledExceptionFilter+0x3e3
05 000000bb`252fecd0 00007ff9`20f140f6 : 000000bb`252ffd80 00007ff9`210001ec 000000bb`252fee10 00000000`00000000 : ntdll!RtlUserThreadStart$filt$0+0xac
06 000000bb`252fed10 00007ff9`20f2906f : 00000000`00000000 000000bb`252ff310 000000bb`252ff9f0 000000bb`252ff9f0 : ntdll!_C_specific_handler+0x96
07 000000bb`252fed80 00007ff9`20eb5bea : 000000bb`252ff9f0 00007ff9`20e80000 00007ff9`20e8485b 000000bb`210001ec : ntdll!RtlpExecuteHandlerForException+0xf
08 000000bb`252fedb0 00007ff9`20f2805e : 00000000`00000000 00000000`00000000 00000000`00000000 ffffffff`ffffffff : ntdll!RtlDispatchException+0x25a
09 000000bb`252ff500 00000000`12345678 : 00007ff6`a4ce1102 00000000`00000000 01000000`00000000 ffffffff`fffffffe : ntdll!KiUserExceptionDispatch+0x2e (TrapFrame @
000000bb`252ff928)
0a 000000bb`252ffc18 00007ff6`a4ce1102 : 00000000`00000000 01000000`00000000 ffffffff`fffffffe 00000000`00000004 : 0x12345678
0b 000000bb`252ffc20 00007ff6`a4ce2c30 : 00000000`00000000 00000000`00000000 00000000`00000000 00000000`00000000 : multiple_exceptions+0x1102
0c 000000bb`252ffc50 00007ff6`a4ced1cd : 00000000`00000000 0000029e`1e70cdc0 00000000`00000000 00000000`00000000 : multiple_exceptions+0x2c30
0d 000000bb`252ffcf0 00007ff9`1f8953e0 : 00000000`00000000 00000000`00000000 00000000`00000000 00000000`00000000 : multiple_exceptions+0xd1cd
0e 000000bb`252ffd50 00007ff9`20e8485b : 00000000`00000000 00000000`00000000 00000000`00000000 00000000`00000000 : kernel32!BaseThreadInitThunk+0x10
0f 000000bb`252ffd80 00000000`00000000 : 00000000`00000000 00000000`00000000 00000000`00000000 00000000`00000000 : ntdll!RtlUserThreadStart+0x2b
```

Note: We see trap frame reference (processor information saved when an exception had occurred).

12.   Setting the current stack frame to #a (the next after the frame #9 where we see the *KiUserExceptionDispatch* function) should show CPU information at the time of the exception:

88

```
0:005> .frame /c a
0a 000000bb`252ffc18 00007ff6`a4ce1102     0x12345678
rax=0000000000000034 rbx=0000000000000000 rcx=0000000000000000
rdx=000000bb252feb80 rsi=0000000000000004 rdi=0000000000000000
rip=0000000012345678 rsp=000000bb252ffc18 rbp=000000bb252ffcc0
 r8=000000bb252feb68  r9=000000bb252ffd80 r10=0000000000000000
r11=0000000000000246 r12=0000000000000000 r13=0000000000000000
r14=0000000000000000 r15=0000000000000000
iopl=0         nv up ei pl zr na po nc
cs=0033  ss=002b  ds=002b  es=002b  fs=0053  gs=002b             efl=00000246
00000000`12345678 ???

0:005> ub 00007ff6`a4ce1102
multiple_exceptions+0x10e4:
00007ff6`a4ce10e4 cmp     ecx,4
00007ff6`a4ce10e7 je      multiple_exceptions+0x10fb (00007ff6`a4ce10fb)
00007ff6`a4ce10e9 cmp     ecx,2
00007ff6`a4ce10ec jne     multiple_exceptions+0x1102 (00007ff6`a4ce1102)
00007ff6`a4ce10ee mov     dword ptr [1],0
00007ff6`a4ce10f9 jmp     multiple_exceptions+0x1102 (00007ff6`a4ce1102)
00007ff6`a4ce10fb mov     eax,12345678h
00007ff6`a4ce1100 call    rax
```

Note: We see an invalid pointer code call. If the address is value less than 64K we also call it NULL Pointer (Code).

We can also double-check this information with the trap frame structure instruction pointer RIP (the **dt** command dumps C/C++ structure fields):

```
09 000000bb`252ff500 00000000`12345678     : 00007ff6`a4ce1102 00000000`00000000 01000000`00000000 ffffffff`fffffffe : ntdll!KiUserExceptionDispatch+0x2e
(TrapFrame @ 000000bb`252ff928)

0:05> dt ntdll!_KTRAP_FRAME RIP 000000bb`252ff928
   +0x168 Rip : 0x12345678
```

13.   Now we check the problem module information and get a stack trace prior to the exception (**lmv m** and **k** commands):

```
0:05> lmv m multiple_exceptions
Browse full module list
start             end               module name
00007ff6`a4ce0000 00007ff6`a4d0c000   multiple_exceptions C (no symbols)
    Loaded symbol image file: multiple-exceptions.exe
    Image path: C:\Work\multiple-exceptions.exe
    Image name: multiple-exceptions.exe
    Browse all global symbols  functions  data  Symbol Reload
    Timestamp:        Mon Oct 28 11:22:33 2024 (671F73F9)
    CheckSum:         00000000
    ImageSize:        0002C000
    Translations:     0000.04b0 0000.04e4 0409.04b0 0409.04e4
    Information from resource tables:

0:005> k
 *** Stack trace for last set context - .thread/.cxr resets it
 # Child-SP          RetAddr           Call Site
0a 000000bb`252ffc18 00007ff6`a4ce1102   0x12345678
0b 000000bb`252ffc20 00007ff6`a4ce2c30   multiple_exceptions+0x1102
0c 000000bb`252ffc50 00007ff6`a4ced1cd   multiple_exceptions+0x2c30
```

```
0d 000000bb`252ffcf0 00007ff9`1f8953e0     multiple_exceptions+0xd1cd
0e 000000bb`252ffd50 00007ff9`20e8485b     kernel32!BaseThreadInitThunk+0x10
0f 000000bb`252ffd80 00000000`00000000     ntdll!RtlUserThreadStart+0x2b
```

14.   We can set symbol file path to see better stack traces:

```
0:05> .sympath+ C:\ARWMDA-Dumps\Symbols\release
Symbol search path is: srv*;C:\ARWMDA-Dumps\Symbols\release
Expanded Symbol search path is:
cache*;SRV*https://msdl.microsoft.com/download/symbols;c:\arwmda-dumps\symbols\release

************ Path validation summary **************
Response                              Time (ms)    Location
Deferred                                           srv*
OK                                                 C:\ARWMDA-Dumps\Symbols\release
```

```
0:005> ~*kL
```

```
   0  Id: 158.ffc Suspend: 0 Teb: 000000bb`248e6000 Unfrozen "main"
 # Child-SP          RetAddr               Call Site
0a 000000bb`2477f768 00007ff9`1e4610ee     ntdll!NtWaitForSingleObject+0x14
0b 000000bb`2477f770 00007ff6`a4ced331     KERNELBASE!WaitForSingleObjectEx+0x8e
0c 000000bb`2477f810 00007ff6`a4ce2381     multiple_exceptions!std::sys::pal::windows::thread::Thread::join+0x21
0d 000000bb`2477f8a0 00007ff6`a4ce2108     multiple_exceptions!ZN3std6thread18JoinInner$LT$T$GT$4join17hd36e1d1226bb5961E+0x21
0e 000000bb`2477f900 00007ff6`a4ce1116
multiple_exceptions!ZN86_$LT$alloc..vec..into_iter..IntoIter$LT$T$C$A$GT$$u20$as$u20$core..ops..drop..Drop$GT$4drop17h8dffdacc0fc38d36E+0x868
0f 000000bb`2477fa20 00007ff6`a4ce10cc     multiple_exceptions!ZN3std3sys9backtrace28__rust_begin_short_backtrace17h10fd792bdcbc8262E+0x36
10 000000bb`2477fa50 00007ff6`a4ce5229
multiple_exceptions!ZN3std2rt10lang_start28_$u7b$$u7b$closure$u7d$$u7d$17h63fd63cfc421acdbE.llvm.18325946273885024129+0xc
11 (Inline Function) --------`--------     multiple_exceptions!std::rt::lang_start_internal::closure$2+0x6
12 (Inline Function) --------`--------     multiple_exceptions!std::panicking::try::do_call+0x6
13 (Inline Function) --------`--------     multiple_exceptions!std::panicking::try+0x6
14 (Inline Function) --------`--------     multiple_exceptions!std::panic::catch_unwind+0x6
15 000000bb`2477fa80 00007ff6`a4ce234c     multiple_exceptions!std::rt::lang_start_internal+0x79
16 000000bb`2477fb40 00007ff6`a4cfa7ac     multiple_exceptions!main+0x2c
17 (Inline Function) --------`--------     multiple_exceptions!invoke_main+0x22
18 000000bb`2477fb80 00007ff9`1f8953e0     multiple_exceptions!__scrt_common_main_seh+0x10c
19 000000bb`2477fbc0 00007ff9`20e8485b     kernel32!BaseThreadInitThunk+0x10
1a 000000bb`2477fbf0 00000000`00000000     ntdll!RtlUserThreadStart+0x2b

   1  Id: 158.ca8 Suspend: 0 Teb: 000000bb`248e8000 Unfrozen
 # Child-SP          RetAddr               Call Site
0a 000000bb`24aff548 00007ff9`20e96cdf     ntdll!NtWaitForWorkViaWorkerFactory+0x14
0b 000000bb`24aff550 00007ff9`1f8953e0     ntdll!TppWorkerThread+0x2df
0c 000000bb`24aff840 00007ff9`20e8485b     kernel32!BaseThreadInitThunk+0x10
0d 000000bb`24aff870 00000000`00000000     ntdll!RtlUserThreadStart+0x2b

   2  Id: 158.1b04 Suspend: 0 Teb: 000000bb`248ea000 Unfrozen
 # Child-SP          RetAddr               Call Site
0a 000000bb`24cff818 00007ff9`20e9d89d     ntdll!NtWaitForAlertByThreadId+0x14
0b 000000bb`24cff820 00007ff9`20edb3fe     ntdll!RtlpWaitOnAddressWithTimeout+0x81
0c 000000bb`24cff850 00007ff9`20edb343     ntdll!RtlpWaitOnAddress+0xae
0d 000000bb`24cff8c0 00007ff9`1e47dd9f     ntdll!RtlWaitOnAddress+0x13
0e 000000bb`24cff900 00007ff6`a4ce5901     KERNELBASE!WaitOnAddress+0x2f
0f (Inline Function) --------`--------     multiple_exceptions!std::sys::sync::thread_parking::futex::Parker::park+0x65
10 (Inline Function) --------`--------     multiple_exceptions!std::thread::Thread::park+0x65
11 000000bb`24cff940 00007ff6`a4ce1107     multiple_exceptions!std::thread::park+0x151
12 000000bb`24cff9b0 00007ff6`a4ce2c30     multiple_exceptions!ZN3std3sys9backtrace28__rust_begin_short_backtrace17h10fd792bdcbc8262E+0x27
13 000000bb`24cff9e0 00007ff6`a4ced1cd     multiple_exceptions!ZN3std6thread7Builder15spawn_unchecked17h913eb9e589eab20fE+0x790
14 (Inline Function) --------`--------     multiple_exceptions!alloc::boxed::impl$48::call_once+0xb
15 (Inline Function) --------`--------     multiple_exceptions!alloc::boxed::impl$48::call_once+0x16
16 000000bb`24cffa80 00007ff9`1f8953e0     multiple_exceptions!std::sys::pal::windows::thread::impl$0::new::thread_start+0x3d
17 000000bb`24cffae0 00007ff9`20e8485b     kernel32!BaseThreadInitThunk+0x10
18 000000bb`24cffb10 00000000`00000000     ntdll!RtlUserThreadStart+0x2b

#  3  Id: 158.1ac8 Suspend: 0 Teb: 000000bb`248ec000 Unfrozen
 # Child-SP          RetAddr               Call Site
0a 000000bb`24efe318 00007ff9`1e46dcd0     ntdll!NtWaitForMultipleObjects+0x14
0b 000000bb`24efe320 00007ff9`1e46dbce     KERNELBASE!WaitForMultipleObjectsEx+0xf0
0c 000000bb`24efe610 00007ff9`1f8ef087     KERNELBASE!WaitForMultipleObjects+0xe
0d 000000bb`24efe650 00007ff9`1f8eeac6     kernel32!WerpReportFaultInternal+0x587
0e 000000bb`24efe770 00007ff9`1e55e503     kernel32!WerpReportFault+0xbe
0f 000000bb`24efe7b0 00007ff9`20f2b0ec     KERNELBASE!UnhandledExceptionFilter+0x3e3
10 000000bb`24efe8d0 00007ff9`20f140f6     ntdll!RtlUserThreadStart$filt$0+0xac
11 000000bb`24efe910 00007ff9`20f2906f     ntdll!_C_specific_handler+0x96
12 000000bb`24efe980 00007ff9`20eb5bea     ntdll!RtlpExecuteHandlerForException+0xf
13 000000bb`24efe9b0 00007ff9`20f2805e     ntdll!RtlDispatchException+0x25a
14 000000bb`24eff100 00007ff6`a4ce10ee     ntdll!KiUserExceptionDispatch+0x2e
15 000000bb`24eff820 00007ff6`a4ce2c30     multiple_exceptions!ZN3std3sys9backtrace28__rust_begin_short_backtrace17h10fd792bdcbc8262E+0xe
16 000000bb`24eff850 00007ff6`a4ced1cd     multiple_exceptions!ZN3std6thread7Builder15spawn_unchecked17h913eb9e589eab20fE+0x790
17 (Inline Function) --------`--------     multiple_exceptions!alloc::boxed::impl$48::call_once+0xb
18 (Inline Function) --------`--------     multiple_exceptions!alloc::boxed::impl$48::call_once+0x16
19 000000bb`24eff8f0 00007ff9`1f8953e0     multiple_exceptions!std::sys::pal::windows::thread::impl$0::new::thread_start+0x3d
1a 000000bb`24eff950 00007ff9`20e8485b     kernel32!BaseThreadInitThunk+0x10
1b 000000bb`24eff980 00000000`00000000     ntdll!RtlUserThreadStart+0x2b
```

```
   4  Id: 158.1ad4 Suspend: 0 Teb: 000000bb`248ee000 Unfrozen
 # Child-SP          RetAddr           Call Site
0a 000000bb`250ffab8 00007ff9`20e9d89d ntdll!NtWaitForAlertByThreadId+0x14
0b 000000bb`250ffac0 00007ff9`20edb3fe ntdll!RtlpWaitOnAddressWithTimeout+0x81
0c 000000bb`250ffaf0 00007ff9`20edb343 ntdll!RtlpWaitOnAddress+0xae
0d 000000bb`250ffb60 00007ff9`1e47dd9f ntdll!RtlWaitOnAddress+0x13
0e 000000bb`250ffba0 00007ff6`a4ce5901 KERNELBASE!WaitOnAddress+0x2f
0f (Inline Function) --------`-------- multiple_exceptions!std::sys::sync::thread_parking::futex::Parker::park+0x65
10 (Inline Function) --------`-------- multiple_exceptions!std::thread::Thread::park+0x65
11 000000bb`250ffbe0 00007ff6`a4ce1107 multiple_exceptions!std::thread::park+0x151
12 000000bb`250ffc50 00007ff6`a4ce2c30 multiple_exceptions!ZN3std3sys9backtrace28__rust_begin_short_backtrace17h10fd792bdcbc8262E+0x27
13 000000bb`250ffc80 00007ff6`a4ced1cd multiple_exceptions!ZN3std6thread7Builder15spawn_unchecked17h913eb9e589eab20fE+0x790
14 (Inline Function) --------`-------- multiple_exceptions!alloc::boxed::impl$48::call_once+0xb
15 (Inline Function) --------`-------- multiple_exceptions!alloc::boxed::impl$48::call_once+0x16
16 000000bb`250ffd20 00007ff9`1f8953e0 multiple_exceptions!std::sys::pal::windows::thread::impl$0::new::thread_start+0x3d
17 000000bb`250ffd80 00007ff9`20e8485b kernel32!BaseThreadInitThunk+0x10
18 000000bb`250ffdb0 00000000`00000000 ntdll!RtlUserThreadStart+0x2b

   5  Id: 158.1acc Suspend: 0 Teb: 000000bb`248f0000 Unfrozen
 # Child-SP          RetAddr           Call Site
0a 000000bb`252feab8 00007ff9`20edb903 ntdll!NtDelayExecution+0x14
0b 000000bb`252feac0 00007ff9`1e43d051 ntdll!RtlDelayExecution+0x43
0c 000000bb`252feaf0 00007ff9`1f8eeaac KERNELBASE!SleepEx+0x71
0d 000000bb`252feb70 00007ff9`1e55e503 kernel32!WerpReportFault+0xa4
0e 000000bb`252febb0 00007ff9`20f2b0ec KERNELBASE!UnhandledExceptionFilter+0x3e3
0f 000000bb`252fecd0 00007ff9`20f140f6 ntdll!RtlUserThreadStart$filt$0+0xac
10 000000bb`252fed10 00007ff9`20f2906f ntdll!_C_specific_handler+0x96
11 000000bb`252fed80 00007ff9`20eb5bea ntdll!RtlpExecuteHandlerForException+0xf
12 000000bb`252fedb0 00007ff9`20f2805e ntdll!RtlDispatchException+0x25a
13 000000bb`252ff500 00000000`12345678 ntdll!KiUserExceptionDispatch+0x2e
14 000000bb`252ffc18 00007ff6`a4ce1102 0x12345678
15 000000bb`252ffc20 00007ff6`a4ce2c30 multiple_exceptions!ZN3std3sys9backtrace28__rust_begin_short_backtrace17h10fd792bdcbc8262E+0x22
16 000000bb`252ffc50 00007ff6`a4ced1cd multiple_exceptions!ZN3std6thread7Builder15spawn_unchecked17h913eb9e589eab20fE+0x790
17 (Inline Function) --------`-------- multiple_exceptions!alloc::boxed::impl$48::call_once+0xb
18 (Inline Function) --------`-------- multiple_exceptions!alloc::boxed::impl$48::call_once+0x16
19 000000bb`252ffcf0 00007ff9`1f8953e0 multiple_exceptions!std::sys::pal::windows::thread::impl$0::new::thread_start+0x3d
1a 000000bb`252ffd50 00007ff9`20e8485b kernel32!BaseThreadInitThunk+0x10
1b 000000bb`252ffd80 00000000`00000000 ntdll!RtlUserThreadStart+0x2b

   6  Id: 158.2090 Suspend: 0 Teb: 000000bb`248f2000 Unfrozen
 # Child-SP          RetAddr           Call Site
0a 000000bb`254ffbd8 00007ff9`20e9d89d ntdll!NtWaitForAlertByThreadId+0x14
0b 000000bb`254ffbe0 00007ff9`20edb3fe ntdll!RtlpWaitOnAddressWithTimeout+0x81
0c 000000bb`254ffc10 00007ff9`20edb343 ntdll!RtlpWaitOnAddress+0xae
0d 000000bb`254ffc80 00007ff9`1e47dd9f ntdll!RtlWaitOnAddress+0x13
0e 000000bb`254ffcc0 00007ff6`a4ce5901 KERNELBASE!WaitOnAddress+0x2f
0f (Inline Function) --------`-------- multiple_exceptions!std::sys::sync::thread_parking::futex::Parker::park+0x65
10 (Inline Function) --------`-------- multiple_exceptions!std::thread::Thread::park+0x65
11 000000bb`254ffd00 00007ff6`a4ce1107 multiple_exceptions!std::thread::park+0x151
12 000000bb`254ffd70 00007ff6`a4ce2c30 multiple_exceptions!ZN3std3sys9backtrace28__rust_begin_short_backtrace17h10fd792bdcbc8262E+0x27
13 000000bb`254ffda0 00007ff6`a4ced1cd multiple_exceptions!ZN3std6thread7Builder15spawn_unchecked17h913eb9e589eab20fE+0x790
14 (Inline Function) --------`-------- multiple_exceptions!alloc::boxed::impl$48::call_once+0xb
15 (Inline Function) --------`-------- multiple_exceptions!alloc::boxed::impl$48::call_once+0x16
16 000000bb`254ffe40 00007ff9`1f8953e0 multiple_exceptions!std::sys::pal::windows::thread::impl$0::new::thread_start+0x3d
17 000000bb`254ffea0 00007ff9`20e8485b kernel32!BaseThreadInitThunk+0x10
```

Note: We also have a memory dump from the debug version: *multiple-exceptions.exe.3592.dmp.* We leave its analysis as a homework exercise.

15.   We close logging before exiting WinDbg:

```
0:005> .logclose
Closing open log file C:\ARWMDA-Dumps\RW4.log
```

Exercise RW5

- **Goal:** Learn how to recognize heap corruption, dump memory contents, follow critical section wait chains, and check error and status codes

- **Patterns:** Exception Thread; Dynamic Memory Corruption (Process Heap); Wait Chain (Critical Sections); Execution Residue (Unmanaged Space, User); Last Error Collection

- \ARWMDA-Dumps\Exercise-RW5.pdf

Exercise RW5

Goal: Learn how to recognize heap corruption, dump memory contents, follow critical section wait chains, and check error and status codes.

Patterns: Exception Thread; Dynamic Memory Corruption (Process Heap); Wait Chain (Critical Sections); Execution Residue (Unmanaged Space, User); Last Error Collection.

1. Launch WinDbg.

2. Open \ARWMDA-Dumps\Process\heap-corruption.exe.6832.dmp.

3. We get the dump file loaded:

```
Loading Dump File [C:\ARWMDA-Dumps\Process\heap-corruption.exe.6832.dmp]
User Mini Dump File with Full Memory: Only application data is available

************* Path validation summary **************
Response                         Time (ms)      Location
Deferred                                        srv*
Symbol search path is: srv
Executable search path is:
Windows 10 Version 22000 UP Free x64
Product: WinNt, suite: SingleUserTS
Edition build lab: 22000.1.amd64fre.co_release.210604-1628
Debug session time: Wed Oct 30 08:55:27.000 2024 (UTC + 0:00)
System Uptime: 0 days 0:11:19.720
Process Uptime: 0 days 0:00:04.000
.......
This dump file has an exception of interest stored in it.
The stored exception information can be accessed via .ecxr
(1ab0.b7c): Unknown exception - code c0000374 (first/second chance not available)
For analysis of this file, run !analyze -v
ntdll!NtWaitForMultipleObjects+0x14:
00007ff9`b2ae4bd4 ret
```

4. Open a log file using the **.logopen** command and load *AppL* symbols (**.sympath+** and **.reload**):

```
0:005> .logopen C:\ARWMDA-Dumps\RW5.log
Opened log file 'C:\ARWMDA-Dumps\RW5.log'

0:005> .sympath+ C:\ARWMDA-Dumps\Symbols\debug
Symbol search path is: srv*;C:\ARWMDA-Dumps\Symbols\debug
Expanded Symbol search path is:
cache*;SRV*https://msdl.microsoft.com/download/symbols;c:\arwmda-dumps\symbols\debug

************* Path validation summary **************
Response                         Time (ms)      Location
Deferred                                        srv*
OK                                              C:\ARWMDA-Dumps\Symbols\debug

0:005> .reload
.......
```

93

5. Type the **kL** command to verify the correctness of the stack trace (we use **L** to suppress the source code information that may clutter the output):

```
0:005> kL
 # Child-SP          RetAddr           Call Site
00 000000d9`699fdb38 00007ff9`b2b291a8 ntdll!NtWaitForMultipleObjects+0x14
01 000000d9`699fdb40 00007ff9`b2b2877e ntdll!WerpWaitForCrashReporting+0xa8
02 000000d9`699fdbc0 00007ff9`b2b27f3b ntdll!RtlReportExceptionHelper+0x33e
03 000000d9`699fdc90 00007ff9`b2b4c104 ntdll!RtlReportException+0x9b
04 000000d9`699fdd10 00007ff9`b2ad40f6 ntdll!RtlReportFatalFailure$filt$0+0x33
05 000000d9`699fdd40 00007ff9`b2ae906f ntdll!_C_specific_handler+0x96
06 000000d9`699fddb0 00007ff9`b2a75bea ntdll!RtlpExecuteHandlerForException+0xf
07 000000d9`699fdde0 00007ff9`b2a72ef1 ntdll!RtlDispatchException+0x25a
08 000000d9`699fe530 00007ff9`b2b4c0c9 ntdll!RtlRaiseException+0x1f1
09 000000d9`699fed10 00007ff9`b2b4c093 ntdll!RtlReportFatalFailure+0x9
0a 000000d9`699fed60 00007ff9`b2b54eb2 ntdll!RtlReportCriticalFailure+0x97
0b 000000d9`699fee50 00007ff9`b2b5519a ntdll!RtlpHeapHandleError+0x12
0c 000000d9`699fee80 00007ff9`b2b5f685 ntdll!RtlpHpHeapHandleError+0x7a
0d 000000d9`699feeb0 00007ff9`b2b54dc0 ntdll!RtlpLogHeapFailure+0x45
0e 000000d9`699feee0 00007ff9`b2a669f5 ntdll!RtlpAnalyzeHeapFailure+0x2fc
0f 000000d9`699fef40 00007ff9`b2a6838e ntdll!RtlpFreeHeap+0xcc5
10 000000d9`699ff0a0 00007ff9`b2a676e1 ntdll!RtlpFreeHeapInternal+0x79e
11 000000d9`699ff160 00007ff6`c7752cfb ntdll!RtlFreeHeap+0x51
12 000000d9`699ff1a0 00007ff6`c77589b0 heap_corruption!alloc::alloc::impl$1::deallocate+0x9b
13 000000d9`699ff240 00007ff6`c7757efe heap_corruption!alloc::boxed::impl$8::drop<array$<i16,100>,alloc::alloc::Global>+0x90
14 000000d9`699ff2d0 00007ff6`c775203c heap_corruption!core::ptr::drop_in_place<alloc::boxed::Box<array$<i16,100>,alloc::alloc::Global> >+0xe
15 000000d9`699ff300 00007ff6`c7752dad heap_corruption!heap_corruption::main::closure$0+0x22c
16 (Inline Function) --------`-------- heap_corruption!core::hint::black_box+0x9
17 000000d9`699ff590 00007ff6`c77550ad heap_corruption!std::sys::backtrace::__rust_begin_short_backtrace<heap_corruption::main::closure_env$0,tuple$<> >+0xd
18 000000d9`699ff5c0 00007ff6`c775566d
heap_corruption!std::thread::impl$0::spawn_unchecked_::closure$1::closure$0<heap_corruption::main::closure_env$0,tuple$<> >+0xd
19 000000d9`699ff5f0 00007ff6`c7756cd3
heap_corruption!core::panic::unwind_safe::impl$25::call_once<tuple$<>,std::thread::impl$0::spawn_unchecked_::closure$1::closure_env$0<heap_corruption::main::c
losure_env$0,tuple$<> >+0xd
1a 000000d9`699ff620 00007ff6`c7755173
heap_corruption!std::panicking::try::do_call<core::panic::unwind_safe::AssertUnwindSafe<std::thread::impl$0::spawn_unchecked_::closure$1::closure_env$0<heap_c
orruption::main::closure_env$0,tuple$<> > >,tuple$<> >+0x23
1b 000000d9`699ff680 00007ff6`c7754c05 heap_corruption!std::thread::impl$7::drop::closure$0<tuple$<> >+0xb3
1c (Inline Function) --------`-------- heap_corruption!std::panicking::try+0x25
1d (Inline Function) --------`-------- heap_corruption!std::panic::catch_unwind+0x25
1e 000000d9`699ff6d0 00007ff6`c775746e heap_corruption!std::thread::impl$0::spawn_unchecked_::closure$1<heap_corruption::main::closure_env$0,tuple$<> >+0x135
1f 000000d9`699ff830 00007ff6`c776353d
heap_corruption!core::ops::function::FnOnce::call_once<std::thread::impl$0::spawn_unchecked_::closure_env$1<heap_corruption::main::closure_env$0,tuple$<> >,tuple$<> >+0xe
20 (Inline Function) --------`-------- heap_corruption!alloc::boxed::impl$48::call_once+0xb
21 (Inline Function) --------`-------- heap_corruption!alloc::boxed::impl$48::call_once+0x16
22 000000d9`699ff870 00007ff9`b18353e0 heap_corruption!std::sys::pal::windows::thread::impl$0::new::thread_start+0x3d
23 000000d9`699ff8d0 00007ff9`b2a4485b kernel32!BaseThreadInitThunk+0x10
24 000000d9`699ff900 00000000`00000000 ntdll!RtlUserThreadStart+0x2b
```

Note: In addition to exception processing, we see heap failure analysis and heap manipulation functions.

6. Let's now double-check our findings with the **!analyze -v** command:

```
0:005> !analyze -v
*******************************************************************************
*                                                                             *
*                        Exception Analysis                                   *
*                                                                             *
*******************************************************************************

KEY_VALUES_STRING: 1

    Key  : Analysis.CPU.mSec
    Value: 390

    Key  : Analysis.Elapsed.mSec
    Value: 3161

    Key  : Analysis.IO.Other.Mb
    Value: 0

    Key  : Analysis.IO.Read.Mb
    Value: 3

    Key  : Analysis.IO.Write.Mb
    Value: 4

    Key  : Analysis.Init.CPU.mSec
    Value: 453

    Key  : Analysis.Init.Elapsed.mSec
    Value: 349520

    Key  : Analysis.Memory.CommitPeak.Mb
    Value: 213
```

```
Key  : Analysis.Version.DbgEng
Value: 10.0.27725.1000

Key  : Analysis.Version.Description
Value: 10.2408.27.01 amd64fre

Key  : Analysis.Version.Ext
Value: 1.2408.27.1

Key  : Failure.Bucket
Value: HEAP_CORRUPTION_c0000374_heap-corruption.exe!alloc::alloc::impl$1::deallocate

Key  : Failure.Hash
Value: {27a16f59-3a07-9406-f076-2f6f31805660}

Key  : Timeline.OS.Boot.DeltaSec
Value: 679

Key  : Timeline.Process.Start.DeltaSec
Value: 4

Key  : WER.OS.Branch
Value: co_release

Key  : WER.OS.Version
Value: 10.0.22000.1


FILE_IN_CAB:  heap-corruption.exe.6832.dmp

NTGLOBALFLAG:  0

APPLICATION_VERIFIER_FLAGS:  0

CONTEXT:  (.ecxr)
rax=0000000000000000 rbx=00000000c0000374 rcx=0000000000000000
rdx=0000000000000000 rsi=0000000000000001 rdi=00007ff9b2bb7780
rip=00007ff9b2b4c0c9 rsp=000000d9699fed10 rbp=000001fbdcd0d810
 r8=0000000000000000  r9=0000000000000000 r10=0000000000000000
r11=0000000000000000 r12=000000007ffe0380 r13=0000000000000001
r14=000001fbdcd0d800 r15=0000000000000000
iopl=0         nv up ei pl nz na po nc
cs=0033  ss=002b  ds=002b  es=002b  fs=0053  gs=002b             efl=00000206
ntdll!RtlReportFatalFailure+0x9:
00007ff9`b2b4c0c9 jmp     ntdll!RtlReportFatalFailure+0xb (00007ff9`b2b4c0cb)
Resetting default scope

EXCEPTION_RECORD:  (.exr -1)
ExceptionAddress: 00007ff9b2b4c0c9 (ntdll!RtlReportFatalFailure+0x0000000000000009)
   ExceptionCode: c0000374
  ExceptionFlags: 00000081
NumberParameters: 1
   Parameter[0]: 00007ff9b2bb7780

PROCESS_NAME:  heap-corruption.exe

ERROR_CODE: (NTSTATUS) 0xc0000374 - A heap has been corrupted.

EXCEPTION_CODE_STR:  c0000374

EXCEPTION_PARAMETER1:  00007ff9b2bb7780

STACK_TEXT:
000000d9`699fed10 00007ff9`b2b4c093     : 000000d9`69a00000 00007ff9`b2bb77d8 00007ff9`b2bc0000 00007ff9`b2a40000 : ntdll!RtlReportFatalFailure+0x9
000000d9`699fed60 00007ff9`b2b54eb2     : 00000000`0000007a 00007ff9`b2bb7780 00000000`00000003 000001fb`dccf0000 : ntdll!RtlReportCriticalFailure+0x97
000000d9`699fee50 00007ff9`b2b5519a     : 00000000`00000003 000001fb`dcd0d810 00000001fb`dccf0000 00000000d9`699feea0 : ntdll!RtlpHeapHandleError+0x12
000000d9`699fee80 00007ff9`b2b5f685     : 000001fb`dccf0000 00000000`00100000 00000000`7d00017c 00007ff9`b075f428 : ntdll!RtlpHpHeapHandleError+0x7a
000000d9`699feeb0 00007ff9`b2b54dc0     : 000001fb`dcd0d780 00007ff9`b2a46800 00000000`00000000 00000000`00000004 : ntdll!RtlpLogHeapFailure+0x45
000000d9`699feee0 00007ff9`b2a669f5     : 000001fb`dccf0000 000001fb`dccf0000 000001fb`dcd0d800 : ntdll!RtlpAnalyzeHeapFailure+0x2fc
000000d9`699fef40 00007ff9`b2a6838e     : 000001fb`dccf0000 000001fb`dcd0d800 000001fb`dcd0d800 000001fb`dccf0000 : ntdll!RtlpFreeHeap+0xcc5
000000d9`699ff0a0 00007ff9`b2a676e1     : 000001fb`dcd0d800 000001fb`dccf0000 00000000d9`699ff380 00000000`00000000 : ntdll!RtlpFreeHeapInternal+0x79e
000000d9`699ff160 00007ff6`c7752cfb     : 000001fb`dccf4a60 00000000`68eaf000 00000000`00000000 00000000`00000000 : ntdll!RtlFreeHeap+0x51
000000d9`699ff1a0 00007ff6`c77589b0     : 000001fb`dcd0d810 000001fb`dcd0d810 000001fb`dcd0d810 000001fb`dcd0d810 :
heap_corruption!alloc::alloc::impl$1::deallocate+0x9b
000000d9`699ff240 00007ff6`c7757efe     : 00000000`00000002 00000000`000000c8 000001fb`dcd0d810 00000000`000000c8 :
heap_corruption!alloc::boxed::impl$8::drop<array$<i16,100>,alloc::alloc::Global>+0x90
000000d9`699ff2d0 00007ff6`c775203c     : 000001fb`dccf5300 00000000`00000000 00000000`00000000 00000000`00000000 :
heap_corruption!core::ptr::drop_in_place<alloc::boxed::Box<array$<i16,100>,alloc::alloc::Global> >+0xe
000000d9`699ff300 00007ff6`c7752dad     : 00000000`00000000 00000000`00000000 00000000`00000000 00000000`00000000 :
heap_corruption!heap_corruption::main::closure$0+0x22c
000000d9`699ff590 00007ff6`c77550ad     : 00000000`00000000 00000000`00000000 00000000`00000000 00000000`00000000 :
heap_corruption!std::sys::backtrace::__rust_begin_short_backtrace<heap_corruption::main::closure_env$0,tuple$<> >+0xd
000000d9`699ff5c0 00007ff6`c775566d     : 00000000`00000000 00000000`00000000 000000d9`699ff690 00007ff6`c775ba84 :
heap_corruption!std::thread::impl$0::spawn_unchecked_::closure$1::closure$0<heap_corruption::main::closure_env$0,tuple$<> >+0xd
000000d9`699ff5f0 00007ff6`c7756cd3     : 00000000`00000000 00000000`00000000 00000000`00000000 000001fb`dcd09ef0 :
heap_corruption!core::panic::unwind_safe::impl$25::call_once<tuple$<>,std::thread::impl$0::spawn_unchecked_::closure$1::closure_env$0<heap_corruption::main::c
losure_env$0,tuple$<> > >+0xd
000000d9`699ff620 00007ff6`c7755173     : 000001fb`dcd09ef0 000001fb`dcd09ef0 000000d9`699ff698 00000000`00000005 :
heap_corruption!std::panicking::try::do_call<core::panic::unwind_safe::AssertUnwindSafe<std::thread::impl$0::spawn_unchecked_::closure$1::closure_env$0<heap_c
orruption::main::closure_env$0,tuple$<> >,tuple$<> >+0x23
000000d9`699ff680 00007ff6`c7754c05     : 00000000`00000000 00000000`00000000 00000000`00000000 00000000`00000000 :
heap_corruption!std::thread::impl$7::drop::closure$0<tuple$<> >+0xb3
000000d9`699ff6d0 00007ff6`c775746e     : 00000000`00001000 00000000`00000104 00000000`00006000 000000d9`699f8000 :
heap_corruption!std::thread::impl$0::spawn_unchecked_::closure$1<heap_corruption::main::closure_env$0,tuple$<> >+0x135
000000d9`699ff830 00007ff6`c776353d     : 00000000`00000000 000001fb`dccf4a60 00000000`00000000 00000000`00000000 :
heap_corruption!core::ops::function::FnOnce::call_once<std::thread::impl$0::spawn_unchecked_::closure_env$1<heap_corruption::main::closure_env$0,tuple$<>
>,tuple$<> >+0xe
```

```
000000d9`699ff870 00007ff9`b18353e0     : 00000000`00000000 00000000`00000000 00000000`00000000 00000000`00000000 :
heap_corruption!std::sys::pal::windows::thread::impl$0::new::thread_start+0x3d
000000d9`699ff8d0 00007ff9`b2a4485b     : 00000000`00000000 00000000`00000000 00000000`00000000 00000000`00000000 : kernel32!BaseThreadInitThunk+0x10
000000d9`699ff900 00000000`00000000     : 00000000`00000000 00000000`00000000 00000000`00000000 00000000`00000000 : ntdll!RtlUserThreadStart+0x2b


STACK_COMMAND:  ~5s; .ecxr ; kb

FAULTING_SOURCE_LINE:  /rustc/eeb90cda1969383f56a2637cbd3037bdf598841c\library\alloc\src\alloc.rs

FAULTING_SOURCE_FILE:  /rustc/eeb90cda1969383f56a2637cbd3037bdf598841c\library\alloc\src\alloc.rs

FAULTING_SOURCE_LINE_NUMBER:  253

FAULTING_SOURCE_CODE:
No source found for '/rustc/eeb90cda1969383f56a2637cbd3037bdf598841c\library\alloc\src\alloc.rs'


SYMBOL_NAME:  heap_corruption!alloc::alloc::impl$1::deallocate+9b

MODULE_NAME: heap_corruption

IMAGE_NAME:  heap-corruption.exe

FAILURE_BUCKET_ID:  HEAP_CORRUPTION_c0000374_heap-corruption.exe!alloc::alloc::impl$1::deallocate

OS_VERSION:  10.0.22000.1

BUILDLAB_STR:  co_release

OSPLATFORM_TYPE:  x64

OSNAME:  Windows 10

FAILURE_ID_HASH:  {27a16f59-3a07-9406-f076-2f6f31805660}

Followup:     MachineOwner
---------
```

Note: We see that WinDbg correctly diagnosed heap corruption and error code 0xc0000374 - A heap has been corrupted. We can also check the process heap for any errors using the **!heap -s -v** command:

```
0:005> !heap -s -v
```

```
*************************************************************************************************
                                  NT HEAP STATS BELOW
*************************************************************************************************
*****************************************************************
*                                                               *
*             HEAP ERROR DETECTED                               *
*                                                               *
*****************************************************************

Details:

Heap address:  000001fbdccf0000
Error address: 000001fbdcd0d800
Last known valid blocks: before - 000001fbdcd0d770, after - 000001fbdcd0d8d0
Error type:    HEAP_FAILURE_BUFFER_OVERRUN
Details:       The heap manager detected an error whose features are
               consistent with a buffer overrun.
Follow-up:     Enable pageheap.

Stack trace:
Stack trace at 0x00007ff9b2bb77d8
    00007ff9b2b5f685: ntdll!RtlpLogHeapFailure+0x45
    00007ff9b2b54dc0: ntdll!RtlpAnalyzeHeapFailure+0x2fc
    00007ff9b2a669f5: ntdll!RtlpFreeHeap+0xcc5
    00007ff9b2a6838e: ntdll!RtlpFreeHeapInternal+0x79e
    00007ff9b2a676e1: ntdll!RtlFreeHeap+0x51
    00007ff6c77552cfb: heap_corruption!alloc::alloc::impl$1::deallocate+0x9b
    00007ff6c77589b0: heap_corruption!alloc::boxed::impl$8::drop<array$<i16,100>,alloc::alloc::Global>+0x90
    00007ff6c7757efe: heap_corruption!core::ptr::drop_in_place<alloc::boxed::Box<array$<i16,100>,alloc::alloc::Global> >+0xe
    00007ff6c775203c: heap_corruption!heap_corruption::main::closure$0+0x22c
    00007ff6c7752dad: heap_corruption!std::sys::backtrace::__rust_begin_short_backtrace<heap_corruption::main::closure_env$0,tuple$<> >+0xd
    00007ff6c77550ad: heap_corruption!std::thread::impl$0::spawn_unchecked_::closure$1::closure$0<heap_corruption::main::closure_env$0,tuple$<> >+0xd
    00007ff6c775566d:
heap_corruption!core::panic::unwind_safe::impl$25::call_once<tuple$<>,std::thread::impl$0::spawn_unchecked_::closure$1::closure_env$0<heap_corruption::main::c
losure_env$0,tuple$<> > >+0xd
    00007ff6c7756cd3:
heap_corruption!std::panicking::try::do_call<core::panic::unwind_safe::AssertUnwindSafe<std::thread::impl$0::spawn_unchecked_::closure$1::closure_env$0<heap_c
orruption::main::closure_env$0,tuple$<> > >,tuple$<> >+0xd
    00007ff6c7755173: heap_corruption!std::thread::impl$7::drop::closure$0<tuple$<> >+0xb3
    00007ff6c7754c05: heap_corruption!std::thread::impl$0::spawn_unchecked_::closure$1<heap_corruption::main::closure_env$0,tuple$<> >+0x135
    00007ff6c775746e:
heap_corruption!core::ops::function::FnOnce::call_once<std::thread::impl$0::spawn_unchecked_::closure_env$1<heap_corruption::main::closure_env$0,tuple$<>
>,tuple$<> >+0xe

LFH Key                 : 0x6d55534b6daab8c5
Termination on corruption : ENABLED
        Heap     Flags   Reserv  Commit  Virt   Free  List   UCR  Virt  Lock  Fast
                          (k)     (k)    (k)     (k) length      blocks cont. heap
-------------------------------------------------------------------------------
```

```
.HEAP 000001fbdccf0000 (Seg 000001fbdccf0000) At 000001fbdcdb9950 Error: invalid block size

000001fbdccf0000 00000002    1048    132    1020     5    4    1    0    3  LFH
.000001fbdcc00000 00008000      64      4     64     2    1    1    0    0
---------------------------------------------------------------------------------
```

Note: The command output shows the last valid heap block before the failure is detected: **000001fbdcd0d770**. Let's check its data:

```
0:005> !heap -x 000001fbdcd0d770
HEAP 000001fbdccf0000 (Seg 000001fbdccf0000) At 000001fbdcdb9950 Error: invalid block size

Entry            User             Heap             Segment            Size PrevSize Unused    Flags
---------------------------------------------------------------------------------------------------
000001fbdcd0d770 000001fbdcd0d780 000001fbdccf0000 000001fbdccf0000     90      7a0     10    busy
```

Since we know this block size (**90**), we can check the next block:

```
0:005> !heap -x 000001fbdcd0d770+90
HEAP 000001fbdccf0000 (Seg 000001fbdccf0000) At 000001fbdcdb9950 Error: invalid block size

Entry            User             Heap             Segment            Size PrevSize Unused    Flags
---------------------------------------------------------------------------------------------------
000001fbdcd0d800 000001fbdcd0d810 000001fbdccf0000 000001fbdccf0000  ac150       90      8    busy
```

Note: Values for **Size** and **PrevSize** are hexadecimal.

We see that its size is very big, but the **PrevSize** looks valid for the previous block we inspected. Let's dump its memory contents:

```
0:005> dc 000001fbdcd0d800
000001fb`dcd0d800  00000000 00000000 92300016 08000c6f  ..........0.o...
000001fb`dcd0d810  00000000 00000000 00000000 00000000  ................
000001fb`dcd0d820  00000000 00000000 00000000 00000000  ................
000001fb`dcd0d830  00000000 00000000 00000000 00000000  ................
000001fb`dcd0d840  00000000 00000000 00000000 00000000  ................
000001fb`dcd0d850  00000000 00000000 00000000 00000000  ................
000001fb`dcd0d860  00000000 00000000 00000000 00000000  ................
000001fb`dcd0d870  00000000 00000000 00000000 00000000  ................

0:005> ? 16
Evaluate expression: 22 = 00000000`00000016
```

We see 22 in the block header (which is 16 bytes, 0x10), which corresponds to match **4** in the source code:

```
for n in 1..=5 {
    let handle = thread::spawn(move || {

        match n {

            2 => unsafe {
                let mut p: Box<[i16; 100]> = Box::new([0; 100]);

                let p_ptr = p.as_mut_ptr();
                *p_ptr.offset(-4) = 11;
            }

            4 => unsafe {
                let mut p: Box<[i16; 100]> = Box::new([0; 100]);
```

```
            let p_ptr = p.as_mut_ptr();
            *p_ptr.offset(-4) = 22;
        }

        _ => ()
    }

});
handles.push(handle);
}
```

Note: -4 in the source code corresponds to **-8** bytes since we have **i16** array elements (**-4** short elements). The correspondence to the source code is more visible if we dump short values (words) using the **dw** command:

```
0:005> dw 000001fbdcd0d800
000001fb`dcd0d800  0000 0000 0000 0000 0016 9230 0c6f 0800
000001fb`dcd0d810  0000 0000 0000 0000 0000 0000 0000 0000
000001fb`dcd0d820  0000 0000 0000 0000 0000 0000 0000 0000
000001fb`dcd0d830  0000 0000 0000 0000 0000 0000 0000 0000
000001fb`dcd0d840  0000 0000 0000 0000 0000 0000 0000 0000
000001fb`dcd0d850  0000 0000 0000 0000 0000 0000 0000 0000
000001fb`dcd0d860  0000 0000 0000 0000 0000 0000 0000 0000
000001fb`dcd0d870  0000 0000 0000 0000 0000 0000 0000 0000
```

000001fb`dcd0d810 address here (**User** from the table header) corresponds to the address returned by C++ *new*. If we try to get the next block information using the corrupt *Size* value, we fail:

```
0:005> !heap -x 000001fbdcd0d800+ac150
HEAP 000001fbdccf0000 (Seg 000001fbdccf0000) At 000001fbdcdb9950 Error: invalid block size
```

The memory for it is also invalid:

```
0:005> dc 000001fbdcd0d800+ac150
000001fb`dcdb9950  ???????? ???????? ???????? ????????  ????????????????
000001fb`dcdb9960  ???????? ???????? ???????? ????????  ????????????????
000001fb`dcdb9970  ???????? ???????? ???????? ????????  ????????????????
000001fb`dcdb9980  ???????? ???????? ???????? ????????  ????????????????
000001fb`dcdb9990  ???????? ???????? ???????? ????????  ????????????????
000001fb`dcdb99a0  ???????? ???????? ???????? ????????  ????????????????
000001fb`dcdb99b0  ???????? ???????? ???????? ????????  ????????????????
000001fb`dcdb99c0  ???????? ???????? ???????? ????????  ????????????????
```

This memory region belongs to the process heap but has not yet been committed:

```
0:005> !address 000001fbdcd0d800+ac150

Mapping file section regions...
Mapping module regions...
Mapping PEB regions...
Mapping TEB and stack regions...
Mapping heap regions...
Mapping page heap regions...
Mapping other regions...
Mapping stack trace database regions...
Mapping activation context regions...
```

```
Usage:                       Heap
Base Address:                000001fb`dcd0f000
End Address:                 000001fb`dcdef000
Region Size:                 00000000`000e0000 ( 896.000 kB)
State:                       00002000          MEM_RESERVE
Protect:                     <info not present at the target>
Type:                        00020000          MEM_PRIVATE
Allocation Base:             000001fb`dccf0000
Allocation Protect:          00000004          PAGE_READWRITE
More info:                   heap owning the address: !heap -s -h 0x1fbdccf0000
More info:                   heap segment
More info:                   heap entry containing the address: !heap -x 0x1fbdcdb9950
```

7.   Let's now check all threads to see if there are any other anomalies:

```
0:005> ~*kL

   0  Id: 1ab0.fc0 Suspend: 0 Teb: 000000d9`68ea5000 Unfrozen "main"
 # Child-SP          RetAddr           Call Site
00 000000d9`690ff758 00007ff9`affa10ee ntdll!NtWaitForSingleObject+0x14
01 000000d9`690ff760 00007ff6`c77636a1 KERNELBASE!WaitForSingleObjectEx+0x8e
02 000000d9`690ff800 00007ff6`c7753cf5 heap_corruption!std::sys::pal::windows::thread::Thread::join+0x21
03 000000d9`690ff890 00007ff6`c7753e9f heap_corruption!std::thread::JoinInner<tuple$<> >::join<tuple$<> >+0x25
04 000000d9`690ff970 00007ff6`c7753b6f heap_corruption!std::thread::JoinHandle<tuple$<> >::join<tuple$<> >+0x1f
05 000000d9`690ff9b0 00007ff6`c77574eb heap_corruption!heap_corruption::main+0x13f
06 000000d9`690ffb20 00007ff6`c7752d8e heap_corruption!core::ops::function::FnOnce::call_once<void (*)(),tuple$<> >+0xb
07 (Inline Function) --------`-------- heap_corruption!core::hint::black_box+0xa
08 000000d9`690ffb60 00007ff6`c7752101 heap_corruption!std::sys::backtrace::__rust_begin_short_backtrace<void (*)(),tuple$<> >+0xe
09 000000d9`690ffba0 00007ff6`c775b639 heap_corruption!std::rt::lang_start::closure$0<tuple$<> >+0x11
0a (Inline Function) --------`-------- heap_corruption!std::rt::lang_start_internal::closure$2+0x6
0b (Inline Function) --------`-------- heap_corruption!std::panicking::try::do_call+0x6
0c (Inline Function) --------`-------- heap_corruption!std::panicking::try+0x6
0d (Inline Function) --------`-------- heap_corruption!std::panic::catch_unwind+0x6
0e 000000d9`690ffbe0 00007ff6`c77520da heap_corruption!std::rt::lang_start_internal+0x79
0f 000000d9`690ffca0 00007ff6`c7753cc9 heap_corruption!std::rt::lang_start<tuple$<> >+0x3a
10 000000d9`690ffd10 00007ff6`c7770bec heap_corruption!main+0x19
11 (Inline Function) --------`-------- heap_corruption!invoke_main+0x22
12 000000d9`690ffd40 00007ff9`b18353e0 heap_corruption!__scrt_common_main_seh+0x10c
13 000000d9`690ffd80 00007ff9`b2a4485b kernel32!BaseThreadInitThunk+0x10
14 000000d9`690ffdb0 00000000`00000000 ntdll!RtlUserThreadStart+0x2b

   1  Id: 1ab0.768 Suspend: 0 Teb: 000000d9`68ea7000 Unfrozen
 # Child-SP          RetAddr           Call Site
00 000000d9`691ff5c8 00007ff9`b2a56cdf ntdll!NtWaitForWorkViaWorkerFactory+0x14
01 000000d9`691ff5d0 00007ff9`b18353e0 ntdll!TppWorkerThread+0x2df
02 000000d9`691ff8c0 00007ff9`b2a4485b kernel32!BaseThreadInitThunk+0x10
03 000000d9`691ff8f0 00000000`00000000 ntdll!RtlUserThreadStart+0x2b

   2  Id: 1ab0.1a50 Suspend: 0 Teb: 000000d9`68ea9000 Unfrozen
 # Child-SP          RetAddr           Call Site
00 000000d9`693ff1c8 00007ff9`b2a5d89d ntdll!NtWaitForAlertByThreadId+0x14
01 000000d9`693ff1d0 00007ff9`b2a5d5c1 ntdll!RtlpWaitOnAddressWithTimeout+0x81
02 000000d9`693ff200 00007ff9`b2a7a7bc ntdll!RtlpWaitOnAddress+0x1a1
03 000000d9`693ff300 00007ff9`b2a7a622 ntdll!RtlpEnterCriticalSectionContended+0x18c
04 000000d9`693ff360 00007ff9`b2a665b8 ntdll!RtlEnterCriticalSection+0x42
05 000000d9`693ff390 00007ff9`b2a6838e ntdll!RtlpFreeHeap+0x888
06 000000d9`693ff4f0 00007ff9`b2a676e1 ntdll!RtlpFreeHeapInternal+0x79e
07 000000d9`693ff5b0 00007ff9`b076218b ntdll!RtlFreeHeap+0x51
08 000000d9`693ff5f0 00007ff9`b077562c ucrtbase!_free_base+0x1b
09 000000d9`693ff620 00007ff9`b2a947ec ucrtbase!destroy_fls+0x3c
0a 000000d9`693ff650 00007ff9`b2a817d3 ntdll!RtlpFlsDataCleanup+0xd8
0b 000000d9`693ff690 00007ff9`b2a448de ntdll!LdrShutdownThread+0x43
0c 000000d9`693ff790 00007ff9`b18353e9 ntdll!RtlExitUserThread+0x3e
0d 000000d9`693ff7d0 00007ff9`b2a4485b kernel32!BaseThreadInitThunk+0x19
0e 000000d9`693ff800 00000000`00000000 ntdll!RtlUserThreadStart+0x2b

   3  Id: 1ab0.1c44 Suspend: 0 Teb: 000000d9`68eab000 Unfrozen
 # Child-SP          RetAddr           Call Site
00 000000d9`695feb48 00007ff9`b2a5d89d ntdll!NtWaitForAlertByThreadId+0x14
01 000000d9`695feb50 00007ff9`b2a5d5c1 ntdll!RtlpWaitOnAddressWithTimeout+0x81
02 000000d9`695feb80 00007ff9`b2a7a7bc ntdll!RtlpWaitOnCriticalSection+0x1a1
03 000000d9`695fec80 00007ff9`b2a7a622 ntdll!RtlpEnterCriticalSectionContended+0x18c
04 000000d9`695fece0 00007ff9`b2a6c5fa ntdll!RtlEnterCriticalSection+0x42
05 000000d9`695fed10 00007ff9`b2a6929c ntdll!RtlpAllocateHeap+0x149a
06 000000d9`695fef70 00007ff6`c7752257 ntdll!RtlpAllocateHeapInternal+0x6ac
07 000000d9`695ff070 00007ff6`c77523b5 heap_corruption!alloc::alloc::alloc+0x67
08 000000d9`695ff0e0 00007ff6`c775218f heap_corruption!alloc::alloc::Global::alloc_impl+0x155
09 (Inline Function) --------`-------- heap_corruption!alloc::alloc::impl$1::allocate+0x2b
0a 000000d9`695ff270 00007ff6`c7751eaf heap_corruption!alloc::alloc::exchange_malloc+0x3f
0b (Inline Function) --------`-------- heap_corruption!alloc::boxed::impl$0::new+0xf
0c 000000d9`695ff300 00007ff6`c7752dad heap_corruption!heap_corruption::main::closure$0+0x9f
0d (Inline Function) --------`-------- heap_corruption!core::hint::black_box+0x9
0e 000000d9`695ff590 00007ff6`c77550ad heap_corruption!std::sys::backtrace::__rust_begin_short_backtrace<heap_corruption::main::closure_env$0,tuple$<>
>+0xd
0f 000000d9`695ff5c0 00007ff6`c775566d
heap_corruption!std::thread::impl$0::spawn_unchecked_::closure$1::closure$0<heap_corruption::main::closure_env$0,tuple$<> >+0xd
```

99

```
10 000000d9`695ff5f0 00007ff6`c7756cd3
heap_corruption!core::panic::unwind_safe::impl$25::call_once<tuple$<>,std::thread::impl$0::spawn_unchecked_::closure$1::closure_env$0<heap_corruption::main::c
losure_env$0,tuple$<> > >+0xd
11 000000d9`695ff620 00007ff6`c7755173
heap_corruption!std::panicking::try::do_call<core::panic::unwind_safe::AssertUnwindSafe<std::thread::impl$0::spawn_unchecked_::closure$1::closure_env$0<heap_c
orruption::main::closure_env$0,tuple$<> > >,tuple$<> >+0x23
12 000000d9`695ff680 00007ff6`c7754c05       heap_corruption!std::thread::impl$7::drop::closure$0<tuple$<> >+0xb3
13 (Inline Function) --------`--------       heap_corruption!std::panicking::try+0x25
14 (Inline Function) --------`--------       heap_corruption!std::panic::catch_unwind+0x25
15 000000d9`695ff6d0 00007ff6`c775746e       heap_corruption!std::thread::impl$0::spawn_unchecked_::closure$1<heap_corruption::main::closure_env$0,tuple$<>
>+0x135
16 000000d9`695ff830 00007ff6`c776353d
heap_corruption!core::ops::function::FnOnce::call_once<std::thread::impl$0::spawn_unchecked_::closure_env$1<heap_corruption::main::closure_env$0,tuple$<>
>,tuple$<> >+0xe
17 (Inline Function) --------`--------       heap_corruption!alloc::boxed::impl$48::call_once+0xb
18 (Inline Function) --------`--------       heap_corruption!alloc::boxed::impl$48::call_once+0x16
19 000000d9`695ff870 00007ff9`b18353e0       heap_corruption!std::sys::pal::windows::thread::impl$0::new::thread_start+0x3d
1a 000000d9`695ff8d0 00007ff9`b2a4485b       kernel32!BaseThreadInitThunk+0x10
1b 000000d9`695ff900 00000000`00000000       ntdll!RtlUserThreadStart+0x2b

    4 Id: 1ab0.1dc0 Suspend: 0 Teb: 000000d9`68ead000 Unfrozen
   # Child-SP          RetAddr           Call Site
00 000000d9`697ff7f8 00007ff9`b2a5d89d       ntdll!NtWaitForAlertByThreadId+0x14
01 000000d9`697ff800 00007ff9`b2a5d5c1       ntdll!RtlpWaitOnAddressWithTimeout+0x81
02 000000d9`697ff830 00007ff9`b2a7a7bc       ntdll!RtlpWaitOnCriticalSection+0x1a1
03 000000d9`697ff930 00007ff9`b2a7a622       ntdll!RtlpEnterCriticalSectionContended+0x18c
04 000000d9`697ff990 00007ff9`b2a665b8       ntdll!RtlEnterCriticalSection+0x42
05 000000d9`697ff9c0 00007ff9`b2a6838e       ntdll!RtlpFreeHeap+0x888
06 000000d9`697ffb20 00007ff9`b2a676e1       ntdll!RtlpFreeHeapInternal+0x79e
07 000000d9`697ffbe0 00007ff9`b076218b       ntdll!RtlFreeHeap+0x51
08 000000d9`697ffc20 00007ff9`b077562c       ucrtbase!_free_base+0x1b
09 000000d9`697ffc50 00007ff9`b2a947ec       ucrtbase!destroy_fls+0x3c
0a 000000d9`697ffc80 00007ff9`b2a817d3       ntdll!RtlpFlsDataCleanup+0xd8
0b 000000d9`697ffcc0 00007ff9`b2a448de       ntdll!LdrShutdownThread+0x43
0c 000000d9`697ffdc0 00007ff9`b18353e9       ntdll!RtlExitUserThread+0x3e
0d 000000d9`697ffe00 00007ff9`b2a4485b       kernel32!BaseThreadInitThunk+0x19
0e 000000d9`697ffe30 00000000`00000000       ntdll!RtlUserThreadStart+0x2b

 # 5 Id: 1ab0.b7c Suspend: 0 Teb: 000000d9`68eaf000 Unfrozen
   # Child-SP          RetAddr           Call Site
00 000000d9`699fdb38 00007ff9`b2b291a8       ntdll!NtWaitForMultipleObjects+0x14
01 000000d9`699fdb40 00007ff9`b2b2877e       ntdll!WerpWaitForCrashReporting+0xa8
02 000000d9`699fdbc0 00007ff9`b2b27f3b       ntdll!RtlReportExceptionHelper+0x33e
03 000000d9`699fdc90 00007ff9`b2b4c104       ntdll!RtlReportException+0x9b
04 000000d9`699fdd10 00007ff9`b2ad40f6       ntdll!RtlReportFatalFailure$filt$0+0x33
05 000000d9`699fdd40 00007ff9`b2ae906f       ntdll!_C_specific_handler+0x96
06 000000d9`699fddb0 00007ff9`b2a75bea       ntdll!RtlpExecuteHandlerForException+0xf
07 000000d9`699fdde0 00007ff9`b2a72ef1       ntdll!RtlDispatchException+0x25a
08 000000d9`699fe530 00007ff9`b2b4c0c9       ntdll!RtlRaiseException+0x1f1
09 000000d9`699fed10 00007ff9`b2b4c093       ntdll!RtlReportFatalFailure+0x9
0a 000000d9`699fed60 00007ff9`b2b54eb2       ntdll!RtlReportCriticalFailure+0x97
0b 000000d9`699fee50 00007ff9`b2b5519a       ntdll!RtlpHeapHandleError+0x12
0c 000000d9`699fee80 00007ff9`b2b5f685       ntdll!RtlpHpHeapHandleError+0x7a
0d 000000d9`699feeb0 00007ff9`b2b54dc0       ntdll!RtlpLogHeapFailure+0x45
0e 000000d9`699feee0 00007ff9`b2a669f5       ntdll!RtlpAnalyzeHeapFailure+0x2fc
0f 000000d9`699fef40 00007ff9`b2a6838e       ntdll!RtlpFreeHeap+0xcc5
10 000000d9`699ff0a0 00007ff9`b2a676e1       ntdll!RtlpFreeHeapInternal+0x79e
11 000000d9`699ff160 00007ff6`c7752cfb       ntdll!RtlFreeHeap+0x51
12 000000d9`699ff1a0 00007ff6`c77589b0       heap_corruption!alloc::alloc::impl$1::deallocate+0x9b
13 000000d9`699ff240 00007ff6`c7757efe       heap_corruption!alloc::boxed::impl$8::drop<array$<i16,100>,alloc::alloc::Global>+0x90
14 000000d9`699ff2d0 00007ff6`c775203c       heap_corruption!core::ptr::drop_in_place<alloc::boxed::Box<array$<i16,100>,alloc::alloc::Global> >+0xe
15 000000d9`699ff300 00007ff6`c7752dad       heap_corruption!heap_corruption::main::closure$0+0x22c
16 (Inline Function) --------`--------       heap_corruption!core::hint::black_box+0x9
17 000000d9`699ff590 00007ff6`c77550ad       heap_corruption!std::sys::backtrace::__rust_begin_short_backtrace<heap_corruption::main::closure_env$0,tuple$<>
>+0xd
18 000000d9`699ff5c0 00007ff6`c775566d
heap_corruption!std::thread::impl$0::spawn_unchecked_::closure$1::closure$0<heap_corruption::main::closure_env$0,tuple$<> >+0xd
19 000000d9`699ff5f0 00007ff6`c7756cd3
heap_corruption!core::panic::unwind_safe::impl$25::call_once<tuple$<>,std::thread::impl$0::spawn_unchecked_::closure$1::closure_env$0<heap_corruption::main::c
losure_env$0,tuple$<> > >+0xd
1a 000000d9`699ff620 00007ff6`c7755173
heap_corruption!std::panicking::try::do_call<core::panic::unwind_safe::AssertUnwindSafe<std::thread::impl$0::spawn_unchecked_::closure$1::closure_env$0<heap_c
orruption::main::closure_env$0,tuple$<> > >,tuple$<> >+0x23
1b 000000d9`699ff680 00007ff6`c7754c05       heap_corruption!std::thread::impl$7::drop::closure$0<tuple$<> >+0xb3
1c (Inline Function) --------`--------       heap_corruption!std::panicking::try+0x25
1d (Inline Function) --------`--------       heap_corruption!std::panic::catch_unwind+0x25
1e 000000d9`699ff6d0 00007ff6`c775746e       heap_corruption!std::thread::impl$0::spawn_unchecked_::closure$1<heap_corruption::main::closure_env$0,tuple$<>
>+0x135
1f 000000d9`699ff830 00007ff6`c776353d
heap_corruption!core::ops::function::FnOnce::call_once<std::thread::impl$0::spawn_unchecked_::closure_env$1<heap_corruption::main::closure_env$0,tuple$<>
>,tuple$<> >+0xe
20 (Inline Function) --------`--------       heap_corruption!alloc::boxed::impl$48::call_once+0xb
21 (Inline Function) --------`--------       heap_corruption!alloc::boxed::impl$48::call_once+0x16
22 000000d9`699ff870 00007ff9`b18353e0       heap_corruption!std::sys::pal::windows::thread::impl$0::new::thread_start+0x3d
23 000000d9`699ff8d0 00007ff9`b2a4485b       kernel32!BaseThreadInitThunk+0x10
24 000000d9`699ff900 00000000`00000000       ntdll!RtlUserThreadStart+0x2b
```

Note: We see that in addition to **Exception Thread** #5, there are threads #2, #3, and #4 that try to allocate or free dynamic memory and are waiting for a critical section.

8. We now check if there is any wait chain, and if there is, what is its owner thread (a thread that entered a critical section and blocked other threads trying to access it)? We can do it using the **!cs -l -o -s** command:

```
0:005> !cs -l -o -s
-----------------------------------------
DebugInfo        = 0x00007ff9b2bb8ed0
Critical section = 0x000001fbdccf02c0 (+0x1FBDCCF02C0)
LOCKED
LockCount        = 0x3
WaiterWoken      = No
OwningThread     = 0x0000000000000b7c
RecursionCount   = 0x1
LockSemaphore    = 0xFFFFFFFF
SpinCount        = 0x0000000000000000
OwningThread DbgId = ~5s
OwningThread Stack =
          Child-SP          RetAddr           : Args to Child                                                          : Call Site
          000000d9`699fdb38 00007ff9`b2b291a8 : 00000000`00000000 00000000`00000000 00000000`00000000 00000000`00000000 :
ntdll!NtWaitForMultipleObjects+0x14
          000000d9`699fdb40 00007ff9`b2b2877e : 00000000`00000000 00000000`00001ab0 000000d9`699fed90 00000000`00001000 :
ntdll!WerpWaitForCrashReporting+0xa8
          000000d9`699fdbc0 00007ff9`b2b27f3b : 00000000`00000000 000000d9`699fe570 00000000`00000000 00000000`00000000 :
ntdll!RtlReportExceptionHelper+0x33e
          000000d9`699fdc90 00007ff9`b2b4c104 : 00007ff9`b2b9f394 000000d9`699fed10 00000000`00000000 00000000`00000000 : ntdll!RtlReportException+0x9b
          000000d9`699fdd10 00007ff9`b2ad40f6 : 000000d9`699fed10 00007ff9`b2bcd8b4 000000d9`699fde40 00000000`00000000 :
ntdll!RtlReportFatalFailure$filt$0+0x33
          000000d9`699fdd40 00007ff9`b2ae906f : 00000000`00000000 000000d9`699fe340 000000d9`699fed90 000000d9`699fed90 : ntdll!_C_specific_handler+0x96
          000000d9`699fddb0 00007ff9`b2a75bea : 000000d9`699fed90 00007ff9`b2a40000 00007ff9`b2b4c0c9 00007ff9`b2bcd8b4 :
ntdll!RtlpExecuteHandlerForException+0xf
          000000d9`699fdde0 00007ff9`b2a72ef1 : 00000000`00000000 000000d9`699febe0 00000000`00000000 00007ff9`b2a72e0b :
ntdll!RtlDispatchException+0x25a
          000000d9`699fe530 00007ff9`b2b4c0c9 : 000004f0`fffffb30 00000000`c0000374 00000000`00000001 000001fb`dccf2ca0 : ntdll!RtlRaiseException+0x1f1
          000000d9`699fed10 00007ff9`b2bb77d8 : 000000d9`69a00000 00007ff9`b2bc0000 00007ff9`b2a40000 00007ff9`b2a70000 : ntdll!RtlReportFatalFailure+0x9
          000000d9`699fed60 00007ff9`b2b54eb2 : 00000000`0000007a 00007ff9`b2bb7780 00000000`00000003 000001fb`dccf0000 :
ntdll!RtlReportCriticalFailure+0x97
          000000d9`699fee50 00007ff9`b2b5519a : 00000000`00000003 000001fb`dcd0d810 000001fb`dccf0000 000000d9`699feea0 : ntdll!RtlpHeapHandleError+0x12
          000000d9`699fee80 00007ff9`b2b5f685 : 000001fb`dccf0000 00000000`00100000 00000000`7d00017c 00007ff9`b075f428 :
ntdll!RtlpHpHeapHandleError+0x7a
          000000d9`699feeb0 00007ff9`b2b54dc0 : 000001fb`dcd0d780 00007ff9`b2a46800 00000000`00000000 00000000`00000004 : ntdll!RtlpLogHeapFailure+0x45
          000000d9`699feee0 00007ff9`b2a669f5 : 000001fb`dccf0000 000001fb`dcd0d800 000001fb`dccf0000 000001fb`dcd0d800 :
ntdll!RtlpAnalyzeHeapFailure+0x2fc
          000000d9`699fef40 00007ff9`b2a6838e : 000001fb`dccf0000 000001fb`dcd0d800 000001fb`dcd0d800 000001fb`dccf0000 : ntdll!RtlpFreeHeap+0xcc5
          000000d9`699ff0a0 00007ff9`b2a676e1 : 000001fb`dcd0d800 000001fb`dccf0000 000000d9`699ff380 00000000`00000000 :
ntdll!RtlpFreeHeapInternal+0x79e
          000000d9`699ff160 00007ff6`c7752cfb : 00000000`00000000 000001fb`dccf4a60 000000d9`68eaf000 00000000`00000000 : ntdll!RtlFreeHeap+0x51
          000000d9`699ff1a0 00007ff6`c77589b0 : 000001fb`dcd0d810 000001fb`dcd0d810 000001fb`dcd0d810 000001fb`dcd0d810 :
heap_corruption!alloc::alloc::impl$1::deallocate+0x9b
          000000d9`699ff240 00007ff6`c7757efe : 00000000`00000002 00000000`000000c8 000001fb`dcd0d810 00000000`000000c8 :
heap_corruption!alloc::boxed::impl$8::drop<array$<i16,100>,alloc::alloc::Global>+0x90
ntdll!RtlpStackTraceDataBase is NULL. Probably the stack traces are not enabled.
```

Note: We see **LockCount** is 3 (means 3 threads are waiting), and **OwningThread** is thread #5 that detected heap corruption. We also see a critical section address and can double-check that threads #2, #3, and #4 are indeed the ones that were waiting (we see it from the execution residue left in the stack region):

```
0:005> ~2kvL
# Child-SP          RetAddr           : Args to Child                                                          : Call Site
00 000000d9`693ff1c8 00007ff9`b2a5d89d : 00000000`00000000 00000000`00000000 00000000`00000000 00007ff9`b2a696fd : ntdll!NtWaitForAlertByThreadId+0x14
01 000000d9`693ff1d0 00007ff9`b2a5d5c1 : 000000d9`68ea43a0 00000000`00000000 00000000`fffffff2 000001fb`dccf02c8 : ntdll!RtlpWaitOnAddressWithTimeout+0x81
02 000000d9`693ff200 00007ff9`b2a7a7bc : 00007ec2`0268e351 00000000`00000000 000001fb`dcd0b500 000001fb`dccf02c0 : ntdll!RtlpWaitOnCriticalSection+0x1a1
03 000000d9`693ff300 00007ff9`b2a7a622 : 00000000`00000000 00000000`00000000 000001fb`dccf0000 00000000`00000000 :
ntdll!RtlpEnterCriticalSectionContended+0x18c
04 000000d9`693ff360 00007ff9`b2a665b8 : 00000000`00000040 000000d9`693ff438 000000d9`693ff3d0 00007ff6`c775b0c1 : ntdll!RtlEnterCriticalSection+0x42
05 000000d9`693ff390 00007ff9`b2a6838e : 000001fb`dccf0000 000001fb`dcd0b590 000001fb`dcd0b590 000001fb`dccf0000 : ntdll!RtlpFreeHeap+0x888
06 000000d9`693ff4f0 00007ff9`b2a676e1 : 000001fb`dcd0b590 000001fb`dccf0000 00000000`00000002 00000000`00000000 : ntdll!RtlpFreeHeapInternal+0x79e
07 000000d9`693ff5b0 00007ff6`b076218b : 000001fb`dcd0b5a0 00000000`00000000 00000000`00000000 000000d9`693ff628 : ntdll!RtlFreeHeap+0x51
08 000000d9`693ff5f0 00007ff6`b077562c : 000001fb`dcd0b968 00000000`00000004 000001fb`00000004 000000d9`693ff620 : ucrtbase!_free_base+0x1b
09 000000d9`693ff620 00007ff9`b2a947ec : 000001fb`dcd0b2d0 00000000`00000013 000001fb`dcd0b2d0 00007ff9`b2a683ba : ucrtbase!destroy_fls+0x3c
0a 000000d9`693ff650 00007ff9`b2a817d3 : 000000d9`68ea9000 00000000`00000000 00000000`00000000 00000000`00000000 : ntdll!RtlpFlsDataCleanup+0xd8
0b 000000d9`693ff690 00007ff9`b2a448de : 000001fb`dccf4d20 00000000`00000000 00000000`00000000 00007ff6`c7774e18 : ntdll!LdrShutdownThread+0x43
0c 000000d9`693ff790 00007ff9`b18353e9 : 00000000`00000000 00000000`00000000 00000000`00000000 00000000`00000000 : ntdll!RtlExitUserThread+0x3e
0d 000000d9`693ff7d0 00007ff9`b2a4485b : 00000000`00000000 00000000`00000000 00000000`00000000 00000000`00000000 : kernel32!BaseThreadInitThunk+0x19
0e 000000d9`693ff800 00000000`00000000 : 00000000`00000000 00000000`00000000 00000000`00000000 00000000`00000000 : ntdll!RtlUserThreadStart+0x2b

0:005> ~3kvL 8
# Child-SP          RetAddr           : Args to Child                                                          : Call Site
00 000000d9`695feb48 00007ff9`b2a5d89d : 00000000`00000000 00000000`00000000 00000000`00000000 00000094`00007ff9 b2a61dfa : ntdll!NtWaitForAlertByThreadId+0x14
01 000000d9`695feb50 00007ff9`b2a5d5c1 : 000000d9`68ea43a0 00000000`00000000 00000000`fffffff6 000001fb`dccf02c8 : ntdll!RtlpWaitOnAddressWithTimeout+0x81
02 000000d9`695feb80 00007ff9`b2a7a7bc : 000001fb`dccf2cd8 00000000`00000000 000000d9`695ff000 000001fb`dccf02c0 : ntdll!RtlpWaitOnCriticalSection+0x1a1
03 000000d9`695fec80 00007ff9`b2a7a622 : 00000000`000000bb 000001fb`dccf0150 000001fb`dccf0000 00000000`00000117 :
ntdll!RtlpEnterCriticalSectionContended+0x18c
04 000000d9`695fece0 00007ff9`b2a6c5fa : 000001fb`dccf24a2 000001fb`dccf0000 00000000`00000002 00000000`00000010 : ntdll!RtlEnterCriticalSection+0x42
05 000000d9`695fed10 00007ff9`b2a6929c : 000001fb`dccf0000 00000000`00000002 00000000`000000c8 00000000`000000d0 : ntdll!RtlpAllocateHeap+0x149a
06 000000d9`695fef70 00007ff6`c7752257 : 00000000`00000000 00000000`00000000 00000000`00000000 00000000`00000000 : ntdll!RtlpAllocateHeapInternal+0x6ac
07 000000d9`695ff070 00007ff6`c77523b5 : 00000000`00000070 ffffffff`ffffffff ffffffff`ffffffff 00007ff9`b2a7fe72 :
heap_corruption!alloc::alloc::alloc+0x67
```

```
0:005> ~4kvL
 # Child-SP          RetAddr           : Args to Child                                                                         : Call Site
00 000000d9`697ff7f8 00007ff9`b2a5d89d : 00000000`00000000 00000000`00000000 00000000`00000000 00007ff9`b2a696fe : ntdll!NtWaitForAlertByThreadId+0x14
01 000000d9`697ff800 00007ff9`b2a5d5c1 : 000000d9`68ea43a0 00000000`00000000 00000000`fffffffa 000001fb`dccf02c8 : ntdll!RtlpWaitOnAddressWithTimeout+0x81
02 000000d9`697ff830 00007ff9`b2a7a7bc : 00007ec2`0228e521 00000000`00000000 000001fb`dcd0c700 000001fb`dccf02c0 : ntdll!RtlpWaitOnCriticalSection+0x1a1
03 000000d9`697ff930 00007ff9`b2a7a622 : 00000000`00000000 00000000`00000000 000001fb`dccf0000 00000000`00000000 :
ntdll!RtlpEnterCriticalSectionContended+0x18c
04 000000d9`697ff990 00007ff9`b2a665b8 : 00000000`00000040 000000d9`697ffa68 000000d9`697ffa00 00007ff6`c775b0c1 : ntdll!RtlEnterCriticalSection+0x42
05 000000d9`697ff9c0 00007ff9`b2a6838e : 000001fb`dccf0000 000001fb`dcd0c710 000001fb`dcd0c710 000001fb`dccf0000 : ntdll!RtlpFreeHeap+0x888
06 000000d9`697ffb20 00007ff9`b2a676e1 : 000001fb`dcd0c710 000001fb`dccf0000 00000000`00000002 00000000`00000000 : ntdll!RtlpFreeHeapInternal+0x79e
07 000000d9`697ffbe0 00007ff9`b076218b : 000001fb`dcd0c720 00000000`00000000 00000000`00000000 000000d9`697ffc58 : ntdll!RtlFreeHeap+0x51
08 000000d9`697ffc20 00007ff9`b077562c : 000001fb`dcd0cae8 00000000`00000004 000001fb`00000004 000000d9`697ffc50 : ucrtbase!_free_base+0x1b
09 000000d9`697ffc50 00007ff9`b2a947ec : 000001fb`dcd0acd0 00000000`00000013 00000000`00000000 00007ff9`b2a683ba : ucrtbase!destroy_fls+0x3c
0a 000000d9`697ffc80 00007ff9`b2a817d3 : 000000d9`68ead000 00000000`00000000 00000000`00000000 00000000`00000000 : ntdll!RtlpFlsDataCleanup+0xd8
0b 000000d9`697ffcc0 00007ff9`b2a448de : 000001fb`dccf4f40 00000000`00000000 00000000`00000000 00007ff6`c7774e18 : ntdll!LdrShutdownThread+0x43
0c 000000d9`697ffdc0 00007ff9`b18353e9 : 00000000`00000000 00000000`00000000 00000000`00000000 00000000`00000000 : ntdll!RtlExitUserThread+0x3e
0d 000000d9`697ffe00 00007ff9`b2a4485b : 00000000`00000000 00000000`00000000 00000000`00000000 00000000`00000000 : kernel32!BaseThreadInitThunk+0x19
0e 000000d9`697ffe30 00000000`00000000 : 00000000`00000000 00000000`00000000 00000000`00000000 00000000`00000000 : ntdll!RtlUserThreadStart+0x2b
```

Note: If values are not visible in the Args to Child sequences, then we can check the stack region range directly:

```
0:005> dp 000000d9`697ff800 000000d9`697ffb20
000000d9`697ff800  00000000`00000000 00000000`00000000
000000d9`697ff810  00000000`00000000 00007ff9`b2a696fd
000000d9`697ff820  00000000`00000000 00007ff9`b2a5d5c1
000000d9`697ff830  000000d9`68ea43a0 00000000`00000000
000000d9`697ff840  00000000`fffffffa 000001fb`dccf02c8
000000d9`697ff850  00000000`00000000 000001fb`dccb0f30
000000d9`697ff860  00000000`00000000 000001fb`dccb0000
000000d9`697ff870  00000000`00000000 000001fb`00000000
000000d9`697ff880  000000d9`68ead000 000001fb`dccf02c8
000000d9`697ff890  00000000`00001dc0 00000000`00000000
000000d9`697ff8a0  000000d9`695febd8 000000d9`697ff888
000000d9`697ff8b0  00000000`00000000 00000000`00000005
000000d9`697ff8c0  00000000`00000000 000000d9`697ff979
000000d9`697ff8d0  000001fb`dccf0000 00007ff9`b2a68d1a
000000d9`697ff8e0  000001fb`dccb0000 00007ff9`00000000
000000d9`697ff8f0  00007ec2`0228ebc1 00000000`00000000
000000d9`697ff900  00000000`00000000 00000000`00000001
000000d9`697ff910  00000000`00000001 00000000`00000001
000000d9`697ff920  00000000`00000000 00007ff9`b2a7a7bc
000000d9`697ff930  00007ec2`0228e521 00000000`00000000
000000d9`697ff940  000001fb`dcd0c700 000001fb`dccf02c0
000000d9`697ff950  00000000`00000000 000001fb`dcd0c710
000000d9`697ff960  00007ff9`b2bbab01 00000000`7ffe0380
000000d9`697ff970  00000000`00000002 000001fb`dcd0c710
000000d9`697ff980  000001fb`dcd0c720 00007ff9`b2a7a622
000000d9`697ff990  00000000`00000000 00000000`00000000
000000d9`697ff9a0  000001fb`dccf0000 00000000`00000000
000000d9`697ff9b0  00000000`00000000 00007ff9`b2a665b8
000000d9`697ff9c0  00000000`00000040 000000d9`697ffa68
000000d9`697ff9d0  000000d9`697ffa00 00007ff6`c775b0c1
000000d9`697ff9e0  00000000`00000000 00000000`00000008
000000d9`697ff9f0  00000000`00000000 00000000`00000000
000000d9`697ffa00  00000000`00000000 00000000`00000001
000000d9`697ffa10  00000000`00000004 000001fb`dcd08c10
000000d9`697ffa20  00000001`697ffa80 00007ff6`c775b2b9
000000d9`697ffa30  00000000`00000000 000000d9`697ffea8
000000d9`697ffa40  00000000`00000000 00000000`00000000
000000d9`697ffa50  00000003`00000000 00000000`00000000
000000d9`697ffa60  00000000`00000000 00000000`00000000
000000d9`697ffa70  000001fb`dccff910 00000000`00000040
000000d9`697ffa80  000001fb`dcd08c50 00007ff6`c77642c0
000000d9`697ffa90  000000d9`697ffb10 00007ff6`c77643c0
000000d9`697ffaa0  00000000`0000027f ffffffff`fffffffe
```

```
000000d9`697ffab0   000000d9`697ffbf0 00007ff6`c7752dad
000000d9`697ffac0   00000000`00000000 00000000`00000000
000000d9`697ffad0   00000000`00000000 00000000`00000000
000000d9`697ffae0   00000003`00000000 00007ff6`c77550ad
000000d9`697ffaf0   00000000`00000000 00000000`00000003
000000d9`697ffb00   00007ff9`b2bbab90 00000000`00000000
000000d9`697ffb10   00000000`00000000 00007ff9`b2a6838e
000000d9`697ffb20   000001fb`dccf0000
```

9.   At the end of this exercise, we check error codes manually (**!error** command):

```
0:005> !error c0000374
Error code: (NTSTATUS) 0xc0000374 (3221226356) - A heap has been corrupted.
```

```
0:005> !error c0000005
Error code: (NTSTATUS) 0xc0000005 (3221225477) - The instruction at 0x%p referenced memory at
0x%p. The memory could not be %s.
```

Note: 0x%p is not "corruption" garbage. It's a formatting instruction (code), and real address values are usually substituted by applications into this generic error code message. Also, sometimes, the codes from the problem machine may not be available on the analysis machine because the **!error** command uses Windows API to get the description.

10.   We can also check the last errors for every thread (most last errors can be ignored – always compare with a normal memory dump):

```
0:005> !gle -all
Last error for thread 0:
LastErrorValue: (Win32) 0xcb (203) - The system could not find the environment option that was entered.
LastStatusValue: (NTSTATUS) 0xc0000100 - Indicates the specified environment variable name was not found
in the specified environment block.

Last error for thread 1:
LastErrorValue: (Win32) 0 (0) - The operation completed successfully.
LastStatusValue: (NTSTATUS) 0 - STATUS_SUCCESS

Last error for thread 2:
LastErrorValue: (Win32) 0xbb (187) - The specified system semaphore name was not found.
LastStatusValue: (NTSTATUS) 0xc000000d - An invalid parameter was passed to a service or function.

Last error for thread 3:
LastErrorValue: (Win32) 0xbb (187) - The specified system semaphore name was not found.
LastStatusValue: (NTSTATUS) 0xc000000d - An invalid parameter was passed to a service or function.

Last error for thread 4:
LastErrorValue: (Win32) 0xbb (187) - The specified system semaphore name was not found.
LastStatusValue: (NTSTATUS) 0xc000000d - An invalid parameter was passed to a service or function.

Last error for thread 5:
LastErrorValue: (Win32) 0xbb (187) - The specified system semaphore name was not found.
LastStatusValue: (NTSTATUS) 0xc000000d - An invalid parameter was passed to a service or function.
```

11.   We close logging before exiting WinDbg:

```
0:005> .logclose
Closing open log file C:\ARWMDA-Dumps\RW5.log
```

Exercise RW6

- **Goal:** Learn how to debug heap corruption using page heap

- **Patterns:** Instrumentation Information

- \ARWMDA-Dumps\Exercise-RW6.pdf

Exercise RW6

Goal: Learn how to debug heap corruption using page heap.

Patterns: Instrumentation Information.

1.   Launch WinDbg.

2.   Open \ARWMDA-Dumps\Process\heap-corruption2.exe.3880.dmp.

3.   We get the dump file loaded:

```
Loading Dump File [C:\ARWMDA-Dumps\Process\heap-corruption2.exe.3880.dmp]
User Mini Dump File with Full Memory: Only application data is available


************* Path validation summary **************
Response                      Time (ms)     Location
Deferred                                    srv*
Symbol search path is: srv*
Executable search path is:
Windows 10 Version 22000 UP Free x64
Product: WinNt, suite: SingleUserTS
Edition build lab: 22000.1.amd64fre.co_release.210604-1628
Debug session time: Wed Oct 30 08:57:35.000 2024 (UTC + 0:00)
System Uptime: 0 days 0:13:27.672
Process Uptime: 0 days 0:00:03.000
.......
This dump file has an exception of interest stored in it.
The stored exception information can be accessed via .ecxr
(f28.1db0): Unknown exception - code c0000374 (first/second chance not available)
For analysis of this file, run !analyze -v
ntdll!NtWaitForMultipleObjects+0x14:
00007ff9`b2ae4bd4 ret
```

4.   Open a log file using the **.logopen** command and load symbols (**.sympath+** and **.reload**):

```
0:003> .logopen C:\ARWMDA-Dumps\RW6.log
Opened log file 'C:\ARWMDA-Dumps\RW6.log'

0:003> .sympath+ C:\ARWMDA-Dumps\Symbols\debug
Symbol search path is: srv*;C:\ARWMDA-Dumps\Symbols\debug
Expanded Symbol search path is:
cache*;SRV*https://msdl.microsoft.com/download/symbols;c:\arwmda-dumps\symbols\debug

************* Path validation summary **************
Response                      Time (ms)     Location
Deferred                                    srv*
OK                                          C:\ARWMDA-Dumps\Symbols\debug

0:003> .reload
........
```

Note: WinDbg may remember symbol and source paths from the previous sessions.

5. Type the **k** command to verify the correctness of the stack trace:

```
0:003> kL
# Child-SP          RetAddr           Call Site
00 00000002`bb5fdd88 00007ff9`b2b291a8 ntdll!NtWaitForMultipleObjects+0x14
01 00000002`bb5fdd90 00007ff9`b2b2877e ntdll!WerpWaitForCrashReporting+0xa8
02 00000002`bb5fde10 00007ff9`b2b27f3b ntdll!RtlReportExceptionHelper+0x33e
03 00000002`bb5fdee0 00007ff9`b2b4c104 ntdll!RtlReportException+0x9b
04 00000002`bb5fdf60 00007ff9`b2ad40f6 ntdll!RtlReportFatalFailure$filt$0+0x33
05 00000002`bb5fdf90 00007ff9`b2ae906f ntdll!_C_specific_handler+0x96
06 00000002`bb5fe000 00007ff9`b2a75bea ntdll!RtlpExecuteHandlerForException+0xf
07 00000002`bb5fe030 00007ff9`b2a72ef1 ntdll!RtlDispatchException+0x25a
08 00000002`bb5fe780 00007ff9`b2b4c0c9 ntdll!RtlRaiseException+0x1f1
09 00000002`bb5fef60 00007ff9`b2b4c093 ntdll!RtlReportFatalFailure+0x9
0a 00000002`bb5fefb0 00007ff9`b2b54eb2 ntdll!RtlReportCriticalFailure+0x97
0b 00000002`bb5ff0a0 00007ff9`b2b5519a ntdll!RtlpHeapHandleError+0x12
0c 00000002`bb5ff0d0 00007ff9`b2b5f685 ntdll!RtlpHpHeapHandleError+0x7a
0d 00000002`bb5ff100 00007ff9`b2aeee1c ntdll!RtlpLogHeapFailure+0x45
0e 00000002`bb5ff130 00007ff9`b2a676e1 ntdll!RtlpFreeHeapInternal+0x8722c
0f 00000002`bb5ff1f0 00007ff7`6ce13c7b ntdll!RtlFreeHeap+0x51
10 00000002`bb5ff230 00007ff7`6ce19226 heap_corruption2!alloc::alloc::impl$1::deallocate+0x9b
11 00000002`bb5ff2d0 00007ff7`6ce185be heap_corruption2!alloc::boxed::impl$8::drop<slice2$<u16>,alloc::alloc::Global>+0xa6
12 00000002`bb5ff370 00007ff7`6ce117d4 heap_corruption2!core::ptr::drop_in_place<alloc::boxed::Box<slice2$<u16>,alloc::alloc::Global> >+0xe
13 00000002`bb5ff3a0 00007ff7`6ce1795d heap_corruption2!heap_corruption2::main::closure$0+0x1d4
14 (Inline Function) --------`-------- heap_corruption2!core::hint::black_box+0x9
15 00000002`bb5ff510 00007ff7`6ce1774d heap_corruption2!std::sys::backtrace::__rust_begin_short_backtrace<heap_corruption2::main::closure_env$0,tuple$<> >+0xd
16 00000002`bb5ff540 00007ff7`6ce1121d heap_corruption2!std::thread::impl$0::spawn_unchecked_::closure$1::closure$0<heap_corruption2::main::closure_env$0,tuple$<> >+0xd
17 00000002`bb5ff570 00007ff7`6ce12f63 heap_corruption2!core::panic::unwind_safe::impl$25::call_once<tuple$<>,std::thread::impl$0::spawn_unchecked_::closure$1::closure_env$0<heap_corruption2::main::closure_env$0,tuple$<> > >+0xd
18 00000002`bb5ff5a0 00007ff7`6ce17813 heap_corruption2!std::panicking::try::do_call<core::panic::unwind_safe::AssertUnwindSafe<std::thread::impl$0::spawn_unchecked_::closure$1::closure_env$0<heap_corruption2::main::closure_env$0,tuple$<> > >,tuple$<> >+0x23
19 00000002`bb5ff600 00007ff7`6ce172a5 heap_corruption2!std::thread::impl$7::drop::closure$0<tuple$<> >+0xb3
1a (Inline Function) --------`-------- heap_corruption2!std::panicking::try+0x25
1b (Inline Function) --------`-------- heap_corruption2!std::panic::catch_unwind+0x25
1c 00000002`bb5ff650 00007ff7`6ce17d3e heap_corruption2!std::thread::impl$0::spawn_unchecked_::closure$1<heap_corruption2::main::closure_env$0,tuple$<> >+0x135
1d 00000002`bb5ff7b0 00007ff7`6ce255cd heap_corruption2!core::ops::function::FnOnce::call_once<std::thread::impl$0::spawn_unchecked_::closure_env$1<heap_corruption2::main::closure_env$0,tuple$<> >,tuple$<> >+0xe
1e (Inline Function) --------`-------- heap_corruption2!alloc::boxed::impl$48::call_once+0xb
1f (Inline Function) --------`-------- heap_corruption2!alloc::boxed::impl$48::call_once+0x16
20 00000002`bb5ff7f0 00007ff9`b18353e0 heap_corruption2!std::sys::pal::windows::thread::impl$0::new::thread_start+0x3d
21 00000002`bb5ff850 00007ff9`b2a4485b kernel32!BaseThreadInitThunk+0x10
22 00000002`bb5ff880 00000000`00000000 ntdll!RtlUserThreadStart+0x2b
```

Note: In addition to exception processing functions, we see heap manipulation functions. So, we check the heap for any errors:

```
0:003> !heap -s -v

********************************************************************************
                          NT HEAP STATS BELOW
********************************************************************************
********************************************************************************
*                                                         *
*              HEAP ERROR DETECTED                        *
*                                                         *
********************************************************************************

Details:

Heap address:  000001769b090000
Error address: 000001769b0950f0
Last known valid blocks: before - 000001769b094940, after - 000001769b095150
Error type:    HEAP_FAILURE_MULTIPLE_ENTRIES_CORRUPTION
Details:       The heap manager detected multiple corrupt heap entries.
Follow-up:     Enable pageheap.

Stack trace:
Stack trace at 0x00007ff9b2bb77d8
    00007ff9b2b5f685: ntdll!RtlpLogHeapFailure+0x45
    00007ff9b2aeee1c: ntdll!RtlpFreeHeapInternal+0x8722c
    00007ff9b2a676e1: ntdll!RtlFreeHeap+0x51
    00007ff76ce13c7b: heap_corruption2!alloc::alloc::impl$1::deallocate+0x9b
    00007ff76ce19226: heap_corruption2!alloc::boxed::impl$8::drop<slice2$<u16>,alloc::alloc::Global>+0xa6
    00007ff76ce185be: heap_corruption2!core::ptr::drop_in_place<alloc::boxed::Box<slice2$<u16>,alloc::alloc::Global> >+0xe
    00007ff76ce117d4: heap_corruption2!heap_corruption2::main::closure$0+0x1d4
    00007ff76ce1795d: heap_corruption2!std::sys::backtrace::__rust_begin_short_backtrace<heap_corruption2::main::closure_env$0,tuple$<> >+0xd
    00007ff76ce1774d: heap_corruption2!std::thread::impl$0::spawn_unchecked_::closure$1::closure$0<heap_corruption2::main::closure_env$0,tuple$<> >+0xd
    00007ff76ce1121d:
heap_corruption2!core::panic::unwind_safe::impl$25::call_once<tuple$<>,std::thread::impl$0::spawn_unchecked_::closure$1::closure_env$0<heap_corruption2::main::closure_env$0,tuple$<> > >+0xd
    00007ff76ce12f63:
heap_corruption2!std::panicking::try::do_call<core::panic::unwind_safe::AssertUnwindSafe<std::thread::impl$0::spawn_unchecked_::closure$1::closure_env$0<heap_corruption2::main::closure_env$0,tuple$<> > >,tuple$<> >+0x23
    00007ff76ce17813: heap_corruption2!std::thread::impl$7::drop::closure$0<tuple$<> >+0xb3
    00007ff76ce172a5: heap_corruption2!std::thread::impl$0::spawn_unchecked_::closure$1<heap_corruption2::main::closure_env$0,tuple$<> >+0x135
```

```
     00007ff76ce17d3e:
heap_corruption2!core::ops::function::FnOnce::call_once<std::thread::impl$0::spawn_unchecked_::closure_env$1<heap_corruption2::main::closure_env$0,tuple$<>
>,tuple$<> >+0xe
     00007ff76ce255cd: heap_corruption2!std::sys::pal::windows::thread::impl$0::new::thread_start+0x3d
     00007ff9b18353e0: kernel32!BaseThreadInitThunk+0x10

LFH Key                 : 0x6e318a42ea49e559
Termination on corruption : ENABLED
        Heap     Flags   Reserv  Commit  Virt   Free List   UCR  Virt  Lock  Fast
                         (k)     (k)     (k)    (k) length       blocks cont. heap
-------------------------------------------------------------------------------
.000001769b090000 00000002   1048    132    1020    3    3     1    0     0   LFH
.000001769ae10000 00008000     64      4      64    2    1     1    0     0
-------------------------------------------------------------------------------
```

Note: This is detected heap corruption, but sometimes, heap corruption results in memory access violation during internal heap manipulation, like when free heap blocks are joined together (heap coalescence). For example, this is a stack trace and **!analyze -v** output from some other crash dump:

```
0:001> kL
ChildEBP RetAddr
0070f2e0 770d0bdd ntdll!NtWaitForMultipleObjects+0x15
0070f37c 7529162d KERNELBASE!WaitForMultipleObjectsEx+0x100
0070f3c4 75291921 kernel32!WaitForMultipleObjectsExImplementation+0xe0
0070f3e0 752b9b2d kernel32!WaitForMultipleObjects+0x18
0070f44c 752b9bca kernel32!WerpReportFaultInternal+0x186
0070f460 752b98f8 kernel32!WerpReportFault+0x70
0070f470 752b9875 kernel32!BasepReportFault+0x20
0070f4fc 77b10df7 kernel32!UnhandledExceptionFilter+0x1af
0070f504 77b10cd4 ntdll!__RtlUserThreadStart+0x62
0070f518 77b10b71 ntdll!_EH4_CallFilterFunc+0x12
0070f540 77ae6ac9 ntdll!_except_handler4+0x8e
0070f564 77ae6a9b ntdll!ExecuteHandler2+0x26
0070f614 77ab010f ntdll!ExecuteHandler+0x24
0070f614 77ad3b30 ntdll!KiUserExceptionDispatcher+0xf
0070f98c 77ad2d07 ntdll!RtlpCoalesceFreeBlocks+0x268
0070fa84 77ad2bf2 ntdll!RtlpFreeHeap+0x1f4
0070faa4 752914d1 ntdll!RtlFreeHeap+0x142
0070fab8 010b11f0 kernel32!HeapFree+0x14
0070faf8 010b1274 ApplicationL!free+0x6e
0070fb30 010b1310 ApplicationL!_callthreadstart+0x1b
0070fb38 75293677 ApplicationL!_threadstart+0x76
0070fb44 77ad9f02 kernel32!BaseThreadInitThunk+0xe
0070fb84 77ad9ed5 ntdll!__RtlUserThreadStart+0x70
0070fb9c 00000000 ntdll!_RtlUserThreadStart+0x1b


0:001> !analyze -v

[...]


EXCEPTION_RECORD:  ffffffff -- (.exr 0xffffffffffffffff)
ExceptionAddress: 77ad3b30 (ntdll!RtlpCoalesceFreeBlocks+0x00000268)
   ExceptionCode: c0000005 (Access violation)
  ExceptionFlags: 00000000
NumberParameters: 2
   Parameter[0]: 00000000
   Parameter[1]: 00000003
Attempt to read from address 00000003

[...]
```

6.   Let's check other threads:

```
0:003> ~*kL

   0 Id: f28.d38 Suspend: 0 Teb: 00000002`bae81000 Unfrozen "main"
 # Child-SP          RetAddr               Call Site
00 00000002`bb0ff7b8 00007ff9`affa10ee     ntdll!NtWaitForSingleObject+0x14
01 00000002`bb0ff7c0 00007ff7`6ce25731     KERNELBASE!WaitForSingleObjectEx+0x8e
02 00000002`bb0ff860 00007ff7`6ce16395     heap_corruption2!std::sys::pal::windows::thread::Thread::join+0x21
03 00000002`bb0ff8f0 00007ff7`6ce1653f     heap_corruption2!std::thread::JoinInner<tuple$<> >::join<tuple$<> >+0x25
04 00000002`bb0ff9d0 00007ff7`6ce1243f     heap_corruption2!std::thread::JoinHandle<tuple$<> >::join<tuple$<> >+0x1f
05 00000002`bb0ffa10 00007ff7`6ce17dfb     heap_corruption2!heap_corruption2::main+0x13f
06 00000002`bb0ffb80 00007ff7`6ce1793e     heap_corruption2!core::ops::function::FnOnce::call_once<void (*)(),tuple$<> >+0xb
07 (Inline Function) --------`--------     heap_corruption2!core::hint::black_box+0xa
08 00000002`bb0ffbc0 00007ff7`6ce14581     heap_corruption2!std::sys::backtrace::__rust_begin_short_backtrace<void (*)(),tuple$<> >+0xe
09 00000002`bb0ffc00 00007ff7`6ce1d419     heap_corruption2!std::rt::lang_start::closure$0<tuple$<> >+0x11
0a (Inline Function) --------`--------     heap_corruption2!std::rt::lang_start_internal::closure$2+0x6
0b (Inline Function) --------`--------     heap_corruption2!std::panicking::try::do_call+0x6
0c (Inline Function) --------`--------     heap_corruption2!std::panicking::try+0x6
0d (Inline Function) --------`--------     heap_corruption2!std::panic::catch_unwind+0x6
0e 00000002`bb0ffc40 00007ff7`6ce1455a     heap_corruption2!std::rt::lang_start_internal+0x79
0f 00000002`bb0ffd00 00007ff7`6ce12599     heap_corruption2!std::rt::lang_start<tuple$<> >+0x3a
10 00000002`bb0ffd70 00007ff7`6ce32c7c     heap_corruption2!main+0x19
11 (Inline Function) --------`--------     heap_corruption2!invoke_main+0x22
12 00000002`bb0ffda0 00007ff9`b18353e0     heap_corruption2!__scrt_common_main_seh+0x10c
13 00000002`bb0ffde0 00007ff9`b2a4485b     kernel32!BaseThreadInitThunk+0x10
14 00000002`bb0ffe10 00000000`00000000     ntdll!RtlUserThreadStart+0x2b

   1 Id: f28.2030 Suspend: 0 Teb: 00000002`bae83000 Unfrozen
 # Child-SP          RetAddr               Call Site
00 00000002`bb1ff978 00007ff9`b2a56cdf     ntdll!NtWaitForWorkViaWorkerFactory+0x14
01 00000002`bb1ff980 00007ff9`b18353e0     ntdll!TppWorkerThread+0x2df
02 00000002`bb1ffc70 00007ff9`b2a4485b     kernel32!BaseThreadInitThunk+0x10
03 00000002`bb1ffca0 00000000`00000000     ntdll!RtlUserThreadStart+0x2b

   2 Id: f28.ddc Suspend: 0 Teb: 00000002`bae85000 Unfrozen
 # Child-SP          RetAddr               Call Site
00 00000002`bb3ff6c8 00007ff9`b2a5d89d     ntdll!NtWaitForAlertByThreadId+0x14
01 00000002`bb3ff6d0 00007ff9`b2a9b3fe     ntdll!RtlpWaitOnAddressWithTimeout+0x81
02 00000002`bb3ff700 00007ff9`b2a9b343     ntdll!RtlpWaitOnAddress+0xae
03 00000002`bb3ff770 00007ff9`affbdd9f     ntdll!RtlWaitOnAddress+0x13
04 00000002`bb3ff7b0 00007ff7`6ce1dc01     KERNELBASE!WaitOnAddress+0x2f
05 (Inline Function) --------`--------     heap_corruption2!std::sys::sync::thread_parking::futex::Parker::park+0x65
06 (Inline Function) --------`--------     heap_corruption2!std::thread::Thread::park+0x65
07 00000002`bb3ff7f0 00007ff7`6ce1163b     heap_corruption2!std::thread::park+0x151
08 00000002`bb3ff860 00007ff7`6ce1795d     heap_corruption2!heap_corruption2::main::closure$0+0x3b
09 (Inline Function) --------`--------     heap_corruption2!core::hint::black_box+0x9
0a 00000002`bb3ff9d0 00007ff7`6ce1774d     heap_corruption2!std::sys::backtrace::__rust_begin_short_backtrace<heap_corruption2::main::closure_env$0,tuple$<>
>+0xd
0b 00000002`bb3ffa00 00007ff7`6ce1121d     heap_corruption2!std::thread::impl$0::spawn_unchecked_::closure$1::closure$0<heap_corruption2::main::closure_env$0,tuple$<> >+0xd
0c 00000002`bb3ffa30 00007ff7`6ce12f63     heap_corruption2!core::panic::unwind_safe::impl$25::call_once<tuple$<>,std::thread::impl$0::spawn_unchecked_::closure$1::closure_env$0<heap_corruption2::main:
:closure_env$0,tuple$<> > >+0xd
0d 00000002`bb3ffa60 00007ff7`6ce17813     heap_corruption2!std::panicking::try::do_call<core::panic::unwind_safe::AssertUnwindSafe<std::thread::impl$0::spawn_unchecked_::closure$1::closure_env$0<heap_
corruption2::main::closure_env$0,tuple$<> > >,tuple$<> >+0x23
0e 00000002`bb3ffac0 00007ff7`6ce172a5     heap_corruption2!std::thread::impl$7::drop::closure$0<tuple$<> >+0xb3
0f (Inline Function) --------`--------     heap_corruption2!std::panicking::try+0x25
10 (Inline Function) --------`--------     heap_corruption2!std::panic::catch_unwind+0x25
11 00000002`bb3ffb10 00007ff7`6ce17d3e     heap_corruption2!std::thread::impl$0::spawn_unchecked_::closure$1<heap_corruption2::main::closure_env$0,tuple$<>
>+0x135
12 00000002`bb3ffc70 00007ff7`6ce255cd     heap_corruption2!core::ops::function::FnOnce::call_once<std::thread::impl$0::spawn_unchecked_::closure_env$1<heap_corruption2::main::closure_env$0,tuple$<>
>,tuple$<> >+0xe
13 (Inline Function) --------`--------     heap_corruption2!alloc::boxed::impl$48::call_once+0xb
14 (Inline Function) --------`--------     heap_corruption2!alloc::boxed::impl$48::call_once+0x16
15 00000002`bb3ffcb0 00007ff9`b18353e0     heap_corruption2!std::sys::pal::windows::thread::impl$0::new::thread_start+0x3d
16 00000002`bb3ffd10 00007ff9`b2a4485b     kernel32!BaseThreadInitThunk+0x10
17 00000002`bb3ffd40 00000000`00000000     ntdll!RtlUserThreadStart+0x2b

#  3 Id: f28.1db0 Suspend: 0 Teb: 00000002`bae87000 Unfrozen
 # Child-SP          RetAddr               Call Site
00 00000002`bb5fdd88 00007ff9`b2b291a8     ntdll!NtWaitForMultipleObjects+0x14
01 00000002`bb5fdd90 00007ff9`b2b2877e     ntdll!WerpWaitForCrashReporting+0xa8
02 00000002`bb5fde10 00007ff9`b2b27f3b     ntdll!RtlReportExceptionHelper+0x33e
03 00000002`bb5fdee0 00007ff9`b2b4c104     ntdll!RtlReportException+0x9b
04 00000002`bb5fdf60 00007ff9`b2ad40f6     ntdll!RtlReportFatalFailure$filt$0+0x33
05 00000002`bb5fdf90 00007ff9`b2ae906f     ntdll!_C_specific_handler+0x96
06 00000002`bb5fe000 00007ff9`b2a75bea     ntdll!RtlpExecuteHandlerForException+0xf
07 00000002`bb5fe030 00007ff9`b2a72ef1     ntdll!RtlDispatchException+0x25a
08 00000002`bb5fe780 00007ff9`b2b4c0c9     ntdll!RtlRaiseException+0x1f1
09 00000002`bb5fef60 00007ff9`b2b4c093     ntdll!RtlReportFatalFailure+0x9
0a 00000002`bb5fefb0 00007ff9`b2b54eb2     ntdll!RtlReportCriticalFailure+0x97
0b 00000002`bb5ff0a0 00007ff9`b2b5519a     ntdll!RtlpHeapHandleError+0x12
0c 00000002`bb5ff0d0 00007ff9`b2b5f685     ntdll!RtlpHpHeapHandleError+0x7a
0d 00000002`bb5ff100 00007ff9`b2aeee1c     ntdll!RtlpLogHeapFailure+0x45
0e 00000002`bb5ff130 00007ff9`b2a676e1     ntdll!RtlpFreeHeapInternal+0x8722c
0f 00000002`bb5ff1f0 00007ff7`6ce13c7b     ntdll!RtlFreeHeap+0x51
10 00000002`bb5ff230 00007ff7`6ce19226     heap_corruption2!alloc::alloc::impl$1::deallocate+0x9b
11 00000002`bb5ff2d0 00007ff7`6ce185be     heap_corruption2!alloc::boxed::impl$8::drop<slice2$<u16>,alloc::alloc::Global>+0xa6
12 00000002`bb5ff370 00007ff7`6ce117d4     heap_corruption2!core::ptr::drop_in_place<alloc::boxed::Box<slice2$<u16>,alloc::alloc::Global> >+0xe
13 00000002`bb5ff3a0 00007ff7`6ce1795d     heap_corruption2!heap_corruption2::main::closure$0+0x1d4
14 (Inline Function) --------`--------     heap_corruption2!core::hint::black_box+0x9
```

```
15 00000002`bb5ff510 00007ff7`6ce1774d     heap_corruption2!std::sys::backtrace::__rust_begin_short_backtrace<heap_corruption2::main::closure_env$0,tuple$<>
>+0xd
16 00000002`bb5ff540 00007ff7`6ce1121d
heap_corruption2!std::thread::impl$0::spawn_unchecked_::closure$1::closure$0<heap_corruption2::main::closure_env$0,tuple$<> >+0xd
17 00000002`bb5ff570 00007ff7`6ce12f63
heap_corruption2!core::panic::unwind_safe::impl$25::call_once<tuple$<>,std::thread::impl$0::spawn_unchecked_::closure$1::closure_env$0<heap_corruption2::main:
:closure_env$0,tuple$<> > >+0xd
18 00000002`bb5ff5a0 00007ff7`6ce17813
heap_corruption2!std::panicking::try::do_call<core::panic::unwind_safe::AssertUnwindSafe<std::thread::impl$0::spawn_unchecked_::closure$1::closure_env$0<heap_
corruption2::main::closure_env$0,tuple$<> > >,tuple$<> >+0x23
19 00000002`bb5ff600 00007ff7`6ce172a5     heap_corruption2!std::thread::impl$7::drop::closure$0<tuple$<> >+0xb3
1a (Inline Function) --------`--------     heap_corruption2!std::panicking::try+0x25
1b (Inline Function) --------`--------     heap_corruption2!std::panic::catch_unwind+0x25
1c 00000002`bb5ff650 00007ff7`6ce17d3e     heap_corruption2!std::thread::impl$0::spawn_unchecked_::closure$1<heap_corruption2::main::closure_env$0,tuple$<>
>+0x135
1d 00000002`bb5ff7b0 00007ff7`6ce255cd
heap_corruption2!core::ops::function::FnOnce::call_once<std::thread::impl$0::spawn_unchecked_::closure_env$1<heap_corruption2::main::closure_env$0,tuple$<>
>,tuple$<> >+0xe
1e (Inline Function) --------`--------     heap_corruption2!alloc::boxed::impl$48::call_once+0xb
1f (Inline Function) --------`--------     heap_corruption2!alloc::boxed::impl$48::call_once+0x16
20 00000002`bb5ff7f0 00007ff9`b18353e0     heap_corruption2!std::sys::pal::windows::thread::impl$0::new::thread_start+0x3d
21 00000002`bb5ff850 00007ff9`b2a4485b     kernel32!BaseThreadInitThunk+0x10
22 00000002`bb5ff880 00000000`00000000     ntdll!RtlUserThreadStart+0x2b

   4  Id: f28.2194 Suspend: 0 Teb: 00000002`bae89000 Unfrozen
 # Child-SP          RetAddr               Call Site
00 00000002`bb7ff158 00007ff9`b2a5d89d     ntdll!NtWaitForAlertByThreadId+0x14
01 00000002`bb7ff160 00007ff9`b2a9b3fe     ntdll!RtlpWaitOnAddressWithTimeout+0x81
02 00000002`bb7ff190 00007ff9`b2a9b343     ntdll!RtlpWaitOnAddress+0xae
03 00000002`bb7ff200 00007ff9`affbdd9f     ntdll!RtlWaitOnAddress+0x13
04 00000002`bb7ff240 00007ff7`6ce1dc01     KERNELBASE!WaitOnAddress+0x2f
05 (Inline Function) --------`--------     heap_corruption2!std::sys::sync::thread_parking::futex::Parker::park+0x65
06 (Inline Function) --------`--------     heap_corruption2!std::thread::Thread::park+0x65
07 00000002`bb7ff280 00007ff7`6ce1163b     heap_corruption2!std::thread::park+0x151
08 00000002`bb7ff2f0 00007ff7`6ce1795d     heap_corruption2!heap_corruption2::main::closure$0+0x3b
09 (Inline Function) --------`--------     heap_corruption2!core::hint::black_box+0x9
0a 00000002`bb7ff460 00007ff7`6ce1774d     heap_corruption2!std::sys::backtrace::__rust_begin_short_backtrace<heap_corruption2::main::closure_env$0,tuple$<>
>+0xd
0b 00000002`bb7ff490 00007ff7`6ce1121d
heap_corruption2!std::thread::impl$0::spawn_unchecked_::closure$1::closure$0<heap_corruption2::main::closure_env$0,tuple$<> >+0xd
0c 00000002`bb7ff4c0 00007ff7`6ce12f63
heap_corruption2!core::panic::unwind_safe::impl$25::call_once<tuple$<>,std::thread::impl$0::spawn_unchecked_::closure$1::closure_env$0<heap_corruption2::main:
:closure_env$0,tuple$<> > >+0xd
0d 00000002`bb7ff4f0 00007ff7`6ce17813
heap_corruption2!std::panicking::try::do_call<core::panic::unwind_safe::AssertUnwindSafe<std::thread::impl$0::spawn_unchecked_::closure$1::closure_env$0<heap_
corruption2::main::closure_env$0,tuple$<> > >,tuple$<> >+0x23
0e 00000002`bb7ff550 00007ff7`6ce172a5     heap_corruption2!std::thread::impl$7::drop::closure$0<tuple$<> >+0xb3
0f (Inline Function) --------`--------     heap_corruption2!std::panicking::try+0x25
10 (Inline Function) --------`--------     heap_corruption2!std::panic::catch_unwind+0x25
11 00000002`bb7ff5a0 00007ff7`6ce17d3e     heap_corruption2!std::thread::impl$0::spawn_unchecked_::closure$1<heap_corruption2::main::closure_env$0,tuple$<>
>+0x135
12 00000002`bb7ff700 00007ff7`6ce255cd
heap_corruption2!core::ops::function::FnOnce::call_once<std::thread::impl$0::spawn_unchecked_::closure_env$1<heap_corruption2::main::closure_env$0,tuple$<>
>,tuple$<> >+0xe
13 (Inline Function) --------`--------     heap_corruption2!alloc::boxed::impl$48::call_once+0xb
14 (Inline Function) --------`--------     heap_corruption2!alloc::boxed::impl$48::call_once+0x16
15 00000002`bb7ff740 00007ff9`b18353e0     heap_corruption2!std::sys::pal::windows::thread::impl$0::new::thread_start+0x3d
16 00000002`bb7ff7a0 00007ff9`b2a4485b     kernel32!BaseThreadInitThunk+0x10
17 00000002`bb7ff7d0 00000000`00000000     ntdll!RtlUserThreadStart+0x2b

   5  Id: f28.1108 Suspend: 0 Teb: 00000002`bae8b000 Unfrozen
 # Child-SP          RetAddr               Call Site
00 00000002`bb9ff808 00007ff7`affa10ee     ntdll!NtWaitForSingleObject+0x14
01 00000002`bb9ff810 00007ff7`6ce1da3d     KERNELBASE!WaitForSingleObjectEx+0x8e
02 (Inline Function) --------`--------     heap_corruption2!std::sys::pal::windows::time::WaitableTimer::wait+0xe
03 (Inline Function) --------`--------     heap_corruption2!std::sys::pal::windows::thread::impl$0::sleep::high_precision_sleep+0x7c
04 (Inline Function) --------`--------     heap_corruption2!std::sys::pal::windows::thread::Thread::sleep+0x89
05 00000002`bb9ff8b0 00007ff7`6ce117e5     heap_corruption2!std::thread::sleep+0x9d
06 00000002`bb9ff920 00007ff7`6ce1795d     heap_corruption2!heap_corruption2::main::closure$0+0x1e5
07 (Inline Function) --------`--------     heap_corruption2!core::hint::black_box+0x9
08 00000002`bb9ffa90 00007ff7`6ce1774d     heap_corruption2!std::sys::backtrace::__rust_begin_short_backtrace<heap_corruption2::main::closure_env$0,tuple$<>
>+0xd
09 00000002`bb9ffac0 00007ff7`6ce1121d
heap_corruption2!std::thread::impl$0::spawn_unchecked_::closure$1::closure$0<heap_corruption2::main::closure_env$0,tuple$<> >+0xd
0a 00000002`bb9ffaf0 00007ff7`6ce12f63
heap_corruption2!core::panic::unwind_safe::impl$25::call_once<tuple$<>,std::thread::impl$0::spawn_unchecked_::closure$1::closure_env$0<heap_corruption2::main:
:closure_env$0,tuple$<> > >+0xd
0b 00000002`bb9ffb20 00007ff7`6ce17813
heap_corruption2!std::panicking::try::do_call<core::panic::unwind_safe::AssertUnwindSafe<std::thread::impl$0::spawn_unchecked_::closure$1::closure_env$0<heap_
corruption2::main::closure_env$0,tuple$<> > >,tuple$<> >+0x23
0c 00000002`bb9ffb80 00007ff7`6ce172a5     heap_corruption2!std::thread::impl$7::drop::closure$0<tuple$<> >+0xb3
0d (Inline Function) --------`--------     heap_corruption2!std::panicking::try+0x25
0e (Inline Function) --------`--------     heap_corruption2!std::panic::catch_unwind+0x25
0f 00000002`bb9ffbd0 00007ff7`6ce17d3e     heap_corruption2!std::thread::impl$0::spawn_unchecked_::closure$1<heap_corruption2::main::closure_env$0,tuple$<>
>+0x135
10 00000002`bb9ffd30 00007ff7`6ce255cd
heap_corruption2!core::ops::function::FnOnce::call_once<std::thread::impl$0::spawn_unchecked_::closure_env$1<heap_corruption2::main::closure_env$0,tuple$<>
>,tuple$<> >+0xe
11 (Inline Function) --------`--------     heap_corruption2!alloc::boxed::impl$48::call_once+0xb
12 (Inline Function) --------`--------     heap_corruption2!alloc::boxed::impl$48::call_once+0x16
13 00000002`bb9ffd70 00007ff9`b18353e0     heap_corruption2!std::sys::pal::windows::thread::impl$0::new::thread_start+0x3d
14 00000002`bb9ffdd0 00007ff9`b2a4485b     kernel32!BaseThreadInitThunk+0x10
15 00000002`bb9ffe00 00000000`00000000     ntdll!RtlUserThreadStart+0x2b

   6  Id: f28.1dac Suspend: 0 Teb: 00000002`bae8d000 Unfrozen
 # Child-SP          RetAddr               Call Site
00 00000002`bbbff148 00007ff9`b2a5d89d     ntdll!NtWaitForAlertByThreadId+0x14
01 00000002`bbbff150 00007ff9`b2a9b3fe     ntdll!RtlpWaitOnAddressWithTimeout+0x81
```

```
02 00000002`bbbff180 00007ff9`b2a9b343     ntdll!RtlpWaitOnAddress+0xae
03 00000002`bbbff1f0 00007ff9`affbdd9f     ntdll!RtlWaitOnAddress+0x13
04 00000002`bbbff230 00007ff7`6ce1dc01     KERNELBASE!WaitOnAddress+0x2f
05 (Inline Function) --------`--------     heap_corruption2!std::sys::sync::thread_parking::futex::Parker::park+0x65
06 (Inline Function) --------`--------     heap_corruption2!std::thread::Thread::park+0x65
07 00000002`bbbff270 00007ff7`6ce1163b     heap_corruption2!std::thread::park+0x151
08 00000002`bbbff2e0 00007ff7`6ce1795d     heap_corruption2!heap_corruption2::main::closure$0+0x3b
09 (Inline Function) --------`--------     heap_corruption2!core::hint::black_box+0x9
0a 00000002`bbbff450 00007ff7`6ce1774d     heap_corruption2!std::sys::backtrace::__rust_begin_short_backtrace<heap_corruption2::main::closure_env$0,tuple$<>
>+0xd
0b 00000002`bbbff480 00007ff7`6ce1121d
heap_corruption2!std::thread::impl$0::spawn_unchecked_::closure$1::closure$0<heap_corruption2::main::closure_env$0,tuple$<> >+0xd
0c 00000002`bbbff4b0 00007ff7`6ce12f63
heap_corruption2!core::panic::unwind_safe::impl$25::call_once<tuple$<>,std::thread::impl$0::spawn_unchecked_::closure$1::closure_env$0<heap_corruption2::main:
:closure_env$0,tuple$<> > >+0xd
0d 00000002`bbbff4e0 00007ff7`6ce17813
heap_corruption2!std::panicking::try::do_call<core::panic::unwind_safe::AssertUnwindSafe<std::thread::impl$0::spawn_unchecked_::closure$1::closure_env$0<heap_
corruption2::main::closure_env$0,tuple$<> >,tuple$<> >+0x23
0e 00000002`bbbff540 00007ff7`6ce172a5     heap_corruption2!std::thread::impl$7::drop::closure$0<tuple$<> >+0xb3
0f (Inline Function) --------`--------     heap_corruption2!std::panicking::try+0x25
10 (Inline Function) --------`--------     heap_corruption2!std::panic::catch_unwind+0x25
11 00000002`bbbff590 00007ff7`6ce17d3e     heap_corruption2!std::thread::impl$0::spawn_unchecked_::closure$1<heap_corruption2::main::closure_env$0,tuple$<>
>+0x135
12 00000002`bbbff6f0 00007ff7`6ce255cd
heap_corruption2!core::ops::function::FnOnce::call_once<std::thread::impl$0::spawn_unchecked_::closure_env$1<heap_corruption2::main::closure_env$0,tuple$<>
>,tuple$<> >+0xe
13 (Inline Function) --------`--------     heap_corruption2!alloc::boxed::impl$48::call_once+0xb
14 (Inline Function) --------`--------     heap_corruption2!alloc::boxed::impl$48::call_once+0x16
15 00000002`bbbff730 00007ff9`b18353e0     heap_corruption2!std::sys::pal::windows::thread::impl$0::new::thread_start+0x3d
16 00000002`bbbff790 00007ff9`b2a4485b     kernel32!BaseThreadInitThunk+0x10
17 00000002`bbbff7c0 00000000`00000000     ntdll!RtlUserThreadStart+0x2b
```

Note: We don't see any other threads having exception or heap processing functions on their call stacks.

7.　　　　In the **!heap** checking command output, we see a follow-up recommendation to **enable pageheap**. This means running the application under conditions when a special version of process heap management runtime is used instead of the default version. It's done using the *gflags* GUI tool from Debugging Tools for Windows (although a command-line version can also be used or even direct registry manipulation). We need to launch the appropriate version of *gflags.exe* based on your process bitness; for example, we use the following Start menu option: Windows Kits \ Global Flags (X64) to launch *gflags.exe* and choose the *Enable page heap* option there in the *Image File* tab for *heap-corruption2.exe*:

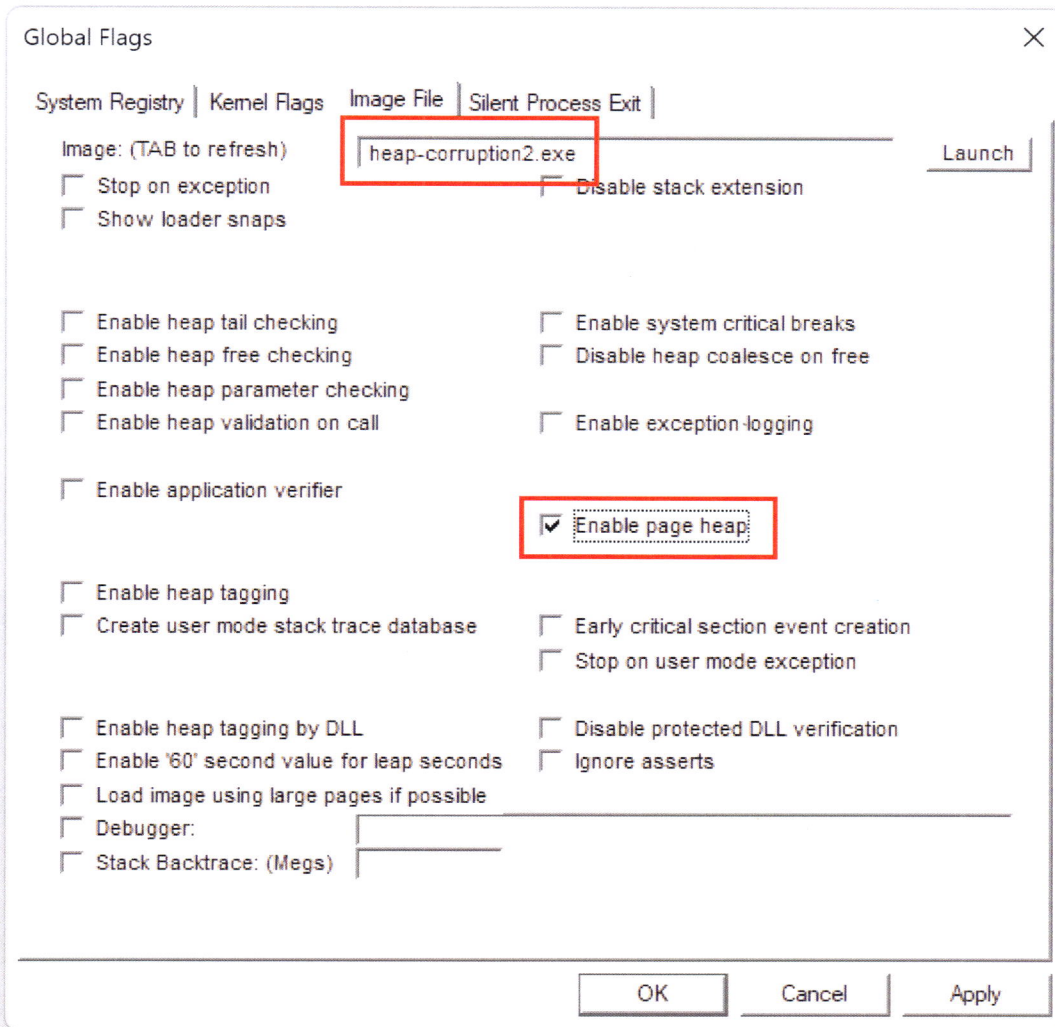

If page heap is enabled, heap entries are created at the end of pages with the next page after the allocated buffer is made inaccessible (reserved), as shown in the picture below:

Subsequent buffer overwrite triggers invalid memory exception, and we can see the exact point of corruption during heap allocation or free instead of heap diagnostics done later. Please also see Debugging.TV episode 0x26 for information about underwrites.

8.   Page heap recommendation was implemented, and the new run of the *heap-corruption2.exe* application resulted in the collection of *heap-corruption2.exe.2884.dmp*. We load this dump in WinDbg:

```
Microsoft (R) Windows Debugger Version 10.0.27725.1000 AMD64
Copyright (c) Microsoft Corporation. All rights reserved.


Loading Dump File [C:\ARWMDA-Dumps\Process\heap-corruption2.exe.2884.dmp]
User Mini Dump File with Full Memory: Only application data is available


************* Path validation summary **************
Response                        Time (ms)      Location
Deferred                                       srv*
Symbol search path is: srv*
Executable search path is:
Windows 10 Version 22000 UP Free x64
Product: WinNt, suite: SingleUserTS
Edition build lab: 22000.1.amd64fre.co_release.210604-1628
Debug session time: Wed Oct 30 09:00:37.000 2024 (UTC + 0:00)
System Uptime: 0 days 0:16:29.396
Process Uptime: 0 days 0:00:04.000
.......
This dump file has an exception of interest stored in it.
The stored exception information can be accessed via .ecxr
(b44.12a8): Access violation - code c0000005 (first/second chance not available)
For analysis of this file, run !analyze -v
ntdll!NtWaitForMultipleObjects+0x14:
00007ff9`b2ae4bd4 ret
```

Note: We see a different exception in this dump: access violation, c0000005.

9.   We provide application symbols and source code path to WinDbg before our next analysis steps:

```
0:005> .logappend C:\ARWMDA-Dumps\RW6.log
Opened log file 'C:\ARWMDA-Dumps\RW6.log'


0:005> .sympath+ C:\ARWMDA-Dumps\Symbols\debug
Symbol search path is: srv*;C:\ARWMDA-Dumps\Symbols\debug
Expanded Symbol search path is:
cache*;SRV*https://msdl.microsoft.com/download/symbols;c:\arwmda-dumps\symbols\debug


************* Path validation summary **************
Response                        Time (ms)      Location
Deferred                                       srv*
OK                                             C:\ARWMDA-Dumps\Symbols\debug

0:005> .srcpath+ C:\ARWMDA-Dumps\Source\heap-corruption2
Source search path is: SRV*;C:\ARWMDA-Dumps\Source\heap-corruption2


************* Path validation summary **************
Response                        Time (ms)      Location
Deferred                                       SRV*
OK                                             C:\ARWMDA-Dumps\Source\heap-corruption2


0:005> .reload
........
```

10. We get the following stack trace, which shows exception processing possibly originating in the function from the *heap_corruption2* module:

```
0:005> kL
 # Child-SP          RetAddr           Call Site
00 000000d2`4ddfe058 00007ff9`affadcd0 ntdll!NtWaitForMultipleObjects+0x14
01 000000d2`4ddfe060 00007ff9`affadbce KERNELBASE!WaitForMultipleObjectsEx+0xf0
02 000000d2`4ddfe350 00007ff9`b188f087 KERNELBASE!WaitForMultipleObjects+0xe
03 000000d2`4ddfe390 00007ff9`b188eac6 kernel32!WerpReportFaultInternal+0x587
04 000000d2`4ddfe4b0 00007ff9`b009e503 kernel32!WerpReportFault+0xbe
05 000000d2`4ddfe4f0 00007ff9`b2aeb0ec KERNELBASE!UnhandledExceptionFilter+0x3e3
06 000000d2`4ddfe610 00007ff9`b2ad40f6 ntdll!RtlUserThreadStart$filt$0+0xac
07 000000d2`4ddfe650 00007ff9`b2ae906f ntdll!_C_specific_handler+0x96
08 000000d2`4ddfe6c0 00007ff9`b2a75bea ntdll!RtlpExecuteHandlerForException+0xf
09 000000d2`4ddfe6f0 00007ff9`b2ae805e ntdll!RtlDispatchException+0x25a
0a 000000d2`4ddfee40 00007ff9`a04a15d8 ntdll!KiUserExceptionDispatch+0x2e
0b 000000d2`4ddff578 00007ff7`6ce117aa VCRUNTIME140!memcpy+0x2e8
0c 000000d2`4ddff580 00007ff7`6ce1795d heap_corruption2!heap_corruption2::main::closure$0+0x1aa
0d (Inline Function) --------`-------- heap_corruption2!core::hint::black_box+0x9
0e 000000d2`4ddff6f0 00007ff7`6ce1774d heap_corruption2!std::sys::backtrace::__rust_begin_short_backtrace<heap_corruption2::main::closure_env$0,tuple$<>
>+0xd
0f 000000d2`4ddff720 00007ff7`6ce1121d
heap_corruption2!std::thread::impl$0::spawn_unchecked_::closure$1::closure$0<heap_corruption2::main::closure_env$0,tuple$<> >+0xd
10 000000d2`4ddff750 00007ff7`6ce12f63
heap_corruption2!core::panic::unwind_safe::impl$25::call_once<tuple$<>,std::thread::impl$0::spawn_unchecked_::closure$1::closure_env$0<heap_corruption2::main:
:closure_env$0,tuple$<> >>+0xd
11 000000d2`4ddff780 00007ff7`6ce17813
heap_corruption2!std::panicking::try::do_call<core::panic::unwind_safe::AssertUnwindSafe<std::thread::impl$0::spawn_unchecked_::closure$1::closure_env$0<heap_
corruption2::main::closure_env$0,tuple$<> >,tuple$<> >+0x23
12 000000d2`4ddff7e0 00007ff7`6ce172a5 heap_corruption2!std::thread::impl$7::drop::closure$0<tuple$<> >+0xb3
13 (Inline Function) --------`-------- heap_corruption2!std::panicking::try+0x25
14 (Inline Function) --------`-------- heap_corruption2!std::panic::catch_unwind+0x25
15 000000d2`4ddff830 00007ff7`6ce17d3e heap_corruption2!std::thread::impl$0::spawn_unchecked_::closure$1<heap_corruption2::main::closure_env$0,tuple$<>
>+0x135
16 000000d2`4ddff990 00007ff7`6ce255cd
heap_corruption2!core::ops::function::FnOnce::call_once<std::thread::impl$0::spawn_unchecked_::closure_env$1<heap_corruption2::main::closure_env$0,tuple$<>
>,tuple$<> >+0xe
17 (Inline Function) --------`-------- heap_corruption2!alloc::boxed::impl$48::call_once+0xb
18 (Inline Function) --------`-------- heap_corruption2!alloc::boxed::impl$48::call_once+0x16
19 000000d2`4ddff9d0 00007ff9`b18353e0 heap_corruption2!std::sys::pal::windows::thread::impl$0::new::thread_start+0x3d
1a 000000d2`4ddffa30 00007ff9`b2a4485b kernel32!BaseThreadInitThunk+0x10
1b 000000d2`4ddffa60 00000000`00000000 ntdll!RtlUserThreadStart+0x2b
```

11. Let's now check the output of the **!analyze -v** command:

```
0:005> !analyze -v
*******************************************************************************
*                                                                             *
*                        Exception Analysis                                   *
*                                                                             *
*******************************************************************************

*** WARNING: Check Image - Checksum mismatch - Dump: 0x24497, File: 0x2c388 - C:\ProgramData\Dbg\sym\VCRUNTIME140.dll\006CB7961b000\VCRUNTIME140.dll
*** WARNING: Check Image - Checksum mismatch - Dump: 0x24497, File: 0x2c388 - C:\ProgramData\Dbg\sym\VCRUNTIME140.dll\006CB7961b000\VCRUNTIME140.dll

KEY_VALUES_STRING: 1

    Key  : AV.Fault
    Value: Write

    Key  : Analysis.CPU.mSec
    Value: 359

    Key  : Analysis.Elapsed.mSec
    Value: 2163

    Key  : Analysis.IO.Other.Mb
    Value: 0

    Key  : Analysis.IO.Read.Mb
    Value: 1

    Key  : Analysis.IO.Write.Mb
    Value: 0

    Key  : Analysis.Init.CPU.mSec
    Value: 296

    Key  : Analysis.Init.Elapsed.mSec
    Value: 325680

    Key  : Analysis.Memory.CommitPeak.Mb
    Value: 234

    Key  : Analysis.Version.DbgEng
    Value: 10.0.27725.1000

    Key  : Analysis.Version.Description
    Value: 10.2408.27.01 amd64fre
```

```
Key  : Analysis.Version.Ext
Value: 1.2408.27.1

Key  : Failure.Bucket
Value: INVALID_POINTER_WRITE_AVRF_c0000005_VCRUNTIME140.dll!memcpy

Key  : Failure.Hash
Value: {4c43fa1c-4438-2fe9-d848-35507a2a9f49}

Key  : Timeline.OS.Boot.DeltaSec
Value: 989

Key  : Timeline.Process.Start.DeltaSec
Value: 4

Key  : WER.OS.Branch
Value: co_release

Key  : WER.OS.Version
Value: 10.0.22000.1


FILE_IN_CAB:  heap-corruption2.exe.2884.dmp

NTGLOBALFLAG:  2000000

APPLICATION_VERIFIER_FLAGS:  0

APPLICATION_VERIFIER_LOADED: 1

CONTEXT:  (.ecxr)
rax=000002045d366fe0 rbx=0000000000000000 rcx=000002045d366fe0
rdx=00007ff76ce3681c rsi=000002045d30aff0 rdi=0000000000000000
rip=00007ff9a04a15d8 rsp=000000d24ddff578 rbp=000000d24ddff600
 r8=000000000000004e  r9=0000000000000060 r10=00007ff9a04a0000
r11=00007ff9a04a15c3 r12=0000000000000000 r13=0000000000000000
r14=0000000000000000 r15=0000000000000000
iopl=0         nv up ei pl nz na po nc
cs=0033  ss=002b  ds=002b  es=002b  fs=0053  gs=002b             efl=00010206
VCRUNTIME140!memcpy+0x2e8:
00007ff9`a04a15d8 vmovdqu ymmword ptr [rcx+r9-40h],ymm1 ds:00000204`5d367000=??
Resetting default scope

EXCEPTION_RECORD:  (.exr -1)
ExceptionAddress: 00007ff9a04a15d8 (VCRUNTIME140!memcpy+0x00000000000002e8)
   ExceptionCode: c0000005 (Access violation)
  ExceptionFlags: 00000000
NumberParameters: 2
   Parameter[0]: 0000000000000001
   Parameter[1]: 000002045d367000
Attempt to write to address 000002045d367000

PROCESS_NAME:  heap-corruption2.exe

WRITE_ADDRESS:  000002045d367000

ERROR_CODE: (NTSTATUS) 0xc0000005 - The instruction at 0x%p referenced memory at 0x%p. The memory could not be %s.

EXCEPTION_CODE_STR:  c0000005

EXCEPTION_PARAMETER1:  0000000000000001

EXCEPTION_PARAMETER2:  000002045d367000

STACK_TEXT:
000000d2`4ddff578 00007ff7`6ce117aa     : 000000d2`4ddff5d0 00000000`00000000 000000d2`4ddff5d0 00000000`00000000 : VCRUNTIME140!memcpy+0x2e8
000000d2`4ddff580 00007ff7`6ce1795d     : 00000000`00000000 00000000`00000000 00000000`00000000 00000000`00000000 :
heap_corruption2!heap_corruption2::main::closure$0+0x1aa
000000d2`4ddff6f0 00007ff7`6ce1774d     : 00000000`00000000 00000000`00000000 00000000`00000000 00000000`00000000 :
heap_corruption2!std::sys::backtrace::__rust_begin_short_backtrace<heap_corruption2::main::closure_env$0,tuple$<> >+0xd
000000d2`4ddff720 00007ff7`6ce1121d     : 00000000`00000000 00000204`5d304fc0 00000000`00000000 00007ff7`6ce1d864 :
heap_corruption2!std::thread::impl$0::spawn_unchecked_::closure$1::closure$0<heap_corruption2::main::closure_env$0,tuple$<> >+0xd
000000d2`4ddff750 00007ff7`6ce12f63     : 00000000`00000000 00000000`00000000 00000000`00000000 00000204`5d304fc0 :
heap_corruption2!core::panic::unwind_safe::impl$25::call_once<tuple$<>,std::thread::impl$0::spawn_unchecked_::closure$1::closure_env$0<heap_corruption2::main:
:closure_env$0,tuple$<> > >+0xd
000000d2`4ddff780 00007ff7`6ce17813     : 00000204`5d304fc0 00000204`5d304fc0 000000d2`4ddff7f8 00000000`00000005 :
heap_corruption2!std::panicking::try::do_call<core::panic::unwind_safe::AssertUnwindSafe<std::thread::impl$0::spawn_unchecked_::closure$1::closure_env$0<heap_
corruption2::main::closure_env$0,tuple$<> > >,tuple$<> >+0x23
000000d2`4ddff7e0 00007ff7`6ce172a5     : 00000000`00000000 00000000`00000000 00000000`00000000 00000000`00000000 :
heap_corruption2!std::thread::impl$7::drop::closure$0<tuple$<> >+0xb3
000000d2`4ddff830 00007ff7`6ce17d3e     : 00000000`00001000 00000000`00000104 00000000`00006000 000000d2`4ddf8000 :
heap_corruption2!std::thread::impl$0::spawn_unchecked_::closure$1<heap_corruption2::main::closure_env$0,tuple$<> >+0x135
000000d2`4ddff990 00007ff7`6ce255cd     : 00000000`00000000 00000204`5d30aff0 00000000`00000000 00000000`00000000 :
heap_corruption2!core::ops::function::FnOnce::call_once<std::thread::impl$0::spawn_unchecked_::closure_env$1<heap_corruption2::main::closure_env$0,tuple$<>
>,tuple$<> >+0xe
000000d2`4ddff9d0 00007ff9`b18353e0     : 00000000`00000000 00000000`00000000 00000000`00000000 00000000`00000000 :
heap_corruption2!std::sys::pal::windows::thread::impl$0::new::thread_start+0x3d
000000d2`4ddffa30 00007ff9`b2a4485b     : 00000000`00000000 00000000`00000000 00000000`00000000 00000000`00000000 : kernel32!BaseThreadInitThunk+0x10
000000d2`4ddffa60 00000000`00000000     : 00000000`00000000 00000000`00000000 00000000`00000000 00000000`00000000 : ntdll!RtlUserThreadStart+0x2b


STACK_COMMAND:  ~5s; .ecxr ; kb

FAULTING_SOURCE_LINE:  d:\a01\_work\43\s\src\vctools\crt\vcruntime\src\string\amd64\memcpy.asm

FAULTING_SOURCE_FILE:  d:\a01\_work\43\s\src\vctools\crt\vcruntime\src\string\amd64\memcpy.asm

FAULTING_SOURCE_LINE_NUMBER:  403
```

```
FAULTING_SOURCE_CODE:
No source found for 'd:\a01\_work\43\s\src\vctools\crt\vcruntime\src\string\amd64\memcpy.asm'

SYMBOL_NAME:  VCRUNTIME140!memcpy+2e8

MODULE_NAME: VCRUNTIME140

IMAGE_NAME:  VCRUNTIME140.dll

FAILURE_BUCKET_ID:  INVALID_POINTER_WRITE_AVRF_c0000005_VCRUNTIME140.dll!memcpy

OS_VERSION:  10.0.22000.1

BUILDLAB_STR:  co_release

OSPLATFORM_TYPE:  x64

OSNAME:  Windows 10

IMAGE_VERSION:  14.31.31103.0

FAILURE_ID_HASH:  {4c43fa1c-4438-2fe9-d848-35507a2a9f49}

Followup:    MachineOwner
---------
```

Note: In addition to exception information that shows an invalid write operation to the 000002045d367000 address.

12.   To see the source code location, we can set the frame:

```
0:005> .frame c
0c 000000d2`4ddff580 00007ff7`6ce1795d     heap_corruption2!heap_corruption2::main::closure$0+0x1aa [C:\ARWMDA-Dumps\heap-corruption2\heap-
corruption2\src\main.rs @ 39]
```

```
main.rs  X                                              ⬍
    17      for n in 1..=5 {                              ▲
    18          let handle = thread::spawn(move || {
    19
    20              match n {
    21
    22                  2 => loop {
    23                      let mut p = vec![0u16; 10].into_boxed_
    24
    25                      unsafe {
    26                          ptr::copy_nonoverlapping(STR.as_p
    27                      }
    28
    29                      thread::sleep(Duration::from_millis(1
    30                  }
    31
    32                  4 => loop {
    33                      let mut p = vec![0u16; 10].into_boxed_
    34
    35                      unsafe {
    36                          ptr::copy_nonoverlapping(STR.as_p
    37                      }
    38
 ⇨  39                      thread::sleep(Duration::from_millis(2
    40                  }
    41
    42                  _ => { thread::park(); }
    43              }
    44
    45          });
    46          handles.push(handle);
    47      }
    48
    49      mod_ab::func();
    50
    51      for handle in handles {
    52          handle.join().unwrap();
    53      }
    54 }
    55                                                       ▼
◄                                                    ►
```

13. We can manually double-check this analysis by setting the frame and non-volatile registers (using the **/c** option to make it current for the stack trace and **/r** to show possible register values):

```
0:005> kc
 # Call Site
00 ntdll!NtWaitForMultipleObjects
01 KERNELBASE!WaitForMultipleObjectsEx
02 KERNELBASE!WaitForMultipleObjects
03 kernel32!WerpReportFaultInternal
04 kernel32!WerpReportFault
05 KERNELBASE!UnhandledExceptionFilter
06 ntdll!RtlUserThreadStart$filt$0
07 ntdll!_C_specific_handler
08 ntdll!RtlpExecuteHandlerForException
09 ntdll!RtlDispatchException
0a ntdll!KiUserExceptionDispatch
0b VCRUNTIME140!memcpy
0c heap_corruption2!heap_corruption2::main::closure$0
0d heap_corruption2!core::hint::black_box
0e heap_corruption2!std::sys::backtrace::__rust_begin_short_backtrace<heap_corruption2::main::closure_env$0,tuple$<> >
0f
heap_corruption2!std::thread::impl$0::spawn_unchecked_::closure$1::closure$0<heap_corruption2::main::closure_env$0,tup
le$<> >
10
heap_corruption2!core::panic::unwind_safe::impl$25::call_once<tuple$<>,std::thread::impl$0::spawn_unchecked_::closure$
1::closure_env$0<heap_corruption2::main::closure_env$0,tuple$<> > >
11
heap_corruption2!std::panicking::try::do_call<core::panic::unwind_safe::AssertUnwindSafe<std::thread::impl$0::spawn_un
checked_::closure$1::closure_env$0<heap_corruption2::main::closure_env$0,tuple$<> > >,tuple$<> >
12 heap_corruption2!std::thread::impl$7::drop::closure$0<tuple$<> >
13 heap_corruption2!std::panicking::try
14 heap_corruption2!std::panic::catch_unwind
15 heap_corruption2!std::thread::impl$0::spawn_unchecked_::closure$1<heap_corruption2::main::closure_env$0,tuple$<> >
16
heap_corruption2!core::ops::function::FnOnce::call_once<std::thread::impl$0::spawn_unchecked_::closure_env$1<heap_corr
uption2::main::closure_env$0,tuple$<> >,tuple$<> >
17 heap_corruption2!alloc::boxed::impl$48::call_once
18 heap_corruption2!alloc::boxed::impl$48::call_once
19 heap_corruption2!std::sys::pal::windows::thread::impl$0::new::thread_start
1a kernel32!BaseThreadInitThunk
1b ntdll!RtlUserThreadStart
```

```
0:005> .frame /r /c b
0b 000000d2`4ddff578 00007ff7`6ce117aa     VCRUNTIME140!memcpy+0x2e8
[d:\a01\_work\43\s\src\vctools\crt\vcruntime\src\string\amd64\memcpy.asm @ 403]
rax=0000000000000002 rbx=0000000000000000 rcx=0000000000000002
rdx=0000000000000002 rsi=000002045d30aff0 rdi=0000000000000000
rip=00007ff9a04a15d8 rsp=000000d24ddff578 rbp=000000d24ddff600
 r8=000000d24ddff39f  r9=0000000000000002 r10=0000000000000014
r11=00007ff76ce1af01 r12=0000000000000000 r13=0000000000000000
r14=0000000000000000 r15=0000000000000000
iopl=0         nv up ei pl zr na po nc
cs=0033  ss=002b  ds=002b  es=002b  fs=0053  gs=002b             efl=00000246
VCRUNTIME140!memcpy+0x2e8:
00007ff9`a04a15d8 vmovdqu ymmword ptr [rcx+r9-40h],ymm1 ds:ffffffff`fffffc4=??
```

```
0:005> kL
  *** Stack trace for last set context - .thread/.cxr resets it
 # Child-SP          RetAddr          Call Site
0b 000000d2`4ddff578 00007ff7`6ce117aa   VCRUNTIME140!memcpy+0x2e8
0c 000000d2`4ddff580 00007ff7`6ce1795d   heap_corruption2!heap_corruption2::main::closure$0+0x1aa
0d (Inline Function) --------`--------   heap_corruption2!core::hint::black_box+0x9
0e 000000d2`4ddff6f0 00007ff7`6ce1774d
heap_corruption2!std::sys::backtrace::__rust_begin_short_backtrace<heap_corruption2::main::closure_env$0,tuple$<>
>+0xd
0f 000000d2`4ddff720 00007ff7`6ce1121d
heap_corruption2!std::thread::impl$0::spawn_unchecked_::closure$1::closure$0<heap_corruption2::main::closure_env$0,tup
le$<> >+0xd
```

116

```
10 000000d2`4ddff750 00007ff7`6ce12f63
heap_corruption2!core::panic::unwind_safe::impl$25::call_once<tuple$<>,std::thread::impl$0::spawn_unchecked_::closure$
1::closure_env$0<heap_corruption2::main::closure_env$0,tuple$<> > >+0xd
11 000000d2`4ddff780 00007ff7`6ce17813
heap_corruption2!std::panicking::try::do_call<core::panic::unwind_safe::AssertUnwindSafe<std::thread::impl$0::spawn_un
checked_::closure$1::closure_env$0<heap_corruption2::main::closure_env$0,tuple$<> > >,tuple$<> >+0x23
12 000000d2`4ddff7e0 00007ff7`6ce172a5      heap_corruption2!std::thread::impl$7::drop::closure$0<tuple$<> >+0xb3
13 (Inline Function) --------`--------      heap_corruption2!std::panicking::try+0x25
14 (Inline Function) --------`--------      heap_corruption2!std::panic::catch_unwind+0x25
15 000000d2`4ddff830 00007ff7`6ce17d3e
heap_corruption2!std::thread::impl$0::spawn_unchecked_::closure$1<heap_corruption2::main::closure_env$0,tuple$<>
>+0x135
16 000000d2`4ddff990 00007ff7`6ce255cd
heap_corruption2!core::ops::function::FnOnce::call_once<std::thread::impl$0::spawn_unchecked_::closure_env$1<heap_corr
uption2::main::closure_env$0,tuple$<> >,tuple$<> >+0xe
17 (Inline Function) --------`--------      heap_corruption2!alloc::boxed::impl$48::call_once+0xb
18 (Inline Function) --------`--------      heap_corruption2!alloc::boxed::impl$48::call_once+0x16
19 000000d2`4ddff9d0 00007ff9`b18353e0
heap_corruption2!std::sys::pal::windows::thread::impl$0::new::thread_start+0x3d
1a 000000d2`4ddffa30 00007ff9`b2a4485b      kernel32!BaseThreadInitThunk+0x10
1b 000000d2`4ddffa60 00000000`00000000      ntdll!RtlUserThreadStart+0x2b
```

Note: What we see is that the calculated memory write address is ffffffff`fffffffc4, not from the stored exception record (this is because of volatile RCX and R9 that are overwritten in subsequent code and calls):

```
0:005> .ecxr
rax=000002045d366fe0 rbx=0000000000000000 rcx=000002045d366fe0
rdx=00007ff76ce3681c rsi=000002045d30aff0 rdi=0000000000000000
rip=00007ff9a04a15d8 rsp=000000d24ddff578 rbp=000000d24ddff600
 r8=000000000000004e  r9=0000000000000060 r10=00007ff9a04a0000
r11=00007ff9a04a15c3 r12=0000000000000000 r13=0000000000000000
r14=0000000000000000 r15=0000000000000000
iopl=0         nv up ei pl nz na po nc
cs=0033  ss=002b  ds=002b  es=002b  fs=0053  gs=002b             efl=00010206
VCRUNTIME140!memcpy+0x2e8:
00007ff9`a04a15d8 vmovdqu ymmword ptr [rcx+r9-40h],ymm1 ds:00000204`5d367000=??
```

14. Let's check the region of memory the invalid write pointer 00000204`5d367000 belongs to:

```
0:005> !address 00000204`5d367000


Mapping file section regions...
Mapping module regions...
Mapping PEB regions...
Mapping TEB and stack regions...
Mapping heap regions...
Mapping page heap regions...
Mapping other regions...
Mapping stack trace database regions...
Mapping activation context regions...

Usage:                  <unknown>
Base Address:           00000204`5d367000
End Address:            00000204`5d368000
Region Size:            00000000`00001000 (   4.000 kB)
State:                  00002000           MEM_RESERVE
Protect:                <info not present at the target>
Type:                   00020000           MEM_PRIVATE
Allocation Base:        00000204`5cff0000
Allocation Protect:     00000001           PAGE_NOACCESS
```

Content source: 0 (invalid), length: 1000

Note: We see that it belongs to a single reserved page that doesn't have physical memory committed to it. Since it is also the start of that page, let's look at the previous byte's region properties:

```
0:005> !address 00000204`5d367000-1

Usage:                  <unknown>
Base Address:           00000204`5d366000
End Address:            00000204`5d367000
Region Size:            00000000`00001000 (    4.000 kB)
State:                  00001000          MEM_COMMIT
Protect:                00000004          PAGE_READWRITE
Type:                   00020000          MEM_PRIVATE
Allocation Base:        00000204`5cff0000
Allocation Protect:     00000001          PAGE_NOACCESS


Content source: 1 (target), length: 1
```

Note: We see that this is also a single page, but it is committed. Let's dump memory contents around the page boundary where we have an invalid write operation:

```
0:005> dc 00000204`5d367000-50
00000204`5d366fb0  00000014 00000000 00001000 00000000  ................
00000204`5d366fc0  00000000 00000000 00000000 00000000  ................
00000204`5d366fd0  5b81af70 00000204 00000000 dcbabbbb  p..[............
00000204`5d366fe0  00650048 006c006c 0020006f 00720043  H.e.l.l.o. .C.r.
00000204`5d366ff0  00730061 00210068 00480020 006c0065  a.s.h.!. .H.e.l.
00000204`5d367000  ???????? ???????? ???????? ????????  ????????????????
00000204`5d367010  ???????? ???????? ???????? ????????  ????????????????
00000204`5d367020  ???????? ???????? ???????? ????????  ????????????????
```

15.   Instead of the **.ecxr** command, we can set context based on *ntdll!KiUserExceptionDispatch* RSP value:

```
0:005> .cxr
```

```
0:005> kL
# Child-SP          RetAddr           Call Site
00 000000d2`4ddfe058 00007ff9`affadcd0 ntdll!NtWaitForMultipleObjects+0x14
01 000000d2`4ddfe060 00007ff9`affadbce KERNELBASE!WaitForMultipleObjectsEx+0xf0
02 000000d2`4ddfe350 00007ff9`b188f087 KERNELBASE!WaitForMultipleObjects+0xe
03 000000d2`4ddfe390 00007ff9`b188eac6 kernel32!WerpReportFaultInternal+0x587
04 000000d2`4ddfe4b0 00007ff9`b009e503 kernel32!WerpReportFault+0xbe
05 000000d2`4ddfe4f0 00007ff9`b2aeb0ec KERNELBASE!UnhandledExceptionFilter+0x3e3
06 000000d2`4ddfe610 00007ff9`b2ad40f6 ntdll!RtlUserThreadStart$filt$0+0xac
07 000000d2`4ddfe650 00007ff9`b2ae906f ntdll!_C_specific_handler+0x96
08 000000d2`4ddfe6c0 00007ff9`b2a75bea ntdll!RtlpExecuteHandlerForException+0xf
09 000000d2`4ddfe6f0 00007ff9`b2ae805e ntdll!RtlDispatchException+0x25a
0a 000000d2`4ddfee40 00007ff9`a04a15d8 ntdll!KiUserExceptionDispatch+0x2e
0b 000000d2`4ddff578 00007ff7`6ce117aa VCRUNTIME140!memcpy+0x2e8
0c 000000d2`4ddff580 00007ff7`6ce1795d heap_corruption2!heap_corruption2::main::closure$0+0x1aa
0d (Inline Function) --------`-------- heap_corruption2!core::hint::black_box+0x9
0e 000000d2`4ddff6f0 00007ff7`6ce1774d heap_corruption2!std::sys::backtrace::__rust_begin_short_backtrace<heap_corruption2::main::closure_env$0,tuple$<> >+0xd
0f 000000d2`4ddff720 00007ff7`6ce1121d heap_corruption2!std::thread::impl$0::spawn_unchecked_::closure$1::closure$0<heap_corruption2::main::closure_env$0,tuple$<> >+0xd
10 000000d2`4ddff750 00007ff7`6ce12f63 heap_corruption2!core::panic::unwind_safe::impl$25::call_once<tuple$<>,std::thread::impl$0::spawn_unchecked_::closure$1::closure_env$0<heap_corruption2::main::closure_env$0,tuple$<> > >+0xd
11 000000d2`4ddff780 00007ff7`6ce17813 heap_corruption2!std::panicking::try::do_call<core::panic::unwind_safe::AssertUnwindSafe<std::thread::impl$0::spawn_unchecked_::closure$1::closure_env$0<heap_corruption2::main::closure_env$0,tuple$<> > >,tuple$<> >+0x23
12 000000d2`4ddff7e0 00007ff7`6ce172a5 heap_corruption2!std::thread::impl$7::drop::closure$0<tuple$<> >+0xb3
13 (Inline Function) --------`-------- heap_corruption2!std::panicking::try+0x25
14 (Inline Function) --------`-------- heap_corruption2!std::panic::catch_unwind+0x25
15 000000d2`4ddff830 00007ff7`6ce17d3e heap_corruption2!std::thread::impl$0::spawn_unchecked_::closure$1<heap_corruption2::main::closure_env$0,tuple$<> >+0x135
```

```
16 000000d2`4ddff990 00007ff7`6ce255cd
heap_corruption2!core::ops::function::FnOnce::call_once<std::thread::impl$0::spawn_unchecked_::closure_env$1<heap_corruption2::main::closure_env$0,tuple$<>
>,tuple$<> >+0xe
17 (Inline Function) --------`--------      heap_corruption2!alloc::boxed::impl$48::call_once+0xb
18 (Inline Function) --------`--------      heap_corruption2!alloc::boxed::impl$48::call_once+0x16
19 000000d2`4ddff9d0 00007ff9`b18353e0     heap_corruption2!std::sys::pal::windows::thread::impl$0::new::thread_start+0x3d
1a 000000d2`4ddffa30 00007ff9`b2a4485b     kernel32!BaseThreadInitThunk+0x10
1b 000000d2`4ddffa60 00000000`00000000     ntdll!RtlUserThreadStart+0x2b
```

`0:005> .cxr 000000d2`4ddfee40`

```
rax=000002045d366fe0 rbx=0000000000000000 rcx=000002045d366fe0
rdx=00007ff76ce3681c rsi=000002045d30aff0 rdi=0000000000000000
rip=00007ff9a04a15d8 rsp=000000d24ddff578 rbp=000000d24ddff600
 r8=000000000000004e  r9=0000000000000060 r10=00007ff9a04a0000
r11=00007ff9a04a15c3 r12=0000000000000000 r13=0000000000000000
r14=0000000000000000 r15=0000000000000000
iopl=0         nv up ei pl nz na po nc
cs=0033  ss=002b  ds=002b  es=002b  fs=0053  gs=002b             efl=00010206
```

`VCRUNTIME140!memcpy+0x2e8:`
`00007ff9`a04a15d8 vmovdqu ymmword ptr [rcx+r9-40h],ymm1 ds:00000204`5d367000=??`

`0:005> .cxr`

16.   Since we identified the buffer overwrite, we now double-check other threads to see if there is something anomalous there as well:

`0:005> ~*kL`

```
   0  Id: b44.ea0 Suspend: 0 Teb: 000000d2`4d273000 Unfrozen "main"
 # Child-SP          RetAddr           Call Site
00 000000d2`4d4ff6a8 00007ff9`affa10ee ntdll!NtWaitForSingleObject+0x14
01 000000d2`4d4ff6b0 00007ff7`6ce25731 KERNELBASE!WaitForSingleObjectEx+0x8e
02 000000d2`4d4ff750 00007ff7`6ce16395 heap_corruption2!std::sys::pal::windows::thread::Thread::join+0x21
03 000000d2`4d4ff7e0 00007ff7`6ce1653f heap_corruption2!std::thread::JoinInner<tuple$<> >::join<tuple$<> >+0x25
04 000000d2`4d4ff8c0 00007ff7`6ce1243f heap_corruption2!std::thread::JoinHandle<tuple$<> >::join<tuple$<> >+0x1f
05 000000d2`4d4ff900 00007ff7`6ce17dfb heap_corruption2!main+0x13f
06 000000d2`4d4ffa70 00007ff7`6ce1793e heap_corruption2!core::ops::function::FnOnce::call_once<void (*)(),tuple$<> >+0xb
07 (Inline Function) --------`-------- heap_corruption2!core::hint::black_box+0xa
08 000000d2`4d4ffab0 00007ff7`6ce14581 heap_corruption2!std::sys::backtrace::__rust_begin_short_backtrace<void (*)(),tuple$<> >+0xe
09 000000d2`4d4ffaf0 00007ff7`6ce1d419 heap_corruption2!std::rt::lang_start::closure$0<tuple$<> >+0x11
0a (Inline Function) --------`-------- heap_corruption2!std::rt::lang_start_internal::closure$2+0x6
0b (Inline Function) --------`-------- heap_corruption2!std::panicking::try::do_call+0x6
0c (Inline Function) --------`-------- heap_corruption2!std::panicking::try+0x6
0d (Inline Function) --------`-------- heap_corruption2!std::panic::catch_unwind+0x6
0e 000000d2`4d4ffb30 00007ff7`6ce1455a heap_corruption2!std::rt::lang_start_internal+0x79
0f 000000d2`4d4ffbf0 00007ff7`6ce12599 heap_corruption2!std::rt::lang_start<tuple$<> >+0x3a
10 000000d2`4d4ffc60 00007ff7`6ce32c7c heap_corruption2!main+0x19
11 (Inline Function) --------`-------- heap_corruption2!invoke_main+0x22
12 000000d2`4d4ffc90 00007ff9`b18353e0 heap_corruption2!__scrt_common_main_seh+0x10c
13 000000d2`4d4ffcd0 00007ff9`b2a4485b kernel32!BaseThreadInitThunk+0x10
14 000000d2`4d4ffd00 00000000`00000000 ntdll!RtlUserThreadStart+0x2b

   1  Id: b44.1ff8 Suspend: 0 Teb: 000000d2`4d275000 Unfrozen
 # Child-SP          RetAddr           Call Site
00 000000d2`4d5ff4c8 00007ff9`b2a56cdf ntdll!NtWaitForWorkViaWorkerFactory+0x14
01 000000d2`4d5ff4d0 00007ff9`b18353e0 ntdll!TppWorkerThread+0x2df
02 000000d2`4d5ff7c0 00007ff9`b2a4485b kernel32!BaseThreadInitThunk+0x10
03 000000d2`4d5ff7f0 00000000`00000000 ntdll!RtlUserThreadStart+0x2b

   2  Id: b44.12e4 Suspend: 0 Teb: 000000d2`4d277000 Unfrozen
 # Child-SP          RetAddr           Call Site
00 000000d2`4d7ff878 00007ff9`b2a5d89d ntdll!NtWaitForAlertByThreadId+0x14
01 000000d2`4d7ff880 00007ff9`b2a9b3fe ntdll!RtlpWaitOnAddressWithTimeout+0x81
02 000000d2`4d7ff8b0 00007ff9`b2a9b343 ntdll!RtlpWaitOnAddress+0xae
03 000000d2`4d7ff920 00007ff9`affbdd9f ntdll!RtlWaitOnAddress+0x13
04 000000d2`4d7ff950 00007ff7`6ce1dc01 KERNELBASE!WaitOnAddress+0x2f
05 (Inline Function) --------`-------- heap_corruption2!std::sys::sync::thread_parking::futex::Parker::park+0x65
06 (Inline Function) --------`-------- heap_corruption2!std::thread::Thread::park+0x65
07 000000d2`4d7ff9a0 00007ff7`6ce1163b heap_corruption2!std::thread::park+0x151
08 000000d2`4d7ffa10 00007ff7`6ce1795d heap_corruption2!main::closure$0+0x3b
09 (Inline Function) --------`-------- heap_corruption2!core::hint::black_box+0x9
0a 000000d2`4d7ffb80 00007ff7`6ce1774d heap_corruption2!std::sys::backtrace::__rust_begin_short_backtrace<heap_corruption2::main::closure_env$0,tuple$<> >+0xd
0b 000000d2`4d7ffbb0 00007ff7`6ce1121d heap_corruption2!std::thread::impl$0::spawn_unchecked_::closure$1::closure$0<heap_corruption2::main::closure_env$0,tuple$<> >+0xd
0c 000000d2`4d7ffbe0 00007ff7`6ce12f63 heap_corruption2!panic::unwind_safe::impl$25::call_once<tuple$<>,std::thread::impl$0::spawn_unchecked_::closure$1::closure_env$0<heap_corruption2::main::closure_env$0,tuple$<> > >+0xd
0d 000000d2`4d7ffc10 00007ff7`6ce17813 heap_corruption2!panicking::try::do_call<core::panic::unwind_safe::AssertUnwindSafe<std::thread::impl$0::spawn_unchecked_::closure$1::closure_env$0<heap_corruption2::main::closure_env$0
,tuple$<> > >,tuple$<> >+0x23
0e 000000d2`4d7ffc70 00007ff7`6ce172a5 heap_corruption2!std::thread::impl$7::drop::closure$0<tuple$<> >+0xb3
0f (Inline Function) --------`-------- heap_corruption2!std::panicking::try+0x25
10 (Inline Function) --------`-------- heap_corruption2!std::panic::catch_unwind+0x25
11 000000d2`4d7ffc0 00007ff7`6ce17d3e heap_corruption2!std::thread::impl$0::spawn_unchecked_::closure$1<heap_corruption2::main::closure_env$0,tuple$<> >+0x135
12 000000d2`4d7ffe20 00007ff7`6ce255cd heap_corruption2!core::ops::function::FnOnce::call_once<std::thread::impl$0::spawn_unchecked_::closure_env$1<heap_corruption2::main::closure_env$0,tuple$<> >,tuple$<> >+0xe
13 (Inline Function) --------`-------- heap_corruption2!alloc::boxed::impl$48::call_once+0xb
14 (Inline Function) --------`-------- heap_corruption2!alloc::boxed::impl$48::call_once+0x16
15 000000d2`4d7ffe60 00007ff9`b18353e0 heap_corruption2!std::sys::pal::windows::thread::impl$0::new::thread_start+0x3d
16 000000d2`4d7ffec0 00007ff9`b2a4485b kernel32!BaseThreadInitThunk+0x10
17 000000d2`4d7ffef0 00000000`00000000 ntdll!RtlUserThreadStart+0x2b

   3  Id: b44.1198 Suspend: 0 Teb: 000000d2`4d279000 Unfrozen
 # Child-SP          RetAddr           Call Site
00 000000d2`4d9fe638 00007ff9`b2a9b903 ntdll!NtDelayExecution+0x14
01 000000d2`4d9fe640 00007ff9`aff7d051 ntdll!RtlDelayExecution+0x43
02 000000d2`4d9fe670 00007ff9`b188eaac KERNELBASE!SleepEx+0x71
03 000000d2`4d9fe6f0 00007ff9`b009e503 kernel32!WerpReportFault+0xa4
04 000000d2`4d9fe730 00007ff9`b2aeb0ec KERNELBASE!UnhandledExceptionFilter+0x3e3
05 000000d2`4d9fe850 00007ff9`b2ad40f6 ntdll!RtlUserThreadStart$filt$0+0xac
```

```
06 000000d2`4d9fe890 00007ff9`b2ae906f     ntdll!_C_specific_handler+0x96
07 000000d2`4d9fe900 00007ff9`b2a75bea     ntdll!RtlpExecuteHandlerForException+0xf
08 000000d2`4d9fe930 00007ff9`b2ae805e     ntdll!RtlDispatchException+0x25a
09 000000d2`4d9ff080 00007ff9`a04a15d8     ntdll!KiUserExceptionDispatch+0x2e
0a 000000d2`4d9ff788 00007ff7`6ce116f1     VCRUNTIME140!memcpy+0x2e8
0b 000000d2`4d9ff790 00007ff7`6ce1795d     heap_corruption2!heap_corruption2::main::closure$0+0xf1
0c (Inline Function) --------`--------     heap_corruption2!core::hint::black_box+0x9
0d 000000d2`4d9ff900 00007ff7`6ce1774d     heap_corruption2!std::sys::backtrace::__rust_begin_short_backtrace<heap_corruption2::main::closure_env$0,tuple$<> >+0xd
0e 000000d2`4d9ff930 00007ff7`6ce1121d     heap_corruption2!std::thread::impl$0::spawn_unchecked_::closure$1::closure$0<heap_corruption2::main::closure_env$0,tuple$<> >+0xd
0f 000000d2`4d9ff960 00007ff7`6ce12f63     heap_corruption2!core::panic::unwind_safe::impl$25::call_once<tuple$<>,std::thread::impl$0::spawn_unchecked_::closure$1::closure_env$0<heap_corruption2::main::closure_env$0,tuple$<> > >+0xd
10 000000d2`4d9ff990 00007ff7`6ce17813     heap_corruption2!std::panicking::try::do_call<core::panic::unwind_safe::AssertUnwindSafe<std::thread::impl$0::spawn_unchecked_::closure$1::closure_env$0<heap_corruption2::main::closure_env$0
,tuple$<> > >,tuple$<> >+0x23
11 000000d2`4d9ff9f0 00007ff7`6ce172a5     heap_corruption2!std::thread::impl$7::drop::closure$0<tuple$<> >+0xb3
12 (Inline Function) --------`--------     heap_corruption2!std::panicking::try+0x25
13 (Inline Function) --------`--------     heap_corruption2!std::panic::catch_unwind+0x25
14 000000d2`4d9ffa40 00007ff7`6ce17d3e     heap_corruption2!std::thread::impl$0::spawn_unchecked_::closure$1<heap_corruption2::main::closure_env$0,tuple$<> >+0x135
15 000000d2`4d9ffba0 00007ff7`6ce255cd     heap_corruption2!core::ops::function::FnOnce::call_once<std::thread::impl$0::spawn_unchecked_::closure_env$1<heap_corruption2::main::closure_env$0,tuple$<> >,tuple$<> >+0xe
16 (Inline Function) --------`--------     heap_corruption2!alloc::boxed::impl$48::call_once+0xb
17 (Inline Function) --------`--------     heap_corruption2!alloc::boxed::impl$48::call_once+0x16
18 000000d2`4d9ffbe0 00007ff9`b18353e0     heap_corruption2!std::sys::pal::windows::thread::impl$0::new::thread_start+0x3d
19 000000d2`4d9ffc40 00007ff9`b2a4485b     kernel32!BaseThreadInitThunk+0x10
1a 000000d2`4d9ffc70 00000000`00000000     ntdll!RtlUserThreadStart+0x2b

    4  Id: b44.1174 Suspend: 0 Teb: 000000d2`4d27b000 Unfrozen
 # Child-SP          RetAddr               Call Site
00 000000d2`4dbff508 00007ff9`b2a5d89d     ntdll!NtWaitForAlertByThreadId+0x14
01 000000d2`4dbff510 00007ff9`b2a9b3fe     ntdll!RtlpWaitOnAddressWithTimeout+0x81
02 000000d2`4dbff540 00007ff9`b2a9b343     ntdll!RtlpWaitOnAddress+0xae
03 000000d2`4dbff5b0 00007ff9`affbdd9f     ntdll!RtlWaitOnAddress+0x13
04 000000d2`4dbff5f0 00007ff7`6ce1dc01     KERNELBASE!WaitOnAddress+0x2f
05 (Inline Function) --------`--------     heap_corruption2!std::sys::sync::thread_parking::futex::Parker::park+0x65
06 (Inline Function) --------`--------     heap_corruption2!std::thread::Thread::park+0x65
07 000000d2`4dbff630 00007ff7`6ce1163b     heap_corruption2!std::thread::park+0x151
08 000000d2`4dbff6a0 00007ff7`6ce1795d     heap_corruption2!heap_corruption2::main::closure$0+0x3b
09 (Inline Function) --------`--------     heap_corruption2!core::hint::black_box+0x9
0a 000000d2`4dbff810 00007ff7`6ce1774d     heap_corruption2!std::sys::backtrace::__rust_begin_short_backtrace<heap_corruption2::main::closure_env$0,tuple$<> >+0xd
0b 000000d2`4dbff840 00007ff7`6ce1121d     heap_corruption2!std::thread::impl$0::spawn_unchecked_::closure$1::closure$0<heap_corruption2::main::closure_env$0,tuple$<> >+0xd
0c 000000d2`4dbff870 00007ff7`6ce12f63     heap_corruption2!core::panic::unwind_safe::impl$25::call_once<tuple$<>,std::thread::impl$0::spawn_unchecked_::closure$1::closure_env$0<heap_corruption2::main::closure_env$0,tuple$<> > >+0xd
0d 000000d2`4dbff8a0 00007ff7`6ce17813     heap_corruption2!std::panicking::try::do_call<core::panic::unwind_safe::AssertUnwindSafe<std::thread::impl$0::spawn_unchecked_::closure$1::closure_env$0<heap_corruption2::main::closure_env$0
,tuple$<> > >,tuple$<> >+0x23
0e 000000d2`4dbff900 00007ff7`6ce172a5     heap_corruption2!std::thread::impl$7::drop::closure$0<tuple$<> >+0xb3
0f (Inline Function) --------`--------     heap_corruption2!std::panicking::try+0x25
10 (Inline Function) --------`--------     heap_corruption2!std::panic::catch_unwind+0x25
11 000000d2`4dbff950 00007ff7`6ce17d3e     heap_corruption2!std::thread::impl$0::spawn_unchecked_::closure$1<heap_corruption2::main::closure_env$0,tuple$<> >+0x135
12 000000d2`4dbffab0 00007ff7`6ce255cd     heap_corruption2!core::ops::function::FnOnce::call_once<std::thread::impl$0::spawn_unchecked_::closure_env$1<heap_corruption2::main::closure_env$0,tuple$<> >,tuple$<> >+0xe
13 (Inline Function) --------`--------     heap_corruption2!alloc::boxed::impl$48::call_once+0xb
14 (Inline Function) --------`--------     heap_corruption2!alloc::boxed::impl$48::call_once+0x16
15 000000d2`4dbffaf0 00007ff9`b18353e0     heap_corruption2!std::sys::pal::windows::thread::impl$0::new::thread_start+0x3d
16 000000d2`4dbffb50 00007ff9`b2a4485b     kernel32!BaseThreadInitThunk+0x10
17 000000d2`4dbffb80 00000000`00000000     ntdll!RtlUserThreadStart+0x2b

#  5  Id: b44.12a8 Suspend: 0 Teb: 000000d2`4d27d000 Unfrozen
 # Child-SP          RetAddr               Call Site
00 000000d2`4ddfe058 00007ff9`affadcd0     ntdll!NtWaitForMultipleObjects+0x14
01 000000d2`4ddfe060 00007ff9`affadbce     KERNELBASE!WaitForMultipleObjectsEx+0xf0
02 000000d2`4ddfe350 00007ff9`b188f087     KERNELBASE!WaitForMultipleObjects+0xe
03 000000d2`4ddfe390 00007ff9`b188eac6     kernel32!WerpReportFaultInternal+0x587
04 000000d2`4ddfe4b0 00007ff9`b009e503     kernel32!WerpReportFault+0xbe
05 000000d2`4ddfe4f0 00007ff9`b2aeb0ec     KERNELBASE!UnhandledExceptionFilter+0x3e3
06 000000d2`4ddfe610 00007ff9`b2ad40f6     ntdll!RtlUserThreadStart$filt$0+0xac
07 000000d2`4ddfe650 00007ff9`b2ae906f     ntdll!_C_specific_handler+0x96
08 000000d2`4ddfe6c0 00007ff9`b2a75bea     ntdll!RtlpExecuteHandlerForException+0xf
09 000000d2`4ddfe6f0 00007ff9`b2ae805e     ntdll!RtlDispatchException+0x25a
0a 000000d2`4ddfee40 00007ff9`a04a15d8     ntdll!KiUserExceptionDispatch+0x2e
0b 000000d2`4ddff578 00007ff7`6ce117aa     VCRUNTIME140!memcpy+0x2e8
0c 000000d2`4ddff580 00007ff7`6ce1795d     heap_corruption2!heap_corruption2::main::closure$0+0x1aa
0d (Inline Function) --------`--------     heap_corruption2!core::hint::black_box+0x9
0e 000000d2`4ddff6f0 00007ff7`6ce1774d     heap_corruption2!std::sys::backtrace::__rust_begin_short_backtrace<heap_corruption2::main::closure_env$0,tuple$<> >+0xd
0f 000000d2`4ddff720 00007ff7`6ce1121d     heap_corruption2!std::thread::impl$0::spawn_unchecked_::closure$1::closure$0<heap_corruption2::main::closure_env$0,tuple$<> >+0xd
10 000000d2`4ddff750 00007ff7`6ce12f63     heap_corruption2!core::panic::unwind_safe::impl$25::call_once<tuple$<>,std::thread::impl$0::spawn_unchecked_::closure$1::closure_env$0<heap_corruption2::main::closure_env$0,tuple$<> > >+0xd
11 000000d2`4ddff780 00007ff7`6ce17813     heap_corruption2!std::panicking::try::do_call<core::panic::unwind_safe::AssertUnwindSafe<std::thread::impl$0::spawn_unchecked_::closure$1::closure_env$0<heap_corruption2::main::closure_env$0
,tuple$<> > >,tuple$<> >+0x23
12 000000d2`4ddff7e0 00007ff7`6ce172a5     heap_corruption2!std::thread::impl$7::drop::closure$0<tuple$<> >+0xb3
13 (Inline Function) --------`--------     heap_corruption2!std::panicking::try+0x25
14 (Inline Function) --------`--------     heap_corruption2!std::panic::catch_unwind+0x25
15 000000d2`4ddff830 00007ff7`6ce17d3e     heap_corruption2!std::thread::impl$0::spawn_unchecked_::closure$1<heap_corruption2::main::closure_env$0,tuple$<> >+0x135
16 000000d2`4ddff990 00007ff7`6ce255cd     heap_corruption2!core::ops::function::FnOnce::call_once<std::thread::impl$0::spawn_unchecked_::closure_env$1<heap_corruption2::main::closure_env$0,tuple$<> >,tuple$<> >+0xe
17 (Inline Function) --------`--------     heap_corruption2!alloc::boxed::impl$48::call_once+0xb
18 (Inline Function) --------`--------     heap_corruption2!alloc::boxed::impl$48::call_once+0x16
19 000000d2`4ddff9d0 00007ff9`b18353e0     heap_corruption2!std::sys::pal::windows::thread::impl$0::new::thread_start+0x3d
1a 000000d2`4ddffa30 00007ff9`b2a4485b     kernel32!BaseThreadInitThunk+0x10
1b 000000d2`4ddffa60 00000000`00000000     ntdll!RtlUserThreadStart+0x2b

    6  Id: b44.1c54 Suspend: 0 Teb: 000000d2`4d27f000 Unfrozen
 # Child-SP          RetAddr               Call Site
00 000000d2`4dfff3e8 00007ff9`b2a5d89d     ntdll!NtWaitForAlertByThreadId+0x14
01 000000d2`4dfff3f0 00007ff9`b2a9b3fe     ntdll!RtlpWaitOnAddressWithTimeout+0x81
02 000000d2`4dfff420 00007ff9`b2a9b343     ntdll!RtlpWaitOnAddress+0xae
03 000000d2`4dfff490 00007ff9`affbdd9f     ntdll!RtlWaitOnAddress+0x13
04 000000d2`4dfff4d0 00007ff7`6ce1dc01     KERNELBASE!WaitOnAddress+0x2f
05 (Inline Function) --------`--------     heap_corruption2!std::sys::sync::thread_parking::futex::Parker::park+0x65
06 (Inline Function) --------`--------     heap_corruption2!std::thread::Thread::park+0x65
07 000000d2`4dfff510 00007ff7`6ce1163b     heap_corruption2!std::thread::park+0x151
08 000000d2`4dfff580 00007ff7`6ce1795d     heap_corruption2!heap_corruption2::main::closure$0+0x3b
09 (Inline Function) --------`--------     heap_corruption2!core::hint::black_box+0x9
0a 000000d2`4dfff6f0 00007ff7`6ce1774d     heap_corruption2!std::sys::backtrace::__rust_begin_short_backtrace<heap_corruption2::main::closure_env$0,tuple$<> >+0xd
0b 000000d2`4dfff720 00007ff7`6ce1121d     heap_corruption2!std::thread::impl$0::spawn_unchecked_::closure$1::closure$0<heap_corruption2::main::closure_env$0,tuple$<> >+0xd
...
0e 000000d2`4dfff7e0 00007ff7`6ce172a5     heap_corruption2!std::thread::impl$7::drop::closure$0<tuple$<> >+0xb3
0f (Inline Function) --------`--------     heap_corruption2!std::panicking::try+0x25
10 (Inline Function) --------`--------     heap_corruption2!std::panic::catch_unwind+0x25
11 000000d2`4dfff830 00007ff7`6ce17d3e     heap_corruption2!std::thread::impl$0::spawn_unchecked_::closure$1<heap_corruption2::main::closure_env$0,tuple$<> >+0x135
12 000000d2`4dfff990 00007ff7`6ce255cd     heap_corruption2!core::ops::function::FnOnce::call_once<std::thread::impl$0::spawn_unchecked_::closure_env$1<heap_corruption2::main::closure_env$0,tuple$<> >,tuple$<> >+0xe
13 (Inline Function) --------`--------     heap_corruption2!alloc::boxed::impl$48::call_once+0xb
14 (Inline Function) --------`--------     heap_corruption2!alloc::boxed::impl$48::call_once+0x16
15 000000d2`4dfff9d0 00007ff9`b18353e0     heap_corruption2!std::sys::pal::windows::thread::impl$0::new::thread_start+0x3d
16 000000d2`4dfffa30 00007ff9`b2a4485b     kernel32!BaseThreadInitThunk+0x10
17 000000d2`4dfffa60 00000000`00000000     ntdll!RtlUserThreadStart+0x2b
```

Note: We see similar exception processing in thread #3.

17.   To see what happened in another thread, we switch to it and do the similar frame analysis that we did for thread #5:

```
0:005> ~3s
ntdll!NtDelayExecution+0x14:
00007ff9`b2ae4704 ret

0:003> .cxr 000000d2`4d9ff080
rax=000002045d36cfe0 rbx=0000000000000000 rcx=000002045d36cfe0
rdx=00007ff76ce3681c rsi=000002045d2faff0 rdi=0000000000000000
rip=00007ff9a04a15d8 rsp=000000d24d9ff788 rbp=000000d24d9ff810
 r8=000000000000004e  r9=0000000000000060 r10=00007ff9a04a0000
r11=00007ff9a04a15c3 r12=0000000000000000 r13=0000000000000000
r14=0000000000000000 r15=0000000000000000
iopl=0         nv up ei pl nz na po nc
cs=0033  ss=002b  ds=002b  es=002b  fs=0053  gs=002b              efl=00010206
VCRUNTIME140!memcpy+0x2e8:
00007ff9`a04a15d8 vmovdqu ymmword ptr [rcx+r9-40h],ymm1 ds:00000204`5d36d000=??


0:003> kL
 *** Stack trace for last set context - .thread/.cxr resets it
 # Child-SP          RetAddr           Call Site
00 000000d2`4d9ff788 00007ff7`6ce116f1 VCRUNTIME140!memcpy+0x2e8
01 000000d2`4d9ff790 00007ff7`6ce1795d heap_corruption2!heap_corruption2::main::closure$0+0xf1
02 (Inline Function) --------`-------- heap_corruption2!core::hint::black_box+0x9
03 000000d2`4d9ff900 00007ff7`6ce1774d heap_corruption2!std::sys::backtrace::__rust_begin_short_backtrace<heap_corruption2::main::closure_env$0,tuple$<>
>+0xd
04 000000d2`4d9ff930 00007ff7`6ce1121d
heap_corruption2!std::thread::impl$0::spawn_unchecked_::closure$1::closure$0<heap_corruption2::main::closure_env$0,tuple$<> >+0xd
05 000000d2`4d9ff960 00007ff7`6ce12f63
heap_corruption2!core::panic::unwind_safe::impl$25::call_once<tuple$<>,std::thread::impl$0::spawn_unchecked_::closure$1::closure_env$0<heap_corruption2::main:
:closure_env$0,tuple$<> > >+0xd
06 000000d2`4d9ff990 00007ff7`6ce17813 heap_corruption2!std::panicking::try::do_call<core::panic::unwind_safe::AssertUnwindSafe<std::thread::impl$0::spawn_unchecked_::closure$1::closure_env$0<heap_
corruption2::main::closure_env$0,tuple$<> > >,tuple$<> >+0x23
07 000000d2`4d9ff9f0 00007ff7`6ce172a5 heap_corruption2!std::thread::impl$7::drop::closure$0<tuple$<> >+0xb3
08 (Inline Function) --------`-------- heap_corruption2!std::panicking::try+0x25
09 (Inline Function) --------`-------- heap_corruption2!std::panic::catch_unwind+0x25
0a 000000d2`4d9ffa40 00007ff7`6ce17d3e heap_corruption2!std::thread::impl$0::spawn_unchecked_::closure$1<heap_corruption2::main::closure_env$0,tuple$<>
>+0x135
0b 000000d2`4d9ffba0 00007ff7`6ce255cd
heap_corruption2!core::ops::function::FnOnce::call_once<std::thread::impl$0::spawn_unchecked_::closure_env$1<heap_corruption2::main::closure_env$0,tuple$<>
>,tuple$<> >+0xe
0c (Inline Function) --------`-------- heap_corruption2!alloc::boxed::impl$48::call_once+0xb
0d (Inline Function) --------`-------- heap_corruption2!alloc::boxed::impl$48::call_once+0x16
0e 000000d2`4d9ffbe0 00007ff9`b18353e0 heap_corruption2!std::sys::pal::windows::thread::impl$0::new::thread_start+0x3d
0f 000000d2`4d9ffc40 00007ff9`b2a4485b kernel32!BaseThreadInitThunk+0x10
10 000000d2`4d9ffc70 00000000`00000000 ntdll!RtlUserThreadStart+0x2b


0:003> dc 00000204`5d36d000-50
00000204`5d36cfb0  00000014 00000000 00001000 00000000  ................
00000204`5d36cfc0  00000000 00000000 00000000 00000000  ................
00000204`5d36cfd0  5b81b020 00000204 00000000 dcbabbbb  ..[.............
00000204`5d36cfe0  00650048 006c006c 0020006f 00720043  H.e.l.l.o. .C.r.
00000204`5d36cff0  00730061 00210068 00480020 006c0065  a.s.h.!. .H.e.l.
00000204`5d36d000  ???????? ???????? ???????? ????????  ?????????????????
00000204`5d36d010  ???????? ???????? ???????? ????????  ?????????????????
00000204`5d36d020  ???????? ???????? ???????? ????????  ?????????????????


0:003> .cxr
Resetting default scope

0:003> kc
 # Call Site
00 ntdll!NtDelayExecution
01 ntdll!RtlDelayExecution
02 KERNELBASE!SleepEx
03 kernel32!WerpReportFault
04 KERNELBASE!UnhandledExceptionFilter
05 ntdll!RtlUserThreadStart$filt$0
06 ntdll!_C_specific_handler
```

```
07 ntdll!RtlpExecuteHandlerForException
08 ntdll!RtlDispatchException
09 ntdll!KiUserExceptionDispatch
0a VCRUNTIME140!memcpy
0b heap_corruption2!heap_corruption2::main::closure$0
0c heap_corruption2!core::hint::black_box
0d heap_corruption2!std::sys::backtrace::__rust_begin_short_backtrace<heap_corruption2::main::closure_env$0,tuple$<> >
0e heap_corruption2!std::thread::impl$0::spawn_unchecked_::closure$1::closure$0<heap_corruption2::main::closure_env$0,tuple$<> >
0f
heap_corruption2!core::panic::unwind_safe::impl$25::call_once<tuple$<>,std::thread::impl$0::spawn_unchecked_::closure$1::closure_env$0<heap_corruption2::main:
:closure_env$0,tuple$<> > >
10
heap_corruption2!std::panicking::try::do_call<core::panic::unwind_safe::AssertUnwindSafe<std::thread::impl$0::spawn_unchecked_::closure$1::closure_env$0<heap_
corruption2::main::closure_env$0,tuple$<> > >,tuple$<> >
11 heap_corruption2!std::thread::impl$7::drop::closure$0<tuple$<> >
12 heap_corruption2!std::panicking::try
13 heap_corruption2!std::panic::catch_unwind
14 heap_corruption2!std::thread::impl$0::spawn_unchecked_::closure$1<heap_corruption2::main::closure_env$0,tuple$<> >
15 heap_corruption2!core::ops::function::FnOnce::call_once<std::thread::impl$0::spawn_unchecked_::closure_env$1<heap_corruption2::main::closure_env$0,tuple$<>
>,tuple$<> >
16 heap_corruption2!alloc::boxed::impl$48::call_once
17 heap_corruption2!alloc::boxed::impl$48::call_once
18 heap_corruption2!std::sys::pal::windows::thread::impl$0::new::thread_start
19 kernel32!BaseThreadInitThunk
1a ntdll!RtlUserThreadStart
```

```
0:003> .frame b
0b 000000d2`4d9ff790 00007ff7`6ce1795d      heap_corruption2!heap_corruption2::main::closure$0+0xf1 [C:\ARWMDA-
Dumps\heap-corruption2\heap-corruption2\src\main.rs @ 29]
```

Note: We see a similar buffer overwrite for a different buffer, and if we set up the source code path correctly, WinDbg would open the source code window and point to the exact location:

```
main.rs  X

17      for n in 1..=5 {
18          let handle = thread::spawn(move || {
19
20              match n {
21
22                  2 => loop {
23                      let mut p = vec![0u16; 10].into_boxed_
24
25                      unsafe {
26                          ptr::copy_nonoverlapping(STR.as_p
27                      }
28
⇒ 29                      thread::sleep(Duration::from_millis(1
30                  }
31
32                  4 => loop {
33                      let mut p = vec![0u16; 10].into_boxed_
34
35                      unsafe {
36                          ptr::copy_nonoverlapping(STR.as_p
37                      }
38
39                      thread::sleep(Duration::from_millis(2
40                  }
41
42                  _ => { thread::park(); }
43              }
44
45          });
46          handles.push(handle);
47      }
48
49      mod_ab::func();
50
51      for handle in handles {
52          handle.join().unwrap();
53      }
54 }
55
```

18.   We close both WinDbg instances.

Exercise RW7

- **Goal:** Learn how to recognize CPU spikes, memory leaks, stack overflow, and handle leaks

- **Patterns:** Active Thread; Spiking Thread; Thread Age; Stack Overflow (User Mode); Near Exception; Memory Leak (Process Heap); Active Space; Handle Leak; Small Value; Punctuated Memory Leak

- \ARWMDA-Dumps\Exercise-RW7.pdf

Exercise RW7

Goal: Learn how to recognize CPU spikes, memory leaks, stack overflow, and handle leaks.

Patterns: Active Thread; Spiking Thread; Thread Age; Memory Leak (Process Heap); Active Space; Handle Leak; Small Value; Punctuated Memory Leak.

1.   It was found that committed memory and the number of handles were increasing, and CPU consumption was high for the *complex-case* application, so the process memory dump was saved using Task Manager:

Name	PID	Status	User name	CPU	Commit size	Handles	Architec...	Descripti
AggregatorHost.exe	3132	Running	SYSTEM	00	1,200 K	101	x64	Aggrega
AM_Delta.exe	2540	Running	SYSTEM	00	968 K	63	x64	AntiMalv
backgroundTaskHost....	82216	Running	User	00	3,540 K	223	x64	Backgrou
complex-case.exe	8128	Running	User	17	121,304 K	20,039	x64	complex
conhost.exe	2428	Running	User	13	6,236 K	185	x64	Console
csrss.exe	604	Running	SYSTEM	00	1,940 K	478	x64	Client Se
csrss.exe	696	Running	SYSTEM	00	2,256 K	347	x64	Client Se
csrss.exe	6972	Running	SYSTEM	00	1,844 K	159	x64	Client Se
ctfmon.exe	3868	Running	User	00	3,580 K	444	x64	CTF Loac
dllhost.exe	3420	Running	SYSTEM	00	3,288 K	212	x64	COM Sur
dllhost.exe	6628	Running	User	00	6,588 K	293	x64	COM Sur
dwm.exe	1384	Running	DWM-1	23	78,620 K	953	x64	Desktop
dwm.exe	6192	Running	DWM-3	00	15,832 K	680	x64	Desktop
explorer.exe	4584	Running	User	00	98,744 K	3,288	x64	Windows
fontdrvhost.exe	992	Running	UMFD-0	00	1,340 K	37	x64	Usermod
fontdrvhost.exe	1000	Running	UMFD-1	00	1,872 K	37	x64	Usermod
fontdrvhost.exe	5532	Running	UMFD-3	00	1,272 K	37	x64	Usermod
LogonUI.exe	6148	Running	SYSTEM	00	17,096 K	659	x64	Windows
Lsalso.exe	844	Running	SYSTEM	00	1,056 K	54	x64	Credenti
lsass.exe	856	Running	SYSTEM	00	6,140 K	1,182	x64	Local Sec
MicrosoftEdgeUpdate...	5800	Running	SYSTEM	01	8,912 K	496	x86	Microsof

2.   Launch WinDbg.

3.   Open \ARWMDA-Dumps\Process\complex-case.DMP.

4.   We get the dump file loaded:

```
Microsoft (R) Windows Debugger Version 10.0.27725.1000 AMD64
Copyright (c) Microsoft Corporation. All rights reserved.


Loading Dump File [C:\ARWMDA-Dumps\Process\complex-case.DMP]
User Mini Dump File with Full Memory: Only application data is available


************* Path validation summary **************
Response                         Time (ms)        Location
Deferred                                          srv*
Symbol search path is: srv*
Executable search path is:
Windows 10 Version 22000 MP (4 procs) Free x64
Product: WinNt, suite: SingleUserTS
Edition build lab: 22000.1.amd64fre.co_release.210604-1628
Debug session time: Thu Nov 28 21:38:49.000 2024 (UTC + 0:00)
System Uptime: 0 days 0:50:54.786
Process Uptime: 0 days 0:38:38.000
......
For analysis of this file, run !analyze -v
ntdll!NtWaitForSingleObject+0x14:
00007ffb`e75a4104 ret
```

5.   Open a log file using the **.logopen** command and load symbols (**.sympath+** and **.reload**):

```
0:000> .logopen C:\ARWMDA-Dumps\RW7.log
Opened log file 'C:\ARWMDA-Dumps\RW7.log'


0:000> .sympath+ C:\ARWMDA-Dumps\Symbols\release
Symbol search path is: srv*;C:\ARWMDA-Dumps\Symbols\release
Expanded Symbol search path is:
cache*;SRV*https://msdl.microsoft.com/download/symbols;c:\arwmda-dumps\symbols\release


************* Path validation summary **************
Response                         Time (ms)        Location
Deferred                                          srv*
OK                                                C:\ARWMDA-Dumps\Symbols\release


0:000> .reload
......
```

Note: WinDbg may remember symbol and source paths from the previous sessions.

6.   Let's start our analysis by looking at all stack traces:

```
0:000> ~*kL 20

.  0  Id: 1fc0.474 Suspend: 0 Teb: 00000099`9cfee000 Unfrozen "main"
 # Child-SP          RetAddr           Call Site
00 00000099`9cd6fa78 00007ffb`e4d110ee     ntdll!NtWaitForSingleObject+0x14
01 00000099`9cd6fa80 00007ff6`6b8ee5a1     KERNELBASE!WaitForSingleObjectEx+0x8e
02 00000099`9cd6fb20 00007ff6`6b8e1021     complex_case!std::sys::pal::windows::thread::Thread::join+0x21
03 00000099`9cd6fbb0 00007ff6`6b8e4298     complex_case!ZN3std6thread18JoinInner$LT$T$GT$4join17he01750eff116e062E+0x21
04 00000099`9cd6fc10 00007ff6`6b8e3536
complex_case!ZN80_$LT$std..io..Write..write_fmt..Adapter$LT$T$GT$$u20$as$u20$core..fmt..Write$GT$9write_str17hcbe9dfd423357c2fE+0x238
05 00000099`9cd6fd30 00007ff6`6b8e2e0c     complex_case!ZN3std3sys9backtrace28__rust_begin_short_backtrace17h2f112179cab5b729E+0x6
```

```
06 00000099`9cd6fd60 00007ff6`6b8e6389
complex_case!ZN3std2rt10lang_start28_$u7b$$u7b$closure$u7d$$u7d$17h06bb858946802ed5E.llvm.805952136491849391+0xc
07 (Inline Function) --------`--------        complex_case!std::rt::lang_start_internal::closure$2+0x6
08 (Inline Function) --------`--------        complex_case!std::panicking::try::do_call+0x6
09 (Inline Function) --------`--------        complex_case!std::panicking::try+0x6
0a (Inline Function) --------`--------        complex_case!std::panic::catch_unwind+0x6
0b 00000099`9cd6fd90 00007ff6`6b8e45bc        complex_case!std::rt::lang_start_internal+0x79
0c 00000099`9cd6fe50 00007ff6`6b8fba1c        complex_case!main+0x2c
0d (Inline Function) --------`--------        complex_case!invoke_main+0x22
0e 00000099`9cd6fe90 00007ffb`e60853e0        complex_case!__scrt_common_main_seh+0x10c
0f 00000099`9cd6fed0 00007ffb`e750485b        kernel32!BaseThreadInitThunk+0x10
10 00000099`9cd6ff00 00000000`00000000        ntdll!RtlUserThreadStart+0x2b

   1  Id: 1fc0.e98 Suspend: 0 Teb: 00000099`9cff6000 Unfrozen
 # Child-SP          RetAddr               Call Site
00 00000099`9d4ffa80 00007ff6`6b8e1f60     complex_case!ZN3std3sys9backtrace28__rust_begin_short_backtrace17h3e8324a489e54ea5E+0x50
01 00000099`9d4ffbe0 00007ff6`6b8ee43d     complex_case!ZN3std6thread7Builder15spawn_unchecked17h6e56a25e80bf8795E+0x790
02 (Inline Function) --------`--------     complex_case!alloc::boxed::impl$48::call_once+0xb
03 (Inline Function) --------`--------     complex_case!alloc::boxed::impl$48::call_once+0x16
04 00000099`9d4ffc80 00007ffb`e60853e0     complex_case!std::sys::pal::windows::thread::impl$0::new::thread_start+0x3d
05 00000099`9d4ffce0 00007ffb`e750485b     kernel32!BaseThreadInitThunk+0x10
06 00000099`9d4ffd10 00000000`00000000     ntdll!RtlUserThreadStart+0x2b

   2  Id: 1fc0.1330 Suspend: 0 Teb: 00000099`9cff8000 Unfrozen
 # Child-SP          RetAddr               Call Site
00 00000099`9d6fcf58 00007ffb`e4cf4da5     ntdll!NtDeviceIoControlFile+0x14
01 00000099`9d6fcf60 00007ffb`e4cf4c3a     KERNELBASE!ConsoleCallServerGeneric+0xe9
02 00000099`9d6fd0c0 00007ff6`6b8ee063     KERNELBASE!WriteConsoleW+0x6a
03 (Inline Function) --------`--------     complex_case!std::sys::pal::windows::stdio::write_u16s+0x2a
04 00000099`9d6fd150 00007ff6`6b8ede45     complex_case!std::sys::pal::windows::stdio::write_valid_utf8_to_console+0xd3
05 00000099`9d6ff1f0 00007ff6`6b8e756f     complex_case!std::sys::pal::windows::stdio::write+0x1d5
06 (Inline Function) --------`--------     complex_case!std::sys::pal::windows::stdio::impl$5::write+0x10
07 (Inline Function) --------`--------     complex_case!std::io::stdio::impl$1::write+0x10
08 00000099`9d6ff2d0 00007ff6`6b8e8180
complex_case!std::io::buffered::bufwriter::BufWriter::flush_buf<std::io::stdio::StdoutRaw>+0x7f
09 00000099`9d6ff370 00007ff6`6b8e95be     complex_case!std::io::stdio::impl$19::write_all+0x150
0a 00000099`9d6ff410 00007ff6`6b8f82bf     complex_case!std::io::Write::write_fmt::impl$0::write_str<std::io::stdio::StdoutLock>+0x1e
0b 00000099`9d6ff460 00007ff6`6b8e7f45     complex_case!core::fmt::write+0x1cf
0c 00000099`9d6ff510 00007ff6`6b8e87f1     complex_case!std::io::stdio::impl$16::write_fmt+0x45
0d 00000099`9d6ff5a0 00007ff6`6b8e36b2     complex_case!std::io::stdio::_print+0x61
0e 00000099`9d6ff650 00007ff6`6b8e1f60     complex_case!ZN3std3sys9backtrace28__rust_begin_short_backtrace17h3e8324a489e54ea5E+0x172
0f 00000099`9d6ff7b0 00007ff6`6b8ee43d     complex_case!ZN3std6thread7Builder15spawn_unchecked17h6e56a25e80bf8795E+0x790
10 (Inline Function) --------`--------     complex_case!alloc::boxed::impl$48::call_once+0xb
11 (Inline Function) --------`--------     complex_case!alloc::boxed::impl$48::call_once+0x16
12 00000099`9d6ff850 00007ffb`e60853e0     complex_case!std::sys::pal::windows::thread::impl$0::new::thread_start+0x3d
13 00000099`9d6ff8b0 00007ffb`e750485b     kernel32!BaseThreadInitThunk+0x10
14 00000099`9d6ff8e0 00000000`00000000     ntdll!RtlUserThreadStart+0x2b

   3  Id: 1fc0.17f4 Suspend: 0 Teb: 00000099`9cffa000 Unfrozen
 # Child-SP          RetAddr               Call Site
00 00000099`9d8ff788 00007ffb`e751d89d     ntdll!NtWaitForAlertByThreadId+0x14
01 00000099`9d8ff790 00007ffb`e755b3fe     ntdll!RtlpWaitOnAddressWithTimeout+0x81
02 00000099`9d8ff7c0 00007ffb`e755b343     ntdll!RtlpWaitOnAddress+0xae
03 00000099`9d8ff830 00007ffb`e4d2dd9f     ntdll!RtlWaitOnAddress+0x13
04 00000099`9d8ff870 00007ff6`6b8e6b71     KERNELBASE!WaitOnAddress+0x2f
05 (Inline Function) --------`--------     complex_case!std::sys::sync::thread_parking::futex::Parker::park+0x65
06 (Inline Function) --------`--------     complex_case!std::thread::Thread::park+0x65
07 00000099`9d8ff8b0 00007ff6`6b8e359c     complex_case!std::thread::park+0x151
08 00000099`9d8ff920 00007ff6`6b8e1f60     complex_case!ZN3std3sys9backtrace28__rust_begin_short_backtrace17h3e8324a489e54ea5E+0x5c
09 00000099`9d8ffa80 00007ff6`6b8ee43d     complex_case!ZN3std6thread7Builder15spawn_unchecked17h6e56a25e80bf8795E+0x790
0a (Inline Function) --------`--------     complex_case!alloc::boxed::impl$48::call_once+0xb
0b (Inline Function) --------`--------     complex_case!alloc::boxed::impl$48::call_once+0x16
0c 00000099`9d8ffb20 00007ffb`e60853e0     complex_case!std::sys::pal::windows::thread::impl$0::new::thread_start+0x3d
0d 00000099`9d8ffb80 00007ffb`e750485b     kernel32!BaseThreadInitThunk+0x10
0e 00000099`9d8ffbb0 00000000`00000000     ntdll!RtlUserThreadStart+0x2b

   4  Id: 1fc0.18c8 Suspend: 0 Teb: 00000099`9cffc000 Unfrozen
 # Child-SP          RetAddr               Call Site
00 00000099`9d928d68 00007ffb`e4d110ee     ntdll!NtWaitForSingleObject+0x14
01 00000099`9d928d70 00007ff6`6b8e69ad     KERNELBASE!WaitForSingleObjectEx+0x8e
02 (Inline Function) --------`--------     complex_case!std::sys::pal::windows::time::WaitableTimer::wait+0xe
03 (Inline Function) --------`--------     complex_case!std::sys::pal::windows::thread::impl$0::sleep::high_precision_sleep+0x7c
04 (Inline Function) --------`--------     complex_case!std::sys::pal::windows::thread::Thread::sleep+0x89
05 00000099`9d928e10 00007ff6`6b8e44c7     complex_case!std::thread::sleep+0x9d
06 00000099`9d928e80 00007ff6`6b8e452e
complex_case!ZN80_$LT$std..io..Write..write_fmt..Adapter$LT$T$GT$$u20$as$u20$core..fmt..Write$GT$9write_str17hcbe9dfd423357c2fE+0x467
07 00000099`9d928f00 00007ff6`6b8e452e
complex_case!ZN80_$LT$std..io..Write..write_fmt..Adapter$LT$T$GT$$u20$as$u20$core..fmt..Write$GT$9write_str17hcbe9dfd423357c2fE+0x4ce
08 00000099`9d928f80 00007ff6`6b8e452e
complex_case!ZN80_$LT$std..io..Write..write_fmt..Adapter$LT$T$GT$$u20$as$u20$core..fmt..Write$GT$9write_str17hcbe9dfd423357c2fE+0x4ce
09 00000099`9d929000 00007ff6`6b8e452e
complex_case!ZN80_$LT$std..io..Write..write_fmt..Adapter$LT$T$GT$$u20$as$u20$core..fmt..Write$GT$9write_str17hcbe9dfd423357c2fE+0x4ce
0a 00000099`9d929080 00007ff6`6b8e452e
complex_case!ZN80_$LT$std..io..Write..write_fmt..Adapter$LT$T$GT$$u20$as$u20$core..fmt..Write$GT$9write_str17hcbe9dfd423357c2fE+0x4ce
```

```
0b 00000099`9d929100 00007ff6`6b8e452e
complex_case!ZN80_$LT$std..io..Write..write_fmt..Adapter$LT$T$GT$$u20$as$u20$core..fmt..Write$GT$9write_str17hcbe9dfd423357c2fE+0x4ce
0c 00000099`9d929180 00007ff6`6b8e452e
complex_case!ZN80_$LT$std..io..Write..write_fmt..Adapter$LT$T$GT$$u20$as$u20$core..fmt..Write$GT$9write_str17hcbe9dfd423357c2fE+0x4ce
0d 00000099`9d929200 00007ff6`6b8e452e
complex_case!ZN80_$LT$std..io..Write..write_fmt..Adapter$LT$T$GT$$u20$as$u20$core..fmt..Write$GT$9write_str17hcbe9dfd423357c2fE+0x4ce
0e 00000099`9d929280 00007ff6`6b8e452e
complex_case!ZN80_$LT$std..io..Write..write_fmt..Adapter$LT$T$GT$$u20$as$u20$core..fmt..Write$GT$9write_str17hcbe9dfd423357c2fE+0x4ce
0f 00000099`9d929300 00007ff6`6b8e452e
complex_case!ZN80_$LT$std..io..Write..write_fmt..Adapter$LT$T$GT$$u20$as$u20$core..fmt..Write$GT$9write_str17hcbe9dfd423357c2fE+0x4ce
10 00000099`9d929380 00007ff6`6b8e452e
complex_case!ZN80_$LT$std..io..Write..write_fmt..Adapter$LT$T$GT$$u20$as$u20$core..fmt..Write$GT$9write_str17hcbe9dfd423357c2fE+0x4ce
11 00000099`9d929400 00007ff6`6b8e452e
complex_case!ZN80_$LT$std..io..Write..write_fmt..Adapter$LT$T$GT$$u20$as$u20$core..fmt..Write$GT$9write_str17hcbe9dfd423357c2fE+0x4ce
12 00000099`9d929480 00007ff6`6b8e452e
complex_case!ZN80_$LT$std..io..Write..write_fmt..Adapter$LT$T$GT$$u20$as$u20$core..fmt..Write$GT$9write_str17hcbe9dfd423357c2fE+0x4ce
13 00000099`9d929500 00007ff6`6b8e452e
complex_case!ZN80_$LT$std..io..Write..write_fmt..Adapter$LT$T$GT$$u20$as$u20$core..fmt..Write$GT$9write_str17hcbe9dfd423357c2fE+0x4ce
14 00000099`9d929580 00007ff6`6b8e452e
complex_case!ZN80_$LT$std..io..Write..write_fmt..Adapter$LT$T$GT$$u20$as$u20$core..fmt..Write$GT$9write_str17hcbe9dfd423357c2fE+0x4ce
15 00000099`9d929600 00007ff6`6b8e452e
complex_case!ZN80_$LT$std..io..Write..write_fmt..Adapter$LT$T$GT$$u20$as$u20$core..fmt..Write$GT$9write_str17hcbe9dfd423357c2fE+0x4ce
16 00000099`9d929680 00007ff6`6b8e452e
complex_case!ZN80_$LT$std..io..Write..write_fmt..Adapter$LT$T$GT$$u20$as$u20$core..fmt..Write$GT$9write_str17hcbe9dfd423357c2fE+0x4ce
17 00000099`9d929700 00007ff6`6b8e452e
complex_case!ZN80_$LT$std..io..Write..write_fmt..Adapter$LT$T$GT$$u20$as$u20$core..fmt..Write$GT$9write_str17hcbe9dfd423357c2fE+0x4ce
18 00000099`9d929780 00007ff6`6b8e452e
complex_case!ZN80_$LT$std..io..Write..write_fmt..Adapter$LT$T$GT$$u20$as$u20$core..fmt..Write$GT$9write_str17hcbe9dfd423357c2fE+0x4ce
19 00000099`9d929800 00007ff6`6b8e452e
complex_case!ZN80_$LT$std..io..Write..write_fmt..Adapter$LT$T$GT$$u20$as$u20$core..fmt..Write$GT$9write_str17hcbe9dfd423357c2fE+0x4ce
1a 00000099`9d929880 00007ff6`6b8e452e
complex_case!ZN80_$LT$std..io..Write..write_fmt..Adapter$LT$T$GT$$u20$as$u20$core..fmt..Write$GT$9write_str17hcbe9dfd423357c2fE+0x4ce
1b 00000099`9d929900 00007ff6`6b8e452e
complex_case!ZN80_$LT$std..io..Write..write_fmt..Adapter$LT$T$GT$$u20$as$u20$core..fmt..Write$GT$9write_str17hcbe9dfd423357c2fE+0x4ce
1c 00000099`9d929980 00007ff6`6b8e452e
complex_case!ZN80_$LT$std..io..Write..write_fmt..Adapter$LT$T$GT$$u20$as$u20$core..fmt..Write$GT$9write_str17hcbe9dfd423357c2fE+0x4ce
1d 00000099`9d929a00 00007ff6`6b8e452e
complex_case!ZN80_$LT$std..io..Write..write_fmt..Adapter$LT$T$GT$$u20$as$u20$core..fmt..Write$GT$9write_str17hcbe9dfd423357c2fE+0x4ce
1e 00000099`9d929a80 00007ff6`6b8e452e
complex_case!ZN80_$LT$std..io..Write..write_fmt..Adapter$LT$T$GT$$u20$as$u20$core..fmt..Write$GT$9write_str17hcbe9dfd423357c2fE+0x4ce
1f 00000099`9d929b00 00007ff6`6b8e452e
complex_case!ZN80_$LT$std..io..Write..write_fmt..Adapter$LT$T$GT$$u20$as$u20$core..fmt..Write$GT$9write_str17hcbe9dfd423357c2fE+0x4ce

   5  Id: 1fc0.22f4 Suspend: 0 Teb: 00000099`9cffe000 Unfrozen
 # Child-SP          RetAddr           Call Site
00 00000099`9dcff958 00007ffb`e4d110ee ntdll!NtWaitForSingleObject+0x14
01 00000099`9dcff960 00007ff6`6b8e69ad KERNELBASE!WaitForSingleObjectEx+0x8e
02 (Inline Function) --------`-------- complex_case!std::sys::pal::windows::time::WaitableTimer::wait+0xe
03 (Inline Function) --------`-------- complex_case!std::sys::pal::windows::thread::impl$0::sleep::high_precision_sleep+0x7c
04 (Inline Function) --------`-------- complex_case!std::sys::pal::windows::thread::Thread::sleep+0x89
05 00000099`9dcffa00 00007ff6`6b8e3749 complex_case!std::thread::sleep+0x9d
06 00000099`9dcffa70 00007ff6`6b8e1f60 complex_case!ZN3std3sys9backtrace28__rust_begin_short_backtrace17h3e8324a489e54ea5E+0x209
07 00000099`9dcffbd0 00007ff6`6b8ee43d complex_case!ZN3std6thread7Builder15spawn_unchecked17h6e56a25e80bf8795E+0x790
08 (Inline Function) --------`-------- complex_case!alloc::boxed::impl$48::call_once+0xb
09 (Inline Function) --------`-------- complex_case!alloc::boxed::impl$48::call_once+0x16
0a 00000099`9dcffc70 00007ffb`e60853e0 complex_case!std::sys::pal::windows::thread::impl$0::new::thread_start+0x3d
0b 00000099`9dcffcd0 00007ffb`e750485b kernel32!BaseThreadInitThunk+0x10
0c 00000099`9dcffd00 00000000`00000000 ntdll!RtlUserThreadStart+0x2b

WARNING: Teb 6 pointer is NULL - defaulting to 00000000`7ffde000
WARNING: 00000000`7ffde000 does not appear to be a TEB
   6  Id: 1fc0.15dfc Suspend: -1 Teb: 00000000`7ffde000 Unfrozen
WARNING: Thread 15dfc context retrieval failure during dump writing, Win32 error 0n31
WARNING: Teb 6 pointer is NULL - defaulting to 00000000`7ffde000
WARNING: 00000000`7ffde000 does not appear to be a TEB
 # Child-SP          RetAddr           Call Site
00 00000000`00000000 00000000`00000000 0x0te
```

Note: We see an active thread #1 and recursive calls in thread #4.

7.   If we switch to thread #1, we see the current CPU instruction is a jump to itself (*loop*). This behavior also corresponds to CPU consumption:

```
0:000> ~1s
complex_case!ZN3std3sys9backtrace28__rust_begin_short_backtrace17h3e8324a489e54ea5E+0x50:
00007ff6`6b8e3590 jmp     complex_case!ZN3std3sys9backtrace28__rust_begin_short_backtrace17h3e8324a489e54ea5E+0x50 (00007ff6`6b8e3590)
```

```
0:001> !runaway f
 User Mode Time
   Thread       Time
     1:e98      0 days 0:23:43.531
     2:1330     0 days 0:00:47.343
     4:18c8     0 days 0:00:11.640
     5:22f4     0 days 0:00:01.031
     6:15dfc     0 days 0:00:00.015
     3:17f4     0 days 0:00:00.000
     0:474      0 days 0:00:00.000
 Kernel Mode Time
   Thread       Time
     2:1330     0 days 0:02:25.437
     1:e98      0 days 0:00:23.281
     4:18c8     0 days 0:00:13.234
     5:22f4     0 days 0:00:04.187
     0:474      0 days 0:00:00.015
     6:15dfc     0 days 0:00:00.000
     3:17f4     0 days 0:00:00.000
 Elapsed Time
   Thread       Time
     0:474      0 days 0:38:37.499
     1:e98      0 days 0:38:37.208
     2:1330     0 days 0:38:37.208
     3:17f4     0 days 0:38:37.208
     4:18c8     0 days 0:38:37.208
     5:22f4     0 days 0:38:37.208
     6:15dfc     0 days 0:00:00.365
```

Note: We see thread #1 was active more in user mode, but thread #2 was active more in kernel mode. Both were created at the same time, with thread #1 spending more than half of its time looping.

8.   We switch to thread #4 and check its full stack trace:

```
0:001> .kframes ffff
Default stack trace depth is 0n65535 frames
```

```
0:001> ~4s
ntdll!NtWaitForSingleObject+0x14:
00007ffb`e75a4104 ret
```

```
0:004> kL
 # Child-SP          RetAddr               Call Site
00 00000099`9d928d68 00007ffb`e4d110ee     ntdll!NtWaitForSingleObject+0x14
01 00000099`9d928d70 00007ff6`6b8e69ad     KERNELBASE!WaitForSingleObjectEx+0x8e
02 (Inline Function) --------`--------     complex_case!std::sys::pal::windows::time::WaitableTimer::wait+0xe
03 (Inline Function) --------`--------     complex_case!std::sys::pal::windows::thread::impl$0::sleep::high_precision_sleep+0x7c
04 (Inline Function) --------`--------     complex_case!std::sys::pal::windows::thread::Thread::sleep+0x89
05 00000099`9d928e10 00007ff6`6b8e44c7     complex_case!std::thread::sleep+0x9d
06 00000099`9d928e80 00007ff6`6b8e452e
complex_case!ZN80_$LT$std..io..Write..write_fmt..Adapter$LT$T$GT$$u20$as$u20$core..fmt..Write$GT$9write_str17hcbe9dfd423357c2fE+0x467
07 00000099`9d928f00 00007ff6`6b8e452e
complex_case!ZN80_$LT$std..io..Write..write_fmt..Adapter$LT$T$GT$$u20$as$u20$core..fmt..Write$GT$9write_str17hcbe9dfd423357c2fE+0x4ce
08 00000099`9d928f80 00007ff6`6b8e452e
complex_case!ZN80_$LT$std..io..Write..write_fmt..Adapter$LT$T$GT$$u20$as$u20$core..fmt..Write$GT$9write_str17hcbe9dfd423357c2fE+0x4ce
09 00000099`9d929000 00007ff6`6b8e452e
complex_case!ZN80_$LT$std..io..Write..write_fmt..Adapter$LT$T$GT$$u20$as$u20$core..fmt..Write$GT$9write_str17hcbe9dfd423357c2fE+0x4ce
0a 00000099`9d929080 00007ff6`6b8e452e
complex_case!ZN80_$LT$std..io..Write..write_fmt..Adapter$LT$T$GT$$u20$as$u20$core..fmt..Write$GT$9write_str17hcbe9dfd423357c2fE+0x4ce
0b 00000099`9d929100 00007ff6`6b8e452e
complex_case!ZN80_$LT$std..io..Write..write_fmt..Adapter$LT$T$GT$$u20$as$u20$core..fmt..Write$GT$9write_str17hcbe9dfd423357c2fE+0x4ce
0c 00000099`9d929180 00007ff6`6b8e452e
complex_case!ZN80_$LT$std..io..Write..write_fmt..Adapter$LT$T$GT$$u20$as$u20$core..fmt..Write$GT$9write_str17hcbe9dfd423357c2fE+0x4ce
0d 00000099`9d929200 00007ff6`6b8e452e
complex_case!ZN80_$LT$std..io..Write..write_fmt..Adapter$LT$T$GT$$u20$as$u20$core..fmt..Write$GT$9write_str17hcbe9dfd423357c2fE+0x4ce
```

```
0e 00000099`9d929280 00007ff6`6b8e452e
complex_case!ZN80_$LT$std..io..Write..write_fmt..Adapter$LT$T$GT$$u20$as$u20$core..fmt..Write$GT$9write_str17hcbe9dfd423357c2fE+0x4ce
...
...
...
3ac8 00000099`9dafef80 00007ff6`6b8e452e
complex_case!ZN80_$LT$std..io..Write..write_fmt..Adapter$LT$T$GT$$u20$as$u20$core..fmt..Write$GT$9write_str17hcbe9dfd423357c2fE+0x4ce
3ac9 00000099`9daff000 00007ff6`6b8e452e
complex_case!ZN80_$LT$std..io..Write..write_fmt..Adapter$LT$T$GT$$u20$as$u20$core..fmt..Write$GT$9write_str17hcbe9dfd423357c2fE+0x4ce
3aca 00000099`9daff080 00007ff6`6b8e452e
complex_case!ZN80_$LT$std..io..Write..write_fmt..Adapter$LT$T$GT$$u20$as$u20$core..fmt..Write$GT$9write_str17hcbe9dfd423357c2fE+0x4ce
3acb 00000099`9daff100 00007ff6`6b8e452e
complex_case!ZN80_$LT$std..io..Write..write_fmt..Adapter$LT$T$GT$$u20$as$u20$core..fmt..Write$GT$9write_str17hcbe9dfd423357c2fE+0x4ce
3acc 00000099`9daff180 00007ff6`6b8e452e
complex_case!ZN80_$LT$std..io..Write..write_fmt..Adapter$LT$T$GT$$u20$as$u20$core..fmt..Write$GT$9write_str17hcbe9dfd423357c2fE+0x4ce
3acd 00000099`9daff200 00007ff6`6b8e452e
complex_case!ZN80_$LT$std..io..Write..write_fmt..Adapter$LT$T$GT$$u20$as$u20$core..fmt..Write$GT$9write_str17hcbe9dfd423357c2fE+0x4ce
3ace 00000099`9daff280 00007ff6`6b8e452e
complex_case!ZN80_$LT$std..io..Write..write_fmt..Adapter$LT$T$GT$$u20$as$u20$core..fmt..Write$GT$9write_str17hcbe9dfd423357c2fE+0x4ce
3acf 00000099`9daff300 00007ff6`6b8e452e
complex_case!ZN80_$LT$std..io..Write..write_fmt..Adapter$LT$T$GT$$u20$as$u20$core..fmt..Write$GT$9write_str17hcbe9dfd423357c2fE+0x4ce
3ad0 00000099`9daff380 00007ff6`6b8e452e
complex_case!ZN80_$LT$std..io..Write..write_fmt..Adapter$LT$T$GT$$u20$as$u20$core..fmt..Write$GT$9write_str17hcbe9dfd423357c2fE+0x4ce
3ad1 00000099`9daff400 00007ff6`6b8e452e
complex_case!ZN80_$LT$std..io..Write..write_fmt..Adapter$LT$T$GT$$u20$as$u20$core..fmt..Write$GT$9write_str17hcbe9dfd423357c2fE+0x4ce
3ad2 00000099`9daff480 00007ff6`6b8e452e
complex_case!ZN80_$LT$std..io..Write..write_fmt..Adapter$LT$T$GT$$u20$as$u20$core..fmt..Write$GT$9write_str17hcbe9dfd423357c2fE+0x4ce
3ad3 00000099`9daff500 00007ff6`6b8e3597
complex_case!ZN80_$LT$std..io..Write..write_fmt..Adapter$LT$T$GT$$u20$as$u20$core..fmt..Write$GT$9write_str17hcbe9dfd423357c2fE+0x4ce
3ad4 00000099`9daff580 00007ff6`6b8e1f60    complex_case!ZN3std3sys9backtrace28__rust_begin_short_backtrace17h3e8324a489e54ea5E+0x57
3ad5 00000099`9daff6e0 00007ff6`6b8ee43d    complex_case!ZN3std6thread7Builder15spawn_unchecked17h6e56a25e80bf8795E+0x790
3ad6 (Inline Function) --------`--------    complex_case!alloc::boxed::impl$48::call_once+0xb
3ad7 (Inline Function) --------`--------    complex_case!alloc::boxed::impl$48::call_once+0x16
3ad8 00000099`9daff780 00007ffb`e60853e0    complex_case!std::sys::pal::windows::thread::impl$0::new::thread_start+0x3d
3ad9 00000099`9daff7e0 00007ffb`e750485b    kernel32!BaseThreadInitThunk+0x10
3ada 00000099`9daff810 00000000`00000000    ntdll!RtlUserThreadStart+0x2b
```

Note: If we disassemble the caller function code for the return address from the *sleep* function, we see the sleep request is for 100ms, and then the code jumps to the beginning of the caller and calls the *sleep* function again. We see a loop here that also correlates with CPU consumption for this thread:

```
0:004> uf 00007ff6`6b8e44c7
complex_case!ZN80_$LT$std..io..Write..write_fmt..Adapter$LT$T$GT$$u20$as$u20$core..fmt..Write$GT$9write_str17hcbe9dfd423357c2fE+0x450:
00007ff6`6b8e44b0 push    rsi
00007ff6`6b8e44b1 push    rdi
00007ff6`6b8e44b2 sub     rsp,68h
00007ff6`6b8e44b6 movaps  xmmword ptr [rsp+50h],xmm6
00007ff6`6b8e44bb xor     ecx,ecx
00007ff6`6b8e44bd mov     edx,5F5E100h
00007ff6`6b8e44c2 call    complex_case!std::thread::sleep (00007ff6`6b8e6910)
00007ff6`6b8e44c7 lea     rsi,[complex_case!anon.64dd45fe3cdeca5ccf89e11d76a8bc89.11.llvm.805952136491849391 (00007ff6`6b8fe650)]
00007ff6`6b8e44ce mov     qword ptr [rsp+20h],rsi
00007ff6`6b8e44d3 mov     qword ptr [rsp+28h],1
00007ff6`6b8e44dc mov     qword ptr [rsp+30h],8
00007ff6`6b8e44e5 xorps   xmm6,xmm6
00007ff6`6b8e44e8 movups  xmmword ptr [rsp+38h],xmm6
00007ff6`6b8e44ed lea     rcx,[rsp+20h]
00007ff6`6b8e44f2 call    complex_case!std::io::stdio::_print (00007ff6`6b8e8790)
00007ff6`6b8e44f7 lea     rdi,[complex_case!anon.64dd45fe3cdeca5ccf89e11d76a8bc89.13.llvm.805952136491849391 (00007ff6`6b8fe670)]
00007ff6`6b8e44fe mov     qword ptr [rsp+20h],rdi
00007ff6`6b8e4503 mov     qword ptr [rsp+28h],1
00007ff6`6b8e450c mov     qword ptr [rsp+30h],8
00007ff6`6b8e4515 movups  xmmword ptr [rsp+38h],xmm6
00007ff6`6b8e451a lea     rcx,[rsp+20h]
00007ff6`6b8e451f call    complex_case!std::io::stdio::_print (00007ff6`6b8e8790)
00007ff6`6b8e4524 call    complex_case!ZN7crate_b5mod_b4func17h2c4118b811a7b92cE (00007ff6`6b8e4610)
00007ff6`6b8e4529 call
complex_case!ZN80_$LT$std..io..Write..write_fmt..Adapter$LT$T$GT$$u20$as$u20$core..fmt..Write$GT$9write_str17hcbe9dfd423357c2fE+0x450
(00007ff6`6b8e44b0)
00007ff6`6b8e452e mov     qword ptr [rsp+20h],rsi
00007ff6`6b8e4533 mov     qword ptr [rsp+28h],1
00007ff6`6b8e453c mov     qword ptr [rsp+30h],8
00007ff6`6b8e4545 movups  xmmword ptr [rsp+38h],xmm6
00007ff6`6b8e454a lea     rcx,[rsp+20h]
00007ff6`6b8e454f call    complex_case!std::io::stdio::_print (00007ff6`6b8e8790)
00007ff6`6b8e4554 mov     qword ptr [rsp+20h],rdi
00007ff6`6b8e4559 mov     qword ptr [rsp+28h],1
00007ff6`6b8e4562 mov     qword ptr [rsp+30h],8
00007ff6`6b8e456b movups  xmmword ptr [rsp+38h],xmm6
00007ff6`6b8e4570 lea     rcx,[rsp+20h]
```

```
00007ff6`6b8e4575 call    complex_case!std::io::stdio::_print (00007ff6`6b8e8790)
00007ff6`6b8e457a movaps  xmm6,xmmword ptr [rsp+50h]
00007ff6`6b8e457f add     rsp,68h
00007ff6`6b8e4583 pop     rdi
00007ff6`6b8e4584 pop     rsi
00007ff6`6b8e4585 jmp     complex_case!ZN7crate_b5mod_b4func17h2c4118b811a7b92cE (00007ff6`6b8e4610)  Branch

complex_case!ZN7crate_b5mod_b4func17h2c4118b811a7b92cE:
00007ff6`6b8e4610 sub     rsp,68h
00007ff6`6b8e4614 movaps  xmmword ptr [rsp+50h],xmm6
00007ff6`6b8e4619 lea     rax,[complex_case!anon.64dd45fe3cdeca5ccf89e11d76a8bc89.13.llvm.805952136491849391+0x2d0 (00007ff6`6b8fe940)]
00007ff6`6b8e4620 mov     qword ptr [rsp+20h],rax
00007ff6`6b8e4625 mov     qword ptr [rsp+28h],1
00007ff6`6b8e462e mov     qword ptr [rsp+30h],8
00007ff6`6b8e4637 xorps   xmm6,xmm6
00007ff6`6b8e463a movups  xmmword ptr [rsp+38h],xmm6
00007ff6`6b8e463f lea     rcx,[rsp+20h]
00007ff6`6b8e4644 call    complex_case!std::io::stdio::_print (00007ff6`6b8e8790)
00007ff6`6b8e4649 lea     rax,[complex_case!anon.64dd45fe3cdeca5ccf89e11d76a8bc89.13.llvm.805952136491849391+0x298 (00007ff6`6b8fe908)]
00007ff6`6b8e4650 mov     qword ptr [rsp+20h],rax
00007ff6`6b8e4655 mov     qword ptr [rsp+28h],1
00007ff6`6b8e465e mov     qword ptr [rsp+30h],8
00007ff6`6b8e4667 movups  xmmword ptr [rsp+38h],xmm6
00007ff6`6b8e466c lea     rcx,[rsp+20h]
00007ff6`6b8e4671 call    complex_case!std::io::stdio::_print (00007ff6`6b8e8790)
00007ff6`6b8e4676 lea     rax,[complex_case!anon.64dd45fe3cdeca5ccf89e11d76a8bc89.13.llvm.805952136491849391+0x2b0 (00007ff6`6b8fe920)]
00007ff6`6b8e467d mov     qword ptr [rsp+20h],rax
00007ff6`6b8e4682 mov     qword ptr [rsp+28h],1
00007ff6`6b8e468b mov     qword ptr [rsp+30h],8
00007ff6`6b8e4694 movups  xmmword ptr [rsp+38h],xmm6
00007ff6`6b8e4699 lea     rcx,[rsp+20h]
00007ff6`6b8e469e call    complex_case!std::io::stdio::_print (00007ff6`6b8e8790)
00007ff6`6b8e46a3 call    complex_case!ZN7crate_c6mod_ca4func17h8bb43d8048892409E (00007ff6`6b8e46c0)
00007ff6`6b8e46a8 movaps  xmm6,xmmword ptr [rsp+50h]
00007ff6`6b8e46ad add     rsp,68h
00007ff6`6b8e46b1 jmp     complex_case!ZN7crate_c6mod_cb4func17h8ed23eaf84b3cc6bE (00007ff6`6b8e4700)  Branch

complex_case!ZN7crate_c6mod_cb4func17h8ed23eaf84b3cc6bE:
00007ff6`6b8e4700 sub     rsp,58h
00007ff6`6b8e4704 lea     rax,[complex_case!anon.64dd45fe3cdeca5ccf89e11d76a8bc89.13.llvm.805952136491849391+0x310 (00007ff6`6b8fe980)]
00007ff6`6b8e470b mov     qword ptr [rsp+28h],rax
00007ff6`6b8e4710 mov     qword ptr [rsp+30h],1
00007ff6`6b8e4719 mov     qword ptr [rsp+38h],8
00007ff6`6b8e4722 xorps   xmm0,xmm0
00007ff6`6b8e4725 movups  xmmword ptr [rsp+40h],xmm0
00007ff6`6b8e472a lea     rcx,[rsp+28h]
00007ff6`6b8e472f call    complex_case!std::io::stdio::_print (00007ff6`6b8e8790)
00007ff6`6b8e4734 nop
00007ff6`6b8e4735 add     rsp,58h
00007ff6`6b8e4739 ret
```

```
0:004> ? 5F5E100 / 0n1000000
Evaluate expression: 100 = 00000000`00000064
```

```
0:004> !runaway f
 User Mode Time
  Thread       Time
     1:e98        0 days 0:23:43.531
     2:1330       0 days 0:00:47.343
     4:18c8       0 days 0:00:11.640
     5:22f4       0 days 0:00:01.031
     6:15dfc       0 days 0:00:00.015
     3:17f4       0 days 0:00:00.000
     0:474        0 days 0:00:00.000
 Kernel Mode Time
  Thread       Time
     2:1330       0 days 0:02:25.437
     1:e98        0 days 0:00:23.281
     4:18c8       0 days 0:00:13.234
     5:22f4       0 days 0:00:04.187
     0:474        0 days 0:00:00.015
     6:15dfc       0 days 0:00:00.000
     3:17f4       0 days 0:00:00.000
 Elapsed Time
```

```
Thread        Time
  0:474       0 days 0:38:37.499
  1:e98       0 days 0:38:37.208
  2:1330      0 days 0:38:37.208
  3:17f4      0 days 0:38:37.208
  4:18c8      0 days 0:38:37.208
  5:22f4      0 days 0:38:37.208
  6:15dfc      0 days 0:00:00.365
```

Note: Eventually, given enough time this thread would hit a stack region boundary (stack overflow).

9.   Since we suspect a memory leak based on Task Manager data, we check the process heap stats:

```
0:004> !heap -s

*************************************************************************************
                            NT HEAP STATS BELOW
*************************************************************************************
LFH Key                   : 0xbbcaa2c8d20abf8c
Termination on corruption : ENABLED
          Heap      Flags   Reserv  Commit  Virt   Free  List   UCR  Virt  Lock  Fast
                             (k)     (k)     (k)    (k) length      blocks cont. heap
-----------------------------------------------------------------------------------
00000219443a0000 00000002    4112    3912    4084    363    20     3    1     1   LFH
00000219441a0000 00008000      64       4      64      2     1     1    0     0
-----------------------------------------------------------------------------------
```

Note: We don't see much heap size increase but check the number of blocks just in case of small allocations.

```
0:004> !heap -s -h 0000219443a0000
Walking the heap 00000219443a0000 ...
 0: Heap 00000219443a0000
   Flags            00000002 - HEAP_GROWABLE
   Reserved memory in segments           4084 (k)
   Commited memory in segments           3904 (k)
   Virtual bytes (correction for large UCR) 4084 (k)
   Free space                             363 (k) (20 blocks)
   External fragmentation        9% (20 free blocks)
   Virtual address fragmentation   4% (3 uncommited ranges)
   Virtual blocks  1 - total 114692 KBytes
   Lock contention 1
   Segments        1

   Low fragmentation heap    0000021944250000
       Metadata usage      6144 bytes
       Statistics:
           Segments created        78
           Segments deleted         9
           Segments reused          0
       Block cache:
            3:        1024 bytes (     2,       0)
            4:        2048 bytes (     4,       0)
            5:        4096 bytes (    18,       1)
            6:        8192 bytes (    10,       1)
            7:       16384 bytes (     9,       0)
            8:       32768 bytes (     8,       0)
            9:       65536 bytes (     8,       0)
```

131

```
      10:          131072 bytes (     12,       0)
```

```
        Buckets info:
   Size   Blocks  Seg  Empty  Aff    Distribution
  -------------------------------------------------
     32      29    1      0    0  (1-29,0-0,0-0,0-0)
     48      19    1      0    0  (1-19,0-0,0-0,0-0)
     64   41684   62      0    0  (62-41684,0-0,0-0,0-0)
     80      24    1      0    0  (1-24,0-0,0-0,0-0)
     96      20    1      0    0  (1-20,0-0,0-0,0-0)
    128      31    1      1    0  (1-31,0-0,0-0,0-0)
    144      13    1      1    0  (1-13,0-0,0-0,0-0)
   2000       8    1      1    0  (1-8,0-0,0-0,0-0)
  -------------------------------------------------
```

Range (bytes)	Default heap Busy	Default heap Free	Front heap Busy	Front heap Free	Unused bytes Total	Unused bytes Average
0 - 1024	125	9	41606	214	501254	12
1024 - 2048	19	1	0	8	275	14
2048 - 3072	1	1	0	0	1	1
3072 - 4096	1	1	0	0	18	18
4096 - 5120	3	1	0	0	48	16
7168 - 8192	1	1	0	0	1	1
8192 - 9216	1	0	0	0	16	16
16384 - 17408	0	1	0	0	0	0
35840 - 36864	0	1	0	0	0	0
40960 - 41984	0	1	0	0	0	0
48128 - 49152	0	1	0	0	0	0
89088 - 90112	0	1	0	0	0	0
114688 - 115712	0	1	0	0	0	0
523264 - 524288	2	0	0	0	16	8
Total	153	20	41606	222	501629	12

Note: We see more than 40,000 blocks of 64 bytes each. If such a problem occurs, one of the troubleshooting steps is to enable **user mode stack trace database** to include all stack traces from threads that were using heap allocation functions. It is usually done by using *gflags.exe* from Debugging Tools for Windows. This procedure had already been done for this application and we look at the corresponding process memory dump later. For now, we list the blocks and dump their content (we break the output after a while):

```
0:004> !heap -s -h 0000219443a0000 -d 0n64

0: Heap 00000219443a0000
  Flags          00000002 - HEAP_GROWABLE
  Low fragmentation heap   0000021944250000
    Metadata usage      6144 bytes
    Statistics:
        Segments created        78
        Segments deleted         9
        Segments reused          0
    Block cache:
            3:          1024 bytes (      2,       0)
            4:          2048 bytes (      4,       0)
            5:          4096 bytes (     18,       1)
            6:          8192 bytes (     10,       1)
            7:         16384 bytes (      9,       0)
            8:         32768 bytes (      8,       0)
            9:         65536 bytes (      8,       0)
           10:        131072 bytes (     12,       0)
```

132

```
       Buckets info:
  Size   Blocks  Seg  Empty  Aff   Distribution
  -----------------------------------------------
    32      29     1     0    0   (1-29,0-0,0-0,0-0)
    48      19     1     0    0   (1-19,0-0,0-0,0-0)
    64   41684    62     0    0   (62-41684,0-0,0-0,0-0)
    80      24     1     0    0   (1-24,0-0,0-0,0-0)
    96      20     1     0    0   (1-20,0-0,0-0,0-0)
   128      31     1     0    0   (1-31,0-0,0-0,0-0)
   144      13     1     0    0   (1-13,0-0,0-0,0-0)
  2000       8     1     0    0   (1-8,0-0,0-0,0-0)
  -----------------------------------------------
0: Segment 00000219443a0000
   Signature:                 0xffeeffee
   Flags:                     0x00000000
   Range:                     0x00000219443a0000 - 0x000002194449f000
   Reserved memory (KBytes):  1020
   Committed memory (KBytes): 996
   LargestUnCommittedRange:   0x0000000000000000
   Number of pages:           255
   Uncommitted pages:         6
   Uncommited ranges:         1
Sub-segment 00000219443a5180
   User blocks:               0x00000219443a4950
   Block size:                0x40
   Block count:               30
   Free blocks:               0
   Size index:                3
   Affinity index:            0
   Lock mask:                 0x1
   Flags:                     0x0
00000219443a4990 00000219443a49a0 00000219443a0000 00000219443a5180    40    -    10  LFH;busy
00000219443a49d0 00000219443a49e0 00000219443a0000 00000219443a5180    40    -    10  LFH;busy
00000219443a4a10 00000219443a4a20 00000219443a0000 00000219443a5180    40    -    10  LFH;busy
00000219443a4a50 00000219443a4a60 00000219443a0000 00000219443a5180    40    -    10  LFH;busy
00000219443a4a90 00000219443a4aa0 00000219443a0000 00000219443a5180    40    -    10  LFH;busy
00000219443a4ad0 00000219443a4ae0 00000219443a0000 00000219443a5180    40    -    10  LFH;busy
00000219443a4b10 00000219443a4b20 00000219443a0000 00000219443a5180    40    -    10  LFH;busy
00000219443a4b50 00000219443a4b60 00000219443a0000 00000219443a5180    40    -    10  LFH;busy
00000219443a4b90 00000219443a4ba0 00000219443a0000 00000219443a5180    40    -    10  LFH;busy
00000219443a4bd0 00000219443a4be0 00000219443a0000 00000219443a5180    40    -    10  LFH;busy
00000219443a4c10 00000219443a4c20 00000219443a0000 00000219443a5180    40    -    10  LFH;busy
00000219443a4c50 00000219443a4c60 00000219443a0000 00000219443a5180    40    -    10  LFH;busy
00000219443a4c90 00000219443a4ca0 00000219443a0000 00000219443a5180    40    -    10  LFH;busy
00000219443a4cd0 00000219443a4ce0 00000219443a0000 00000219443a5180    40    -    10  LFH;busy
00000219443a4d10 00000219443a4d20 00000219443a0000 00000219443a5180    40    -    10  LFH;busy
00000219443a4d50 00000219443a4d60 00000219443a0000 00000219443a5180    40    -    10  LFH;busy
00000219443a4d90 00000219443a4da0 00000219443a0000 00000219443a5180    40    -    10  LFH;busy
00000219443a4dd0 00000219443a4de0 00000219443a0000 00000219443a5180    40    -    10  LFH;busy
00000219443a4e10 00000219443a4e20 00000219443a0000 00000219443a5180    40    -    10  LFH;busy
00000219443a4e50 00000219443a4e60 00000219443a0000 00000219443a5180    40    -    10  LFH;busy
00000219443a4e90 00000219443a4ea0 00000219443a0000 00000219443a5180    40    -    10  LFH;busy
00000219443a4ed0 00000219443a4ee0 00000219443a0000 00000219443a5180    40    -    10  LFH;busy
00000219443a4f10 00000219443a4f20 00000219443a0000 00000219443a5180    40    -    10  LFH;busy
00000219443a4f50 00000219443a4f60 00000219443a0000 00000219443a5180    40    -    10  LFH;busy
00000219443a4f90 00000219443a4fa0 00000219443a0000 00000219443a5180    40    -    10  LFH;busy
00000219443a4fd0 00000219443a4fe0 00000219443a0000 00000219443a5180    40    -    10  LFH;busy
00000219443a5010 00000219443a5020 00000219443a0000 00000219443a5180    40    -    10  LFH;busy
00000219443a5050 00000219443a5060 00000219443a0000 00000219443a5180    40    -    10  LFH;busy
00000219443a5090 00000219443a50a0 00000219443a0000 00000219443a5180    40    -    10  LFH;busy
00000219443a50d0 00000219443a50e0 00000219443a0000 00000219443a5180    40    -    10  LFH;busy
Sub-segment 00000219443a51c0
   User blocks:               0x00000219443a5560
   Block size:                0x40
   Block count:               62
   Free blocks:               0
   Size index:                3
   Affinity index:            0
   Lock mask:                 0x1
   Flags:                     0x0
00000219443a55a0 00000219443a55b0 00000219443a0000 00000219443a51c0    40    -     8  LFH;busy
00000219443a55e0 00000219443a55f0 00000219443a0000 00000219443a51c0    40    -    10  LFH;busy
00000219443a5620 00000219443a5630 00000219443a0000 00000219443a51c0    40    -    10  LFH;busy
00000219443a5660 00000219443a5670 00000219443a0000 00000219443a51c0    40    -     8  LFH;busy
```

```
00000219443a56a0  00000219443a56b0  00000219443a0000  00000219443a51c0  40  -  10  LFH;busy
00000219443a56e0  00000219443a56f0  00000219443a0000  00000219443a51c0  40  -  10  LFH;busy
00000219443a5720  00000219443a5730  00000219443a0000  00000219443a51c0  40  -  10  LFH;busy
00000219443a5760  00000219443a5770  00000219443a0000  00000219443a51c0  40  -  17  LFH;busy
00000219443a57a0  00000219443a57b0  00000219443a0000  00000219443a51c0  40  -   8  LFH;busy
00000219443a57e0  00000219443a57f0  00000219443a0000  00000219443a51c0  40  -  10  LFH;busy
00000219443a5820  00000219443a5830  00000219443a0000  00000219443a51c0  40  -   8  LFH;busy
...
...
...
0000021944471200  0000021944471210  00000219443a0000  00000219443a9f50  40  -  10  LFH;busy
0000021944471240  0000021944471250  00000219443a0000  00000219443a9f50  40  -   8  LFH;busy
0000021944471280  0000021944471290  00000219443a0000  00000219443a9f50  40  -   8  LFH;busy
00000219444712c0  00000219444712d0  00000219443a0000  00000219443a9f50  40  -   8  LFH;busy
0000021944471300  0000021944471310  00000219443a0000  00000219443a9f50  40  -  10  LFH;busy
0000021944471340  0000021944471350  00000219443a0000  00000219443a9f50  40  -   8  LFH;busy
0000021944471380  0000021944471390  00000219443a0000  00000219443a9f50  40  -  10  LFH;busy
00000219444713c0  00000219444713d0  00000219443a0000  00000219443a9f50  40  -  10  LFH;busy
0000021944471400  0000021944471410  00000219443a0000  00000219443a9f50  40  -   8  LFH;busy
0000021944471440  0000021944471450  00000219443a0000  00000219443a9f50  40  -   8  LFH;busy
0000021944471480  0000021944471490  00000219443a0000  00000219443a9f50  40  -   8  LFH;busy
...
...
...

0:004> dp 0000021944471480
00000219`44471480  00000219`44440600  88048c00`1030cec4
00000219`44471490  00000000`00000001  00000000`00000001
00000219`444714a0  00000000`00000002  00000000`00000000
00000219`444714b0  00000000`00000000  00000000`0000263c
00000219`444714c0  00000219`44440400  88048d19`103ccec0
00000219`444714d0  00000000`00000001  00000000`00000001
00000219`444714e0  00000000`00000002  00000000`00000000
00000219`444714f0  00000000`00000000  00000000`00002654

0:004> dc 0000021944471440
00000219`44471440  00003100 00000000 1034cec8 88048b19  .1........4.....
00000219`44471450  00000001 00000000 00000001 00000000  ................
00000219`44471460  00000002 00000000 00000000 00000000  ................
00000219`44471470  00000000 00000000 00002653 00000000  ........S&......
00000219`44471480  44440600 00000219 1030cec4 88048c00  ..DD......0.....
00000219`44471490  00000001 00000000 00000001 00000000  ................
00000219`444714a0  00000002 00000000 00000000 00000000  ................
00000219`444714b0  00000000 00000000 0000263c 00000000  ........<&......

0:004> dps 0000021944471400
00000219`44471400  00000219`4443fc90
00000219`44471408  88048a19`1048cecc
00000219`44471410  00000000`00000001
00000219`44471418  00000000`00000001
00000219`44471420  00000000`00000002
00000219`44471428  00000000`00000000
00000219`44471430  00000000`00000000
00000219`44471438  00000000`00002643
00000219`44471440  00000000`00003100
00000219`44471448  88048b19`1034cec8
00000219`44471450  00000000`00000001
00000219`44471458  00000000`00000001
00000219`44471460  00000000`00000002
00000219`44471468  00000000`00000000
00000219`44471470  00000000`00000000
00000219`44471478  00000000`00002653
```

Note: We don't see any character or symbolic data. But we see the increasing values inside that may correlate with the observed hande leak:

```
0:004> !handle 263c
Handle 000000000000263c
  Type                Thread

0:004> !handle 2653
Handle 0000000000002653
  Type                Thread

0:004> !handle 2643
Handle 0000000000002643
  Type                Thread
```

10.   We also check the handle table:

```
0:004> !handle
Handle 0000000000000004
  Type                Event
Handle 0000000000000008
  Type                Event
Handle 000000000000000c
  Type                Event
Handle 0000000000000010
  Type                WaitCompletionPacket
Handle 0000000000000014
  Type                IoCompletion
Handle 0000000000000018
  Type                TpWorkerFactory
Handle 000000000000001c
  Type                IRTimer
Handle 0000000000000020
  Type                WaitCompletionPacket
Handle 0000000000000024
  Type                IRTimer
Handle 0000000000000028
  Type                WaitCompletionPacket
Handle 000000000000002c
  Type
Handle 0000000000000030
  Type
Handle 0000000000000034
  Type
Handle 0000000000000038
  Type
Handle 000000000000003c
  Type                Directory
Handle 0000000000000040
  Type                Event
Handle 0000000000000044
  Type                Event
Handle 0000000000000048
  Type                File
Handle 000000000000004c
  Type                Semaphore
Handle 0000000000000050
  Type                File
```

```
Handle 0000000000000054
    Type                ALPC Port
Handle 0000000000000058
    Type                File
Handle 000000000000005c
    Type                File
Handle 0000000000000060
    Type                File
Handle 0000000000000064
    Type                File
Handle 0000000000000068
    Type
Handle 000000000000006c
    Type                Mutant
Handle 0000000000000070
    Type                Directory
Handle 0000000000000074
    Type                Semaphore
Handle 0000000000000078
    Type
Handle 000000000000007c
    Type
Handle 0000000000000080
    Type                Key
Handle 0000000000000084
    Type                IoCompletion
Handle 0000000000000088
    Type                TpWorkerFactory
Handle 000000000000008c
    Type                IRTimer
Handle 0000000000000090
    Type                WaitCompletionPacket
Handle 0000000000000094
    Type                IRTimer
Handle 0000000000000098
    Type                WaitCompletionPacket
Handle 000000000000009c
    Type                Thread
Handle 00000000000000a0
    Type                Thread
Handle 00000000000000a4
    Type                Key
Handle 00000000000000a8
    Type                Thread
Handle 00000000000000ac
    Type                Thread
Handle 00000000000000b0
    Type                Thread
Handle 00000000000000b4
    Type                Thread
Handle 00000000000000b8
    Type                Thread
Handle 00000000000000bc
    Type                Thread
Handle 00000000000000c0
    Type                Thread
Handle 00000000000000c4
    Type                Thread
Handle 00000000000000c8
```

```
   Type              Thread
Handle 00000000000000cc
   Type              Thread
Handle 00000000000000d0
   Type              Thread
Handle 00000000000000d4
   Type              Thread
Handle 00000000000000d8
   Type              Thread
...
...
...
Handle 0000000000014634
   Type              Thread
Handle 0000000000014638
   Type              Thread
Handle 000000000001463c
   Type              Thread
Handle 0000000000014644
   Type              Thread
Handle 0000000000014648
   Type              Thread
Handle 000000000001464c
   Type              Thread
Handle 0000000000014650
   Type              Thread
Handle 0000000000014654
   Type              Thread
Handle 0000000000014658
   Type              IRTimer
20804 Handles
Type                 Count
None                 14
Event                5
File                 6
Directory            2
Mutant               1
Semaphore            2
Key                  2
Thread               20762
IoCompletion         2
TpWorkerFactory      2
ALPC Port            1
WaitCompletionPacket 5
```

Note: We have a similar number of thread handles as the total number of handles in Task Manager. To trace handle creation to modules and functions, we can enable Application Verifier in *gflags.exe*. This procedure had already been done for this application and we look at the corresponding process memory dump later.

11.   We may think we identified all the leaks, but we may recall that the app was sequentially doubling its memory consumption after periods of the same memory size. Also, the combined size of 64-byte allocations is far less than the overall size of the heap. By looking at virtual memory allocation stats, we identify the large heap block allocated via *VirtualAlloc*:

```
0:004> !address -summary
```

Mapping file section regions...
Mapping module regions...
Mapping PEB regions...
Mapping TEB and stack regions...
WARNING: Thread 15dfc context retrieval failure during dump writing, Win32 error 0n31
WARNING: Teb 6 pointer is NULL - defaulting to 00000000`7ffde000
WARNING: 00000000`7ffde000 does not appear to be a TEB
WARNING: Teb 6 pointer is NULL - defaulting to 00000000`7ffde000
WARNING: 00000000`7ffde000 does not appear to be a TEB
Mapping heap regions...
Mapping page heap regions...
Mapping other regions...
Mapping stack trace database regions...
Mapping activation context regions...

--- Usage Summary ---------------	RgnCount	----------- Total Size --------	%ofBusy	%ofTotal
Free	27	7ffe`f54c3000 (127.996 TB)		100.00%
<unknown>	19	1`0242e000 (4.035 GB)	96.84%	0.00%
Heap	36	0`07423000 (116.137 MB)	2.72%	0.00%
Stack	18	0`00b00000 (11.000 MB)	0.26%	0.00%
Image	34	0`007a6000 (7.648 MB)	0.18%	0.00%
Other	4	0`00029000 (164.000 kB)	0.00%	0.00%
TEB	6	0`0000c000 (48.000 kB)	0.00%	0.00%
PEB	1	0`00001000 (4.000 kB)	0.00%	0.00%

--- Type Summary (for busy) ------	RgnCount	----------- Total Size --------	%ofBusy	%ofTotal
MEM_PRIVATE	71	1`0a13b000 (4.157 GB)	99.77%	0.00%
MEM_IMAGE	34	0`007a6000 (7.648 MB)	0.18%	0.00%
MEM_MAPPED	13	0`0024c000 (2.297 MB)	0.05%	0.00%

--- State Summary ---------------	RgnCount	----------- Total Size --------	%ofBusy	%ofTotal
MEM_FREE	27	7ffe`f54c3000 (127.996 TB)		100.00%
MEM_RESERVE	20	1`02c46000 (4.043 GB)	97.03%	0.00%
MEM_COMMIT	98	0`07ee7000 (126.902 MB)	2.97%	0.00%

--- Protect Summary (for commit) -	RgnCount	----------- Total Size --------	%ofBusy	%ofTotal
PAGE_READWRITE	40	0`075e2000 (117.883 MB)	2.76%	0.00%
PAGE_READONLY	31	0`004b9000 (4.723 MB)	0.11%	0.00%
PAGE_EXECUTE_READ	6	0`00418000 (4.094 MB)	0.10%	0.00%
PAGE_READWRITE	PAGE_GUARD	6	0`00024000 (144.000 kB)	0.00%	0.00%
PAGE_NOACCESS	12	0`0000c000 (48.000 kB)	0.00%	0.00%
PAGE_WRITECOPY	3	0`00004000 (16.000 kB)	0.00%	0.00%

--- Largest Region by Usage -----------	Base Address --------	Region Size ----------
Free	219`5244f000	7ddb`001f1000 (125.855 TB)
<unknown>	7ff4`52740000	1`00020000 (4.000 GB)
Heap	219`4b44d000	0`07001000 (112.004 MB)
Stack	99`9d300000	0`001f8000 (1.969 MB)
Image	7ffb`e4e41000	0`001b6000 (1.711 MB)
Other	219`441c0000	0`0001f000 (124.000 kB)
TEB	99`9cfee000	0`00002000 (8.000 kB)
PEB	99`9cfed000	0`00001000 (4.000 kB)

Note: We can also find it by filtering larger and larger busy blocks:

```
0:004> !heap -flt r 0n100000 0n1000000
    _HEAP @ 219443a0000
            HEAP_ENTRY Size Prev Flags           UserPtr UserSize - state
        00000219445e4010 1c07 0000  [00]  00000219445e4020   1c060 - (free)
        0000021944688010 c001 1c07  [00]  0000021944688020   c0000 - (busy)
        unknown!printable
    _HEAP @ 219441a0000

0:004> !heap -flt r 0n100000 0n10000000
    _HEAP @ 219443a0000
            HEAP_ENTRY Size Prev Flags           UserPtr UserSize - state
        00000219445e4010 1c07 0000  [00]  00000219445e4020   1c060 - (free)
        0000021944688010 c001 1c07  [00]  0000021944688020   c0000 - (busy)
        unknown!printable
    _HEAP @ 219441a0000

0:004> !heap -flt r 0n100000 0n100000000
    _HEAP @ 219443a0000
            HEAP_ENTRY Size Prev Flags           UserPtr UserSize - state
        00000219445e4010 1c07 0000  [00]  00000219445e4020   1c060 - (free)
        0000021944688010 c001 1c07  [00]  0000021944688020   c0000 - (busy)
        unknown!printable
    _HEAP @ 219441a0000

0:004> !heap -flt r 0n100000 0n1000000000
    _HEAP @ 219443a0000
            HEAP_ENTRY Size Prev Flags           UserPtr UserSize - state
        00000219445e4010 1c07 0000  [00]  00000219445e4020   1c060 - (free)
        0000021944688010 c001 1c07  [00]  0000021944688020   c0000 - (busy)
        unknown!printable
        000002194b44d030 700100 c001  [00]   000002194b44d040   7000000 - (busy VirtualAlloc)
    _HEAP @ 219441a0000

0:004> dc 000002194b44d030 L100
00000219`4b44d030  00000000 00000000 b1f0ddd0 04000000  ...............
00000219`4b44d040  00000001 00000000 00000048 00000065  ........H...e...
00000219`4b44d050  0000006c 0000006c 0000006f 00000020  l...l...o... ...
00000219`4b44d060  0000004c 00000065 00000061 0000006b  L...e...a...k...
00000219`4b44d070  00000021 00000000 00000002 00000000  !...............
00000219`4b44d080  00000048 00000065 0000006c 0000006c  H...e...l...l...
00000219`4b44d090  0000006f 00000020 0000004c 00000065  o... ...L...e...
00000219`4b44d0a0  00000061 0000006b 00000021 00000000  a...k...!.......
00000219`4b44d0b0  00000003 00000000 00000048 00000065  ........H...e...
00000219`4b44d0c0  0000006c 0000006c 0000006f 00000020  l...l...o... ...
00000219`4b44d0d0  0000004c 00000065 00000061 0000006b  L...e...a...k...
00000219`4b44d0e0  00000021 00000000 00000004 00000000  !...............
00000219`4b44d0f0  00000048 00000065 0000006c 0000006c  H...e...l...l...
00000219`4b44d100  0000006f 00000020 0000004c 00000065  o... ...L...e...
00000219`4b44d110  00000061 0000006b 00000021 00000000  a...k...!.......
00000219`4b44d120  00000005 00000000 00000048 00000065  ........H...e...
00000219`4b44d130  0000006c 0000006c 0000006f 00000020  l...l...o... ...
00000219`4b44d140  0000004c 00000065 00000061 0000006b  L...e...a...k...
00000219`4b44d150  00000021 00000000 00000006 00000000  !...............
00000219`4b44d160  00000048 00000065 0000006c 0000006c  H...e...l...l...
00000219`4b44d170  0000006f 00000020 0000004c 00000065  o... ...L...e...
00000219`4b44d180  00000061 0000006b 00000021 00000000  a...k...!.......
00000219`4b44d190  00000007 00000000 00000048 00000065  ........H...e...
00000219`4b44d1a0  0000006c 0000006c 0000006f 00000020  l...l...o... ...
00000219`4b44d1b0  0000004c 00000065 00000061 0000006b  L...e...a...k...
```

```
00000219`4b44d1c0  00000021 00000000 00000008 00000000  !...............
00000219`4b44d1d0  00000048 00000065 0000006c 0000006c  H...e...l...l...
00000219`4b44d1e0  0000006f 00000020 0000004c 00000065  o... ...L...e...
00000219`4b44d1f0  00000061 0000006b 00000021 00000000  a...k...!.......
00000219`4b44d200  00000009 00000000 00000048 00000065  .......H...e...
00000219`4b44d210  0000006c 0000006c 0000006f 00000020  l...l...o... ...
00000219`4b44d220  0000004c 00000065 00000061 0000006b  L...e...a...k...
00000219`4b44d230  00000021 00000000 0000000a 00000000  !...............
00000219`4b44d240  00000048 00000065 0000006c 0000006c  H...e...l...l...
00000219`4b44d250  0000006f 00000020 0000004c 00000065  o... ...L...e...
00000219`4b44d260  00000061 0000006b 00000021 00000000  a...k...!.......
00000219`4b44d270  0000000b 00000000 00000048 00000065  .......H...e...
00000219`4b44d280  0000006c 0000006c 0000006f 00000020  l...l...o... ...
00000219`4b44d290  0000004c 00000065 00000061 0000006b  L...e...a...k...
00000219`4b44d2a0  00000021 00000000 0000000c 00000000  !...............
00000219`4b44d2b0  00000048 00000065 0000006c 0000006c  H...e...l...l...
00000219`4b44d2c0  0000006f 00000020 0000004c 00000065  o... ...L...e...
00000219`4b44d2d0  00000061 0000006b 00000021 00000000  a...k...!.......
00000219`4b44d2e0  0000000d 00000000 00000048 00000065  .......H...e...
00000219`4b44d2f0  0000006c 0000006c 0000006f 00000020  l...l...o... ...
00000219`4b44d300  0000004c 00000065 00000061 0000006b  L...e...a...k...
00000219`4b44d310  00000021 00000000 0000000e 00000000  !...............
00000219`4b44d320  00000048 00000065 0000006c 0000006c  H...e...l...l...
00000219`4b44d330  0000006f 00000020 0000004c 00000065  o... ...L...e...
00000219`4b44d340  00000061 0000006b 00000021 00000000  a...k...!.......
00000219`4b44d350  0000000f 00000000 00000048 00000065  .......H...e...
00000219`4b44d360  0000006c 0000006c 0000006f 00000020  l...l...o... ...
00000219`4b44d370  0000004c 00000065 00000061 0000006b  L...e...a...k...
00000219`4b44d380  00000021 00000000 00000010 00000000  !...............
00000219`4b44d390  00000048 00000065 0000006c 0000006c  H...e...l...l...
00000219`4b44d3a0  0000006f 00000020 0000004c 00000065  o... ...L...e...
00000219`4b44d3b0  00000061 0000006b 00000021 00000000  a...k...!.......
00000219`4b44d3c0  00000011 00000000 00000048 00000065  .......H...e...
00000219`4b44d3d0  0000006c 0000006c 0000006f 00000020  l...l...o... ...
00000219`4b44d3e0  0000004c 00000065 00000061 0000006b  L...e...a...k...
00000219`4b44d3f0  00000021 00000000 00000012 00000000  !...............
00000219`4b44d400  00000048 00000065 0000006c 0000006c  H...e...l...l...
00000219`4b44d410  0000006f 00000020 0000004c 00000065  o... ...L...e...
00000219`4b44d420  00000061 0000006b 00000021 00000000  a...k...!.......
```

12.   We applied x64 *gflags.exe* settings to our executable, rerun it for a few minutes, and then saved a new memory dump using Task Manager (don't forget to clear settings after troubleshooting):

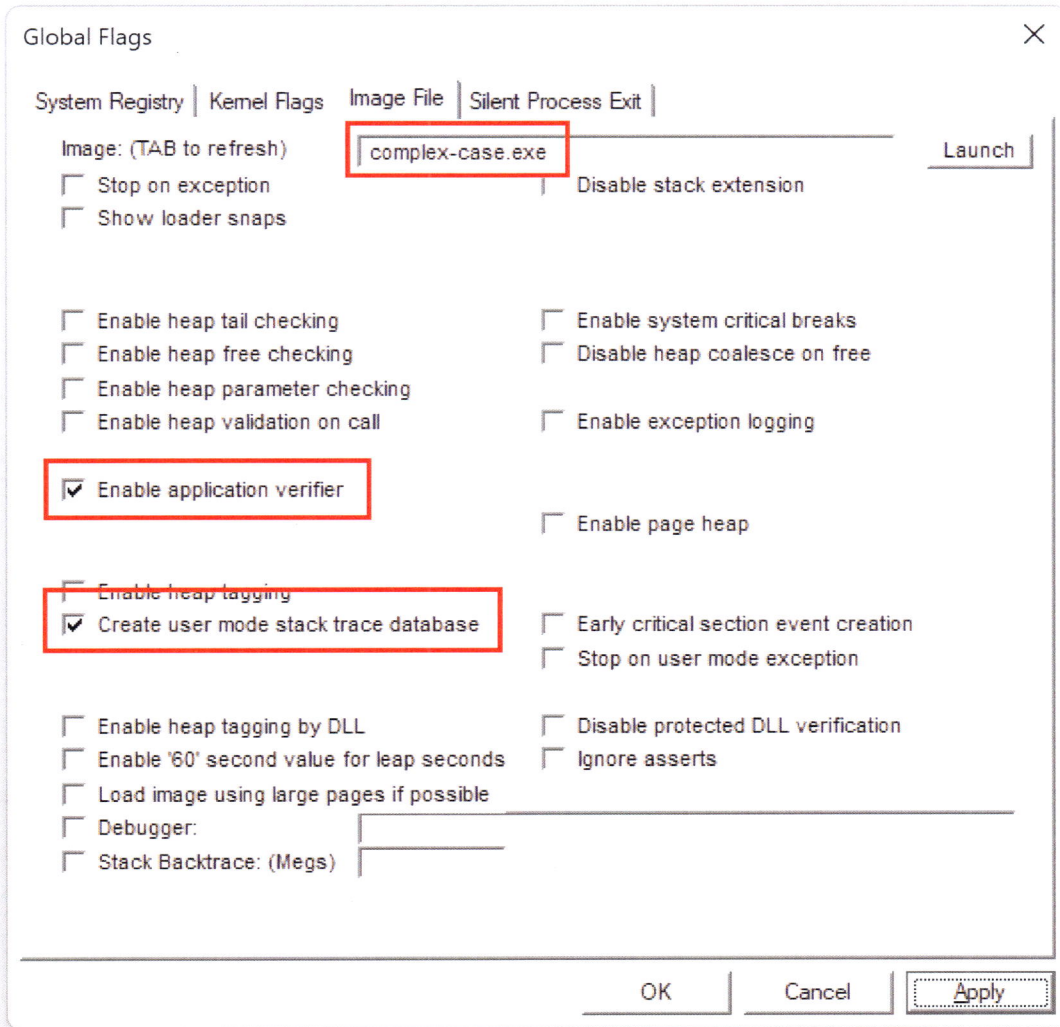

Global Flags

System Registry | Kernel Flags | Image File | Silent Process Exit

Image: (TAB to refresh)   complex-case.exe   Launch

☐ Stop on exception   ☐ Disable stack extension
☐ Show loader snaps

☐ Enable heap tail checking   ☐ Enable system critical breaks
☐ Enable heap free checking   ☐ Disable heap coalesce on free
☐ Enable heap parameter checking
☐ Enable heap validation on call   ☐ Enable exception logging

☑ Enable application verifier

                                 ☐ Enable page heap

☐ Enable heap tagging
☑ Create user mode stack trace database   ☐ Early critical section event creation
                                 ☐ Stop on user mode exception

☐ Enable heap tagging by DLL   ☐ Disable protected DLL verification
☐ Enable '60' second value for leap seconds   ☐ Ignore asserts
☐ Load image using large pages if possible
☐ Debugger:
☐ Stack Backtrace: (Megs)

                    OK   Cancel   Apply

13.   Launch another instance of WinDbg.

14.   Open \ARWMDA-Dumps\Process\complex-case2.DMP.

15.   We get the dump file loaded:

```
Microsoft (R) Windows Debugger Version 10.0.27725.1000 AMD64
Copyright (c) Microsoft Corporation. All rights reserved.


Loading Dump File [C:\ARWMDA-Dumps\Process\complex-case2.DMP]
User Mini Dump File with Full Memory: Only application data is available


************* Path validation summary **************
Response                    Time (ms)      Location
Deferred                                   srv*
Symbol search path is: srv*
Executable search path is:
Windows 10 Version 22000 MP (4 procs) Free x64
```

```
Product: WinNt, suite: SingleUserTS
Edition build lab: 22000.1.amd64fre.co_release.210604-1628
Debug session time: Sat Nov 30 16:42:50.000 2024 (UTC + 0:00)
System Uptime: 0 days 0:08:11.619
Process Uptime: 0 days 0:05:31.000
........
For analysis of this file, run !analyze -v
ntdll!NtWaitForSingleObject+0x14:
00007ffc`647c4104 ret
```

16.   Open a log file using the **.logopen** command and load symbols (**.symfix** and **.reload**):

```
0:000> .logappend C:\ARWMDA-Dumps\RW7.log
Opened log file 'C:\ARWMDA-Dumps\RW7.log'
```

```
0:000> .sympath+ C:\ARWMDA-Dumps\Symbols\release
Symbol search path is: srv*;C:\ARWMDA-Dumps\Symbols\release
Expanded Symbol search path is:
cache*;SRV*https://msdl.microsoft.com/download/symbols;c:\arwmda-dumps\symbols\release
```

```
************* Path validation summary **************
Response                        Time (ms)   Location
Deferred                                    srv*
OK                                          C:\ARWMDA-Dumps\Symbols\release
```

```
0:000> .reload
......
```

Note: WinDbg may remember symbol and source paths from the previous sessions.

17.   Let's look at saved stack traces for handles:

```
0:000> !htrace
--------------------------------------
Handle = 0x00000000000031f8 - CLOSE
Thread ID = 0x0000000000005044, Process ID = 0x000000000000215c

0x00007ffc647c4264: ntdll!NtClose+0x0000000000000014
0x00007ffc40c4465b: verifier!AVrfpNtClose+0x000000000000005b
0x00007ffc61c70d0f: KERNELBASE!CloseHandle+0x000000000000004f
0x00007ffc40c440e7: verifier!AVrfpCloseHandleCommon+0x00000000000000b7
0x00007ffc40c443fd: verifier!AVrfpKernelbaseCloseHandle+0x000000000000001d
0x00007ffc40c440e7: verifier!AVrfpCloseHandleCommon+0x00000000000000b7
0x00007ffc40c443c8: verifier!AVrfpKernel32CloseHandle+0x0000000000000028
0x00007ff75a0c69b9: complex_case!std::thread::sleep+0x00000000000000a9
0x00007ff75a0c3520: complex_case!ZN3std3sys9backtrace28__rust_begin_short_backtrace17h0b873ad0682fe542E+0x0000000000000010
0x00007ff75a0c226b: complex_case!ZN3std6thread7Builder15spawn_unchecked17h6e56a25e80bf8795E+0x0000000000000a9b
0x00007ff75a0ce43d: complex_case!std::sys::pal::windows::thread::impl$0::new::thread_start+0x000000000000003d
0x00007ffc40c43bae: verifier!AVrfpStandardThreadFunction+0x000000000000004e
0x00007ffc63e053e0: kernel32!BaseThreadInitThunk+0x0000000000000010
0x00007ffc6472485b: ntdll!RtlUserThreadStart+0x000000000000002b
--------------------------------------
Handle = 0x00000000000031f8 - OPEN
Thread ID = 0x0000000000005044, Process ID = 0x000000000000215c

0x00007ffc647c5994: ntdll!NtCreateTimer2+0x0000000000000014
0x00007ffc61c833ef: KERNELBASE!CreateWaitableTimerExW+0x00000000000000bf
0x00007ff75a0c6947: complex_case!std::thread::sleep+0x0000000000000037
0x00007ff75a0c3520: complex_case!ZN3std3sys9backtrace28__rust_begin_short_backtrace17h0b873ad0682fe542E+0x0000000000000010
0x00007ff75a0c226b: complex_case!ZN3std6thread7Builder15spawn_unchecked17h6e56a25e80bf8795E+0x0000000000000a9b
0x00007ff75a0ce43d: complex_case!std::sys::pal::windows::thread::impl$0::new::thread_start+0x000000000000003d
0x00007ffc40c43bae: verifier!AVrfpStandardThreadFunction+0x000000000000004e
0x00007ffc63e053e0: kernel32!BaseThreadInitThunk+0x0000000000000010
0x00007ffc6472485b: ntdll!RtlUserThreadStart+0x000000000000002b
--------------------------------------
Handle = 0x00000000000031f0 - OPEN
Thread ID = 0x0000000000000e2c, Process ID = 0x000000000000215c
```

```
0x00007ffc647c5994: ntdll!NtCreateTimer2+0x0000000000000014
0x00007ffc61c833ef: KERNELBASE!CreateWaitableTimerExW+0x00000000000000bf
0x00007ff75a0c6947: complex_case!std::thread::sleep+0x0000000000000037
0x00007ff75a0c3749: complex_case!ZN3std3sys9backtrace28__rust_begin_short_backtrace17h3e8324a489e54ea5E+0x0000000000000209
0x00007ff75a0c1f60: complex_case!ZN3std6thread7Builder15spawn_unchecked17h6e56a25e80bf8795E+0x0000000000000790
0x00007ff75a0ce43d: complex_case!std::sys::pal::windows::thread::impl$0::new::thread_start+0x000000000000003d
0x00007ffc40c43bae: verifier!AVrfpStandardThreadFunction+0x000000000000004e
0x00007ffc63e053e0: kernel32!BaseThreadInitThunk+0x0000000000000010
0x00007ffc6472485b: ntdll!RtlUserThreadStart+0x000000000000002b
-------------------------------------
Handle = 0x000000000000031fc - OPEN
Thread ID = 0x0000000000000e2c, Process ID = 0x000000000000215c

0x00007ffc647c5934: ntdll!NtCreateThreadEx+0x0000000000000014
0x00007ffc61c83c3f: KERNELBASE!CreateRemoteThreadEx+0x000000000000029f
0x00007ffc61d797fb: KERNELBASE!CreateThread+0x000000000000003b
0x00007ffc40c437df: verifier!AVrfpCreateThread+0x00000000000000cf
0x00007ff75a0ce2d1: complex_case!std::sys::pal::windows::thread::Thread::new+0x0000000000000071
0x00007ff75a0c13eb: complex_case!ZN3std6thread7Builder15spawn_unchecked17h4b51093272731609E+0x00000000000002ab
0x00007ff75a0c3760: complex_case!ZN3std3sys9backtrace28__rust_begin_short_backtrace17h3e8324a489e54ea5E+0x0000000000000220
0x00007ff75a0c1f60: complex_case!ZN3std6thread7Builder15spawn_unchecked17h6e56a25e80bf8795E+0x0000000000000790
0x00007ff75a0ce43d: complex_case!std::sys::pal::windows::thread::impl$0::new::thread_start+0x000000000000003d
0x00007ffc40c43bae: verifier!AVrfpStandardThreadFunction+0x000000000000004e
0x00007ffc63e053e0: kernel32!BaseThreadInitThunk+0x0000000000000010
-------------------------------------
...
...
...
andle = 0x0000000000002414 - OPEN
Thread ID = 0x000000000000466c, Process ID = 0x000000000000215c

0x00007ffc647c5994: ntdll!NtCreateTimer2+0x0000000000000014
0x00007ffc61c833ef: KERNELBASE!CreateWaitableTimerExW+0x00000000000000bf
0x00007ff75a0c6947: complex_case!std::thread::sleep+0x0000000000000037
0x00007ff75a0c3520: complex_case!ZN3std3sys9backtrace28__rust_begin_short_backtrace17h0b873ad0682fe542E+0x0000000000000010
0x00007ff75a0c226b: complex_case!ZN3std6thread7Builder15spawn_unchecked17h6e56a25e80bf8795E+0x0000000000000a9b
0x00007ff75a0ce43d: complex_case!std::sys::pal::windows::thread::impl$0::new::thread_start+0x000000000000003d
0x00007ffc40c43bae: verifier!AVrfpStandardThreadFunction+0x000000000000004e
0x00007ffc63e053e0: kernel32!BaseThreadInitThunk+0x0000000000000010
0x00007ffc6472485b: ntdll!RtlUserThreadStart+0x000000000000002b
-------------------------------------
Handle = 0x0000000000000027e0 - OPEN
Thread ID = 0x0000000000000e2c, Process ID = 0x000000000000215c

0x00007ffc647c5994: ntdll!NtCreateTimer2+0x0000000000000014
0x00007ffc61c833ef: KERNELBASE!CreateWaitableTimerExW+0x00000000000000bf
0x00007ff75a0c6947: complex_case!std::thread::sleep+0x0000000000000037
0x00007ff75a0c3749: complex_case!ZN3std3sys9backtrace28__rust_begin_short_backtrace17h3e8324a489e54ea5E+0x0000000000000209
0x00007ff75a0c1f60: complex_case!ZN3std6thread7Builder15spawn_unchecked17h6e56a25e80bf8795E+0x0000000000000790
0x00007ff75a0ce43d: complex_case!std::sys::pal::windows::thread::impl$0::new::thread_start+0x000000000000003d
0x00007ffc40c43bae: verifier!AVrfpStandardThreadFunction+0x000000000000004e
0x00007ffc63e053e0: kernel32!BaseThreadInitThunk+0x0000000000000010
0x00007ffc6472485b: ntdll!RtlUserThreadStart+0x000000000000002b

-------------------------------------
Parsed 0x1000 stack traces.
Dumped 0x1000 stack traces.
```

Note: We can also check the traces for the most recent handles:

```
0:000> !handle
Handle 0000000000000004
  Type             Event
Handle 0000000000000008
  Type             Event
Handle 000000000000000c
  Type             Key
Handle 0000000000000010
  Type             Thread
Handle 0000000000000014
  Type             Thread
Handle 0000000000000018
  Type             Thread
Handle 000000000000001c
  Type             Thread
```

```
Handle 0000000000000020
   Type            Thread
Handle 0000000000000024
...
...
...
Handle 00000000000033b4
   Type            Thread
Handle 00000000000033c4
   Type            Thread
Handle 00000000000033d4
   Type            Thread
Handle 00000000000033e4
   Type            Thread
Handle 00000000000033f4
   Type            Thread
3151 Handles
Type                    Count
None                    19
Event                   6
File                    6
Directory               2
Mutant                  1
Semaphore               6
Key                     3
Thread                  3098
IoCompletion            2
TpWorkerFactory         2
ALPC Port               1
WaitCompletionPacket    5
```

```
0:000> !htrace 33f4
--------------------------------------
Handle = 0x00000000000033f4 - OPEN
Thread ID = 0x0000000000000e2c, Process ID = 0x000000000000215c

0x00007ffc647c5934: ntdll!NtCreateThreadEx+0x0000000000000014
0x00007ffc61c83c3f: KERNELBASE!CreateRemoteThreadEx+0x000000000000029f
0x00007ffc61d797fb: KERNELBASE!CreateThread+0x000000000000003b
0x00007ffc40c437df: verifier!AVrfpCreateThread+0x00000000000000cf
0x00007ff75a0ce2d1: complex_case!std::sys::pal::windows::thread::Thread::new+0x0000000000000071
0x00007ff75a0c13eb: complex_case!ZN3std6thread7Builder15spawn_unchecked17h4b51093272731609E+0x00000000000002ab
0x00007ff75a0c3760: complex_case!ZN3std3sys9backtrace28__rust_begin_short_backtrace17h3e8324a489e54ea5E+0x0000000000000220
0x00007ff75a0c1f60: complex_case!ZN3std6thread7Builder15spawn_unchecked17h6e56a25e80bf8795E+0x0000000000000790
0x00007ff75a0ce43d: complex_case!std::sys::pal::windows::thread::impl$0::new::thread_start+0x000000000000003d
0x00007ffc40c43bae: verifier!AVrfpStandardThreadFunction+0x000000000000004e
0x00007ffc63e053e0: kernel32!BaseThreadInitThunk+0x0000000000000010

--------------------------------------
Parsed 0x1000 stack traces.
Dumped 0x1 stack traces.
```

18.   Now we track heap allocation again:

```
0:000> !heap -s

*******************************************************************************
                          NT HEAP STATS BELOW
*******************************************************************************
LFH Key                   : 0x5388df4979365f6c
Termination on corruption : ENABLED
          Heap     Flags   Reserv  Commit  Virt   Free  List   UCR  Virt  Lock  Fast
                           (k)     (k)     (k)    (k)  length       blocks cont. heap
          -------------------------------------------------------------------------
```

```
00000254d1310000 00000002    16364  12916  16364       4    4    5    0    4
00000254d12e0000 00001002     3124   1420   3124       3    2    3    0    0
00000254d12b0000 00008000       64      4     64       2    1    1    0    0
```

Note: We don't see much heap size increase but check the number of blocks just in case of small allocations.

```
0:000> !heap -s -h 00000254d1310000
Walking the heap 00000254d1310000 .....
 0: Heap 00000254d1310000
    Flags             00000002 - HEAP_GROWABLE
    Reserved memory in segments               16364 (k)
    Commited memory in segments               12916 (k)
    Virtual bytes (correction for large UCR) 12916 (k)
    Free space                                    4 (k) (4 blocks)
    External fragmentation           0% (4 free blocks)
    Virtual address fragmentation    0% (5 uncommited ranges)
    Virtual blocks  0 - total 0 KBytes
    Lock contention 4
    Segments        1

                    Default heap    Front heap      Unused bytes
    Range (bytes)   Busy  Free     Busy   Free     Total  Average
-------------------------------------------------------------------
      0 -    1024  34605    3        0      0    1259578    36
   1024 -    2048     22    0        0      0        724    32
   2048 -    3072   3102    0        0      0      99424    32
   3072 -    4096      5    1        0      0        188    37
   4096 -    5120      4    0        0      0        128    32
   5120 -    6144      1    0        0      0         40    40
   6144 -    7168      1    0        0      0         32    32
   7168 -    8192      1    0        0      0         32    32
  12288 -   13312      1    0        0      0         32    32
  14336 -   15360      1    0        0      0         32    32
  19456 -   20480      1    0        0      0         40    40
  24576 -   25600      1    0        0      0         32    32
  28672 -   29696      1    0        0      0         32    32
  29696 -   30720      1    0        0      0         32    32
  38912 -   39936      1    0        0      0         40    40
  49152 -   50176      1    0        0      0         32    32
  57344 -   58368      1    0        0      0         32    32
-------------------------------------------------------------------
    Total           37750    4        0      0    1360450    36

0:000> !heap -flt r 0n1 0n1024
    _DPH_HEAP_ROOT @ 254d01e1000
    Freed and decommitted blocks
      DPH_HEAP_BLOCK : VirtAddr VirtSize
    Busy allocations
      DPH_HEAP_BLOCK : UserAddr  UserSize - VirtAddr VirtSize
    _HEAP @ 254d1310000
            HEAP_ENTRY Size Prev Flags         UserPtr UserSize - state
        00000254d1310850 0017 0000  [00]   00000254d13108a0    00100 - (busy)
        00000254d13109c0 0016 0017  [00]   00000254d1310a10    000f0 - (busy)
        00000254d1310b20 0025 0016  [00]   00000254d1310b70    001d8 - (busy)
        00000254d1310d70 0025 0025  [00]   00000254d1310dc0    001d8 - (busy)
        00000254d1310fc0 000c 0025  [00]   00000254d1311010    00048 - (busy)
        00000254d1311080 0008 000c  [00]   00000254d13110d0    00004 - (busy)
        00000254d1311100 0008 0008  [00]   00000254d1311150    00010 - (busy)
```

```
00000254d1311180 000a 0008  [00]  00000254d13111d0  00030 - (free DelayedFree)
00000254d1311220 0017 000a  [00]  00000254d1311270  00100 - (busy)
    unknown!noop
00000254d1311390 0017 0017  [00]  00000254d13113e0  00100 - (busy)
00000254d1311500 0017 0017  [00]  00000254d1311550  00100 - (busy)
00000254d1312370 0017 0017  [00]  00000254d13123c0  00100 - (busy)
00000254d13124e0 000a 0017  [00]  00000254d1312530  00030 - (free DelayedFree)
00000254d1312580 000a 000a  [00]  00000254d13125d0  00030 - (free DelayedFree)
00000254d1312620 000a 000a  [00]  00000254d1312670  00030 - (free DelayedFree)
00000254d13126c0 000a 000a  [00]  00000254d1312710  00030 - (free DelayedFree)
00000254d1312760 000a 000a  [00]  00000254d13127b0  00030 - (free DelayedFree)
00000254d1312800 000a 000a  [00]  00000254d1312850  00030 - (free DelayedFree)
00000254d13128a0 000a 000a  [00]  00000254d13128f0  00030 - (free DelayedFree)
00000254d1312940 000a 000a  [00]  00000254d1312990  00030 - (free DelayedFree)
00000254d13129e0 000a 000a  [00]  00000254d1312a30  00030 - (free DelayedFree)
00000254d1312a80 000a 000a  [00]  00000254d1312ad0  00030 - (free DelayedFree)
00000254d1312b20 000a 000a  [00]  00000254d1312b70  00030 - (free DelayedFree)
00000254d1312bc0 000a 000a  [00]  00000254d1312c10  00030 - (free DelayedFree)
00000254d1312c60 000a 000a  [00]  00000254d1312cb0  00030 - (free DelayedFree)
00000254d1312d00 000a 000a  [00]  00000254d1312d50  00030 - (free DelayedFree)
00000254d1312da0 000a 000a  [00]  00000254d1312df0  00030 - (free DelayedFree)
00000254d1312e40 000a 000a  [00]  00000254d1312e90  00030 - (free DelayedFree)
00000254d1312ee0 000a 000a  [00]  00000254d1312f30  00030 - (free DelayedFree)
00000254d1312f80 000a 000a  [00]  00000254d1312fd0  00030 - (free DelayedFree)
00000254d1313020 000a 000a  [00]  00000254d1313070  00030 - (free DelayedFree)
00000254d13130c0 000a 000a  [00]  00000254d1313110  00030 - (free DelayedFree)
00000254d1313160 000a 000a  [00]  00000254d13131b0  00030 - (free DelayedFree)
00000254d1313200 000a 000a  [00]  00000254d1313250  00030 - (free DelayedFree)
00000254d13132a0 000a 000a  [00]  00000254d13132f0  00030 - (free DelayedFree)
00000254d1313340 000a 000a  [00]  00000254d1313390  00030 - (free DelayedFree)
00000254d13133e0 000a 000a  [00]  00000254d1313430  00030 - (free DelayedFree)
00000254d1313480 000a 000a  [00]  00000254d13134d0  00030 - (free DelayedFree)
00000254d1313520 000a 000a  [00]  00000254d1313570  00030 - (free DelayedFree)
00000254d13135c0 000a 000a  [00]  00000254d1313610  00030 - (free DelayedFree)
00000254d1313660 000a 000a  [00]  00000254d13136b0  00030 - (free DelayedFree)
00000254d1313700 000a 000a  [00]  00000254d1313750  00030 - (free DelayedFree)
00000254d13137a0 000a 000a  [00]  00000254d13137f0  00030 - (free DelayedFree)
00000254d1313840 000a 000a  [00]  00000254d1313890  00030 - (free DelayedFree)
00000254d13138e0 000a 000a  [00]  00000254d1313930  00030 - (free DelayedFree)
00000254d1313980 000a 000a  [00]  00000254d13139d0  00030 - (free DelayedFree)
00000254d1313a20 000a 000a  [00]  00000254d1313a70  00030 - (free DelayedFree)
00000254d1313ac0 000a 000a  [00]  00000254d1313b10  00030 - (free DelayedFree)
00000254d1313b60 000a 000a  [00]  00000254d1313bb0  00030 - (free DelayedFree)
00000254d1313c00 000a 000a  [00]  00000254d1313c50  00030 - (free DelayedFree)
00000254d1313ca0 000a 000a  [00]  00000254d1313cf0  00030 - (free DelayedFree)
00000254d1313d40 000a 000a  [00]  00000254d1313d90  00030 - (free DelayedFree)
00000254d1313de0 000a 000a  [00]  00000254d1313e30  00030 - (free DelayedFree)
00000254d1313e80 000a 000a  [00]  00000254d1313ed0  00030 - (free DelayedFree)
00000254d1313f20 000a 000a  [00]  00000254d1313f70  00030 - (free DelayedFree)
00000254d1313fc0 000a 000a  [00]  00000254d1314010  00030 - (free DelayedFree)
00000254d1314060 000a 000a  [00]  00000254d13140b0  00030 - (free DelayedFree)
00000254d1314100 000a 000a  [00]  00000254d1314150  00030 - (free DelayedFree)
00000254d13141a0 000a 000a  [00]  00000254d13141f0  00030 - (free DelayedFree)
00000254d1314240 000a 000a  [00]  00000254d1314290  00030 - (free DelayedFree)
00000254d13142e0 000a 000a  [00]  00000254d1314330  00030 - (free DelayedFree)
00000254d1314380 000a 000a  [00]  00000254d13143d0  00030 - (free DelayedFree)
00000254d1314420 000a 000a  [00]  00000254d1314470  00030 - (free DelayedFree)
00000254d13144c0 000a 000a  [00]  00000254d1314510  00030 - (free DelayedFree)
00000254d1314560 000a 000a  [00]  00000254d13145b0  00030 - (free DelayedFree)
```

```
00000254d1314600 000a 000a  [00]  00000254d1314650  00030 - (free DelayedFree)
00000254d13146a0 000a 000a  [00]  00000254d13146f0  00030 - (free DelayedFree)
00000254d1314740 000a 000a  [00]  00000254d1314790  00030 - (free DelayedFree)
00000254d13147e0 000a 000a  [00]  00000254d1314830  00030 - (free DelayedFree)
00000254d1314880 000a 000a  [00]  00000254d13148d0  00030 - (free DelayedFree)
00000254d1314920 000a 000a  [00]  00000254d1314970  00030 - (free DelayedFree)
00000254d13149c0 000a 000a  [00]  00000254d1314a10  00030 - (free DelayedFree)
00000254d1314a60 000a 000a  [00]  00000254d1314ab0  00030 - (free DelayedFree)
00000254d1314b00 000a 000a  [00]  00000254d1314b50  00030 - (free DelayedFree)
00000254d1314ba0 000a 000a  [00]  00000254d1314bf0  00030 - (free DelayedFree)
00000254d1314c40 000a 000a  [00]  00000254d1314c90  00030 - (free DelayedFree)
00000254d1314ce0 000a 000a  [00]  00000254d1314d30  00030 - (free DelayedFree)
00000254d1314d80 000a 000a  [00]  00000254d1314dd0  00030 - (free DelayedFree)
00000254d1314e20 000a 000a  [00]  00000254d1314e70  00030 - (free DelayedFree)
00000254d1314ec0 000a 000a  [00]  00000254d1314f10  00030 - (free DelayedFree)
00000254d1314f60 000a 000a  [00]  00000254d1314fb0  00030 - (free DelayedFree)
00000254d1315000 000a 000a  [00]  00000254d1315050  00030 - (free DelayedFree)
00000254d1315820 000b 000a  [00]  00000254d1315870  0003c - (busy)
    unknown!noop
00000254d13158d0 000a 000b  [00]  00000254d1315920  00030 - (busy)
    unknown!noop
00000254d1315970 000e 000a  [00]  00000254d13159c0  00062 - (busy)
    unknown!noop
00000254d1315a50 001b 000e  [00]  00000254d1315aa0  00138 - (busy)
00000254d1315c00 000c 001b  [00]  00000254d1315c50  00050 - (busy)
    unknown!noop
00000254d1315cc0 001b 000c  [00]  00000254d1315d10  00138 - (busy)
00000254d1315e70 000c 001b  [00]  00000254d1315ec0  00050 - (busy)
00000254d1315f30 0009 000c  [00]  00000254d1315f80  0001a - (free DelayedFree)
00000254d1315fc0 002b 0009  [00]  00000254d1316010  00238 - (busy)
00000254d1316270 001b 002b  [00]  00000254d13162c0  00138 - (busy)
00000254d1316420 000c 001b  [00]  00000254d1316470  00050 - (busy)
00000254d13164e0 000c 000c  [00]  00000254d1316530  00048 - (busy)
    ntdll!AVrfpVerifierProvidersList
00000254d13165a0 000a 000c  [00]  00000254d13165f0  00030 - (busy)
00000254d1316640 000a 000a  [00]  00000254d1316690  00030 - (busy)
00000254d13166e0 000a 000a  [00]  00000254d1316730  00030 - (busy)
00000254d1316780 000a 000a  [00]  00000254d13167d0  00030 - (busy)
00000254d1316820 000a 000a  [00]  00000254d1316870  00030 - (busy)
00000254d13168c0 000a 000a  [00]  00000254d1316910  00030 - (busy)
00000254d1316960 000a 000a  [00]  00000254d13169b0  00030 - (busy)
00000254d131b6b0 000a 000a  [00]  00000254d131b700  00030 - (busy)
00000254d1325000 000a 000a  [00]  00000254d1325050  00030 - (busy)
00000254d13250a0 000a 000a  [00]  00000254d13250f0  00030 - (busy)
00000254d1325140 000a 000a  [00]  00000254d1325190  00030 - (busy)
00000254d132d3a0 0012 000a  [00]  00000254d132d3f0  000aa - (free DelayedFree)
00000254d132d4c0 0012 0012  [00]  00000254d132d510  000ac - (free DelayedFree)
00000254d132d5e0 0012 0012  [00]  00000254d132d630  000ac - (free DelayedFree)
00000254d132d700 0009 0012  [00]  00000254d132d750  0001c - (busy)
00000254d132d790 0012 0009  [00]  00000254d132d7e0  000ac - (free DelayedFree)
00000254d132d8b0 0008 0012  [00]  00000254d132d900  0000c - (free DelayedFree)
00000254d132d930 000c 0008  [00]  00000254d132d980  00046 - (busy)
00000254d132d9f0 0012 000c  [00]  00000254d132da40  000ac - (free DelayedFree)
00000254d132db10 0008 0012  [00]  00000254d132db60  0000c - (free DelayedFree)
00000254d132db90 0008 0008  [00]  00000254d132dbe0  0000e - (free DelayedFree)
00000254d132dc10 0009 0008  [00]  00000254d132dc60  00018 - (free DelayedFree)
00000254d132dca0 0012 0009  [00]  00000254d132dcf0  000aa - (free DelayedFree)
00000254d132ddc0 000c 0012  [00]  00000254d132de10  00046 - (busy)
00000254d132de80 0008 000c  [00]  00000254d132ded0  00010 - (busy)
```

```
00000254d132df00 0015 0008 [00]   00000254d132df50 000d6 - (busy)
00000254d132e050 0015 0015 [00]   00000254d132e0a0 000d6 - (free DelayedFree)
00000254d132e1a0 001d 0015 [00]   00000254d132e1f0 00154 - (free DelayedFree)
00000254d132e370 0012 001d [00]   00000254d132e3c0 000aa - (free DelayedFree)
00000254d132e490 0027 0012 [00]   00000254d132e4e0 001fe - (free DelayedFree)
00000254d132e700 0012 0027 [00]   00000254d132e750 000aa - (free DelayedFree)
00000254d132e820 0012 0012 [00]   00000254d132e870 000aa - (free DelayedFree)
00000254d132e940 0012 0012 [00]   00000254d132e990 000aa - (free DelayedFree)
00000254d132ea60 0012 0012 [00]   00000254d132eab0 000aa - (free DelayedFree)
00000254d132eb80 0012 0012 [00]   00000254d132ebd0 000aa - (free DelayedFree)
00000254d132eca0 0012 0012 [00]   00000254d132ecf0 000aa - (free DelayedFree)
00000254d132edc0 0012 0012 [00]   00000254d132ee10 000aa - (free DelayedFree)
00000254d132eee0 0012 0012 [00]   00000254d132ef30 000aa - (free DelayedFree)
00000254d132f000 0012 0012 [00]   00000254d132f050 000aa - (free DelayedFree)
00000254d132f120 0012 0012 [00]   00000254d132f170 000aa - (free DelayedFree)
00000254d132f240 0012 0012 [00]   00000254d132f290 000aa - (free DelayedFree)
00000254d132f360 0009 0012 [00]   00000254d132f3b0 00018 - (busy)
    verifier!tlgEnableCallback <PERF> (verifier+0x0)
00000254d132f3f0 000b 0009 [00]   00000254d132f440 0003d - (busy)
    unknown!noop
00000254d132f4a0 000e 000b [00]   00000254d132f4f0 0006c - (busy)
    unknown!printable
00000254d132f580 000c 000e [00]   00000254d132f5d0 0004d - (busy)
    unknown!printable
00000254d132f640 0014 000c [00]   00000254d132f690 000c8 - (busy)
00000254d132f780 000b 0014 [00]   00000254d132f7d0 0003a - (busy)
    unknown!noop
00000254d132f830 000c 000b [00]   00000254d132f880 0004d - (busy)
    unknown!noop
00000254d132f8f0 0014 000c [00]   00000254d132f940 000c8 - (busy)
00000254d1330750 000a 0014 [00]   00000254d13307a0 00028 - (busy)
00000254d13307f0 0008 000a [00]   00000254d1330840 00008 - (busy)
00000254d1330870 000a 0008 [00]   00000254d13308c0 00030 - (busy)
00000254d1330910 000a 000a [00]   00000254d1330960 00030 - (busy)
00000254d13312b0 000a 000a [00]   00000254d1331300 00030 - (busy)
00000254d1331350 000a 000a [00]   00000254d13313a0 00030 - (busy)
00000254d13313f0 000a 000a [00]   00000254d1331440 00030 - (busy)
...
...
...
00000254d531be90 000f 0010 [00]   00000254d531bee0 00080 - (free DelayedFree)
00000254d531bf80 000b 000f [00]   00000254d531bfd0 00040 - (free DelayedFree)
00000254d531c030 000b 000b [00]   00000254d531c080 00038 - (busy)
00000254d531c0e0 000a 000b [00]   00000254d531c130 00030 - (busy)
00000254d531c180 0009 000a [00]   00000254d531c1d0 00018 - (free DelayedFree)
00000254d531c210 0008 0009 [00]   00000254d531c260 00010 - (free DelayedFree)
00000254d531c290 000d 0008 [00]   00000254d531c2e0 00058 - (free DelayedFree)
00000254d531c360 000e 000d [00]   00000254d531c3b0 00070 - (free DelayedFree)
00000254d531c440 0009 000e [00]   00000254d531c490 00018 - (free DelayedFree)
00000254d531c4d0 000d 0009 [00]   00000254d531c520 00058 - (free DelayedFree)
00000254d531c5a0 0010 000d [00]   00000254d531c5f0 00088 - (free DelayedFree)
00000254d531cea0 000f 0010 [00]   00000254d531cef0 00080 - (free DelayedFree)
00000254d531cf90 000b 000f [00]   00000254d531cfe0 00040 - (free DelayedFree)
00000254d531d040 000b 000b [00]   00000254d531d090 00038 - (busy)
00000254d531d0f0 000a 000b [00]   00000254d531d140 00030 - (busy)
00000254d531d190 0009 000a [00]   00000254d531d1e0 00018 - (free DelayedFree)
00000254d531d220 0008 0009 [00]   00000254d531d270 00010 - (free DelayedFree)
00000254d531d2a0 000d 0008 [00]   00000254d531d2f0 00058 - (free DelayedFree)
00000254d531d370 000e 000d [00]   00000254d531d3c0 00070 - (free DelayedFree)
```

```
      00000254d531d450 0009 000e  [00]   00000254d531d4a0      00018 - (free DelayedFree)
      00000254d531d4e0 000d 0009  [00]   00000254d531d530      00058 - (free DelayedFree)
      00000254d531d5b0 0010 000d  [00]   00000254d531d600      00088 - (free DelayedFree)
      00000254d531deb0 000f 0010  [00]   00000254d531df00      00080 - (free DelayedFree)
      00000254d531dfa0 000b 000f  [00]   00000254d531dff0      00040 - (free DelayedFree)
      00000254d531e050 000b 000b  [00]   00000254d531e0a0      00038 - (busy)
      00000254d531e100 000a 000b  [00]   00000254d531e150      00030 - (busy)
      00000254d531e1a0 0009 000a  [00]   00000254d531e1f0      00018 - (free DelayedFree)
      00000254d531e230 0008 0009  [00]   00000254d531e280      00010 - (free DelayedFree)
      00000254d531e2b0 000d 0008  [00]   00000254d531e300      00058 - (free DelayedFree)
      00000254d531e380 000e 000d  [00]   00000254d531e3d0      00070 - (free DelayedFree)
      00000254d531e460 0009 000e  [00]   00000254d531e4b0      00018 - (free DelayedFree)
      00000254d531e4f0 000d 0009  [00]   00000254d531e540      00058 - (free DelayedFree)
      00000254d531e5c0 0010 000d  [00]   00000254d531e610      00088 - (free DelayedFree)
      00000254d531eec0 0010 0010  [00]   00000254d531ef10      00080 - (free DelayedFree)
      00000254d531efc0 000b 0010  [00]   00000254d531f010      00040 - (free DelayedFree)
      00000254d531f070 000b 000b  [00]   00000254d531f0c0      00038 - (busy)
      00000254d531f120 000a 000b  [00]   00000254d531f170      00030 - (busy)
      00000254d531f1c0 0009 000a  [00]   00000254d531f210      00018 - (free DelayedFree)
      00000254d531f250 0008 0009  [00]   00000254d531f2a0      00010 - (free DelayedFree)
      00000254d531f2d0 000d 0008  [00]   00000254d531f320      00058 - (free DelayedFree)
      00000254d531f3a0 000e 000d  [00]   00000254d531f3f0      00070 - (free DelayedFree)
      00000254d531f480 0009 000e  [00]   00000254d531f4d0      00018 - (free DelayedFree)
      00000254d531f510 000d 0009  [00]   00000254d531f560      00058 - (free DelayedFree)
      00000254d531f5e0 0010 000d  [00]   00000254d531f630      00088 - (free DelayedFree)
      00000254d531fee0 000f 0010  [00]   00000254d531ff30      00080 - (free DelayedFree)
      00000254d531ffd0 000b 000f  [00]   00000254d5320020      00040 - (free DelayedFree)
    _DPH_HEAP_ROOT @ 254d1411000
    Freed and decommitted blocks
      DPH_HEAP_BLOCK : VirtAddr VirtSize
    Busy allocations
      DPH_HEAP_BLOCK : UserAddr  UserSize - VirtAddr VirtSize
    _HEAP @ 254d12e0000
...
...
...
```

Note: We need to finish till the end to see the most recent entries. We see many uniform trace entries of 38 and 30 szie in the first heap and dump some of them:

```
0:000> dp 00000254d531f070
00000254`d531f070  00000000`00000000 284a7822`4c19156a
00000254`d531f080  00000254`abcdaaaa 80000254`d01e1000
00000254`d531f090  00000000`00000038 00000000`00000088
00000254`d531f0a0  00000254`d531f150 00000254`d531e130
00000254`d531f0b0  00000254`cea18b60 dcbaaaaa`00000000
00000254`d531f0c0  00000000`00000001 00000000`00000001
00000254`d531f0d0  00000000`00000002 00007ffc`40c440e7
00000254`d531f0e0  00000000`00000001 00000000`00000c1b

0:000> !handle c1b
Handle 0000000000000c1b
  Type              Thread
```

Note: To find out which address is a pointer to the heap stack trace, we check if it belongs to the region of the *Stack Trace Database*:

```
0:000> !address

Mapping file section regions...
Mapping module regions...
Mapping PEB regions...
Mapping TEB and stack regions...
Mapping heap regions...
Mapping page heap regions...
Mapping other regions...
Mapping stack trace database regions...
Mapping activation context regions...

        BaseAddress      EndAddress+1        RegionSize     Type       State                 Protect             Usage
-----------------------------------------------------------------------------------------------------------------------------
+        0`00000000        0`7ffe0000        0`7ffe0000             MEM_FREE    PAGE_NOACCESS                  Free
+        0`7ffe0000        0`7ffe1000        0`00001000 MEM_PRIVATE MEM_COMMIT  PAGE_READONLY                  Other      [User Shared Data]
+        0`7ffe1000        0`7ffe7000        0`00006000             MEM_FREE    PAGE_NOACCESS                  Free
+        0`7ffe7000        0`7ffe8000        0`00001000 MEM_PRIVATE MEM_COMMIT  PAGE_READONLY                  <unknown>  [............M6.]
+        0`7ffe8000       eb`d8200000       eb`58218000             MEM_FREE    PAGE_NOACCESS                  Free
+       eb`d8200000       eb`d820a000        0`0000a000 MEM_PRIVATE MEM_RESERVE                                <unknown>
        eb`d820a000       eb`d820c000        0`00002000 MEM_PRIVATE MEM_COMMIT  PAGE_READWRITE                 TEB        [~6; 215c.3f20]
        eb`d820c000       eb`d835a000        0`0014e000 MEM_PRIVATE MEM_RESERVE                                <unknown>
        eb`d835a000       eb`d835b000        0`00001000 MEM_PRIVATE MEM_COMMIT  PAGE_READWRITE                 PEB        [215c]
        eb`d835b000       eb`d835d000        0`00002000 MEM_PRIVATE MEM_COMMIT  PAGE_READWRITE                 TEB        [~0; 215c.1e0c]
        eb`d835d000       eb`d8361000        0`00004000 MEM_PRIVATE MEM_RESERVE                                <unknown>
        eb`d8361000       eb`d8363000        0`00002000 MEM_PRIVATE MEM_COMMIT  PAGE_READWRITE                 TEB        [~1; 215c.12ac]
        eb`d8363000       eb`d8365000        0`00002000 MEM_PRIVATE MEM_COMMIT  PAGE_READWRITE                 TEB        [~2; 215c.12a4]
        eb`d8365000       eb`d8367000        0`00002000 MEM_PRIVATE MEM_COMMIT  PAGE_READWRITE                 TEB        [~3; 215c.804]
        eb`d8367000       eb`d8369000        0`00002000 MEM_PRIVATE MEM_COMMIT  PAGE_READWRITE                 TEB        [~4; 215c.7a4]
        eb`d8369000       eb`d836b000        0`00002000 MEM_PRIVATE MEM_COMMIT  PAGE_READWRITE                 TEB        [~5; 215c.e2c]
        eb`d836b000       eb`d8400000        0`00095000 MEM_PRIVATE MEM_RESERVE                                <unknown>
+       eb`d8400000       eb`d84f5000        0`000f5000 MEM_PRIVATE MEM_RESERVE                                Stack      [~0; 215c.1e0c]
        eb`d84f5000       eb`d84fb000        0`00006000 MEM_PRIVATE MEM_COMMIT  PAGE_READWRITE | PAGE_GUARD    Stack      [~0; 215c.1e0c]
        eb`d84fb000       eb`d8500000        0`00005000 MEM_PRIVATE MEM_COMMIT  PAGE_READWRITE                 Stack      [~0; 215c.1e0c]
+       eb`d8500000       eb`d85fb000        0`000fb000 MEM_PRIVATE MEM_RESERVE                                Stack      [~6; 215c.3f20]
        eb`d85fb000       eb`d85fe000        0`00003000 MEM_PRIVATE MEM_COMMIT  PAGE_READWRITE | PAGE_GUARD    Stack      [~6; 215c.3f20]
        eb`d85fe000       eb`d8600000        0`00002000 MEM_PRIVATE MEM_COMMIT  PAGE_READWRITE                 Stack      [~6; 215c.3f20]
+       eb`d8600000       eb`d8700000        0`00100000             MEM_FREE    PAGE_NOACCESS                  Free
+       eb`d8700000       eb`d88f8000        0`001f8000 MEM_PRIVATE MEM_RESERVE                                Stack      [~1; 215c.12ac]
        eb`d88f8000       eb`d88fe000        0`00006000 MEM_PRIVATE MEM_COMMIT  PAGE_READWRITE | PAGE_GUARD    Stack      [~1; 215c.12ac]
        eb`d88fe000       eb`d8900000        0`00002000 MEM_PRIVATE MEM_COMMIT  PAGE_READWRITE                 Stack      [~1; 215c.12ac]
+       eb`d8900000       eb`d8af7000        0`001f7000 MEM_PRIVATE MEM_RESERVE                                Stack      [~2; 215c.12a4]
        eb`d8af7000       eb`d8afd000        0`00006000 MEM_PRIVATE MEM_COMMIT  PAGE_READWRITE | PAGE_GUARD    Stack      [~2; 215c.12a4]
        eb`d8afd000       eb`d8b00000        0`00003000 MEM_PRIVATE MEM_COMMIT  PAGE_READWRITE                 Stack      [~2; 215c.12a4]
+       eb`d8b00000       eb`d8cf8000        0`001f8000 MEM_PRIVATE MEM_RESERVE                                Stack      [~3; 215c.804]
        eb`d8cf8000       eb`d8cfe000        0`00006000 MEM_PRIVATE MEM_COMMIT  PAGE_READWRITE | PAGE_GUARD    Stack      [~3; 215c.804]
        eb`d8cfe000       eb`d8d00000        0`00002000 MEM_PRIVATE MEM_COMMIT  PAGE_READWRITE                 Stack      [~3; 215c.804]
+       eb`d8d00000       eb`d8eb0000        0`001b0000 MEM_PRIVATE MEM_RESERVE                                Stack      [~4; 215c.7a4]
        eb`d8eb0000       eb`d8eb6000        0`00006000 MEM_PRIVATE MEM_COMMIT  PAGE_READWRITE | PAGE_GUARD    Stack      [~4; 215c.7a4]
        eb`d8eb6000       eb`d8f00000        0`0004a000 MEM_PRIVATE MEM_COMMIT  PAGE_READWRITE                 Stack      [~4; 215c.7a4]
+       eb`d8f00000       eb`d90f8000        0`001f8000 MEM_PRIVATE MEM_RESERVE                                Stack      [~5; 215c.e2c]
        eb`d90f8000       eb`d90fe000        0`00006000 MEM_PRIVATE MEM_COMMIT  PAGE_READWRITE | PAGE_GUARD    Stack      [~5; 215c.e2c]
        eb`d90fe000       eb`d9100000        0`00002000 MEM_PRIVATE MEM_COMMIT  PAGE_READWRITE                 Stack      [~5; 215c.e2c]
+       eb`d9100000      254`ce930000      168`f5830000             MEM_FREE    PAGE_NOACCESS                  Free
+      254`ce930000      254`ce932000        0`00002000 MEM_PRIVATE MEM_COMMIT  PAGE_READWRITE                 <unknown>  [................]
+      254`ce932000      254`ce940000        0`0000e000             MEM_FREE    PAGE_NOACCESS                  Free
+      254`ce940000      254`ce942000        0`00002000 MEM_PRIVATE MEM_COMMIT  PAGE_READWRITE                 <unknown>  [................]
+      254`ce942000      254`ce950000        0`0000e000             MEM_FREE    PAGE_NOACCESS                  Free
+      254`ce950000      254`ce96f000        0`0001f000 MEM_MAPPED  MEM_COMMIT  PAGE_READONLY                  Other      [API Set Map]
+      254`ce96f000      254`ce970000        0`00001000             MEM_FREE    PAGE_NOACCESS                  Free
+      254`ce970000      254`ce974000        0`00004000 MEM_MAPPED  MEM_COMMIT  PAGE_READONLY                  Other      [System Default Activation Context Data]
+      254`ce974000      254`ce980000        0`0000c000             MEM_FREE    PAGE_NOACCESS                  Free
+      254`ce980000      254`ce982000        0`00002000 MEM_PRIVATE MEM_COMMIT  PAGE_READWRITE                 <unknown>  [................]
+      254`ce982000      254`ce990000        0`0000e000             MEM_FREE    PAGE_NOACCESS                  Free
+      254`ce990000      254`ce9a1000        0`00011000 MEM_MAPPED  MEM_COMMIT  PAGE_READONLY                  <unknown>  [................]
+      254`ce9a1000      254`ce9b0000        0`0000f000             MEM_FREE    PAGE_NOACCESS                  Free
+      254`ce9b0000      254`ce9c1000        0`00011000 MEM_MAPPED  MEM_COMMIT  PAGE_READONLY                  <unknown>  [................]
+      254`ce9c1000      254`ce9d0000        0`0000f000             MEM_FREE    PAGE_NOACCESS                  Free
+      254`ce9d0000      254`ce9d3000        0`00003000 MEM_MAPPED  MEM_COMMIT  PAGE_READONLY                  <unknown>  [........0...P...]
+      254`ce9d3000      254`ce9e0000        0`0000d000             MEM_FREE    PAGE_NOACCESS                  Free
+      254`ce9e0000      254`cea1a000        0`0003a000 MEM_PRIVATE MEM_COMMIT  PAGE_READWRITE                 Other      [Stack Trace Database]
       254`cea1a000      254`d01df000        0`017c5000 MEM_PRIVATE MEM_RESERVE                                Other      [Stack Trace Database]
       254`d01df000      254`d01e0000        0`00001000 MEM_PRIVATE MEM_COMMIT  PAGE_READWRITE                 Other      [Stack Trace Database]
+      254`d01e0000      254`d01e1000        0`00001000 MEM_PRIVATE MEM_COMMIT  PAGE_READONLY                  PageHeap   [PageHeap: 254d01e1000; NormalHeap: 254d1310000]
       254`d01e1000      254`d01e3000        0`00002000 MEM_PRIVATE MEM_COMMIT  PAGE_READWRITE                 PageHeap   [PageHeap: 254d01e1000; NormalHeap: 254d1310000]
       254`d01e3000      254`d0249000        0`00066000 MEM_PRIVATE MEM_RESERVE                                PageHeap   [PageHeap: 254d01e1000; NormalHeap: 254d1310000]
       254`d0249000      254`d070a000        0`004c1000 MEM_PRIVATE MEM_COMMIT  PAGE_READWRITE                 PageHeap   [PageHeap: 254d01e1000; NormalHeap: 254d1310000]
       254`d070a000      254`d070b000        0`00001000 MEM_PRIVATE MEM_RESERVE                                PageHeap   [PageHeap: 254d01e1000; NormalHeap: 254d1310000]
       254`d070b000      254`d0bcc000        0`004c1000 MEM_PRIVATE MEM_COMMIT  PAGE_READWRITE                 PageHeap   [PageHeap: 254d01e1000; NormalHeap: 254d1310000]
       254`d0bcc000      254`d0bcd000        0`00001000 MEM_PRIVATE MEM_RESERVE                                PageHeap   [PageHeap: 254d01e1000; NormalHeap: 254d1310000]
       254`d0bcd000      254`d0c66000        0`00099000 MEM_PRIVATE MEM_COMMIT  PAGE_READWRITE                 PageHeap   [PageHeap: 254d01e1000; NormalHeap: 254d1310000]
       254`d0c66000      254`d0c67000        0`00001000 MEM_PRIVATE MEM_RESERVE                                PageHeap   [PageHeap: 254d01e1000; NormalHeap: 254d1310000]
       254`d0c67000      254`d0d00000        0`00099000 MEM_PRIVATE MEM_COMMIT  PAGE_READWRITE                 PageHeap   [PageHeap: 254d01e1000; NormalHeap: 254d1310000]
       254`d0d00000      254`d0d01000        0`00001000 MEM_PRIVATE MEM_RESERVE                                PageHeap   [PageHeap: 254d01e1000; NormalHeap: 254d1310000]
       254`d0d01000      254`d0d9a000        0`00099000 MEM_PRIVATE MEM_COMMIT  PAGE_READWRITE                 PageHeap   [PageHeap: 254d01e1000; NormalHeap: 254d1310000]
       254`d0d9a000      254`d0d9b000        0`00001000 MEM_PRIVATE MEM_RESERVE                                PageHeap   [PageHeap: 254d01e1000; NormalHeap: 254d1310000]
       254`d0d9b000      254`d0e34000        0`00099000 MEM_PRIVATE MEM_COMMIT  PAGE_READWRITE                 PageHeap   [PageHeap: 254d01e1000; NormalHeap: 254d1310000]
       254`d0e34000      254`d0e35000        0`00001000 MEM_PRIVATE MEM_RESERVE                                PageHeap   [PageHeap: 254d01e1000; NormalHeap: 254d1310000]
       254`d0e35000      254`d0e5c000        0`00027000 MEM_PRIVATE MEM_COMMIT  PAGE_READWRITE                 PageHeap   [PageHeap: 254d01e1000; NormalHeap: 254d1310000]
       254`d0e5c000      254`d11e0000        0`00384000 MEM_PRIVATE MEM_RESERVE                                PageHeap   [PageHeap: 254d01e1000; NormalHeap: 254d1310000]
+      254`d11e0000      254`d12ae000        0`000ce000 MEM_MAPPED  MEM_COMMIT  PAGE_READONLY                  <unknown>  [................]
+      254`d12ae000      254`d12b0000        0`00002000             MEM_FREE    PAGE_NOACCESS                  Free
+      254`d12b0000      254`d12c0000        0`00010000 MEM_MAPPED  MEM_COMMIT  PAGE_READWRITE                 Heap       [ID: 2; Handle: 00000254d12b0000; Type: Segment]
+      254`d12c0000      254`d12c3000        0`00003000 MEM_MAPPED  MEM_COMMIT  PAGE_READONLY                  <unknown>  [........0...P...]
+      254`d12c3000      254`d12e0000        0`0001d000             MEM_FREE    PAGE_NOACCESS                  Free
+      254`d12e0000      254`d12ef000        0`0000f000 MEM_PRIVATE MEM_COMMIT  PAGE_READWRITE                 Heap       [ID: 1; Handle: 00000254d12e0000; Type: Segment]
       254`d12ef000      254`d12f0000        0`00001000 MEM_PRIVATE MEM_RESERVE                                <unknown>
+      254`d12f0000      254`d1301000        0`00011000 MEM_MAPPED  MEM_COMMIT  PAGE_READONLY                  <unknown>  [................]
+      254`d1301000      254`d1310000        0`0000f000             MEM_FREE    PAGE_NOACCESS                  Free
+      254`d1310000      254`d140f000        0`000ff000 MEM_PRIVATE MEM_COMMIT  PAGE_READWRITE                 Heap       [ID: 0; Handle: 00000254d1310000; Type: Segment]
       254`d140f000      254`d1410000        0`00001000 MEM_PRIVATE MEM_RESERVE                                <unknown>
+      254`d1410000      254`d1411000        0`00001000 MEM_PRIVATE MEM_COMMIT  PAGE_READONLY                  PageHeap   [PageHeap: 254d1411000; NormalHeap: 254d12e0000]
       254`d1411000      254`d1412000        0`00001000 MEM_PRIVATE MEM_COMMIT  PAGE_READWRITE                 PageHeap   [PageHeap: 254d1411000; NormalHeap: 254d12e0000]
       254`d1412000      254`d2410000        0`00ffe000 MEM_PRIVATE MEM_RESERVE                                PageHeap   [PageHeap: 254d1411000; NormalHeap: 254d12e0000]
+      254`d2410000      254`d250f000        0`000ff000 MEM_PRIVATE MEM_COMMIT  PAGE_READWRITE                 Heap       [ID: 1; Handle: 00000254d12e0000; Type: Segment]
       254`d250f000      254`d2510000        0`00001000 MEM_PRIVATE MEM_RESERVE                                <unknown>
+      254`d2510000      254`d2617000        0`00107000 MEM_PRIVATE MEM_COMMIT  PAGE_READWRITE                 <unknown>  [.........p......]
+      254`d2617000      254`d2620000        0`00009000             MEM_FREE    PAGE_NOACCESS                  Free
+      254`d2620000      254`d2751000        0`00131000 MEM_PRIVATE MEM_COMMIT  PAGE_READWRITE                 <unknown>  [................]
+      254`d2751000      254`d2760000        0`0000f000             MEM_FREE    PAGE_NOACCESS                  Free
+      254`d2760000      254`d2771000        0`00011000 MEM_MAPPED  MEM_COMMIT  PAGE_READONLY                  <unknown>  [................]
+      254`d2771000      254`d2780000        0`0000f000             MEM_FREE    PAGE_NOACCESS                  Free
+      254`d2780000      254`d287f000        0`000ff000 MEM_PRIVATE MEM_COMMIT  PAGE_READWRITE                 Heap       [ID: 0; Handle: 00000254d1310000; Type: Segment]
       254`d287f000      254`d2880000        0`00001000 MEM_PRIVATE MEM_RESERVE                                <unknown>
+      254`d2880000      254`d2a7f000        0`001ff000 MEM_PRIVATE MEM_COMMIT  PAGE_READWRITE                 Heap       [ID: 0; Handle: 00000254d1310000; Type: Segment]
       254`d2a7f000      254`d2a80000        0`00001000 MEM_PRIVATE MEM_RESERVE                                <unknown>
```

```
+        254`d2a80000      254`d3a80000        0`01000000 MEM_PRIVATE MEM_RESERVE                                    PageHeap   [PageHeap: 254d01e1000; NormalHeap: 254d1310000]
+        254`d3a80000      254`d3e7f000        0`003ff000 MEM_PRIVATE MEM_COMMIT  PAGE_READWRITE                     Heap       [ID: 0; Handle: 00000254d1310000; Type: Segment]
         254`d3e7f000      254`d3e80000        0`00001000 MEM_PRIVATE MEM_RESERVE                                    <unknown>
+        254`d3e80000      254`d4c82000        0`00e02000 MEM_PRIVATE MEM_RESERVE                                    PageHeap   [PageHeap: 254d01e1000; NormalHeap: 254d1310000]
         254`d4c82000      254`d4c9b000        0`00019000 MEM_PRIVATE MEM_COMMIT  PAGE_READWRITE                     PageHeap   [PageHeap: 254d01e1000; NormalHeap: 254d1310000]
         254`d4c9b000      254`d4e80000        0`001e5000 MEM_PRIVATE MEM_RESERVE                                    PageHeap   [PageHeap: 254d01e1000; NormalHeap: 254d1310000]
+        254`d4e80000      254`d5321000        0`004a1000 MEM_PRIVATE MEM_COMMIT  PAGE_READWRITE                     Heap       [ID: 0; Handle: 00000254d1310000; Type: Segment]
         254`d5321000      254`d567f000        0`0035e000 MEM_PRIVATE MEM_RESERVE                                    Heap       [ID: 0; Handle: 00000254d1310000; Type: Segment]
         254`d567f000      254`d5680000        0`00001000 MEM_PRIVATE MEM_RESERVE                                    <unknown>
+        254`d5680000      254`d56d5000        0`00055000 MEM_PRIVATE MEM_COMMIT  PAGE_READWRITE                     Heap       [ID: 1; Handle: 00000254d12e0000; Type: Segment]
         254`d56d5000      254`d587f000        0`001aa000 MEM_PRIVATE MEM_RESERVE                                    Heap       [ID: 1; Handle: 00000254d12e0000; Type: Segment]
         254`d587f000      254`d5880000        0`00001000 MEM_PRIVATE MEM_RESERVE                                    <unknown>
+        254`d5880000      254`d7481000        0`01c01000 MEM_PRIVATE MEM_COMMIT  PAGE_READWRITE                     PageHeap   [PageHeap: 254d01e1000; NormalHeap: 254d1310000]
         254`d7481000      254`d7490000        0`0000f000 MEM_PRIVATE MEM_RESERVE                                    PageHeap   [PageHeap: 254d01e1000; NormalHeap: 254d1310000]
+        254`d7490000     7ff4`bcb20000     7d9f`e5690000             MEM_FREE    PAGE_NOACCESS                      Free
+       7ff4`bcb20000     7ff4`bcb25000        0`00005000 MEM_MAPPED  MEM_COMMIT  PAGE_READONLY                      Other      [Read Only Shared Memory]
        7ff4`bcb25000     7ff4`bcc20000        0`000fb000 MEM_MAPPED  MEM_RESERVE                                    <unknown>
+       7ff4`bcc20000     7ff5`bcc40000        1`00020000 MEM_PRIVATE MEM_RESERVE                                    <unknown>
+       7ff5`bcc40000     7ff5`bec40000        0`02000000 MEM_PRIVATE MEM_RESERVE                                    <unknown>
        7ff5`bec40000     7ff5`bec41000        0`00001000 MEM_PRIVATE MEM_COMMIT  PAGE_READWRITE                     <unknown>  [................]
+       7ff5`bec41000     7ff5`bec50000        0`0000f000             MEM_FREE    PAGE_NOACCESS                      Free
+       7ff5`bec50000     7ff5`bec51000        0`00001000 MEM_MAPPED  MEM_COMMIT  PAGE_READONLY                      <unknown>  [................]
+       7ff5`bec51000     7ff7`5a0c0000        1`9b46f000             MEM_FREE    PAGE_NOACCESS                      Free
+       7ff7`5a0c0000     7ff7`5a0c1000        0`00001000 MEM_IMAGE   MEM_COMMIT  PAGE_READONLY                      Image      [complex_case; "C:\Work\complex-case.exe"]
        7ff7`5a0c1000     7ff7`5a0de000        0`0001d000 MEM_IMAGE   MEM_COMMIT  PAGE_EXECUTE_READ                  Image      [complex_case; "C:\Work\complex-case.exe"]
        7ff7`5a0de000     7ff7`5a0ea000        0`0000c000 MEM_IMAGE   MEM_COMMIT  PAGE_READONLY                      Image      [complex_case; "C:\Work\complex-case.exe"]
        7ff7`5a0ea000     7ff7`5a0eb000        0`00001000 MEM_IMAGE   MEM_COMMIT  PAGE_READWRITE                     Image      [complex_case; "C:\Work\complex-case.exe"]
        7ff7`5a0eb000     7ff7`5a0ee000        0`00003000 MEM_IMAGE   MEM_COMMIT  PAGE_READONLY                      Image      [complex_case; "C:\Work\complex-case.exe"]
+       7ff7`5a0ee000     7ffc`40c20000        4`e6b32000             MEM_FREE    PAGE_NOACCESS                      Free
+       7ffc`40c20000     7ffc`40c21000        0`00001000 MEM_IMAGE   MEM_COMMIT  PAGE_READONLY                      Image      [verifier; "C:\Windows\System32\verifier.dll"]
        7ffc`40c21000     7ffc`40c4c000        0`0002b000 MEM_IMAGE   MEM_COMMIT  PAGE_EXECUTE_READ                  Image      [verifier; "C:\Windows\System32\verifier.dll"]
        7ffc`40c4c000     7ffc`40c56000        0`0000a000 MEM_IMAGE   MEM_COMMIT  PAGE_READONLY                      Image      [verifier; "C:\Windows\System32\verifier.dll"]
        7ffc`40c56000     7ffc`40c5e000        0`00008000 MEM_IMAGE   MEM_COMMIT  PAGE_READWRITE                     Image      [verifier; "C:\Windows\System32\verifier.dll"]
        7ffc`40c5e000     7ffc`40c5f000        0`00001000 MEM_IMAGE   MEM_COMMIT  PAGE_WRITECOPY                     Image      [verifier; "C:\Windows\System32\verifier.dll"]
        7ffc`40c5f000     7ffc`40c68000        0`00009000 MEM_IMAGE   MEM_COMMIT  PAGE_READWRITE                     Image      [verifier; "C:\Windows\System32\verifier.dll"]
        7ffc`40c68000     7ffc`40c6f000        0`00007000 MEM_IMAGE   MEM_COMMIT  PAGE_WRITECOPY                     Image      [verifier; "C:\Windows\System32\verifier.dll"]
        7ffc`40c6f000     7ffc`40c71000        0`00002000 MEM_IMAGE   MEM_COMMIT  PAGE_READWRITE                     Image      [verifier; "C:\Windows\System32\verifier.dll"]
        7ffc`40c71000     7ffc`40c96000        0`00025000 MEM_IMAGE   MEM_COMMIT  PAGE_READONLY                      Image      [verifier; "C:\Windows\System32\verifier.dll"]
+       7ffc`40c96000     7ffc`537c0000        0`12b2a000             MEM_FREE    PAGE_NOACCESS                      Free
+       7ffc`537c0000     7ffc`537c1000        0`00001000 MEM_IMAGE   MEM_COMMIT  PAGE_READONLY                      Image      [VCRUNTIME140; "C:\Windows\System32\VCRUNTIME140.dll"]
        7ffc`537c1000     7ffc`537d1000        0`00010000 MEM_IMAGE   MEM_COMMIT  PAGE_EXECUTE_READ                  Image      [VCRUNTIME140; "C:\Windows\System32\VCRUNTIME140.dll"]
        7ffc`537d1000     7ffc`537d6000        0`00005000 MEM_IMAGE   MEM_COMMIT  PAGE_READONLY                      Image      [VCRUNTIME140; "C:\Windows\System32\VCRUNTIME140.dll"]
        7ffc`537d6000     7ffc`537d7000        0`00001000 MEM_IMAGE   MEM_COMMIT  PAGE_READWRITE                     Image      [VCRUNTIME140; "C:\Windows\System32\VCRUNTIME140.dll"]
        7ffc`537d7000     7ffc`537db000        0`00004000 MEM_IMAGE   MEM_COMMIT  PAGE_READONLY                      Image      [VCRUNTIME140; "C:\Windows\System32\VCRUNTIME140.dll"]
+       7ffc`537db000     7ffc`5ec10000        0`0b435000             MEM_FREE    PAGE_NOACCESS                      Free
+       7ffc`5ec10000     7ffc`5ec11000        0`00001000 MEM_IMAGE   MEM_COMMIT  PAGE_READONLY                      Image      [apphelp; "C:\Windows\System32\apphelp.dll"]
        7ffc`5ec11000     7ffc`5ec5f000        0`0004e000 MEM_IMAGE   MEM_COMMIT  PAGE_EXECUTE_READ                  Image      [apphelp; "C:\Windows\System32\apphelp.dll"]
        7ffc`5ec5f000     7ffc`5ec81000        0`00022000 MEM_IMAGE   MEM_COMMIT  PAGE_READONLY                      Image      [apphelp; "C:\Windows\System32\apphelp.dll"]
        7ffc`5ec81000     7ffc`5ec84000        0`00003000 MEM_IMAGE   MEM_COMMIT  PAGE_READWRITE                     Image      [apphelp; "C:\Windows\System32\apphelp.dll"]
        7ffc`5ec84000     7ffc`5eca1000        0`0001d000 MEM_IMAGE   MEM_COMMIT  PAGE_READONLY                      Image      [apphelp; "C:\Windows\System32\apphelp.dll"]
+       7ffc`5eca1000     7ffc`61c30000        0`02f8f000             MEM_FREE    PAGE_NOACCESS                      Free
+       7ffc`61c30000     7ffc`61c31000        0`00001000 MEM_IMAGE   MEM_COMMIT  PAGE_READONLY                      Image      [KERNELBASE; "C:\Windows\System32\KERNELBASE.dll"]
        7ffc`61c31000     7ffc`61db1000        0`00180000 MEM_IMAGE   MEM_COMMIT  PAGE_EXECUTE_READ                  Image      [KERNELBASE; "C:\Windows\System32\KERNELBASE.dll"]
        7ffc`61db1000     7ffc`61f67000        0`001b6000 MEM_IMAGE   MEM_COMMIT  PAGE_READONLY                      Image      [KERNELBASE; "C:\Windows\System32\KERNELBASE.dll"]
        7ffc`61f67000     7ffc`61f6c000        0`00005000 MEM_IMAGE   MEM_COMMIT  PAGE_READWRITE                     Image      [KERNELBASE; "C:\Windows\System32\KERNELBASE.dll"]
        7ffc`61f6c000     7ffc`61fb5000        0`00049000 MEM_IMAGE   MEM_COMMIT  PAGE_READONLY                      Image      [KERNELBASE; "C:\Windows\System32\KERNELBASE.dll"]
+       7ffc`61fb5000     7ffc`62090000        0`000db000             MEM_FREE    PAGE_NOACCESS                      Free
+       7ffc`62090000     7ffc`62091000        0`00001000 MEM_IMAGE   MEM_COMMIT  PAGE_READONLY                      Image      [ucrtbase; "C:\Windows\System32\ucrtbase.dll"]
        7ffc`62091000     7ffc`62154000        0`000c3000 MEM_IMAGE   MEM_COMMIT  PAGE_EXECUTE_READ                  Image      [ucrtbase; "C:\Windows\System32\ucrtbase.dll"]
        7ffc`62154000     7ffc`6218f000        0`0003b000 MEM_IMAGE   MEM_COMMIT  PAGE_READONLY                      Image      [ucrtbase; "C:\Windows\System32\ucrtbase.dll"]
        7ffc`6218f000     7ffc`62192000        0`00003000 MEM_IMAGE   MEM_COMMIT  PAGE_READWRITE                     Image      [ucrtbase; "C:\Windows\System32\ucrtbase.dll"]
        7ffc`62192000     7ffc`621a1000        0`0000f000 MEM_IMAGE   MEM_COMMIT  PAGE_READONLY                      Image      [ucrtbase; "C:\Windows\System32\ucrtbase.dll"]
+       7ffc`621a1000     7ffc`63df0000        0`01c4f000             MEM_FREE    PAGE_NOACCESS                      Free
+       7ffc`63df0000     7ffc`63df1000        0`00001000 MEM_IMAGE   MEM_COMMIT  PAGE_READONLY                      Image      [kernel32; "C:\Windows\System32\kernel32.dll"]
        7ffc`63df1000     7ffc`63e6e000        0`0007d000 MEM_IMAGE   MEM_COMMIT  PAGE_EXECUTE_READ                  Image      [kernel32; "C:\Windows\System32\kernel32.dll"]
        7ffc`63e6e000     7ffc`63ea2000        0`00034000 MEM_IMAGE   MEM_COMMIT  PAGE_READONLY                      Image      [kernel32; "C:\Windows\System32\kernel32.dll"]
        7ffc`63ea2000     7ffc`63ea3000        0`00001000 MEM_IMAGE   MEM_COMMIT  PAGE_READWRITE                     Image      [kernel32; "C:\Windows\System32\kernel32.dll"]
        7ffc`63ea3000     7ffc`63ea4000        0`00001000 MEM_IMAGE   MEM_COMMIT  PAGE_WRITECOPY                     Image      [kernel32; "C:\Windows\System32\kernel32.dll"]
        7ffc`63ea4000     7ffc`63ead000        0`00009000 MEM_IMAGE   MEM_COMMIT  PAGE_READONLY                      Image      [kernel32; "C:\Windows\System32\kernel32.dll"]
+       7ffc`63ead000     7ffc`64720000        0`00873000             MEM_FREE    PAGE_NOACCESS                      Free
+       7ffc`64720000     7ffc`64721000        0`00001000 MEM_IMAGE   MEM_COMMIT  PAGE_READONLY                      Image      [ntdll; "C:\Windows\System32\ntdll.dll"]
        7ffc`64721000     7ffc`6484c000        0`0012b000 MEM_IMAGE   MEM_COMMIT  PAGE_EXECUTE_READ                  Image      [ntdll; "C:\Windows\System32\ntdll.dll"]
        7ffc`6484c000     7ffc`64894000        0`00048000 MEM_IMAGE   MEM_COMMIT  PAGE_READONLY                      Image      [ntdll; "C:\Windows\System32\ntdll.dll"]
        7ffc`64894000     7ffc`64895000        0`00001000 MEM_IMAGE   MEM_COMMIT  PAGE_READWRITE                     Image      [ntdll; "C:\Windows\System32\ntdll.dll"]
        7ffc`64895000     7ffc`64897000        0`00002000 MEM_IMAGE   MEM_COMMIT  PAGE_WRITECOPY                     Image      [ntdll; "C:\Windows\System32\ntdll.dll"]
        7ffc`64897000     7ffc`6489f000        0`00008000 MEM_IMAGE   MEM_COMMIT  PAGE_READWRITE                     Image      [ntdll; "C:\Windows\System32\ntdll.dll"]
        7ffc`6489f000     7ffc`648a0000        0`00001000 MEM_IMAGE   MEM_COMMIT  PAGE_WRITECOPY                     Image      [ntdll; "C:\Windows\System32\ntdll.dll"]
        7ffc`648a0000     7ffc`6492a000        0`0008a000 MEM_IMAGE   MEM_COMMIT  PAGE_READONLY                      Image      [ntdll; "C:\Windows\System32\ntdll.dll"]
+       7ffc`6492a000     7fff`ffff0000        3`9b6c6000             MEM_FREE    PAGE_NOACCESS                      Free
```

```
0:000> dps 00000254`cea18b60
00000254`cea18b60  00000000`00000000
00000254`cea18b68  000e0000`00006fff
00000254`cea18b70  00007ffc`40c22743 verifier!AVrfDebugPageHeapAllocate+0x403
00000254`cea18b78  00007ffc`648241cc ntdll!RtlDebugAllocateHeap+0x48
00000254`cea18b80  00007ffc`647de1a2 ntdll!RtlpAllocateHeap+0x93042
00000254`cea18b88  00007ffc`6474929c ntdll!RtlpAllocateHeapInternal+0x6ac
00000254`cea18b90  00007ffc`40c4084d verifier!AVrfpRtlAllocateHeap+0x11d
00000254`cea18b98  00007ff7`5a0c6db8 complex_case!std::thread::Thread::new_inner+0x48
[/rustc/eeb90cda1969383f56a2637cbd3037bdf598841c/library\std\src\thread\mod.rs @ 1402]
00000254`cea18ba0  00007ff7`5a0c6d5b complex_case!std::thread::Thread::new_unnamed+0x1b
[/rustc/eeb90cda1969383f56a2637cbd3037bdf598841c/library\std\src\thread\mod.rs @ 1388]
00000254`cea18ba8  00007ff7`5a0c11c6 complex_case!ZN3std6thread7Builder15spawn_unchecked17h4b51093272731609E+0x86
00000254`cea18bb0  00007ff7`5a0c3760 complex_case!ZN3std3sys9backtrace28__rust_begin_short_backtrace17h3e8324a489e54ea5E+0x220
00000254`cea18bb8  00007ff7`5a0c1f60 complex_case!ZN3std6thread7Builder15spawn_unchecked17h6e56a25e80bf8795E+0x790
00000254`cea18bc0  00007ff7`5a0ce43d complex_case!std::sys::pal::windows::thread::impl$0::new::thread_start+0x3d
[/rustc/eeb90cda1969383f56a2637cbd3037bdf598841c/library\std\src\sys\pal\windows\thread.rs @ 58]
00000254`cea18bc8  00007ffc`40c43bae verifier!AVrfpStandardThreadFunction+0x4e
00000254`cea18bd0  00007ffc`63e053e0 kernel32!BaseThreadInitThunk+0x10
00000254`cea18bd8  00007ffc`6472485b ntdll!RtlUserThreadStart+0x2b
```

```
0:000> dp 00000254d531f120
00000254`d531f120  00000000`00000000 204a7822`4d19156b
00000254`d531f130  00000254`abcdaaaa 80000254`d01e1000
```

```
00000254`d531f140   00000000`00000030 00000000`00000080
00000254`d531f150   00000254`d01e1168 00000254`d531f0a0
00000254`d531f160   00000254`cea18be0 dcbaaaaa`00000000
00000254`d531f170   00000000`00000001 00000000`00000001
00000254`d531f180   00000000`00000000 00000000`00000001
00000254`d531f190   00000000`00000000 00000000`00000000
```

```
0:000> dps 00000254`cea18be0
00000254`cea18be0  00000000`00000000
00000254`cea18be8  000c0000`00005fff
00000254`cea18bf0  00007ffc`40c22743 verifier!AVrfDebugPageHeapAllocate+0x403
00000254`cea18bf8  00007ffc`648241cc ntdll!RtlDebugAllocateHeap+0x48
00000254`cea18c00  00007ffc`647de1a2 ntdll!RtlpAllocateHeap+0x93042
00000254`cea18c08  00007ffc`6474929c ntdll!RtlpAllocateHeapInternal+0x6ac
00000254`cea18c10  00007ffc`40c4084d verifier!AVrfpRtlAllocateHeap+0x11d
00000254`cea18c18  00007ff7`5a0c12de complex_case!ZN3std6thread7Builder15spawn_unchecked17h4b51093272731609E+0x19e
00000254`cea18c20  00007ff7`5a0c3760 complex_case!ZN3std3sys9backtrace28__rust_begin_short_backtrace17h3e8324a489e54ea5E+0x220
00000254`cea18c28  00007ff7`5a0c1f60 complex_case!ZN3std6thread7Builder15spawn_unchecked17h6e56a25e80bf8795E+0x790
00000254`cea18c30  00007ff7`5a0ce43d complex_case!std::sys::pal::windows::thread::impl$0::new::thread_start+0x3d
[/rustc/eeb90cda1969383f56a2637cbd3037bdf598841c/library\std\src\sys\pal\windows\thread.rs @ 58]
00000254`cea18c38  00007ffc`40c43bae verifier!AVrfpStandardThreadFunction+0x4e
00000254`cea18c40  00007ffc`63e053e0 kernel32!BaseThreadInitThunk+0x10
00000254`cea18c48  00007ffc`6472485b ntdll!RtlUserThreadStart+0x2b
00000254`cea18c50  00000000`00000000
00000254`cea18c58  000b0000`00005fff
```

19.   Finally, we find the stack trace for the largest heap block:

```
0:000> !address -summary
```

--- Usage Summary ---------------	RgnCount	----------- Total Size --------	%ofBusy	%ofTotal
Free	30	7ffe`f3d76000 (127.996 TB)		100.00%
<unknown>	30	1`0266d000 (4.038 GB)	96.36%	0.00%
PageHeap	26	0`05c10000 (92.062 MB)	2.15%	0.00%
Other	7	0`01829000 (24.160 MB)	0.56%	0.00%
Heap	11	0`01318000 (19.094 MB)	0.45%	0.00%
Stack	21	0`00c00000 (12.000 MB)	0.28%	0.00%
Image	48	0`008ad000 (8.676 MB)	0.20%	0.00%
TEB	7	0`0000e000 (56.000 kB)	0.00%	0.00%
PEB	1	0`00001000 (4.000 kB)	0.00%	0.00%

--- Type Summary (for busy) ------	RgnCount	----------- Total Size --------	%ofBusy	%ofTotal
MEM_PRIVATE	90	1`0b781000 (4.179 GB)	99.74%	0.00%
MEM_IMAGE	48	0`008ad000 (8.676 MB)	0.20%	0.00%
MEM_MAPPED	13	0`0024c000 (2.297 MB)	0.05%	0.00%

--- State Summary ---------------	RgnCount	----------- Total Size --------	%ofBusy	%ofTotal
MEM_FREE	30	7ffe`f3d76000 (127.996 TB)		100.00%
MEM_RESERVE	38	1`07f44000 (4.124 GB)	98.43%	0.00%
MEM_COMMIT	113	0`04336000 (67.211 MB)	1.57%	0.00%

--- Protect Summary (for commit) -	RgnCount	----------- Total Size --------	%ofBusy	%ofTotal
PAGE_READWRITE	54	0`03947000 (57.277 MB)	1.33%	0.00%
PAGE_READONLY	39	0`0052b000 (5.168 MB)	0.12%	0.00%
PAGE_EXECUTE_READ	8	0`00491000 (4.566 MB)	0.11%	0.00%
PAGE_READWRITE | PAGE_GUARD	7	0`00027000 (156.000 kB)	0.00%	0.00%
PAGE_WRITECOPY	5	0`0000c000 (48.000 kB)	0.00%	0.00%

--- Largest Region by Usage -----------	Base Address --------	Region Size ----------
Free	254`d7490000	7d9f`e5690000 (125.625 TB)
<unknown>	7ff4`bcc20000	1`00020000 (4.000 GB)
PageHeap	254`d5880000	0`01c01000 (28.004 MB)
Other	254`cea1a000	0`017c5000 (23.770 MB)

```
Heap                        254`d4e80000      0`004a1000 (    4.629 MB)
Stack                        eb`d8700000      0`001f8000 (    1.969 MB)
Image                      7ffc`61db1000      0`001b6000 (    1.711 MB)
TEB                          eb`d820a000      0`00002000 (    8.000 kB)
PEB                          eb`d835a000      0`00001000 (    4.000 kB)

0:000> dps 254`d5880000 L246
00000254`d5880000  eeeeeeee`eeeeeeee
00000254`d5880008  00000254`d01e2820
00000254`d5880010  00000000`00000000
00000254`d5880018  00000000`00000000
00000254`d5880020  00000000`00000000
00000254`d5880028  00000000`00000000
00000254`d5880030  00000000`00000000
00000254`d5880038  00000000`00000000
00000254`d5880040  00000000`00000000
00000254`d5880048  00000000`00000000
00000254`d5880050  00000000`00000000
00000254`d5880058  00000000`00000000
00000254`d5880060  00000000`00000000
00000254`d5880068  00000000`00000000
00000254`d5880070  00000000`00000000
00000254`d5880078  00000000`00000000
00000254`d5880080  00000000`00000000
00000254`d5880088  00000000`00000000
00000254`d5880090  00000000`00000000
00000254`d5880098  00000000`00000000
00000254`d58800a0  00000000`00000000
00000254`d58800a8  00000000`00000000
00000254`d58800b0  00000000`00000000
00000254`d58800b8  00000000`00000000
00000254`d58800c0  00000000`00000000
00000254`d58800c8  00000000`00000000
00000254`d58800d0  00000000`00000000
00000254`d58800d8  00000000`00000000
00000254`d58800e0  00000000`00000000
00000254`d58800e8  00000000`00000000
00000254`d58800f0  00000000`00000000
00000254`d58800f8  00000000`00000000
00000254`d5880100  00000000`00000000
00000254`d5880108  00000000`00000000
00000254`d5880110  00000000`00000000
00000254`d5880118  00000000`00000000
00000254`d5880120  00000000`00000000
00000254`d5880128  00000000`00000000
00000254`d5880130  00000000`00000000
00000254`d5880138  00000000`00000000
00000254`d5880140  00000000`00000000
00000254`d5880148  00000000`00000000
00000254`d5880150  00000000`00000000
00000254`d5880158  00000000`00000000
00000254`d5880160  00000000`00000000
00000254`d5880168  00000000`00000000
00000254`d5880170  00000000`00000000
00000254`d5880178  00000000`00000000
00000254`d5880180  00000000`00000000
00000254`d5880188  00000000`00000000
00000254`d5880190  00000000`00000000
00000254`d5880198  00000000`00000000
```

```
00000254`d58801a0    00000000`00000000
00000254`d58801a8    00000000`00000000
00000254`d58801b0    00000000`00000000
00000254`d58801b8    00000000`00000000
00000254`d58801c0    00000000`00000000
00000254`d58801c8    00000000`00000000
00000254`d58801d0    00000000`00000000
00000254`d58801d8    00000000`00000000
00000254`d58801e0    00000000`00000000
00000254`d58801e8    00000000`00000000
00000254`d58801f0    00000000`00000000
00000254`d58801f8    00000000`00000000
00000254`d5880200    00000000`00000000
00000254`d5880208    00000000`00000000
00000254`d5880210    00000000`00000000
00000254`d5880218    00000000`00000000
00000254`d5880220    00000000`00000000
00000254`d5880228    00000000`00000000
00000254`d5880230    00000000`00000000
00000254`d5880238    00000000`00000000
00000254`d5880240    00000000`00000000
00000254`d5880248    00000000`00000000
00000254`d5880250    00000000`00000000
00000254`d5880258    00000000`00000000
00000254`d5880260    00000000`00000000
00000254`d5880268    00000000`00000000
00000254`d5880270    00000000`00000000
00000254`d5880278    00000000`00000000
00000254`d5880280    00000000`00000000
00000254`d5880288    00000000`00000000
00000254`d5880290    00000000`00000000
00000254`d5880298    00000000`00000000
00000254`d58802a0    00000000`00000000
00000254`d58802a8    00000000`00000000
00000254`d58802b0    00000000`00000000
00000254`d58802b8    00000000`00000000
00000254`d58802c0    00000000`00000000
00000254`d58802c8    00000000`00000000
00000254`d58802d0    00000000`00000000
00000254`d58802d8    00000000`00000000
00000254`d58802e0    00000000`00000000
00000254`d58802e8    00000000`00000000
00000254`d58802f0    00000000`00000000
00000254`d58802f8    00000000`00000000
00000254`d5880300    00000000`00000000
00000254`d5880308    00000000`00000000
00000254`d5880310    00000000`00000000
00000254`d5880318    00000000`00000000
00000254`d5880320    00000000`00000000
00000254`d5880328    00000000`00000000
00000254`d5880330    00000000`00000000
00000254`d5880338    00000000`00000000
00000254`d5880340    00000000`00000000
00000254`d5880348    00000000`00000000
00000254`d5880350    00000000`00000000
00000254`d5880358    00000000`00000000
00000254`d5880360    00000000`00000000
00000254`d5880368    00000000`00000000
00000254`d5880370    00000000`00000000
```

```
00000254`d5880378  00000000`00000000
00000254`d5880380  00000000`00000000
00000254`d5880388  00000000`00000000
00000254`d5880390  00000000`00000000
00000254`d5880398  00000000`00000000
00000254`d58803a0  00000000`00000000
00000254`d58803a8  00000000`00000000
00000254`d58803b0  00000000`00000000
00000254`d58803b8  00000000`00000000
00000254`d58803c0  00000000`00000000
00000254`d58803c8  00000000`00000000
00000254`d58803d0  00000000`00000000
00000254`d58803d8  00000000`00000000
00000254`d58803e0  00000000`00000000
00000254`d58803e8  00000000`00000000
00000254`d58803f0  00000000`00000000
00000254`d58803f8  00000000`00000000
00000254`d5880400  00000000`00000000
00000254`d5880408  00000000`00000000
00000254`d5880410  00000000`00000000
00000254`d5880418  00000000`00000000
00000254`d5880420  00000000`00000000
00000254`d5880428  00000000`00000000
00000254`d5880430  00000000`00000000
00000254`d5880438  00000000`00000000
00000254`d5880440  00000000`00000000
00000254`d5880448  00000000`00000000
00000254`d5880450  00000000`00000000
00000254`d5880458  00000000`00000000
00000254`d5880460  00000000`00000000
00000254`d5880468  00000000`00000000
00000254`d5880470  00000000`00000000
00000254`d5880478  00000000`00000000
00000254`d5880480  00000000`00000000
00000254`d5880488  00000000`00000000
00000254`d5880490  00000000`00000000
00000254`d5880498  00000000`00000000
00000254`d58804a0  00000000`00000000
00000254`d58804a8  00000000`00000000
00000254`d58804b0  00000000`00000000
00000254`d58804b8  00000000`00000000
00000254`d58804c0  00000000`00000000
00000254`d58804c8  00000000`00000000
00000254`d58804d0  00000000`00000000
00000254`d58804d8  00000000`00000000
00000254`d58804e0  00000000`00000000
00000254`d58804e8  00000000`00000000
00000254`d58804f0  00000000`00000000
00000254`d58804f8  00000000`00000000
00000254`d5880500  00000000`00000000
00000254`d5880508  00000000`00000000
00000254`d5880510  00000000`00000000
00000254`d5880518  00000000`00000000
00000254`d5880520  00000000`00000000
00000254`d5880528  00000000`00000000
00000254`d5880530  00000000`00000000
00000254`d5880538  00000000`00000000
00000254`d5880540  00000000`00000000
00000254`d5880548  00000000`00000000
```

```
00000254`d5880550    00000000`00000000
00000254`d5880558    00000000`00000000
00000254`d5880560    00000000`00000000
00000254`d5880568    00000000`00000000
00000254`d5880570    00000000`00000000
00000254`d5880578    00000000`00000000
00000254`d5880580    00000000`00000000
00000254`d5880588    00000000`00000000
00000254`d5880590    00000000`00000000
00000254`d5880598    00000000`00000000
00000254`d58805a0    00000000`00000000
00000254`d58805a8    00000000`00000000
00000254`d58805b0    00000000`00000000
00000254`d58805b8    00000000`00000000
00000254`d58805c0    00000000`00000000
00000254`d58805c8    00000000`00000000
00000254`d58805d0    00000000`00000000
00000254`d58805d8    00000000`00000000
00000254`d58805e0    00000000`00000000
00000254`d58805e8    00000000`00000000
00000254`d58805f0    00000000`00000000
00000254`d58805f8    00000000`00000000
00000254`d5880600    00000000`00000000
00000254`d5880608    00000000`00000000
00000254`d5880610    00000000`00000000
00000254`d5880618    00000000`00000000
00000254`d5880620    00000000`00000000
00000254`d5880628    00000000`00000000
00000254`d5880630    00000000`00000000
00000254`d5880638    00000000`00000000
00000254`d5880640    00000000`00000000
00000254`d5880648    00000000`00000000
00000254`d5880650    00000000`00000000
00000254`d5880658    00000000`00000000
00000254`d5880660    00000000`00000000
00000254`d5880668    00000000`00000000
00000254`d5880670    00000000`00000000
00000254`d5880678    00000000`00000000
00000254`d5880680    00000000`00000000
00000254`d5880688    00000000`00000000
00000254`d5880690    00000000`00000000
00000254`d5880698    00000000`00000000
00000254`d58806a0    00000000`00000000
00000254`d58806a8    00000000`00000000
00000254`d58806b0    00000000`00000000
00000254`d58806b8    00000000`00000000
00000254`d58806c0    00000000`00000000
00000254`d58806c8    00000000`00000000
00000254`d58806d0    00000000`00000000
00000254`d58806d8    00000000`00000000
00000254`d58806e0    00000000`00000000
00000254`d58806e8    00000000`00000000
00000254`d58806f0    00000000`00000000
00000254`d58806f8    00000000`00000000
00000254`d5880700    00000000`00000000
00000254`d5880708    00000000`00000000
00000254`d5880710    00000000`00000000
00000254`d5880718    00000000`00000000
00000254`d5880720    00000000`00000000
```

```
00000254`d5880728    00000000`00000000
00000254`d5880730    00000000`00000000
00000254`d5880738    00000000`00000000
00000254`d5880740    00000000`00000000
00000254`d5880748    00000000`00000000
00000254`d5880750    00000000`00000000
00000254`d5880758    00000000`00000000
00000254`d5880760    00000000`00000000
00000254`d5880768    00000000`00000000
00000254`d5880770    00000000`00000000
00000254`d5880778    00000000`00000000
00000254`d5880780    00000000`00000000
00000254`d5880788    00000000`00000000
00000254`d5880790    00000000`00000000
00000254`d5880798    00000000`00000000
00000254`d58807a0    00000000`00000000
00000254`d58807a8    00000000`00000000
00000254`d58807b0    00000000`00000000
00000254`d58807b8    00000000`00000000
00000254`d58807c0    00000000`00000000
00000254`d58807c8    00000000`00000000
00000254`d58807d0    00000000`00000000
00000254`d58807d8    00000000`00000000
00000254`d58807e0    00000000`00000000
00000254`d58807e8    00000000`00000000
00000254`d58807f0    00000000`00000000
00000254`d58807f8    00000000`00000000
00000254`d5880800    00000000`00000000
00000254`d5880808    00000000`00000000
00000254`d5880810    00000000`00000000
00000254`d5880818    00000000`00000000
00000254`d5880820    00000000`00000000
00000254`d5880828    00000000`00000000
00000254`d5880830    00000000`00000000
00000254`d5880838    00000000`00000000
00000254`d5880840    00000000`00000000
00000254`d5880848    00000000`00000000
00000254`d5880850    00000000`00000000
00000254`d5880858    00000000`00000000
00000254`d5880860    00000000`00000000
00000254`d5880868    00000000`00000000
00000254`d5880870    00000000`00000000
00000254`d5880878    00000000`00000000
00000254`d5880880    00000000`00000000
00000254`d5880888    00000000`00000000
00000254`d5880890    00000000`00000000
00000254`d5880898    00000000`00000000
00000254`d58808a0    00000000`00000000
00000254`d58808a8    00000000`00000000
00000254`d58808b0    00000000`00000000
00000254`d58808b8    00000000`00000000
00000254`d58808c0    00000000`00000000
00000254`d58808c8    00000000`00000000
00000254`d58808d0    00000000`00000000
00000254`d58808d8    00000000`00000000
00000254`d58808e0    00000000`00000000
00000254`d58808e8    00000000`00000000
00000254`d58808f0    00000000`00000000
00000254`d58808f8    00000000`00000000
```

```
00000254`d5880900   00000000`00000000
00000254`d5880908   00000000`00000000
00000254`d5880910   00000000`00000000
00000254`d5880918   00000000`00000000
00000254`d5880920   00000000`00000000
00000254`d5880928   00000000`00000000
00000254`d5880930   00000000`00000000
00000254`d5880938   00000000`00000000
00000254`d5880940   00000000`00000000
00000254`d5880948   00000000`00000000
00000254`d5880950   00000000`00000000
00000254`d5880958   00000000`00000000
00000254`d5880960   00000000`00000000
00000254`d5880968   00000000`00000000
00000254`d5880970   00000000`00000000
00000254`d5880978   00000000`00000000
00000254`d5880980   00000000`00000000
00000254`d5880988   00000000`00000000
00000254`d5880990   00000000`00000000
00000254`d5880998   00000000`00000000
00000254`d58809a0   00000000`00000000
00000254`d58809a8   00000000`00000000
00000254`d58809b0   00000000`00000000
00000254`d58809b8   00000000`00000000
00000254`d58809c0   00000000`00000000
00000254`d58809c8   00000000`00000000
00000254`d58809d0   00000000`00000000
00000254`d58809d8   00000000`00000000
00000254`d58809e0   00000000`00000000
00000254`d58809e8   00000000`00000000
00000254`d58809f0   00000000`00000000
00000254`d58809f8   00000000`00000000
00000254`d5880a00   00000000`00000000
00000254`d5880a08   00000000`00000000
00000254`d5880a10   00000000`00000000
00000254`d5880a18   00000000`00000000
00000254`d5880a20   00000000`00000000
00000254`d5880a28   00000000`00000000
00000254`d5880a30   00000000`00000000
00000254`d5880a38   00000000`00000000
00000254`d5880a40   00000000`00000000
00000254`d5880a48   00000000`00000000
00000254`d5880a50   00000000`00000000
00000254`d5880a58   00000000`00000000
00000254`d5880a60   00000000`00000000
00000254`d5880a68   00000000`00000000
00000254`d5880a70   00000000`00000000
00000254`d5880a78   00000000`00000000
00000254`d5880a80   00000000`00000000
00000254`d5880a88   00000000`00000000
00000254`d5880a90   00000000`00000000
00000254`d5880a98   00000000`00000000
00000254`d5880aa0   00000000`00000000
00000254`d5880aa8   00000000`00000000
00000254`d5880ab0   00000000`00000000
00000254`d5880ab8   00000000`00000000
00000254`d5880ac0   00000000`00000000
00000254`d5880ac8   00000000`00000000
00000254`d5880ad0   00000000`00000000
```

```
00000254`d5880ad8    00000000`00000000
00000254`d5880ae0    00000000`00000000
00000254`d5880ae8    00000000`00000000
00000254`d5880af0    00000000`00000000
00000254`d5880af8    00000000`00000000
00000254`d5880b00    00000000`00000000
00000254`d5880b08    00000000`00000000
00000254`d5880b10    00000000`00000000
00000254`d5880b18    00000000`00000000
00000254`d5880b20    00000000`00000000
00000254`d5880b28    00000000`00000000
00000254`d5880b30    00000000`00000000
00000254`d5880b38    00000000`00000000
00000254`d5880b40    00000000`00000000
00000254`d5880b48    00000000`00000000
00000254`d5880b50    00000000`00000000
00000254`d5880b58    00000000`00000000
00000254`d5880b60    00000000`00000000
00000254`d5880b68    00000000`00000000
00000254`d5880b70    00000000`00000000
00000254`d5880b78    00000000`00000000
00000254`d5880b80    00000000`00000000
00000254`d5880b88    00000000`00000000
00000254`d5880b90    00000000`00000000
00000254`d5880b98    00000000`00000000
00000254`d5880ba0    00000000`00000000
00000254`d5880ba8    00000000`00000000
00000254`d5880bb0    00000000`00000000
00000254`d5880bb8    00000000`00000000
00000254`d5880bc0    00000000`00000000
00000254`d5880bc8    00000000`00000000
00000254`d5880bd0    00000000`00000000
00000254`d5880bd8    00000000`00000000
00000254`d5880be0    00000000`00000000
00000254`d5880be8    00000000`00000000
00000254`d5880bf0    00000000`00000000
00000254`d5880bf8    00000000`00000000
00000254`d5880c00    00000000`00000000
00000254`d5880c08    00000000`00000000
00000254`d5880c10    00000000`00000000
00000254`d5880c18    00000000`00000000
00000254`d5880c20    00000000`00000000
00000254`d5880c28    00000000`00000000
00000254`d5880c30    00000000`00000000
00000254`d5880c38    00000000`00000000
00000254`d5880c40    00000000`00000000
00000254`d5880c48    00000000`00000000
00000254`d5880c50    00000000`00000000
00000254`d5880c58    00000000`00000000
00000254`d5880c60    00000000`00000000
00000254`d5880c68    00000000`00000000
00000254`d5880c70    00000000`00000000
00000254`d5880c78    00000000`00000000
00000254`d5880c80    00000000`00000000
00000254`d5880c88    00000000`00000000
00000254`d5880c90    00000000`00000000
00000254`d5880c98    00000000`00000000
00000254`d5880ca0    00000000`00000000
00000254`d5880ca8    00000000`00000000
```

```
00000254`d5880cb0    00000000`00000000
00000254`d5880cb8    00000000`00000000
00000254`d5880cc0    00000000`00000000
00000254`d5880cc8    00000000`00000000
...
00000254`d5880e20    00000000`00000000
00000254`d5880e28    00000000`00000000
00000254`d5880e30    00000000`00000000
00000254`d5880e38    00000000`00000000
00000254`d5880e40    00000000`00000000
00000254`d5880e48    00000000`00000000
00000254`d5880e50    00000000`00000000
00000254`d5880e58    00000000`00000000
00000254`d5880e60    00000000`00000000
00000254`d5880e68    00000000`00000000
00000254`d5880e70    00000000`00000000
00000254`d5880e78    00000000`00000000
00000254`d5880e80    00000000`00000000
00000254`d5880e88    00000000`00000000
00000254`d5880e90    00000000`00000000
00000254`d5880e98    00000000`00000000
00000254`d5880ea0    00000000`00000000
00000254`d5880ea8    00000000`00000000
00000254`d5880eb0    00000000`00000000
00000254`d5880eb8    00000000`00000000
00000254`d5880ec0    00000000`00000000
00000254`d5880ec8    00000000`00000000
00000254`d5880ed0    00000000`00000000
00000254`d5880ed8    00000000`00000000
00000254`d5880ee0    00000000`00000000
00000254`d5880ee8    00000000`00000000
00000254`d5880ef0    00000000`00000000
00000254`d5880ef8    00000000`00000000
00000254`d5880f00    00000000`00000000
00000254`d5880f08    00000000`00000000
00000254`d5880f10    00000000`00000000
00000254`d5880f18    00000000`00000000
00000254`d5880f20    00000000`00000000
00000254`d5880f28    00000000`00000000
00000254`d5880f30    00000000`00000000
00000254`d5880f38    00000000`00000000
00000254`d5880f40    00000000`00000000
00000254`d5880f48    00000000`00000000
00000254`d5880f50    00000000`00000000
00000254`d5880f58    00000000`00000000
00000254`d5880f60    00000000`00000000
00000254`d5880f68    00000000`00000000
00000254`d5880f70    00000000`00000000
00000254`d5880f78    00000000`00000000
00000254`d5880f80    00000000`00000000
00000254`d5880f88    00000000`00000000
00000254`d5880f90    00000000`00000000
00000254`d5880f98    00000000`00000000
00000254`d5880fa0    00000000`00000000
00000254`d5880fa8    00000000`00000000
00000254`d5880fb0    00000000`00000000
00000254`d5880fb8    00000000`00000000
00000254`d5880fc0    00000000`abcdbbbb
00000254`d5880fc8    00000254`d01e1000
```

```
00000254`d5880fd0  00000000`01c00000
00000254`d5880fd8  00000000`01c01000
00000254`d5880fe0  00000000`00000000
00000254`d5880fe8  00000000`00000000
00000254`d5880ff0  00000254`cea19450
00000254`d5880ff8  dcbabbbb`00000000
00000254`d5881000  00000000`00000001
00000254`d5881008  00000065`00000048
00000254`d5881010  0000006c`0000006c
00000254`d5881018  00000020`0000006f
00000254`d5881020  00000065`0000004c
00000254`d5881028  0000006b`00000061
00000254`d5881030  00000254`00000021
00000254`d5881038  00000000`00000002
00000254`d5881040  00000065`00000048
00000254`d5881048  0000006c`0000006c
00000254`d5881050  00000020`0000006f
00000254`d5881058  00000065`0000004c
00000254`d5881060  0000006b`00000061
00000254`d5881068  00000254`00000021
00000254`d5881070  00000000`00000003
00000254`d5881078  00000065`00000048
00000254`d5881080  0000006c`0000006c
00000254`d5881088  00000020`0000006f
00000254`d5881090  00000065`0000004c
00000254`d5881098  0000006b`00000061
00000254`d58810a0  00000254`00000021
00000254`d58810a8  00000000`00000004
00000254`d58810b0  00000065`00000048
00000254`d58810b8  0000006c`0000006c
00000254`d58810c0  00000020`0000006f
00000254`d58810c8  00000065`0000004c
00000254`d58810d0  0000006b`00000061
00000254`d58810d8  00000254`00000021
00000254`d58810e0  00000000`00000005
00000254`d58810e8  00000065`00000048
00000254`d58810f0  0000006c`0000006c
00000254`d58810f8  00000020`0000006f
00000254`d5881100  00000065`0000004c
00000254`d5881108  0000006b`00000061
00000254`d5881110  00000254`00000021
00000254`d5881118  00000000`00000006
00000254`d5881120  00000065`00000048
00000254`d5881128  0000006c`0000006c
00000254`d5881130  00000020`0000006f
00000254`d5881138  00000065`0000004c
00000254`d5881140  0000006b`00000061
00000254`d5881148  00000254`00000021
00000254`d5881150  00000000`00000007
00000254`d5881158  00000065`00000048
00000254`d5881160  0000006c`0000006c
00000254`d5881168  00000020`0000006f
00000254`d5881170  00000065`0000004c
00000254`d5881178  0000006b`00000061
00000254`d5881180  00000254`00000021
00000254`d5881188  00000000`00000008
00000254`d5881190  00000065`00000048
00000254`d5881198  0000006c`0000006c
00000254`d58811a0  00000020`0000006f
```

```
00000254`d58811a8    00000065`0000004c
00000254`d58811b0    0000006b`00000061
00000254`d58811b8    00000254`00000021
00000254`d58811c0    00000000`00000009
00000254`d58811c8    00000065`00000048
00000254`d58811d0    0000006c`0000006c
00000254`d58811d8    00000020`0000006f
00000254`d58811e0    00000065`0000004c
00000254`d58811e8    0000006b`00000061
00000254`d58811f0    00000254`00000021
00000254`d58811f8    00000000`0000000a
00000254`d5881200    00000065`00000048
00000254`d5881208    0000006c`0000006c
00000254`d5881210    00000020`0000006f
00000254`d5881218    00000065`0000004c
00000254`d5881220    0000006b`00000061
00000254`d5881228    00000254`00000021
```

```
0:000> dps 00000254`cea19450
00000254`cea19450  00000000`00000000
00000254`cea19458  000d0000`00006801
00000254`cea19460  00007ffc`40c2340c verifier!AVrfDebugPageHeapReAllocate+0x1cc
00000254`cea19468  00007ffc`64825a32 ntdll!RtlDebugReAllocateHeap+0x52
00000254`cea19470  00007ffc`647dca3e ntdll!RtlpReAllocateHeapInternal+0x98486
00000254`cea19478  00007ffc`6474458a ntdll!RtlReAllocateHeap+0x5a
00000254`cea19480  00007ffc`40c40fea verifier!AVrfpRtlReAllocateHeap+0x1fa
00000254`cea19488  00007ff7`5a0c3263
complex_case!ZN4core5array69_$LT$impl$u20$core..fmt..Debug$u20$for$u20$$u5b$T$u3b$$u20$N$u5d$$GT$3fmt17h319b7c3a0af6f58fE+0x173
00000254`cea19490  00007ff7`5a0c333f complex_case!ZN5alloc7raw_vec19RawVec$LT$T$C$A$GT$8grow_one17h03a23c82c10e5c9eE+0x7f
00000254`cea19498  00007ff7`5a0c36e9 complex_case!ZN3std3sys9backtrace28__rust_begin_short_backtrace17h3e8324a489e54ea5E+0x1a9
00000254`cea194a0  00007ff7`5a0c1f60 complex_case!ZN3std6thread7Builder15spawn_unchecked17h6e56a25e80bf8795E+0x790
00000254`cea194a8  00007ff7`5a0ce43d complex_case!std::sys::pal::windows::thread::impl$0::new::thread_start+0x3d
[/rustc/eeb90cda1969383f56a2637cbd3037bdf598841c/library\std\src\sys\pal\windows\thread.rs @ 58]
00000254`cea194b0  00007ffc`40c43bae verifier!AVrfpStandardThreadFunction+0x4e
00000254`cea194b8  00007ffc`63e053e0 kernel32!BaseThreadInitThunk+0x10
00000254`cea194c0  00007ffc`6472485b ntdll!RtlUserThreadStart+0x2b
00000254`cea194c8  00007ffc`6472485b ntdll!RtlUserThreadStart+0x2b
```

```
0:000> dc 00000254`d5881008
00000254`d5881008  00000048 00000065 0000006c 0000006c  H...e...l...l...
00000254`d5881018  0000006f 00000020 0000004c 00000065  o... ...L...e...
00000254`d5881028  00000061 0000006b 00000021 00000254  a...k...!...T...
00000254`d5881038  00000002 00000000 00000048 00000065  ........H...e...
00000254`d5881048  0000006c 0000006c 0000006f 00000020  l...l...o... ...
00000254`d5881058  0000004c 00000065 00000061 0000006b  L...e...a...k...
00000254`d5881068  00000021 00000254 00000003 00000000  !...T...........
00000254`d5881078  00000048 00000065 0000006c 0000006c  H...e...l...l...
```

20.   We can also use the **!heap -l** command to find memory leaks. Now, we close both instances of WinDbg.

Exercise RW8

- **Goal:** Learn how to recognize waits and deadlocks, dump and analyze raw stack data

- **Patterns:** Deadlock (Futex)

- \ARWMDA-Dumps\Exercise-RW8.pdf

Goal: Learn how to recognize waits and deadlocks, dump and analyze raw stack data.

Patterns: Deadlock (Futex).

1.   Launch WinDbg.

2.   Open \ARWMDA-Dumps\Process\deadlock.DMP.

3.   We get the dump file loaded:

```
Microsoft (R) Windows Debugger Version 10.0.27725.1000 AMD64
Copyright (c) Microsoft Corporation. All rights reserved.


Loading Dump File [C:\ARWMDA-Dumps\Process\deadlock.DMP]
User Mini Dump File with Full Memory: Only application data is available


************* Path validation summary **************
Response                        Time (ms)      Location
Deferred                                       srv*
Symbol search path is: srv*
Executable search path is:
Windows 10 Version 22000 MP (4 procs) Free x64
Product: WinNt, suite: SingleUserTS
Edition build lab: 22000.1.amd64fre.co_release.210604-1628
Debug session time: Sun Dec  1 20:25:48.000 2024 (UTC + 0:00)
System Uptime: 0 days 0:03:22.198
Process Uptime: 0 days 0:01:06.000
.......
For analysis of this file, run !analyze -v
ntdll!NtWaitForSingleObject+0x14:
00007ffa`d5ac4104 ret
```

4.   Open a log file and load application symbols:

```
0:000> .logopen C:\ARWMDA-Dumps\RW8.log
Opened log file 'C:\ARWMDA-Dumps\RW8.log'

0:000> .sympath+ C:\ARWMDA-Dumps\Symbols\release
Symbol search path is: srv*;C:\ARWMDA-Dumps\Symbols\release
Expanded Symbol search path is:
cache*;SRV*https://msdl.microsoft.com/download/symbols;c:\arwmda-dumps\symbols\release

************* Path validation summary **************
Response                        Time (ms)      Location
Deferred                                       srv*
OK                                             C:\ARWMDA-Dumps\Symbols\release

0:004> .reload
...........
```

Note: WinDbg may remember symbol and source paths from the previous sessions.

5.   Since it was reported that the application was hanging, we looked at its stack traces to find any waiting threads:

```
0:000> ~*kL

.  0  Id: 318.314 Suspend: 0 Teb: 000000b9`003af000 Unfrozen "main"
 # Child-SP          RetAddr               Call Site
00 000000b9`001cf6a8 00007ffa`d33510ee     ntdll!NtWaitForSingleObject+0x14
01 000000b9`001cf6b0 00007ff7`a534d2d1     KERNELBASE!WaitForSingleObjectEx+0x8e
02 000000b9`001cf750 00007ff7`a5341021     deadlock!std::sys::pal::windows::thread::Thread::join+0x21
03 000000b9`001cf7e0 00007ff7`a5343b5d     deadlock!ZN3std6thread18JoinInner$LT$T$GT$4join17h4ee8eb9e65ea5d47E+0x21
04 000000b9`001cf840 00007ff7`a5343106     deadlock!ZN4core3ptr42drop_in_place$LT$std..io..error..Error$GT$17h70f2bc589075172fE.llvm.7025607320133951313+0x48d
05 000000b9`001cf930 00007ff7`a53430ec     deadlock!ZN3std2io5Write9write_fmt17h3bf5d50606710bf5E+0xe6
06 000000b9`001cf960 00007ff7`a5345d89     deadlock!ZN3std2io5Write9write_fmt17h3bf5d50606710bf5E+0xcc
07 (Inline Function) --------`--------     deadlock!std::rt::lang_start_internal::closure$2+0x6
08 (Inline Function) --------`--------     deadlock!std::panicking::try::do_call+0x6
09 (Inline Function) --------`--------     deadlock!std::panicking::try+0x6
0a (Inline Function) --------`--------     deadlock!std::panic::catch_unwind+0x6
0b 000000b9`001cf990 00007ff7`a5343e6c     deadlock!std::rt::lang_start_internal+0x79
0c 000000b9`001cfa50 00007ff7`a535a6ec     deadlock!main+0x2c
0d (Inline Function) --------`--------     deadlock!invoke_main+0x22
0e 000000b9`001cfa90 00007ffa`d44c53e0     deadlock!__scrt_common_main_seh+0x10c
0f 000000b9`001cfad0 00007ff7`d5a2485b     kernel32!BaseThreadInitThunk+0x10
10 000000b9`001cfb00 00000000`00000000     ntdll!RtlUserThreadStart+0x2b

   1  Id: 318.1e10 Suspend: 0 Teb: 000000b9`003b5000 Unfrozen
 # Child-SP          RetAddr               Call Site
00 000000b9`007ff598 00007ffa`d5a3d89d     ntdll!NtWaitForAlertByThreadId+0x14
01 000000b9`007ff5a0 00007ffa`d5a7b3fe     ntdll!RtlpWaitOnAddressWithTimeout+0x81
02 000000b9`007ff5d0 00007ffa`d5a7b343     ntdll!RtlpWaitOnAddress+0xae
03 000000b9`007ff640 00007ffa`d336dd9f     ntdll!RtlWaitOnAddress+0x13
04 000000b9`007ff680 00007ff7`a535b744     KERNELBASE!WaitOnAddress+0x2f
05 (Inline Function) --------`--------     deadlock!std::sys::pal::windows::futex::wait_on_address+0x18
06 (Inline Function) --------`--------     deadlock!std::sys::pal::windows::futex::futex_wait+0x18
07 000000b9`007ff6c0 00007ff7`a5343469     deadlock!std::sys::sync::mutex::futex::Mutex::lock_contended+0x84
08 000000b9`007ff720 00007ff7`a53423a3     deadlock!ZN3std3sys9backtrace28__rust_begin_short_backtrace17h143869be3e2b58f2E+0x89
09 000000b9`007ff7b0 00007ff7`a534d16d     deadlock!ZN3std6thread7Builder15spawn_unchecked17hb55d1af939eec8acE+0xb63
0a (Inline Function) --------`--------     deadlock!alloc::boxed::impl$48::call_once+0xb
0b (Inline Function) --------`--------     deadlock!alloc::boxed::impl$48::call_once+0x16
0c 000000b9`007ff860 00007ffa`d44c53e0     deadlock!std::sys::pal::windows::thread::impl$0::new::thread_start+0x3d
0d 000000b9`007ff8c0 00007ff7`d5a2485b     kernel32!BaseThreadInitThunk+0x10
0e 000000b9`007ff8f0 00000000`00000000     ntdll!RtlUserThreadStart+0x2b

   2  Id: 318.1df8 Suspend: 0 Teb: 000000b9`003b7000 Unfrozen
 # Child-SP          RetAddr               Call Site
00 000000b9`009ffb88 00007ffa`d5a3d89d     ntdll!NtWaitForAlertByThreadId+0x14
01 000000b9`009ffb90 00007ffa`d5a7b3fe     ntdll!RtlpWaitOnAddressWithTimeout+0x81
02 000000b9`009ffbc0 00007ffa`d5a7b343     ntdll!RtlpWaitOnAddress+0xae
03 000000b9`009ffc30 00007ffa`d336dd9f     ntdll!RtlWaitOnAddress+0x13
04 000000b9`009ffc70 00007ff7`a535b744     KERNELBASE!WaitOnAddress+0x2f
05 (Inline Function) --------`--------     deadlock!std::sys::pal::windows::futex::wait_on_address+0x18
06 (Inline Function) --------`--------     deadlock!std::sys::pal::windows::futex::futex_wait+0x18
07 000000b9`009ffcb0 00007ff7`a5343199     deadlock!std::sys::sync::mutex::futex::Mutex::lock_contended+0x84
08 000000b9`009ffd10 00007ff7`a5342003     deadlock!ZN3std3sys9backtrace28__rust_begin_short_backtrace17h1370fa1b5a06339fE+0x89
09 000000b9`009ffda0 00007ff7`a534d16d     deadlock!ZN3std6thread7Builder15spawn_unchecked17hb55d1af939eec8acE+0x7c3
0a (Inline Function) --------`--------     deadlock!alloc::boxed::impl$48::call_once+0xb
0b (Inline Function) --------`--------     deadlock!alloc::boxed::impl$48::call_once+0x16
0c 000000b9`009ffe50 00007ffa`d44c53e0     deadlock!std::sys::pal::windows::thread::impl$0::new::thread_start+0x3d
0d 000000b9`009ffeb0 00007ff7`d5a2485b     kernel32!BaseThreadInitThunk+0x10
0e 000000b9`009ffee0 00000000`00000000     ntdll!RtlUserThreadStart+0x2b
```

Note: Since we have two threads waiting on futexes (fast user space mutexes) and nothing else except the main thread, which looks normal, we suspect a deadlock.

6.   Let's check the futex address thread #1 is waiting on.

```
0:000> ~1s
ntdll!NtWaitForAlertByThreadId+0x14:
00007ffa`d5ac7bf4 ret

0:001> kL
 # Child-SP          RetAddr               Call Site
00 000000b9`007ff598 00007ffa`d5a3d89d     ntdll!NtWaitForAlertByThreadId+0x14
01 000000b9`007ff5a0 00007ffa`d5a7b3fe     ntdll!RtlpWaitOnAddressWithTimeout+0x81
02 000000b9`007ff5d0 00007ffa`d5a7b343     ntdll!RtlpWaitOnAddress+0xae
03 000000b9`007ff640 00007ffa`d336dd9f     ntdll!RtlWaitOnAddress+0x13
04 000000b9`007ff680 00007ff7`a535b744     KERNELBASE!WaitOnAddress+0x2f
05 (Inline Function) --------`--------     deadlock!std::sys::pal::windows::futex::wait_on_address+0x18
06 (Inline Function) --------`--------     deadlock!std::sys::pal::windows::futex::futex_wait+0x18
07 000000b9`007ff6c0 00007ff7`a5343469     deadlock!std::sys::sync::mutex::futex::Mutex::lock_contended+0x84
08 000000b9`007ff720 00007ff7`a53423a3     deadlock!ZN3std3sys9backtrace28__rust_begin_short_backtrace17h143869be3e2b58f2E+0x89
```

```
09 000000b9`007ff7b0 00007ff7`a534d16d     deadlock!ZN3std6thread7Builder15spawn_unchecked17hb55d1af939eec8acE+0xb63
0a (Inline Function) --------`--------     deadlock!alloc::boxed::impl$48::call_once+0xb
0b (Inline Function) --------`--------     deadlock!alloc::boxed::impl$48::call_once+0x16
0c 000000b9`007ff860 00007ffa`d44c53e0     deadlock!std::sys::pal::windows::thread::impl$0::new::thread_start+0x3d
0d 000000b9`007ff8c0 00007ffa`d5a2485b     kernel32!BaseThreadInitThunk+0x10
0e 000000b9`007ff8f0 00000000`00000000     ntdll!RtlUserThreadStart+0x2b
```

```
0:001> .frame /c 8
```
```
08 000000b9`007ff720 00007ff7`a53423a3
deadlock!ZN3std3sys9backtrace28__rust_begin_short_backtrace17h143869be3e2b58f2E+0x89
rax=00000000000001dc rbx=00007ff7a53681c8 rcx=00000248b1e61430
rdx=0000000000000000 rsi=00000248b1e613a0 rdi=00000248b1e61430
rip=00007ff7a5343469 rsp=000000b9007ff720 rbp=000000b9007ff780
 r8=000000b9007ff7f8  r9=000000b9007ff830 r10=0000000000000000
r11=0000000000000246 r12=0000000000000000 r13=0000000000000000
r14=00000248b1e61420 r15=0000000000000000
iopl=0         nv up ei pl zr na po nc
cs=0033  ss=002b  ds=002b  es=002b  fs=0053  gs=002b             efl=00000246
deadlock!ZN3std3sys9backtrace28__rust_begin_short_backtrace17h143869be3e2b58f2E+0x89:
00007ff7`a5343469 mov     rax,qword ptr [rbx] ds:00007ff7`a53681c8=0000000000000000
```

```
0:000> uf 00007ff7`a5343469
deadlock!ZN3std3sys9backtrace28__rust_begin_short_backtrace17h143869be3e2b58f2E:
00007ff7`a53433e0 push    rbp
00007ff7`a53433e1 push    r14
00007ff7`a53433e3 push    rsi
00007ff7`a53433e4 push    rdi
00007ff7`a53433e5 push    rbx
00007ff7`a53433e6 sub     rsp,60h
00007ff7`a53433ea lea     rbp,[rsp+60h]
00007ff7`a53433ef mov     qword ptr [rbp-8],0FFFFFFFFFFFFFFFEh
00007ff7`a53433f7 mov     rsi,rcx
00007ff7`a53433fa mov     qword ptr [rbp-20h],rcx
00007ff7`a53433fe mov     qword ptr [rbp-18h],rdx
00007ff7`a5343402 lea     rdi,[rcx+10h]
00007ff7`a5343406 mov     cl,1
00007ff7`a5343408 xor     eax,eax
00007ff7`a534340a lock cmpxchg byte ptr [rsi+10h],cl
00007ff7`a534340f je      deadlock!ZN3std3sys9backtrace28__rust_begin_short_backtrace17h143869be3e2b58f2E+0x39 (00007ff7`a5343419)  Branch

deadlock!ZN3std3sys9backtrace28__rust_begin_short_backtrace17h143869be3e2b58f2E+0x31:
00007ff7`a5343411 mov     rcx,rdi
00007ff7`a5343414 call    deadlock!std::sys::sync::mutex::futex::Mutex::lock_contended (00007ff7`a535b6c0)

deadlock!ZN3std3sys9backtrace28__rust_begin_short_backtrace17h143869be3e2b58f2E+0x39:
00007ff7`a5343419 mov     rbx,qword ptr [deadlock!_imp__ZN3std9panicking11panic_count18GLOBAL_PANIC_COUNT17hb7d1c2d819ed605cE (00007ff7`a5368038)]
00007ff7`a5343420 mov     rax,qword ptr [rbx]
00007ff7`a5343423 shl     rax,1
00007ff7`a5343426 test    rax,rax
00007ff7`a5343429 je      deadlock!ZN3std3sys9backtrace28__rust_begin_short_backtrace17h143869be3e2b58f2E+0xac (00007ff7`a534348c)  Branch

deadlock!ZN3std3sys9backtrace28__rust_begin_short_backtrace17h143869be3e2b58f2E+0x4b:
00007ff7`a534342b call    deadlock!std::panicking::panic_count::is_zero_slow_path (00007ff7`a535b5f0)
00007ff7`a5343430 xor     al,1
00007ff7`a5343432 mov     dword ptr [rbp-0Ch],eax
00007ff7`a5343435 mov     qword ptr [rbp-28h],rdi
00007ff7`a5343439 movzx   eax,byte ptr [rsi+11h]
00007ff7`a534343d test    al,al
00007ff7`a534343f jne     deadlock!ZN3std3sys9backtrace28__rust_begin_short_backtrace17h143869be3e2b58f2E+0xbf (00007ff7`a534349f)  Branch

deadlock!ZN3std3sys9backtrace28__rust_begin_short_backtrace17h143869be3e2b58f2E+0x61:
00007ff7`a5343441 xor     ecx,ecx
00007ff7`a5343443 mov     edx,2FAF080h
00007ff7`a5343448 call    deadlock!std::thread::sleep (00007ff7`a5346310)
00007ff7`a534344d mov     r14,qword ptr [rbp-18h]
00007ff7`a5343451 lea     rdi,[r14+10h]
00007ff7`a5343455 mov     cl,1
00007ff7`a5343457 xor     eax,eax
00007ff7`a5343459 lock cmpxchg byte ptr [r14+10h],cl
00007ff7`a534345f je      deadlock!ZN3std3sys9backtrace28__rust_begin_short_backtrace17h143869be3e2b58f2E+0x89 (00007ff7`a5343469)  Branch

deadlock!ZN3std3sys9backtrace28__rust_begin_short_backtrace17h143869be3e2b58f2E+0x81:
00007ff7`a5343461 mov     rcx,rdi
00007ff7`a5343464 call    deadlock!std::sys::sync::mutex::futex::Mutex::lock_contended (00007ff7`a535b6c0)

deadlock!ZN3std3sys9backtrace28__rust_begin_short_backtrace17h143869be3e2b58f2E+0x89:
00007ff7`a5343469 mov     rax,qword ptr [rbx]
00007ff7`a534346c shl     rax,1
00007ff7`a534346f test    rax,rax
00007ff7`a5343472 je      deadlock!ZN3std3sys9backtrace28__rust_begin_short_backtrace17h143869be3e2b58f2E+0xfa (00007ff7`a53434da)  Branch

deadlock!ZN3std3sys9backtrace28__rust_begin_short_backtrace17h143869be3e2b58f2E+0x94:
00007ff7`a5343474 call    deadlock!std::panicking::panic_count::is_zero_slow_path (00007ff7`a535b5f0)
00007ff7`a5343479 movzx   ecx,byte ptr [r14+11h]
00007ff7`a534347e test    cl,cl
00007ff7`a5343480 jne     deadlock!ZN3std3sys9backtrace28__rust_begin_short_backtrace17h143869be3e2b58f2E+0x199 (00007ff7`a5343579)  Branch
```

```
deadlock!ZN3std3sys9backtrace28__rust_begin_short_backtrace17h143869be3e2b58f2E+0xa6:
00007ff7`a5343486 test    al,al
00007ff7`a5343488 jne     deadlock!ZN3std3sys9backtrace28__rust_begin_short_backtrace17h143869be3e2b58f2E+0x107 (00007ff7`a53434e7)  Branch

deadlock!ZN3std3sys9backtrace28__rust_begin_short_backtrace17h143869be3e2b58f2E+0xaa:
00007ff7`a534348a jmp     deadlock!ZN3std3sys9backtrace28__rust_begin_short_backtrace17h143869be3e2b58f2E+0x123 (00007ff7`a5343503)  Branch

deadlock!ZN3std3sys9backtrace28__rust_begin_short_backtrace17h143869be3e2b58f2E+0xac:
00007ff7`a534348c mov     dword ptr [rbp-0Ch],0
00007ff7`a5343493 mov     qword ptr [rbp-28h],rdi
00007ff7`a5343497 movzx   eax,byte ptr [rsi+11h]
00007ff7`a534349b test    al,al
00007ff7`a534349d je      deadlock!ZN3std3sys9backtrace28__rust_begin_short_backtrace17h143869be3e2b58f2E+0x61 (00007ff7`a5343441)  Branch

deadlock!ZN3std3sys9backtrace28__rust_begin_short_backtrace17h143869be3e2b58f2E+0xbf:
00007ff7`a534349f mov     rax,qword ptr [rbp-28h]
00007ff7`a53434a3 mov     qword ptr [rbp-38h],rax
00007ff7`a53434a7 mov     eax,dword ptr [rbp-0Ch]
00007ff7`a53434aa mov     byte ptr [rbp-30h],al
00007ff7`a53434ad lea     rax,[deadlock!anon.326e3e11907f6038199e4e734391f949.7.llvm.7025607320133951313+0x1a0 (00007ff7`a535d778)]
00007ff7`a53434b4 mov     qword ptr [rsp+20h],rax
00007ff7`a53434b9 lea     rcx,[deadlock!anon.326e3e11907f6038199e4e734391f949.7.llvm.7025607320133951313+0x88 (00007ff7`a535d660)]
00007ff7`a53434c0 lea     r9,[deadlock!anon.326e3e11907f6038199e4e734391f949.7.llvm.7025607320133951313+0xb8 (00007ff7`a535d690)]
00007ff7`a53434c7 lea     r8,[rbp-38h]
00007ff7`a53434cb mov     edx,2Bh
00007ff7`a53434d0 call    deadlock!core::result::unwrap_failed (00007ff7`a535c690)

deadlock!ZN3std3sys9backtrace28__rust_begin_short_backtrace17h143869be3e2b58f2E+0xfa:
00007ff7`a53434da movzx   eax,byte ptr [r14+11h]
00007ff7`a53434df test    al,al
00007ff7`a53434e1 jne     deadlock!ZN3std3sys9backtrace28__rust_begin_short_backtrace17h143869be3e2b58f2E+0x19d (00007ff7`a534357d)  Branch

deadlock!ZN3std3sys9backtrace28__rust_begin_short_backtrace17h143869be3e2b58f2E+0x107:
00007ff7`a53434e7 add     r14,11h
00007ff7`a53434eb mov     rax,qword ptr [rbx]
00007ff7`a53434ee shl     rax,1
00007ff7`a53434f1 test    rax,rax
00007ff7`a53434f4 je      deadlock!ZN3std3sys9backtrace28__rust_begin_short_backtrace17h143869be3e2b58f2E+0x123 (00007ff7`a5343503)  Branch

deadlock!ZN3std3sys9backtrace28__rust_begin_short_backtrace17h143869be3e2b58f2E+0x116:
00007ff7`a53434f6 call    deadlock!std::panicking::panic_count::is_zero_slow_path (00007ff7`a535b5f0)
00007ff7`a53434fb test    al,al
00007ff7`a53434fd jne     deadlock!ZN3std3sys9backtrace28__rust_begin_short_backtrace17h143869be3e2b58f2E+0x123 (00007ff7`a5343503)  Branch

deadlock!ZN3std3sys9backtrace28__rust_begin_short_backtrace17h143869be3e2b58f2E+0x11f:
00007ff7`a53434ff mov     byte ptr [r14],1

deadlock!ZN3std3sys9backtrace28__rust_begin_short_backtrace17h143869be3e2b58f2E+0x123:
00007ff7`a5343503 xor     eax,eax
00007ff7`a5343505 xchg    al,byte ptr [rdi]
00007ff7`a5343507 cmp     al,2
00007ff7`a5343509 jne     deadlock!ZN3std3sys9backtrace28__rust_begin_short_backtrace17h143869be3e2b58f2E+0x133 (00007ff7`a5343513)  Branch

deadlock!ZN3std3sys9backtrace28__rust_begin_short_backtrace17h143869be3e2b58f2E+0x12b:
00007ff7`a534350b mov     rcx,rdi
00007ff7`a534350e call    deadlock!std::sys::sync::mutex::futex::Mutex::wake (00007ff7`a535b780)

deadlock!ZN3std3sys9backtrace28__rust_begin_short_backtrace17h143869be3e2b58f2E+0x133:
00007ff7`a5343513 cmp     byte ptr [rbp-0Ch],0
00007ff7`a5343517 mov     rdi,qword ptr [rbp-28h]
00007ff7`a534351b je      deadlock!ZN3std3sys9backtrace28__rust_begin_short_backtrace17h143869be3e2b58f2E+0x17f (00007ff7`a534355f)  Branch

deadlock!ZN3std3sys9backtrace28__rust_begin_short_backtrace17h143869be3e2b58f2E+0x13d:
00007ff7`a534351d xor     eax,eax
00007ff7`a534351f xchg    al,byte ptr [rdi]
00007ff7`a5343521 cmp     al,2
00007ff7`a5343523 jne     deadlock!ZN3std3sys9backtrace28__rust_begin_short_backtrace17h143869be3e2b58f2E+0x14d (00007ff7`a534352d)  Branch

deadlock!ZN3std3sys9backtrace28__rust_begin_short_backtrace17h143869be3e2b58f2E+0x145:
00007ff7`a5343525 mov     rcx,rdi
00007ff7`a5343528 call    deadlock!std::sys::sync::mutex::futex::Mutex::wake (00007ff7`a535b780)

deadlock!ZN3std3sys9backtrace28__rust_begin_short_backtrace17h143869be3e2b58f2E+0x14d:
00007ff7`a534352d mov     rax,qword ptr [rbp-20h]
00007ff7`a5343531 lock dec qword ptr [rax]
00007ff7`a5343535 jne     deadlock!ZN3std3sys9backtrace28__rust_begin_short_backtrace17h143869be3e2b58f2E+0x160 (00007ff7`a5343540)  Branch

deadlock!ZN3std3sys9backtrace28__rust_begin_short_backtrace17h143869be3e2b58f2E+0x157:
00007ff7`a5343537 lea     rcx,[rbp-20h]
00007ff7`a534353b call    deadlock!ZN5alloc4sync16Arc$LT$T$C$A$GT$9drop_slow17h0b761e990f3e7b1dE (00007ff7`a5343fc0)

deadlock!ZN3std3sys9backtrace28__rust_begin_short_backtrace17h143869be3e2b58f2E+0x160:
00007ff7`a5343540 mov     rax,qword ptr [rbp-18h]
00007ff7`a5343544 lock dec qword ptr [rax]
00007ff7`a5343548 jne     deadlock!ZN3std3sys9backtrace28__rust_begin_short_backtrace17h143869be3e2b58f2E+0x173 (00007ff7`a5343553)  Branch

deadlock!ZN3std3sys9backtrace28__rust_begin_short_backtrace17h143869be3e2b58f2E+0x16a:
00007ff7`a534354a lea     rcx,[rbp-18h]
00007ff7`a534354e call    deadlock!ZN5alloc4sync16Arc$LT$T$C$A$GT$9drop_slow17h0b761e990f3e7b1dE (00007ff7`a5343fc0)

deadlock!ZN3std3sys9backtrace28__rust_begin_short_backtrace17h143869be3e2b58f2E+0x173:
00007ff7`a5343553 nop
00007ff7`a5343554 add     rsp,60h
00007ff7`a5343558 pop     rbx
00007ff7`a5343559 pop     rdi
00007ff7`a534355a pop     rsi
00007ff7`a534355b pop     r14
00007ff7`a534355d pop     rbp
```

```
00007ff7`a534355e ret

deadlock!ZN3std3sys9backtrace28__rust_begin_short_backtrace17h143869be3e2b58f2E+0x17f:
00007ff7`a534355f mov     rax,qword ptr [rbx]
00007ff7`a5343562 shl     rax,1
00007ff7`a5343565 test    rax,rax
00007ff7`a5343568 je      deadlock!ZN3std3sys9backtrace28__rust_begin_short_backtrace17h143869be3e2b58f2E+0x13d (00007ff7`a534351d)  Branch

deadlock!ZN3std3sys9backtrace28__rust_begin_short_backtrace17h143869be3e2b58f2E+0x18a:
00007ff7`a534356a call    deadlock!std::panicking::panic_count::is_zero_slow_path (00007ff7`a535b5f0)
00007ff7`a534356f test    al,al
00007ff7`a5343571 jne     deadlock!ZN3std3sys9backtrace28__rust_begin_short_backtrace17h143869be3e2b58f2E+0x13d (00007ff7`a534351d)  Branch

deadlock!ZN3std3sys9backtrace28__rust_begin_short_backtrace17h143869be3e2b58f2E+0x193:
00007ff7`a5343573 mov     byte ptr [rsi+11h],1
00007ff7`a5343577 jmp     deadlock!ZN3std3sys9backtrace28__rust_begin_short_backtrace17h143869be3e2b58f2E+0x13d (00007ff7`a534351d)  Branch

deadlock!ZN3std3sys9backtrace28__rust_begin_short_backtrace17h143869be3e2b58f2E+0x199:
00007ff7`a5343579 xor     al,1
00007ff7`a534357b jmp     deadlock!ZN3std3sys9backtrace28__rust_begin_short_backtrace17h143869be3e2b58f2E+0x19f (00007ff7`a534357f)  Branch

deadlock!ZN3std3sys9backtrace28__rust_begin_short_backtrace17h143869be3e2b58f2E+0x19d:
00007ff7`a534357d xor     eax,eax

deadlock!ZN3std3sys9backtrace28__rust_begin_short_backtrace17h143869be3e2b58f2E+0x19f:
00007ff7`a534357f mov     qword ptr [rbp-38h],rdi
00007ff7`a5343583 mov     byte ptr [rbp-30h],al
00007ff7`a5343586 lea     rax,[deadlock!anon.326e3e11907f6038199e4e734391f949.7.llvm.7025607320133951313+0x1b8 (00007ff7`a535d790)]
00007ff7`a534358d mov     qword ptr [rsp+20h],rax
00007ff7`a5343592 lea     rcx,[deadlock!anon.326e3e11907f6038199e4e734391f949.7.llvm.7025607320133951313+0x88 (00007ff7`a535d660)]
00007ff7`a5343599 lea     r9,[deadlock!anon.326e3e11907f6038199e4e734391f949.7.llvm.7025607320133951313+0xb8 (00007ff7`a535d690)]
00007ff7`a53435a0 lea     r8,[rbp-38h]
00007ff7`a53435a4 mov     edx,2Bh
00007ff7`a53435a9 call    deadlock!core::result::unwrap_failed (00007ff7`a535c690)
```

```
0:001> dp rbp-18 L1
000000b9`007ff768   00000248`b1e61420
```

7. Let's check the futex address thread #2 is waiting on.

```
0:001> ~2s
ntdll!NtWaitForAlertByThreadId+0x14:
00007ffa`d5ac7bf4 ret
```

```
0:002> kL
 # Child-SP          RetAddr               Call Site
00 000000b9`009ffb88 00007ffa`d5a3d89d     ntdll!NtWaitForAlertByThreadId+0x14
01 000000b9`009ffb90 00007ffa`d5a7b3fe     ntdll!RtlpWaitOnAddressWithTimeout+0x81
02 000000b9`009ffbc0 00007ffa`d5a7b343     ntdll!RtlpWaitOnAddress+0xae
03 000000b9`009ffc30 00007ffa`d336dd9f     ntdll!RtlWaitOnAddress+0x13
04 000000b9`009ffc70 00007ff7`a535b744     KERNELBASE!WaitOnAddress+0x2f
05 (Inline Function) --------`--------     deadlock!std::sys::pal::windows::futex::wait_on_address+0x18
06 (Inline Function) --------`--------     deadlock!std::sys::pal::windows::futex::futex_wait+0x18
07 000000b9`009ffcb0 00007ff7`a5343199     deadlock!std::sys::sync::mutex::futex::Mutex::lock_contended+0x84
08 000000b9`009ffd10 00007ff7`a5342003     deadlock!ZN3std3sys9backtrace28__rust_begin_short_backtrace17h1370fa1b5a06339fE+0x89
09 000000b9`009ffda0 00007ff7`a534d16d     deadlock!ZN3std6thread7Builder15spawn_unchecked17hb55d1af939eec8acE+0x7c3
0a (Inline Function) --------`--------     deadlock!alloc::boxed::impl$48::call_once+0xb
0b (Inline Function) --------`--------     deadlock!alloc::boxed::impl$48::call_once+0x16
0c 000000b9`009ffe50 00007ffa`d44c53e0     deadlock!std::sys::pal::windows::thread::impl$0::new::thread_start+0x3d
0d 000000b9`009ffeb0 00007ffa`d5a2485b     kernel32!BaseThreadInitThunk+0x10
0e 000000b9`009ffee0 00000000`00000000     ntdll!RtlUserThreadStart+0x2b
```

```
0:002> uf 00007ff7`a5343199
deadlock!ZN3std3sys9backtrace28__rust_begin_short_backtrace17h1370fa1b5a06339fE:
00007ff7`a5343110 push    rbp
00007ff7`a5343111 push    r14
00007ff7`a5343113 push    rsi
00007ff7`a5343114 push    rdi
00007ff7`a5343115 push    rbx
00007ff7`a5343116 sub     rsp,60h
00007ff7`a534311a lea     rbp,[rsp+60h]
00007ff7`a534311f mov     qword ptr [rbp-8],0FFFFFFFFFFFFFFFEh
00007ff7`a5343127 mov     rsi,rcx
00007ff7`a534312a mov     qword ptr [rbp-20h],rcx
00007ff7`a534312e mov     qword ptr [rbp-18h],rdx
00007ff7`a5343132 lea     rdi,[rcx+10h]
00007ff7`a5343136 mov     cl,1
00007ff7`a5343138 xor     eax,eax
00007ff7`a534313a lock cmpxchg byte ptr [rsi+10h],cl
00007ff7`a534313f je      deadlock!ZN3std3sys9backtrace28__rust_begin_short_backtrace17h1370fa1b5a06339fE+0x39 (00007ff7`a5343149)  Branch

deadlock!ZN3std3sys9backtrace28__rust_begin_short_backtrace17h1370fa1b5a06339fE+0x31:
00007ff7`a5343141 mov     rcx,rdi
00007ff7`a5343144 call    deadlock!std::sys::sync::mutex::futex::Mutex::lock_contended (00007ff7`a535b6c0)

deadlock!ZN3std3sys9backtrace28__rust_begin_short_backtrace17h1370fa1b5a06339fE+0x39:
```

```
00007ff7`a5343149 mov      rbx,qword ptr [deadlock!_imp__ZN3std9panicking11panic_count18GLOBAL_PANIC_COUNT17hb7d1c2d819ed605cE (00007ff7`a5368038)]
00007ff7`a5343150 mov      rax,qword ptr [rbx]
00007ff7`a5343153 shl      rax,1
00007ff7`a5343156 test     rax,rax
00007ff7`a5343159 je       deadlock!ZN3std3sys9backtrace28__rust_begin_short_backtrace17h1370fa1b5a06339fE+0xac (00007ff7`a53431bc)  Branch

deadlock!ZN3std3sys9backtrace28__rust_begin_short_backtrace17h1370fa1b5a06339fE+0x4b:
00007ff7`a534315b call     deadlock!std::panicking::panic_count::is_zero_slow_path (00007ff7`a535b5f0)
00007ff7`a5343160 xor      al,1
00007ff7`a5343162 mov      dword ptr [rbp-0Ch],eax
00007ff7`a5343165 mov      qword ptr [rbp-28h],rdi
00007ff7`a5343169 movzx    eax,byte ptr [rsi+11h]
00007ff7`a534316d test     al,al
00007ff7`a534316f jne      deadlock!ZN3std3sys9backtrace28__rust_begin_short_backtrace17h1370fa1b5a06339fE+0xbf (00007ff7`a53431cf)  Branch

deadlock!ZN3std3sys9backtrace28__rust_begin_short_backtrace17h1370fa1b5a06339fE+0x61:
00007ff7`a5343171 xor      ecx,ecx
00007ff7`a5343173 mov      edx,2FAF080h
00007ff7`a5343178 call     deadlock!std::thread::sleep (00007ff7`a5346310)
00007ff7`a534317d mov      r14,qword ptr [rbp-18h]
00007ff7`a5343181 lea      rdi,[r14+10h]
00007ff7`a5343185 mov      cl,1
00007ff7`a5343187 xor      eax,eax
00007ff7`a5343189 lock cmpxchg byte ptr [r14+10h],cl
00007ff7`a534318f je       deadlock!ZN3std3sys9backtrace28__rust_begin_short_backtrace17h1370fa1b5a06339fE+0x89 (00007ff7`a5343199)  Branch

deadlock!ZN3std3sys9backtrace28__rust_begin_short_backtrace17h1370fa1b5a06339fE+0x81:
00007ff7`a5343191 mov      rcx,rdi
00007ff7`a5343194 call     deadlock!std::sys::sync::mutex::futex::Mutex::lock_contended (00007ff7`a535b6c0)

deadlock!ZN3std3sys9backtrace28__rust_begin_short_backtrace17h1370fa1b5a06339fE+0x89:
00007ff7`a5343199 mov      rax,qword ptr [rbx]
00007ff7`a534319c shl      rax,1
00007ff7`a534319f test     rax,rax
00007ff7`a53431a2 je       deadlock!ZN3std3sys9backtrace28__rust_begin_short_backtrace17h1370fa1b5a06339fE+0xfa (00007ff7`a534320a)  Branch

deadlock!ZN3std3sys9backtrace28__rust_begin_short_backtrace17h1370fa1b5a06339fE+0x94:
00007ff7`a53431a4 call     deadlock!std::panicking::panic_count::is_zero_slow_path (00007ff7`a535b5f0)
00007ff7`a53431a9 movzx    ecx,byte ptr [r14+11h]
00007ff7`a53431ae test     cl,cl
00007ff7`a53431b0 jne      deadlock!ZN3std3sys9backtrace28__rust_begin_short_backtrace17h1370fa1b5a06339fE+0x199 (00007ff7`a53432a9)  Branch

deadlock!ZN3std3sys9backtrace28__rust_begin_short_backtrace17h1370fa1b5a06339fE+0xa6:
00007ff7`a53431b6 test     al,al
00007ff7`a53431b8 jne      deadlock!ZN3std3sys9backtrace28__rust_begin_short_backtrace17h1370fa1b5a06339fE+0x107 (00007ff7`a5343217)  Branch

deadlock!ZN3std3sys9backtrace28__rust_begin_short_backtrace17h1370fa1b5a06339fE+0xaa:
00007ff7`a53431ba jmp      deadlock!ZN3std3sys9backtrace28__rust_begin_short_backtrace17h1370fa1b5a06339fE+0x123 (00007ff7`a5343233)  Branch

deadlock!ZN3std3sys9backtrace28__rust_begin_short_backtrace17h1370fa1b5a06339fE+0xac:
00007ff7`a53431bc mov      dword ptr [rbp-0Ch],0
00007ff7`a53431c3 mov      qword ptr [rbp-28h],rdi
00007ff7`a53431c7 movzx    eax,byte ptr [rsi+11h]
00007ff7`a53431cb test     al,al
00007ff7`a53431cd je       deadlock!ZN3std3sys9backtrace28__rust_begin_short_backtrace17h1370fa1b5a06339fE+0x61 (00007ff7`a5343171)  Branch

deadlock!ZN3std3sys9backtrace28__rust_begin_short_backtrace17h1370fa1b5a06339fE+0xbf:
00007ff7`a53431cf mov      rax,qword ptr [rbp-28h]
00007ff7`a53431d3 mov      qword ptr [rbp-38h],rax
00007ff7`a53431d7 mov      eax,dword ptr [rbp-0Ch]
00007ff7`a53431da mov      byte ptr [rbp-30h],al
00007ff7`a53431dd lea      rax,[deadlock!anon.326e3e11907f6038199e4e734391f949.7.llvm.7025607320133951313+0x1d0 (00007ff7`a535d7a8)]
00007ff7`a53431e4 mov      qword ptr [rsp+20h],rax
00007ff7`a53431e9 lea      rcx,[deadlock!anon.326e3e11907f6038199e4e734391f949.7.llvm.7025607320133951313+0x88 (00007ff7`a535d660)]
00007ff7`a53431f0 lea      r9,[deadlock!anon.326e3e11907f6038199e4e734391f949.7.llvm.7025607320133951313+0xb8 (00007ff7`a535d690)]
00007ff7`a53431f7 lea      r8,[rbp-38h]
00007ff7`a53431fb mov      edx,2Bh
00007ff7`a5343200 call     deadlock!core::result::unwrap_failed (00007ff7`a535c690)

deadlock!ZN3std3sys9backtrace28__rust_begin_short_backtrace17h1370fa1b5a06339fE+0xfa:
00007ff7`a534320a movzx    eax,byte ptr [r14+11h]
00007ff7`a534320f test     al,al
00007ff7`a5343211 jne      deadlock!ZN3std3sys9backtrace28__rust_begin_short_backtrace17h1370fa1b5a06339fE+0x19d (00007ff7`a53432ad)  Branch

deadlock!ZN3std3sys9backtrace28__rust_begin_short_backtrace17h1370fa1b5a06339fE+0x107:
00007ff7`a5343217 add      r14,11h
00007ff7`a534321b mov      rax,qword ptr [rbx]
00007ff7`a534321e shl      rax,1
00007ff7`a5343221 test     rax,rax
00007ff7`a5343224 je       deadlock!ZN3std3sys9backtrace28__rust_begin_short_backtrace17h1370fa1b5a06339fE+0x123 (00007ff7`a5343233)  Branch

deadlock!ZN3std3sys9backtrace28__rust_begin_short_backtrace17h1370fa1b5a06339fE+0x116:
00007ff7`a5343226 call     deadlock!std::panicking::panic_count::is_zero_slow_path (00007ff7`a535b5f0)
00007ff7`a534322b test     al,al
00007ff7`a534322d jne      deadlock!ZN3std3sys9backtrace28__rust_begin_short_backtrace17h1370fa1b5a06339fE+0x123 (00007ff7`a5343233)  Branch

deadlock!ZN3std3sys9backtrace28__rust_begin_short_backtrace17h1370fa1b5a06339fE+0x11f:
00007ff7`a534322f mov      byte ptr [r14],1

deadlock!ZN3std3sys9backtrace28__rust_begin_short_backtrace17h1370fa1b5a06339fE+0x123:
00007ff7`a5343233 xor      eax,eax
00007ff7`a5343235 xchg     al,byte ptr [rdi]
00007ff7`a5343237 cmp      al,2
00007ff7`a5343239 jne      deadlock!ZN3std3sys9backtrace28__rust_begin_short_backtrace17h1370fa1b5a06339fE+0x133 (00007ff7`a5343243)  Branch

deadlock!ZN3std3sys9backtrace28__rust_begin_short_backtrace17h1370fa1b5a06339fE+0x12b:
00007ff7`a534323b mov      rcx,rdi
00007ff7`a534323e call     deadlock!std::sys::sync::mutex::futex::Mutex::wake (00007ff7`a535b780)
```

```
deadlock!ZN3std3sys9backtrace28__rust_begin_short_backtrace17h1370fa1b5a06339fE+0x133:
00007ff7`a5343243 cmp     byte ptr [rbp-0Ch],0
00007ff7`a5343247 mov     rdi,qword ptr [rbp-28h]
00007ff7`a534324b je      deadlock!ZN3std3sys9backtrace28__rust_begin_short_backtrace17h1370fa1b5a06339fE+0x17f (00007ff7`a534328f)  Branch

deadlock!ZN3std3sys9backtrace28__rust_begin_short_backtrace17h1370fa1b5a06339fE+0x13d:
00007ff7`a534324d xor     eax,eax
00007ff7`a534324f xchg    al,byte ptr [rdi]
00007ff7`a5343251 cmp     al,2
00007ff7`a5343253 jne     deadlock!ZN3std3sys9backtrace28__rust_begin_short_backtrace17h1370fa1b5a06339fE+0x14d (00007ff7`a534325d)  Branch

deadlock!ZN3std3sys9backtrace28__rust_begin_short_backtrace17h1370fa1b5a06339fE+0x145:
00007ff7`a5343255 mov     rcx,rdi
00007ff7`a5343258 call    deadlock!std::sys::sync::mutex::futex::Mutex::wake (00007ff7`a535b780)

deadlock!ZN3std3sys9backtrace28__rust_begin_short_backtrace17h1370fa1b5a06339fE+0x14d:
00007ff7`a534325d mov     rax,qword ptr [rbp-20h]
00007ff7`a5343261 lock dec qword ptr [rax]
00007ff7`a5343265 jne     deadlock!ZN3std3sys9backtrace28__rust_begin_short_backtrace17h1370fa1b5a06339fE+0x160 (00007ff7`a5343270)  Branch

deadlock!ZN3std3sys9backtrace28__rust_begin_short_backtrace17h1370fa1b5a06339fE+0x157:
00007ff7`a5343267 lea     rcx,[rbp-20h]
00007ff7`a534326b call    deadlock!ZN5alloc4sync16Arc$LT$T$C$A$GT$9drop_slow17h0b761e990f3e7b1dE (00007ff7`a5343fc0)

deadlock!ZN3std3sys9backtrace28__rust_begin_short_backtrace17h1370fa1b5a06339fE+0x160:
00007ff7`a5343270 mov     rax,qword ptr [rbp-18h]
00007ff7`a5343274 lock dec qword ptr [rax]
00007ff7`a5343278 jne     deadlock!ZN3std3sys9backtrace28__rust_begin_short_backtrace17h1370fa1b5a06339fE+0x173 (00007ff7`a5343283)  Branch

deadlock!ZN3std3sys9backtrace28__rust_begin_short_backtrace17h1370fa1b5a06339fE+0x16a:
00007ff7`a534327a lea     rcx,[rbp-18h]
00007ff7`a534327e call    deadlock!ZN5alloc4sync16Arc$LT$T$C$A$GT$9drop_slow17h0b761e990f3e7b1dE (00007ff7`a5343fc0)

deadlock!ZN3std3sys9backtrace28__rust_begin_short_backtrace17h1370fa1b5a06339fE+0x173:
00007ff7`a5343283 nop
00007ff7`a5343284 add     rsp,60h
00007ff7`a5343288 pop     rbx
00007ff7`a5343289 pop     rdi
00007ff7`a534328a pop     rsi
00007ff7`a534328b pop     r14
00007ff7`a534328d pop     rbp
00007ff7`a534328e ret

deadlock!ZN3std3sys9backtrace28__rust_begin_short_backtrace17h1370fa1b5a06339fE+0x17f:
00007ff7`a534328f mov     rax,qword ptr [rbx]
00007ff7`a5343292 shl     rax,1
00007ff7`a5343295 test    rax,rax
00007ff7`a5343298 je      deadlock!ZN3std3sys9backtrace28__rust_begin_short_backtrace17h1370fa1b5a06339fE+0x13d (00007ff7`a534324d)  Branch

deadlock!ZN3std3sys9backtrace28__rust_begin_short_backtrace17h1370fa1b5a06339fE+0x18a:
00007ff7`a534329a call    deadlock!std::panicking::panic_count::is_zero_slow_path (00007ff7`a535b5f0)
00007ff7`a534329f test    al,al
00007ff7`a53432a1 jne     deadlock!ZN3std3sys9backtrace28__rust_begin_short_backtrace17h1370fa1b5a06339fE+0x13d (00007ff7`a534324d)  Branch

deadlock!ZN3std3sys9backtrace28__rust_begin_short_backtrace17h1370fa1b5a06339fE+0x193:
00007ff7`a53432a3 mov     byte ptr [rsi+11h],1
00007ff7`a53432a7 jmp     deadlock!ZN3std3sys9backtrace28__rust_begin_short_backtrace17h1370fa1b5a06339fE+0x13d (00007ff7`a534324d)  Branch

deadlock!ZN3std3sys9backtrace28__rust_begin_short_backtrace17h1370fa1b5a06339fE+0x199:
00007ff7`a53432a9 xor     al,1
00007ff7`a53432ab jmp     deadlock!ZN3std3sys9backtrace28__rust_begin_short_backtrace17h1370fa1b5a06339fE+0x19f (00007ff7`a53432af)  Branch

deadlock!ZN3std3sys9backtrace28__rust_begin_short_backtrace17h1370fa1b5a06339fE+0x19d:
00007ff7`a53432ad xor     eax,eax

deadlock!ZN3std3sys9backtrace28__rust_begin_short_backtrace17h1370fa1b5a06339fE+0x19f:
00007ff7`a53432af mov     qword ptr [rbp-38h],rdi
00007ff7`a53432b3 mov     byte ptr [rbp-30h],al
00007ff7`a53432b6 lea     rax,[deadlock!anon.326e3e11907f6038199e4e734391f949.7.llvm.7025607320133951313+0x1e8 (00007ff7`a535d7c0)]
00007ff7`a53432bd mov     qword ptr [rsp+20h],rax
00007ff7`a53432c2 lea     rcx,[deadlock!anon.326e3e11907f6038199e4e734391f949.7.llvm.7025607320133951313+0x88 (00007ff7`a535d660)]
00007ff7`a53432c9 lea     r9,[deadlock!anon.326e3e11907f6038199e4e734391f949.7.llvm.7025607320133951313+0xb8 (00007ff7`a535d690)]
00007ff7`a53432d0 lea     r8,[rbp-38h]
00007ff7`a53432d4 mov     edx,2Bh
00007ff7`a53432d9 call    deadlock!core::result::unwrap_failed (00007ff7`a535c690)
```

```
0:002> .frame /c 8
08 000000b9`009ffd10 00007ff7`a5342003
deadlock!ZN3std3sys9backtrace28__rust_begin_short_backtrace17h1370fa1b5a06339fE+0x89
rax=00000000000001dc rbx=00007ff7a53681c8 rcx=00000248b1e613b0
rdx=0000000000000000 rsi=00000248b1e61420 rdi=00000248b1e613b0
rip=00007ff7a5343199 rsp=000000b9009ffd10 rbp=000000b9009ffd70
 r8=0000000000000003  r9=0000000000000018 r10=0000000000000000
r11=e0000000001ffbff r12=0000000000000000 r13=0000000000000000
r14=00000248b1e613a0 r15=0000000000000000
iopl=0         nv up ei pl zr na po nc
cs=0033  ss=002b  ds=002b  es=002b  fs=0053  gs=002b              efl=00000246
deadlock!ZN3std3sys9backtrace28__rust_begin_short_backtrace17h1370fa1b5a06339fE+0x89:
```

```
00007ff7`a5343199 mov     rax,qword ptr [rbx] ds:00007ff7`a53681c8=0000000000000000

0:002> dp rbp-18 L1
000000b9`009ffd58  00000248`b1e613a0
```

Note: We see **thread #1** is waiting on `00000248`b1e61420` and **thread #2** is waiting on `00000248`b1e613a0`.

8.   We now check these addresses in thread #1 execution residue:

```
0:002> ~1s
ntdll!NtWaitForAlertByThreadId+0x14:
00007ffa`d5ac7bf4 ret
0:001> !teb
TEB at 000000b9003b5000
    ExceptionList:        0000000000000000
    StackBase:            000000b900800000
    StackLimit:           000000b9007fe000
    SubSystemTib:         0000000000000000
    FiberData:            0000000000001e00
    ArbitraryUserPointer: 0000000000000000
    Self:                 000000b9003b5000
    EnvironmentPointer:   0000000000000000
    ClientId:             0000000000000318 . 0000000000001e10
    RpcHandle:            0000000000000000
    Tls Storage:          00000248b1e5c050
    PEB Address:          000000b9003ae000
    LastErrorValue:       0
    LastStatusValue:      c000000d
    Count Owned Locks:    0
    HardErrorMode:        0

0:001> dps 000000b9007fe000 000000b900800000
...
...
...
000000b9`007ff6c0  00000000`00000000
000000b9`007ff6c8  00000000`000000c4
000000b9`007ff6d0  00000000`00000000
000000b9`007ff6d8  00000248`00000000
000000b9`007ff6e0  000000b9`007ff770
000000b9`007ff6e8  02ffffff`fff85ee0
000000b9`007ff6f0  00007ff7`a53681c8 deadlock!ZN3std9panicking11panic_count18GLOBAL_PANIC_COUNT17hb7d1c2d819ed605cE
000000b9`007ff6f8  00000248`b1e61430
000000b9`007ff700  00000248`b1e613a0
000000b9`007ff708  00000248`b1e61420
000000b9`007ff710  000000b9`007ff780
000000b9`007ff718  00007ff7`a5343469
deadlock!ZN3std3sys9backtrace28__rust_begin_short_backtrace17h143869be3e2b58f2E+0x89
000000b9`007ff720  00000000`00000000
000000b9`007ff728  00000000`00000000
000000b9`007ff730  00000000`00000000
000000b9`007ff738  00000000`00000000
000000b9`007ff740  00000000`00000000
000000b9`007ff748  00000000`00000000
000000b9`007ff750  00000000`00000000
000000b9`007ff758  00000248`b1e613b0
000000b9`007ff760  00000248`b1e613a0
000000b9`007ff768  00000248`b1e61420
000000b9`007ff770  00000000`007ff778
000000b9`007ff778  ffffffff`fffffffe
000000b9`007ff780  00000000`00000000
000000b9`007ff788  00000248`b1e61420
000000b9`007ff790  00000248`b1e613a0
000000b9`007ff798  00000000`00000000
000000b9`007ff7a0  000000b9`007ff830
```

```
000000b9`007ff7a8  00007ff7`a53423a3 deadlock!ZN3std6thread7Builder15spawn_unchecked17hb55d1af939eec8acE+0xb63
000000b9`007ff7b0  00000000`00000000
000000b9`007ff7b8  00000000`00000000
000000b9`007ff7c0  00000000`00000000
000000b9`007ff7c8  00000000`00000000
000000b9`007ff7d0  00000000`00000000
000000b9`007ff7d8  00000000`00000000
000000b9`007ff7e0  00000248`b1e613a0
000000b9`007ff7e8  00000248`b1e61420
000000b9`007ff7f0  00000000`00000000
000000b9`007ff7f8  00007ffa`d33742f5 KERNELBASE!SetThreadStackGuarantee+0x105
000000b9`007ff800  00000000`00000000
000000b9`007ff808  00000000`00000000
000000b9`007ff820  01010001`01001000
...
...
...
```

9.   We now check the same addresses in thread #2 execution residue:

```
0:001> ~2s
ntdll!NtWaitForAlertByThreadId+0x14:
00007ffa`d5ac7bf4 ret
```

```
0:002> !teb
TEB at 000000b9003b7000
    ExceptionList:        0000000000000000
    StackBase:            000000b900a00000
    StackLimit:           000000b9009ff000
    SubSystemTib:         0000000000000000
    FiberData:            0000000000001e00
    ArbitraryUserPointer: 0000000000000000
    Self:                 000000b9003b7000
    EnvironmentPointer:   0000000000000000
    ClientId:             0000000000000318 . 0000000000001df8
    RpcHandle:            0000000000000000
    Tls Storage:          00000248b1e5c780
    PEB Address:          000000b9003ae000
    LastErrorValue:       0
    LastStatusValue:      c000000d
    Count Owned Locks:    0
    HardErrorMode:        0
```

```
0:002> dps 000000b9009ff000 000000b900a00000
...
...
...
000000b9`009ffcb8  00000000`000000c0
000000b9`009ffcc0  00000000`00000000
000000b9`009ffcc8  00000248`00000000
000000b9`009ffcd0  000000b9`009ffd60
000000b9`009ffcd8  02ffffff`fff85ee0
000000b9`009ffce0  00007ff7`a53681c8 deadlock!ZN3std9panicking11panic_count18GLOBAL_PANIC_COUNT17hb7d1c2d819ed605cE
000000b9`009ffce8  00000248`b1e613b0
000000b9`009ffcf0  00000248`b1e61420
000000b9`009ffcf8  00000248`b1e613a0
000000b9`009ffd00  000000b9`009ffd70
000000b9`009ffd08  00007ff7`a5343199
deadlock!ZN3std3sys9backtrace28__rust_begin_short_backtrace17h1370fa1b5a06339fE+0x89
000000b9`009ffd10  00000000`00000000
000000b9`009ffd18  00000000`00000000
000000b9`009ffd20  00000000`00000000
000000b9`009ffd28  00000000`00000000
000000b9`009ffd30  00000000`00000000
000000b9`009ffd38  00000000`00000000
000000b9`009ffd40  00000000`00000000
```

```
000000b9`009ffd48    00000248`b1e61430
000000b9`009ffd50    00000248`b1e61420
000000b9`009ffd58    00000248`b1e613a0
000000b9`009ffd60    00000000`009ffd68
000000b9`009ffd68    ffffffff`fffffffe
000000b9`009ffd70    00000000`00000000
000000b9`009ffd78    00000248`b1e613a0
000000b9`009ffd80    00000248`b1e61420
000000b9`009ffd88    00000000`00000000
000000b9`009ffd90    000000b9`009ffe20
000000b9`009ffd98    00007ff7`a5342003 deadlock!ZN3std6thread7Builder15spawn_unchecked17hb55d1af939eec8acE+0x7c3
000000b9`009ffda0    00000000`00000000
000000b9`009ffda8    00000000`00000000
000000b9`009ffdb0    00000000`00000000
000000b9`009ffdb8    00000000`00000000
000000b9`009ffdc0    00000000`00000000
000000b9`009ffdc8    00000000`00000000
000000b9`009ffdd0    00000248`b1e61420
000000b9`009ffdd8    00000248`b1e613a0
000000b9`009ffde0    00000000`00000000
000000b9`009ffde8    00007ffa`d33742f5 KERNELBASE!SetThreadStackGuarantee+0x105
000000b9`009ffdf0    00000000`00000000
000000b9`009ffdf8    00000000`00000000
...
...
...
```

Note: We see both addresses in both threads but in the opposite order. Thus, we can hyposthesize that **thread #1** owns 00000248`b1e613a0 and is waiting on 00000248`b1e61420, and **thread #2** owns 00000248`b1e61420 and is waiting on 00000248`b1e613a0. The acquisition and waiting in opposite order caused the deadlock.

10.   We close logging before exiting WinDbg:

```
0:002> .logclose
Closing open log file C:\ARWMDA-Dumps\RW8.log
```

Complete Memory Dumps

Exercises RC1 – RC2

All exercises were modeled on real-life examples using specially constructed applications. Complete memory dumps for Exercises RC1 – RC2 were saved from the Windows 11 system under Hyper-V. In this section, we learn more than 10 memory analysis patterns.

Memory Spaces

- Complete memory == Physical memory
- We always see the current process space
- Kernel space is the same for any process

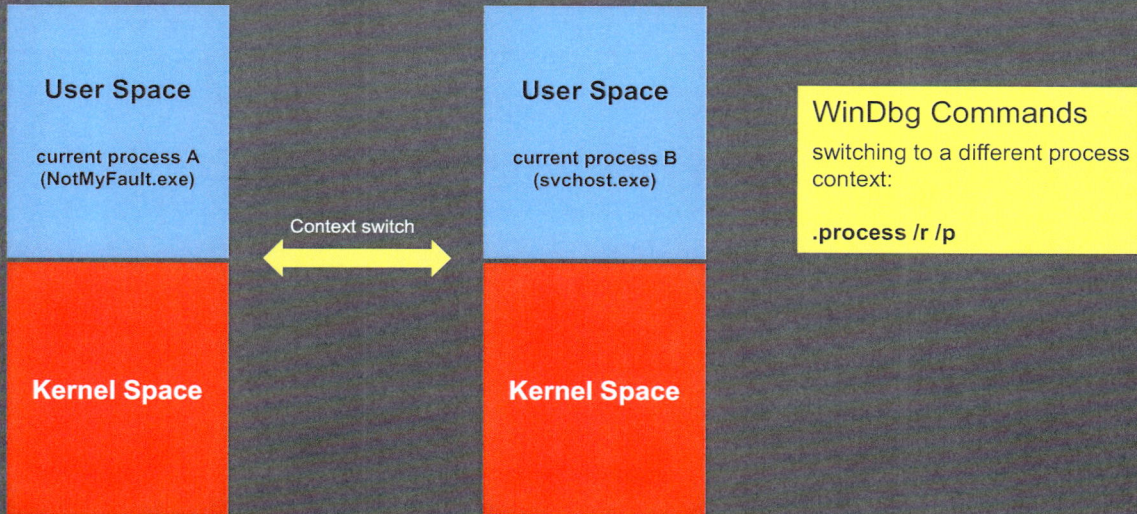

User Space

current process A
(NotMyFault.exe)

Context switch ←→

Kernel Space

User Space

current process B
(svchost.exe)

Kernel Space

WinDbg Commands

switching to a different process context:

.process /r /p

Major Challenges

- Multiple processes (user spaces) to examine
- User space view needs to be correct when we examine another thread

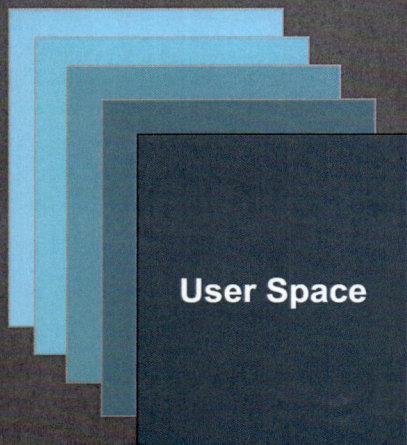

User Space

WinDbg Commands
dump all stack traces:
!process 0 3f

Common Commands

- **.logopen <file>**
  Opens a log file to save all subsequent output

- View commands
  Dump everything or selected processes and threads (context changes automatically)

- Switch commands
  Switch to a specific process or thread for a fine-grain analysis

View Commands

- **!process 0 3f**
  Lists all processes (including times, environment, modules) and their thread stack traces

- **!process 0 1f**
  The same as the previous command but without PEB information (more secure)

- **!process <address> 3f or !process <address> 1f**
  The same as the previous commands but only for an individual process

- **!thread <address> 3f**
  Shows thread information and stack trace

- **!thread <address> 36**
  The same as the previous command but shows the first 4 parameters for every function

Switch Commands

- **.process /r /p <address>**

  Switches to a specified process. Its context becomes current. Reloads symbol files for user space. Now we can use commands like !cs

  ```
  0: kd> .process /r /p fffffa80044d8b30
  Implicit process is now fffffa80`044d8b30
  Loading User Symbols
  ..............................
  ```

- **.thread <address>**

  Switches to a specified thread. Assumes the current process context

  Now we can use commands like k*

- **.thread /r /p <address>**

  The same as the previous command but makes the thread process context current and reloads symbol files for user space:

  ```
  0: kd> .thread /r /p fffffa80051b7060
  Implicit thread is now fffffa80`051b7060
  Implicit process is now fffffa80`044d8b30
  Loading User Symbols
  ..............................
  ```

Fiber Bindle Memory Dump

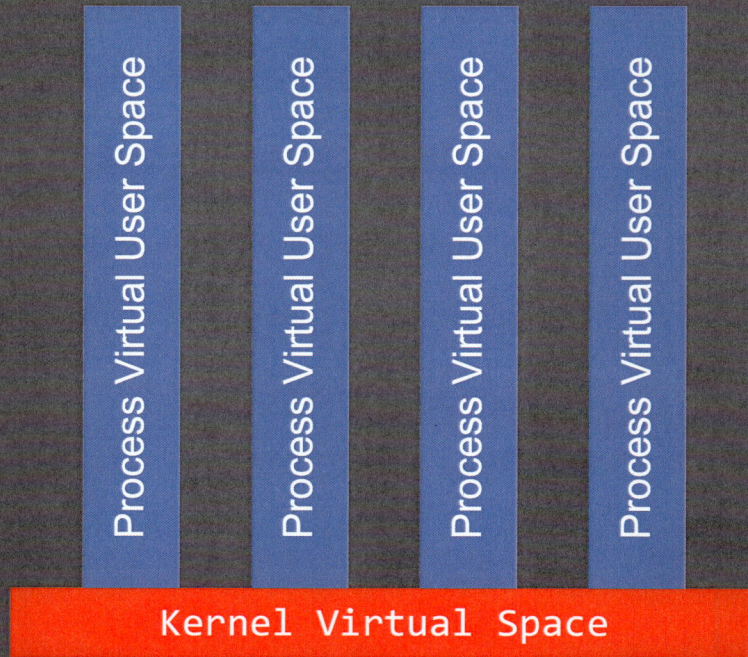

Exercise RC1

- **Goal:** Learn how to get various information related to processes, threads, and modules

- **Patterns:** Stack Trace Collection (Unmanaged Space); Incorrect Stack Trace; Truncated Stack Trace; Dual Stack Trace; Raw Stack Trace; Coincidental Symbolic Information; Source Stack Trace

- \ARWMDA-Dumps\Exercise-RC1.pdf

Goal: Learn how to get various information related to processes, threads, and modules.

Patterns: Stack Trace Collection (Unmanaged Space); Incorrect Stack Trace; Truncated Stack Trace; Dual Stack Trace; Raw Stack Trace; Coincidental Symbolic Information; Source Stack Trace.

1.   Launch WinDbg.

2.   Open \ARWMDA-Dumps\Complete\MEMORY-normal.DMP.

3.   We get the dump file loaded:

```
Microsoft (R) Windows Debugger Version 10.0.27725.1000 AMD64
Copyright (c) Microsoft Corporation. All rights reserved.


Loading Dump File [C:\ARWMDA-Dumps\Complete\MEMORY-normal.DMP]
Kernel Bitmap Dump File: Full address space is available


************* Path validation summary **************
Response                         Time (ms)      Location
Deferred                                        srv*
Symbol search path is: srv*
Executable search path is:
Windows 10 Kernel Version 22000 MP (4 procs) Free x64
Product: WinNt, suite: TerminalServer SingleUserTS
Edition build lab: 22000.1.amd64fre.co_release.210604-1628
Kernel base = 0xfffff801`4621d000 PsLoadedModuleList = 0xfffff801`46e46850
Debug session time: Sat Nov 23 14:38:07.918 2024 (UTC + 0:00)
System Uptime: 0 days 0:04:32.192
Loading Kernel Symbols
...........................................................
...........................................................
.........................................
Loading User Symbols
.................................
Loading unloaded module list
...........
For analysis of this file, run !analyze -v
nt!KeBugCheckEx:
fffff801`4663c1d0 mov      qword ptr [rsp+8],rcx ss:0018:ffffa389`469cd680=000000000000000a
```

4.   We open a log file:

```
0: kd> .logopen C:\ARWMDA-Dumps\Complete\MEMORY-normal.log
Opened log file 'C:\ARWMDA-Dumps\Complete\MEMORY-normal.log'
```

5.   We check the current thread running on the current processor (**k** command):

```
0: kd> k
 # Child-SP          RetAddr           Call Site
00 ffffa389`469cd678 fffff801`46651c29 nt!KeBugCheckEx
01 ffffa389`469cd680 fffff801`4664d261 nt!KiBugCheckDispatch+0x69
02 ffffa389`469cd7c0 fffff801`67471530 nt!KiPageFault+0x461
03 ffffa389`469cd950 fffff801`67471e2d myfault+0x1530
04 ffffa389`469cd980 fffff801`67471f88 myfault+0x1e2d
05 ffffa389`469cdad0 fffff801`464c9325 myfault+0x1f88
06 ffffa389`469cdb10 fffff801`4694ea69 nt!IofCallDriver+0x55
07 ffffa389`469cdb50 fffff801`4694e589 nt!IopSynchronousServiceTail+0x479
08 ffffa389`469cdc00 fffff801`4694d846 nt!IopXxxControlFile+0xd29
09 ffffa389`469cdd40 fffff801`466512d5 nt!NtDeviceIoControlFile+0x56
0a ffffa389`469cddb0 00007ffe`a1ca4164 nt!KiSystemServiceCopyEnd+0x25
0b 00000089`a8d7ee98 00007ffe`9f7135bb ntdll!NtDeviceIoControlFile+0x14
0c 00000089`a8d7eea0 00007ffe`a1775e91 KERNELBASE!DeviceIoControl+0x6b
0d 00000089`a8d7ef10 00007ff6`c15226ce KERNEL32!DeviceIoControlImplementation+0x81
0e 00000089`a8d7ef60 00007ffe`a15b48ab notmyfault64+0x26ce
0f 00000089`a8d7f060 00007ffe`a15b40fb USER32!UserCallDlgProcCheckWow+0x14b
10 00000089`a8d7f140 00007ffe`a15f9a59 USER32!DefDlgProcWorker+0xcb
11 00000089`a8d7f200 00007ffe`a15b1cac USER32!DefDlgProcA+0x39
12 00000089`a8d7f240 00007ffe`a15b17fc USER32!UserCallWinProcCheckWow+0x33c
13 00000089`a8d7f3b0 00007ffe`a15c4c2d USER32!DispatchClientMessage+0x9c
14 00000089`a8d7f410 00007ffe`a1ca8004 USER32!_fnDWORD+0x3d
15 00000089`a8d7f470 00007ffe`9f4c1434 ntdll!KiUserCallbackDispatcherContinue
16 00000089`a8d7f4f8 00007ffe`a15b092f win32u!NtUserMessageCall+0x14
17 00000089`a8d7f500 00007ffe`a15b0797 USER32!SendMessageWorker+0x12f
18 00000089`a8d7f5a0 00007ffe`8ea250bf USER32!SendMessageW+0x137
19 00000089`a8d7f600 00007ffe`8ea58822 COMCTL32!Button_ReleaseCapture+0xbb
1a 00000089`a8d7f630 00007ffe`a15b1cac COMCTL32!Button_WndProc+0x802
1b 00000089`a8d7f740 00007ffe`a15b0f06 USER32!UserCallWinProcCheckWow+0x33c
1c 00000089`a8d7f8b0 00007ffe`a15b60e4 USER32!DispatchMessageWorker+0x2a6
1d 00000089`a8d7f930 00007ffe`8ea05f9f USER32!IsDialogMessageW+0x104
1e 00000089`a8d7f990 00007ffe`8ea05e48 COMCTL32!Prop_IsDialogMessage+0x4b
1f 00000089`a8d7f9d0 00007ffe`8ea05abd COMCTL32!_RealPropertySheet+0x2c0
20 00000089`a8d7faa0 00007ffe`8ead0803 COMCTL32!_PropertySheet+0x49
21 00000089`a8d7fad0 00007ff6`c1523415 COMCTL32!PropertySheetA+0x53
22 00000089`a8d7fb70 00007ff6`c1525c68 notmyfault64+0x3415
23 00000089`a8d7fda0 00007ffe`a17753e0 notmyfault64+0x5c68
24 00000089`a8d7fde0 00007ffe`a1c0485b KERNEL32!BaseThreadInitThunk+0x10
25 00000089`a8d7fe10 00000000`00000000 ntdll!RtlUserThreadStart+0x2b
```

Note: We see the kernel stack (in red), and we also see a user space portion (in blue) because the dump is complete and includes both user space and kernel space (unless paged out). Sometimes, due to the absence of symbol files, stack traces are incomplete or truncated.

6.   To see the stack trace of the current thread of the current process on the current CPU, use the **!thread** command:

```
0: kd> !thread
THREAD ffffe70808f5b080  Cid 1f40.1250  Teb: 00000089a8ede000 Win32Thread: ffffe7080b49c3b0 RUNNING on processor 0
IRP List:
    ffffe70804c48370: (0006,0118) Flags: 00060000  Mdl: 00000000
Not impersonating
DeviceMap                 ffffa88ee7ae5070
Owning Process            ffffe7080ac390c0       Image:         notmyfault64.exe
Attached Process          N/A            Image:         N/A
Wait Start TickCount      17420          Ticks: 0
Context Switch Count      2940           IdealProcessor: 2
UserTime                  00:00:00.187
KernelTime                00:00:00.437
Win32 Start Address notmyfault64 (0x00007ff6c1525b0c)
Stack Init ffffa389469cdfb0 Current ffffa389469ccf70
Base ffffa389469ce000 Limit ffffa389469c8000 Call 0000000000000000
Priority 12 BasePriority 8 Foreground Boost 2 IoPriority 2 PagePriority 5
Part of process with FOREGROUND Priority
Child-SP          RetAddr           : Args to Child                                                           : Call Site
ffffa389`469cd678 fffff801`46651c29 : 00000000`0000000a ffffa88e`e64ec010 00000000`00000002 00000000`00000000 : nt!KeBugCheckEx
ffffa389`469cd680 fffff801`4664d261 : ffffa389`469cd878 ffffa389`469cd7fc ffffa88e`e64e6fe0 fffff801`46569f77 : nt!KiBugCheckDispatch+0x69
ffffa389`469cd7c0 fffff801`67471530 : 00000000`00000000 fffffe708`04b2f1f0 00000000`00000000 00000000`00000000 : nt!KiPageFault+0x461 (TrapFrame @
ffffa389`469cd7c0)
ffffa389`469cd950 fffff801`67471e2d : fffffe708`ef08581e 00000000`000000f0 00000000`00000000 00000000`00000000 : myfault+0x1530
ffffa389`469cd980 fffff801`67471f88 : 00000000`00000000 fffff801`4694fee1 00004e11`00000b65 fffffe708`000048c2 : myfault+0x1e2d
ffffa389`469cda00 fffff801`464c9325 : 00000000`00000002 00000000`00000001 fffffe708`08f5b080 00000000`00000000 : myfault+0x1f88
ffffa389`469cdb10 fffff801`4694ea69 : 00000000`00000000 00000000`00000000 ffffa389`469cdbd0 fffff801`464c7e54 : nt!IofCallDriver+0x55
ffffa389`469cdb50 fffff801`4694e589 : fffffe708`00000000 ffffa389`469cdea0 00000000`00000001 00000000`83360018 : nt!IopSynchronousServiceTail+0x479
ffffa389`469cdc00 fffff801`4694d846 : 00000000`00000000 00000000`00000000 00000000`00000000 00000000`00000000 : nt!IopXxxControlFile+0xd29
ffffa389`469cdd40 fffff801`466512d5 : 00000000`00000000 00000000`00000000 00000000`00000000 00000000`00000000 : nt!NtDeviceIoControlFile+0x56
ffffa389`469cddb0 00007ffe`a1ca4164 : 00007ffe`9f7135bb 00000000`000704dc 00000014`00000048 00001fd5`05f58c7d : nt!KiSystemServiceCopyEnd+0x25 (TrapFrame
@ ffffa389`469cde20)
00000089`a8d7ee98 00007ffe`9f7135bb : 00000000`000704dc 00000014`00000048 00001fd5`05f58c7d 00000000`00000000 : ntdll!NtDeviceIoControlFile+0x14
00000089`a8d7eea0 00007ffe`a1775e91 : 00000000`83360018 00000000`00000000 00000000`00000000 00007ffe`a15f9c89 : KERNELBASE!DeviceIoControl+0x6b
00000089`a8d7ef10 00007ff6`c15226ce : 00000000`00020500 00000089`a8d7eff9 00000089`a8d7eff9 00000000`00000000 :
KERNEL32!DeviceIoControlImplementation+0x81
00000089`a8d7ef60 00007ffe`a15b48ab : 00000000`00000001 00000000`00000001 00000000`00000001 00000000`00000002 : notmyfault64+0x26ce
00000089`a8d7f060 00007ffe`a15b40fb : 00000000`00000000 00007ff6`c1522570 00000000`00000111 00000238`8004d880 : USER32!UserCallDlgProcCheckWow+0x14b
00000089`a8d7f140 00007ffe`a15f9a59 : 00000000`0002050e 00000000`000000f3 00000000`0002050e 00000000`00000000 : USER32!DefDlgProcWorker+0xcb
00000089`a8d7f200 00007ffe`a15b1cac : 00000000`00000001 00000000`00000000 00000000`00000001 00000000`00000000 : USER32!DefDlgProcA+0x39
00000089`a8d7f240 00007ffe`a15b17fc : 00000238`ff1b7cc0 00007ffe`a1ca3e00 00000000`0002050e 00000238`00000111 : USER32!UserCallWinProcCheckWow+0x33c
00000089`a8d7f3b0 00007ffe`a15c4c2d : 00000000`00000000 00000000`00000000 00000000`000003f9 00000000`000c0000 : USER32!DispatchClientMessage+0x9c
00000089`a8d7f410 00007ffe`a1ca8004 : 00000000`00000000 00000000`00000000 00000000`00000000 00000000`00000000 : USER32!_fnDWORD+0x3d
00000089`a8d7f470 00007ffe`9f4c1434 : 00007ffe`a15b092f 00000000`00000000 00007ffe`a15c4c45 00000000`00000000 : ntdll!KiUserCallbackDispatcherContinue
(TrapFrame @ 00000089`a8d7f338)
00000089`a8d7f4f8 00007ffe`a15b092f : 00000000`00000000 00007ffe`a15c4c45 00000000`00000000 00000000`00000000 : win32u!NtUserMessageCall+0x14
00000089`a8d7f500 00007ffe`9f4cb2d4 : 00000000`00000000 00000000`000003f9 00000000`0002050e 00000000`00000000 : USER32!SendMessageWorker+0x12f
00000089`a8d7f5a0 00007ffe`8ea250bf : 00000238`ff1b8cd0 00000000`00000001 00000000`50010001 00000000`00000001 : USER32!SendMessageW+0x137
00000089`a8d7f600 00007ffe`8ea58822 : 00000000`00000202 00000089`a8d7f6d9 00000000`00000000 00000000`00000000 : COMCTL32!Button_ReleaseCapture+0xbb
00000089`a8d7f630 00007ffe`a15b1cac : 00000000`00000000 00000000`80000000 00000000`00000001 00000000`00000000 : COMCTL32!Button_WndProc+0x802
00000089`a8d7f740 00007ffe`a15b0f06 : 00000000`00000000 00007ffe`8ea58020 00000000`0002050e 00007ffe`00000202 : USER32!UserCallWinProcCheckWow+0x33c
00000089`a8d7f8b0 00007ffe`a15b60e4 : 00007ffe`8ea58020 00000000`00000000 00000238`80048bf0 00000000`0002050e : USER32!DispatchMessageWorker+0x2a6
00000089`a8d7f930 00007ffe`8ea05f9f : 00000238`ff178410 00000089`a8d7fa39 00000000`00000100 00000000`000203c4 : USER32!IsDialogMessageW+0x104
00000089`a8d7f990 00007ffe`8ea05e48 : 00000238`ff165980 00000089`a8d7fa39 00000000`00000000 100396a3`00000001 : COMCTL32!Prop_IsDialogMessage+0x4b
00000089`a8d7f9d0 00007ffe`8ea05abd : 00000089`a8d7faf0 00000089`a8d7faf0 00007ff6`c1520000 00000238`ff178410 : COMCTL32!_RealPropertySheet+0x2c0
00000089`a8d7faa0 00007ffe`8ead0803 : 00000238`ff178410 00000089`a8d7fbd0 00007ffe`a1069170 00760065`00000000 : COMCTL32!_PropertySheet+0x49
00000089`a8d7fad0 00007ff6`c1523415 : 00007ff6`c1520000 00000238`ff172080 00000089`a8d7fc70 00000089`a8d7fc70 : COMCTL32!PropertySheetA+0x53
00000089`a8d7fb70 00007ff6`c1525c68 : 00000000`00000000 00000000`00000000 00000000`00000001 00000000`00000001 : notmyfault64+0x3415
00000089`a8d7fda0 00007ffe`a17753e0 : 00000000`00000000 00000000`00000000 00000000`00000000 00000000`00000000 : notmyfault64+0x5c68
00000089`a8d7fde0 00007ffe`a1c0485b : 00000000`00000000 00000000`00000000 00000000`00000000 00000000`00000000 : KERNEL32!BaseThreadInitThunk+0x10
00000089`a8d7fe10 00000000`00000000 : 00000000`00000000 00000000`00000000 00000000`00000000 00000000`00000000 : ntdll!RtlUserThreadStart+0x2b
```

7.   The version command shows additional information:

```
0: kd> version
Windows 10 Kernel Version 22000 MP (4 procs) Free x64
Product: WinNt, suite: TerminalServer SingleUserTS
Edition build lab: 22000.1.amd64fre.co_release.210604-1628
Kernel base = 0xfffff801`4621d000 PsLoadedModuleList = 0xfffff801`46e46850
Debug session time: Sat Nov 23 14:38:07.918 2024 (UTC + 0:00)
System Uptime: 0 days 0:04:32.192
64-bit Kernel bitmap dump: C:\ARWMDA-Dumps\Complete\MEMORY-normal.DMP
```

[...]

8.   Now we check loaded modules and their timestamps using **lmt** command:

```
0: kd> lmt
start             end               module name
00007ff6`c1520000 00007ff6`c1562000 notmyfault64  Fri Jun  9 03:43:10 2017 (593A0B3E)
00007ffe`84f90000 00007ffe`84ff9000 Oleacc    D4726D59 (This is a reproducible build file hash, not a timestamp)
00007ffe`8e9d0000 00007ffe`8ec75000 COMCTL32  7B1156C1 (This is a reproducible build file hash, not a timestamp)
00007ffe`8f2e0000 00007ffe`8f38e000 TextShaping  4AED9582 (This is a reproducible build file hash, not a timestamp)
00007ffe`8fac0000 00007ffe`8fbec000 textinputframework  13CE190B (This is a reproducible build file hash, not a timestamp)
00007ffe`98f90000 00007ffe`992fd000 CoreUIComponents  578E8F6C (This is a reproducible build file hash, not a timestamp)
00007ffe`9ad70000 00007ffe`9aea2000 CoreMessaging  E056FF75 (This is a reproducible build file hash, not a timestamp)
00007ffe`9bb00000 00007ffe`9bb91000 apphelp   F8DFA076 (This is a reproducible build file hash, not a timestamp)
00007ffe`9c770000 00007ffe`9c81c000 uxtheme   DE2F24ED (This is a reproducible build file hash, not a timestamp)
00007ffe`9cfe0000 00007ffe`9d147000 wintypes  Tue Oct  8 01:53:04 1996 (3259A5F0)
00007ffe`9e0e0000 00007ffe`9e0f8000 kernel_appcore  90A828D2 (This is a reproducible build file hash, not a timestamp)
00007ffe`9e750000 00007ffe`9e75c000 CRYPTBASE  14759998 (This is a reproducible build file hash, not a timestamp)
00007ffe`9f070000 00007ffe`9f10d000 msvcp_win  Wed Nov 12 03:53:59 1986 (1FB7FD57)
00007ffe`9f110000 00007ffe`9f22c000 gdi32full  3772588A (This is a reproducible build file hash, not a timestamp)
00007ffe`9f230000 00007ffe`9f341000 ucrtbase  00E78CE9 (This is a reproducible build file hash, not a timestamp)
00007ffe`9f4c0000 00007ffe`9f4e6000 win32u    Fri Jul 18 13:38:10 2031 (73C2C6B2)
00007ffe`9f4f0000 00007ffe`9f56f000 bcryptPrimitives  A6F742A6 (This is a reproducible build file hash, not a timestamp)
00007ffe`9f5e0000 00007ffe`9f607000 bcrypt    D4036918 (This is a reproducible build file hash, not a timestamp)
00007ffe`9f6d0000 00007ffe`9fa55000 KERNELBASE  Wed May 12 21:26:00 1999 (3739E3D8)
00007ffe`9fa60000 00007ffe`9fdd6000 combase   E6E0BFEF (This is a reproducible build file hash, not a timestamp)
00007ffe`9fde0000 00007ffe`9feb6000 OLEAUT32  75801AEB (This is a reproducible build file hash, not a timestamp)
00007ffe`9fee0000 00007ffe`9ffcc000 COMDLG32  B62D71FC (This is a reproducible build file hash, not a timestamp)
00007ffe`a00d0000 00007ffe`a0101000 IMM32     A830D784 (This is a reproducible build file hash, not a timestamp)
00007ffe`a02d0000 00007ffe`a032d000 SHLWAPI   5D809272 (This is a reproducible build file hash, not a timestamp)
00007ffe`a0330000 00007ffe`a044d000 MSCTF     B693B13B (This is a reproducible build file hash, not a timestamp)
00007ffe`a08c0000 00007ffe`a1086000 SHELL32   ***** Invalid (8E3DCBFC)
00007ffe`a1090000 00007ffe`a11b0000 RPCRT4    2A8F41B1 (This is a reproducible build file hash, not a timestamp)
00007ffe`a11b0000 00007ffe`a1261000 ADVAPI32  Mon Oct 12 04:08:11 2026 (6ACC4F1B)
00007ffe`a1300000 00007ffe`a13a2000 sechost   80B4BF25 (This is a reproducible build file hash, not a timestamp)
00007ffe`a1440000 00007ffe`a152a000 shcore    ***** Invalid (D85EBCF4)
00007ffe`a15a0000 00007ffe`a174c000 USER32    42176440 (This is a reproducible build file hash, not a timestamp)
00007ffe`a1760000 00007ffe`a181d000 KERNEL32  1B24EDA6 (This is a reproducible build file hash, not a timestamp)
00007ffe`a19c0000 00007ffe`a1a63000 msvcrt    90483ED2 (This is a reproducible build file hash, not a timestamp)
00007ffe`a1a70000 00007ffe`a1a99000 GDI32     47353A16 (This is a reproducible build file hash, not a timestamp)
00007ffe`a1c00000 00007ffe`a1e0a000 ntdll     77DA5A19 (This is a reproducible build file hash, not a timestamp)
ffff9010`08d70000 ffff9010`08e1a000 win32k    F12684B7 (This is a reproducible build file hash, not a timestamp)
ffff9010`09000000 ffff9010`093ad000 win32kfull  D669AD20 (This is a reproducible build file hash, not a timestamp)
ffff9010`09400000 ffff9010`09445000 cdd       228D01D3 (This is a reproducible build file hash, not a timestamp)
ffff9010`09fb0000 ffff9010`0a2db000 win32kbase  5E7DB7B2 (This is a reproducible build file hash, not a timestamp)
fffff801`45de0000 fffff801`46163000 mcupdate_GenuineIntel  3AFA5B4A (This is a reproducible build file hash, not a timestamp)
fffff801`46170000 fffff801`46176000 hal       EE778D5D (This is a reproducible build file hash, not a timestamp)
fffff801`46180000 fffff801`46192000 kdstub    DA07C766 (This is a reproducible build file hash, not a timestamp)
fffff801`461a0000 fffff801`461e6000 kdcom     135D2C69 (This is a reproducible build file hash, not a timestamp)
fffff801`461f0000 fffff801`461fb000 BOOTVID   F9005FA9 (This is a reproducible build file hash, not a timestamp)
fffff801`4621d000 fffff801`47264000 nt        2A4F46B3 (This is a reproducible build file hash, not a timestamp)
fffff801`47b00000 fffff801`47b28000 tm        EA75A61C (This is a reproducible build file hash, not a timestamp)
fffff801`47b30000 fffff801`47b9e000 CLFS      D8915809 (This is a reproducible build file hash, not a timestamp)
fffff801`47ba0000 fffff801`47bba000 PSHED     B186E628 (This is a reproducible build file hash, not a timestamp)
fffff801`47bc0000 fffff801`47cce000 clipsp    Thu Sep  5 10:34:57 2024 (66D97B41)
fffff801`47cd0000 fffff801`47d43000 FLTMGR    43AFD083 (This is a reproducible build file hash, not a timestamp)
fffff801`47d50000 fffff801`47d7a000 ksecdd    4FFDFD9D (This is a reproducible build file hash, not a timestamp)
fffff801`47d80000 fffff801`47de4000 msrpc     C312302E (This is a reproducible build file hash, not a timestamp)
fffff801`47df0000 fffff801`47dfe000 cmimcext  44830797 (This is a reproducible build file hash, not a timestamp)
fffff801`47e00000 fffff801`47e14000 werkernel  A1002A9B (This is a reproducible build file hash, not a timestamp)
fffff801`47e20000 fffff801`47e2c000 ntosext   E8A42C19 (This is a reproducible build file hash, not a timestamp)
fffff801`47e30000 fffff801`47f19000 CI        EDFFE010 (This is a reproducible build file hash, not a timestamp)
fffff801`47f20000 fffff801`47fdd000 cng       6D662EBF (This is a reproducible build file hash, not a timestamp)
fffff801`47fe0000 fffff801`480b3000 Wdf01000  AA914C07 (This is a reproducible build file hash, not a timestamp)
fffff801`480c0000 fffff801`480d4000 WDFLDR    9772E9CF (This is a reproducible build file hash, not a timestamp)
fffff801`480e0000 fffff801`480ed000 PRM       635DFAED (This is a reproducible build file hash, not a timestamp)
fffff801`480f0000 fffff801`48116000 acpiex    6EA4C7B4 (This is a reproducible build file hash, not a timestamp)
fffff801`48120000 fffff801`48132000 WppRecorder  040C9450 (This is a reproducible build file hash, not a timestamp)
fffff801`48140000 fffff801`4814e000 msseccore  0A62297B (This is a reproducible build file hash, not a timestamp)
fffff801`48150000 fffff801`4816b000 SgrmAgent  6A6260BA (This is a reproducible build file hash, not a timestamp)
fffff801`48170000 fffff801`4817a000 lxss      CCCB6FD2 (This is a reproducible build file hash, not a timestamp)
fffff801`48180000 fffff801`48291000 LXCORE    9CDFF202 (This is a reproducible build file hash, not a timestamp)
fffff801`482a0000 fffff801`4836c000 ACPI      9993EE17 (This is a reproducible build file hash, not a timestamp)
fffff801`48370000 fffff801`4837c000 WMILIB    50EF2C8D (This is a reproducible build file hash, not a timestamp)
fffff801`48390000 fffff801`48403000 intelpep  BA74A520 (This is a reproducible build file hash, not a timestamp)
fffff801`48410000 fffff801`48427000 WindowsTrustedRT  FBFE0729 (This is a reproducible build file hash, not a timestamp)
fffff801`48430000 fffff801`48440000 IntelPMT  2EEF2CE8 (This is a reproducible build file hash, not a timestamp)
fffff801`48450000 fffff801`4845b000 WindowsTrustedRTProxy  511A675B (This is a reproducible build file hash, not a timestamp)
fffff801`48460000 fffff801`48475000 pcw       33D0336B (This is a reproducible build file hash, not a timestamp)
fffff801`48480000 fffff801`48497000 vdrvroot  1D57ABB7 (This is a reproducible build file hash, not a timestamp)
fffff801`484a0000 fffff801`484cf000 pdc       5FC847CC (This is a reproducible build file hash, not a timestamp)
fffff801`484d0000 fffff801`484e7000 CEA       4388A4C9 (This is a reproducible build file hash, not a timestamp)
fffff801`484f0000 fffff801`48522000 partmgr   371F386A (This is a reproducible build file hash, not a timestamp)
fffff801`48530000 fffff801`485ff000 spaceport  48173FBF (This is a reproducible build file hash, not a timestamp)
fffff801`48600000 fffff801`4861b000 volmgr    BE64E26A (This is a reproducible build file hash, not a timestamp)
```

```
fffff801`48620000 fffff801`48683000   volmgrx    Mon Dec 24 13:36:11 2018 (5C20E0CB)
fffff801`48690000 fffff801`486c3000   vmbus      8CD3CC3A (This is a reproducible build file hash, not a timestamp)
fffff801`486d0000 fffff801`486fa000   hvsocket   6B8E8359 (This is a reproducible build file hash, not a timestamp)
fffff801`48700000 fffff801`4879d000   NETIO      79584749 (This is a reproducible build file hash, not a timestamp)
fffff801`487a0000 fffff801`48921000   NDIS       8D49FE7F (This is a reproducible build file hash, not a timestamp)
fffff801`48930000 fffff801`48955000   vmbkmcl    FB5AF5ED (This is a reproducible build file hash, not a timestamp)
fffff801`48960000 fffff801`48973000   winhv      530962A9 (This is a reproducible build file hash, not a timestamp)
fffff801`48980000 fffff801`4899e000   mountmgr   FA75996D (This is a reproducible build file hash, not a timestamp)
fffff801`489a0000 fffff801`489c2000   EhStorClass 2CCA47B8 (This is a reproducible build file hash, not a timestamp)
fffff801`489d0000 fffff801`489eb000   fileinfo   0144422D (This is a reproducible build file hash, not a timestamp)
fffff801`489f0000 fffff801`48a33000   Wof        0A72D6CA (This is a reproducible build file hash, not a timestamp)
fffff801`48a40000 fffff801`48ad6000   WdFilter   2D17164C (This is a reproducible build file hash, not a timestamp)
fffff801`48ae0000 fffff801`48df1000   Ntfs       96E2CB2C (This is a reproducible build file hash, not a timestamp)
fffff801`48e00000 fffff801`48e12000   storvsc    41D45A1D (This is a reproducible build file hash, not a timestamp)
fffff801`48e20000 fffff801`48f02000   storport   CCED8F5F (This is a reproducible build file hash, not a timestamp)
fffff801`48f10000 fffff801`48f1d000   Fs_Rec     ***** Invalid (AE0F16E9)
fffff801`48f20000 fffff801`48f4d000   fse        2C2593C7 (This is a reproducible build file hash, not a timestamp)
fffff801`48f50000 fffff801`48fd1000   fwpkclnt   4E2A2814 (This is a reproducible build file hash, not a timestamp)
fffff801`48fe0000 fffff801`49013000   ksecpkg    709C330D (This is a reproducible build file hash, not a timestamp)
fffff801`49020000 fffff801`49338000   tcpip      DFFD5357 (This is a reproducible build file hash, not a timestamp)
fffff801`49340000 fffff801`49370000   wfplwfs    E692EB1C (This is a reproducible build file hash, not a timestamp)
fffff801`49380000 fffff801`4938e000   VmsProxy   AA60D882 (This is a reproducible build file hash, not a timestamp)
fffff801`49390000 fffff801`4939f000   VmsProxyHNic  6D1CBCDE (This is a reproducible build file hash, not a timestamp)
fffff801`493a0000 fffff801`49472000   fvevol     630AA60E (This is a reproducible build file hash, not a timestamp)
fffff801`49480000 fffff801`4948b000   volume     A21DB093 (This is a reproducible build file hash, not a timestamp)
fffff801`49490000 fffff801`49503000   volsnap    3112A7C7 (This is a reproducible build file hash, not a timestamp)
fffff801`49510000 fffff801`4955f000   rdyboost   679861A9 (This is a reproducible build file hash, not a timestamp)
fffff801`49560000 fffff801`49586000   mup        27ABAFBF (This is a reproducible build file hash, not a timestamp)
fffff801`49590000 fffff801`495a2000   iorate     09C64CE2 (This is a reproducible build file hash, not a timestamp)
fffff801`495d0000 fffff801`495ef000   disk       00D7CA81 (This is a reproducible build file hash, not a timestamp)
fffff801`495f0000 fffff801`49666000   CLASSPNP   D3DFE540 (This is a reproducible build file hash, not a timestamp)
fffff801`49a40000 fffff801`49ab3000   msquic     Fri Jan 12 21:55:59 2024 (65A1B56F)
fffff801`49af0000 fffff801`49b20000   cdrom      766B7F2D (This is a reproducible build file hash, not a timestamp)
fffff801`49b30000 fffff801`49b45000   filecrypt  F9D07A7A (This is a reproducible build file hash, not a timestamp)
fffff801`49b50000 fffff801`49b5e000   tbs        B7E220C3 (This is a reproducible build file hash, not a timestamp)
fffff801`49b60000 fffff801`49b6a000   Null       ***** Invalid (A41489EF)
fffff801`49b70000 fffff801`49b7a000   Beep       4D5648BF (This is a reproducible build file hash, not a timestamp)
fffff801`49b80000 fffff801`49fee000   dxgkrnl    5FEC2D6C (This is a reproducible build file hash, not a timestamp)
fffff801`49ff0000 fffff801`4a00e000   watchdog   58566D7C (This is a reproducible build file hash, not a timestamp)
fffff801`4a010000 fffff801`4a025000   BasicDisplay  39B04BC4 (This is a reproducible build file hash, not a timestamp)
fffff801`4a030000 fffff801`4a041000   BasicRender  2BC4E0FA (This is a reproducible build file hash, not a timestamp)
fffff801`4a050000 fffff801`4a06c000   Npfs       6AC5B004 (This is a reproducible build file hash, not a timestamp)
fffff801`4a070000 fffff801`4a081000   Msfs       050BF92B (This is a reproducible build file hash, not a timestamp)
fffff801`4a090000 fffff801`4a0b5000   CimFS      B250C149 (This is a reproducible build file hash, not a timestamp)
fffff801`4a0c0000 fffff801`4a0e3000   tdx        B4EE93B1 (This is a reproducible build file hash, not a timestamp)
fffff801`4a0f0000 fffff801`4a100000   TDI        0C29C965 (This is a reproducible build file hash, not a timestamp)
fffff801`4a110000 fffff801`4a16a000   netbt      7A93255D (This is a reproducible build file hash, not a timestamp)
fffff801`4a170000 fffff801`4a184000   afunix     F9F43A03 (This is a reproducible build file hash, not a timestamp)
fffff801`4a190000 fffff801`4a236000   afd        9609B293 (This is a reproducible build file hash, not a timestamp)
fffff801`4a240000 fffff801`4a25a000   vwififlt   AE9945C8 (This is a reproducible build file hash, not a timestamp)
fffff801`4a260000 fffff801`4a28b000   pacer      D9D36A67 (This is a reproducible build file hash, not a timestamp)
fffff801`4a290000 fffff801`4a2a3000   ndiscap    884BF1ED (This is a reproducible build file hash, not a timestamp)
fffff801`4a2b0000 fffff801`4a2c4000   netbios    6EEE9A65 (This is a reproducible build file hash, not a timestamp)
fffff801`4a2d0000 fffff801`4a386000   Vid        F1B61CCD (This is a reproducible build file hash, not a timestamp)
fffff801`4a390000 fffff801`4a3b3000   winhvr     44FF1051 (This is a reproducible build file hash, not a timestamp)
fffff801`4a3c0000 fffff801`4a43b000   rdbss      82A2DBB1 (This is a reproducible build file hash, not a timestamp)
fffff801`4a440000 fffff801`4a4d6000   csc        AE01C4F2 (This is a reproducible build file hash, not a timestamp)
fffff801`4a4e0000 fffff801`4a4f2000   nsiproxy   5B7A4012 (This is a reproducible build file hash, not a timestamp)
fffff801`4a500000 fffff801`4a50f000   npsvctrig  FCE748E0 (This is a reproducible build file hash, not a timestamp)
fffff801`4a510000 fffff801`4a520000   mssmbios   E6EAE99D (This is a reproducible build file hash, not a timestamp)
fffff801`4a530000 fffff801`4a53a000   gpuenergydrv  369BA49C (This is a reproducible build file hash, not a timestamp)
fffff801`4a540000 fffff801`4a56d000   dfsc       0CFBE935 (This is a reproducible build file hash, not a timestamp)
fffff801`4a5a0000 fffff801`4a60d000   fastfat    E8B47B68 (This is a reproducible build file hash, not a timestamp)
fffff801`4a610000 fffff801`4a628000   bam        A1451E1B (This is a reproducible build file hash, not a timestamp)
fffff801`4a630000 fffff801`4a683000   ahcache    34DD12CD (This is a reproducible build file hash, not a timestamp)
fffff801`4a690000 fffff801`4a6c7000   storvsp    F95AFC19 (This is a reproducible build file hash, not a timestamp)
fffff801`4a6d0000 fffff801`4a6f7000   vmbkmclr   4C95270A (This is a reproducible build file hash, not a timestamp)
fffff801`4a700000 fffff801`4a70d000   NdisVirtualBus  7C5FA602 (This is a reproducible build file hash, not a timestamp)
fffff801`4a710000 fffff801`4a72e000   hvservice  2E19FA24 (This is a reproducible build file hash, not a timestamp)
fffff801`4a730000 fffff801`4a743000   CompositeBus  ECFE8F40 (This is a reproducible build file hash, not a timestamp)
fffff801`4a750000 fffff801`4a75e000   kdnic      6F4C908A (This is a reproducible build file hash, not a timestamp)
fffff801`4a760000 fffff801`4a776000   umbus      7C36A743 (This is a reproducible build file hash, not a timestamp)
fffff801`4a780000 fffff801`4a795000   CAD        B1D4D535 (This is a reproducible build file hash, not a timestamp)
fffff801`4a7a0000 fffff801`4a7b5000   dmvsc      7C89FCB9 (This is a reproducible build file hash, not a timestamp)
fffff801`4a7c0000 fffff801`4a7ce000   VMBusHID   7163AD91 (This is a reproducible build file hash, not a timestamp)
fffff801`4a7d0000 fffff801`4a813000   HIDCLASS   95579DF3 (This is a reproducible build file hash, not a timestamp)
fffff801`4a820000 fffff801`4a833000   HIDPARSE   DFD5985A (This is a reproducible build file hash, not a timestamp)
fffff801`4a840000 fffff801`4a84c000   hyperkbd   E1F1CB69 (This is a reproducible build file hash, not a timestamp)
fffff801`4a850000 fffff801`4a864000   kbdclass   6FA2173F (This is a reproducible build file hash, not a timestamp)
fffff801`4a870000 fffff801`4a880000   HyperVideo  90AE33D4 (This is a reproducible build file hash, not a timestamp)
fffff801`4a890000 fffff801`4a8a1000   CmBatt     AA6A0739 (This is a reproducible build file hash, not a timestamp)
fffff801`4a8b0000 fffff801`4a8c8000   BATTC      20B84CAF (This is a reproducible build file hash, not a timestamp)
fffff801`4a8d0000 fffff801`4a8db000   vmgencounter  EB2DAFA4 (This is a reproducible build file hash, not a timestamp)
fffff801`4a8e0000 fffff801`4a92c000   intelppm   85B5A1B8 (This is a reproducible build file hash, not a timestamp)
```

```
fffff801`4a930000 fffff801`4a967000   vpcivsp    31596080 (This is a reproducible build file hash, not a timestamp)
fffff801`4a970000 fffff801`4a97c000   swenum     F62F1994 (This is a reproducible build file hash, not a timestamp)
fffff801`4a9d0000 fffff801`4a9f3000   crashdmp   8D9363E5 (This is a reproducible build file hash, not a timestamp)
fffff801`4f800000 fffff801`4f902000   dxgmms2    59EEB35A (This is a reproducible build file hash, not a timestamp)
fffff801`4f910000 fffff801`4f91d000   rdpvideominiport  3AF83E68 (This is a reproducible build file hash, not a timestamp)
fffff801`4f920000 fffff801`4f94f000   rdpdr      0D0652B8 (This is a reproducible build file hash, not a timestamp)
fffff801`4f950000 fffff801`4f977000   tsusbhub   2A54B94F (This is a reproducible build file hash, not a timestamp)
fffff801`4f980000 fffff801`4f9a6000   bowser     2BA6F817 (This is a reproducible build file hash, not a timestamp)
fffff801`4f9b0000 fffff801`4fa32000   ks         57FEC922 (This is a reproducible build file hash, not a timestamp)
fffff801`4fa40000 fffff801`4fa4f000   rdpbus     BD8B4E4D (This is a reproducible build file hash, not a timestamp)
fffff801`4fa50000 fffff801`4fa60000   mouhid     E5C292FD (This is a reproducible build file hash, not a timestamp)
fffff801`4fa70000 fffff801`4fa84000   mouclass   E5804605 (This is a reproducible build file hash, not a timestamp)
fffff801`4fab0000 fffff801`4fac0000   dump_diskdump  2B89D48E (This is a reproducible build file hash, not a timestamp)
fffff801`4faf0000 fffff801`4fb02000   dump_storvsc   41D45A1D (This is a reproducible build file hash, not a timestamp)
fffff801`4fb10000 fffff801`4fb35000   dump_vmbkmcl   FB5AF5ED (This is a reproducible build file hash, not a timestamp)
fffff801`4fb60000 fffff801`4fb7d000   dump_dumpfve   CC83E9F5 (This is a reproducible build file hash, not a timestamp)
fffff801`4fb80000 fffff801`4fb9c000   monitor    B69D294B (This is a reproducible build file hash, not a timestamp)
fffff801`4fba0000 fffff801`4fbab000   vmgid      69D0A17B (This is a reproducible build file hash, not a timestamp)
fffff801`61800000 fffff801`61885000   cldflt     F7B493E8 (This is a reproducible build file hash, not a timestamp)
fffff801`61890000 fffff801`618aa000   storqosflt 25F123C9 (This is a reproducible build file hash, not a timestamp)
fffff801`618b0000 fffff801`618d9000   bindflt    F69B37A8 (This is a reproducible build file hash, not a timestamp)
fffff801`618e0000 fffff801`618f8000   lltdio     281A4957 (This is a reproducible build file hash, not a timestamp)
fffff801`61900000 fffff801`61918000   mslldp     F7A73DC1 (This is a reproducible build file hash, not a timestamp)
fffff801`61920000 fffff801`6193b000   rspndr     37CA927E (This is a reproducible build file hash, not a timestamp)
fffff801`61940000 fffff801`61bc6000   vmswitch   BFE1FC1A (This is a reproducible build file hash, not a timestamp)
fffff801`61bd0000 fffff801`61bed000   wanarp     19E3B2D4 (This is a reproducible build file hash, not a timestamp)
fffff801`61c40000 fffff801`61cdd000   mrxsmb     5D6F6901 (This is a reproducible build file hash, not a timestamp)
fffff801`61ce0000 fffff801`61d29000   mrxsmb20   525796BA (This is a reproducible build file hash, not a timestamp)
fffff801`61d30000 fffff801`61d5c000   luafv      828F1DB8 (This is a reproducible build file hash, not a timestamp)
fffff801`61d60000 fffff801`61d98000   wcifs      A60B478F (This is a reproducible build file hash, not a timestamp)
fffff801`67200000 fffff801`67228000   Ndu        24EB76BF (This is a reproducible build file hash, not a timestamp)
fffff801`67230000 fffff801`672fe000   peauth     E1BC348A (This is a reproducible build file hash, not a timestamp)
fffff801`67300000 fffff801`67314000   tcpipreg   37803DC6 (This is a reproducible build file hash, not a timestamp)
fffff801`67320000 fffff801`67333000   condrv     12793F73 (This is a reproducible build file hash, not a timestamp)
fffff801`67340000 fffff801`6735d000   WdNisDrv   CEFCB763 (This is a reproducible build file hash, not a timestamp)
fffff801`67360000 fffff801`6736f000   terminpt   628D7DB4 (This is a reproducible build file hash, not a timestamp)
fffff801`673f0000 fffff801`67445000   WUDFRd     3379B41B (This is a reproducible build file hash, not a timestamp)
fffff801`67450000 fffff801`67461000   IndirectKmd   04A56B8C (This is a reproducible build file hash, not a timestamp)
fffff801`67470000 fffff801`67478000   myfault    Fri Jun  9 03:40:12 2017 (593A0A8C)
fffff801`680c0000 fffff801`6825f000   HTTP       726B9091 (This is a reproducible build file hash, not a timestamp)
fffff801`68260000 fffff801`6827b000   mpsdrv     340730AF (This is a reproducible build file hash, not a timestamp)
fffff801`68280000 fffff801`682db000   srvnet     A82EE6B0 (This is a reproducible build file hash, not a timestamp)
fffff801`682e0000 fffff801`682f4000   mmcss      C84340FC (This is a reproducible build file hash, not a timestamp)
fffff801`68300000 fffff801`683d2000   srv2       64642898 (This is a reproducible build file hash, not a timestamp)

Unloaded modules:
fffff801`673d0000 fffff801`673e2000   IndirectKmd.sys
    Timestamp: unavailable (00000000)
    Checksum:  00000000
    ImageSize:  00012000
fffff801`67370000 fffff801`673c6000   WUDFRd.sys
    Timestamp: unavailable (00000000)
    Checksum:  00000000
    ImageSize:  00056000
fffff801`49a20000 fffff801`49a31000   dump_storport.sys
    Timestamp: unavailable (00000000)
    Checksum:  00000000
    ImageSize:  00011000
fffff801`49a60000 fffff801`49a73000   dump_storvsc.sys
    Timestamp: unavailable (00000000)
    Checksum:  00000000
    ImageSize:  00013000
fffff801`49a80000 fffff801`49aa6000   dump_vmbkmcl.sys
    Timestamp: unavailable (00000000)
    Checksum:  00000000
    ImageSize:  00026000
fffff801`49ad0000 fffff801`49aee000   dump_dumpfve.sys
    Timestamp: unavailable (00000000)
    Checksum:  00000000
    ImageSize:  0001E000
fffff801`4a690000 fffff801`4a6da000   vmbusr.sys
    Timestamp: unavailable (00000000)
    Checksum:  00000000
    ImageSize:  0004A000
```

Note: All loaded process modules (DLLs) are also seen in addition to kernel modules because this is a complete memory dump.

9.   For complete memory dumps, the most useful strategy is to dump all processes and threads into a log file. This can be done by using **!process 0 3f** command. This command can be time-consuming. We now just look at the found *normal.exe* output:

```
0: kd> !process 0 3f
**** NT ACTIVE PROCESS DUMP ****

[...]

PROCESS ffffe7080ad590c0
    SessionId: 1  Cid: 1158    Peb: cddc53d000  ParentCid: 11f8
    DirBase: 79396002  ObjectTable: ffffa88ee88a9740  HandleCount: 49.
    Image: normal.exe
    VadRoot ffffe7080b607580 Vads 34 Clone 0 Private 144. Modified 0. Locked 6.
    DeviceMap ffffa88ee736eeb0
    Token                             ffffa88ee8ef0060
    ElapsedTime                       00:00:09.161
    UserTime                          00:00:00.000
    KernelTime                        00:00:00.000
    QuotaPoolUsage[PagedPool]         25072
    QuotaPoolUsage[NonPagedPool]      5064
    Working Set Sizes (now,min,max)  (815, 50, 345) (3260KB, 200KB, 1380KB)
    PeakWorkingSetSize                772
    VirtualSize                       4154 Mb
    PeakVirtualSize                   4154 Mb
    PageFaultCount                    817
    MemoryPriority                    BACKGROUND
    BasePriority                      8
    CommitCharge                      197
    Job                               ffffe70809f64300

    PEB at 000000cddc53d000
    InheritedAddressSpace:     No
    ReadImageFileExecOptions:  No
    BeingDebugged:             No
    ImageBaseAddress:          00007ff6cf3f0000
    NtGlobalFlag:              400
    NtGlobalFlag2:             0
    Ldr                        00007ffea1d7a140
    Ldr.Initialized:           Yes
    Ldr.InInitializationOrderModuleList: 0000020ca2d32070 . 0000020ca2d39070
    Ldr.InLoadOrderModuleList:          0000020ca2d321f0 . 0000020ca2d39050
    Ldr.InMemoryOrderModuleList:        0000020ca2d32200 . 0000020ca2d39060
              Base TimeStamp                     Module
          7ff6cf3f0000 670be4f6 Oct 13 16:19:18 2024 C:\Work\normal.exe
          7ffea1c00000 77da5a19 Sep 20 04:10:17 2033 C:\WINDOWS\SYSTEM32\ntdll.dll
          7ffea1760000 1b24eda6 Jun 06 22:22:46 1984 C:\WINDOWS\System32\KERNEL32.DLL
          7ffe9f6d0000 3739e3d8 May 12 21:26:00 1999 C:\WINDOWS\System32\KERNELBASE.dll
          7ffe9f230000 00e78ce9 Jun 25 16:14:49 1970 C:\WINDOWS\System32\ucrtbase.dll
          7ffe91cf0000 006cb796 Mar 24 11:08:06 1970 C:\WINDOWS\SYSTEM32\VCRUNTIME140.dll
    SubSystemData:      0000000000000000
    ProcessHeap:        0000020ca2d30000
    ProcessParameters:  0000020ca2d36570
    CurrentDirectory:   'C:\Work\'
    WindowTitle:  'C:\Work\normal.exe'
    ImageFile:    'C:\Work\normal.exe'
    CommandLine:  '"C:\Work\normal.exe" '
    DllPath:      '< Name not readable >'
    Environment:  0000020ca2d311f0
        =::=::\
        ALLUSERSPROFILE=C:\ProgramData
        APPDATA=C:\Users\User\AppData\Roaming
        CommonProgramFiles=C:\Program Files\Common Files
        CommonProgramFiles(x86)=C:\Program Files (x86)\Common Files
        CommonProgramW6432=C:\Program Files\Common Files
        COMPUTERNAME=WINDEV2204EVAL
        ComSpec=C:\WINDOWS\system32\cmd.exe
        DriverData=C:\Windows\System32\Drivers\DriverData
        FPS_BROWSER_APP_PROFILE_STRING=Internet Explorer
        FPS_BROWSER_USER_PROFILE_STRING=Default
        HOMEDRIVE=C:
```

```
HOMEPATH=\Users\User
LOCALAPPDATA=C:\Users\User\AppData\Local
LOGONSERVER=\\WINDEV2204EVAL
NUMBER_OF_PROCESSORS=4
OneDrive=C:\Users\User\OneDrive
OS=Windows_NT

Path=C:\Windows\system32;C:\Windows;C:\Windows\System32\Wbem;C:\Windows\System32\WindowsPowerShell\v1.0\;C:\Windows\Sy
stem32\OpenSSH\;C:\Program Files\Microsoft SQL Server\150\Tools\Binn\;C:\Program Files\Microsoft SQL Server\Client
SDK\ODBC\170\Tools\Binn\;C:\Program
Files\dotnet\;C:\Users\User\AppData\Local\Microsoft\WindowsApps;C:\Users\User\.dotnet\tools
PATHEXT=.COM;.EXE;.BAT;.CMD;.VBS;.VBE;.JS;.JSE;.WSF;.WSH;.MSC
PROCESSOR_ARCHITECTURE=AMD64
PROCESSOR_IDENTIFIER=Intel64 Family 6 Model 142 Stepping 10, GenuineIntel
PROCESSOR_LEVEL=6
PROCESSOR_REVISION=8e0a
ProgramData=C:\ProgramData
ProgramFiles=C:\Program Files
ProgramFiles(x86)=C:\Program Files (x86)
ProgramW6432=C:\Program Files
PSModulePath=C:\Program Files\WindowsPowerShell\Modules;C:\WINDOWS\system32\WindowsPowerShell\v1.0\Modules
PUBLIC=C:\Users\Public
SESSIONNAME=Console
SystemDrive=C:
SystemRoot=C:\WINDOWS
TEMP=C:\Users\User\AppData\Local\Temp
TMP=C:\Users\User\AppData\Local\Temp
USERDOMAIN=WINDEV2204EVAL
USERDOMAIN_ROAMINGPROFILE=WINDEV2204EVAL
USERNAME=User
USERPROFILE=C:\Users\User
windir=C:\WINDOWS


        THREAD ffffe708090790c0  Cid 1158.1cb8  Teb: 000000cddc53e000 Win32Thread: 0000000000000000 WAIT: (Executive)
KernelMode Alertable
            ffffe7080a14be88  NotificationEvent
        IRP List:
            ffffe708079022b0: (0006,0358) Flags: 00060030  Mdl: 00000000
        Not impersonating
        DeviceMap                 ffffa88ee736eeb0
        Owning Process            ffffe7080ad590c0       Image:          normal.exe
        Attached Process          N/A                    Image:          N/A
        Wait Start TickCount      16864                  Ticks: 556 (0:00:00:08.687)
        Context Switch Count      40                     IdealProcessor: 2
        UserTime                  00:00:00.000
        KernelTime                00:00:00.015
Unable to load image C:\Work\normal.exe, Win32 error 0n2
*** WARNING: Unable to verify checksum for normal.exe
        Win32 Start Address normal (0x00007ff6cf411dfc)
        Stack Init ffffa38943c3ec70 Current ffffa38943c3e3e0
        Base ffffa38943c3f000 Limit ffffa38943c39000 Call 0000000000000000
        Priority 9  BasePriority 8  IoPriority 2  PagePriority 5
        Child-SP          RetAddr             Call Site
        ffffa389`43c3e420 fffff801`464d04e7    nt!KiSwapContext+0x76
        ffffa389`43c3e560 fffff801`464d2399    nt!KiSwapThread+0x3a7
        ffffa389`43c3e640 fffff801`464cc2b4    nt!KiCommitThreadWait+0x159
        ffffa389`43c3e6e0 fffff801`46634b14    nt!KeWaitForSingleObject+0x234
        ffffa389`43c3e7d0 fffff801`4694ec58    nt!IopWaitForSynchronousIoEvent+0x50
        ffffa389`43c3e810 fffff801`4694e589    nt!IopSynchronousServiceTail+0x668
        ffffa389`43c3e8c0 fffff801`4694d846    nt!IopXxxControlFile+0xd29
        ffffa389`43c3ea00 fffff801`466512d5    nt!NtDeviceIoControlFile+0x56
        ffffa389`43c3ea70 00007ffe`a1ca4164    nt!KiSystemServiceCopyEnd+0x25 (TrapFrame @ ffffa389`43c3eae0)
        000000cd`dc36d3c8 00007ffe`9f704da5    ntdll!NtDeviceIoControlFile+0x14
        000000cd`dc36d3d0 00007ffe`9f784c5d    KERNELBASE!ConsoleCallServerGeneric+0xe9
        000000cd`dc36d530 00007ffe`9f784aba    KERNELBASE!ReadConsoleInternal+0x18d
        000000cd`dc36d680 00007ff6`cf4043cb    KERNELBASE!ReadConsoleW+0x1a
        000000cd`dc36d6c0 00000000`00000000    normal+0x143cb


        THREAD ffffe70808f4e080  Cid 1158.15d4  Teb: 000000cddc540000 Win32Thread: 0000000000000000 WAIT: (WrQueue)
UserMode Alertable
            ffffe7080c2dbac0  QueueObject
        Not impersonating
        DeviceMap                 ffffa88ee736eeb0
```

```
      Owning Process            ffffe7080ad590c0      Image:           normal.exe
      Attached Process          N/A              Image:        N/A
      Wait Start TickCount      16864            Ticks: 556 (0:00:00:08.687)
      Context Switch Count      7                IdealProcessor: 1
      UserTime                  00:00:00.000
      KernelTime                00:00:00.000
      Win32 Start Address ntdll!TppWorkerThread (0x00007ffea1c16a00)
      Stack Init ffffa389468d1c70 Current ffffa389468d1370
      Base ffffa389468d2000 Limit ffffa389468cc000 Call 0000000000000000
      Priority 8  BasePriority 8  IoPriority 2  PagePriority 5
      Child-SP          RetAddr            Call Site
      ffffa389`468d13b0 fffff801`464d04e7  nt!KiSwapContext+0x76
      ffffa389`468d14f0 fffff801`464d2399  nt!KiSwapThread+0x3a7
      ffffa389`468d15d0 fffff801`464d5256  nt!KiCommitThreadWait+0x159
      ffffa389`468d1670 fffff801`464d4c68  nt!KeRemoveQueueEx+0x2b6
      ffffa389`468d1720 fffff801`464d7f24  nt!IoRemoveIoCompletion+0x98
      ffffa389`468d1840 fffff801`466512d5  nt!NtWaitForWorkViaWorkerFactory+0xdf4
      ffffa389`468d1a70 00007ffe`a1ca7c54  nt!KiSystemServiceCopyEnd+0x25 (TrapFrame @ ffffa389`468d1ae0)
      000000cd`dc6ff4a8 00007ffe`a1c16cdf  ntdll!NtWaitForWorkViaWorkerFactory+0x14
      000000cd`dc6ff4b0 00007ffe`a17753e0  ntdll!TppWorkerThread+0x2df
      000000cd`dc6ff7a0 00007ffe`a1c0485b  KERNEL32!BaseThreadInitThunk+0x10
      000000cd`dc6ff7d0 00000000`00000000  ntdll!RtlUserThreadStart+0x2b

        THREAD ffffe708099960c0  Cid 1158.201c  Teb: 000000cddc542000 Win32Thread: 0000000000000000 WAIT: (WrQueue)
UserMode Alertable
          ffffe7080c2dbac0  QueueObject
      Not impersonating
      DeviceMap                 ffffa88ee736eeb0
      Owning Process            ffffe7080ad590c0      Image:           normal.exe
      Attached Process          N/A              Image:        N/A
      Wait Start TickCount      16864            Ticks: 556 (0:00:00:08.687)
      Context Switch Count      3                IdealProcessor: 3
      UserTime                  00:00:00.000
      KernelTime                00:00:00.000
      Win32 Start Address ntdll!TppWorkerThread (0x00007ffea1c16a00)
      Stack Init ffffa389468f4c70 Current ffffa389468f4370
      Base ffffa389468f5000 Limit ffffa389468ef000 Call 0000000000000000
      Priority 8  BasePriority 8  IoPriority 2  PagePriority 5
      Child-SP          RetAddr            Call Site
      ffffa389`468f43b0 fffff801`464d04e7  nt!KiSwapContext+0x76
      ffffa389`468f44f0 fffff801`464d2399  nt!KiSwapThread+0x3a7
      ffffa389`468f45d0 fffff801`464d5256  nt!KiCommitThreadWait+0x159
      ffffa389`468f4670 fffff801`464d4c68  nt!KeRemoveQueueEx+0x2b6
      ffffa389`468f4720 fffff801`464d7f24  nt!IoRemoveIoCompletion+0x98
      ffffa389`468f4840 fffff801`466512d5  nt!NtWaitForWorkViaWorkerFactory+0xdf4
      ffffa389`468f4a70 00007ffe`a1ca7c54  nt!KiSystemServiceCopyEnd+0x25 (TrapFrame @ ffffa389`468f4ae0)
      000000cd`dc7ffbc8 00007ffe`a1c16cdf  ntdll!NtWaitForWorkViaWorkerFactory+0x14
      000000cd`dc7ffbd0 00007ffe`a17753e0  ntdll!TppWorkerThread+0x2df
      000000cd`dc7ffec0 00007ffe`a1c0485b  KERNEL32!BaseThreadInitThunk+0x10
      000000cd`dc7ffef0 00000000`00000000  ntdll!RtlUserThreadStart+0x2b

        THREAD ffffe70808f33080  Cid 1158.1294  Teb: 000000cddc544000 Win32Thread: 0000000000000000 WAIT:
(UserRequest) UserMode Non-Alertable
          ffffe70809b28900  Timer2SynchronizationObject
      Not impersonating
      DeviceMap                 ffffa88ee736eeb0
      Owning Process            ffffe7080ad590c0      Image:           normal.exe
      Attached Process          N/A              Image:        N/A
      Wait Start TickCount      16864            Ticks: 556 (0:00:00:08.687)
      Context Switch Count      6                IdealProcessor: 0
      UserTime                  00:00:00.000
      KernelTime                00:00:00.000
      Win32 Start Address normal (0x00007ff6cf4046a0)
      Stack Init ffffa389468fbc70 Current ffffa389468fb650
      Base ffffa389468fc000 Limit ffffa389468f6000 Call 0000000000000000
      Priority 8  BasePriority 8  IoPriority 2  PagePriority 5
      Child-SP          RetAddr            Call Site
      ffffa389`468fb690 fffff801`464d04e7  nt!KiSwapContext+0x76
      ffffa389`468fb7d0 fffff801`464d2399  nt!KiSwapThread+0x3a7
      ffffa389`468fb8b0 fffff801`464cc2b4  nt!KiCommitThreadWait+0x159
      ffffa389`468fb950 fffff801`469fd22b  nt!KeWaitForSingleObject+0x234
      ffffa389`468fba40 fffff801`469fd15a  nt!ObWaitForSingleObject+0xbb
      ffffa389`468fbaa0 fffff801`466512d5  nt!NtWaitForSingleObject+0x6a
      ffffa389`468fbae0 00007ffe`a1ca4104  nt!KiSystemServiceCopyEnd+0x25 (TrapFrame @ ffffa389`468fbae0)
```

```
000000cd`dc9ff638 00007ffe`9f7210ee     ntdll!NtWaitForSingleObject+0x14
000000cd`dc9ff640 00007ff6`cf3fbf2d     KERNELBASE!WaitForSingleObjectEx+0x8e
000000cd`dc9ff6e0 00000000`000000b4     normal+0xbf2d
000000cd`dc9ff6e8 00000000`00000000     0xb4

    THREAD ffffe7080aae6080  Cid 1158.1d9c  Teb: 000000cddc546000 Win32Thread: 0000000000000000 WAIT:
(UserRequest) UserMode Non-Alertable
        ffffe70809b28a10  Timer2SynchronizationObject
    Not impersonating
    DeviceMap                 ffffa88ee736eeb0
    Owning Process            ffffe7080ad590c0       Image:          normal.exe
    Attached Process          N/A               Image:        N/A
    Wait Start TickCount      16864             Ticks: 556 (0:00:00:08.687)
    Context Switch Count      3                 IdealProcessor: 2
    UserTime                  00:00:00.000
    KernelTime                00:00:00.000
    Win32 Start Address normal (0x00007ff6cf4046a0)
    Stack Init ffffa38946909c70 Current ffffa38946909650
    Base ffffa3894690a000 Limit ffffa38946904000 Call 0000000000000000
    Priority 9  BasePriority 8  IoPriority 2  PagePriority 5
    Child-SP          RetAddr           Call Site
    ffffa389`46909690 fffff801`464d04e7     nt!KiSwapContext+0x76
    ffffa389`469097d0 fffff801`464d2399     nt!KiSwapThread+0x3a7
    ffffa389`469098b0 fffff801`464cc2b4     nt!KiCommitThreadWait+0x159
    ffffa389`46909950 fffff801`469fd22b     nt!KeWaitForSingleObject+0x234
    ffffa389`46909a40 fffff801`469fd15a     nt!ObWaitForSingleObject+0xbb
    ffffa389`46909aa0 fffff801`466512d5     nt!NtWaitForSingleObject+0x6a
    ffffa389`46909ae0 00007ffe`a1ca4104     nt!KiSystemServiceCopyEnd+0x25 (TrapFrame @ ffffa389`46909ae0)
    000000cd`dcbffab8 00007ffe`9f7210ee     ntdll!NtWaitForSingleObject+0x14
    000000cd`dcbffac0 00007ff6`cf3fbf2d     KERNELBASE!WaitForSingleObjectEx+0x8e
    000000cd`dcbffb60 00000000`000000b8     normal+0xbf2d
    000000cd`dcbffb68 00000000`00000000     0xb8

    THREAD ffffe70809c72080  Cid 1158.128c  Teb: 000000cddc548000 Win32Thread: 0000000000000000 WAIT:
(UserRequest) UserMode Non-Alertable
        ffffe70809b29b10  Timer2SynchronizationObject
    Not impersonating
    DeviceMap                 ffffa88ee736eeb0
    Owning Process            ffffe7080ad590c0       Image:          normal.exe
    Attached Process          N/A               Image:        N/A
    Wait Start TickCount      16864             Ticks: 556 (0:00:00:08.687)
    Context Switch Count      3                 IdealProcessor: 1
    UserTime                  00:00:00.000
    KernelTime                00:00:00.000
    Win32 Start Address normal (0x00007ff6cf4046a0)
    Stack Init ffffa38946910c70 Current ffffa38946910650
    Base ffffa38946911000 Limit ffffa3894690b000 Call 0000000000000000
    Priority 9  BasePriority 8  IoPriority 2  PagePriority 5
    Child-SP          RetAddr           Call Site
    ffffa389`46910690 fffff801`464d04e7     nt!KiSwapContext+0x76
    ffffa389`469107d0 fffff801`464d2399     nt!KiSwapThread+0x3a7
    ffffa389`469108b0 fffff801`464cc2b4     nt!KiCommitThreadWait+0x159
    ffffa389`46910950 fffff801`469fd22b     nt!KeWaitForSingleObject+0x234
    ffffa389`46910a40 fffff801`469fd15a     nt!ObWaitForSingleObject+0xbb
    ffffa389`46910aa0 fffff801`466512d5     nt!NtWaitForSingleObject+0x6a
    ffffa389`46910ae0 00007ffe`a1ca4104     nt!KiSystemServiceCopyEnd+0x25 (TrapFrame @ ffffa389`46910ae0)
    000000cd`dcdff318 00007ffe`9f7210ee     ntdll!NtWaitForSingleObject+0x14
    000000cd`dcdff320 00007ff6`cf3fbf2d     KERNELBASE!WaitForSingleObjectEx+0x8e
    000000cd`dcdff3c0 00000000`000000bc     normal+0xbf2d
    000000cd`dcdff3c8 00000000`00000000     0xbc

    THREAD ffffe7080a9d8080  Cid 1158.1270  Teb: 000000cddc54a000 Win32Thread: 0000000000000000 WAIT:
(UserRequest) UserMode Non-Alertable
        ffffe70808cbc090  Timer2SynchronizationObject
    Not impersonating
    DeviceMap                 ffffa88ee736eeb0
    Owning Process            ffffe7080ad590c0       Image:          normal.exe
    Attached Process          N/A               Image:        N/A
    Wait Start TickCount      16866             Ticks: 554 (0:00:00:08.656)
    Context Switch Count      3                 IdealProcessor: 3
    UserTime                  00:00:00.000
    KernelTime                00:00:00.000
    Win32 Start Address normal (0x00007ff6cf4046a0)
    Stack Init ffffa38946917c70 Current ffffa38946917650
```

```
          Base ffffa38946918000 Limit ffffa38946912000 Call 0000000000000000
          Priority 9  BasePriority 8  IoPriority 2  PagePriority 5
          Child-SP          RetAddr           Call Site
          ffffa389`46917690 fffff801`464d04e7  nt!KiSwapContext+0x76
          ffffa389`469177d0 fffff801`464d2399  nt!KiSwapThread+0x3a7
          ffffa389`469178b0 fffff801`464cc2b4  nt!KiCommitThreadWait+0x159
          ffffa389`46917950 fffff801`469fd22b  nt!KeWaitForSingleObject+0x234
          ffffa389`46917a40 fffff801`469fd15a  nt!ObWaitForSingleObject+0xbb
          ffffa389`46917aa0 fffff801`466512d5  nt!NtWaitForSingleObject+0x6a
          ffffa389`46917ae0 00007ffe`a1ca4104  nt!KiSystemServiceCopyEnd+0x25 (TrapFrame @ ffffa389`46917ae0)
          000000cd`dcfff708 00007ffe`9f7210ee  ntdll!NtWaitForSingleObject+0x14
          000000cd`dcfff710 00007ff6`cf3fbf2d  KERNELBASE!WaitForSingleObjectEx+0x8e
          000000cd`dcfff7b0 00000000`000000c0  normal+0xbf2d
          000000cd`dcfff7b8 00000000`00000000  0xc0

            THREAD ffffe70808e47080  Cid 1158.2550  Teb: 000000cddc54c000 Win32Thread: 0000000000000000 WAIT:
(UserRequest) UserMode Non-Alertable
            ffffe70808cbbe70  Timer2SynchronizationObject
          Not impersonating
          DeviceMap                 ffffa88ee736eeb0
          Owning Process            ffffe7080ad590c0        Image:          normal.exe
          Attached Process          N/A            Image:          N/A
          Wait Start TickCount      16866          Ticks: 554 (0:00:00:08.656)
          Context Switch Count      3              IdealProcessor: 0
          UserTime                  00:00:00.000
          KernelTime                00:00:00.000
          Win32 Start Address normal (0x00007ff6cf4046a0)
          Stack Init ffffa38946925c70 Current ffffa38946925650
          Base ffffa38946926000 Limit ffffa38946920000 Call 0000000000000000
          Priority 9  BasePriority 8  IoPriority 2  PagePriority 5
          Child-SP          RetAddr           Call Site
          ffffa389`46925690 fffff801`464d04e7  nt!KiSwapContext+0x76
          ffffa389`469257d0 fffff801`464d2399  nt!KiSwapThread+0x3a7
          ffffa389`469258b0 fffff801`464cc2b4  nt!KiCommitThreadWait+0x159
          ffffa389`46925950 fffff801`469fd22b  nt!KeWaitForSingleObject+0x234
          ffffa389`46925a40 fffff801`469fd15a  nt!ObWaitForSingleObject+0xbb
          ffffa389`46925aa0 fffff801`466512d5  nt!NtWaitForSingleObject+0x6a
          ffffa389`46925ae0 00007ffe`a1ca4104  nt!KiSystemServiceCopyEnd+0x25 (TrapFrame @ ffffa389`46925ae0)
          000000cd`dd1ff378 00007ffe`9f7210ee  ntdll!NtWaitForSingleObject+0x14
          000000cd`dd1ff380 00007ff6`cf3fbf2d  KERNELBASE!WaitForSingleObjectEx+0x8e
          000000cd`dd1ff420 00000000`000000c4  normal+0xbf2d
          000000cd`dd1ff428 00000000`00000000  0xc4
```

[...]

Note: We see user space stack traces, although they look truncated. We also see loaded process DLLs paths and environment information, like a computer name (where the memory dump came from).

10.   Using **.process /r /p** *<address>* and **.thread** *<address>* commands to change the current process and thread:

```
0: kd> .process /r /p ffffe7080ad590c0
Implicit process is now ffffe7080ad590c0
Loading User Symbols
......

************* Symbol Loading Error Summary *************
Module name          Error
WdFilter             The system cannot find the file specified
myfault              The system cannot find the file specified

You can troubleshoot most symbol related issues by turning on symbol loading diagnostics (!sym
noisy) and repeating the command that caused symbols to be loaded.
You should also verify that your symbol search path (.sympath) is correct.

0: kd> .thread ffffe708090790c0
Implicit thread is now ffffe708090790c0
```

```
0: kd> k
  *** Stack trace for last set context - .thread/.cxr resets it
 # Child-SP          RetAddr               Call Site
00 ffffa389`43c3e420 fffff801`464d04e7     nt!KiSwapContext+0x76
01 ffffa389`43c3e560 fffff801`464d2399     nt!KiSwapThread+0x3a7
02 ffffa389`43c3e640 fffff801`464cc2b4     nt!KiCommitThreadWait+0x159
03 ffffa389`43c3e6e0 fffff801`46634b14     nt!KeWaitForSingleObject+0x234
04 ffffa389`43c3e7d0 fffff801`4694ec58     nt!IopWaitForSynchronousIoEvent+0x50
05 ffffa389`43c3e810 fffff801`4694e589     nt!IopSynchronousServiceTail+0x668
06 ffffa389`43c3e8c0 fffff801`4694d846     nt!IopXxxControlFile+0xd29
07 ffffa389`43c3ea00 fffff801`466512d5     nt!NtDeviceIoControlFile+0x56
08 ffffa389`43c3ea70 00007ffe`a1ca4164     nt!KiSystemServiceCopyEnd+0x25
09 000000cd`dc36d3c8 00007ffe`9f704da5     ntdll!NtDeviceIoControlFile+0x14
0a 000000cd`dc36d3d0 00007ffe`9f784c5d     KERNELBASE!ConsoleCallServerGeneric+0xe9
0b 000000cd`dc36d530 00007ffe`9f784aba     KERNELBASE!ReadConsoleInternal+0x18d
0c 000000cd`dc36d680 00007ff6`cf4043cb     KERNELBASE!ReadConsoleW+0x1a
0d 000000cd`dc36d6c0 00000000`00000000     normal+0x143cb
```

Note: /r /p is important in the complete memory dumps because when we change the current process, we must change the whole virtual to physical memory mapping (kernel space remains the same for all processes) and reload user space symbols because DLLs and their mapping change too. However, the *normal* module stack trace portion is truncated because we didn't specify the symbol file.

```
0: kd> lmv m normal
Browse full module list
start             end               module name
00007ff6`cf3f0000 00007ff6`cf428000   normal   C (no symbols)
    Loaded symbol image file: normal.exe
    Image path: C:\Work\normal.exe
    Image name: normal.exe
    Browse all global symbols  functions  data  Symbol Reload
    Timestamp:        Sun Oct 13 16:19:18 2024 (670BE4F6)
    CheckSum:         00000000
    ImageSize:        00038000
    Translations:     0000.04b0 0000.04e4 0409.04b0 0409.04e4
    Information from resource tables:
```

Note: From the timestamp of the normal module, we see it is a debug build.

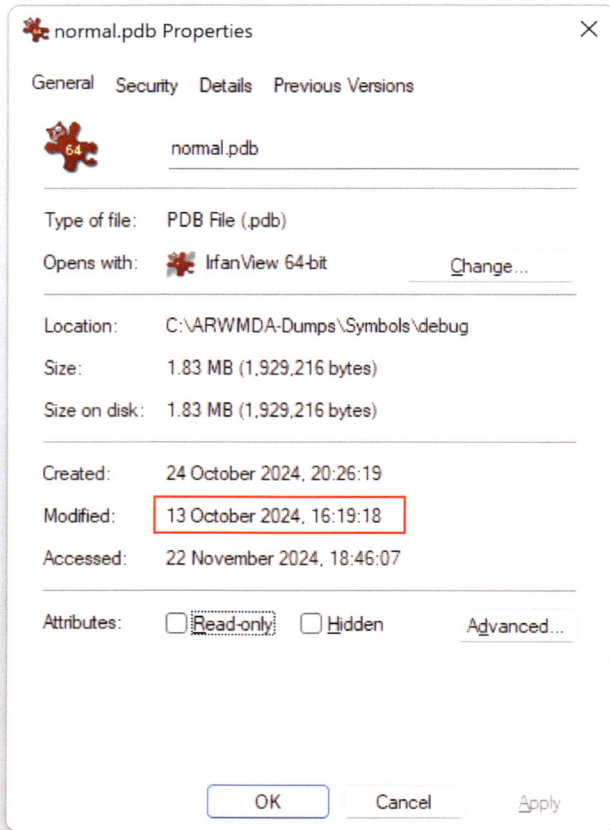

```
0: kd> .sympath+ C:\ARWMDA-Dumps\Symbols\debug
Symbol search path is: srv*;C:\ARWMDA-Dumps\Symbols\debug
Expanded Symbol search path is:
cache*;SRV*https://msdl.microsoft.com/download/symbols;c:\arwmda-dumps\symbols\debug

************* Path validation summary **************
Response                        Time (ms)       Location
Deferred                                        srv*
OK                                              C:\ARWMDA-Dumps\Symbols\debug

0: kd> kL
 *** Stack trace for last set context - .thread/.cxr resets it
 # Child-SP          RetAddr           Call Site
00 ffffa389`43c3e420 fffff801`464d04e7  nt!KiSwapContext+0x76
01 ffffa389`43c3e560 fffff801`464d2399  nt!KiSwapThread+0x3a7
02 ffffa389`43c3e640 fffff801`464cc2b4  nt!KiCommitThreadWait+0x159
03 ffffa389`43c3e6e0 fffff801`46634b14  nt!KeWaitForSingleObject+0x234
04 ffffa389`43c3e7d0 fffff801`4694ec58  nt!IopWaitForSynchronousIoEvent+0x50
05 ffffa389`43c3e810 fffff801`4694e589  nt!IopSynchronousServiceTail+0x668
06 ffffa389`43c3e8c0 fffff801`4694d846  nt!IopXxxControlFile+0xd29
07 ffffa389`43c3ea00 fffff801`466512d5  nt!NtDeviceIoControlFile+0x56
08 ffffa389`43c3ea70 00007ffe`a1ca4164  nt!KiSystemServiceCopyEnd+0x25
09 000000cd`dc36d3c8 00007ffe`9f704da5  ntdll!NtDeviceIoControlFile+0x14
0a 000000cd`dc36d3d0 00007ffe`9f784c5d  KERNELBASE!ConsoleCallServerGeneric+0xe9
0b 000000cd`dc36d530 00007ffe`9f784aba  KERNELBASE!ReadConsoleInternal+0x18d
0c 000000cd`dc36d680 00007ff6`cf4043cb  KERNELBASE!ReadConsoleW+0x1a
0d (Inline Function) --------`--------  normal!std::sys::pal::windows::stdio::read_u16s+0x4e
0e 000000cd`dc36d6c0 00000000`00000000  normal!std::sys::pal::windows::stdio::read_u16s_fixup_surrogates+0xcb
```

194

Note: We still see the truncated stack trace, probably due to inlined functions. We can either compare it to a process memory dump taken before triggering the complete memory dump (fiber dump memory dump) or look at raw stack symbolic data.

11.   Let's get the user space stack region boundary and dump symbolic references:

```
0: kd> !teb
TEB at 000000cddc53e000
    ExceptionList:         0000000000000000
    StackBase:             000000cddc370000
    StackLimit:            000000cddc36d000
    SubSystemTib:          0000000000000000
    FiberData:             0000000000001e00
    ArbitraryUserPointer:  0000000000000000
    Self:                  000000cddc53e000
    EnvironmentPointer:    0000000000000000
    ClientId:              0000000000001158 . 0000000000001cb8
    RpcHandle:             0000000000000000
    Tls Storage:           0000020ca2d323a0
    PEB Address:           000000cddc53d000
    LastErrorValue:        0
    LastStatusValue:       c0000100
    Count Owned Locks:     0
    HardErrorMode:         0
```

```
0: kd> dpS 000000cddc36d000 000000cddc370000
00007ffe`9f704db6 KERNELBASE!ConsoleCallServerGeneric+0xfa
00007ffe`9f71bf4c KERNELBASE!MultiByteToWideChar+0x15c
00007ffe`9f704da5 KERNELBASE!ConsoleCallServerGeneric+0xe9
00007ffe`9f704c3a KERNELBASE!WriteConsoleW+0x6a
00007ff6`cf4176d0 normal!_xmm+0xfc0
00007ff6`cf403e23 normal!std::sys::pal::windows::stdio::write_valid_utf8_to_console+0xd3
[/rustc/eeb90cda1969383f56a2637cbd3037bdf598841c/library\std\src\sys\pal\windows\stdio.rs @ 194]
00007ff6`cf4176d0 normal!_xmm+0xfc0
00007ffe`9f784c5d KERNELBASE!ReadConsoleInternal+0x18d
00007ff6`cf4176d0 normal!_xmm+0xfc0
00007ffe`9f732eba KERNELBASE!GetConsoleMode+0xfa
00007ffe`a17766f0 KERNEL32!GetLastErrorStub
00007ffe`a1783a40 KERNEL32!ReadConsoleW
00007ffe`9f784aba KERNELBASE!ReadConsoleW+0x1a
00007ff6`cf4043cb normal!std::sys::pal::windows::stdio::read_u16s_fixup_surrogates+0xcb
[/rustc/eeb90cda1969383f56a2637cbd3037bdf598841c/library\std\src\sys\pal\windows\stdio.rs @ 318]
00007ffe`a1c74149 ntdll!RtlIntegerToChar+0xb9
00007ff6`cf423188 normal!ZN3std6thread7Builder16spawn_unchecked_28_$u7b$$u7b$closure$u7d$$u7d$3MIN17h5c25c6e0b107703eE+0x40
00007ff6`cf42318a normal!ZN3std6thread7Builder16spawn_unchecked_28_$u7b$$u7b$closure$u7d$$u7d$3MIN17h5c25c6e0b107703eE+0x42
00007ff6`cf40419f normal!std::sys::pal::windows::stdio::impl$2::read+0x19f
[/rustc/eeb90cda1969383f56a2637cbd3037bdf598841c/library\std\src\sys\pal\windows\stdio.rs @ 284]
00007ffe`9f705ec9 KERNELBASE!OpenSortingKey+0x45
00007ff6`cf423188 normal!ZN3std6thread7Builder16spawn_unchecked_28_$u7b$$u7b$closure$u7d$$u7d$3MIN17h5c25c6e0b107703eE+0x40
00007ff6`cf423188 normal!ZN3std6thread7Builder16spawn_unchecked_28_$u7b$$u7b$closure$u7d$$u7d$3MIN17h5c25c6e0b107703eE+0x40
00007ffe`9f706470 KERNELBASE!NlsConvertIntegerToString+0xac
00007ffe`9f709818 KERNELBASE!StringCchCopyW+0x24
00007ffe`9f705ec9 KERNELBASE!OpenSortingKey+0x45
00007ffe`a1c9a319 ntdll!guard_check_icall+0xd
00007ffe`a1c967c1 ntdll!bsearch+0x81
00007ffe`9f7098fc KERNELBASE!QueryRegValue+0x7c
00007ffe`a1ce0a7f ntdll!LdrpQueryIllegalCWDDevices+0x24b
00007ffe`9f7060dd KERNELBASE!QueryRegSortVersionDll+0xc9
00007ffe`a1c9b5fb ntdll!write_char+0x27
00007ffe`a1c9b5b0 ntdll!woutput_l+0x8f0
00007ffe`9f9301f8 KERNELBASE!`string'+0x30
00007ffe`a1c41503 ntdll!LdrpFindLoadedDllByNameLockHeld+0x14f
00007ffe`a1d79dc0 ntdll!LdrpHashTable+0x40
00007ffe`a1c48b5b ntdll!ApiSetpSearchForApiSet+0xdb
00007ffe`9f7098fc KERNELBASE!QueryRegValue+0x7c
00007ffe`a1c3fc5a ntdll!LdrpIncrementModuleLoadCount+0x36
00007ffe`9f70379f KERNELBASE!QueryRegDefaultSortingVersion+0xc3
00007ffe`a1c3ba15 ntdll!LdrpLoadDllInternal+0xd5
00007ffe`9f71d21c KERNELBASE!LCMapStringEx+0x2fc
00007ffe`9f72a0ab KERNELBASE!WideCharToMultiByte+0x39b
00007ffe`9f236dfc ucrtbase!_acrt_WideCharToMultiByte+0x3c
00007ffe`9f236b9b ucrtbase!__acrt_LCMapStringA_stat+0x297
00007ffe`9f2fc278 ucrtbase!`string'
00007ffe`9f71cf20 KERNELBASE!LCMapStringEx
00007ffe`9f230001 ucrtbase!_acrt_update_multibyte_info <PERF> (ucrtbase+0x1)
00007ffe`9f245e30 ucrtbase!_acrt_DllMain
00007ffe`9f32fc90 ucrtbase!_globallocalestatus+0x10
00007ffe`9f2366a5 ucrtbase!_acrt_LCMapStringA+0x71
00007ffe`9f32f0c0 ucrtbase!_acrt_initial_locale_data
```

```
00007ffe`9f230000 ucrtbase!_acrt_update_multibyte_info <PERF> (ucrtbase+0x0)
00007ffe`9f236602 ucrtbase!setSBUpLow+0x172
00007ffe`9f32fc90 ucrtbase!_globallocalestatus+0x10
00007ffe`a1c455fb ntdll!RtlDosApplyFileIsolationRedirection_Ustr+0x30b
00007ffe`a1c21dfa ntdll!RtlpFindEntry+0x3a
00007ffe`a1c2b7bb ntdll!RtlpAllocateHeap+0x65b
00007ffe`a1c219c9 ntdll!RtlpHeapAddListEntry+0x9d
00007ffe`a1c2b7bb ntdll!RtlpAllocateHeap+0x65b
00007ffe`91d00003 VCRUNTIME140!__isa_available_init+0x193 [d:\a01\_work\43\s\src\vctools\crt\vcstartup\src\misc\amd64\cpu_disp.c @ 162]
00007ffe`a1c41363 ntdll!LdrpFindLoadedDllByName+0x123
00007ffe`a1c21dfa ntdll!RtlpFindEntry+0x3a
00007ffe`a1c261b1 ntdll!RtlpFreeHeap+0x481
00007ffe`a1c1c289 ntdll!RtlpQueryInformationActivationContextBasicInformation+0x4d
00007ffe`91d01588 VCRUNTIME140!`string'
00007ffe`a1c1bd6a ntdll!RtlQueryInformationActivationContext+0x15a
00007ffe`a1c283ba ntdll!RtlpFreeHeapInternal+0x7ca
00007ffe`a1c283ba ntdll!RtlpFreeHeapInternal+0x7ca
00007ff6`cf4046a0 normal!std::sys::pal::windows::thread::impl$0::new::thread_start
[/rustc/eeb90cda1969383f56a2637cbd3037bdf598841c/library\std\src\sys\pal\windows\thread.rs @ 52]
00007ffe`a1c276e1 ntdll!RtlFreeHeap+0x51
00007ffe`a1c24fbe ntdll!RtlpReAllocateHeap+0x72e
00007ffe`91d01600 VCRUNTIME140!`string'+0x38
00007ffe`a1c2b7bb ntdll!RtlpAllocateHeap+0x65b
00007ffe`a1c24730 ntdll!RtlpReAllocateHeapInternal+0x178
00007ffe`a1c28d1a ntdll!RtlpAllocateHeapInternal+0x12a
00007ffe`a1c461a6 ntdll!RtlpFindUnicodeStringInSection+0x1d6
00007ffe`a1c296fd ntdll!RtlpLowFragHeapAllocFromContext+0x1cd
00007ff6`cf423141 normal!_rust_no_alloc_shim_is_unstable
00007ffe`a2458a ntdll!RtlReAllocateHeap+0x5a
00007ff6`cf4157c0 normal!impl$<std::io::Write::write_fmt::Adapter<std::sys::pal::windows::stdio::Stderr>, core::fmt::Write>::vtable$+0x328
00007ff6`cf3f234c normal!alloc::alloc::Global::grow_impl+0x6fc [/rustc/eeb90cda1969383f56a2637cbd3037bdf598841c\library\alloc\src\alloc.rs @ 220]
00007ff6`cf4157c0 normal!impl$<std::io::Write::write_fmt::Adapter<std::sys::pal::windows::stdio::Stderr>, core::fmt::Write>::vtable$+0x328
00007ffe`a1c296fd ntdll!RtlpLowFragHeapAllocFromContext+0x1cd
00007ff6`cf3f1c23 normal!alloc::alloc::Global::alloc_impl+0x2a3 [/rustc/eeb90cda1969383f56a2637cbd3037bdf598841c\library\alloc\src\alloc.rs @ 185]
00007ff6`cf4157c0 normal!impl$<std::io::Write::write_fmt::Adapter<std::sys::pal::windows::stdio::Stderr>, core::fmt::Write>::vtable$+0x328
00007ffe`a1c21dfa ntdll!RtlpFindEntry+0x3a
00007ffe`a1c23372 ntdll!RtlpInsertFreeBlock+0x19e
00007ffe`a1c21dfa ntdll!RtlpFindEntry+0x3a
00007ffe`a1c2b7bb ntdll!RtlpAllocateHeap+0x65b
00007ff6`cf416548 normal!impl$<alloc::boxed::Box<dyn$<core::any::Any,core::marker::Send>,alloc::alloc::Global>, core::fmt::Debug>::vtable$+0x5b8
00007ff6`cf403c05 normal!std::sys::pal::windows::stdio::write+0x1d5 [/rustc/eeb90cda1969383f56a2637cbd3037bdf598841c/library\std\src\sys\pal\windows\stdio.rs
@ 168]
00007ff6`cf416528 normal!impl$<alloc::boxed::Box<dyn$<core::any::Any,core::marker::Send>,alloc::alloc::Global>, core::fmt::Debug>::vtable$+0x598
00007ff6`cf4231c9 normal!ZN3std6thread7Builder16spawn_unchecked_28_$u7b$$u7b$closure$u7d$$u7d$3MIN17h5c25c6e0b107703eE+0x81
00007ff6`cf416548 normal!impl$<alloc::boxed::Box<dyn$<core::any::Any,core::marker::Send>,alloc::alloc::Global>, core::fmt::Debug>::vtable$+0x5b8
00007ff6`cf3fdf9c normal!std::io::Write::write_all<std::sys::pal::windows::stdio::Stdout>+0x6c
00007ff6`cf403d60 normal!std::sys::pal::windows::stdio::write_valid_utf8_to_console+0x10
[/rustc/eeb90cda1969383f56a2637cbd3037bdf598841c/library\std\src\sys\pal\windows\stdio.rs @ 171]
00007ff6`cf416528 normal!impl$<alloc::boxed::Box<dyn$<core::any::Any,core::marker::Send>,alloc::alloc::Global>, core::fmt::Debug>::vtable$+0x598
00007ff6`cf4231b0 normal!ZN3std6thread7Builder16spawn_unchecked_28_$u7b$$u7b$closure$u7d$$u7d$3MIN17h5c25c6e0b107703eE+0x68
00007ff6`cf416548 normal!impl$<alloc::boxed::Box<dyn$<core::any::Any,core::marker::Send>,alloc::alloc::Global>, core::fmt::Debug>::vtable$+0x5b8
00007ff6`cf423198 normal!ZN3std6thread7Builder16spawn_unchecked_28_$u7b$$u7b$closure$u7d$$u7d$3MIN17h5c25c6e0b107703eE+0x50
00007ff6`cf3fd80f normal!std::io::stdio::impl$19::write_all+0x19f [/rustc/eeb90cda1969383f56a2637cbd3037bdf598841c/library\std\src\io\stdio.rs @ 813]
00007ff6`cf4231b0 normal!ZN3std6thread7Builder16spawn_unchecked_28_$u7b$$u7b$closure$u7d$$u7d$3MIN17h5c25c6e0b107703eE+0x68
00007ff6`cf423198 normal!ZN3std6thread7Builder16spawn_unchecked_28_$u7b$$u7b$closure$u7d$$u7d$3MIN17h5c25c6e0b107703eE+0x50
00007ffe`a1c2929c ntdll!RtlpAllocateHeapInternal+0x6ac
00007ff6`cf40e60f normal!core::fmt::write+0x1cf [/rustc/eeb90cda1969383f56a2637cbd3037bdf598841c/library\core\src\fmt\mod.rs @ 1207]
00007ff6`cf3fec0e normal!std::io::Write::write_fmt::impl$0::write_str<std::io::stdio::StdoutLock>+0x1e
[/rustc/eeb90cda1969383f56a2637cbd3037bdf598841c/library\std\src\io\mod.rs @ 1816]
00007ff6`cf423198 normal!ZN3std6thread7Builder16spawn_unchecked_28_$u7b$$u7b$closure$u7d$$u7d$3MIN17h5c25c6e0b107703eE+0x50
00007ffe`91cf0000 VCRUNTIME140!__ImageBase
00007ffe`91cf1b41 VCRUNTIME140!memset+0x1a1 [d:\a01\_work\43\s\src\vctools\crt\vcruntime\src\string\amd64\memset.asm @ 303]
00007ff6`cf3fed57 normal!std::io::read_until<std::io::buffered::bufreader::BufReader<std::io::stdio::StdinRaw> >+0x67
[/rustc/eeb90cda1969383f56a2637cbd3037bdf598841c/library\std\src\io\mod.rs @ 2091]
00007ff6`cf413775
normal!std::sys::once::futex::Once::call<std::sync::once::impl$2::call_once_force::closure_env$0<std::sync::once_lock::impl$0::initialize::closure_env$0
<std::sync::mutex::Mutex<std::io::buffered::bufreader::BufReader<std::io::stdio::StdinRaw>
>,std::sync::once_lock::impl$0::get_or_init::closure_env$0<std::sync::mutex::Mutex<std::io::buffered::bufreader::BufReader<std::io::stdio::StdinRaw>
>,std::io::stdio::stdin::closure_env$0>,never$> > >+0xe5 [/rustc/eeb90cda1969383f56a2637cbd3037bdf598841c/library\std\src\sys\sync\once\futex.rs @ 124]
00007ff6`cf423188 normal!ZN3std6thread7Builder16spawn_unchecked_28_$u7b$$u7b$closure$u7d$$u7d$3MIN17h5c25c6e0b107703eE+0x40
00007ff6`cf423160 normal!ZN3std6thread7Builder16spawn_unchecked_28_$u7b$$u7b$closure$u7d$$u7d$3MIN17h5c25c6e0b107703eE+0x18
00007ff6`cf423158 normal!ZN3std6thread7Builder16spawn_unchecked_28_$u7b$$u7b$closure$u7d$$u7d$3MIN17h5c25c6e0b107703eE+0x10
00007ff6`cf3fd3f5 normal!std::io::stdio::Stdin::read_line+0x65 [/rustc/eeb90cda1969383f56a2637cbd3037bdf598841c/library\std\src\io\stdio.rs @ 399]
00007ff6`cf412d9f normal!std::sync::once_lock::OnceLock::initialize<std::sync::mutex::Mutex<std::io::buffered::bufreader::BufReader<std::io::stdio::StdinRaw>
>,std::sync::once_lock::impl$0::get_or_init::closure_env$0<std::sync::mutex::Mutex<std::io::buffered::bufreader::BufReader<std::io::stdio::StdinRaw>
>,std::io::stdio::stdin::closure_env$0>,never$>+0x3f [/rustc/eeb90cda1969383f56a2637cbd3037bdf598841c/library\std\src\sync\once_lock.rs @ 497]
00007ff6`cf423198 normal!ZN3std6thread7Builder16spawn_unchecked_28_$u7b$$u7b$closure$u7d$$u7d$3MIN17h5c25c6e0b107703eE+0x50
00007ff6`cf423158 normal!ZN3std6thread7Builder16spawn_unchecked_28_$u7b$$u7b$closure$u7d$$u7d$3MIN17h5c25c6e0b107703eE+0x10
00007ff6`cf415f18 normal!impl$<std::rt::lang_start::closure_env$0<tuple$<> >, core::ops::function::Fn<tuple$<> > >::vtable$
00007ff6`cf3f936e normal!crate_c::mod_cb::func+0x5e [C:\ARWMDA-Dumps\normal\crate_c\src\mod_cb.rs @ 6]
00007ff6`cf3fde31 normal!std::io::stdio::_print+0x61 [/rustc/eeb90cda1969383f56a2637cbd3037bdf598841c/library\std\src\io\stdio.rs @ 1227]
00007ff6`cf4175b0 normal!_xmm+0xea0
00007ff6`cf423198 normal!ZN3std6thread7Builder16spawn_unchecked_28_$u7b$$u7b$closure$u7d$$u7d$3MIN17h5c25c6e0b107703eE+0x50
00007ff6`cf416558 normal!impl$<alloc::boxed::Box<dyn$<core::any::Any,core::marker::Send>,alloc::alloc::Global>, core::fmt::Debug>::vtable$+0x5c8
00007ff6`cf423158 normal!ZN3std6thread7Builder16spawn_unchecked_28_$u7b$$u7b$closure$u7d$$u7d$3MIN17h5c25c6e0b107703eE+0x10
00007ff6`cf3f8dde normal!crate_b::mod_b::func+0x2e [C:\ARWMDA-Dumps\normal\crate_b\src\mod_b.rs @ 11]
00007ff6`cf3fde31 normal!std::io::stdio::_print+0x61 [/rustc/eeb90cda1969383f56a2637cbd3037bdf598841c/library\std\src\io\stdio.rs @ 1227]
00007ff6`cf3f5fd7 normal!alloc::raw_vec::RawVec<std::thread::JoinHandle<tuple$<> >,alloc::alloc::Global>::grow_one<std::thread::JoinHandle<tuple$<>
>,alloc::alloc::Global>+0x17 [/rustc/eeb90cda1969383f56a2637cbd3037bdf598841c\library\alloc\src\raw_vec.rs @ 364]
00007ff6`cf4175b0 normal!_xmm+0xea0
00007ff6`cf4164d8 normal!impl$<alloc::boxed::Box<dyn$<core::any::Any,core::marker::Send>,alloc::alloc::Global>, core::fmt::Debug>::vtable$+0x548
00007ff6`cf3f26f4 normal!normal::mod_aa::func+0x24 [C:\ARWMDA-Dumps\normal\normal\src\mod_aa.rs @ 6]
00007ff6`cf3f250c normal!alloc::vec::Vec<std::thread::JoinHandle<tuple$<> >,alloc::alloc::Global>::push<std::thread::JoinHandle<tuple$<>
>,alloc::alloc::Global>+0x4c [/rustc/eeb90cda1969383f56a2637cbd3037bdf598841c\library\alloc\src\vec\mod.rs @ 2003]
```

196

```
00007ff6`cf3f3f93 normal!std::thread::spawn<normal::main::closure_env$0,tuple$<> >+0x93
[/rustc/eeb90cda1969383f56a2637cbd3037bdf598841c\library\std\src\thread\mod.rs @ 694]
00007ff6`cf4175b0 normal!_xmm+0xea0
00007ff6`cf4157e0 normal!impl$<std::io::Write::write_fmt::Adapter<std::sys::pal::windows::stdio::Stderr>, core::fmt::Write>::vtable$+0x348
00007ff6`cf3f2fb4 normal!normal::mod_ab::func+0x24 [C:\ARWMDA-Dumps\normal\normal\src\mod_ab.rs @ 6]
00007ff6`cf415a98 normal!impl$<ref$<usize>, core::fmt::Debug>::vtable$+0x188
00007ff6`cf3f6780 normal!normal::main+0x90 [C:\ARWMDA-Dumps\normal\normal\src\main.rs @ 20]
00007ff6`cf3fb391 normal!alloc::raw_vec::finish_grow<alloc::alloc::Global>+0x61 [/rustc/eeb90cda1969383f56a2637cbd3037bdf598841c\library\alloc\src\raw_vec.rs
@ 593]
00007ff6`cf405460 normal!std::sys::thread_local::native::eager::destroy<core::cell::once::OnceCell<std::thread::Thread> >
[/rustc/eeb90cda1969383f56a2637cbd3037bdf598841c\library\std\src\sys\thread_local\native\eager.rs @ 63]
00007ff6`cf405560 normal!std::sys::thread_local::destructors::list::register+0x90
[/rustc/eeb90cda1969383f56a2637cbd3037bdf598841c\library\std\src\sys\thread_local\destructors\list.rs @ 17]
00007ffe`a1c276e1 ntdll!RtlFreeHeap+0x51
00007ff6`cf3f74db normal!core::ops::function::FnOnce::call_once<void (*)(),tuple$<> >+0xb
[/rustc/eeb90cda1969383f56a2637cbd3037bdf598841c\library\core\src\ops\function.rs @ 250]
00007ff6`cf412e97 normal!std::sys::pal::windows::alloc::process_heap_init_and_alloc+0x17
[/rustc/eeb90cda1969383f56a2637cbd3037bdf598841c\library\std\src\sys\pal\windows\alloc.rs @ 117]
00007ff6`cf3f66f0 normal!normal::main [C:\ARWMDA-Dumps\normal\normal\src\main.rs @ 7]
00007ff6`cf3f184e normal!std::sys::backtrace::__rust_begin_short_backtrace<void (*)(),tuple$<> >+0xe
[/rustc/eeb90cda1969383f56a2637cbd3037bdf598841c\library\std\src\sys\backtrace.rs @ 155]
00007ff6`cf3fc198 normal!std::thread::Thread::new_inner+0x48 [/rustc/eeb90cda1969383f56a2637cbd3037bdf598841c\library\std\src\thread\mod.rs @ 1402]
00007ff6`cf410000 normal!core::str::count::char_count_general_case [/rustc/eeb90cda1969383f56a2637cbd3037bdf598841c\library\core\src\str\count.rs @ 135]
00007ff6`cf3f66f0 normal!normal::main [C:\ARWMDA-Dumps\normal\normal\src\main.rs @ 7]
00007ff6`cf3f63d1 normal!std::rt::lang_start::closure$0<tuple$<> >+0x11 [/rustc/eeb90cda1969383f56a2637cbd3037bdf598841c\library\std\src\rt.rs @ 162]
00007ff6`cf3fb909 normal!std::rt::lang_start_internal+0x79 [/rustc/eeb90cda1969383f56a2637cbd3037bdf598841c\library\std\src\rt.rs @ 141]
00007ff6`cf415f18 normal!impl$<std::rt::lang_start::closure_env$0<tuple$<> >, core::ops::function::Fn<tuple$<> > >::vtable$
00007ffe`9f253403 ucrtbase!needs_trail_byte+0x17
00007ffe`a1c06800 ntdll!RtlSetLastWin32Error+0x40
00007ffe`9f253485 ucrtbase!parse_command_line<char>+0x71
00007ffe`9f330f60 ucrtbase!commode+0x10
00007ffe`9f72cc8b KERNELBASE!FlsGetValue+0x1b
00007ffe`9f72cc8b KERNELBASE!FlsGetValue+0x1b
00007ff6`cf3f63aa normal!std::rt::lang_start<tuple$<> >+0x3a [/rustc/eeb90cda1969383f56a2637cbd3037bdf598841c\library\std\src\rt.rs @ 161]
00007ffe`9f24bf85 ucrtbase!__crt_state_management::get_current_state_index+0x29
00007ff6`cf415300 normal!__guard_xfg_dispatch_icall_fptr
00007ff6`cf415330 normal!__xc_z
00007ff6`cf3f66f0 normal!normal::main [C:\ARWMDA-Dumps\normal\normal\src\main.rs @ 7]
00007ff6`cf3f66f0 normal!normal::main [C:\ARWMDA-Dumps\normal\normal\src\main.rs @ 7]
00007ff6`cf415328 normal!pre_cpp_initializer
00007ff6`cf3f6979 normal!main+0x19
00007ff6`cf411d8c normal!__scrt_common_main_seh+0x10c [D:\a\_work\1\s\src\vctools\crt\vcstartup\src\startup\exe_common.inl @ 288]
00007ff6`cf411e05 normal!mainCRTStartup+0x9 [D:\a\_work\1\s\src\vctools\crt\vcstartup\src\startup\exe_main.cpp @ 17]
00007ffe`a17753e0 KERNEL32!BaseThreadInitThunk+0x10
00007ffe`a1c0485b ntdll!RtlUserThreadStart+0x2b
```

Note: To check that the symbolic return address is not coincidental, use backward disassembly to verify that the previous CPU instruction is the call instruction:

```
0: kd> ub 00007ff6`cf3f2fb4
normal!std::process::impl$57::report+0xf:
00007ff6`cf3f2f8f int      3
normal!normal::mod_ab::func [C:\ARWMDA-Dumps\normal\normal\src\mod_ab.rs @ 3]:
00007ff6`cf3f2f90 sub      rsp,58h
00007ff6`cf3f2f94 lea      rcx,[rsp+28h]
00007ff6`cf3f2f99 lea      rdx,[normal!impl$<ref$<usize>, core::fmt::Debug>::vtable$+0x188 (00007ff6`cf415a98)]
00007ff6`cf3f2fa0 call     normal!core::fmt::Arguments::new_const<1> (00007ff6`cf3f92a0)
00007ff6`cf3f2fa5 lea      rcx,[rsp+28h]
00007ff6`cf3f2faa call     normal!std::io::stdio::_print (00007ff6`cf3fddd0)
00007ff6`cf3f2faf call     normal!normal::mod_aa::func (00007ff6`cf3f26d0)
```

12.   Let's now see how the **.trap** command shows user mode/kernel mode transitions:

```
0: kd> kvL
*** Stack trace for last set context - .thread/.cxr resets it
# Child-SP          RetAddr           : Args to Child                                                        : Call Site
00 ffffa389`43c3e420 fffff801`464d04e7 : 00000000`0000000b ffffbe01`ffffffff fffb900`00000000 fffe708`04918158 : nt!KiSwapContext+0x76
01 ffffa389`43c3e560 fffff801`464d2399 : fffe708`0a53dc20 fffe708`0a53dd00 ffffa389`43c3e740 fffe708`00000002 : nt!KiSwapThread+0x3a7
02 ffffa389`43c3e640 fffff801`464cc2b4 : 00000000`00000000 fffff801`00000000 fffe708`00000000 00000000`00000000 : nt!KiCommitThreadWait+0x159
03 ffffa389`43c3e6e0 fffff801`46634b14 : fffe708`0a14be88 7b62542b`00000000 fffe708`00000000 00000000`00000001 : nt!KeWaitForSingleObject+0x234
04 ffffa389`43c3e7d0 fffff801`4694ec58 : 00000000`00000002 ffffa389`43c3e890 fffe708`0a14bdf0 fffe708`079022b0 : nt!IopWaitForSynchronousIoEvent+0x50
05 ffffa389`43c3e810 fffff801`4694e589 : 00000000`00500016 ffffa389`43c3eb60 00000000`00000005 00000000`00500016 : nt!IopSynchronousServiceTail+0x668
06 ffffa389`43c3e8c0 fffff801`4694d846 : 00007ffe`9f784aa0 00000000`00000000 00000000`00000000 00000000`00000000 : nt!IopXxxControlFile+0xd29
07 ffffa389`43c3ea00 fffff801`466512d5 : 00000000`00000000 00000000`00000000 00000000`00000000 000000cd`dc36f3f8 : nt!NtDeviceIoControlFile+0x56
08 ffffa389`43c3ea70 00007ffe`a1ca4164 : 00007ffe`9f704da5 000000cd`dc36d4f0 00007ffe`9f704c3a 00000000`00000000 : nt!KiSystemServiceCopyEnd+0x25
(TrapFrame @ ffffa389`43c3eae0)
09 000000cd`dc36d3c8 00007ffe`9f704da5 : 000000cd`dc36d4f0 00007ffe`9f704c3a 00000000`00000000 00000000`00000008 : ntdll!NtDeviceIoControlFile+0x14
0a 000000cd`dc36d3d0 00007ffe`9f784c5d : 00000000`00000000 00000000`00000000 00000000`00000000 00007ff6`cf4176d0 :
KERNELBASE!ConsoleCallServerGeneric+0xe9
0b 000000cd`dc36d530 00007ffe`9f784aba : 00000000`00000000 00000000`00000000 00000000`0000005c 00000001`00000001 : KERNELBASE!ReadConsoleInternal+0x18d
0c 000000cd`dc36d680 00007ffe`a1c74149 : 00000000`00000000 00007ffe`a1c74149 00000000`00000000 00000000`00000005 : KERNELBASE!ReadConsoleW+0x1a
0d (Inline Function) --------`-------- : --------`-------- --------`-------- --------`-------- --------`-------- :
normal!std::sys::pal::windows::stdio::read_u16s+0x4e (Inline Function @ 00007ff6`cf4043cb)
0e 000000cd`dc36d6c0 00000000`00000000 : 00007ffe`a1c74149 00000000`00000000 00000000`00000005 000000cd`dc36d6f0 :
normal!std::sys::pal::windows::stdio::read_u16s_fixup_surrogates+0xcb
```

```
0: kd> .trap ffffa389`43c3eae0
NOTE: The trap frame does not contain all registers.
Some register values may be zeroed or incorrect.
rax=0000000000000000 rbx=0000000000000000 rcx=0000000000000000
rdx=0000000000000000 rsi=0000000000000000 rdi=0000000000000000
rip=00007ffea1ca4164 rsp=000000cddc36d3c8 rbp=000000cddc36d4d0
 r8=0000000000000000  r9=0000000000000000 r10=0000000000000000
r11=0000000000000000 r12=0000000000000000 r13=0000000000000000
r14=0000000000000000 r15=0000000000000000
iopl=0         nv up ei pl zr na po nc
ntdll!NtDeviceIoControlFile+0x14:
0033:00007ffe`a1ca4164 ret
```

```
0: kd> kL
  *** Stack trace for last set context - .thread/.cxr resets it
 # Child-SP          RetAddr               Call Site
00 000000cd`dc36d3c8 00007ffe`9f704da5     ntdll!NtDeviceIoControlFile+0x14
01 000000cd`dc36d3d0 00007ffe`9f784c5d     KERNELBASE!ConsoleCallServerGeneric+0xe9
02 000000cd`dc36d530 00007ffe`9f784aba     KERNELBASE!ReadConsoleInternal+0x18d
03 000000cd`dc36d680 00007ff6`cf4043cb     KERNELBASE!ReadConsoleW+0x1a
04 (Inline Function) --------`--------     normal!std::sys::pal::windows::stdio::read_u16s+0x4e
05 000000cd`dc36d6c0 00000000`00000000     normal!std::sys::pal::windows::stdio::read_u16s_fixup_surrogates+0xcb
```

13.   The importance of changing mapping and reloading symbols is illustrated using this exercise. First, we revert to the original NotMyFault process:

```
0: kd> .process
Implicit process is now ffffe708`0ac390c0
```

We then see the incomplete and wrong stack trace because the current thread hasn't changed:

```
0: kd> k
  *** Stack trace for last set context - .thread/.cxr resets it
 # Child-SP          RetAddr               Call Site
00 000000cd`dc36d3c8 00000000`00000000     ntdll!NtDeviceIoControlFile+0x14
```

Now, we restore the original current thread from NotMyFault, but something in the stack trace is not quite right (it doesn't resemble the original in parts):

```
0: kd> .thread
Implicit thread is now ffffe708`08f5b080
```

```
0: kd> k
 # Child-SP          RetAddr               Call Site
00 ffffa389`469cd678 fffff801`46651c29     nt!KeBugCheckEx
01 ffffa389`469cd680 fffff801`4664d261     nt!KiBugCheckDispatch+0x69
02 ffffa389`469cd7c0 fffff801`67471530     nt!KiPageFault+0x461
03 ffffa389`469cd950 fffff801`67471e2d     myfault+0x1530
04 ffffa389`469cd980 fffff801`67471f88     myfault+0x1e2d
05 ffffa389`469cdad0 fffff801`464c9325     myfault+0x1f88
06 ffffa389`469cdb10 fffff801`4694ea69     nt!IofCallDriver+0x55
07 ffffa389`469cdb50 fffff801`4694e589     nt!IopSynchronousServiceTail+0x479
08 ffffa389`469cdc00 fffff801`4694d846     nt!IopXxxControlFile+0xd29
09 ffffa389`469cdd40 fffff801`466512d5     nt!NtDeviceIoControlFile+0x56
0a ffffa389`469cddb0 00007ffe`a1ca4164     nt!KiSystemServiceCopyEnd+0x25
0b 00000089`a8d7ee98 00007ffe`9f7135bb     ntdll!NtDeviceIoControlFile+0x14
0c 00000089`a8d7eea0 00007ffe`a1775e91     KERNELBASE!DeviceIoControl+0x6b
```

```
0d 00000089`a8d7ef10 00007ff6`c15226ce     KERNEL32!DeviceIoControlImplementation+0x81
0e 00000089`a8d7ef60 00000000`00020500     0x00007ff6`c15226ce
0f 00000089`a8d7ef68 00000089`a8d7eff9     0x20500
10 00000089`a8d7ef70 00000089`a8d7eff9     0x00000089`a8d7eff9
11 00000089`a8d7ef78 00000000`00000000     0x00000089`a8d7eff9
```

We now restore the current process context again but with specifying **/r /p** parameters:

```
0: kd> .process /r /p
Implicit process is now ffffe708`0ac390c0
Loading User Symbols
...................................

************* Symbol Loading Error Summary *************
Module name           Error
SharedUserData        No error - symbol load deferred
myfault               The system cannot find the file specified
```

You can troubleshoot most symbol related issues by turning on symbol loading diagnostics (!sym noisy) and repeating the command that caused symbols to be loaded.
You should also verify that your symbol search path (.sympath) is correct.

```
0: kd> k
 # Child-SP          RetAddr             Call Site
00 ffffa389`469cd678 fffff801`46651c29   nt!KeBugCheckEx
01 ffffa389`469cd680 fffff801`4664d261   nt!KiBugCheckDispatch+0x69
02 ffffa389`469cd7c0 fffff801`67471530   nt!KiPageFault+0x461
03 ffffa389`469cd950 fffff801`67471e2d   myfault+0x1530
04 ffffa389`469cd980 fffff801`67471f88   myfault+0x1e2d
05 ffffa389`469cdad0 fffff801`464c9325   myfault+0x1f88
06 ffffa389`469cdb10 fffff801`4694ea69   nt!IofCallDriver+0x55
07 ffffa389`469cdb50 fffff801`4694e589   nt!IopSynchronousServiceTail+0x479
08 ffffa389`469cdc00 fffff801`4694d846   nt!IopXxxControlFile+0xd29
09 ffffa389`469cdd40 fffff801`466512d5   nt!NtDeviceIoControlFile+0x56
0a ffffa389`469cddb0 00007ffe`a1ca4164   nt!KiSystemServiceCopyEnd+0x25
0b 00000089`a8d7ee98 00007ffe`9f7135bb   ntdll!NtDeviceIoControlFile+0x14
0c 00000089`a8d7eea0 00007ffe`a1775e91   KERNELBASE!DeviceIoControl+0x6b
0d 00000089`a8d7ef10 00007ff6`c15226ce   KERNEL32!DeviceIoControlImplementation+0x81
0e 00000089`a8d7ef60 00007ffe`a15b48ab   notmyfault64+0x26ce
0f 00000089`a8d7f060 00007ffe`a15b40fb   USER32!UserCallDlgProcCheckWow+0x14b
10 00000089`a8d7f140 00007ffe`a15f9a59   USER32!DefDlgProcWorker+0xcb
11 00000089`a8d7f200 00007ffe`a15b1cac   USER32!DefDlgProcA+0x39
12 00000089`a8d7f240 00007ffe`a15b17fc   USER32!UserCallWinProcCheckWow+0x33c
13 00000089`a8d7f3b0 00007ffe`a15c4c2d   USER32!DispatchClientMessage+0x9c
14 00000089`a8d7f410 00007ffe`a1ca8004   USER32!_fnDWORD+0x3d
15 00000089`a8d7f470 00007ffe`9f4c1434   ntdll!KiUserCallbackDispatcherContinue
16 00000089`a8d7f4f8 00007ffe`a15b092f   win32u!NtUserMessageCall+0x14
17 00000089`a8d7f500 00007ffe`a15b0797   USER32!SendMessageWorker+0x12f
18 00000089`a8d7f5a0 00007ffe`8ea250bf   USER32!SendMessageW+0x137
19 00000089`a8d7f600 00007ffe`8ea58822   COMCTL32!Button_ReleaseCapture+0xbb
1a 00000089`a8d7f630 00007ffe`a15b1cac   COMCTL32!Button_WndProc+0x802
1b 00000089`a8d7f740 00007ffe`a15b0f06   USER32!UserCallWinProcCheckWow+0x33c
1c 00000089`a8d7f8b0 00007ffe`a15b60e4   USER32!DispatchMessageWorker+0x2a6
1d 00000089`a8d7f930 00007ffe`8ea05f9f   USER32!IsDialogMessageW+0x104
1e 00000089`a8d7f990 00007ffe`8ea05e48   COMCTL32!Prop_IsDialogMessage+0x4b
1f 00000089`a8d7f9d0 00007ffe`8ea05abd   COMCTL32!_RealPropertySheet+0x2c0
20 00000089`a8d7faa0 00007ffe`8ead0803   COMCTL32!_PropertySheet+0x49
21 00000089`a8d7fad0 00007ff6`c1523415   COMCTL32!PropertySheetA+0x53
22 00000089`a8d7fb70 00007ff6`c1525c68   notmyfault64+0x3415
```

```
23 00000089`a8d7fda0  00007ffe`a17753e0    notmyfault64+0x5c68
24 00000089`a8d7fde0  00007ffe`a1c0485b    KERNEL32!BaseThreadInitThunk+0x10
25 00000089`a8d7fe10  00000000`00000000    ntdll!RtlUserThreadStart+0x2b
```

14.   If we want to see the particular stack trace using the **!thread** *<address>* command, we shouldn't forget about mapping, too:

```
0: kd> !thread ffffe708090790c0
THREAD ffffe708090790c0  Cid 1158.1cb8  Teb: 000000cddc53e000 Win32Thread: 0000000000000000 WAIT: (Executive) KernelMode Alertable
    ffffe7080a14be88  NotificationEvent
IRP List:
    ffffe708079022b0: (0006,0358) Flags: 00060030  Mdl: 00000000
Not impersonating
DeviceMap               ffffa88ee736eeb0
Owning Process          ffffe7080ad590c0      Image:        normal.exe
Attached Process        N/A            Image:        N/A
Wait Start TickCount    16864          Ticks: 556 (0:00:00:08.687)
Context Switch Count    40             IdealProcessor: 2
UserTime                00:00:00.000
KernelTime              00:00:00.015
Win32 Start Address 0x00007ff6cf411dfc
Stack Init ffffa38943c3ec70 Current ffffa38943c3e3e0
Base ffffa38943c3f000 Limit ffffa38943c39000 Call 0000000000000000
Priority 9  BasePriority 8  IoPriority 2  PagePriority 5
Child-SP          RetAddr           : Args to Child                                                         : Call Site
ffffa389`43c3e420 fffff801`464d04e7 : 00000000`0000000b ffffbe01`ffffffff ffffb900`00000000 ffffe708`04918158 : nt!KiSwapContext+0x76
ffffa389`43c3e560 fffff801`464d2399 : ffffe708`0a53dc20 ffffe708`0a53dd00 ffffa389`43c3e740 ffffe708`00000002 : nt!KiSwapThread+0x3a7
ffffa389`43c3e640 fffff801`464cc2b4 : 00000000`00000000 fffff801`00000000 ffffe708`00000000 00000000`00000000 : nt!KiCommitThreadWait+0x159
ffffa389`43c3e6e0 fffff801`46634b14 : ffffe708`0a14be88 7b62542b`00000000 ffffe708`00000000 00000000`00000001 : nt!KeWaitForSingleObject+0x234
ffffa389`43c3e7d0 fffff801`4694ec58 : 00000000`00000002 ffffa389`43c3e890 ffffe708`0a14bdf0 ffffe708`079022b0 : nt!IopWaitForSynchronousIoEvent+0x50
ffffa389`43c3e810 fffff801`4694e589 : 00000000`00500016 ffffa389`43c3eb60 00000000`00000005 00000000`00500016 : nt!IopSynchronousServiceTail+0x668
ffffa389`43c3e8c0 fffff801`4694d846 : 00007ffe`9f784aa0 00000000`00000000 00000000`00000000 00000000`00000000 : nt!IopXxxControlFile+0xd29
ffffa389`43c3ea00 fffff801`466512d5 : 00000000`00000000 00000000`00000000 00000000`00000000 000000cd`dc36f3f8 : nt!NtDeviceIoControlFile+0x56
ffffa389`43c3ea70 00007ffe`a1ca4164 : 00000000`00000000 00000000`00000000 00000000`00000000 00000000`00000000 : nt!KiSystemServiceCopyEnd+0x25 (TrapFrame
@ ffffa389`43c3eae0)
000000cd`dc36d3c8 00000000`00000000 : 00000000`00000000 00000000`00000000 00000000`00000000 00000000`00000000 : ntdll!NtDeviceIoControlFile+0x14
```

Note: We don't see user space part of the *normal.exe* thread. **3f** parameter does the right thing:

```
0: kd> !thread ffffe708090790c0 3f
THREAD ffffe708090790c0  Cid 1158.1cb8  Teb: 000000cddc53e000 Win32Thread: 0000000000000000 WAIT: (Executive)
KernelMode Alertable
    ffffe7080a14be88  NotificationEvent
IRP List:
    ffffe708079022b0: (0006,0358) Flags: 00060030  Mdl: 00000000
Not impersonating
DeviceMap                 ffffa88ee736eeb0
Owning Process            ffffe7080ad590c0      Image:        normal.exe
Attached Process          N/A          Image:        N/A
Wait Start TickCount      16864        Ticks: 556 (0:00:00:08.687)
Context Switch Count      40           IdealProcessor: 2
UserTime                  00:00:00.000
KernelTime                00:00:00.015
Unable to load image C:\Work\normal.exe, Win32 error 0n2
*** WARNING: Unable to verify checksum for normal.exe
Win32 Start Address normal!mainCRTStartup (0x00007ff6cf411dfc)
Stack Init ffffa38943c3ec70 Current ffffa38943c3e3e0
Base ffffa38943c3f000 Limit ffffa38943c39000 Call 0000000000000000
Priority 9  BasePriority 8  IoPriority 2  PagePriority 5
Child-SP          RetAddr           Call Site
ffffa389`43c3e420 fffff801`464d04e7 nt!KiSwapContext+0x76
ffffa389`43c3e560 fffff801`464d2399 nt!KiSwapThread+0x3a7
ffffa389`43c3e640 fffff801`464cc2b4 nt!KiCommitThreadWait+0x159
ffffa389`43c3e6e0 fffff801`46634b14 nt!KeWaitForSingleObject+0x234
ffffa389`43c3e7d0 fffff801`4694ec58 nt!IopWaitForSynchronousIoEvent+0x50
ffffa389`43c3e810 fffff801`4694e589 nt!IopSynchronousServiceTail+0x668
ffffa389`43c3e8c0 fffff801`4694d846 nt!IopXxxControlFile+0xd29
ffffa389`43c3ea00 fffff801`466512d5 nt!NtDeviceIoControlFile+0x56
ffffa389`43c3ea70 00007ffe`a1ca4164 nt!KiSystemServiceCopyEnd+0x25 (TrapFrame @ ffffa389`43c3eae0)
000000cd`dc36d3c8 00007ffe`9f704da5 ntdll!NtDeviceIoControlFile+0x14
000000cd`dc36d3d0 00007ffe`9f784c5d KERNELBASE!ConsoleCallServerGeneric+0xe9
000000cd`dc36d530 00007ffe`9f784aba KERNELBASE!ReadConsoleInternal+0x18d
000000cd`dc36d680 00007ff6`cf4043cb KERNELBASE!ReadConsoleW+0x1a
(Inline Function) --------`-------- normal!std::sys::pal::windows::stdio::read_u16s+0x4e (Inline Function @
00007ff6`cf4043cb) [/rustc/eeb90cda1969383f56a2637cbd3037bdf598841c/library/std/src/sys/pal/windows/stdio.rs @ 352]
```

```
000000cd`dc36d6c0 00000000`00000000     normal!std::sys::pal::windows::stdio::read_u16s_fixup_surrogates+0xcb
[/rustc/eeb90cda1969383f56a2637cbd3037bdf598841c/library\std\src\sys\pal\windows\stdio.rs @ 318]
```

Note: However, we don't see the first 4 stack trace parameters (like in the **kv** command). We can use the **36** parameter here to achieve that:

```
0: kd> !thread ffffe708090790c0 36
THREAD ffffe708090790c0  Cid 1158.1cb8  Teb: 000000cddc53e000 Win32Thread: 0000000000000000 WAIT: (Executive) KernelMode Alertable
    ffffe7080a14be88  NotificationEvent
IRP List:
    ffffe708079022b0: (0006,0358) Flags: 00060030  Mdl: 00000000
Not impersonating
DeviceMap                 ffffa88ee736eeb0
Owning Process            ffffe7080ad590c0       Image:         normal.exe
Attached Process          N/A             Image:         N/A
Wait Start TickCount      16864           Ticks: 556 (0:00:00:08.687)
Context Switch Count      40              IdealProcessor: 2
UserTime                  00:00:00.000
KernelTime                00:00:00.015
Unable to load image C:\Work\normal.exe, Win32 error 0n2
*** WARNING: Unable to verify checksum for normal.exe
Win32 Start Address normal!mainCRTStartup (0x00007ff6cf411dfc)
Stack Init ffffa38943c3ec70 Current ffffa38943c3e3e0
Base ffffa38943c3f000 Limit ffffa38943c39000 Call 0000000000000000
Priority 9  BasePriority 8  IoPriority 2  PagePriority 5
Child-SP          RetAddr           : Args to Child                                                           : Call Site
ffffa389`43c3e420 fffff801`464d04e7 : 00000000`0000000b ffffbe01`ffffffff fffb900`00000000 ffffe708`04918158 : nt!KiSwapContext+0x76
ffffa389`43c3e560 fffff801`464d2399 : ffffe708`0a53dc20 ffffe708`0a53dd00 ffffa389`43c3e740 ffffe708`00000002 : nt!KiSwapThread+0x3a7
ffffa389`43c3e640 fffff801`464cc2b4 : 00000000`00000000 fffff801`00000000 ffffe708`00000000 00000000`00000000 : nt!KiCommitThreadWait+0x159
ffffa389`43c3e6e0 fffff801`46634b14 : ffffe708`0a14be88 7b62542b`00000000 ffffe708`00000000 00000000`00000001 : nt!KeWaitForSingleObject+0x234
ffffa389`43c3e7d0 fffff801`4694ec58 : 00000000`00000002 ffffa389`43c3e890 ffffe708`0a14bdf0 ffffe708`079022b0 : nt!IopWaitForSynchronousIoEvent+0x50
ffffa389`43c3e810 fffff801`4694e589 : 00000000`00500016 ffffa389`43c3eb60 00000000`00000005 00000000`00500016 : nt!IopSynchronousServiceTail+0x668
ffffa389`43c3e8c0 fffff801`4694d846 : 00007ffe`9f784aa0 00000000`00000000 00000000`00000000 00000000`00000000 : nt!IopXxxControlFile+0xd29
ffffa389`43c3ea00 fffff801`466512d5 : 00000000`00000000 00000000`00000000 00000000`00000000 000000cd`dc36f3f8 : nt!NtDeviceIoControlFile+0x56
ffffa389`43c3ea70 00007ffe`a1ca4164 : 00007ffe`9f704da5 000000cd`dc36d4f0 00007ffe`9f704c3a 00000000`00000000 : nt!KiSystemServiceCopyEnd+0x25 (TrapFrame
@ ffffa389`43c3eae0)
000000cd`dc36d3c8 00007ffe`9f704da5 : 000000cd`dc36d4f0 00007ffe`9f704c3a 00000000`00000000 00000000`00000008 : ntdll!NtDeviceIoControlFile+0x14
000000cd`dc36d3d0 00007ffe`9f784c5d : 00000000`00000000 00000000`00000000 00007ff6`cf4176d0 : KERNELBASE!ConsoleCallServerGeneric+0xe9
000000cd`dc36d530 00007ffe`9f784aba : 00000000`00000000 00000000`00000000 0000005c`00000001`00000001 : KERNELBASE!ReadConsoleInternal+0x18d
000000cd`dc36d680 00007ff6`cf4043cb : 00000000`00000000 00007ffe`a1c74149 00000000`00000000 00000000`00000005 : KERNELBASE!ReadConsoleW+0x1a
(Inline Function) --------`-------- : --------`-------- --------`-------- --------`-------- --------`-------- :
normal!std::sys::pal::windows::stdio::read_u16s+0x4e (Inline Function @ 00007ff6`cf4043cb)
[/rustc/eeb90cda1969383f56a2637cbd3037bdf598841c/library\std\src\sys\pal\windows\stdio.rs @ 352]
000000cd`dc36d6c0 00000000`00000000 : 00007ffe`a1c74149 00000000`00000000 00000000`00000005 000000cd`dc36d6f0 :
normal!std::sys::pal::windows::stdio::read_u16s_fixup_surrogates+0xcb
[/rustc/eeb90cda1969383f56a2637cbd3037bdf598841c/library\std\src\sys\pal\windows\stdio.rs @ 318]
```

15.   The current process context is still NotMyFault, as we restored (set) it last time again. So, the current thread is still the one from that process:

```
0: kd> k
 # Child-SP          RetAddr           Call Site
00 ffffa389`469cd678 fffff801`46651c29 nt!KeBugCheckEx
01 ffffa389`469cd680 fffff801`4664d261 nt!KiBugCheckDispatch+0x69
02 ffffa389`469cd7c0 fffff801`67471530 nt!KiPageFault+0x461
03 ffffa389`469cd950 fffff801`67471e2d myfault+0x1530
04 ffffa389`469cd980 fffff801`67471f88 myfault+0x1e2d
05 ffffa389`469cdad0 fffff801`464c9325 myfault+0x1f88
06 ffffa389`469cdb10 fffff801`4694ea69 nt!IofCallDriver+0x55
07 ffffa389`469cdb50 fffff801`4694e589 nt!IopSynchronousServiceTail+0x479
08 ffffa389`469cdc00 fffff801`4694d846 nt!IopXxxControlFile+0xd29
09 ffffa389`469cdd40 fffff801`466512d5 nt!NtDeviceIoControlFile+0x56
0a ffffa389`469cddb0 00007ffe`a1ca4164 nt!KiSystemServiceCopyEnd+0x25
0b 00000089`a8d7ee98 00007ffe`9f7135bb ntdll!NtDeviceIoControlFile+0x14
0c 00000089`a8d7eea0 00007ffe`a1775e91 KERNELBASE!DeviceIoControl+0x6b
0d 00000089`a8d7ef10 00007ff6`c15226ce KERNEL32!DeviceIoControlImplementation+0x81
0e 00000089`a8d7ef60 00007ffe`a15b48ab notmyfault64+0x26ce
0f 00000089`a8d7f060 00007ffe`a15b40fb USER32!UserCallDlgProcCheckWow+0x14b
10 00000089`a8d7f140 00007ffe`a15f9a59 USER32!DefDlgProcWorker+0xcb
11 00000089`a8d7f200 00007ffe`a15b1cac USER32!DefDlgProcA+0x39
12 00000089`a8d7f240 00007ffe`a15b17fc USER32!UserCallWinProcCheckWow+0x33c
13 00000089`a8d7f3b0 00007ffe`a15c4c2d USER32!DispatchClientMessage+0x9c
```

```
14  00000089`a8d7f410 00007ffe`a1ca8004     USER32!_fnDWORD+0x3d
15  00000089`a8d7f470 00007ffe`9f4c1434     ntdll!KiUserCallbackDispatcherContinue
16  00000089`a8d7f4f8 00007ffe`a15b092f     win32u!NtUserMessageCall+0x14
17  00000089`a8d7f500 00007ffe`a15b0797     USER32!SendMessageWorker+0x12f
18  00000089`a8d7f5a0 00007ffe`8ea250bf     USER32!SendMessageW+0x137
19  00000089`a8d7f600 00007ffe`8ea58822     COMCTL32!Button_ReleaseCapture+0xbb
1a  00000089`a8d7f630 00007ffe`a15b1cac     COMCTL32!Button_WndProc+0x802
1b  00000089`a8d7f740 00007ffe`a15b0f06     USER32!UserCallWinProcCheckWow+0x33c
1c  00000089`a8d7f8b0 00007ffe`a15b60e4     USER32!DispatchMessageWorker+0x2a6
1d  00000089`a8d7f930 00007ffe`8ea05f9f     USER32!IsDialogMessageW+0x104
1e  00000089`a8d7f990 00007ffe`8ea05e48     COMCTL32!Prop_IsDialogMessage+0x4b
1f  00000089`a8d7f9d0 00007ffe`8ea05abd     COMCTL32!_RealPropertySheet+0x2c0
20  00000089`a8d7faa0 00007ffe`8ead0803     COMCTL32!_PropertySheet+0x49
21  00000089`a8d7fad0 00007ff6`c1523415     COMCTL32!PropertySheetA+0x53
22  00000089`a8d7fb70 00007ff6`c1525c68     notmyfault64+0x3415
23  00000089`a8d7fda0 00007ffe`a17753e0     notmyfault64+0x5c68
24  00000089`a8d7fde0 00007ffe`a1c0485b     KERNEL32!BaseThreadInitThunk+0x10
25  00000089`a8d7fe10 00000000`00000000     ntdll!RtlUserThreadStart+0x2b
```

Note: If we want to make a particular thread current and at the same time make its process current, too, we need to use **/r /p** parameters for the **.thread** command:

```
0: kd> .thread /r /p ffffe708090790c0
Implicit thread is now ffffe708`090790c0
Implicit process is now ffffe708`0ad590c0
Loading User Symbols
......

************* Symbol Loading Error Summary **************
Module name           Error
SharedUserData        No error - symbol load deferred
myfault               The system cannot find the file specified

You can troubleshoot most symbol related issues by turning on symbol loading diagnostics (!sym
noisy) and repeating the command that caused symbols to be loaded.
You should also verify that your symbol search path (.sympath) is correct.
```

```
0: kd> k
 *** Stack trace for last set context - .thread/.cxr resets it
 # Child-SP          RetAddr           Call Site
00 ffffa389`43c3e420 fffff801`464d04e7  nt!KiSwapContext+0x76
01 ffffa389`43c3e560 fffff801`464d2399  nt!KiSwapThread+0x3a7
02 ffffa389`43c3e640 fffff801`464cc2b4  nt!KiCommitThreadWait+0x159
03 ffffa389`43c3e6e0 fffff801`46634b14  nt!KeWaitForSingleObject+0x234
04 ffffa389`43c3e7d0 fffff801`4694ec58  nt!IopWaitForSynchronousIoEvent+0x50
05 ffffa389`43c3e810 fffff801`4694e589  nt!IopSynchronousServiceTail+0x668
06 ffffa389`43c3e8c0 fffff801`4694d846  nt!IopXxxControlFile+0xd29
07 ffffa389`43c3ea00 fffff801`466512d5  nt!NtDeviceIoControlFile+0x56
08 ffffa389`43c3ea70 00007ffe`a1ca4164  nt!KiSystemServiceCopyEnd+0x25
09 000000cd`dc36d3c8 00007ffe`9f704da5  ntdll!NtDeviceIoControlFile+0x14
0a 000000cd`dc36d3d0 00007ffe`9f784c5d  KERNELBASE!ConsoleCallServerGeneric+0xe9
0b 000000cd`dc36d530 00007ffe`9f784aba  KERNELBASE!ReadConsoleInternal+0x18d
0c 000000cd`dc36d680 00007ff6`cf4043cb  KERNELBASE!ReadConsoleW+0x1a
0d (Inline Function) --------`--------  normal!std::sys::pal::windows::stdio::read_u16s+0x4e
[/rustc/eeb90cda1969383f56a2637cbd3037bdf598841c/library/std/src/sys/pal/windows/stdio.rs @ 352]
0e 000000cd`dc36d6c0 00000000`00000000  normal!std::sys::pal::windows::stdio::read_u16s_fixup_surrogates+0xcb
[/rustc/eeb90cda1969383f56a2637cbd3037bdf598841c/library/std/src/sys/pal/windows/stdio.rs @ 318]
```

Note: In conclusion, **!process** *<address>* 3f and **!thread** *<address>* 3f just show the right stack traces without changing the current process and thread, but **.thread /r /p** *<address>* and **.process /r /p** *<address>* make them current.

16.	Finally, we check various kernel pool stats to compare later with the problem memory dump in Exercise RC2 (NonPaged Pool is dynamic memory like heap for kernel structures, for example, processes and threads):

```
0: kd> !vm
unable to get nt!PspSessionIdBitmap
Page File: \??\C:\pagefile.sys
  Current:    2359296 Kb  Free Space:    2149352 Kb
  Minimum:    2359296 Kb  Maximum:       6291456 Kb
Page File: \??\C:\swapfile.sys
  Current:     262144 Kb  Free Space:     255236 Kb
  Minimum:     262144 Kb  Maximum:       3139540 Kb
No Name for Paging File
  Current:    8384484 Kb  Free Space:    7826296 Kb
  Minimum:    8384484 Kb  Maximum:       8384484 Kb

Physical Memory:          523257 (    2093028 Kb)
Available Pages:           50392 (     201568 Kb)
ResAvail Pages:           430708 (    1722832 Kb)
Locked IO Pages:               0 (          0 Kb)
Free System PTEs:     4295193947 (17180775788 Kb)

******* 111736 kernel stack PTE allocations have failed ******


******* 1 kernel stack growth attempts have failed ******

Modified Pages:                5 (         20 Kb)
Modified PF Pages:             0 (          0 Kb)
Modified No Write Pages:     349 (       1396 Kb)
NonPagedPool Usage:          110 (        440 Kb)
NonPagedPoolNx Usage:      20931 (      83724 Kb)
NonPagedPool Max:     4294967296 (17179869184 Kb)
PagedPool Usage:           29126 (     116504 Kb)
PagedPool Maximum:    4294967296 (17179869184 Kb)
Processor Commit:            599 (       2396 Kb)
Unable to read nt!_LIST_ENTRY.Flink at 0000000000000000
Shared Commit:             69503 (     278012 Kb)
Kernel Stacks:             11178 (      44712 Kb)
Pages For MDLs:             3169 (      12676 Kb)
ContigMem Pages:               3 (         12 Kb)
Partition Pages:               0 (          0 Kb)
Pages For AWE:                 0 (          0 Kb)
NonPagedPool Commit:       20667 (      82668 Kb)
PagedPool Commit:          29126 (     116504 Kb)
Driver Commit:             12302 (      49208 Kb)
Boot Commit:                3265 (      13060 Kb)
PFN Array Commit:           7165 (      28660 Kb)
SmallNonPagedPtesCommit:     458 (       1832 Kb)
SlabAllocatorPages:            0 (          0 Kb)
SkPagesInUnchargedSlabs:       0 (          0 Kb)
CrossPartitionCommit:          0 (          0 Kb)
System PageTables:          2852 (      11408 Kb)
ProcessLockedFilePages:       18 (         72 Kb)
Pagefile Hash Pages:         165 (        660 Kb)
Sum System Commit:        160470 (     641880 Kb)
Total Private:            434387 (    1737548 Kb)
Misc/Transient Commit:      9051 (      36204 Kb)
Committed pages:          603908 (    2415632 Kb)
```

```
Commit limit:           1113081 (    4452324 Kb)

  Pid ImageName                  Commit   SharedCommit      Debt

  be4 MsMpEng.exe             263748 Kb      2236 Kb      0 Kb
 11f8 explorer.exe            132980 Kb     64072 Kb      0 Kb
  438 svchost.exe             129344 Kb      6396 Kb      0 Kb
  424 svchost.exe             127092 Kb     65808 Kb      0 Kb
 14f4 SearchHost.exe          117216 Kb     13896 Kb      0 Kb
  5f4 svchost.exe              74940 Kb      1832 Kb      0 Kb
  494 svchost.exe              68548 Kb      2184 Kb      0 Kb
  51c dwm.exe                  61928 Kb    125852 Kb      0 Kb
 1cc0 TiWorker.exe             54740 Kb      1880 Kb      0 Kb
  c78 svchost.exe              41916 Kb      2160 Kb      0 Kb
 1d28 setup.exe                35048 Kb      1832 Kb      0 Kb
 1b5c MoUsoCoreWorker.exe      27652 Kb      2152 Kb      0 Kb
 1f5c GameBar.exe              24268 Kb      3180 Kb      0 Kb
  45c svchost.exe              21412 Kb      1836 Kb      0 Kb
 14fc StartMenuExperienceHost. 20692 Kb      9048 Kb      0 Kb
  b30 svchost.exe              17904 Kb      2152 Kb      0 Kb
 10ac dwm.exe                  16556 Kb     11364 Kb      0 Kb
 1040 SearchIndexer.exe        16324 Kb      2704 Kb      0 Kb
 1cb4 TextInputHost.exe        15204 Kb      3852 Kb      0 Kb
 19f0 XboxGameBarWidgets.exe    14636 Kb     21896 Kb      0 Kb
 20ac OneDrive.exe             13624 Kb      3308 Kb      0 Kb
 1d10 LogonUI.exe              13512 Kb      8412 Kb      0 Kb
   7c Registry                 13280 Kb         0 Kb      0 Kb
 17d0 backgroundTaskHost.exe   12740 Kb     10092 Kb      0 Kb
 1acc backgroundTaskHost.exe   12632 Kb     10092 Kb      0 Kb
 18b0 VSIXConfigurationUpdater  12184 Kb      2260 Kb      0 Kb
 1e78 backgroundTaskHost.exe   10864 Kb      2544 Kb      0 Kb
  3c8 svchost.exe              10852 Kb      2244 Kb      0 Kb
 11c0 svchost.exe              10696 Kb      1828 Kb      0 Kb
  4c0 svchost.exe              10120 Kb      2564 Kb      0 Kb
  a40 svchost.exe               9624 Kb      1824 Kb      0 Kb
  b14 svchost.exe               9304 Kb      2492 Kb      0 Kb
  e24 RuntimeBroker.exe         9136 Kb      2504 Kb      0 Kb
  c30 sppsvc.exe                8116 Kb      1804 Kb      0 Kb
  ba0 svchost.exe               7972 Kb      1852 Kb      0 Kb
  730 svchost.exe               7928 Kb      1864 Kb      0 Kb
  b60 MpDefenderCoreService.ex   7840 Kb      1872 Kb      0 Kb
 1b3c smartscreen.exe           7784 Kb      2500 Kb      0 Kb
  a20 spoolsv.exe               7564 Kb      1852 Kb      0 Kb
 1fb4 OneDriveSetup.exe         7164 Kb      2300 Kb      0 Kb
  e54 WmiPrvSE.exe              6840 Kb      1832 Kb      0 Kb
 2298 audiodg.exe               6804 Kb      1824 Kb      0 Kb
  388 svchost.exe               6592 Kb       696 Kb      0 Kb
 1554 RuntimeBroker.exe         6384 Kb      2600 Kb      0 Kb
 27e0 conhost.exe               6368 Kb     10640 Kb      0 Kb
 1950 SgrmBroker.exe            6296 Kb       220 Kb      0 Kb
 16f8 dllhost.exe               6252 Kb      2324 Kb      0 Kb
  f34 sihost.exe                6136 Kb      2480 Kb      0 Kb
  c3c taskhostw.exe             6020 Kb      3404 Kb      0 Kb
  354 lsass.exe                 6008 Kb       248 Kb      0 Kb
  2d4 OneDriveSetup.exe         5932 Kb      2220 Kb      0 Kb
 1b98 conhost.exe               5780 Kb      3800 Kb      0 Kb
 1bf8 conhost.exe               5776 Kb      3800 Kb      0 Kb
 2470 XboxPcAppFT.exe           5628 Kb      2484 Kb      0 Kb
  958 svchost.exe               5340 Kb      2576 Kb      0 Kb
```

```
  15b0 RuntimeBroker.exe              5168 Kb      3424 Kb      0 Kb
   f04 WmiPrvSE.exe                   4772 Kb      1864 Kb      0 Kb
   504 svchost.exe                    4660 Kb      1844 Kb      0 Kb
   568 NisSrv.exe                     4256 Kb      1824 Kb      0 Kb
   334 services.exe                   4204 Kb       240 Kb      0 Kb
  1990 MicrosoftEdge_X64_131.0.       4124 Kb      1828 Kb      0 Kb
  1220 GameBarFTServer.exe            3976 Kb      2484 Kb      0 Kb
  1954 SecurityHealthService.ex       3744 Kb      1864 Kb      0 Kb
  20e8 rdpclip.exe                    3724 Kb      3136 Kb      0 Kb
   e80 TabTip.exe                     3696 Kb      2228 Kb      0 Kb
  1ab4 MicrosoftEdgeUpdate.exe        3640 Kb      1868 Kb      0 Kb
  2094 WUDFHost.exe                   3584 Kb     55996 Kb      0 Kb
   b28 svchost.exe                    3544 Kb      1956 Kb      0 Kb
...
   3e8 fontdrvhost.exe                1356 Kb       228 Kb      0 Kb
   3d4 fontdrvhost.exe                1280 Kb       228 Kb      0 Kb
   1e4 smss.exe                       1108 Kb       132 Kb      0 Kb
   348 LsaIso.exe                      972 Kb       128 Kb      0 Kb
  1158 normal.exe                      788 Kb       228 Kb      0 Kb
   bf0 wlms.exe                        760 Kb       232 Kb      0 Kb
   580 MemCompression                  468 Kb         0 Kb      0 Kb
    48 Secure System                   188 Kb         0 Kb      0 Kb
  1070 OneDrive.exe                     92 Kb         0 Kb      0 Kb
  1ba4 TabTip.exe                       84 Kb         0 Kb      0 Kb
  20e0 MoNotificationUx.exe             80 Kb         0 Kb      0 Kb
  1198 userinit.exe                     80 Kb         0 Kb      0 Kb
   340 taskhostw.exe                    80 Kb         0 Kb      0 Kb
   220 MoNotificationUx.exe             80 Kb         0 Kb      0 Kb
  1b6c MoNotificationUx.exe             76 Kb         0 Kb      0 Kb
     4 System                           40 Kb       296 Kb      0 Kb

0: kd> !poolused 2
....
 Sorting by NonPaged Pool Consumed

           NonPaged            Paged
 Tag    Allocs     Used     Allocs     Used
 
 EtwB     230    7454976       10    212992    Etw Buffer , Binary: nt!etw
 Thre    1909    5130368        0         0    Thread objects , Binary: nt!ps
 smNp     698    2859008        0         0    ReadyBoost store node pool allocations , Binary: nt!store or rdyboost.sys
 EtwR   12500    2749216        0         0    Etw KM RegEntry , Binary: nt!etw
 NtxF    6926    2548768        0         0    FCB_NONPAGED              NtfsFcbNonpagedDataLookasideList , Binary: ntfs.sys
 KDNF    1537    2459200        0         0    Network Kernel Debug Adapter FRAME , Binary: kdnic.sys
 CDmp      21    2451184        0         0    Crashdump driver , Binary: crashdmp.sys
 UxSE     100    2329600        0         0    UNKNOWN pooltag 'UxSE', please update pooltag.txt
 File    5098    2025312        0         0    File objects
 Vad    11899    1903840        0         0    Mm virtual address descriptors , Binary: nt!mm
 Even   14692    1891616        0         0    Event objects
 MmCa    2541    1802592        0         0    Mm control areas for mapped files , Binary: nt!mm
 smCB     419    1716224        0         0    ReadyBoost allocations , Binary: nt!store or rdyboost.sys
 FMsl    8022    1668576        0         0    STREAM_LIST_CTRL structure , Binary: fltmgr.sys
 ALPC    2624    1563744        0         0    ALPC port objects , Binary: nt!alpc
 Pool       8    1474560        0         0    Pool tables, etc.
 smBt     350    1433600        0         0    ReadyBoost various B+Tree allocations , Binary: nt!store or rdyboost.sys
 Mdl     2205    1394352        0         0    Io, Mdls
 MmPb       3    1118208        0         0    Paging file bitmaps , Binary: nt!mm
 AfdB     183     970192        0         0    Afd data buffer , Binary: afd.sys
 KDNr    1537     935424        0         0    Network Kernel Debug Adapter RECV-NBL , Binary: kdnic.sys
 EtwG    2063     924224        0         0    Etw Guid , Binary: nt!etw
 MmCi    1407     917632        0         0    Mm control areas for images , Binary: nt!mm
...
...
...
```

17.   We close logging before exiting WinDbg:

```
0: kd> .logclose
Closing open log file C:\ARWMDA-Dumps\Complete\MEMORY-normal.log
```

Exercise RC2

- **Goal:** Learn how to recognize various abnormal software behavior patterns in a physical memory context

- **Patterns:** Handle Leak; Stack Trace Collection (CPUs); Active Thread; Spiking Thread

- \ARWMDA-Dumps\Exercise-RC2.pdf

Exercise RC2

Goal: Learn how to recognize various abnormal software behavior patterns in a physical memory context.

Patterns: Handle Leak; Stack Trace Collection (CPUs); Active Thread; Spiking Thread.

1.   Launch WinDbg.

2.   Open \ARWMDA-Dumps\Complete\MEMORY-abnormal.DMP.

3.   We get the dump file loaded:

```
Microsoft (R) Windows Debugger Version 10.0.27725.1000 AMD64
Copyright (c) Microsoft Corporation. All rights reserved.


Loading Dump File [C:\ARWMDA-Dumps\Complete\MEMORY-abnormal.DMP]
Kernel Bitmap Dump File: Full address space is available


************* Path validation summary **************
Response                        Time (ms)      Location
Deferred                                       srv*
Symbol search path is: srv*
Executable search path is:
Windows 10 Kernel Version 22000 MP (4 procs) Free x64
Product: WinNt, suite: TerminalServer SingleUserTS
Edition build lab: 22000.1.amd64fre.co_release.210604-1628
Kernel base = 0xfffff802`1521c000 PsLoadedModuleList = 0xfffff802`15e45850
Debug session time: Thu Nov 28 21:40:17.104 2024 (UTC + 0:00)
System Uptime: 0 days 0:52:22.038
Loading Kernel Symbols
...............................................................
...............................................................
...........................................
Loading User Symbols
..................................
Loading unloaded module list
...............
For analysis of this file, run !analyze -v
nt!KeBugCheckEx:
fffff802`1563b1d0 mov     qword ptr [rsp+8],rcx ss:0018:fffffa0f`b574b680=000000000000000a
```

4.   We open a log file and set the symbol path:

```
0: kd> .logopen C:\ARWMDA-Dumps\Complete\MEMORY-abnormal.log
Opened log file 'C:\ARWMDA-Dumps\Complete\MEMORY-abnormal.log '

0: kd> .sympath+ C:\ARWMDA-Dumps\Symbols\release
Symbol search path is: srv*;C:\ARWMDA-Dumps\Symbols\release
Expanded Symbol search path is:
cache*;SRV*https://msdl.microsoft.com/download/symbols;c:\arwmda-dumps\symbols\release

************* Path validation summary **************
Response                        Time (ms)      Location
```

5.   Because we know the problem description that the handle consumption was increasing for the *complex-case.exe* process, we jump straight to memory statistics:

```
0: kd> !vm
unable to get nt!PspSessionIdBitmap
Page File: \??\C:\pagefile.sys
  Current:    2710412 Kb  Free Space:    2045092 Kb
  Minimum:    2359296 Kb  Maximum:       6291456 Kb
Page File: \??\C:\swapfile.sys
  Current:     262144 Kb  Free Space:     262136 Kb
  Minimum:     262144 Kb  Maximum:       3139536 Kb
No Name for Paging File
  Current:    8384480 Kb  Free Space:    7137552 Kb
  Minimum:    8384480 Kb  Maximum:       8384480 Kb

Physical Memory:           523256 (    2093024 Kb)
Available Pages:            39495 (     157980 Kb)
ResAvail Pages:           399750 (    1599000 Kb)
Locked IO Pages:               0 (          0 Kb)
Free System PTEs:     4295023195 (17180092780 Kb)

******* 192905 kernel stack PTE allocations have failed ******


******* 1 kernel stack growth attempts have failed ******

Modified Pages:             9901 (      39604 Kb)
Modified PF Pages:          8936 (      35744 Kb)
Modified No Write Pages:      54 (        216 Kb)
NonPagedPool Usage:          118 (        472 Kb)
NonPagedPoolNx Usage:      53607 (     214428 Kb)
NonPagedPool Max:     4294967296 (17179869184 Kb)
PagedPool Usage:           66718 (     266872 Kb)
PagedPool Maximum:    4294967296 (17179869184 Kb)
Processor Commit:            800 (       3200 Kb)
Unable to read nt!_LIST_ENTRY.Flink at 0000000000000000
Shared Commit:             66944 (     267776 Kb)
Kernel Stacks:              8616 (      34464 Kb)
Pages For MDLs:             3170 (      12680 Kb)
ContigMem Pages:               3 (         12 Kb)
Partition Pages:               0 (          0 Kb)
Pages For AWE:                 0 (          0 Kb)
NonPagedPool Commit:       53353 (     213412 Kb)
PagedPool Commit:          66718 (     266872 Kb)
Driver Commit:             12317 (      49268 Kb)
Boot Commit:                3265 (      13060 Kb)
PFN Array Commit:           7165 (      28660 Kb)
SmallNonPagedPtesCommit:     458 (       1832 Kb)
SlabAllocatorPages:            0 (          0 Kb)
SkPagesInUnchargedSlabs:       0 (          0 Kb)
CrossPartitionCommit:          0 (          0 Kb)
System PageTables:          5283 (      21132 Kb)
ProcessLockedFilePages:       24 (         96 Kb)
Pagefile Hash Pages:         601 (       2404 Kb)
Sum System Commit:        228717 (     914868 Kb)
```

```
Total Private:               599506 (    2398024 Kb)
Misc/Transient Commit:         8471 (      33884 Kb)
Committed pages:             836694 (    3346776 Kb)
Commit limit:               1200859 (    4803436 Kb)

  Pid ImageName                      Commit   SharedCommit      Debt

  5e0 MsMpEng.exe                 914340 Kb      2252 Kb      0 Kb
13d38 TiWorker.exe                150876 Kb      1896 Kb      0 Kb
 1680 SearchHost.exe              134336 Kb     19256 Kb      0 Kb
  430 svchost.exe                 124016 Kb     45584 Kb      0 Kb
 1fc0 complex-case.exe            121620 Kb       228 Kb      0 Kb
 11e8 explorer.exe                113808 Kb    108076 Kb      0 Kb
  568 dwm.exe                      91248 Kb    149564 Kb      0 Kb
  438 svchost.exe                  77472 Kb      6016 Kb      0 Kb
  488 svchost.exe                  74812 Kb      2196 Kb      0 Kb
 1104 svchost.exe                  59200 Kb      2176 Kb      0 Kb
 1f80 OneDrive.exe                 48192 Kb      4348 Kb      0 Kb
  fc0 MoUsoCoreWorker.exe          29416 Kb      2168 Kb      0 Kb
  468 svchost.exe                  19728 Kb      1836 Kb      0 Kb
 1094 StartMenuExperienceHost.     19640 Kb      4716 Kb      0 Kb
 1804 LogonUI.exe                  17096 Kb      8432 Kb      0 Kb
  b2c svchost.exe                  17052 Kb      2168 Kb      0 Kb
 1cfc SearchIndexer.exe            16744 Kb      2720 Kb      0 Kb
 1830 dwm.exe                      15832 Kb      6276 Kb      0 Kb
 2360 TextInputHost.exe            14764 Kb      3932 Kb      0 Kb
  6bc svchost.exe                  13832 Kb      1824 Kb      0 Kb
  b1c svchost.exe                  13276 Kb      1956 Kb      0 Kb
 1a8c svchost.exe                  11228 Kb      2176 Kb      0 Kb
  3cc svchost.exe                  10488 Kb      2260 Kb      0 Kb
  4d0 svchost.exe                  10324 Kb      2564 Kb      0 Kb
  a00 svchost.exe                   9748 Kb      1824 Kb      0 Kb
  dac svchost.exe                   9284 Kb      2572 Kb      0 Kb
 2710 MpDefenderCoreService.ex      9192 Kb      1896 Kb      0 Kb
14128 backgroundTaskHost.exe        8880 Kb      2692 Kb      0 Kb
  aec svchost.exe                   8356 Kb      1868 Kb      0 Kb
  e54 taskhostw.exe                 8324 Kb      3552 Kb      0 Kb
1508c smartscreen.exe               7840 Kb      2580 Kb      0 Kb
  ac8 SgrmBroker.exe                7636 Kb       220 Kb      0 Kb
  a44 sppsvc.exe                    7176 Kb      1804 Kb      0 Kb
16a48 audiodg.exe                   6980 Kb      1824 Kb      0 Kb
  9c0 spoolsv.exe                   6784 Kb      1868 Kb      0 Kb
   7c Registry                      6748 Kb         0 Kb      0 Kb
 19e4 dllhost.exe                   6648 Kb      2404 Kb      0 Kb
 1870 RuntimeBroker.exe             6524 Kb      3596 Kb      0 Kb
  224 svchost.exe                   6412 Kb       568 Kb      0 Kb
  97c conhost.exe                   6280 Kb     10720 Kb      0 Kb
  358 lsass.exe                     6228 Kb       248 Kb      0 Kb
  d7c sihost.exe                    5900 Kb      2564 Kb      0 Kb
1503c RuntimeBroker.exe             5872 Kb      2600 Kb      0 Kb
  190 svchost.exe                   5532 Kb      1828 Kb      0 Kb
 180c RuntimeBroker.exe             5520 Kb      2676 Kb      0 Kb
 2568 msteamsupdate.exe             5500 Kb      2688 Kb      0 Kb
 b388 taskhostw.exe                 5448 Kb      3520 Kb      0 Kb
  50c svchost.exe                   4368 Kb      1844 Kb      0 Kb
 1778 TabTip.exe                    3948 Kb      2596 Kb      0 Kb
  338 services.exe                  3924 Kb       240 Kb      0 Kb
 17c0 rdpclip.exe                   3752 Kb      3216 Kb      0 Kb
  f1c ctfmon.exe                    3724 Kb      3216 Kb      0 Kb
```

```
1658 svchost.exe                  3692 Kb        2568 Kb        0 Kb
1f88 NisSrv.exe                   3480 Kb        1824 Kb        0 Kb
1740 WUDFHost.exe                 3440 Kb       55996 Kb        0 Kb
 5c0 svchost.exe                  3380 Kb        1828 Kb        0 Kb
1f20 SecurityHealthService.ex     3376 Kb        1880 Kb        0 Kb
 d5c dllhost.exe                  3344 Kb        2004 Kb        0 Kb
 530 svchost.exe                  2928 Kb        1868 Kb        0 Kb
2368 svchost.exe                  2912 Kb        1824 Kb        0 Kb
1198 svchost.exe                  2824 Kb        2156 Kb        0 Kb
 308 winlogon.exe                 2704 Kb        3580 Kb        0 Kb
 788 svchost.exe                  2692 Kb        1820 Kb        0 Kb
 2b8 csrss.exe                    2268 Kb       84504 Kb        0 Kb
 900 svchost.exe                  2260 Kb        1828 Kb        0 Kb
18ac svchost.exe                  2196 Kb        2564 Kb        0 Kb
1b80 winlogon.exe                 2188 Kb        3048 Kb        0 Kb
100b8 MpCmdRun.exe                2124 Kb        1820 Kb        0 Kb
2b1c MpSigStub.exe                2012 Kb        1864 Kb        0 Kb
 fc4 MicrosoftEdgeUpdate.exe      1968 Kb        1880 Kb        0 Kb
16b24 notmyfault64.exe            1944 Kb        3844 Kb        0 Kb
 6d8 svchost.exe                  1932 Kb        1868 Kb        0 Kb
 25c csrss.exe                    1932 Kb        6332 Kb        0 Kb
```

Note: We notice a significant increase in nonpaged pool usage compared to Exercise RC1.

6.   We check nonpaged pool tag usage:

```
0: kd> !poolused 2
....
Sorting by NonPaged Pool Consumed

            NonPaged          Paged
Tag    Allocs     Used    Allocs     Used
Thre    23052  61962752        0        0    Thread objects , Binary: nt!ps
NtxF    20429   7517872        0        0    FCB_NONPAGED               NtfsFcbNonpagedDataLookasideList , Binary: ntfs.sys
EtwB      229   7475456       10   212992    Etw Buffer , Binary: nt!etw
smNp     1610   6594560        0        0    ReadyBoost store node pool allocations , Binary: nt!store or rdyboost.sys
Even    44499   5707264        0        0    Event objects
smCB     1244   5095424        0        0    ReadyBoost allocations , Binary: nt!store or rdyboost.sys
FMsl    18654   3880032        0        0    STREAM_LIST_CTRL structure , Binary: fltmgr.sys
smBt      825   3379200        0        0    ReadyBoost various B+Tree allocations , Binary: nt!store or rdyboost.sys
HVD.        3   3146576        0        0    UNKNOWN pooltag ' HVD', please update pooltag.txt
File     6957   2765616        0        0    File objects
Pool        8   2555904        0        0    Pool tables, etc.
KDNF     1537   2459200        0        0    Network Kernel Debug Adapter FRAME , Binary: kdnic.sys
CDmp       21   2451200        0        0    Crashdump driver , Binary: crashdmp.sys
EtwR    10842   2377728        0        0    Etw KM RegEntry , Binary: nt!etw
UxSE      100   2329600        0        0    UNKNOWN pooltag 'UxSE', please update pooltag.txt
MmCa     4657   1749824        0        0    Mm control areas for mapped files , Binary: nt!mm
Mdl      2217   1733952        0        0    Io, Mdls
Vad     10389   1662240        0        0    Mm virtual address descriptors , Binary: nt!mm
ALPC     2379   1418480        0        0    ALPC port objects , Binary: nt!alpc
MmPb        3   1118208        0        0    Paging file bitmaps , Binary: nt!mm
CcSc     1752   1093248        0        0    Cache Manager Shared Cache Map , Binary: nt!cc
KDNr     1537    935424        0        0    Network Kernel Debug Adapter RECV-NBL , Binary: kdnic.sys
VadS    11574    925920        0        0    Mm virtual address descriptors (short) , Binary: nt!mm
EtwG     2034    911232        0        0    Etw Guid , Binary: nt!etw
MmCi     1282    841280        0        0    Mm control areas for images , Binary: nt!mm
```

Note: As you can guess correctly '**Thre**' pool tag corresponds to thread objects. If we open *MEMORY-normal.DMP*, we would see much less amount of thread objects:

```
Thre     1909   5130368        0        0    Thread objects , Binary: nt!ps
```

Now, we see more than 20,000 thread objects, certainly an indication of a thread handle leak.

7.   We also get another process list:

```
1: kd> !process 0 0
**** NT ACTIVE PROCESS DUMP ****
PROCESS ffff838758ce2040
    SessionId: none  Cid: 0004    Peb: 00000000  ParentCid: 0000
    DirBase: 007d5002  ObjectTable: ffffc481d2835800  HandleCount: 2952.
    Image: System

PROCESS ffff838758e13080
    SessionId: none  Cid: 0048    Peb: 00000000  ParentCid: 0004
    DirBase: 00eeb002  ObjectTable: ffffc481d2824dc0  HandleCount:    0.
    Image: Secure System

PROCESS ffff838758cb0080
    SessionId: none  Cid: 007c    Peb: 00000000  ParentCid: 0004
    DirBase: 0060e002  ObjectTable: ffffc481d2809100  HandleCount:    0.
    Image: Registry

PROCESS ffff838759c620c0
    SessionId: none  Cid: 01d8    Peb: 2171cb1000  ParentCid: 0004
    DirBase: 0a066002  ObjectTable: ffffc481d4ab0340  HandleCount:   60.
    Image: smss.exe

PROCESS ffff83875c2f8080
    SessionId: 0  Cid: 025c    Peb: d1fc472000  ParentCid: 024c
    DirBase: 4d122002  ObjectTable: ffffc481d633a980  HandleCount:  466.
    Image: csrss.exe

PROCESS ffff83875d659080
    SessionId: 0  Cid: 02a4    Peb: 65bedfe000  ParentCid: 024c
    DirBase: 4d221002  ObjectTable: ffffc481d4e1e980  HandleCount:  155.
    Image: wininit.exe

PROCESS ffff83875d662140
    SessionId: 1  Cid: 02b8    Peb: a84502b000  ParentCid: 029c
    DirBase: 4449d002  ObjectTable: ffffc481d4aaf6c0  HandleCount:  352.
    Image: csrss.exe

PROCESS ffff83875d6f3080
    SessionId: 1  Cid: 0308    Peb: 1a2e0af000  ParentCid: 029c
    DirBase: 53949002  ObjectTable: ffffc481d4aaf9c0  HandleCount:  277.
    Image: winlogon.exe

PROCESS ffff83875d7411c0
    SessionId: 0  Cid: 0338    Peb: 5365ee6000  ParentCid: 02a4
    DirBase: 4c4c7002  ObjectTable: ffffc481d4aafd00  HandleCount:  451.
    Image: services.exe

PROCESS ffff83875d6f2080
    SessionId: 0  Cid: 034c    Peb: 9880625000  ParentCid: 02a4
    DirBase: 15c1f002  ObjectTable: ffffc481d6339380  HandleCount:   54.
    Image: LsaIso.exe

PROCESS ffff83875d765080
    SessionId: 0  Cid: 0358    Peb: b44ae9e000  ParentCid: 02a4
    DirBase: 4c4b0002  ObjectTable: ffffc481d633a4c0  HandleCount: 1190.
    Image: lsass.exe
```

```
PROCESS ffff83875d77c0c0
    SessionId: 0  Cid: 03cc    Peb: 3d03d88000  ParentCid: 0338
    DirBase: 15b40002  ObjectTable: ffffc481d6339840  HandleCount: 1312.
    Image: svchost.exe

PROCESS ffff83875d780080
    SessionId: 0  Cid: 03e0    Peb: ba38d06000  ParentCid: 02a4
    DirBase: 54c98002  ObjectTable: ffffc481d64b1200  HandleCount:  37.
    Image: fontdrvhost.exe

PROCESS ffff83875d77d080
    SessionId: 1  Cid: 03e8    Peb: f4ab80c000  ParentCid: 0308
    DirBase: 109ec002  ObjectTable: ffffc481d64b1840  HandleCount:  37.
    Image: fontdrvhost.exe

PROCESS ffff83875d40a080
    SessionId: 0  Cid: 0224    Peb: f835ce3000  ParentCid: 0338
    DirBase: 4011d002  ObjectTable: ffffc481d64b1080  HandleCount: 1044.
    Image: svchost.exe

PROCESS ffff83875d4ab080
    SessionId: 0  Cid: 0430    Peb: aaafaa0000  ParentCid: 0338
    DirBase: 3518f002  ObjectTable: ffffc481d666f340  HandleCount: 794.
    Image: svchost.exe

PROCESS ffff83875d4a8080
    SessionId: 0  Cid: 0438    Peb: c05f399000  ParentCid: 0338
    DirBase: 318b6002  ObjectTable: ffffc481d666fc80  HandleCount: 2676.
    Image: svchost.exe

PROCESS ffff83875d5840c0
    SessionId: 0  Cid: 0468    Peb: a89178d000  ParentCid: 0338
    DirBase: 3429d002  ObjectTable: ffffc481d666e080  HandleCount: 815.
    Image: svchost.exe

PROCESS ffff83875d587080
    SessionId: 0  Cid: 0488    Peb: 6b0fab000  ParentCid: 0338
    DirBase: 32053002  ObjectTable: ffffc481d67584c0  HandleCount: 1207.
    Image: svchost.exe

PROCESS ffff83875d59a080
    SessionId: 0  Cid: 04d0    Peb: 7829a31000  ParentCid: 0338
    DirBase: 27538002  ObjectTable: ffffc481d67587c0  HandleCount: 579.
    Image: svchost.exe

PROCESS ffff83875d5e0080
    SessionId: 0  Cid: 050c    Peb: 5d8c1b3000  ParentCid: 0338
    DirBase: 295c6002  ObjectTable: ffffc481d6757e80  HandleCount: 804.
    Image: svchost.exe

PROCESS ffff83875de29080
    SessionId: 0  Cid: 0530    Peb: 533984b000  ParentCid: 0338
    DirBase: 23839002  ObjectTable: ffffc481d666f640  HandleCount: 279.
    Image: svchost.exe

PROCESS ffff83875de27100
    SessionId: 1  Cid: 0568    Peb: d5bbdb4000  ParentCid: 0308
    DirBase: 27c6e002  ObjectTable: ffffc481d6757380  HandleCount: 1003.
```

```
        Image: dwm.exe

PROCESS ffff83875dee3080
    SessionId: 0  Cid: 0634    Peb: bdd9974000  ParentCid: 0338
    DirBase: 225e8002  ObjectTable: ffffc481d6757d00  HandleCount: 159.
    Image: VSSVC.exe

PROCESS ffff83875dedc080
    SessionId: 0  Cid: 0654    Peb: 60db0c8000  ParentCid: 0338
    DirBase: 1f671002  ObjectTable: ffffc481d4e1e180  HandleCount: 184.
    Image: svchost.exe

PROCESS ffff83875df6e080
    SessionId: 0  Cid: 06bc    Peb: cba9a06000  ParentCid: 0338
    DirBase: 1c21f002  ObjectTable: ffffc481d6757200  HandleCount: 451.
    Image: svchost.exe

PROCESS ffff83875df6c080
    SessionId: 0  Cid: 06d8    Peb: c06d24e000  ParentCid: 0338
    DirBase: 3f4c2002  ObjectTable: ffffc481d6757080  HandleCount: 219.
    Image: svchost.exe

PROCESS ffff83875d760080
    SessionId: 0  Cid: 0788    Peb: d9e9a4f000  ParentCid: 0338
    DirBase: 1a808002  ObjectTable: ffffc481d6b169c0  HandleCount: 278.
    Image: svchost.exe

PROCESS ffff838759964040
    SessionId: none  Cid: 07ac    Peb: 00000000  ParentCid: 0004
    DirBase: 1f34a002  ObjectTable: ffffc481d6b17b00  HandleCount:   0.
    Image: MemCompression

PROCESS ffff83875e031080
    SessionId: 0  Cid: 07f0    Peb: 606326d000  ParentCid: 0338
    DirBase: 1b6da002  ObjectTable: ffffc481d6b16540  HandleCount: 186.
    Image: svchost.exe

PROCESS ffff83875e091080
    SessionId: 0  Cid: 05c0    Peb: 7e80bc6000  ParentCid: 0338
    DirBase: 523ad002  ObjectTable: ffffc481d6b16380  HandleCount: 326.
    Image: svchost.exe

PROCESS ffff838758d85080
    SessionId: 0  Cid: 08f8    Peb: 44d6e7e000  ParentCid: 0338
    DirBase: 4f221002  ObjectTable: ffffc481d6b18c40  HandleCount: 148.
    Image: svchost.exe

PROCESS ffff838758d83080
    SessionId: 0  Cid: 0900    Peb: 3c425db000  ParentCid: 0338
    DirBase: 518fb002  ObjectTable: ffffc481d661fe80  HandleCount: 401.
    Image: svchost.exe

PROCESS ffff83875e3020c0
    SessionId: 0  Cid: 09c0    Peb: 00fc2000  ParentCid: 0338
    DirBase: 52f31002  ObjectTable: ffffc481d6b18dc0  HandleCount: 560.
    Image: spoolsv.exe

PROCESS ffff83875e49b0c0
    SessionId: 0  Cid: 0a00    Peb: 5e9c404000  ParentCid: 0338
```

```
        DirBase: 494d2002  ObjectTable: ffffc481d6b17800  HandleCount: 417.
        Image: svchost.exe

    PROCESS ffff83875e5cc0c0
        SessionId: 0  Cid: 0aec    Peb: b406576000  ParentCid: 0338
        DirBase: 52f67002  ObjectTable: ffffc481d6b198c0  HandleCount: 315.
        Image: svchost.exe

    PROCESS ffff83875e1e8080
        SessionId: 0  Cid: 0b1c    Peb: 57bd455000  ParentCid: 0338
        DirBase: 42ea1002  ObjectTable: ffffc481d71ab540  HandleCount: 432.
        Image: svchost.exe

    PROCESS ffff83875e1f7080
        SessionId: 0  Cid: 0b2c    Peb: 5697fdd000  ParentCid: 0338
        DirBase: 4bddc002  ObjectTable: ffffc481d71ad900  HandleCount: 620.
        Image: svchost.exe

    PROCESS ffff83875e4aa080
        SessionId: 0  Cid: 0b78    Peb: eff9ae000  ParentCid: 0338
        DirBase: 4a9e4002  ObjectTable: ffffc481d71addc0  HandleCount: 145.
        Image: sqlwriter.exe

    PROCESS ffff83875e466080
        SessionId: 0  Cid: 0bc0    Peb: 3df31c1000  ParentCid: 0338
        DirBase: 4cd5b002  ObjectTable: ffffc481d71ab080  HandleCount:  68.
        Image: wlms.exe

    PROCESS ffff83875e3990c0
        SessionId: 0  Cid: 0a44    Peb: 6db6d7c000  ParentCid: 0338
        DirBase: 4cb18002  ObjectTable: ffffc481d71ab9c0  HandleCount: 265.
        Image: sppsvc.exe

    PROCESS ffff83875e7ca080
        SessionId: 0  Cid: 0c3c    Peb: e2ed3ca000  ParentCid: 0b2c
        DirBase: 4f8ea002  ObjectTable: ffffc481d71ab200  HandleCount: 101.
        Image: AggregatorHost.exe

    PROCESS ffff83875e7e3080
        SessionId: 0  Cid: 0c70    Peb: e3c78af000  ParentCid: 0338
        DirBase: 50e23002  ObjectTable: ffffc481d71ac980  HandleCount: 231.
        Image: svchost.exe

    PROCESS ffff83875e906080
        SessionId: 0  Cid: 0d5c    Peb: ad27fe3000  ParentCid: 03cc
        DirBase: 2148b002  ObjectTable: ffffc481d781edc0  HandleCount: 212.
        Image: dllhost.exe

    PROCESS ffff83875e909080
        SessionId: 1  Cid: 0d7c    Peb: 5239549000  ParentCid: 0438
        DirBase: 2dc34002  ObjectTable: ffffc481d781c6c0  HandleCount: 539.
        Image: sihost.exe

    PROCESS ffff83875e9d50c0
        SessionId: 1  Cid: 0dac    Peb: dbaaf2a000  ParentCid: 0338
        DirBase: 21143002  ObjectTable: ffffc481d781e900  HandleCount: 679.
        Image: svchost.exe

    PROCESS ffff83875e9e7080
```

```
        SessionId: 1  Cid: 0e54     Peb: 4f652ee000  ParentCid: 0438
        DirBase: 2aed6002  ObjectTable: ffffc481d781fbc0  HandleCount: 320.
        Image: taskhostw.exe

PROCESS ffff83875eb0e080
        SessionId: 1  Cid: 0f1c     Peb: 8495346000  ParentCid: 0488
        DirBase: 58a38002  ObjectTable: ffffc481d781f580  HandleCount: 463.
        Image: ctfmon.exe

PROCESS ffff83875ecf4080
        SessionId: 0  Cid: 10a8     Peb: 57ece1b000  ParentCid: 03cc
        DirBase: 57fa9002  ObjectTable: ffffc481d7c89c40  HandleCount: 161.
        Image: SppExtComObj.Exe

PROCESS ffff83875ecd60c0
        SessionId: 0  Cid: 1104     Peb: 225a463000  ParentCid: 0338
        DirBase: 0717f002  ObjectTable: ffffc481d7c884c0  HandleCount: 904.
        Image: svchost.exe

PROCESS ffff83875ed89080
        SessionId: 1  Cid: 1184     Peb: 5304300000  ParentCid: 0308
        DirBase: 185a2002  ObjectTable: 00000000  HandleCount:   0.
        Image: userinit.exe

PROCESS ffff83875ed88080
        SessionId: 0  Cid: 1198     Peb: f787c2b000  ParentCid: 0338
        DirBase: 0c06d002  ObjectTable: ffffc481d7c87b80  HandleCount: 203.
        Image: svchost.exe

PROCESS ffff83875ec0c0c0
        SessionId: 1  Cid: 11e8     Peb: 00606000  ParentCid: 1184
        DirBase: 064da002  ObjectTable: ffffc481d7c8a100  HandleCount: 4143.
        Image: explorer.exe

PROCESS ffff83875f083080
        SessionId: 0  Cid: 0fc0     Peb: a27645c000  ParentCid: 0438
        DirBase: 60f80002  ObjectTable: ffffc481d7c8e740  HandleCount: 698.
        Image: MoUsoCoreWorker.exe

PROCESS ffff83875f890080
        SessionId: 1  Cid: 1658     Peb: 7045fd7000  ParentCid: 0338
        DirBase: 6912b002  ObjectTable: ffffc481d8a04300  HandleCount: 331.
        Image: svchost.exe

PROCESS ffff83875e8660c0
        SessionId: 1  Cid: 1094     Peb: 4854023000  ParentCid: 03cc
        DirBase: 768ea002  ObjectTable: ffffc481d8a07cc0  HandleCount: 659.
        Image: StartMenuExperienceHost.exe

PROCESS ffff83875ff290c0
        SessionId: 1  Cid: 180c     Peb: cbdca21000  ParentCid: 03cc
        DirBase: 5b2be002  ObjectTable: ffffc481d8a07340  HandleCount: 288.
        Image: RuntimeBroker.exe

PROCESS ffff83875fc420c0
        SessionId: 1  Cid: 1870     Peb: f01e2e8000  ParentCid: 03cc
        DirBase: 50fd9002  ObjectTable: ffffc481d8a07040  HandleCount: 501.
        Image: RuntimeBroker.exe
```

```
PROCESS ffff8387600af0c0
    SessionId: 1  Cid: 18ac      Peb: c90c747000  ParentCid: 0338
    DirBase: 0b683002  ObjectTable: ffffc481d71ac340  HandleCount: 167.
    Image: svchost.exe

PROCESS ffff83875fe44080
    SessionId: 1  Cid: 19e4      Peb: 33ed8cd000  ParentCid: 03cc
    DirBase: 4fbfe002  ObjectTable: ffffc481d8a09440  HandleCount: 298.
    Image: dllhost.exe

PROCESS ffff83875fe45080
    SessionId: 0  Cid: 1a8c      Peb: bd0b6e2000  ParentCid: 0338
    DirBase: 507b7002  ObjectTable: ffffc481d8a08940  HandleCount: 1421.
    Image: svchost.exe

PROCESS ffff83875d681080
    SessionId: 3  Cid: 1b3c      Peb: fa8f701000  ParentCid: 1adc
    DirBase: 6e7e4002  ObjectTable: ffffc481ddeec800  HandleCount: 159.
    Image: csrss.exe

PROCESS ffff83875ff9f080
    SessionId: 3  Cid: 1b80      Peb: aa3a03a000  ParentCid: 1adc
    DirBase: 175c8002  ObjectTable: ffffc481ddeebb80  HandleCount: 207.
    Image: winlogon.exe

PROCESS ffff83875fa8f080
    SessionId: 3  Cid: 1804      Peb: ab262b4000  ParentCid: 1b80
    DirBase: 75e89002  ObjectTable: ffffc481ddeeb200  HandleCount: 659.
    Image: LogonUI.exe

PROCESS ffff83875ff9e080
    SessionId: 3  Cid: 1830      Peb: 2f28cd0000  ParentCid: 1b80
    DirBase: 647ef002  ObjectTable: ffffc481ddeec4c0  HandleCount: 680.
    Image: dwm.exe

PROCESS ffff83875fcdb080
    SessionId: 3  Cid: 159c      Peb: 9fe8b8b000  ParentCid: 1b80
    DirBase: 1aa7b002  ObjectTable: ffffc481ddeec680  HandleCount:  37.
    Image: fontdrvhost.exe

PROCESS ffff83875f9430c0
    SessionId: 1  Cid: 044c      Peb: f8bcb5a000  ParentCid: 0fc0
    DirBase: 17a2a002  ObjectTable: 00000000  HandleCount:  0.
    Image: MoNotificationUx.exe

PROCESS ffff83875f0d1080
    SessionId: 0  Cid: 1740      Peb: 71239b1000  ParentCid: 0338
    DirBase: 76e14002  ObjectTable: ffffc481ddeebd00  HandleCount: 337.
    Image: WUDFHost.exe

PROCESS ffff83875e73e080
    SessionId: 1  Cid: 17c0      Peb: c19ff4d000  ParentCid: 0430
    DirBase: 0aa04002  ObjectTable: ffffc481d8a04ac0  HandleCount: 469.
    Image: rdpclip.exe

PROCESS ffff838760a650c0
    SessionId: 0  Cid: 1cfc      Peb: 52d5d83000  ParentCid: 0338
    DirBase: 699d3002  ObjectTable: ffffc481ddeec040  HandleCount: 694.
    Image: SearchIndexer.exe
```

```
PROCESS ffff83875fc250c0
    SessionId: 1  Cid: 1560    Peb: f2b1255000  ParentCid: 17c0
    DirBase: 4096e002  ObjectTable: ffffc481ddeedac0  HandleCount: 141.
    Image: rdpinput.exe

PROCESS ffff83875f0b80c0
    SessionId: 1  Cid: 1778    Peb: cd8218b000  ParentCid: 0488
    DirBase: 06063002  ObjectTable: ffffc481ddeece40  HandleCount: 316.
    Image: TabTip.exe

PROCESS ffff83875fc070c0
    SessionId: 0  Cid: 0190    Peb: 2e2f4a4000  ParentCid: 0338
    DirBase: 3edce002  ObjectTable: ffffc481d8a04600  HandleCount: 359.
    Image: svchost.exe

PROCESS ffff838760b57080
    SessionId: 1  Cid: 1f04    Peb: f35ce2000  ParentCid: 11e8
    DirBase: 105f9002  ObjectTable: ffffc481ddeeb3c0  HandleCount: 182.
    Image: SecurityHealthSystray.exe

PROCESS ffff83875c4da080
    SessionId: 0  Cid: 1f20    Peb: c6acdf8000  ParentCid: 0338
    DirBase: 1803a002  ObjectTable: ffffc481ddeed600  HandleCount: 379.
    Image: SecurityHealthService.exe

PROCESS ffff83875fdc2080
    SessionId: 1  Cid: 1f80    Peb: 86e728f000  ParentCid: 11e8
    DirBase: 1b188002  ObjectTable: ffffc481ddeeb540  HandleCount: 911.
    Image: OneDrive.exe

PROCESS ffff83875fd760c0
    SessionId: 0  Cid: 210c    Peb: a264641000  ParentCid: 0338
    DirBase: 4e645002  ObjectTable: ffffc481ddeef540  HandleCount: 214.
    Image: svchost.exe

PROCESS ffff83875ff80080
    SessionId: 1  Cid: 2360    Peb: 40bf6bd000  ParentCid: 03cc
    DirBase: 40603002  ObjectTable: ffffc481ddeedc40  HandleCount: 745.
    Image: TextInputHost.exe

PROCESS ffff83875cba00c0
    SessionId: 0  Cid: 0ac8    Peb: 9d7ac7d000  ParentCid: 0338
    DirBase: 5f9df002  ObjectTable: ffffc481daf3ab40  HandleCount: 119.
    Image: SgrmBroker.exe

PROCESS ffff83875988f0c0
    SessionId: 0  Cid: 21dc    Peb: 964eb83000  ParentCid: 0338
    DirBase: 18c60002  ObjectTable: ffffc481daf35840  HandleCount: 121.
    Image: uhssvc.exe

PROCESS ffff83875f8e90c0
    SessionId: 0  Cid: 1468    Peb: 2124fb1000  ParentCid: 0338
    DirBase: 3634a002  ObjectTable: ffffc481daf35a00  HandleCount: 210.
    Image: svchost.exe

PROCESS ffff83875c7af0c0
    SessionId: 0  Cid: 2368    Peb: 5e90b1000  ParentCid: 0338
    DirBase: 2fa24002  ObjectTable: ffffc481ddeeed80  HandleCount: 228.
```

```
       Image: svchost.exe

  PROCESS ffff83875f29f080
      SessionId: 1  Cid: 2568    Peb: bd2e3dd000  ParentCid: 03cc
      DirBase: 0d39a002  ObjectTable: ffffc481dacf7100  HandleCount: 499.
      Image: msteamsupdate.exe

  PROCESS ffff83875fb8c0c0
      SessionId: 0  Cid: 0fc4    Peb: 00cab000  ParentCid: 0aa4
      DirBase: 26120002  ObjectTable: ffffc481daf3b180  HandleCount: 213.
      Image: MicrosoftEdgeUpdate.exe

  PROCESS ffff83875fdcb100
      SessionId: 0  Cid: 1460    Peb: 1c0eb7d000  ParentCid: 0338
      DirBase: 2ee01002  ObjectTable: ffffc481ddeeb6c0  HandleCount: 140.
      Image: svchost.exe

  PROCESS ffff83875c6840c0
      SessionId: 1  Cid: 1680    Peb: 9fe48a9000  ParentCid: 03cc
  DeepFreeze
      DirBase: 10786002  ObjectTable: ffffc481dacf4840  HandleCount: 1615.
      Image: SearchHost.exe

  PROCESS ffff8387598a80c0
      SessionId: 0  Cid: 2710    Peb: 959e13d000  ParentCid: 0338
      DirBase: 4d5ac002  ObjectTable: ffffc481dc1b9800  HandleCount: 491.
      Image: MpDefenderCoreService.exe

  PROCESS ffff838760eb10c0
      SessionId: 0  Cid: 05e0    Peb: 1291bff000  ParentCid: 0338
      DirBase: 23793002  ObjectTable: ffffc481dc1bb440  HandleCount: 1032.
      Image: MsMpEng.exe

  PROCESS ffff8387603820c0
      SessionId: 0  Cid: 1f88    Peb: 5f197df000  ParentCid: 0338
      DirBase: 09f4e002  ObjectTable: ffffc481ddef1180  HandleCount: 208.
      Image: NisSrv.exe

  PROCESS ffff83875fce00c0
      SessionId: 0  Cid: 2b8c    Peb: 7317e3f000  ParentCid: 0438
      DirBase: 4d66c002  ObjectTable: ffffc481d8a03800  HandleCount: 148.
      Image: wuauclt.exe

  PROCESS ffff83875f2280c0
      SessionId: 0  Cid: 09ec    Peb: baf7a7e000  ParentCid: 2b8c
      DirBase: 5a3d0002  ObjectTable: ffffc481dc1bdb40  HandleCount:  63.
      Image: AM_Delta.exe

  PROCESS ffff83875afce0c0
      SessionId: 0  Cid: 2b1c    Peb: 5664f2d000  ParentCid: 2b8c
      DirBase: 32ad8002  ObjectTable: ffffc481dacf6140  HandleCount:  98.
      Image: MpSigStub.exe

  PROCESS ffff83875f4130c0
      SessionId: 1  Cid: 1fc0    Peb: 999cfed000  ParentCid: 11e8
      DirBase: 5d787002  ObjectTable: ffffc481d8a04dc0  HandleCount: 21575.
      Image: complex-case.exe

  PROCESS ffff83875f3020c0
```

```
    SessionId: 1  Cid: 097c    Peb: 296bb24000  ParentCid: 1fc0
    DirBase: 5e3d6002  ObjectTable: ffffc481daf356c0  HandleCount: 187.
    Image: conhost.exe

PROCESS ffff8387653cd080
    SessionId: 1  Cid: b388    Peb: c279e4b000  ParentCid: 0438
    DirBase: 72fb3002  ObjectTable: ffffc481e0f69e40  HandleCount: 336.
    Image: taskhostw.exe

PROCESS ffff8387668b6080
    SessionId: 0  Cid: 100b8   Peb: 470c087000  ParentCid: 10074
    DirBase: 50c1d002  ObjectTable: ffffc481e0584180  HandleCount: 109.
    Image: MpCmdRun.exe

PROCESS ffff838767b49080
    SessionId: 0  Cid: 13cf8   Peb: b082dc2000  ParentCid: 0338
    DirBase: 641b3002  ObjectTable: ffffc481dc1c00c0  HandleCount: 137.
    Image: TrustedInstaller.exe

PROCESS ffff838767b4c080
    SessionId: 0  Cid: 13d38   Peb: 5732857000  ParentCid: 03cc
    DirBase: 60815002  ObjectTable: ffffc481dc1bfdc0  HandleCount: 335.
    Image: TiWorker.exe

PROCESS ffff838767c92080
    SessionId: 1  Cid: 14128   Peb: b35f017000  ParentCid: 03cc
    DirBase: 2e907002  ObjectTable: ffffc481e058a700  HandleCount: 423.
    Image: backgroundTaskHost.exe

PROCESS ffff8387681e90c0
    SessionId: 1  Cid: 1503c   Peb: ce69933000  ParentCid: 03cc
    DirBase: 2f27d002  ObjectTable: ffffc481dc1b9040  HandleCount: 282.
    Image: RuntimeBroker.exe

PROCESS ffff83876842b0c0
    SessionId: 1  Cid: 1508c   Peb: 8e1b407000  ParentCid: 03cc
    DirBase: 0cead002  ObjectTable: ffffc481e05823c0  HandleCount: 420.
    Image: smartscreen.exe

PROCESS ffff838768bf80c0
    SessionId: 0  Cid: 16a48   Peb: 8777b50000  ParentCid: 05c0
    DirBase: 70ddd002  ObjectTable: ffffc481dc1b8700  HandleCount: 299.
    Image: audiodg.exe

PROCESS ffff838768c770c0
    SessionId: 1  Cid: 16b04   Peb: e7e22f0000  ParentCid: 0488
    DirBase: 3bde1002  ObjectTable: 00000000  HandleCount:   0.
    Image: TabTip.exe

PROCESS ffff838768c880c0
    SessionId: 1  Cid: 16b24   Peb: ad6d512000  ParentCid: 11e8
    DirBase: 2e60a002  ObjectTable: ffffc481d8a03b00  HandleCount: 177.
    Image: notmyfault64.exe
```

Note: We see more than 20,000 handles for the complex-case.exe process, which correlates with the thread pool leak we saw previously. We can check that with the process handle table. We list only handles that have the Thread handle type (we break the listing after some time):

```
0: kd> !handle -1 3 ffff83875f4130c0 Thread

Searching for handles of type Thread

PROCESS ffff83875f4130c0
    SessionId: 1  Cid: 1fc0    Peb: 999cfed000  ParentCid: 11e8
    DirBase: 5d787002  ObjectTable: ffffc481d8a04dc0  HandleCount: 21575.
    Image: complex-case.exe

Handle table at ffffc481d8a04dc0 with 21575 entries in use

009c: Object: ffff83875e0d0080  GrantedAccess: 001fffff (Protected) (Audit) Entry:
ffffc481de424270
Object: ffff83875e0d0080  Type: (ffff838758ce0900) Thread
    ObjectHeader: ffff83875e0d0050 (new version)
        HandleCount: 1  PointerCount: 1

00a0: Object: ffff838758d72080  GrantedAccess: 001fffff (Protected) (Audit) Entry:
ffffc481de424280
Object: ffff838758d72080  Type: (ffff838758ce0900) Thread
    ObjectHeader: ffff838758d72050 (new version)
        HandleCount: 1  PointerCount: 1

00a8: Object: ffff83875e7ce080  GrantedAccess: 001fffff (Protected) (Audit) Entry:
ffffc481de4242a0
Object: ffff83875e7ce080  Type: (ffff838758ce0900) Thread
    ObjectHeader: ffff83875e7ce050 (new version)
        HandleCount: 1  PointerCount: 65537

00ac: Object: ffff83875de41080  GrantedAccess: 001fffff (Protected) (Audit) Entry:
ffffc481de4242b0
Object: ffff83875de41080  Type: (ffff838758ce0900) Thread
    ObjectHeader: ffff83875de41050 (new version)
        HandleCount: 1  PointerCount: 29200

00b0: Object: ffff83875fd99080  GrantedAccess: 001fffff (Protected) (Audit) Entry:
ffffc481de4242c0
Object: ffff83875fd99080  Type: (ffff838758ce0900) Thread
    ObjectHeader: ffff83875fd99050 (new version)
        HandleCount: 1  PointerCount: 32769

00b4: Object: ffff83875de4d080  GrantedAccess: 001fffff (Protected) (Audit) Entry:
ffffc481de4242d0
Object: ffff83875de4d080  Type: (ffff838758ce0900) Thread
    ObjectHeader: ffff83875de4d050 (new version)
        HandleCount: 1  PointerCount: 30999

00b8: Object: ffff83875de47080  GrantedAccess: 001fffff (Protected) (Audit) Entry:
ffffc481de4242e0
Object: ffff83875de47080  Type: (ffff838758ce0900) Thread
    ObjectHeader: ffff83875de47050 (new version)
        HandleCount: 1  PointerCount: 32768

00bc: Object: ffff83875c092080  GrantedAccess: 001fffff (Protected) (Audit) Entry:
ffffc481de4242f0
Object: ffff83875c092080  Type: (ffff838758ce0900) Thread
    ObjectHeader: ffff83875c092050 (new version)
        HandleCount: 1  PointerCount: 1
```

```
00c0: Object: ffff838760a78080  GrantedAccess: 001fffff (Protected) (Audit) Entry:
ffffc481de424300
Object: ffff838760a78080  Type: (ffff838758ce0900) Thread
    ObjectHeader: ffff838760a78050 (new version)
        HandleCount: 1  PointerCount: 1

00c4: Object: ffff83875c21b080  GrantedAccess: 001fffff (Protected) (Audit) Entry:
ffffc481de424310
Object: ffff83875c21b080  Type: (ffff838758ce0900) Thread
    ObjectHeader: ffff83875c21b050 (new version)
        HandleCount: 1  PointerCount: 1

00c8: Object: ffff83875fa4c080  GrantedAccess: 001fffff (Protected) (Audit) Entry:
ffffc481de424320
Object: ffff83875fa4c080  Type: (ffff838758ce0900) Thread
    ObjectHeader: ffff83875fa4c050 (new version)
        HandleCount: 1  PointerCount: 1

00cc: Object: ffff83875c088080  GrantedAccess: 001fffff (Protected) (Audit) Entry:
ffffc481de424330
Object: ffff83875c088080  Type: (ffff838758ce0900) Thread
    ObjectHeader: ffff83875c088050 (new version)
        HandleCount: 1  PointerCount: 1

00d0: Object: ffff83875fbed080  GrantedAccess: 001fffff (Protected) (Audit) Entry:
ffffc481de424340
Object: ffff83875fbed080  Type: (ffff838758ce0900) Thread
    ObjectHeader: ffff83875fbed050 (new version)
        HandleCount: 1  PointerCount: 1

[...]

0600: Object: ffff83875c080080  GrantedAccess: 001fffff (Protected) (Audit) Entry:
ffffc481df2fb800
Object: ffff83875c080080  Type: (ffff838758ce0900) Thread
    ObjectHeader: ffff83875c080050 (new version)
        HandleCount: 1  PointerCount: 1

0604: Object: ffff83875ff41080  GrantedAccess: 001fffff (Protected) (Audit) Entry:
ffffc481df2fb810
Object: ffff83875ff41080  Type: (ffff838758ce0900) Thread
    ObjectHeader: ffff83875ff41050 (new version)
        HandleCount: 1  PointerCount: 1

0608: Object: ffff83875fdca080  GrantedAccess: 001fffff (Protected) (Audit) Entry:
ffffc481df2fb820
Object: ffff83875fdca080  Type: (ffff838758ce0900) Thread
    ObjectHeader: ffff83875fdca050 (new version)
        HandleCount: 1  PointerCount: 1

060c: Object: ffff83875c176080  GrantedAccess: 001fffff (Protected) (Audit) Entry:
ffffc481df2fb830
Object: ffff83875c176080  Type: (ffff838758ce0900) Thread
    ObjectHeader: ffff83875c176050 (new version)
        HandleCount: 1  PointerCount: 1

0610: Object: ffff83875f809300  GrantedAccess: 001fffff (Protected) (Audit) Entry:
ffffc481df2fb840
Object: ffff83875f809300  Type: (ffff838758ce0900) Thread
```

```
    ObjectHeader: ffff83875f8092d0 (new version)
        HandleCount: 1  PointerCount: 1


0614: Object: ffff83875f8c9080  GrantedAccess: 001fffff (Protected) (Audit) Entry:
ffffc481df2fb850
Object: ffff83875f8c9080  Type: (ffff838758ce0900) Thread
    ObjectHeader: ffff83875f8c9050 (new version)
        HandleCount: 1  PointerCount: 1


0618: Object: ffff83875f38a5c0  GrantedAccess: 001fffff (Protected) Entry: ffffc481df2fb860
Object: ffff83875f38a5c0  Type: (ffff838758ce0900) Thread
    ObjectHeader: ffff83875f38a590 (new version)
        HandleCount: 1  PointerCount: 1


061c: Object: ffff83875c0ae080  GrantedAccess: 001fffff (Protected) (Audit) Entry:
ffffc481df2fb870
Object: ffff83875c0ae080  Type: (ffff838758ce0900) Thread
    ObjectHeader: ffff83875c0ae050 (new version)
        HandleCount: 1  PointerCount: 1


0620: Object: ffff83875f31f080  GrantedAccess: 001fffff (Protected) (Audit) Entry:
ffffc481df2fb880
Object: ffff83875f31f080  Type: (ffff838758ce0900) Thread
    ObjectHeader: ffff83875f31f050 (new version)
        HandleCount: 1  PointerCount: 1
```

[...]

```
0: kd> !thread ffff83875f31f080 3f
THREAD ffff83875f31f080  Cid 1fc0.1f44  Teb: 0000000000000000 Win32Thread: 0000000000000000 TERMINATED
Not impersonating
DeviceMap                 ffffc481d7808870
Owning Process            ffff83875f4130c0        Image:          complex-case.exe
Attached Process          N/A          Image:      N/A
Wait Start TickCount      49492        Ticks: 151598 (0:00:39:28.718)
Context Switch Count      4            IdealProcessor: 0
UserTime                  00:00:00.000
KernelTime                00:00:00.000
Unable to load image C:\Work\complex-case.exe, Win32 error 0n2
*** WARNING: Unable to verify checksum for complex-case.exe
Win32 Start Address complex_case!std::sys::pal::windows::thread::impl$0::new::thread_start (0x00007ff66b8ee400)
Stack Init 0000000000000000 Current fffffa0fb46dd670
Base fffffa0fb46de000 Limit fffffa0fb46d8000 Call 0000000000000000
Priority 8  BasePriority 8  IoPriority 2  PagePriority 5
```

8.   We now check for any running threads:

```
0: kd> !running

System Processors:  (000000000000000f)
  Idle Processors:  (0000000000000000)

     Prcbs            Current          (pri) Next          (pri) Idle
  0  fffff8021400f180 ffff838768cbd0c0 (12)                     fffff80215f51bc0  ...............
  1  ffffd480bd4dd180 ffff8387678bf080 ( 9)                     ffffd480bd4e9140  ...............
  2  ffffd480bd5c0180 ffff83875efe0080 ( 9)                     ffffd480bd5cc140  ...............
  3  ffffd480bd697180 ffff83875e7ce080 ( 8)                     ffffd480bd6a3140  ...............
```

Note: The thread running on the first processor (CPU #0) is a thread from NotMyFault used to generate a bugcheck and save this dump file:

222

```
0: kd> !thread ffff838768cbd0c0 3f
THREAD ffff838768cbd0c0  Cid 16b24.16b28  Teb: 000000ad6d513000 Win32Thread: ffff838760b954c0 RUNNING on processor 0
IRP List:
    ffff83875cc992d0: (0006,0118) Flags: 00060000  Mdl: 00000000
Not impersonating
DeviceMap                 ffffc481d7809130
Owning Process            ffff838768c880c0       Image:         notmyfault64.exe
Attached Process          N/A            Image:         N/A
Wait Start TickCount      201089         Ticks: 1 (0:00:00.015)
Context Switch Count      1680           IdealProcessor: 2
UserTime                  00:00:00.015
KernelTime                00:00:00.140
Unable to load image C:\NotMyFault\notmyfault64.exe, Win32 error 0n2
Win32 Start Address notmyfault64 (0x00007ff7ea105b0c)
Stack Init fffffa0fb574bfb0 Current fffffa0fb6846ce0
Base fffffa0fb574c000 Limit fffffa0fb5746000 Call 0000000000000000
Priority 12  BasePriority 8  Foreground Boost 2  IoPriority 2  PagePriority 5
Part of process with FOREGROUND Priority
Child-SP          RetAddr           Call Site
fffffa0f`b574b678 fffff802`15650c29 nt!KeBugCheckEx
fffffa0f`b574b680 fffff802`1564c261 nt!KiBugCheckDispatch+0x69
fffffa0f`b574b7c0 fffff802`37621530 nt!KiPageFault+0x461 (TrapFrame @ fffffa0f`b574b7c0)
fffffa0f`b574b950 fffff802`37621e2d myfault+0x1530
fffffa0f`b574b980 fffff802`37621f88 myfault+0x1e2d
fffffa0f`b574bad0 fffff802`154c8325 myfault+0x1f88
fffffa0f`b574bb10 fffff802`1594da69 nt!IofCallDriver+0x55
fffffa0f`b574bb50 fffff802`1594d589 nt!IopSynchronousServiceTail+0x479
fffffa0f`b574bc00 fffff802`1594c846 nt!IopXxxControlFile+0xd29
fffffa0f`b574bd40 fffff802`156502d5 nt!NtDeviceIoControlFile+0x56
fffffa0f`b574bdb0 00007ffb`e75a4164 nt!KiSystemServiceCopyEnd+0x25 (TrapFrame @ fffffa0f`b574be20)
000000ad`6d6fee88 00007ffb`e4d035bb ntdll!NtDeviceIoControlFile+0x14
000000ad`6d6fee90 00007ffb`e6085e91 KERNELBASE!DeviceIoControl+0x6b
000000ad`6d6fef00 00007ff7`ea1026ce KERNEL32!DeviceIoControlImplementation+0x81
000000ad`6d6fef50 00007ffb`e6a048ab notmyfault64+0x26ce
000000ad`6d6ff050 00007ffb`e6a040fb USER32!UserCallDlgProcCheckWow+0x14b
000000ad`6d6ff130 00007ffb`e6a49a59 USER32!DefDlgProcWorker+0xcb
000000ad`6d6ff1f0 00007ffb`e6a01cac USER32!DefDlgProcA+0x39
000000ad`6d6ff230 00007ffb`e6a017fc USER32!UserCallWinProcCheckWow+0x33c
000000ad`6d6ff3a0 00007ffb`e6a14c2d USER32!DispatchClientMessage+0x9c
000000ad`6d6ff400 00007ffb`e75a8004 USER32!_fnDWORD+0x3d
000000ad`6d6ff460 00007ffb`e5211434 ntdll!KiUserCallbackDispatcherContinue (TrapFrame @ 000000ad`6d6ff328)
000000ad`6d6ff4e8 00007ffb`e6a0092f win32u!NtUserMessageCall+0x14
000000ad`6d6ff4f0 00007ffb`e6a00797 USER32!SendMessageWorker+0x12f
000000ad`6d6ff590 00007ffb`d47b50bf USER32!SendMessageW+0x137
000000ad`6d6ff5f0 00007ffb`d47e8822 COMCTL32!Button_ReleaseCapture+0xbb
000000ad`6d6ff620 00007ffb`e6a01cac COMCTL32!Button_WndProc+0x802
000000ad`6d6ff730 00007ffb`e6a00f06 USER32!UserCallWinProcCheckWow+0x33c
000000ad`6d6ff8a0 00007ffb`e6a060e4 USER32!DispatchMessageWorker+0x2a6
000000ad`6d6ff920 00007ffb`d4795f9f USER32!IsDialogMessageW+0x104
000000ad`6d6ff980 00007ffb`d4795e48 COMCTL32!Prop_IsDialogMessage+0x4b
000000ad`6d6ff9c0 00007ffb`d4795abd COMCTL32!_RealPropertySheet+0x2c0
000000ad`6d6ffa90 00007ffb`d4860803 COMCTL32!_PropertySheet+0x49
000000ad`6d6ffac0 00007ff7`ea103415 COMCTL32!PropertySheetA+0x53
000000ad`6d6ffb60 00007ff7`ea105c68 notmyfault64+0x3415
000000ad`6d6ffd90 00007ffb`e60853e0 notmyfault64+0x5c68
000000ad`6d6ffdd0 00007ffb`e750485b KERNEL32!BaseThreadInitThunk+0x10
000000ad`6d6ffe00 00000000`00000000 ntdll!RtlUserThreadStart+0x2b
```

Note: We now check the threads running on CPU#1 and CPU#2:

```
0: kd> !thread ffff8387678bf080 3f
THREAD ffff8387678bf080  Cid 14128.14388  Teb: 000000b35f026000 Win32Thread: ffff838760baba70 RUNNING on processor 1
Not impersonating
DeviceMap                 ffffc481d7808870
Owning Process            ffff838767c92080       Image:         backgroundTaskHost.exe
Attached Process          N/A            Image:         N/A
Wait Start TickCount      201089         Ticks: 1 (0:00:00.015)
Context Switch Count      16293          IdealProcessor: 0
UserTime                  00:00:00.796
KernelTime                00:00:01.093
Win32 Start Address ntdll!TppWorkerThread (0x00007ffbe7516a00)
```

```
Stack Init fffffa0fb5afbc70 Current fffffa0fb5afb440
Base fffffa0fb5afc000 Limit fffffa0fb5af6000 Call 0000000000000000
Priority 9 BasePriority 8 IoPriority 2 PagePriority 5
Scheduling Group: ffff8387678a3090 KSCB: ffff8387678a32b8 rank 2
Child-SP          RetAddr           Call Site
000000b3`5f4fd828 00007ffb`e52525e1 ucrtbase!_security_check_cookie+0xe
000000b3`5f4fd830 00007ffb`e525231b
ucrtbase!__crt_stdio_output::output_processor<wchar_t,__crt_stdio_output::string_output_adapter<wchar_t>,__crt_stdio_o
utput::standard_base<wchar_t,__crt_stdio_output::string_output_adapter<wchar_t> > >::state_case_type+0x1b1
000000b3`5f4fd8b0 00007ffb`e525204f
ucrtbase!__crt_stdio_output::output_processor<wchar_t,__crt_stdio_output::string_output_adapter<wchar_t>,__crt_stdio_o
utput::standard_base<wchar_t,__crt_stdio_output::string_output_adapter<wchar_t> > >::process+0x17b
000000b3`5f4fd8f0 00007ffb`e525e1ef ucrtbase!__stdio_common_vswprintf+0x13f
000000b3`5f4fde40 00007ffb`e525e182 ucrtbase!__crt_state_management::wrapped_invoke<int (__cdecl*)(unsigned
__int64,wchar_t * __ptr64,unsigned __int64,wchar_t const * __ptr64,__crt_locale_pointers * __ptr64,char *
__ptr64),unsigned __int64,wchar_t * __ptr64,unsigned __int64,wchar_t const * __ptr64,__crt_locale_pointers *
__ptr64,char * __ptr64,int>+0x5f
000000b3`5f4fde90 00007ffb`e5c8267d ucrtbase!o___stdio_common_vswprintf+0x32
(Inline Function) --------`-------- combase!_vsnwprintf_l+0x25 (Inline Function @ 00007ffb`e5c8267d)
[minkernel\crts\ucrt\inc\corecrt_wstdio.h @ 1062]
000000b3`5f4fdee0 00007ffb`e5c102bc combase!_vsnwprintf+0x45 [minkernel\crts\ucrt\inc\corecrt_wstdio.h @ 1131]
(Inline Function) --------`-------- combase!StringVPrintfWorkerW+0x17 (Inline Function @ 00007ffb`e5c102bc)
[onecore\external\shared\inc\strsafe.h @ 10140]
(Inline Function) --------`-------- combase!StringCchVPrintfW+0x2b (Inline Function @ 00007ffb`e5c102bc)
[onecore\external\shared\inc\strsafe.h @ 4565]
000000b3`5f4fdf20 00007ffb`e5c0ff8e combase!FormatTraceMessage+0xbc [onecore\com\combase\ih\comtracefmt.h @ 180]
000000b3`5f4fe1c0 00007ffb`e5c0fc27 combase!ComTraceMessageWorker+0xe2
[onecore\com\combase\common\internal\comtraceworker.cxx @ 103]
000000b3`5f4fe280 00007ffb`e5bed199 combase!ComTraceHr+0x2f [onecore\com\combase\ih\comtrace.h @ 164]
000000b3`5f4fe2d0 00007ffb`e5bf0950 combase!CWinRTActivationStoreCatalog::GetRuntimeClassInfo+0x8f9
[onecore\com\combase\catalog\storecat.cxx @ 415]
000000b3`5f4fe3e0 00007ffb`e5bd6fef combase!CComCatalog::GetRuntimeClassInfoFromPackageScopedCatalog+0x430
[onecore\com\combase\catalog\catalog.cxx @ 1802]
000000b3`5f4fe4c0 00007ffb`e5bee4d1 combase!CComCatalog::GetRuntimeClassInfo+0x4cf
[onecore\com\combase\catalog\catalog.cxx @ 1466]
(Inline Function) --------`-------- combase!WinRTGetRuntimeClassInfo+0x112 (Inline Function @ 00007ffb`e5bee4d1)
[onecore\com\combase\inc\WinRTGetRuntimeClassInfo.hpp @ 38]
000000b3`5f4fe610 00007ffb`d7b76f13 combase!_RoGetActivationFactory+0x2e1
[onecore\com\combase\winrtbase\winrtbase.cpp @ 921]
000000b3`5f4fea30 00007ffb`c43d2907 wincorlib!GetActivationFactoryByPCWSTR+0x293
000000b3`5f4feb40 00007ffb`c43cb53f
ContentDeliveryManager_Background!ContentManagementSDK::Placement::Placement+0x53
000000b3`5f4feba0 00007ffb`c44df28f
ContentDeliveryManager_Background!CreativeFramework::ContentManager::ContentManager::ResolveMismatchedPlacementRenderS
tateIfNeeded+0x24f
000000b3`5f4fed60 00007ffb`c44e15d8
ContentDeliveryManager_Background!<lambda_046557a4efd8ef42bb705bcdae5c9a94>::operator()+0x197
000000b3`5f4fee30 00007ffb`c449e575
ContentDeliveryManager_Background!std::_Func_impl<std::_Callable_obj<<lambda_046557a4efd8ef42bb705bcdae5c9a94>,0>,std:
:allocator<std::_Func_class<void,std::shared_ptr<ContentDeliveryManager::Background::ITaskThreadExecutionContext>,std:
:shared_ptr<ContentDeliveryManager::Background::CorrelationVectorWrapper>,std::_Nil,std::_Nil,std::_Nil,std::_Nil,std:
:_Nil>
>,void,std::shared_ptr<ContentDeliveryManager::Background::ITaskThreadExecutionContext>,std::shared_ptr<ContentDeliver
yManager::Background::CorrelationVectorWrapper>,std::_Nil,std::_Nil,std::_Nil,std::_Nil,std::_Nil>::_Do_call+0x68
000000b3`5f4fee80 00007ffb`c44e0a6e
ContentDeliveryManager_Background!std::_Func_class<void,std::shared_ptr<ContentDeliveryManager::Background::ITaskThrea
dExecutionContext>,std::shared_ptr<ContentDeliveryManager::Background::CorrelationVectorWrapper>,std::_Nil,std::_Nil,s
td::_Nil,std::_Nil,std::_Nil>::operator()+0x49
000000b3`5f4feed0 00000000`00000000
ContentDeliveryManager_Background!ContentDeliveryManager::Background::Details::RunContentDeliveryManagerBackgroundTask
Worker<ContentDeliveryManager::Background::ContentDeliveryManagerTelemetry::MaintenanceTaskActivity,ContentDeliveryMan
ager::Background::MaintenanceTask>+0x692


0: kd> !thread ffff83875efe0080 3f
THREAD ffff83875efe0080  Cid 097c.1598  Teb: 000000296bb2d000 Win32Thread: ffff8387599d1500 RUNNING on processor 2
Not impersonating
DeviceMap                 ffffc481d7808870
Owning Process            ffff83875f3020c0     Image:          conhost.exe
Attached Process          N/A         Image:          N/A
Wait Start TickCount      201090      Ticks: 0
Context Switch Count      4425253     IdealProcessor: 2
UserTime                  00:01:21.312
KernelTime                00:02:48.718
```

```
Win32 Start Address conhost!ConsoleIoThread (0x00007ff73e3191e0)
Stack Init fffffa0fb2bccc70 Current fffffa0fb2bcc650
Base fffffa0fb2bcd000 Limit fffffa0fb2bc7000 Call 0000000000000000
Priority 9  BasePriority 8  IoPriority 2  PagePriority 5
Child-SP          RetAddr           Call Site
00000029`6bd7e7f8 00007ff7`3e36f9b9     conhost!Microsoft::Console::Render::Renderer::TriggerCircling
00000029`6bd7e800 00007ff7`3e3823ce     conhost!ScreenBufferRenderTarget::TriggerCircling+0x69
00000029`6bd7e830 00007ff7`3e36910b     conhost!TextBuffer::IncrementCircularBuffer+0x3e
00000029`6bd7e880 00007ff7`3e347f4b     conhost!StreamScrollRegion+0x1f
00000029`6bd7e8b0 00007ff7`3e31feb6     conhost!AdjustCursorPosition+0x26f5b
00000029`6bd7e9d0 00007ff7`3e31edff     conhost!WriteCharsLegacy+0x1006
00000029`6bd7f1c0 00007ff7`3e31ed20     conhost!DoWriteConsole+0x8f
00000029`6bd7f250 00007ff7`3e3316dd     conhost!WriteConsoleWImplHelper+0x70
00000029`6bd7f290 00007ff7`3e3196f8     conhost!ApiRoutines::WriteConsoleWImpl+0x6d
00000029`6bd7f300 00007ff7`3e32b5c3     conhost!ApiDispatchers::ServerWriteConsole+0x178
00000029`6bd7f3d0 00007ff7`3e3192de     conhost!ApiSorter::ConsoleDispatchRequest+0x1b3
00000029`6bd7f4c0 00007ffb`e60853e0     conhost!ConsoleIoThread+0xfe
00000029`6bd7f750 00007ffb`e750485b     KERNEL32!BaseThreadInitThunk+0x10
00000029`6bd7f780 00000000`00000000     ntdll!RtlUserThreadStart+0x2b
```

Note: These are not processes we are interested in. We now check the threads running on CPU#3:

```
0: kd> !thread ffff83875e7ce080 3f
THREAD ffff83875e7ce080  Cid 1fc0.0e98  Teb: 000000999cff6000 Win32Thread: 0000000000000000 RUNNING on processor 3
Not impersonating
DeviceMap                 ffffc481d7808870
Owning Process            ffff83875f4130c0       Image:         complex-case.exe
Attached Process          N/A            Image:         N/A
Wait Start TickCount      201089         Ticks: 1 (0:00:00.015)
Context Switch Count      3401614        IdealProcessor: 2
UserTime                  00:24:34.390
KernelTime                00:00:24.093
Unable to load image C:\Work\complex-case.exe, Win32 error 0n2
*** WARNING: Unable to verify checksum for complex-case.exe
Win32 Start Address complex_case!std::sys::pal::windows::thread::impl$0::new::thread_start (0x00007ff66b8ee400)
Stack Init fffffa0fb2c12c70 Current fffffa0fb2c12960
Base fffffa0fb2c13000 Limit fffffa0fb2c0d000 Call 0000000000000000
Priority 8  BasePriority 8  IoPriority 2  PagePriority 5
Child-SP          RetAddr           Call Site
00000099`9d4ffa80 00007ff6`6b8e1f60     complex_case!ZN3std3sys9backtrace28__rust_begin_short_backtrace17h3e8324a489e54ea5E+0x50
00000099`9d4ffbe0 00007ff6`6b8ee43d     complex_case!ZN3std6thread7Builder15spawn_unchecked17h6e56a25e80bf8795E+0x790
(Inline Function) --------`--------     complex_case!alloc::boxed::impl$48::call_once+0xb (Inline Function @
00007ff6`6b8ee43d) [/rustc/eeb90cda1969383f56a2637cbd3037bdf598841c/library\alloc\src\boxed.rs @ 2070]
(Inline Function) --------`--------     complex_case!alloc::boxed::impl$48::call_once+0x16 (Inline Function @
00007ff6`6b8ee43d) [/rustc/eeb90cda1969383f56a2637cbd3037bdf598841c/library\alloc\src\boxed.rs @ 2070]
00000099`9d4ffc80 00007ffb`e60853e0     complex_case!std::sys::pal::windows::thread::impl$0::new::thread_start+0x3d
[/rustc/eeb90cda1969383f56a2637cbd3037bdf598841c/library\std\src\sys\pal\windows\thread.rs @ 58]
00000099`9d4ffce0 00007ffb`e750485b     KERNEL32!BaseThreadInitThunk+0x10
00000099`9d4ffd10 00000000`00000000     ntdll!RtlUserThreadStart+0x2b
```

Note: We see it belongs to **complex-case.exe** and consumed a lot of **UserTime** compared to the process uptime (**ElapsedTime**):

```
0: kd> !process ffff83875f4130c0 1
PROCESS ffff83875f4130c0
    SessionId: 1  Cid: 1fc0     Peb: 999cfed000  ParentCid: 11e8
    DirBase: 5d787002  ObjectTable: ffffc481d8a04dc0  HandleCount: 21575.
    Image: complex-case.exe
    VadRoot ffff838760ee9870 Vads 37 Clone 0 Private 30346. Modified 32281. Locked 3.
    DeviceMap ffffc481d7808870
    Token                             ffffc481da0b8670
    ElapsedTime                       00:40:05.604
    UserTime                          00:00:00.000
    KernelTime                        00:00:00.000
    QuotaPoolUsage[PagedPool]         373152
```

```
QuotaPoolUsage[NonPagedPool]        5440
Working Set Sizes (now,min,max)  (32599, 50, 345) (130396KB, 200KB, 1380KB)
PeakWorkingSetSize                  32508
VirtualSize                         4273 Mb
PeakVirtualSize                     4325 Mb
PageFaultCount                      197844
MemoryPriority                      BACKGROUND
BasePriority                        8
CommitCharge                        30405
Job                                 ffff83875f0886b0
```

9.   Now we look at the **complex-case** process threads:

```
0: kd> !process ffff83875f4130c0 3f
PROCESS ffff83875f4130c0
    SessionId: 1  Cid: 1fc0    Peb: 999cfed000  ParentCid: 11e8
    DirBase: 5d787002  ObjectTable: ffffc481d8a04dc0  HandleCount: 21575.
    Image: complex-case.exe
    VadRoot ffff838760ee9870 Vads 37 Clone 0 Private 30346. Modified 32281. Locked 3.
    DeviceMap ffffc481d7808870
    Token                             ffffc481da0b8670
    ElapsedTime                       00:40:05.604
    UserTime                          00:00:00.000
    KernelTime                        00:00:00.000
    QuotaPoolUsage[PagedPool]         373152
    QuotaPoolUsage[NonPagedPool]      5440
    Working Set Sizes (now,min,max)  (32599, 50, 345) (130396KB, 200KB, 1380KB)
    PeakWorkingSetSize                32508
    VirtualSize                       4273 Mb
    PeakVirtualSize                   4325 Mb
    PageFaultCount                    197844
    MemoryPriority                    BACKGROUND
    BasePriority                      8
    CommitCharge                      30405
    Job                               ffff83875f0886b0

    PEB at 000000999cfed000
    InheritedAddressSpace:    No
    ReadImageFileExecOptions: No
    BeingDebugged:            No
    ImageBaseAddress:         00007ff66b8e0000
    NtGlobalFlag:             400
    NtGlobalFlag2:            0
    Ldr                       00007ffbe767a140
    Ldr.Initialized:          Yes
    Ldr.InInitializationOrderModuleList: 00000219443a2070 . 00000219443a90a0
    Ldr.InLoadOrderModuleList:           00000219443a21f0 . 00000219443a9080
    Ldr.InMemoryOrderModuleList:         00000219443a2200 . 00000219443a9090
              Base TimeStamp                     Module
        7ff66b8e0000 6748d9ad Nov 28 20:59:25 2024 C:\Work\complex-case.exe
        7ffbe7500000 77da5a19 Sep 20 04:10:17 2033 C:\WINDOWS\SYSTEM32\ntdll.dll
        7ffbe6070000 1b24eda6 Jun 06 22:22:46 1984 C:\WINDOWS\System32\KERNEL32.DLL
        7ffbe4cc0000 3739e3d8 May 12 21:26:00 1999 C:\WINDOWS\System32\KERNELBASE.dll
        7ffbe5240000 00e78ce9 Jun 25 16:14:49 1970 C:\WINDOWS\System32\ucrtbase.dll
        7ffbd94a0000 006cb796 Mar 24 11:08:06 1970 C:\WINDOWS\SYSTEM32\VCRUNTIME140.dll
SubSystemData:     0000000000000000
ProcessHeap:       00000219443a0000
ProcessParameters: 00000219443a6570
CurrentDirectory:  'C:\Work\'
WindowTitle:  'C:\Work\complex-case.exe'
ImageFile:    'C:\Work\complex-case.exe'
CommandLine:  '"C:\Work\complex-case.exe" '
DllPath:      '< Name not readable >'
Environment:  00000219443a11f0
   =::=::\
   ALLUSERSPROFILE=C:\ProgramData
   APPDATA=C:\Users\User\AppData\Roaming
   CommonProgramFiles=C:\Program Files\Common Files
   CommonProgramFiles(x86)=C:\Program Files (x86)\Common Files
   CommonProgramW6432=C:\Program Files\Common Files
   COMPUTERNAME=WINDEV2204EVAL
   ComSpec=C:\WINDOWS\system32\cmd.exe
   DriverData=C:\Windows\System32\Drivers\DriverData
   FPS_BROWSER_APP_PROFILE_STRING=Internet Explorer
   FPS_BROWSER_USER_PROFILE_STRING=Default
   HOMEDRIVE=C:
   HOMEPATH=\Users\User
   LOCALAPPDATA=C:\Users\User\AppData\Local
   LOGONSERVER=\\WINDEV2204EVAL
   NUMBER_OF_PROCESSORS=4
   OneDrive=C:\Users\User\OneDrive
   OS=Windows_NT
   Path=C:\Windows\system32;C:\Windows;C:\Windows\System32\Wbem;C:\Windows\System32\WindowsPowerShell\v1.0\;C:\Windows\System32\OpenSSH\;C:\Program
Files\Microsoft SQL Server\150\Tools\Binn\;C:\Program Files\Microsoft SQL Server\Client SDK\ODBC\170\Tools\Binn\;C:\Program
Files\dotnet\;C:\Users\User\AppData\Local\Microsoft\WindowsApps;C:\Users\User\.dotnet\tools
   PATHEXT=.COM;.EXE;.BAT;.CMD;.VBS;.VBE;.JS;.JSE;.WSF;.WSH;.MSC
   PROCESSOR_ARCHITECTURE=AMD64
   PROCESSOR_IDENTIFIER=Intel64 Family 6 Model 142 Stepping 10, GenuineIntel
```

```
PROCESSOR_LEVEL=6
PROCESSOR_REVISION=8e0a
ProgramData=C:\ProgramData
ProgramFiles=C:\Program Files
ProgramFiles(x86)=C:\Program Files (x86)
ProgramW6432=C:\Program Files
PSModulePath=C:\Program Files\WindowsPowerShell\Modules;C:\WINDOWS\system32\WindowsPowerShell\v1.0\Modules
PUBLIC=C:\Users\Public
SESSIONNAME=Console
SystemDrive=C:
SystemRoot=C:\WINDOWS
TEMP=C:\Users\User\AppData\Local\Temp
TMP=C:\Users\User\AppData\Local\Temp
USERDOMAIN=WINDEV2204EVAL
USERDOMAIN_ROAMINGPROFILE=WINDEV2204EVAL
USERNAME=User
USERPROFILE=C:\Users\User
windir=C:\WINDOWS


    THREAD ffff83875f951080  Cid 1fc0.0474  Teb: 000000999cfee000 Win32Thread: 0000000000000000 WAIT: (UserRequest) UserMode Non-Alertable
        ffff83875e7ce080  Thread
    Not impersonating
    DeviceMap                 ffffc481d7808870
    Owning Process            ffff83875f4130c0       Image:         complex-case.exe
    Attached Process          N/A           Image:         N/A
    Wait Start TickCount      195730        Ticks: 5360 (0:00:01:23.750)
    Context Switch Count      50            IdealProcessor: 2
    UserTime                  00:00:00.000
    KernelTime                00:00:00.015
Unable to load image C:\Work\complex-case.exe, Win32 error 0n2
*** WARNING: Unable to verify checksum for complex-case.exe
    Win32 Start Address complex_case!mainCRTStartup (0x00007ff66b8fba8c)
    Stack Init fffffa0fb63b4c70 Current fffffa0fb63b4650
    Base fffffa0fb63b5000 Limit fffffa0fb63af000 Call 0000000000000000
    Priority 9  BasePriority 8  IoPriority 2  PagePriority 5
    Child-SP          RetAddr           Call Site
    fffffa0f`b63b4690 fffff802`154cf4e7 nt!KiSwapContext+0x76
    fffffa0f`b63b47d0 fffff802`154d1399 nt!KiSwapThread+0x3a7
    fffffa0f`b63b48b0 fffff802`154cb2b4 nt!KiCommitThreadWait+0x159
    fffffa0f`b63b4950 fffff802`159fc22b nt!KeWaitForSingleObject+0x234
    fffffa0f`b63b4a40 fffff802`159fc15a nt!ObWaitForSingleObject+0xbb
    fffffa0f`b63b4aa0 fffff802`156502d5 nt!NtWaitForSingleObject+0x6a
    fffffa0f`b63b4ae0 00007ffb`e75a4104 nt!KiSystemServiceCopyEnd+0x25 (TrapFrame @ fffffa0f`b63b4ae0)
    00000099`9cd6fa78 00007ffb`e4d110ee ntdll!NtWaitForSingleObject+0x14
    00000099`9cd6fa80 00007ff6`6b8ee5a1 KERNELBASE!WaitForSingleObjectEx+0x8e
    00000099`9cd6fb20 00007ff6`6b8e1021 complex_case!std::sys::pal::windows::thread::Thread::join+0x21
[/rustc/eeb90cda1969383f56a2637cbd3037bdf598841c/library\std\src\sys\pal\windows\thread.rs @ 83]
    00000099`9cd6fbb0 00007ff6`6b8e4298 complex_case!ZN3std6thread18JoinInner$LT$T$GT$4join17he01750eff116e062E+0x21
    00000099`9cd6fc10 00007ff6`6b8e3536
complex_case!ZN80_$LT$std..io..Write..write_fmt..Adapter$LT$T$GT$$u20$as$u20$core..fmt..Write$GT$9write_str17hcbe9dfd423357c2fE+0x238
    00000099`9cd6fd30 00007ff6`6b8e2e0c complex_case!ZN3std3sys9backtrace28__rust_begin_short_backtrace17h2f112179cab5b729E+0x6
    00000099`9cd6fd60 00007ff6`6b8e6389
complex_case!ZN3std2rt10lang_start28_$u7b$$u7b$closure$u7d$$u7d$17h06bb858946802ed5E.llvm.805952136491849391+0xc
        (Inline Function) --------`-------- complex_case!std::rt::lang_start_internal::closure$2+0x6 (Inline Function @ 00007ff6`6b8e6389)
[/rustc/eeb90cda1969383f56a2637cbd3037bdf598841c/library\std\src\rt.rs @ 141]
        (Inline Function) --------`-------- complex_case!std::panicking::try::do_call+0x6 (Inline Function @ 00007ff6`6b8e6389)
[/rustc/eeb90cda1969383f56a2637cbd3037bdf598841c/library\std\src\panicking.rs @ 557]
        (Inline Function) --------`-------- complex_case!std::panicking::try+0x6 (Inline Function @ 00007ff6`6b8e6389)
[/rustc/eeb90cda1969383f56a2637cbd3037bdf598841c/library\std\src\panicking.rs @ 521]
        (Inline Function) --------`-------- complex_case!std::panic::catch_unwind+0x6 (Inline Function @ 00007ff6`6b8e6389)
[/rustc/eeb90cda1969383f56a2637cbd3037bdf598841c/library\std\src\panic.rs @ 350]
    00000099`9cd6fd90 00007ff6`6b8e45bc complex_case!std::rt::lang_start_internal+0x79
[/rustc/eeb90cda1969383f56a2637cbd3037bdf598841c/library\std\src\rt.rs @ 141]
    00000099`9cd6fe50 00007ff6`6b8fba1c complex_case!main+0x2c
        (Inline Function) --------`-------- complex_case!invoke_main+0x22 (Inline Function @ 00007ff6`6b8fba1c)
[D:\a\_work\1\s\src\vctools\crt\vcstartup\src\startup\exe_common.inl @ 78]
    00000099`9cd6fe90 00007ffb`e60853e0 complex_case!__scrt_common_main_seh+0x10c [D:\a\_work\1\s\src\vctools\crt\vcstartup\src\startup\exe_common.inl
@ 288]
    00000099`9cd6fed0 00007ffb`e750485b KERNEL32!BaseThreadInitThunk+0x10
    00000099`9cd6ff00 00000000`00000000 ntdll!RtlUserThreadStart+0x2b


    THREAD ffff83875e7ce080  Cid 1fc0.0e98  Teb: 000000999cff6000 Win32Thread: 0000000000000000 RUNNING on processor 3
    Not inpersonating
    DeviceMap                 ffffc481d7808870
    Owning Process            ffff83875f4130c0       Image:         complex-case.exe
    Attached Process          N/A           Image:         N/A
    Wait Start TickCount      201089        Ticks: 1 (0:00:00.015)
    Context Switch Count      3401614       IdealProcessor: 2
    UserTime                  00:24:34.390
    KernelTime                00:00:24.093
    Win32 Start Address complex_case!std::sys::pal::windows::thread::impl$0::new::thread_start (0x00007ff66b8ee400)
    Stack Init fffffa0fb2c12c70 Current fffffa0fb2c12960
    Base =fffffa0fb2c13000 Limit fffffa0fb2c0d000 Call 0000000000000000
    Priority 8  BasePriority 8  IoPriority 2  PagePriority 5
    Child-SP          RetAddr           Call Site
    00000099`9d4ffa80 00007ff6`6b8e1f60 complex_case!ZN3std3sys9backtrace28__rust_begin_short_backtrace17h3e8324a489e54ea5E+0x50
    00000099`9d4ffbe0 00007ff6`6b8ee43d complex_case!ZN3std6thread7Builder15spawn_unchecked17h6e56a25e80bf8795E+0x790
        (Inline Function) --------`-------- complex_case!alloc::boxed::impl$48::call_once+0xb (Inline Function @ 00007ff6`6b8ee43d)
[/rustc/eeb90cda1969383f56a2637cbd3037bdf598841c/library\alloc\src\boxed.rs @ 2070]
        (Inline Function) --------`-------- complex_case!alloc::boxed::impl$48::call_once+0x16 (Inline Function @ 00007ff6`6b8ee43d)
[/rustc/eeb90cda1969383f56a2637cbd3037bdf598841c/library\alloc\src\boxed.rs @ 2070]
    00000099`9d4ffc80 00007ffb`e60853e0 complex_case!std::sys::pal::windows::thread::impl$0::new::thread_start+0x3d
[/rustc/eeb90cda1969383f56a2637cbd3037bdf598841c/library\std\src\sys\pal\windows\thread.rs @ 58]
    00000099`9d4ffce0 00007ffb`e750485b KERNEL32!BaseThreadInitThunk+0x10
    00000099`9d4ffd10 00000000`00000000 ntdll!RtlUserThreadStart+0x2b


    THREAD ffff83875de41080  Cid 1fc0.1330  Teb: 000000999cff8000 Win32Thread: 0000000000000000 WAIT: (Executive) KernelMode Alertable
```

```
        ffff83875a51edd8  NotificationEvent
    IRP List:
        ffff8387688295b0: (0006,0160) Flags: 00060030  Mdl: 00000000
    Not impersonating
    DeviceMap                  ffffc481d7808870
    Owning Process             ffff83875f4130c0      Image:          complex-case.exe
    Attached Process           N/A            Image:        N/A
    Wait Start TickCount       201090         Ticks: 0
    Context Switch Count       4329409        IdealProcessor: 1
    UserTime                   00:00:49.156
    KernelTime                 00:02:30.640
    Win32 Start Address complex_case!std::sys::pal::windows::thread::impl$0::new::thread_start (0x00007ff66b8ee400)
    Stack Init ffffffa0fb2c19c70 Current ffffffa0fb2c193e0
    Base ffffffa0fb2c1a000 Limit ffffffa0fb2c14000 Call 0000000000000000
    Priority 9 BasePriority 8 IoPriority 2 PagePriority 5
    Child-SP          RetAddr           Call Site
    ffffffa0f`b2c19420 fffff802`154cf4e7 nt!KiSwapContext+0x76
    ffffffa0f`b2c19560 fffff802`154d1399 nt!KiSwapThread+0x3a7
    ffffffa0f`b2c19640 fffff802`154cb2b4 nt!KiCommitThreadWait+0x159
    ffffffa0f`b2c196e0 fffff802`15633b14 nt!KeWaitForSingleObject+0x234
    ffffffa0f`b2c197d0 fffff802`1594dc58 nt!IopWaitForSynchronousIoEvent+0x50
    ffffffa0f`b2c19810 fffff802`1594d589 nt!IopSynchronousServiceTail+0x668
    ffffffa0f`b2c198c0 fffff802`1594c846 nt!IopXxxControlFile+0xd29
    ffffffa0f`b2c19a00 fffff802`156502d5 nt!NtDeviceIoControlFile+0x56
    ffffffa0f`b2c19a70 00007ffb`e75a4164 nt!KiSystemServiceCopyEnd+0x25 (TrapFrame @ ffffffa0f`b2c19ae0)
    00000099`9d6fcf58 00007ffb`e4cf4da5 ntdll!NtDeviceIoControlFile+0x14
    00000099`9d6fcf60 00007ffb`e4c4c3a ntdll!NtDeviceIoControlFile+0x14
    00000099`9d6fcf60 00007ffb`e4c4c3a KERNELBASE!ConsoleCallServerGeneric+0xe9
    00000099`9d6fd0c0 00007ff6`6b8ee063 KERNELBASE!WriteConsoleW+0x6a
       (Inline Function) --------`-------- complex_case!std::sys::pal::windows::stdio::write_u16s+0x2a (Inline Function @ 00007ff6`6b8ee063)
    [/rustc/eeb90cda1969383f56a2637cbd3037bdf598841c/library\std\src\sys\pal\windows\stdio.rs @ 231]
    00000099`9d6fd150 00007ff6`6b8ede45 complex_case!std::sys::pal::windows::stdio::write_valid_utf8_to_console+0xd3
    [/rustc/eeb90cda1969383f56a2637cbd3037bdf598841c/library\std\src\sys\pal\windows\stdio.rs @ 194]
    00000099`9d6ff1f0 00007ff6`6b8e756f complex_case!std::sys::pal::windows::stdio::write+0x1d5
    [/rustc/eeb90cda1969383f56a2637cbd3037bdf598841c/library\std\src\sys\pal\windows\stdio.rs @ 168]
       (Inline Function) --------`-------- complex_case!std::sys::pal::windows::stdio::impl$5::write+0x10 (Inline Function @ 00007ff6`6b8e756f)
    [/rustc/eeb90cda1969383f56a2637cbd3037bdf598841c/library\std\src\sys\pal\windows\stdio.rs @ 422]
       (Inline Function) --------`-------- complex_case!std::io::stdio::impl$1::write+0x10 (Inline Function @ 00007ff6`6b8e756f)
    [/rustc/eeb90cda1969383f56a2637cbd3037bdf598841c/library\std\src\io\stdio.rs @ 128]
    00000099`9d6ff2d0 00007ff6`6b8e8180 complex_case!std::io::buffered::bufwriter::BufWriter::flush_buf<std::io::stdio::StdoutRaw>+0x7f
    [/rustc/eeb90cda1969383f56a2637cbd3037bdf598841c/library\std\src\io\buffered\bufwriter.rs @ 228]
    00000099`9d6ff370 00007ff6`6b8e95be complex_case!std::io::stdio::impl$19::write_all+0x150
    [/rustc/eeb90cda1969383f56a2637cbd3037bdf598841c/library\std\src\io\stdio.rs @ 813]
    00000099`9d6ff410 00007ff6`6b8f82bf complex_case!std::io::Write::write_fmt<std::io::stdio::StdoutLock>+0x1e
    [/rustc/eeb90cda1969383f56a2637cbd3037bdf598841c/library\std\src\io\mod.rs @ 1816]
    00000099`9d6ff460 00007ff6`6b8e7f45 complex_case!core::fmt::write+0x1cf
    [/rustc/eeb90cda1969383f56a2637cbd3037bdf598841c/library\core\src\fmt\mod.rs @ 1207]
    00000099`9d6ff510 00007ff6`6b8e87f1 complex_case!std::io::stdio::impl$16::write_fmt+0x45
    [/rustc/eeb90cda1969383f56a2637cbd3037bdf598841c/library\std\src\io\stdio.rs @ 787]
    00000099`9d6ff5a0 00007ff6`6b8e36b2 complex_case!std::io::stdio::_print+0x61
    [/rustc/eeb90cda1969383f56a2637cbd3037bdf598841c/library\std\src\io\stdio.rs @ 1227]
    00000099`9d6ff650 00007ff6`6b8e1f60 complex_case!ZN3std3sys9backtrace28__rust_begin_short_backtrace17h3e8324a489e54ea5E+0x172
    00000099`9d6ff7b0 00007ff6`6b8ee43d complex_case!ZN3std6thread7Builder15spawn_unchecked17h6e56a25e80bf8795E+0x790
       (Inline Function) --------`-------- complex_case!alloc::boxed::impl$48::call_once+0xb (Inline Function @ 00007ff6`6b8ee43d)
    [/rustc/eeb90cda1969383f56a2637cbd3037bdf598841c/library\alloc\src\boxed.rs @ 2070]
       (Inline Function) --------`-------- complex_case!alloc::boxed::impl$48::call_once+0x16 (Inline Function @ 00007ff6`6b8ee43d)
    [/rustc/eeb90cda1969383f56a2637cbd3037bdf598841c/library\alloc\src\boxed.rs @ 2070]
    00000099`9d6ff850 00007ffb`e60853e0 complex_case!std::sys::pal::windows::thread::impl$0::new::thread_start+0x3d
    [/rustc/eeb90cda1969383f56a2637cbd3037bdf598841c/library\std\src\sys\pal\windows\thread.rs @ 58]
    00000099`9d6ff8b0 00007ffb`e750485b KERNEL32!BaseThreadInitThunk+0x10
    00000099`9d6ff8e0 00000000`00000000 ntdll!RtlUserThreadStart+0x2b

    THREAD ffff83875fd99080 Cid 1fc0.17f4 Teb: 000000999cffa000 Win32Thread: 0000000000000000 WAIT: (WrAlertByThreadId) UserMode Non-Alertable
        00002219443a59e0 Unknown
    Not impersonating
    DeviceMap                  ffffc481d7808870
    Owning Process             ffff83875f4130c0      Image:          complex-case.exe
    Attached Process           N/A            Image:        N/A
    Wait Start TickCount       195730         Ticks: 5360 (0:00:01:23.750)
    Context Switch Count       10             IdealProcessor: 3
    UserTime                   00:00:00.000
    KernelTime                 00:00:00.000
    Win32 Start Address complex_case!std::sys::pal::windows::thread::impl$0::new::thread_start (0x00007ff66b8ee400)
    Stack Init ffffffa0fb2c29c70 Current ffffffa0fb2c29750
    Base ffffffa0fb2c2a000 Limit ffffffa0fb2c24000 Call 0000000000000000
    Priority 9 BasePriority 8 IoPriority 2 PagePriority 5
    Child-SP          RetAddr           Call Site
    ffffffa0f`b2c29790 fffff802`154cf4e7 nt!KiSwapContext+0x76
    ffffffa0f`b2c298d0 fffff802`154d1399 nt!KiSwapThread+0x3a7
    ffffffa0f`b2c299b0 fffff802`15433bc8 nt!KiCommitThreadWait+0x159
    ffffffa0f`b2c29a50 fffff802`158aff30 nt!KeWaitForAlertByThreadId+0xc4
    ffffffa0f`b2c29ab0 fffff802`156502d5 nt!NtWaitForAlertByThreadId+0x30
    ffffffa0f`b2c29ae0 00007ffb`e75a7bf4 nt!KiSystemServiceCopyEnd+0x25 (TrapFrame @ ffffffa0f`b2c29ae0)
    00000099`9d8ff788 00007ffb`e751d89d ntdll!NtWaitForAlertByThreadId+0x14
    00000099`9d8ff790 00007ffb`e755b3fe ntdll!RtlpWaitOnAddressWithTimeout+0x81
    00000099`9d8ff7c0 00007ffb`e755b343 ntdll!RtlpWaitOnAddress+0xae
    00000099`9d8ff830 00007ff6`e4d2dd9f ntdll!RtlWaitOnAddress+0x13
    00000099`9d8ff870 00007ff6`6b8e6b71 KERNELBASE!WaitOnAddress+0x2f
       (Inline Function) --------`-------- complex_case!std::sys::sync::thread_parking::futex::Parker::park+0x65 (Inline Function @ 00007ff6`6b8e6b71)
    [/rustc/eeb90cda1969383f56a2637cbd3037bdf598841c/library\std\src\sys\sync\thread_parking\futex.rs @ 55]
       (Inline Function) --------`-------- complex_case!std::thread::Thread::park+0x65 (Inline Function @ 00007ff6`6b8e6b71)
    [/rustc/eeb90cda1969383f56a2637cbd3037bdf598841c/library\std\src\thread\mod.rs @ 1419]
    00000099`9d8ff8b0 00007ff6`6b8e359c complex_case!std::thread::park+0x151
    [/rustc/eeb90cda1969383f56a2637cbd3037bdf598841c/library\std\src\thread\mod.rs @ 1126]
    00000099`9d8ff920 00007ff6`6b8e1f60 complex_case!ZN3std3sys9backtrace28__rust_begin_short_backtrace17h3e8324a489e54ea5E+0x5c
    00000099`9d8ffa80 00007ff6`6b8ee43d complex_case!ZN3std6thread7Builder15spawn_unchecked17h6e56a25e80bf8795E+0x790
       (Inline Function) --------`-------- complex_case!alloc::boxed::impl$48::call_once+0xb (Inline Function @ 00007ff6`6b8ee43d)
    [/rustc/eeb90cda1969383f56a2637cbd3037bdf598841c/library\alloc\src\boxed.rs @ 2070]
```

```
        (Inline Function) --------`--------      complex_case!alloc::boxed::impl$48::call_once+0x16 (Inline Function @ 00007ff6`6b8ee43d)
[/rustc/eeb90cda1969383f56a2637cbd3037bdf598841c/library\alloc\src\boxed.rs @ 2070]
        00000099`9d8ffb20 00007ffb`e60853e0      complex_case!std::sys::pal::windows::thread::impl$0::new::thread_start+0x3d
[/rustc/eeb90cda1969383f56a2637cbd3037bdf598841c/library\std\src\sys\pal\windows\thread.rs @ 58]
        00000099`9d8ffb80 00007ffb`e750485b      KERNEL32!BaseThreadInitThunk+0x10
        00000099`9d8ffbb0 00000000`00000000      ntdll!RtlUserThreadStart+0x2b

        THREAD ffff83875de4d080  Cid 1fc0.18c8  Teb: 000000999cffc000 Win32Thread: 0000000000000000 WAIT: (UserRequest) UserMode Non-Alertable
            ffff838763a43210  Timer2SynchronizationObject
        Not impersonating
        DeviceMap                 ffffc481d7808870
        Owning Process            ffff83875f4130c0      Image:         complex-case.exe
        Attached Process          N/A           Image:         N/A
        Wait Start TickCount      201088        Ticks: 2 (0:00:00:00.031)
        Context Switch Count      498670        IdealProcessor: 0
        UserTime                  00:00:12.031
        KernelTime                00:00:13.609
        Win32 Start Address complex_case!std::sys::pal::windows::thread::impl$0::new::thread_start (0x00007ff66b8ee400)
        Stack Init fffffa0fb2c3ec70 Current fffffa0fb2c3e650
        Base fffffa0fb2c3f000 Limit fffffa0fb2c39000 Call 0000000000000000
        Priority 9  BasePriority 8  IoPriority 2  PagePriority 5
        Child-SP          RetAddr           Call Site
        fffffa0f`b2c3e690 fffff802`154cf4e7  nt!KiSwapContext+0x76
        fffffa0f`b2c3e7d0 fffff802`154d1399  nt!KiSwapThread+0x3a7
        fffffa0f`b2c3e8b0 fffff802`154cb2b4  nt!KiCommitThreadWait+0x159
        fffffa0f`b2c3e950 fffff802`159fc22b  nt!KeWaitForSingleObject+0x234
        fffffa0f`b2c3ea40 fffff802`159fc15a  nt!ObWaitForSingleObject+0xbb
        fffffa0f`b2c3eaa0 fffff802`156502d5  nt!NtWaitForSingleObject+0x6a
        fffffa0f`b2c3eae0 00007ffb`e75a4104  nt!KiSystemServiceCopyEnd+0x25 (TrapFrame @ fffffa0f`b2c3eae0)
        00000099`9d918068 00007ffb`e4d110ee  ntdll!NtWaitForSingleObject+0x14
        00000099`9d918070 00007ff6`6b8e69ad  KERNELBASE!WaitForSingleObjectEx+0x8e
        (Inline Function) --------`--------      complex_case!std::sys::pal::windows::time::WaitableTimer::wait+0xe (Inline Function @ 00007ff6`6b8e69ad)
[/rustc/eeb90cda1969383f56a2637cbd3037bdf598841c/library\std\src\sys\pal\windows\time.rs @ 254]
        (Inline Function) --------`--------      complex_case!std::sys::pal::windows::thread::impl$0::sleep::high_precision_sleep+0x7c (Inline Function @
00007ff6`6b8e69ad) [/rustc/eeb90cda1969383f56a2637cbd3037bdf598841c/library\std\src\sys\pal\windows\thread.rs @ 101]
        (Inline Function) --------`--------      complex_case!std::sys::pal::windows::thread::Thread::sleep+0x89 (Inline Function @ 00007ff6`6b8e69ad)
[/rustc/eeb90cda1969383f56a2637cbd3037bdf598841c/library\std\src\sys\pal\windows\thread.rs @ 106]
        00000099`9d918110 00007ff6`6b8e44c7  complex_case!std::thread::sleep+0x9d
[/rustc/eeb90cda1969383f56a2637cbd3037bdf598841c/library\std\src\thread\mod.rs @ 930]
        00000099`9d918180 00007ff6`6b8e452e
complex_case!ZN80_$LT$std..io..Write..write_fmt..Adapter$LT$T$GT$$u20$as$u20$core..fmt..Write$GT$9write_str17hcbe9dfd423357c2fE+0x467
        00000099`9d918200 00007ff6`6b8e452e
complex_case!ZN80_$LT$std..io..Write..write_fmt..Adapter$LT$T$GT$$u20$as$u20$core..fmt..Write$GT$9write_str17hcbe9dfd423357c2fE+0x4ce
        00000099`9d918280 00007ff6`6b8e452e
complex_case!ZN80_$LT$std..io..Write..write_fmt..Adapter$LT$T$GT$$u20$as$u20$core..fmt..Write$GT$9write_str17hcbe9dfd423357c2fE+0x4ce
        00000099`9d918300 00007ff6`6b8e452e
complex_case!ZN80_$LT$std..io..Write..write_fmt..Adapter$LT$T$GT$$u20$as$u20$core..fmt..Write$GT$9write_str17hcbe9dfd423357c2fE+0x4ce
        00000099`9d918380 00007ff6`6b8e452e
complex_case!ZN80_$LT$std..io..Write..write_fmt..Adapter$LT$T$GT$$u20$as$u20$core..fmt..Write$GT$9write_str17hcbe9dfd423357c2fE+0x4ce
        00000099`9d918400 00007ff6`6b8e452e
complex_case!ZN80_$LT$std..io..Write..write_fmt..Adapter$LT$T$GT$$u20$as$u20$core..fmt..Write$GT$9write_str17hcbe9dfd423357c2fE+0x4ce
        00000099`9d918480 00007ff6`6b8e452e
complex_case!ZN80_$LT$std..io..Write..write_fmt..Adapter$LT$T$GT$$u20$as$u20$core..fmt..Write$GT$9write_str17hcbe9dfd423357c2fE+0x4ce
        00000099`9d918500 00007ff6`6b8e452e
complex_case!ZN80_$LT$std..io..Write..write_fmt..Adapter$LT$T$GT$$u20$as$u20$core..fmt..Write$GT$9write_str17hcbe9dfd423357c2fE+0x4ce
        00000099`9d918580 00007ff6`6b8e452e
complex_case!ZN80_$LT$std..io..Write..write_fmt..Adapter$LT$T$GT$$u20$as$u20$core..fmt..Write$GT$9write_str17hcbe9dfd423357c2fE+0x4ce
        00000099`9d918600 00007ff6`6b8e452e
complex_case!ZN80_$LT$std..io..Write..write_fmt..Adapter$LT$T$GT$$u20$as$u20$core..fmt..Write$GT$9write_str17hcbe9dfd423357c2fE+0x4ce
        00000099`9d918680 00007ff6`6b8e452e
complex_case!ZN80_$LT$std..io..Write..write_fmt..Adapter$LT$T$GT$$u20$as$u20$core..fmt..Write$GT$9write_str17hcbe9dfd423357c2fE+0x4ce
        00000099`9d918700 00007ff6`6b8e452e
complex_case!ZN80_$LT$std..io..Write..write_fmt..Adapter$LT$T$GT$$u20$as$u20$core..fmt..Write$GT$9write_str17hcbe9dfd423357c2fE+0x4ce
        00000099`9d918780 00007ff6`6b8e452e
complex_case!ZN80_$LT$std..io..Write..write_fmt..Adapter$LT$T$GT$$u20$as$u20$core..fmt..Write$GT$9write_str17hcbe9dfd423357c2fE+0x4ce
        00000099`9d918800 00007ff6`6b8e452e
complex_case!ZN80_$LT$std..io..Write..write_fmt..Adapter$LT$T$GT$$u20$as$u20$core..fmt..Write$GT$9write_str17hcbe9dfd423357c2fE+0x4ce
        00000099`9d918880 00007ff6`6b8e452e
complex_case!ZN80_$LT$std..io..Write..write_fmt..Adapter$LT$T$GT$$u20$as$u20$core..fmt..Write$GT$9write_str17hcbe9dfd423357c2fE+0x4ce
        00000099`9d918900 00007ff6`6b8e452e
complex_case!ZN80_$LT$std..io..Write..write_fmt..Adapter$LT$T$GT$$u20$as$u20$core..fmt..Write$GT$9write_str17hcbe9dfd423357c2fE+0x4ce
        00000099`9d918980 00007ff6`6b8e452e
complex_case!ZN80_$LT$std..io..Write..write_fmt..Adapter$LT$T$GT$$u20$as$u20$core..fmt..Write$GT$9write_str17hcbe9dfd423357c2fE+0x4ce
        00000099`9d918a00 00007ff6`6b8e452e
complex_case!ZN80_$LT$std..io..Write..write_fmt..Adapter$LT$T$GT$$u20$as$u20$core..fmt..Write$GT$9write_str17hcbe9dfd423357c2fE+0x4ce
        00000099`9d918a80 00007ff6`6b8e452e
complex_case!ZN80_$LT$std..io..Write..write_fmt..Adapter$LT$T$GT$$u20$as$u20$core..fmt..Write$GT$9write_str17hcbe9dfd423357c2fE+0x4ce
        00000099`9d918b00 00007ff6`6b8e452e
complex_case!ZN80_$LT$std..io..Write..write_fmt..Adapter$LT$T$GT$$u20$as$u20$core..fmt..Write$GT$9write_str17hcbe9dfd423357c2fE+0x4ce
        00000099`9d918b80 00007ff6`6b8e452e
complex_case!ZN80_$LT$std..io..Write..write_fmt..Adapter$LT$T$GT$$u20$as$u20$core..fmt..Write$GT$9write_str17hcbe9dfd423357c2fE+0x4ce
        00000099`9d918c00 00007ff6`6b8e452e
complex_case!ZN80_$LT$std..io..Write..write_fmt..Adapter$LT$T$GT$$u20$as$u20$core..fmt..Write$GT$9write_str17hcbe9dfd423357c2fE+0x4ce
        00000099`9d918c80 00007ff6`6b8e452e
complex_case!ZN80_$LT$std..io..Write..write_fmt..Adapter$LT$T$GT$$u20$as$u20$core..fmt..Write$GT$9write_str17hcbe9dfd423357c2fE+0x4ce
        00000099`9d918d00 00007ff6`6b8e452e
complex_case!ZN80_$LT$std..io..Write..write_fmt..Adapter$LT$T$GT$$u20$as$u20$core..fmt..Write$GT$9write_str17hcbe9dfd423357c2fE+0x4ce
        00000099`9d918d80 00007ff6`6b8e452e
complex_case!ZN80_$LT$std..io..Write..write_fmt..Adapter$LT$T$GT$$u20$as$u20$core..fmt..Write$GT$9write_str17hcbe9dfd423357c2fE+0x4ce
        00000099`9d918e00 00007ff6`6b8e452e
complex_case!ZN80_$LT$std..io..Write..write_fmt..Adapter$LT$T$GT$$u20$as$u20$core..fmt..Write$GT$9write_str17hcbe9dfd423357c2fE+0x4ce
        00000099`9d918e80 00007ff6`6b8e452e
complex_case!ZN80_$LT$std..io..Write..write_fmt..Adapter$LT$T$GT$$u20$as$u20$core..fmt..Write$GT$9write_str17hcbe9dfd423357c2fE+0x4ce

        THREAD ffff83875de47080  Cid 1fc0.22f4  Teb: 000000999cffe000 Win32Thread: 0000000000000000 WAIT: (UserRequest) UserMode Non-Alertable
            ffff838763a44200  Timer2SynchronizationObject
        Not impersonating
        DeviceMap                 ffffc481d7808870
```

```
Owning Process          ffff83875f4130c0   Image:          complex-case.exe
Attached Process        N/A           Image:      N/A
Wait Start TickCount    201088        Ticks: 2 (0:00:00.031)
Context Switch Count     45681        IdealProcessor: 2
UserTime                00:00:01.031
KernelTime              00:00:04.218
Win32 Start Address complex_case!std::sys::pal::windows::thread::impl$0::new::thread_start (0x00007ff66b8ee400)
Stack Init fffffa0fb2c4cc70 Current fffffa0fb2c4c650
Base fffffa0fb2c4d000 Limit fffffa0fb2c47000 Call 0000000000000000
Priority 11 BasePriority 8 Unusual Boost 3 IoPriority 2 PagePriority 5
Child-SP          RetAddr           Call Site
fffffa0f`b2c4c690 fffff802`154cf4e7 nt!KiSwapContext+0x76
fffffa0f`b2c4c7d0 fffff802`154d1399 nt!KiSwapThread+0x3a7
fffffa0f`b2c4c8b0 fffff802`154cb2b4 nt!KiCommitThreadWait+0x159
fffffa0f`b2c4c950 fffff802`159fc22b nt!KeWaitForSingleObject+0x234
fffffa0f`b2c4ca40 fffff802`159fc15a nt!ObWaitForSingleObject+0xbb
fffffa0f`b2c4caa0 fffff802`156502d5 nt!NtWaitForSingleObject+0x6a
fffffa0f`b2c4cae0 00007ffb`e75a4104 nt!KiSystemServiceCopyEnd+0x25 (TrapFrame @ fffffa0f`b2c4cae0)
00000099`9dcff958 00007ffb`e4d110ee ntdll!NtWaitForSingleObject+0x14
00000099`9dcff960 00007ff6`6b8e69ad KERNELBASE!WaitForSingleObjectEx+0x8e
        (Inline Function) --------`-------- complex_case!std::sys::pal::windows::time::WaitableTimer::wait+0xe (Inline Function @ 00007ff6`6b8e69ad)
[/rustc/eeb90cda1969383f56a2637cbd3037bdf598841c/library\std\src\sys\pal\windows\time.rs @ 254]
        (Inline Function) --------`-------- complex_case!std::sys::pal::windows::thread::impl$0::sleep::high_precision_sleep+0x7c (Inline Function @
00007ff6`6b8e69ad) [/rustc/eeb90cda1969383f56a2637cbd3037bdf598841c/library\std\src\sys\pal\windows\thread.rs @ 101]
        (Inline Function) --------`-------- complex_case!std::sys::pal::windows::thread::Thread::sleep+0x89 (Inline Function @ 00007ff6`6b8e69ad)
[/rustc/eeb90cda1969383f56a2637cbd3037bdf598841c/library\std\src\sys\pal\windows\thread.rs @ 106]
00000099`9dcffa00 00007ff6`6b8e3749 complex_case!std::thread::sleep+0x9d
[/rustc/eeb90cda1969383f56a2637cbd3037bdf598841c/library\std\src\thread\mod.rs @ 930]
00000099`9dcffa70 00007ff6`6b8e1f60 complex_case!ZN3std3sys9backtrace28__rust_begin_short_backtrace17h3e8324a489e54ea5E+0x209
00000099`9dcffbd0 00007ff6`6b8ee43d complex_case!ZN3std6thread7Builder15spawn_unchecked17h6e56a25e80bf8795E+0x790
        (Inline Function) --------`-------- complex_case!alloc::boxed::impl$48::call_once+0xb (Inline Function @ 00007ff6`6b8ee43d)
[/rustc/eeb90cda1969383f56a2637cbd3037bdf598841c/library\alloc\src\boxed.rs @ 2070]
        (Inline Function) --------`-------- complex_case!alloc::boxed::impl$48::call_once+0x16 (Inline Function @ 00007ff6`6b8ee43d)
[/rustc/eeb90cda1969383f56a2637cbd3037bdf598841c/library\alloc\src\boxed.rs @ 2070]
00000099`9dcffc70 00007ffb`e60853e0 complex_case!std::sys::pal::windows::thread::impl$0::new::thread_start+0x3d
[/rustc/eeb90cda1969383f56a2637cbd3037bdf598841c/library\std\src\sys\pal\windows\thread.rs @ 58]
00000099`9dcffcd0 00007ffb`e750485b KERNEL32!BaseThreadInitThunk+0x10
00000099`9dcffd00 00000000`00000000 ntdll!RtlUserThreadStart+0x2b

THREAD ffff838768bc20c0 Cid 1fc0.16a40 Teb: 000000999cf00000 Win32Thread: 0000000000000000 WAIT: (UserRequest) UserMode Non-Alertable
    ffff838763a44310  Timer2SynchronizationObject
Not impersonating
DeviceMap               ffffc481d7808870
Owning Process          ffff83875f4130c0   Image:          complex-case.exe
Attached Process        N/A           Image:      N/A
Wait Start TickCount    201089        Ticks: 1 (0:00:00.015)
Context Switch Count     4            IdealProcessor: 3
...
...
...
```

10.   We can switch to thread user space context (don't forget to reload user space symbols):

```
0: kd> .process /r /p ffff83875f4130c0
Implicit process is now ffff8387`5f4130c0
Loading User Symbols
......

************* Symbol Loading Error Summary **************
Module name             Error
myfault                 The system cannot find the file specified

You can troubleshoot most symbol related issues by turning on symbol loading diagnostics (!sym
noisy) and repeating the command that caused symbols to be loaded.
You should also verify that your symbol search path (.sympath) is correct.
```

```
0: kd> .trap fffffa0f`b2c3eae0
NOTE: The trap frame does not contain all registers.
Some register values may be zeroed or incorrect.
rax=0000000000000000 rbx=0000000000000000 rcx=0000000000000000
rdx=0000000000000000 rsi=0000000000000000 rdi=0000000000000000
rip=00007ffbe75a4104 rsp=000000999d918068 rbp=000000999d918150
 r8=0000000000000000  r9=0000000000000000 r10=0000000000000000
r11=0000000000000000 r12=0000000000000000 r13=0000000000000000
r14=0000000000000000 r15=0000000000000000
iopl=0         nv up ei pl zr na po nc
ntdll!NtWaitForSingleObject+0x14:
0033:00007ffb`e75a4104 ret
```

```
0: kd> .reload
Loading Kernel Symbols
.............................................................
.............................................................
.......................................
Loading User Symbols
......
Loading unloaded module list
...............

0: kd> kL 10
 # Child-SP          RetAddr               Call Site
00 00000099`9d918068 00007ffb`e4d110ee     ntdll!NtWaitForSingleObject+0x14
01 00000099`9d918070 00007ff6`6b8e69ad     KERNELBASE!WaitForSingleObjectEx+0x8e
02 (Inline Function) --------`--------     complex_case!std::sys::pal::windows::time::WaitableTimer::wait+0xe
03 (Inline Function) --------`--------     complex_case!std::sys::pal::windows::thread::impl$0::sleep::high_precision_sleep+0x7c
04 (Inline Function) --------`--------     complex_case!std::sys::pal::windows::thread::Thread::sleep+0x89
05 00000099`9d918110 00007ff6`6b8e44c7     complex_case!std::thread::sleep+0x9d
06 00000099`9d918180 00007ff6`6b8e452e
complex_case!ZN80_$LT$std..io..Write..write_fmt..Adapter$LT$T$GT$$u20$as$u20$core..fmt..Write$GT$9write_str17hcbe9dfd423357c2fE+0x467
07 00000099`9d918200 00007ff6`6b8e452e
complex_case!ZN80_$LT$std..io..Write..write_fmt..Adapter$LT$T$GT$$u20$as$u20$core..fmt..Write$GT$9write_str17hcbe9dfd423357c2fE+0x4ce
08 00000099`9d918280 00007ff6`6b8e452e
complex_case!ZN80_$LT$std..io..Write..write_fmt..Adapter$LT$T$GT$$u20$as$u20$core..fmt..Write$GT$9write_str17hcbe9dfd423357c2fE+0x4ce
09 00000099`9d918300 00007ff6`6b8e452e
complex_case!ZN80_$LT$std..io..Write..write_fmt..Adapter$LT$T$GT$$u20$as$u20$core..fmt..Write$GT$9write_str17hcbe9dfd423357c2fE+0x4ce
0a 00000099`9d918380 00007ff6`6b8e452e
complex_case!ZN80_$LT$std..io..Write..write_fmt..Adapter$LT$T$GT$$u20$as$u20$core..fmt..Write$GT$9write_str17hcbe9dfd423357c2fE+0x4ce
0b 00000099`9d918400 00007ff6`6b8e452e
complex_case!ZN80_$LT$std..io..Write..write_fmt..Adapter$LT$T$GT$$u20$as$u20$core..fmt..Write$GT$9write_str17hcbe9dfd423357c2fE+0x4ce
0c 00000099`9d918480 00007ff6`6b8e452e
complex_case!ZN80_$LT$std..io..Write..write_fmt..Adapter$LT$T$GT$$u20$as$u20$core..fmt..Write$GT$9write_str17hcbe9dfd423357c2fE+0x4ce
0d 00000099`9d918500 00007ff6`6b8e452e
complex_case!ZN80_$LT$std..io..Write..write_fmt..Adapter$LT$T$GT$$u20$as$u20$core..fmt..Write$GT$9write_str17hcbe9dfd423357c2fE+0x4ce
0e 00000099`9d918580 00007ff6`6b8e452e
complex_case!ZN80_$LT$std..io..Write..write_fmt..Adapter$LT$T$GT$$u20$as$u20$core..fmt..Write$GT$9write_str17hcbe9dfd423357c2fE+0x4ce
0f 00000099`9d918600 00007ff6`6b8e452e
complex_case!ZN80_$LT$std..io..Write..write_fmt..Adapter$LT$T$GT$$u20$as$u20$core..fmt..Write$GT$9write_str17hcbe9dfd423357c2fE+0x4ce
```

11.   If there is no trap (a thread is already in user space) we can just switch to it:

```
0: kd> .thread /r /p ffff83875e7ce080
Implicit thread is now ffff8387`5e7ce080
Implicit process is now ffff8387`5f4130c0
Loading User Symbols
.Unable to load image C:\Work\complex-case.exe, Win32 error 0n2
*** WARNING: Unable to verify checksum for complex-case.exe
.....

0: kd> kL 10
 # Child-SP          RetAddr               Call Site
00 00000099`9d4ffa80 00007ff6`6b8e1f60     complex_case!ZN3std3sys9backtrace28__rust_begin_short_backtrace17h3e8324a489e54ea5E+0x50
01 00000099`9d4ffbe0 00007ff6`6b8ee43d     complex_case!ZN3std6thread7Builder15spawn_unchecked17h6e56a25e80bf8795E+0x790
02 (Inline Function) --------`--------     complex_case!alloc::boxed::impl$48::call_once+0xb
03 (Inline Function) --------`--------     complex_case!alloc::boxed::impl$48::call_once+0x16
04 00000099`9d4ffc80 00007ffb`e60853e0     complex_case!std::sys::pal::windows::thread::impl$0::new::thread_start+0x3d
05 00000099`9d4ffce0 00007ffb`e750485b     KERNEL32!BaseThreadInitThunk+0x10
06 00000099`9d4ffd10 00000000`00000000     ntdll!RtlUserThreadStart+0x2b
```

12.   Also, we can carry out the heap analysis (via the **!heap** command) like we did in Exercise RW7 (not include due to the same output here).

13.   We close logging before exiting WinDbg:

```
0: kd> .logclose
Closing open log file C:\ARWMDA-Dumps\Complete\MEMORY-abnormal.log
```

Additional Resources

- WinDbg Help / WinDbg.org (quick links)
- DumpAnalysis.org / SoftwareDiagnostics.Institute / PatternDiagnostics.com
- Debugging.TV / YouTube.com/DebuggingTV / YouTube.com/PatternDiagnostics
- Principles of Memory Dump Analysis
- Fundamentals of Physical Memory Analysis: Anniversary Edition
- Encyclopedia of Crash Dump Analysis Patterns, 3rd edition
- Memory Thinking for Rust
- Accelerated Windows API for Software Diagnostics
- Memory Dump Analysis Anthology (Diagnomicon)

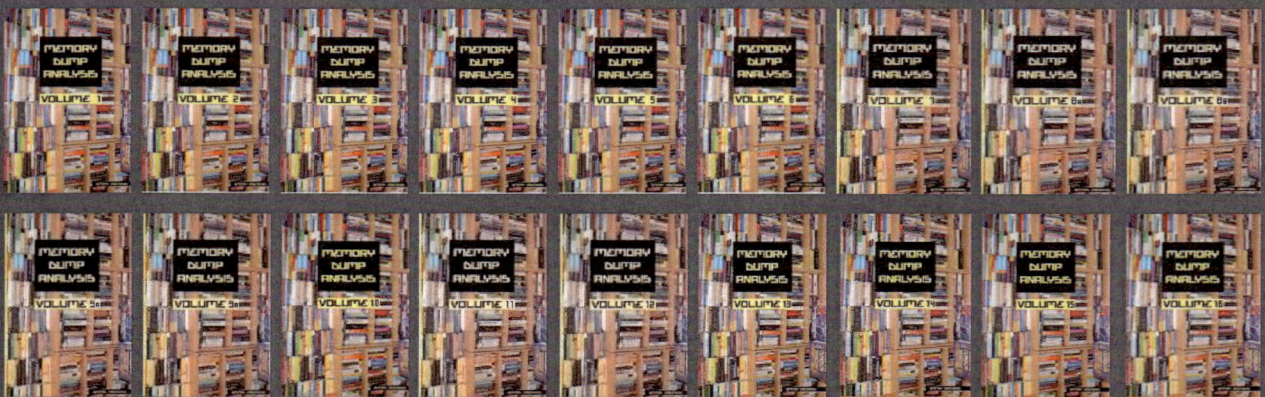

Additional learning and reference resources:

WinDbg quick links
http://WinDbg.org

Software Diagnostics Institute
https://www.dumpanalysis.org

Debugging.TV
http://debugging.tv

Pattern Diagnostics Seminars
https://www.youtube.com/PatternDiagnostics

Software Diagnostics Services
https://www.patterndiagnostics.com

Principles of Memory Dump Analysis
https://www.dumpanalysis.org/principles-memory-dump-analysis-book

Fundamentals of Physical Memory Analysis: Anniversary Edition
https://www.dumpanalysis.org/FCMDA-book

Encyclopedia of Crash Dump Analysis Patterns, 3rd edition
https://www.patterndiagnostics.com/encyclopedia-crash-dump-analysis-patterns

Memory Dump Analysis Anthology (Diagnomicon)
https://www.patterndiagnostics.com/mdaa-volumes

Memory Thinking for Rust

https://www.patterndiagnostics.com/memory-thinking-rust

Accelerated Windows API for Software Diagnostics

https://www.patterndiagnostics.com/accelerated-windows-api-book